TCP/IP with Windows NT Illustrated

McGraw-Hill Series on Computer Communications (Selected Titles)

ISBN	AUTHOR	TITLE
0-07-005147-X	Bates	*Voice and Data Communications Handbook*
0-07-005669-2	Benner	*Fibre Channel: Gigabit Communications and I/O for Computer Networks*
0-07-005560-2	Black	*TCP/IP and Related Protocols, 2/e*
0-07-005590-4	Black	*Frame Relay Networks: Specifications and Implementati 2/e*
0-07-006730-3	Blakeley/Harris/Lewis	*Messaging/Queuing using the MQI*
0-07-011486-2	Chiong	*SNA Interconnections: Bridging and Routing SNA in Hierarchical, Peer, and High-Speed Networks*
0-07-020359-8	Feit	*SNMP: A Guide to Network Management*
0-07-024043-4	Goralski	*Introduction to ATM Networking*
0-07-034249-0	Kessler	*ISDN: Concepts, Facilities, and Services, 3/e*
0-07-035968-7	Kumar	*Broadband Communications*
0-07-041051-8	Matusow	*SNA, APPN, HPR and TCP/IP Integration*
0-07-0603362-6	McDysan/Spohn	*ATM: Theory and Applications*
0-07-044362-9	Muller	*Network Planning Procurement and Management*
0-07-046380-8	Nemzow	*The Ethernet Management Guide, 3/e*
0-07-049663-3	Peterson	*TCP/IP Networking: A Guide to the IBM Environment*
0-07-051506-9	Ranade/Sackett	*Introduction to SNA Networking, 2/e*
0-07-054991-6	Saunders	*The McGraw-Hill High-Speed LANs Handbook*
0-07-057639-4	Simonds	*Network Security: Data and Voice Communications*
0-07-060363-4	Spohn	*Data Network Design, 2/e*
0-07-069416-8	Summers	*ISDN Implementor's Guide*
0-07-063263-4	Taylor	*The McGraw-Hill Internetworking Handbook*
0-07-063301-0	Taylor	*McGraw-Hill Internetworking Command Reference*
0-07-063639-7	Terplan	*Effective Management of Local Area Networks, 2/e*
0-07-065766-1	Udupa	*Network Management System Essentials*

To order or receive additional information on these or any other McGraw-Hill titles, please call 1-800-822-8158 in the United States. In other countries, contact your local McGraw-Hill representative.

KEY = WM16X

TCP/IP with Windows NT Illustrated

Teresa Bisaillon
Brad Werner

McGraw-Hill
New York San Francisco Washington, D.C. Auckland Bogotá
Caracas Lisbon London Madrid Mexico City Milan
Montreal New Delhi San Juan Singapore
Sydney Tokyo Toronto

Library of Congress Cataloging-in-Publication Data

Bisaillon, Teresa
TCP/IP with Windows NT illustrated / Teresa Bisaillon, Brad Werner.
p. cm.
Includes index.
ISBN 0-07-913648-6
1. TCP/IP (Computer network protocol) 2. Microsoft Windows NT.
I. Werner, Brad. II. Title.
TK5105.585.B53 1998
005.7'13769--dc21

97-41022
CIP

McGraw-Hill

A Division of The ***McGraw-Hill*** *Companies*

2 3 4 5 7 8 9 0 DOC/DOC 9 0 2 1 0 9 8

ISBN 0-07-913648-6

The sponsoring editor for this book was Steven Elliot. This book was set in Vendome ICG and ITC Eras by Werner Training and Consulting, Inc. using Adobe FrameMaker 5.1 on an Apple Power Macintosh.

Printed and bound by R. R. Donnelley & Sons Company.

Contents at a Glance

Part One — The Foundation

Chapter 1. TCP/IP Architecture 3
Chapter 2. IP Addressing and Datagram Transmission 53
Chapter 3. IP Subnetting 97
Chapter 4. Windows NT Networking — Under the Hood 137
Chapter 5. Installing and Configuring TCP/IP on NT 173

Part Two — The Details

Chapter 6. Examining Network Traffic Using Network Monitor ... 207
Chapter 7. NT Server as an IP Router 245
Chapter 8. Using Steelhead as a RIPv2 Router 293
Chapter 9. Remotely Accessing the Corporate Network 333
Chapter 10. Securely Accessing the Corporate Network Using PPTP 365
Chapter 11. Domain Name Resolution 405
Chapter 12. Internet Access Using Proxy Server 445
Chapter 13. Advanced DNS Configuration 493
Chapter 14. Securing Web Traffic using SSL and IIS 521
Chapter 15. DHCP 569
Chapter 16. NetBIOS Name Resolution 615
Chapter 17. Monitoring Using SNMP 657

Table of Contents

Preface .... **xix**

- What's it all about? xx
- Who's this book for? xxi
- Where do I start? xxiii
- Conventions xxiii
- Caveat xxiv

Chapter 1. TCP/IP Architecture **3**

- TCP/IP Layer Model 4
  - TCP/IP and the OSI Model 4
- Process Layer Protocols 5
- Host-to-Host Layer Protocols 9
  - Ports and Sockets 9
  - Transmission Control Protocol (TCP) 13
  - TCP Segments 14
  - TCP Segment Flags 16
  - TCP Segment Options 17
  - TCP Connection Setup (Three-Step Handshake) 18
  - Passing Process Layer Information over TCP 22
  - TCP Connection Termination (Four-Step Teardown) 24
  - User Datagram Protocol (UDP) 26
- Internet Layer Protocols 27
  - Internet Protocol (IP) 27
  - Internet Control Message Protocol (ICMP) 29
  - Address Resolution Protocol (ARP) 29
  - Other Internetwork Layer Protocols 29
- Network Interface Layer Protocols 30
  - IP Over Everything 30
  - Network Interface Example — Ethernet 31
  - Logical Link Control (LLC) Sublayer 35
  - 802.2 LLC Header Layout 36
  - 802.2 SNAP (SubNetwork Access Protocol) 36
  - Binding 39
- The Big Picture 40
  - TCP/IP Protocol Numbering Scheme 40
  - Data Encapsulation 44
- Politics of the Internet 46
  - Request for Comments (RFC) 46
  - Administration of the Internet 47
- High-Level Addressing 49
  - IP Addresses 49
- Summary 50

Further Reading 51

Chapter 2. IP Addressing and Datagram Transmission 53

Why Do We Have IP Addresses, and What Do We Use Them For? 54
- Common Numbering 54
- Labeling Each Interface 55
- Binding Addresses to an Interface 55
- Example of Bound Addresses 56
- Using Bound IP Addresses to Communicate 57
- Multiple Interfaces 58

Anatomy of an IP Address 58
- Writing Out IP Address Values 59
- Classes of Networks 60
- Network Identifiers 62
- IP Networks and Broadcast Addresses 64
- Multicast IP Addresses 65
- Non-routable Networks 66

Sending IP Datagrams 66
- Local vs. Remote Destinations 67
- Sending IP Datagrams to Local Destinations 68
- Sending IP Datagrams to Remote Destinations 69

Obtaining Hardware Addresses 72
- The ARP Cache 74
- An ARP Cache Example 75
- ARP Cache Registry Values 76
- Broadcast Packets 77
- Using ARP in a Routed Network 78

IP Header Fields 79
- IP Version Number 81
- IP Header Length 81
- Precedence 82
- Type of Service 83
- Total IP Length 83
- Datagram Identifier 84
- Fragmentation Fields 84
- Time to Live 85
- Protocol 85
- Checksum 86
- Source IP Address 87
- Target IP Address 87

Transmitting "Big" Datagrams 87
- Fragmentation 88
- Reassembly 89

Internet Control Message Protocol (ICMP) 90
- Destination Unreachable Exception 91
- Time Exceeded Exception 92
- Diagnostic Echo Service 93

Summary 93

Further Reading 94

Chapter 3. IP Subnetting 97

How Big Can a Network Be? 98
- Subnets and Routing 99

Subnetting Basics 100
- Address Space 101
- Five–Step Procedure for Subnetting 102

Subnetting Example 103
- Step 1: Plan Logical Network Divisions 103
- Step 2: Divide Network Address Space into Subnets 105
- Step 3: Partition Locally Administered Field 108
- Step 4: Assign IP Addresses to Each Interface 109
- Step 5: Convince IP to Use the Subnet Field 112
- Example Conclusion 114

Subnet Details 115
- Interpreting the Subnet Mask 116
- Default Subnet Mask 117
- Another Subnet Example 118

Calculating the Number of Subnets and Hosts 119
- Class C Subnetting Table 119
- Class B Subnetting Table 120
- Class A Subnetting Table 121

Rules of Subnetting 122

Address Utilization 123
- Lost Addresses 125
- Maximum Number of Addresses 126
- Effective Number of Addresses 126
- Class C Subnetting Example 127

Calculating Subnetted IP Addresses 128
- Step-by-Step Address Calculation 129
- Applying the Procedure for the Whole Network 131
- Comparing Subnet Fields 132

Summary 134

Further Reading 134

Chapter 4. Windows NT Networking — Under the Hood 137

NT Networking Overview 138

Application Layer 141
- User Interface 141

Service Layer 142
- Application Interface 142
- Windows Sockets Library 144
- Remote Procedure Call (RPC) 150
- NetBIOS Library 152
- Server Message Block (SMB) 154
- Named Pipe Library 156

Mail Slot Library ... 157
Windows 32-bit Networking (WNet) ... 157
General Input/Output Method ... 159
Emulation Layer ... 160
Kernel Interface ... 160
Windows Sockets Emulator ... 161
NetBIOS Emulator ... 161
Server Service ... 161
I/O Services ... 162
Redirector ... 162
Transport Layer ... 163
Transport Driver Interface (TDI) ... 164
Transmission Control Protocol (TCP) ... 166
User Datagram Protocol (UDP) ... 166
NetBIOS over TCP/IP (NBT) ... 167
Raw IP Interface ... 167
NetBEUI Frame (NBF) ... 168
NetWare Link (NWLink) ... 168
NetBIOS over IPX (NBNWLink) ... 168
Network Interface Layer ... 169
Network Device Interface Specification (NDIS) ... 169
Summary ... 170
Further Reading ... 171

Chapter 5. Installing and Configuring TCP/IP on NT ... 173

Installation Overview ... 174
Installing TCP/IP ... 174
Configuring TCP/IP ... 174
Testing TCP/IP ... 176
Example Network ... 176
Installing TCP/IP ... 177
Network Control Panel ... 177
TCP/IP Installation ... 178
Configuring TCP/IP ... 180
TCP/IP Configuration Dialog ... 180
IP Address Configuration ... 181
Multiple IP Addresses per NIC ... 183
Multiple Gateways ... 183
PPTP Filtering ... 184
TCP/IP Security Configuration ... 184
DNS Tab ... 187
WINS Address Tab ... 188
DHCP Relay Tab ... 189
Routing Tab ... 190
Testing the Installation ... 190
Wntipcfg ... 192
Ping ... 193
Where TCP/IP Parameters are Stored in NT ... 195

Traversing the Registry Tree ... 197
Adding Registry Parameters using Regedit.exe ... 199
Summary ... 202
Further Reading ... 203

Chapter 6. Examining Network Traffic Using Network Monitor ... 207

Microsoft Network Monitor ... 208
Statistics Dialog ... 209
Example Capture: Ping Packets ... 210
Network Monitor Packet Decode ... 212
ARP Request Packet ... 213
ARP Reply Packet ... 215
ICMP Echo Request Packet ... 216
Address Database ... 218
Loading the Address Database ... 220
Configuring Passwords and Assigning Network Card Descriptions ... 221
Filtering Packets that Are Displayed ... 223
Filtering by Address ... 225
Filtering by Protocol Type ... 226
Filtering by Protocol Property ... 227
Filtering Packets During Capture ... 228
Filtering on SAP/ETYPE During Capture ... 230
Filtering on Addresses During Capture ... 231
Filtering on Pattern Matches During Capture ... 231
Loading Capture Filters ... 232
Selecting the Network to Monitor ... 233
Selecting the NIC to Monitor ... 234
Monitoring a Dialup Connection ... 235
Monitoring a Remote Network ... 236
TCPIP.INI Configuration File ... 239
Why Monitor? ... 241
Using Network Monitor Throughout This Book ... 242
Summary ... 242
Further Reading ... 243

Chapter 7. NT Server as an IP Router ... 245

Why Do We Route? ... 246
Communication Between Hosts on Different Networks ... 246
Communication Between Hosts on Different Subnets ... 247
Simple IP Routing Example ... 248
Broadcast Datagrams ... 249
Routing Process ... 250
Updating Routing Tables using Routing Protocols ... 251
Enabling IP Routing ... 253
Static IP Routing ... 253
Manipulating the Routing Table Using the Route Command ... 254
Example Network with Static Routes ... 255

Interpreting the Routing Table 256
Routing Tables for Multihomed Machines 258
Routing Tables with Static Routes Added 259
Persistent Routes 261
Review of IP Communication 262
RIP Operation 264
What Do the Routers Know Initially? 265
First RIP Message 267
Router B Updates Routing Table 268
Another RIP Exchange 268
Routers A and C Update Tables 270
Yet Another Routing Exchange 270
Router B Updates Its Table (Again) 271
What Do RIP Version 1 Messages Look Like? 273
Does RIP Always Advertise All Known Routes? 275
How Does RIP Construct a Route from an Advertisement? 276
Installing RIP Version 1 277
RIP Registry Entries 278
RIP Version 1 Packet Captures 279
RIP Message from ENG_RTR onto Backbone 281
RIP Message from SALES_RTR onto Backbone 282
RIP Message from ENG_RTR onto Subnet 10.1.3.0 283
RIP Message from SALES_RTR onto Subnet 10.1.4.0 284
Testing Routes 284
Tracert Operation 286
Summary 290
Further Reading 291

Chapter 8. Using Steelhead as a RIPv2 Router 293

Why Was It Called "Steelhead"? 294
Hardware Routing 294
Kernel Routing Table 296
IP Routing Protocols Supported by RRAS 299
RIPv2 Improvements Upon RIPv1 299
RIPv2 Operation 300
What Do RIPv2 Messages Look Like? 300
How Does RIPv2 Construct a Route From an Advertisement? 303
Installing RRAS 305
RRAS Manager 307
Installing and Configuring RIPv2 307
Installing RIP 308
Configuring RIP 309
RIPv2 Security Configuration 310
Routing Domains 311
Interface Configuration 313
Interface Properties 314
RIP Interface: General Tab 314
RIP Interface: Security Tab 317

RIP Interface: Neighbors Tab 318
RIP Interface: Advanced Tab 321
Starting the Router 323
RIP Version 2 Packet Captures 325
RIPv2 Message from ENG_RTR onto Subnet 10.1.3.0 326
RIPv2 Message from SALES_RTR onto Subnet 10.1.4.0 327
RIPv2 Message from ENG_RTR onto Backbone 328
RIPv2 Message from SALES_RTR onto Backbone 329
Summary 329
Further Reading 330

Chapter 9. Remotely Accessing the Corporate Network 333

Options for Remotely Accessing the Corporate Network 334
Private Direct-Dial Access to a Corporate Network 335
Connecting a Single Machine to the Corporate Network Using the Internet 336
Connecting a Remote Office to the Corporate Network Using the Internet 337
PPP Operation 338
PPP Framing 339
Multiprotocol Data Link 340
PPP Link Phases 341
Phase 1 — PPP Link Establishment 342
Phase 2 — Authentication 343
Phase 3 — Network Layer Protocol Link Establishment 345
Private Direct-Dial Access to a Corporate Network 348
Who is the RAS Server and Who is the RAS Client? 349
Potential Security Problems with Remote Access 350
Overview of Installation Steps for NT 4.0 RAS 350
Client Step 1: Install and Configure RAS Service 351
Client Step 2: Create Phonebook Entry for Corporate RAS Server 353
Server Step 1: Install and Configure RAS Service 355
Server Step 2: Allow Users Dialin Access 359
Server Step 3: Configure RAS Service to Start Automatically 360
Testing the RAS Client and Server 361
Summary 362
Further Reading 362

Chapter 10. Securely Accessing the Corporate Network Using PPTP 365

Tunneling and VPNs 366
What is a PPTP Tunnel Made of? 368
How Does PPTP Make the Tunnel? 372
Details of Tunneling with GRE 377
Connecting a Single Machine to the Corporate Network Using the Internet 380
Overview of PPTP Installation and Configuration Steps (NT 4.0) 381
Client Step 1: Install PPTP protocol 382
Client Step 2: Configure the RAS VPN Device 383
Client Step 3: Create a Phonebook Entry for the PPTP Server 386
Server Step 1: Install PPTP 389

Server Step 2: Configure a RAS VPN Device 390
Testing the PPTP Connection 393
Connecting a Remote Office to the Corporate Network Using the Internet 394
Install Steelhead (RRAS) on Both Servers 395
Using RRAS Admin to Check the Connection 396
Kernel Routing Tables 397
Routes Prior to Dialup Connection 398
Routes After Dialup Connection 398
Routes After Tunnel Creation 401
Summary 402
Further Reading 403

Chapter 11. Domain Name Resolution 405

The Host File 406
Domain Name System (DNS) 408
Order of Name Resolution Methods 409
Domain Names 410
The Domain Name Tree 411
DNS in the Internet 412
Packet Captures of DNS Queries 416
Example Name Query/Name Reply Packets 417
Configuring a Client to Use DNS 419
Installing Microsoft DNS Service 420
DNS Manager 421
Basic DNS Configuration 422
DNS Record Types 426
Adding Domains 427
Adding Hosts 428
Reverse Lookup: in-addr.arpa Domain 429
Adding Hosts Revisited — with PTR Records 432
Testing the DNS Server Using Nslookup 435
Debug Option to Nslookup 438
DNS Domain and Searchlist 439
Summary 443
Further Reading 444

Chapter 12. Internet Access Using Proxy Server 445

Hypertext Transfer Protocol (HTTP) 446
HTTP Messages 447
Parsing an HTTP Request 447
HTTP Packet Exchange 448
Internet Access Options 450
Using NT Server 4.0 to Access the Internet 450
Using Steelhead Router to Access the Internet 451
Using Proxy Server to Access the Internet 452
Current Network Diagram 453
How Proxy Servers Work 454

Firewalls 455
Filtering Router as a Firewall 455
Proxy Server as a Firewall 458
Example of Proxy Operation 460
Types of Proxies 461
Proxy Side Effects 462
Hybrid Firewalls 463
Mapping Clients to Servers 464
Non-transparent Client Configuration 466
Proxy Server 2.0 Services 467
Web Proxy 468
WinSock Proxy 470
SOCKS Proxy 471
Client Configuration 472
Web Proxy Clients 472
SOCKS Proxy Clients 474
WinSock Proxy Clients 474
Comparison of Web/SOCKS/WinSock Proxy Protocols 476
Understanding Proxy through Packet Traces 478
Automatic Configuration Using a Startup Script 479
What Does Web Proxy Really Look Like? 482
How Are Non-Web Clients (e.g. Telnet) Proxied? 486
Summary 491
Further Reading 492

Chapter 13. Advanced DNS Configuration 493

Forwarding DNS Queries to Other DNS Servers 495
Review of Name Resolution 496
Forwarding Queries 499
Sending Queries to the Root Servers 501
Forwarding Resolution Requests to WINS Servers 503
Zone Transfers 503
Configuration of a Secondary DNS Server 504
Zone Transfer Process 506
Notify Lists and Restricting Zone Transfers 507
Zone Transfer Packet Captures 508
Configuring Zone Transfer and Cache Timers 509
Configuring Multihomed DNS Servers 511
Configuring DNS to Load From the Boot File 512
Cache-Only DNS 515
Configuring a Caching DNS for Use by Proxy Server 518
Summary 520
Further Reading 520

Chapter 14. Securing Web Traffic using SSL and IIS 521

Cryptography Concepts 522
Hashes 524

Message Digest Types 526
Checking Message Integrity 528
Is Your Cryptography Symmetric? 529
Symmetric Key Cryptography (a.k.a Secret Key Cryptography) 529
Public Key Cryptography 530
Authenticating a Message 533
Hybrid Key Cryptography 534
Digital Certificates 536
Identifying Users and Resources 538
Secure Sockets Layer (SSL) Operation 540
SSL Handshake 541
SSL Packet Trace 543
IIS Management 544
Configuring IIS 4.0 Using the Microsoft Management Console 545
IIS Security Checks 546
IIS Anonymous User 547
NT Challenge Response 548
Local User Authentication 548
User Authentication using a Remote SAM Database 549
Controlling IIS Access by User or Group 551
Configuring IIS to Use Multiple IP Addresses 553
Steps to Enable SSL on IIS 559
Step 1: Creating a New Key and Certificate Request 560
Step 2: Send the Request to a Certificate Authority 562
Step 3: Install Certificate Using Key Manager 562
Step 4: Select the Directories Which Will Use SSL 565
Testing SSL Access 566
Summary 567
Further Reading 568

Chapter 15. DHCP 569

Methods of IP Address Assignment 570
Reverse Address Resolution Protocol (RARP) 571
Bootstrap Protocol (BootP) 571
Dynamic Host Configuration Protocol (DHCP) 572
Configuring Clients to Use DHCP 573
Confirming the Dynamic Assignment: ipconfig /all 574
Testing Tool: ipconfig /release and /renew 575
DHCP Scopes and Options 576
Installing and Managing DHCP Server 577
DHCP Scope Properties 578
Viewing Active DHCP Leases 581
Client Reservation in DHCP 583
Assigning DHCP Options 584
Selecting Options to Configure 585
Assigning Values to Options 587
Adding a New DHCP Option Type 588
DHCP Logging 589

IP Address Conflict Detection ... 590
DHCP Database Record States ... 592
How Records are Released ... 592
After Lease Release ... 593
Obtaining a Lease ... 594
Four-Step Initial Leasing Process ... 594
Example Lease Scenario ... 595
DHCP Discover ... 596
DHCP Offer ... 597
DHCP Request ... 599
DHCP Acknowledgment ... 600
Extending Lease Time ... 601
DHCP Reboot Sequence ... 602
Using DHCP in Routed Networks ... 603
DHCP Relay Agent ... 603
Configuring DHCP Relay Agent Using Steelhead ... 605
Relay Agent Operation ... 605
Backing Up and Restoring the DHCP Database ... 610
Backing up the DHCP Servers ... 611
Summary ... 612
Further Reading ... 613

Chapter 16. NetBIOS Name Resolution ... 615

Why We Need NetBIOS Name Resolution ... 616
How Long Will NetBIOS Be Used? ... 617
Browsing ... 618
Current Network Diagram for Foobar.com ... 619
NetBIOS Over TCP/IP (NetBT) ... 620
Microsoft NetBIOS Names ... 621
Methods of Resolution ... 623
The LMHOSTS File ... 624
Windows Internet Name Service (WINS) Operation ... 625
Packet Decode of Name Queries ... 626
Broadcast Query Packets ... 628
NetBIOS Name Cache ... 630
Using the Hosts File to Resolve NetBIOS Name Queries ... 632
Using DNS to Resolve NetBIOS Name Queries ... 632
NetBT Node Types ... 632
The Complete Search List ... 634
Client Configuration ... 634
WINS Proxy ... 637
WINS Manager ... 639
Understanding the WINS Database ... 640
How is the WINS Database Populated? ... 640
NetBIOS Name Registration ... 641
Name Registration Packet Decode ... 643
Viewing the WINS Database ... 644
Viewing the WINS Database with Client Records ... 646

WINS Database Records ... 647
WINS Name Renewal ... 648
WINS Name Release ... 649
Backing up and Restoring the WINS Database ... 651
DNS and WINS Integration ... 652
Forwarding Requests from DNS to WINS Servers ... 653
Summary ... 655
Further Reading ... 656

Chapter 17. Monitoring Using SNMP ... 657

Network Management Concepts ... 658
Management Areas ... 658
Managing Networks with SNMP ... 660
SNMP Operations ... 661
SNMP Simplicity ... 663
SNMP Managed Information ... 664
Structure of Management Information ... 666
Loading MIBs ... 667
How to Select Information — Object Identifiers (OIDs) ... 669
Object Class and Instance ... 670
Simplifying Class and Instance for SNMP ... 673
Get Next ... 675
How the Tree Was Built ... 677
Grafting onto the Tree ... 679
Installing the SNMP Agent on NT ... 681
SNMP Agent Properties ... 684
SNMP Communities ... 685
SNMP Trap Configuration ... 686
SNMP Security ... 687
SNMP Utilities and Files ... 689
SNMP MIB Files ... 689
SNMP Utilities ... 690
SNMP Utility (snmputil.exe) ... 690
Summary ... 692
Further Reading ... 693
Network Diagram ... 710
Contents of the Companion CD ... 711
Where to Begin ... 711
RFCs ... 711
Packet Captures ... 711

Preface

Welcome to the wonderful world of networking.

intranet sockets Windows NT UNIX World-Wide Web Internet TCP/IP RFC RPC OSI Ethernet PPP

Are you swimming in a sea of buzzwords, acronyms, and technomumbo-jumbo? Stop now! Read this book. Slay the dragons of the deep sea of internetworking.

What's it all about?

TCP/IP is the common name for the protocols of the Internet. These protocols are also used in many corporate networks, households, factories and labs. They have their roots in a government network which was developed in the late 1960s, and got their current names around 1980. They support many services such as video conferencing, electronic mail, audio and video webcasts, and interactive collaboration of people around the globe — just to name a few. This family of computer and information networking protocols has been "intruding" into television and telephone markets and has spawned new markets such as the world-wide web. Traditionally, these protocols were supported on minicomputers and mainframes, often as a part of the UNIX operating system. For roughly eight years, these protocols have been available on desktop and minicomputer servers running Macintosh and Windows operating systems as well.

Windows NT 4.0 is an operating system from Microsoft which runs on desktop and server computers. It is much more advanced than previous versions of Windows, and sports features from a rich heritage of VMS, UNIX, MacOS, and earlier Windows operating systems.

TCP/IP with Windows NT Illustrated covers administration, management, and features of the Internet protocol suite (TCP/IP) as it is implemented in Microsoft Windows NT 4.0.

There is a wealth of information in this book on internetworking your Windows NT systems with UNIX, MacOS, Windows 95 and other systems. The network packets themselves are analyzed using Microsoft's Network Analyzer such that you will understand the workings of Microsoft TCP/I.P in depth.

Who's this book for?

This book is primarily targeted at system administrators, network administrators, and systems engineers. This book is a user's guide for networking with Windows NT for those with a technical background.

The level of expertise required to read this book is intermediate, in that general knowledge of data communications is required to read this book.

However, this book contains many illustrations of the operations of networks. Explanations are given in easy-to-understand terms. There aren't many mathematical formulas in this book — that would make for dry reading.

Installing the TCP/IP software on NT is the *simple* part of the process — it is the configuring and the troubleshooting that is the complicated part. The person managing the network needs to have a design in order to use TCP/IP. This book gives detailed information as to the workings of TCP/IP applications on NT, such that the network administrator can effectively design and manage a TCP/IP network.

An analogy...

> Say you were put in charge of designing a roller-coaster for a new amusement park. You would have to have a design of how to assemble all the pieces, and would have to know many details in order to ensure that it would work properly — the strength of the steel, the speed of the cars, the maximum number of people that it would carry, etc. Once you have the design, the structure would have to be built, but if you have a good design, that process should be simple. After it is built, you are put in charge of monitoring it daily for proper operation: making sure the motors don't get overheated, the beams don't become warped, and too many teenagers don't jump in one car. If any of these problems occur, you need to act immediately to fix the problem, or a major disaster could occur.
>
> The design and implementation of a computer network is similar. A good design is needed, as well as methods to monitor the network. If you have a poor design, or if you do not regularly monitor the system, things WILL fall apart.
>
> So if network administrators want to tame the wild roller-coaster ride of managing a TCP/IP network, they need to buy this book. ;-)

Networking isn't typically considered to be a trivial topic. However, that doesn't mean that it has to be explained in complex terms. Sure, we could speak in tongues and mathematical equations and make it look like it's really complex. That kind of thing may be appropriate for some audiences. But perhaps you picked up this book without wanting to have a translator, a calculus book and physics book handy to help you read it. We've tried to explain the topics covered in this book in straight-forward terms and use lots of illustrations and analogies.

If you have any suggestions on ways we could improve the explanations, please let us know so we can improve it. You can email us with comments at **book@wernerconsulting.com**.

Where do I start?

If you are new to networking with TCP/IP, we suggest you start with **Part 1: The Foundation**. Those 5 chapters are meant as a good foundation for the remainder of the book.

If you've used TCP/IP for a bit, and understand IP addressing and subnetting, we suggest you skip ahead to **Part 2: The Details**. These chapters are an in-depth analysis of the many networking features of NT.

Note for programmers: you may find especially interesting chapter 4: Windows NT Networking— Under the Hood. It talks about the various APIs available in NT, as well as how all the pieces fit together.

Conventions

The following typographical conventions are used throughout this book:

Alerts

Some paragraphs will be of particular importance thus will be marked with the alert! symbol. There may be words added beneath the symbol for at-a-glance indication of the type of message.

CD

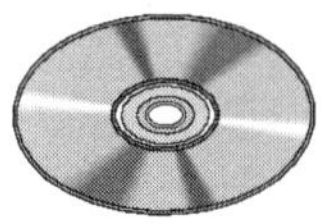
somefile.cap

Throughout the book, there are Network Monitor packet captures which are described in the text. Most of these captures have been saved onto the compact disc (CD) that comes with the book. These will be noted in the text, and indicated with the CD-ROM icon, as shown on the left. The name of the capture file is given beneath the CD icon.

Command

Identifies commands and command parameters.

Domain names

Domain names and file names are shown in this typeface.

definition: terms are sometimes defined in the side margin.

Definition

New terms and phrases are shown in this style, and definitions are sometimes placed in the side margin, as shown on the left.

italic

Italic is used for screen, menu and button names, as well as to highlight certain phrases.

Caveat

This information is intended to be correct. It is not intended to be a rendering of engineering services. Use this book as a guide. Neither the authors nor the publisher are responsible for any error, omission, or assumed liability based on the information contained in this book.

All trademarks, copyrights, slogans, and logos are the property of their respective holders. No material was used intentionally without reference.

The enclosed Compact Disc isn't intended to say anything bizarre if played backward. If you find anything, let us know. ;-)

Part One

The Foundation

1 TCP/IP Architecture

This chapter provides an overview of the TCP/IP architecture. The layers of the TCP/IP architecture are described and the interrelationships are shown. Administration and standardization of TCP/IP and the Internet are discussed.

TCP/IP Layer Model

The name *TCP/IP* is used to refer to a family of communications protocols. As with most modern networking protocols, TCP/IP may be described as a stack of layered functions.

The TCP/IP stack can be broken down into four layers:

- Process Layer
- Host-to-Host Layer
- Internet Layer
- Network Interface Layer

TCP/IP and the OSI Model

The functionality in each of these four layers of the TCP/IP stack corresponds to one or more layers in the **Open Systems Interconnect (OSI)**[1] stack as shown in Figure 1.1. Notice however that the correlation is not always on a dividing line: for example, the TCP/IP host-to-host layer has similar functionality as the OSI layer 5 (Session) and part of the OSI layer 4 (Transport).

1. The Open Systems Interconnect (OSI) is a suite of standards and recommendations developed by the International Organization for Standardization (ISO) and International Telecommunications Union (ITU). The OSI Basic Reference Model (BRM) specifies a division of the functions for data communications into a seven layer model. Other communications architectures, such as TCP/IP, are often compared with the OSI BRM.

Figure 1.1
The four layers of the TCP/IP stack don't correspond directly to the seven layers of the OSI model.

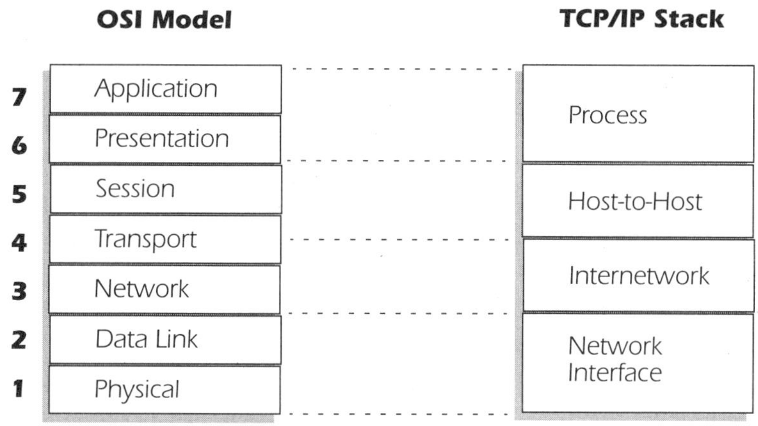

Each one of the TCP/IP layers contains one or more protocols, which we'll examine now. The names shown above are the standard names, but we'll often refer to some of the layers by other names. For instance, the process layer is often called the application layer, and the host-to-host layer is often called the transport layer. Let's look at these layers from the top down.

Process Layer Protocols

At the top of the TCP/IP stack are several protocols which provide communications services. Each of these protocols provides presentation and application layer functions. There can be hundreds or even thousands of different application layer protocols running over TCP/IP.

process: context for execution of an instance of a software application.

What we sometimes call the TCP/IP application layer is actually called the process layer. This is because the applications which implement communications protocols are implemented as **processes** under operating systems such as UNIX, where much of the TCP/IP evolution has occurred. Windows NT has threads and tasks rather than processes for different execution contexts.

So what do these protocols do? A few of the most common process layer protocols running over TCP/IP are shown in Figure 1.2.

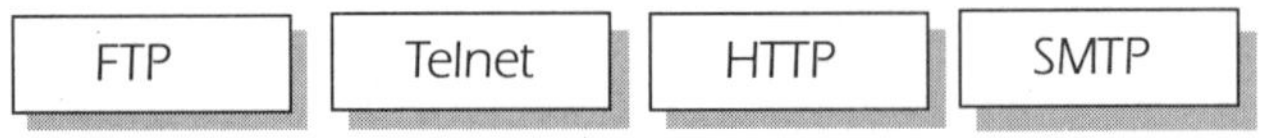

Figure 1.2
Some of the most common process layer protocols.

- The *File Transfer Protocol (FTP)* supports the transfer of files between computers. The client application allows the user to store and retrieve files from a potentially remote server computer.

server: a process offering access to information

- *Telnet*[2] allows for remote login sessions between computers. As telnet supports a text-oriented mode of communications, the user interface usually presents a command prompt style of interaction— you type commands and are presented with responses.

client: a process which uses access methods to work with information provided by a server.

- The *HyperText Transfer Protocol (HTTP)* exchanges hypertext documents to support the World Wide Web. Rather than accessing a number of files with FTP and having to know how they work together and having to run Telnet to interact with a remote computer, HTTP fuses the two concepts together. More importantly, the methods for interacting with a remote computer are standardized so that universal graphical interfaces can more easily be built on top of the transfer protocol.

- The *Simple Mail Transfer Protocol (SMTP)* exchanges electronic mail messages between computers. This is a specialized form of file transfer used for sending messages to an electronic post office (or mail exchange) and between electronic post offices.

client application: the piece of software which implements the client role in communications.

These protocols are used by applications to transmit data from point to point. There are often two roles for each protocol. One side of the connection will be the **client application**, the other side will be the **server application** as shown in Figure 1.3. The **client** and **server** negotiate how they will communicate. For example, Telnet negotiations between the client and server will select terminal emulation type among other things.

2. NT itself does not contain a telnet server application. In order to allow users to telnet into an NT box, you must obtain third-party telnet server software.

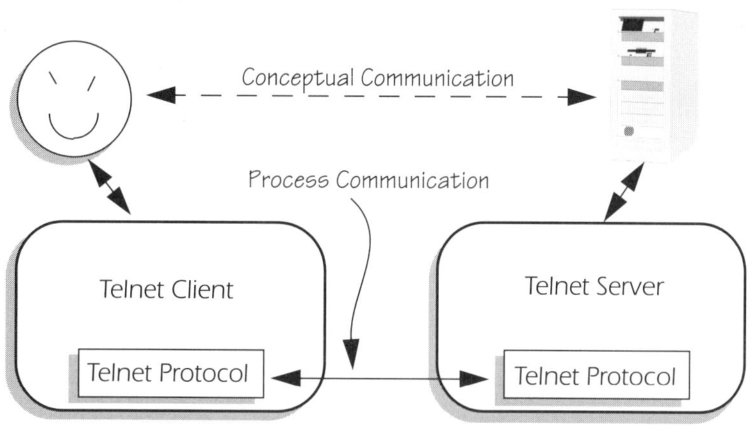

Figure 1.3 Client-Server relationship for Telnet.

server application: the piece of software which implements the server role in communications.

Telnet provides emulation of a teletype connection to a host computer via the network. The name "telnet" is short for TELetype over the NETwork. We run client application software which implements the Telnet protocol. Another piece of software implements the Telnet server to allow our client to connect into the host computer.

There is more to the Telnet service than the protocol itself. Several messages are defined in the protocol to handle negotiation of how the virtual teletype terminal presented to the client user should operate. Then the protocol takes on the role of passing the user data between the client and server.

Both the Telnet client and server applications may render the view of the terminal in a vendor-specific manner. Some Telnet clients simply pass the text to be displayed to the current text flow that the application runs in. In windowed environments, Telnet clients often provide a window which serves as the text backdrop with a terminal emulator.

The other process layer protocols shown in Figure 1.2 constitute some applications which implement the appropriate services. There may be different roles played on the client side versus the server side.

Some applications use more than one process layer protocol. For example, most web browsers implement several process layer protocols so that you may access information using whichever one is appropriate, as shown in Figure 1.4. A single application may use multiple protocols, and they may in fact be used simultaneously. Furthermore, any one protocol could be used in multiple connections simultaneously[3], and these connections could be to one server or to many servers.

Figure 1.4 Multiple client protocols can be used by a web browser.

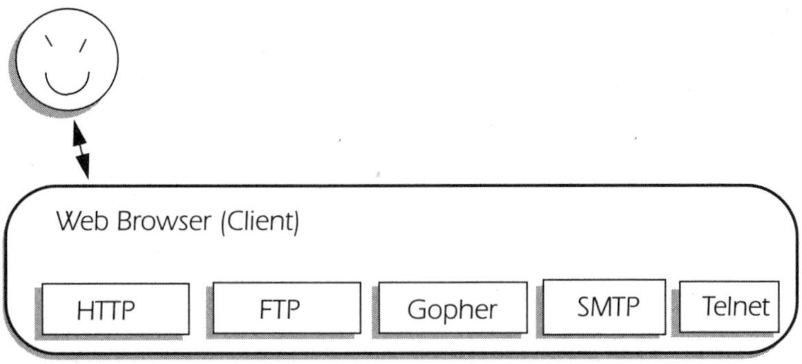

Let's take a look at some other process layer protocols which often work behind the scenes. These protocols are shown in Figure 1.5.

Figure 1.5 Some additional process layer protocols.

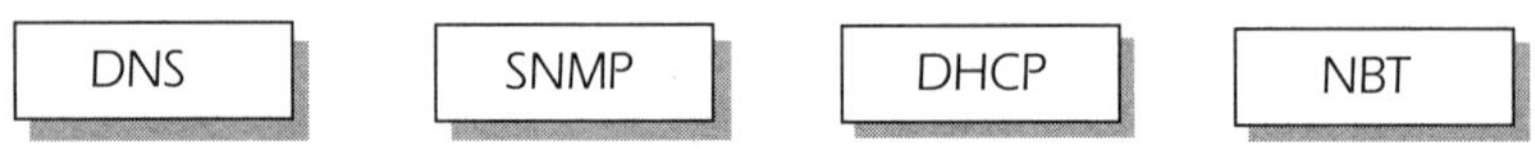

- The *Domain Name System (DNS)* translates hierarchical domain names (e.g. mcgraw-hill.com) to IP addresses. This is commonly used by applications so that the users and applications can deal with names rather than numbers.
- The *Dynamic Host Configuration Protocol (DHCP)* supplies configuration information for hosts, such as IP address assignment. DHCP is typically used upon boot as well as at periodic intervals thereafter.
- The *Simple Network Management Protocol (SNMP)* can be used to remotely administer network devices running TCP/IP. SNMP is often implemented in management stations which allow you to centralize many control and monitoring functions in your network.
- *NetBIOS over TCP/IP (NBT)* is the protocol used by NT that allows the NetBIOS interface to send datagrams using UDP and IP.

---

3. Simultaneity of multiple protocols may depend on operating system features such as multiprocessing, multitasking, or multithreading. The degree to which this is done and whether the protocols work together is an implementation issue.

Implementations of some of these protocols are often embedded within applications which we use directly. Others are implemented in services which are not directly tied to one application. In some cases, the use of the protocol is so integral to the operation of the computer that we often don't think of it as a separate piece of software.

We've seen some short descriptions for the application layer protocols in the last few diagrams. Remember that these are just a few examples, and that there are many more protocols at this layer. There are dozens of standard process layer protocols which run over TCP/IP, and hundreds if not thousands of proprietary process layer protocols for TCP/IP networks.

Host-to-Host Layer Protocols

A machine can have multiple users, and each user could have multiple simultaneous TCP/IP connections. Just how does TCP/IP keep all of these conversations straight? The conversations are kept separate using host-to-host layer protocols. The host-to-host layer of the TCP/IP stack is sometimes called the transport layer, although it isn't strictly equivalent to the OSI model's transport layer.

Ports and Sockets

port: a communication endpoint within a given machine.

The transport[4] layer protocols provide services which allow multiple communications endpoints to exist on a machine[5]. Each of these endpoints is called a **port**.

4. With TCP/IP networking, the transport layer is also known as the "host-to-host" layer because there once were devices called Interface Message Processors (IMPs) which talked to host computers at this layer. The transport layers were the lowest layer actually running on the host, thus it was the lowest layer of host-to-host communication.

5. More specifically, there may be many ports per network interface. We'll see shortly that a given machine may also have more than one network interface.

port number: the identifier used to refer to a given port relative to a network interface.

Let's consider an analogy. Assume that a network address is like a street address. In the world of networking, a message destined for a particular end station on a network gets there by using that station's network address. In the "real" world, you can get to a certain building by using a street address. Once you've gotten to a certain building, you may also have a suite number or office number to further direct you. You can get to a certain room in the building by going through a particular door or window. Another name for a door or window is a portal, or port. So back in the networking world, once you (the message) have arrived at a certain end station, you (the message) get to a certain endpoint by going through a particular port. Note that an host-to-host port is similar to a physical port on a minicomputer or mainframe, just logical.

socket address: the combination of a port number and an IP address.

To get to a certain room in a certain building, you would need to combine the street address with an indication of which door to go in (e.g. suite number). Similarly, the combination of a TCP/IP network address (called simply an IP address) and a **port number** is called a **socket address**[6].

socket: a communication endpoint within a network.

A **socket** is simply a conceptual place that you plug into the network (Figure 1.6). A socket is the pairing of a network interface and a port. Keep in mind that it's a *logical*, not a physical, port. Sockets are used by both servers and clients alike.

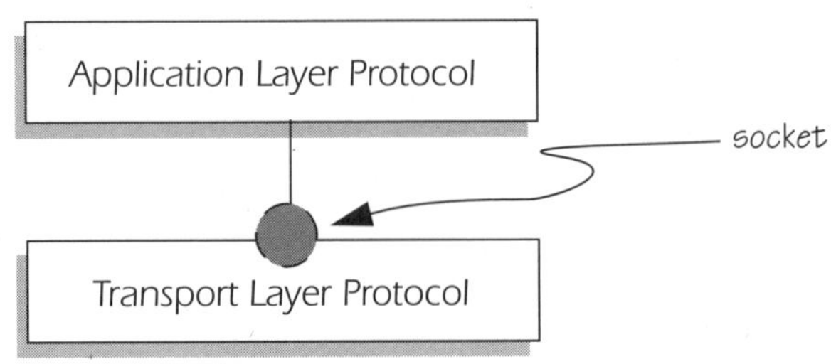

Figure 1.6 An application protocol plugs into the transport layer using a communications socket.

You can have many sockets on a given end station. Each of these sockets may be used by an application layer protocol. Having many ports (thus sockets) per machine allows many services and/or many users to simultaneously communicate through a machine.

6. Socket addresses actually come in many flavors, but for the TCP/IP or UDP/IP family of sockets being discussed here, the address is a port number and IP address.

well-known port: a port with a published or standardized number for access to a specific service.

The host-to-host layer protocols support a range of port numbers[7], from 0 to 65535, as shown in Figure 1.7. Part of the range is allocated for use by well-known services such as Telnet, FTP, and SMTP. Port numbers 0-1023 are allocated as **well-known ports** (a.k.a. *named* ports). Ports 1024-65535 may be **registered** to other services. If one of these "high-numbered" ports has not been reserved on a given machine, it is available to be **randomly assigned** to a process requesting a port which is not well-known.

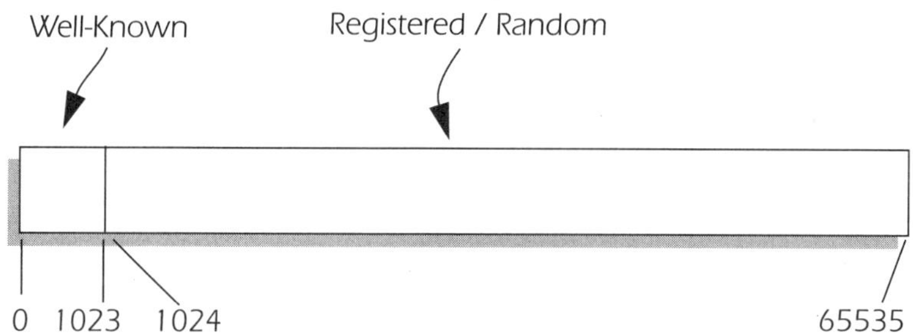

Figure 1.7 Port numbers range from 0-65535. Certain ranges of numbers are assigned for well-known services or applications.

registered ports: ports assigned to particular applications on particular machines.

In general, well-known ports are used by servers and random ports are used by clients. Notable exceptions to this rule include RIP messages, DHCP and BOOTP transactions. Because random ports are typically used for a short time by transient applications, they are often called ephemeral ports.

Communications schemes that use sockets were designed to support several address families. One of these address families is the Internet family of sockets.

random port: ports which use neither a well-known or registered port number may have a number randomly assigned by the operating system.

The sockets design is a standard application programming interface (API) for accessing network facilities. The first implementation of the sockets API[8] can be found in the U. C. Berkeley versions of UNIX. This implementation has been ported to other operating systems and embedded systems which use TCP/IP. Other versions of UNIX also (or alternately) support other transport layer interfaces. A comparable transport layer interface was defined by the POSIX standardization effort. It is called the Transport Layer Interface (TLI). Windows NT interfaces are discussed in the Windows NT Networking chapter.

---

7. Ports are numbered in a way similar to the data link layer Link Service Access Points (LSAPs). Actually, in the OSI model access to the transport layer is done via Transport Service Access Points (TSAPs). These are similar to sockets.
8. Versions of UNIX such as 4.2 BSD and 2.9.1 BSD supported TCP/IP with sockets in the early 1980s.

Each transport layer protocol may support communications for several applications simultaneously, as shown in Figure 1.8. Each application uses a socket address derived from an IP address and a port number.

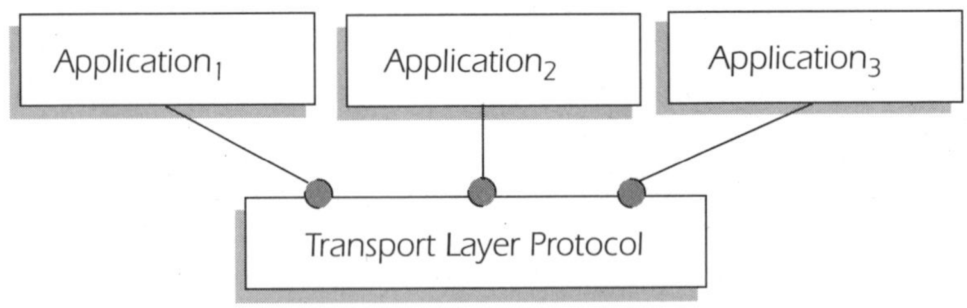

Figure 1.8 Many applications plug into a transport layer protocol.

You probably have some idea about where the different doors in certain kinds of buildings would lead. In a house, the front door may lead into a living room or foyer, whereas the back door may lead into the kitchen. In a manufacturing plant, the front door probably leads to a reception area and the back door (or dock) may land you in shipping and receiving. Where do the different ports in the transport layer lead you? The ports which get you to the most commonly used applications are called well-known ports. But just as the front door in different types of buildings (e.g. house vs. factory) may lead you to different kinds of rooms, the port number, when associated with either TCP or UDP, may lead you to a different application. TCP and UDP have separate port address spaces.

The two common transport protocols in the TCP/IP family are the Transmission Control Protocol (TCP) and the User Datagram Protocol (UDP) (Figure 1.9). The Internet protocol stack is typically called TCP/IP which implies TCP encapsulated by IP. This doesn't mean that if a machine supports TCP/IP that it doesn't support UDP — it's simply easier to write TCP/IP than [applications]/{TCP,UDP}/IP/[network access layers]!

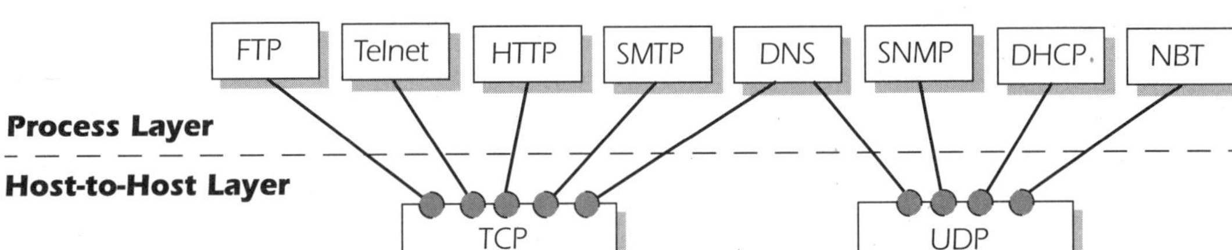

Figure 1.9 TCP and UDP transport protocols support many applications.

An application is typically designed to use either TCP or UDP. Some applications (such as DNS) have the option of using either TCP or UDP at run-time. As we saw with the web browser example in Figure 1.4 on page 8, an application could be using several process layer protocols at once.

TCP and UDP provide very different services. TCP is the more complex of the two. We'll look at TCP first, after which UDP will seem quite simple in comparison.

Transmission Control Protocol (TCP)

TCP provides a connection-oriented transmission of streams of data. The classic analogy used for TCP's style of connection orientation is to a traditional person-to-person voice phone call.

- People usually answer ("initialize") the phone call with an exchange of hellos.
- With some types of conversation, one person may talk a lot more than the other.
- You can be silent for a long time, but the connection is still there.
- When both parties are finished talking, they say goodbye and hang up.

There are of course many differences between TCP and traditional voice service, but the basics are the same.

When an application chooses to communicate using TCP's services, TCP establishes a connection between the source and the destination process. These processes may be running on the same machine, or on different machines. Once the connection is established, the application may transfer data over the connection. TCP connections are bidirectional. The TCP software on each side of the connection maintains information about the connection until the communicating processes (or an unrecoverable error) terminate the connection.

Along with its connection orientation, TCP also provides reliable service. TCP keeps track of the data that is sent, sends acknowledgments for the data, and retransmits data if necessary. This is analogous to people asking each other to repeat what they hadn't clearly heard on the phone. TCP provides this kind of service transparently to the process layer protocols.

Note that TCP cannot be used for multicast or broadcast types of applications due to the single process to process (i.e. point-to-point) nature of the connection. An application process would have to relay the information itself over independent connections. Many servers support several simultaneous connections with different clients. A given user may also run more than one client connection to the same server if necessary.

TCP Segments

segment: the transmission unit for TCP.

Each message which TCP sends is called a **segment**. A segment consists of a TCP header and possibly some process layer information.

As shown in Figure 1.10, there are nine standard TCP header fields and four[9] reserved bits. This standard header may be extended with options. The standard TCP header takes up twenty octets, while a fully loaded TCP header (with the maximum space for options) would be sixty octets in length. The data from the process layer protocol follows the header.

Figure 1.10 Standard TCP header layout — five 32-bit words.

bits 0-3	bits 4-7	bits 8-11	bits 12-15	bits 16-19	bits 20-23	bits 24-27	bits 28-31
Source Port				Target Port			
Segment Sequence Number							
Acknowledgment Number							
THL	Resv.	Flags		Window Size			
Checksum				Urgent Data Size			

TCP deals with the segment headers in 32-bit "chunks," or 32-bit words. Therefore, the standard 20 octet header takes up five 32-bit words. The TCP Header Length (THL) field is a four-bit field which is used to specify the number of 32-bit words which are in the header. The THL value must be at least five because the first five words are standard. THL values

9. There are six reserved bits if you count the two reserved flag bits.

six through fifteen specify that following the first five standard words, there may be between one and eleven extra words in the header for use by TCP options.

The TCP header fields are described as follows:

- The *Source Port* specifies a logical end-point on the system transmitting the segment. Recall that the source port number is part of the source socket address.
- The *Target Port* specifies a logical end-point on the system intended to receive the segment. Recall that the target port number is part of the target socket address.
- A *Segment Sequence Number* is actually an octet offset within the source data stream.
- An *Acknowledgment Number* is also an octet offset, but within the target's data stream rather than the source data stream.
- As mentioned earlier, the *TCP Header Length* specifies the length of the header, indicating if there are options or not. There are four reserved bits after the THL (and then two more reserved flags, making a total of six reserved bits).
- A group of six *Flags* specifies a number of special indications with respect to this connection. These are described in the next section.
- The *Window Size* indicates how many octets may be received by the sender for purposes of flow control. In other words, this is the amount of available receive buffer space for this connection on the host machine sending this segment.
- A *Checksum* is computed over the segment header and the process layer protocol data carried in the segment and this value is transmitted in the segment header. The receiver will compute the checksum and compare to this field to confirm that the segment has been received unaltered.
- The *Urgent Data Size* specifies an offset in octets from the segment sequence number where non-urgent data begins. In other words, if this value is non-zero then the sender is transmitting in urgent data mode — all of the urgent data is not necessarily transmitted in this segment.

Urgent data may be sent by an application using TCP to signal that special processing of this information is desired. Because the transmission of urgent data on a TCP connection shares the same sequence number space as "non-urgent" data, the connection is said to be in urgent data mode when transferring this data. Thus normal data may not be passed simultaneously, therefore the urgent data mode is not an out of band mode, but only a way of marking special (i.e. urgent) data.

TCP Segment Flags

Each TCP segment header has a flags field which contains six one bit indicator flags. Figure 1.11 shows the layout of these flags, with bit numbers within the fourth TCP segment header word.

Figure 1.11
TCP Segment Flags.

bit 8	bit 9	bit 10	bit 11	bit 12	bit 13	bit 14	bit 15
reserved		URG	ACK	PSH	RST	SYN	FIN

Each of these flags is described as follows. The notation *set* without a specific value implies a flag value of one, whereas the notation *clear* without a specific value implies a value of zero.

- An *urgent mode indicator* (URG) specifies that the urgent data size field contains a valid offset which may be added to the segment sequence number to yield the *urgent data pointer*. The urgent data size field is to be ignored if the URG flag is zero.
- The *valid acknowledgment indicator* (ACK) specifies that the acknowledgment number is to be used by the receiver.
- The delivery of the data in a segment may be pushed to the upper-layer protocol at the receiver with some priority if the *push indicator* (PSH) flag is set to one. This flag is set by the sending TCP software when the sending application requests a push. In this case, the sending TCP forces all pending outbound data to be flushed through toward the receiver. Otherwise, TCP normally waits some amount of time for a buffer to fill before sending for greater efficiency.

- It may be necessary to reset a connection without using the normal tear-down procedure. The *reset indication* (RST) informs the receiver that the sender is giving up on the connection. This also can be used to indicate that no process is listening to the requested port during connection setup.
- During the setup of any TCP connection (as we'll describe shortly) a receiver must synchronize its understanding of the segment sequence numbers which are to be sent to it. The *sequence number synchronization indication* (SYN) is set when the value in the sequence number field is to be used as an *initial sequence number.*
- When the process at either side of the connection is done sending data, it may specify the final segment in which data is sent. The *final data indication* (FIN) flag must be set in such a segment.

These flags are *not* mutually exclusive, thus more than one flag bit may be set in a given segment. Segments with a certain flag are sometimes called by the name of the flag, for instance a segment with the SYN flag set is often called a SYN segment, and one with FIN set is called a FIN segment.

TCP Segment Options

At certain times during a connection there may be a need to pass options at the end of the segment header. This is normally the case for the first segment in each direction during connection establishment.

The TCP header length (THL) field may specify a value greater than five when a header longer than the standard form (e.g. Table 1.10) is necessary to carry options. THL values of 6 to 15 (hex F) signify that up to eleven options words are present at the end of the segment header.

There may be more than one option in the options area. Each option[10] consists of the following pieces:

- The *option code* specifies which kind of option is present.

10. As we'll see shortly, the "end of list" and "no operation" options don't have a length or value field, but are wholly specified in one octet.

- The *option length* indicates the number of octets in the option, including the option code and length itself.
- Finally, the *option value* takes zero or more octets, as specified by the option length minus two.

Options are processed until the space for options is exhausted. The option length is specified explicitly in the segment so that if a receiver does not know how to process an option, it may skip past it. A sender may pad the options area with null options to round the options up to an even 32-bit size.

- The *End of List (EOL)* option has a code of zero (0). There is no length or value portion, thus the EOL takes only one octet. It may be used to pad the options area and to end the processing of the list.
- The *No Operation (NOP)* option has a code of one (1). Like EOL, the NOP is only one octet with no length or value. It may be used in the middle of an option list to align subsequent options to an even 32-bit alignment.
- The *Maximum Segment Size (MSS)* option has a code of two (2). This option may be specified on a SYN segment. The value for MSS specifies the greatest number of octets which may be received in a single segment on this connection. If no MSS option is present on the SYN segment, the receiver of the SYN may assume a default MSS of 536 octets.

Some other options you may encounter on various systems are the window size shift, timestamp, options relating to selective acknowledgment. However, these are beyond the scope of this book.

TCP Connection Setup (Three-Step Handshake)

Before a pair of processes may pass any process layer information across a connection, they must request that TCP set up the connection.

The connection setup procedure involves three segments being exchanged — it is called a 3-step handshake. Once the connection is established, data can be transmitted back and forth over the TCP connection. When there is no further data to send, the connection is torn down using a 4-step (4 segment) teardown sequence.

Why do we do a handshake to set up a connection? Imagine this:

You go into a certain room in your house and open up the blinds. This way you can hear if anyone comes up and taps on your window.

Your friends down the street want to talk with you. If they lived next door to you, they'd throw rocks at your window, but that's a different protocol. Because they live too far away to throw rocks, they send a carrier pigeon with a little note attached to his leg. [Step 1] It's a kinder, gentler protocol. There are some interesting things about how this message is sent.

- The window which your friend sent the pigeon out of was on the upper floor of his house, in a room picked at random, that wasn't being used for pigeon transfer.
- The note tied to the pigeon is blue, and written on the note is some big number that your friend picked at random (732), but he also wrote it down so that he remembers it.
- Your friend leaves the window wide open so that the pigeon can get back in.

Figure 1.12 Carrier pigeon tapping at the window. Notice the message attached to its leg.

The carrier pigeon (tcp) taps at your window (Figure 1.12). You look at the pigeon and notice a blue note attached to its leg. You're not too busy doing other things, so you open the window and take a look at the note (and feed the pigeon). Why is the note blue? The color of the note is a little flag which let's you know that your friend wants to start a conversation. You note that random number on the note — that's the number that your friend wants to start using to identify each message he sends to you. That's really all your friend wanted to say (so far) — to indicate that he wants to have a conversation. You note this number (732) that he has asked you to synchronize to. You treat this indication as though it is one little piece of information. So you prepare a response with an indication that you're acknowledging that the next thing you expect from him will be a message starting at number 733 (you write this in green). You also pick a number (let's say **9764**, which you write in blue) that you'll start counting at for information which you send back. You attach this response to the pigeon's leg and send it on its way. [Step 2] You leave your window open all the way so the pigeon can get back in.

The trusty carrier pigeon flies right in your friend's window (because it's wide open) and delivers the message. You friend takes a look. Hmm, it's got a number written in blue: **9764** — he notes that that's the number you picked to start counting information which you send to him. He also sees that you've acknowledged (in green) that the next thing you expect from him will start with a sequence number 733. Good. That means he doesn't have to start all over again. He wants to make sure that you know he got this, so he sends back a message acknowledging that the next thing he expects from you will start with the number **9765**. He sends this (written in green of course) back to you, care of the friendly pigeon. [Step 3]

This process is summarized in Figure 1.13 which shows the exchange of these three messages.

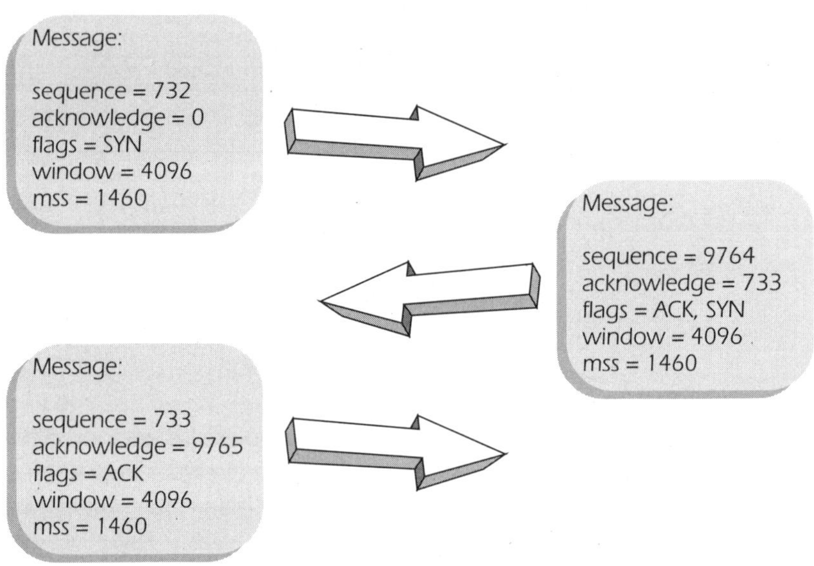

Figure 1.13
This is the flow of the messages in the three-way handshake between your friend and you via carrier pigeon.

Now the two of you can start communicating back and forth, actually sending information if you want, but we'll get to that later. First, let's get back to the details of TCP.

What information is exchanged in this three-step TCP connection set-up handshake? Before the first step occurs, a process must listen at a particular socket address.

1. Then the first segment is sent from the process initiating (or actively opening) the connection to the socket address of the listening process. This segment has the SYN flag bit set and an initial sequence number in the Segment Sequence Number field. This is sometimes referred to as the original SYN because it is used to start a connection. The amount of memory available for receiving information on this connection is placed in the Window Size field. An option is added to specify the Maximum Segment Size (MSS) which may be received.
2. Next, the recipient acknowledges this original SYN by responding with its own SYN segment. This segment is sent back from the responding machine to the originating machine at the originating port. Both the ACK and SYN flag bits are set. The acknowledgment number is set to one greater than the original SYN's sequence number. The segment sequence number is set to a random number which the responding side selects.
3. Finally, the originator acknowledges the responding SYN by sending back a segment with the ACK flag set. SYN is not set again because the two sides are now synchronized. The acknowledgment number is set to one greater than the segment sequence number from the responding SYN. The segment sequence number is set to one greater than the original SYN's segment sequence number, so that it equals the acknowledged number in the responding SYN.

Once both sides are synchronized in this way, the connection is said to be established. Any process layer information which had been passed in the handshake segments would have been buffered by TCP. Now that the connection is established, that buffered information is passed up to the process layer. The process layer information sent in subsequent segments will be passed up the stack.

Figure 1.14 shows a summary of this three step handshake. This figure utilizes an illustration technique called *ladder diagramming*.

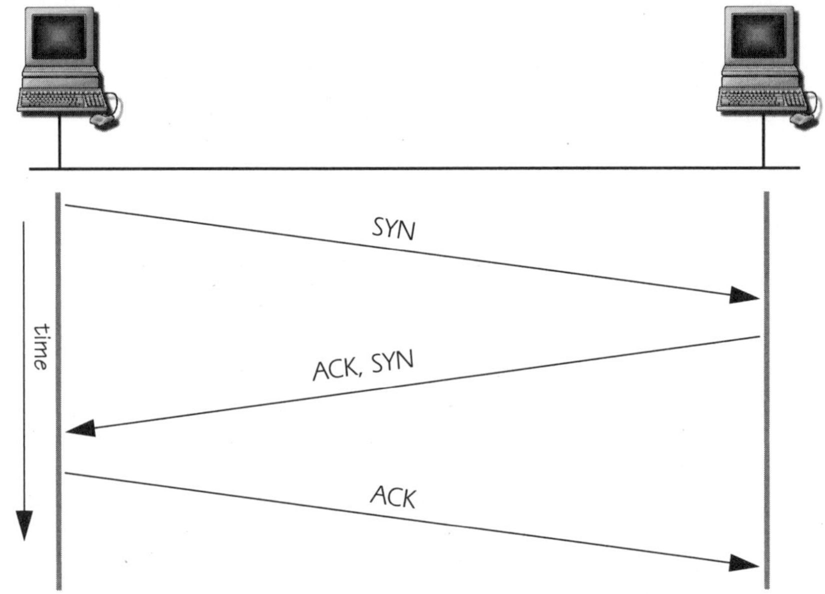

Figure 1.14
Summary of the TCP handshake shown as a ladder diagram.

In the ladder diagram, the timeline is from top to bottom. The messages sent between the network interfaces take some time to transmit, thus the arrows go down the page. The messages going back and forth between interfaces resemble the rungs of a ladder, with the interface lines as the rails.

Passing Process Layer Information over TCP

How do the sequence numbers work once the connection is established? Let's go back to the carrier pigeon example for a moment.[11]

How much information can be passed between you and your friend using the carrier pigeon method? All in all, a virtually unlimited amount. But not all at once. The carrier pigeon can only carry so much information at a time. Even if you were employing the services of an awesome carrier pigeon, your window is only so big, so only so much can fit in the window at a time. Let's take a look at these two factors in a little more detail.

11. Actually there is also a different story about carrier pigeons which has to do with IP. This is entirely unrelated. See [RFC1149].

maximum segment size: the largest payload that will be accepted in one TCP segment.

Assume that you measure the amount that the pigeon can carry by the length of a strip of paper that you roll up. Let's say that a given pigeon that you're using can carry a strip of paper which is up to 1460 mm (just under five feet) long. You know this because you've tested this pigeon before and know that if someone tries to send you a message which is longer, the pigeon gets too tired and will miss your window. This could cause inefficiencies in your network. So whenever you start a connection, in your SYN message you want to tell the other side not to send you a message longer than 1460 mm. This is the **maximum segment size (MSS)**. If you're using an average carrier pigeon which can carry a maximum segment size of 536 mm, then you don't have to explicitly state an MSS in your SYN segment (i.e. 536 is the default MSS). Both parties have to restrict the size of the segments they transmit to not be larger than what the other party has said they can receive.

Everything that the pigeon brings in your window it puts on the window sill. When you receive some information and haven't had time to read it yet, you shut your window (which opens/closes sideways) enough so that a later message won't run into what you've already received. When you get a chance to read the information, you open your window by the amount you've read. How does this affect what the pigeon can bring to you?

Let's say that you have a pretty big window — 4096 mm wide. Let's also assume that your MSS is 1460 mm. If you receive a segment which is of the maximum size, 1460 mm, you would close your window that much, leaving it open 2636 mm. Now let's say that you receive another segment which is also 1460 mm. You'd close your window again by that much, leaving it open 1176 mm. When you receive this information you'd be sending back acknowledgments. In each ACK segment, you note your current window size, which is how far your window is open.

Your peer also keeps track of how much it's filled up of the open width of your window that it last heard. So whether or not your peer has gotten an ACK from you indicating a window size of 1176 mm, it knows that size. The next segment he sends you will be at most 1176 mm long, and not up to 1460 mm because you wouldn't have enough room. Each side will send— at most— the minimum of the current window size and maximum segment size that it's heard the other side request.

maximum transmission unit:
the largest chunk of data that may be sent across a data link.

How does TCP differ in behavior from our pigeon network? To begin with, TCP sends information in octets rather than on paper measured in millimeters. Your receive window size is a memory buffer. The maximum segment size is derived from the **maximum transmission unit (MTU)** for the link you're receiving on. In some cases, the MSS may be based on a path MTU, which is the minimum MTU along the path of the connection. The MTU will be discussed in more detail in the section on Network Interface Layer Protocols.

TCP Connection Termination (Four-Step Teardown)

When you and your friend are done sending information back and forth, you can close down the connection. Just how is this done? With a four-step teardown process, of course! Examine Figure 1.15.

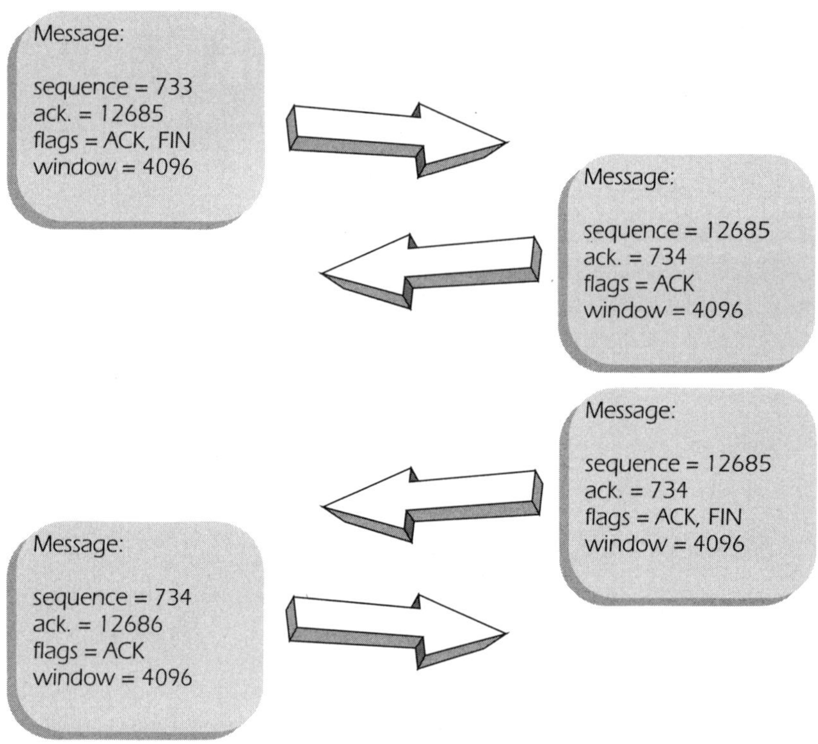

Figure 1.15
This is the flow of the messages in the four step teardown between your friend and you via carrier pigeon.

Whomever finishes talking first sends a FIN segment [Step 1]. This could be either party. We'll call this original FIN.

The other side acknowledges receipt of the original FIN. [Step 2] As with the SYN indication, the FIN counts as one virtual octet with respect to sequence numbers and acknowledgment numbers.

The side which responded to the FIN with an ACK could continue sending information as long as it needs to. The original FIN side will only send ACKs back, as it has declared that it is FINished sending process layer information. This condition is called a half-closed connection.

At some point, the side which responded to the FIN with an ACK will decide that it too is done sending information on this connection. It will send a FIN to the original FIN end. [Step 3] This is the responding FIN.

The original FIN side receives the responding FIN and sends back an ACK for the FIN (acknowledgment number one greater than the sequence number of the FIN) [Step 4].

The connection is now effectively closed. There is a short delay before the TCP software actually closes the connection.

A ladder diagram summarizing the four step teardown is shown in Figure 1.16

Figure 1.16 Summary of the TCP teardown shown as a ladder diagram.

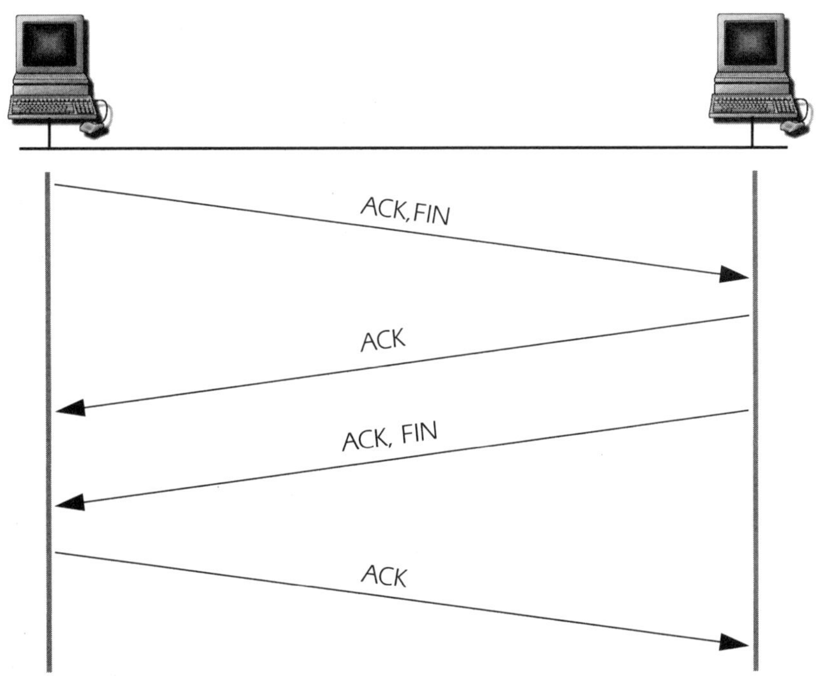

User Datagram Protocol (UDP)

In contrast to TCP's connection-oriented communication mode of operation, UDP provides connectionless transmission of data. Sending of data over UDP does not require a three segment startup, or a four segment teardown — data can be sent in the very first UDP packet.

However, UDP does not provide a reliable service since it does not send acknowledgments and does not retransmit data. It is the responsibility of the process layer protocol using UDP to decide if it important to track the data sent, and retransmit when necessary.

Each message passed by UDP is called a **datagram**.

datagram: the transmission unit for UDP.

Returning to the analogy of buildings and doors being like IP addresses and ports, let's look at what this means for UDP. Consider the following:

1. You go to a room with a window.
2. You write a message to someone.
3. You put the message in an envelope, with the address of the intended recipient and your return address.
4. You throw the envelope out the window.
5. You hope that the wind carries it to its destination.

Hmm, that's an interesting process. Why would you want to do something like this in real life? Because you don't have to call someone, hope that they're home and they answer the phone, then they say "hello", then you say "Hi this is me. I want to talk.", then they say "OK, let's talk.", then you say "OK", and then you can send your message. If it's a short message, it's really not worth all of the hassle. After all, having a phone is more expensive than having a window. Unless you live by a baseball field or golf course.

Let's step through the same process with the UDP protocol.

1. Ask UDP for a socket.
2. Write a message.
3. Determine where to send the message.
4. Pass the message to UDP.
5. You hope that the datagram reaches its destination.

So just what does UDP write on the envelope that your message goes in? Figure 1.17 shows the UDP header format.

bit 0-3	bit 4-7	bit 8-11	bit 12-15	bit 16-19	bit 20-23	bit 24-27	bit 28-31
Source Port				Target Port			
Length				Checksum			

Figure 1.17
UDP header layout.

It looks as though UDP is much simpler than TCP, just by looking at the differences in the TCP and UDP headers. UDP has only four fields in its header compared with TCP's nine. UDP does not support options, and does not perform segmentation.

UDP's four field header format simply fits in two 32-bit words. The first two fields are the same as for TCP — the source and target port numbers. The Internet Layer provides a datagram service which attempts to deliver datagrams to a target machine. This User Datagram Protocol simply uses the port numbers to extend the Internet Layer datagram service so that many services and users may use the same machine.

Internet Layer Protocols

The most notable protocol at the internet layer is the Internet Protocol (IP) itself. Two other protocols that work in conjunction with IP is the Internet Control Message Protocol (ICMP) and the Address Resolution Protocol (ARP).

Internet Protocol (IP)

IP provides a communications service for the transport protocols at the internetwork level (Figure 1.18). IP also carries other protocols, such as ICMP and OSPF, which help IP do its job. In other words, IP handles the routing of information from a source system, potentially through several intermediate networks, and finally to the destination end system. IP accepts information from a transport protocol at the source. The peer IP at the target passes the information up to the appropriate transport protocol. UDP and TCP ports can be compared with IP access points. Access points are used by IP to determine which transport or help protocol the datagram being processed belongs to.

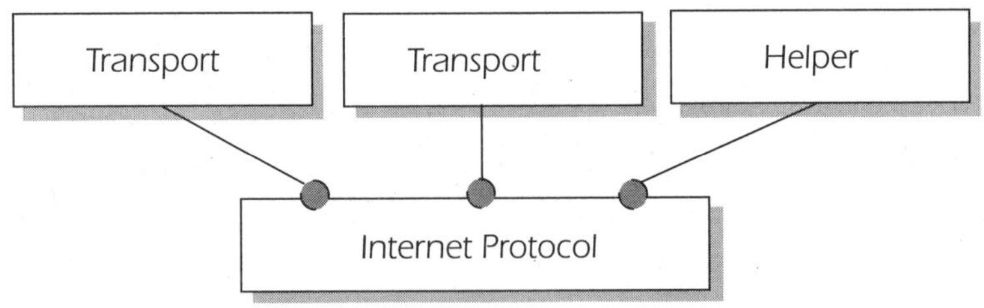

Figure 1.18 Several transport protocols run over the Internet Protocol (IP).

IP itself is a packet switching protocol. Packets are routed to the next "switch" using the destination IP address. IP fragments packets based upon the transmission media's MTU. IP also is responsible for obtaining hardware addresses for the associated IP addresses; IP uses the Address Resolution Protocol (ARP) to obtain this information. The way in which IP does routing is discussed in the IP routing chapter. Many of the aspects of how IP works will make sense after reading that chapter.

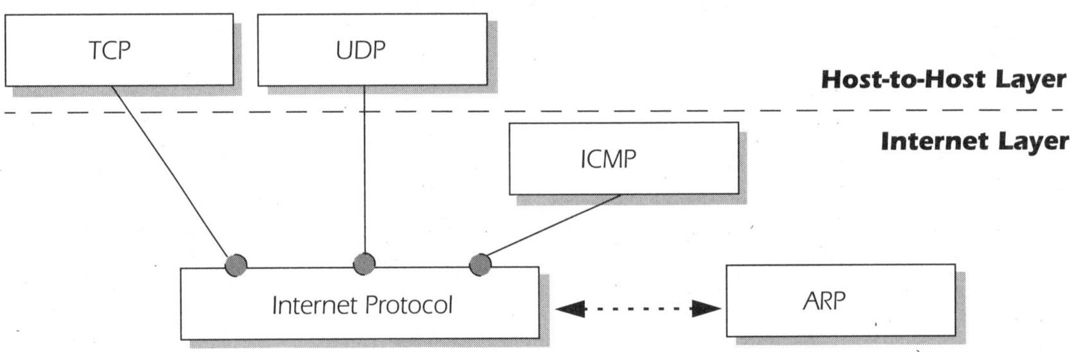

Figure 1.19 TCP and UDP run over the Internet Protocol (IP).

Figure 1.19 shows only a sampling of protocols which run over IP. Of particular interest are TCP and UDP because these host-to-host protocols are used most often. Also shown in the diagram are ICMP and ARP. Note that ICMP runs over IP in the same manner that TCP and UDP do, however because ICMP helps out IP so intimately, ICMP is considered a part of the Internet layer. The Address Resolution Protocol (ARP) runs in parallel to IP, but does not use IP to send information. Beside ICMP, some other protocols, such as OSPF and EGP, run over IP yet because they help IP (e.g. distribute routing information) and don't provide upper layer transport, they are also at the Internet layer.

Internet Control Message Protocol (ICMP)

The primary role of the Internet Control Message Protocol (ICMP) is to notify the sender of an IP datagram that there was an error in the delivery of that datagram — for example, the destination was unreachable. Several types of routing and delivery errors and are reported by ICMP messages. Also, course corrections (i.e. routing updates) are signalled by ICMP with its redirect messages.

ICMP is also used in network testing: for example, the echo request/echo reply ICMP message is used by the user command ***ping*** to test network connectivity. Timestamp request/reply messages may also be used by ping. ICMP and ping will be discussed further in the "IP Addressing and Datagram Transmission" chapter.

ICMP also provides flow control with its source quench message type.

Address Resolution Protocol (ARP)

The Address Resolution Protocol (ARP) is used by IP to resolve network addresses. In order for IP to encapsulate the IP packet in, for example, an Ethernet packet, IP needs to obtain the Ethernet hardware address of the target. ARP is used to obtain a hardware address from an IP address. The details are discussed in the "IP Addressing and Datagram Transmission" chapter (Chapter 2).

Other Internetwork Layer Protocols

There are several other protocols which may be used at the internetwork layer. Some of these, such as IGRP, OSPF, EGP, and BGP provide distribution of routing information. Others, such as IGMP and RSVP, provide services to IP for advanced features. These protocols run over IP, but like ICMP are considered a part of the Internet Layer rather than the host-to-host layer due to the function they perform.

Network Interface Layer Protocols

Everything below IP is considered a *network interface*. The Network Interface Layer presents the Internet Layer (and IP in particular) with one or more ways to interface to the network.

IP Over Everything

There are many physical and data link protocols that can be used to transmit IP. In fact, one of the goals of the designers of IP was to make IP very portable — the saying goes: "IP Over Everything."[12]

Figure 1.20 shows just a few of the most common network interfaces. The example machine has an Ethernet interface, an FDDI interface, an AAL5 over ATM interface, and a PPP over ISDN interface. Notice that IP runs over all of these interfaces. ARP runs over those interfaces which require address resolution.[13]

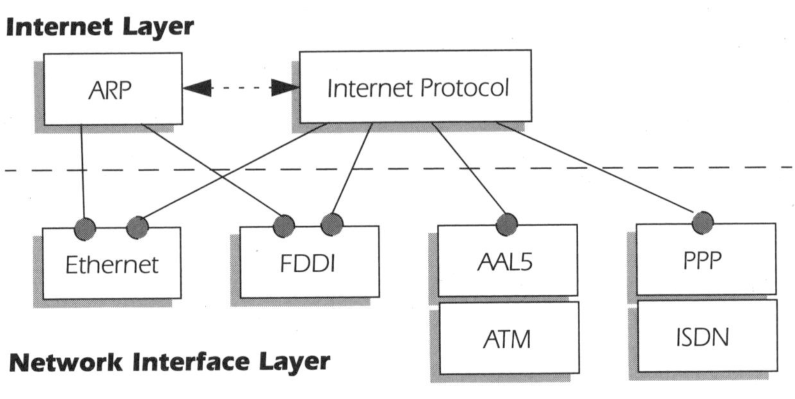

Figure 1.20
IP can transmitted using many different types of network interfaces, such as Ethernet, FDDI, AAL5, and PPP.

12. Huitema, Christian. IPv6: the New Internet Protocol.

13. RFC 1577 provides a means to run a kind of address resolution over ATM interfaces. Also not shown in Figure 1.20 are encapsulations such as SNAP, which are discussed later.

The Network Interface Layer is also called the Network Access Layer. Network Interface Layer protocols which may run under IP include, but are not limited to:

- DIX[14] Ethernet & 802.3 Ethernet, Fast Ethernet, and Gigabit Ethernet
- Token Ring, both 4Mbps and 16Mbps
- Fiber Distributed Data Interface (FDDI)
- Serial Line IP (SLIP)
- Point-to-Point Protocol (PPP)
- Frame Relay
- Asynchronous Transfer Mode (ATM)
- Switched Multimegabit Data Service

Note that the point-to-point protocol (PPP) may be used on top of just about any synchronous or asynchronous character-oriented media, such as phone line modems (V.32, V.34, et al), wireless modems, the Integrated Services Digital Network (ISDN), cable modems, and so on.

Network Interface Example — Ethernet

Each of the technologies at the data link layer which may be used as network interfaces have their own peculiarities. Rather than presenting an exposition of several of these, we'll use the most common technology used in local area networks (LANs) — Ethernet. The IEEE 802.3 (i.e. Ethernet) standard is a Medium Access Control (MAC) layer protocol.

The IEEE 802 view of the data link layer is a two sublayer model, as shown in Figure 1.21. The lower sublayer is the MAC sublayer. The upper sublayer is the logical link control (LLC) sublayer.

14. After Xerox had worked with Ethernet for while, they teamed up with Digital and Intel to form the Ethernet II standard. Ethernet II is often called DIX Ethernet as an abbreviation for the three organizations.

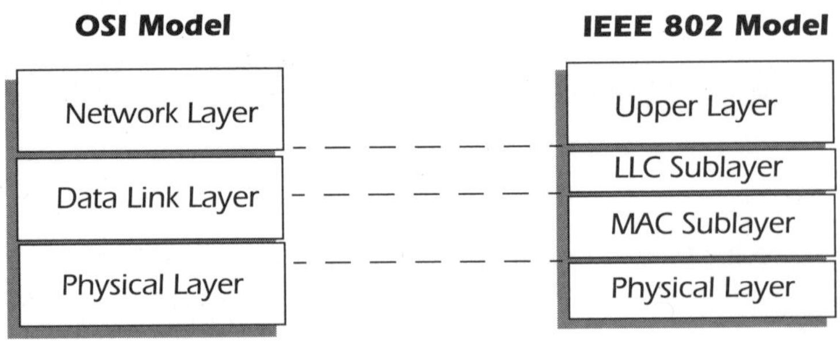

Figure 1.21 The data link layer maps to two sublayers — the MAC and LLC sublayers.

Ethernet uses a *contention-based* method of accessing transmission media which is based in part on systems such as ALOHA[15] and the telegraph[16]. The term *carrier sense multiple access* with *collision detection* (CSMA/CD) is used to describe access schemes such as Ethernet. Just what is CSMA/CD?

Imagine that you live in a neighborhood in which every house has a big hedge at the end of the driveway so that you can't see down the street. When you want to make a trip to the grocery store, you hop in your golf cart (it's a small neighborhood), go to the end of the driveway and listen. Why do you listen? Because the street that your driveway goes to isn't dedicated to you, but is a *multiple access* street, and there could be someone else driving down it, so you listen for other golf carts (*carrier sense*).

Assuming that you don't hear another golf cart nearby, you'll pull out into the street toward your destination. Normally you'd get to your destination, however sometimes you run into another golf cart that had pulled out at pretty near the same time as you had! You know this because your golf cart is smaller than it should be (*runt*), bigger than it should be (*giant*), or simply has an integrity problem (CRC error) — thus *collision detection*! Note that there is also an electrical form of collision detection.

In the event of such a collision, you go back to your garage and fix the cart, which takes you a different amount of time than your neighbor's repairs. You then try again. So this access method is pretty efficient for low-trafficked neighborhoods, however everyone in your neighborhood could spend more time repairing your carts than going places if there is a lot of demand for travel. That's CSMA/CD.

---

15. At the root of shared channel access schemes is discussion of the University of Hawaii's ALOHA network, yet there is more information in people's memories and in books than on the campus — refer to [Tannenbaum1989] §3.2 and §3.7.1 for an introduction.
16. Telegraph systems share many characteristics with Ethernet. For a review of telegraph systems see [Goralski1995] §1.1 which discusses The "Telegraph Transfer Mode" Network.

There are two standardized flavors of Ethernet: the original Ethernet specification created by Digital, Intel and Xerox (DIX Ethernet), and the IEEE specification of Ethernet, called 802.3 (which is commonly called 802.3 Ethernet). DIX Ethernet is also called Ethernet II because version 2 of the specification is used. The generic term for both is Ethernet. Both can be, and often are, transmitted across the same cable.

The difference between the two kinds of frames is found in octets 13 and 14 of the header. Octets 13 and 14 in DIX Ethernet (a.k.a. Ethernet II) specify a *protocol type* — a 16-bit (2 octet) number that identifies the upper layer protocol which the Ethernet frame is carrying. A list of these protocol types is found in RFC 1700, the Assigned Numbers RFC, where they are called *EtherType* values. Protocol type values are greater than 1500 (05dc hex).

In contrast, octets 13 and 14 of the 802.3 header represent the *length* of payload data found in the Ethernet frame. This field will have a value of 1500 (05dc hex) or less.

So octets 13 and 14 may be used to determine whether the frame is an Ethernet II or 802.3 frame. Values less than or equal to 05dc (hex) are used in 802.3 frames, and values greater than 05dc (hex) are used in Ethernet II frames. Just where does this differentiating value of 05dc (hex) come from? Figure 1.22 states that the maximum size payload allowed in Ethernet frames is 1500 octets (05dc hex). This characteristic is used to allow us to differentiate the two types based on two distinct ranges of numbers, the 802.3 data length and the Ethernet II EtherType.

Figure 1.22 The dividing line between 802.3 and Ethernet II frame types is based on the maximum size of an Ethernet payload.

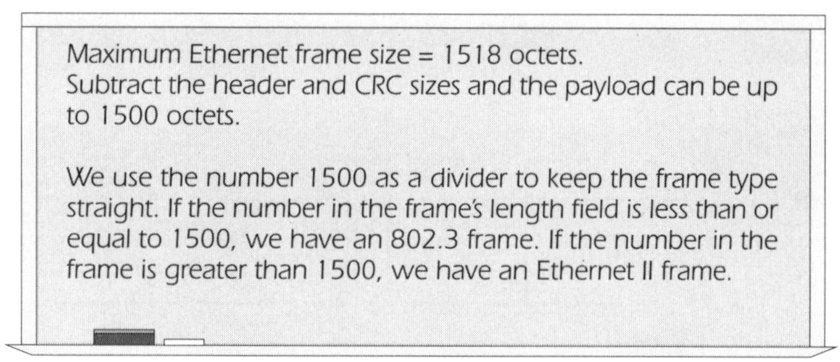

Some low numbers (less than 1500) had been used for EtherType codes prior to the standardization of 802.3; these have been reassigned to higher numbers in order to allow the two types of Ethernet framing to coexist on the same network segment. A few EtherType values are shown in Table 1.2 on page 38. The minimum payload size in Ethernet is 46 octets, thus counting in the header and CRC overhead, the minimum size for a frame is 64 octets.

Both types of Ethernet framing may be used over various types of cabling, and are specified with a 10 Mbps transfer rate. Newer versions of Ethernet such as 802.3u (fast Ethernet) and 802.3z (gigabit Ethernet) have different physical characteristics but use the same framing. The frame layouts shown in Figure 1.23 and Figure 1.24 only depict the part of the frame often seen in Ethernet driver software.

Figure 1.23 DIX Ethernet frame header layout.

6 octets	6 octets	2 octets	46-1500 octets	4 octets
Target Hardware Address	Source Hardware Address	Protocol Type	Payload Data	CRC

Figure 1.24 802.3 Ethernet frame header layout.

6 octets	6 octets	2 octets	46-1500 octets	4 octets
Target Hardware Address	Source Hardware Address	Data Length	802.2 header and Payload Data	CRC

Prior to the target address are 64 bits of *preamble*, shown as eight octets, yet you may see references which show that for 802.3 the first seven are called preamble followed by a one octet start frame delimiter (SFD). The remainder of the frame is as we have shown previously. Following each Ethernet frame is a required interval of silence which is called an *inter-frame gap* (IFG), which for the 10 Mbps versions of Ethernet is 9.6 μs or 96 bit times. We've shown the inter-frame gap in Figure 1.25 as though it was part of the frame so that we can account for the time in network utilization calculations.

Figure 1.25 Overall Ethernet frame layout.

8 octets	6 octets	6 octets	2 octets	46-1500 octets	4 octets	12 octets
Preamble	Target Hardware Address	Source Hardware Address	Data Length	802.2 header and Payload Data	CRC	Inter-Frame Gap

Logical Link Control (LLC) Sublayer

Along with the rest of the 802 LAN standards, the IEEE defined a standardized format for the link layer, called the 802.2 framing format. The 802.2 framing format is a common format used by 802.3 (Ethernet), 802.4 (Token Bus), 802.5 (Token Ring), and the standard forms for other media. The 802.2 LLC framing is contained within the MAC layer framing. Using the analogy of a painting with an physical frame, the 802.2 LLC framing is like a matte which shows between the frame and the painting, as shown in Figure 1.26.

Figure 1.26
Framing a message with matting.

LSAP:
the interface between network and data link layer protocols.

One of the functions of the LLC sublayer is to identify a number of **Link Service Access Points (LSAPs)**. An LSAP defines the interface between the upper side of the LLC sublayer, which happens to be the upper side of the data link layer, and the next higher layer, which is the network layer. Because there may be a number of LSAPs, there may be a number of network layer entities (i.e. different network layer protocols) on a computer.

Figure 1.27 shows an example of an LLC sublayer with three LSAPs. Thus, in this example, three distinct network layers or protocol families may be supported!

Figure 1.27
The LLC sublayer supports many link service access points (LSAPs), such as the three network layer entities.

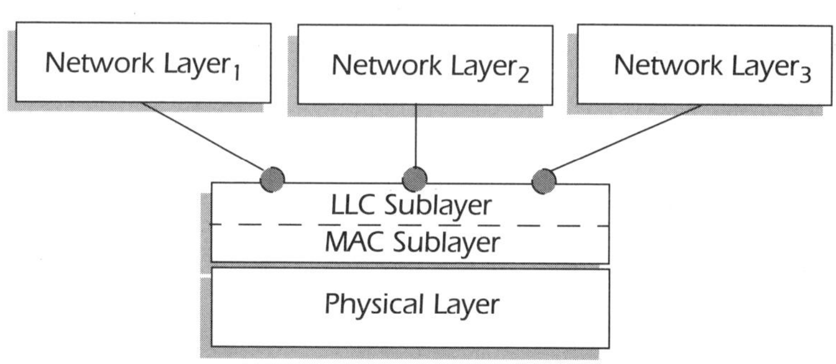

802.2 LLC Header Layout

Logical Link Control headers are composed of three fields (Figure 1.28). Each field is usually one octet. The first of these is the Destination Service Access Point (DSAP), followed by the Source Service Access Point (SSAP), and finally the control field.

Figure 1.28
Layout of 802.2 Logical Link Control header.

1 octet	1 octet	1-2 octets	0-n octets
Destination Service Access Point	Source Service Access Point	Control	Payload Data

The IEEE and various vendors have specified several Link Service Access Point (LSAP) values to correspond to different type of network platforms. These values are used for the DSAP and SSAP fields in 802.2 headers. Table 1.1 shows just a few of the values.

Table 1.1
Link Service Access Point (LSAP) values for 802.2 headers.

LSAP name	Binary	Hexadecimal
Null LSAP	00000000	00
IBM SNA	00000100	04
X.25	01111110	7E
SNAP	10101010	AA
Banyan VINES	10111100	BC
Novell NetWare	11100000	E0
IBM NetBIOS	11110000	F0
ISO Network Layer Protocol	11111110	FE

802.2 SNAP (SubNetwork Access Protocol)

SNAP: used to carry more detailed protocol type values than LSAP addresses.

During the development of LLC, an LSAP value was assigned for carrying the Internet Protocol (IP). This value is not used. Instead, for carrying the IP over 802 MACs such as 802.3 Ethernet, the 802.2 LLC is used and an LSAP called the **SubNetwork Access Protocol (SNAP)** is selected. Note that because DIX Ethernet already has a protocol type (EtherType) in its header, it does not use LLC or SNAP. The LSAP value for SNAP is AA (hex). Because IP is connectionless, all information is passed as unnumbered information (UI) frames, thus the LLC control field is set to a value of three. The LLC header fields are set to values of AA, AA, and 03 respectively.

SNAP headers follow the LLC header on 802.3 Ethernet. This is like using double-matting when framing a painting, as shown in Figure 1.29.

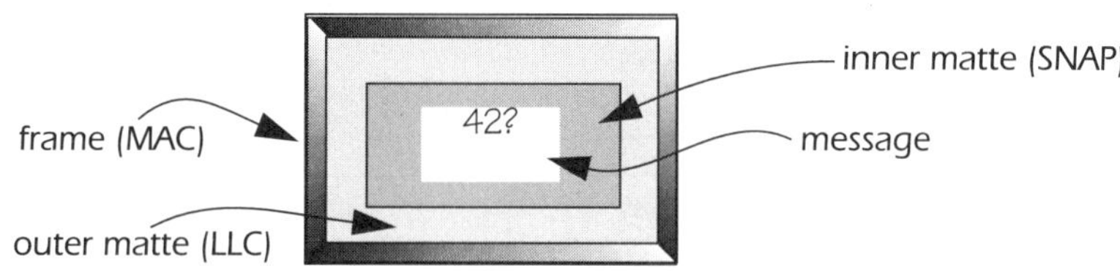

Figure 1.29 Framing a message with double matting.

The SNAP header is five octets long (Figure 1.30). It contains a three octet organization code (24 bits). The type field is the next two octets (16 bits), and identifies the next layer (network) protocol. Values for the type field are selected by the identified organization. The values for the organization code are in the format of IEEE Organizationally Unique Identifiers (OUI) and are also used as the first three octets of 802 MAC (e.g. Ethernet) unicast addresses.

Figure 1.30 Layout of SNAP header.

3 octets	2 octets
Organizationally Unique Identifier	Protocol for Payload

For carrying IP in SNAP, the OUI value of 000000 is used. This effectively specifies the IEEE. The values for the protocol type field in the SNAP header are the same as the values for the Ethernet II protocol type field. These protocol type values are referred to as EtherTypes. Some of the values are shown in Table 1.2.

Table 1.2
Some common EtherType values.

Decimal	Hexadecimal	Protocol Type
0-1500	0000-05DC	IEEE 802.3
1536	0600	Xerox XNS IDP
2048	0800	Internet IP
2053	0805	ITU-T X.25
2054	0806	Internet ARP
24579	6003	DEC DECnet
32821	8035	Internet RARP
32981	80D5	IBM SNA
32923	809B	Kinetics EtherTalk
33079-33080	8137-8138	Novell

So effectively, the SNAP header allows us to carry IP and other network protocols over all 802-style MACs (802.3, Token Ring, FDDI, etc.) as they would be carried over Ethernet II, as shown in Figure 1.31.

Figure 1.31
Layout of 802.3 Ethernet frame with 802.2 and SNAP headers.

6 octets	6 octets	2 octets	8 octets	38-1492 octets	4 octets
Target Hardware Address	Source Hardware Address	Data Length	802.2 & SNAP header	Payload Data	CRC

When comparing IP over Ethernet II vs. 802.3, note that it takes eight more octets to use a SNAP header to specify an EtherType than a raw EtherType with Ethernet II. Recall that one of the purposes of the 802.2 LLC is to provide support for multiple upper layer protocols, yet the LSAP addresses (DSAP, SSAP) are only eight bits. SNAP was created to provide the ability to support many more protocols as they are registered by many different authorities. The OUI specifies the registration authority for the protocol, and the remaining sixteen bits specify the protocol number, such as an EtherType.

Binding

binding: the pairing of an Internet layer protocol with a network interface device driver.

Each network interface may have one or more *bindings*, which are associations between the Internet Layer protocols and the Network Interface Layer protocols. In other words, a binding is a network interface layer service access point (SAP). (We don't usually use OSI terminology with the Internet protocols.) Functionally, a binding instructs its associated network interface layer protocol (e.g. DIX Ethernet) to take incoming frames which match certain criteria and pass them up to a specific Internet layer protocol (e.g. IP). The binding also works the other way, instructing an Internet layer protocol (e.g. IP) as to which datagrams should be sent over a particular network interface layer protocol (e.g. Ethernet).

There are several different implementation methods used for creating and describing bindings. One of these is the Network Device Interface Specification (NDIS). We'll see more information on NDIS in the chapter on Windows NT network specifics.

For more information about the interaction between IP and the network interface layer protocols, see the IP Addressing chapter (chapter 2).

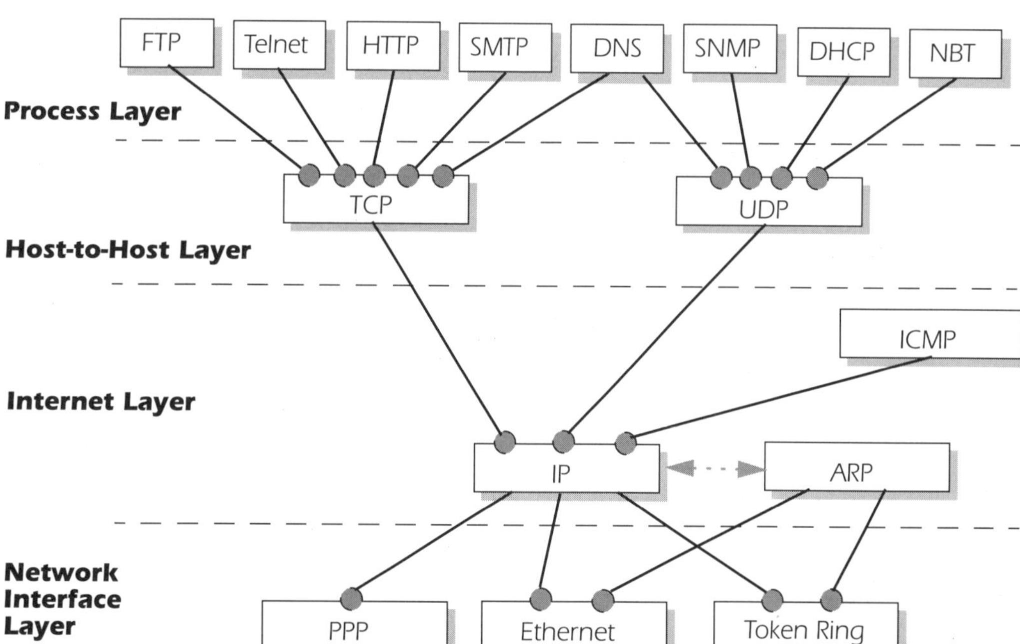

Figure 1.32 Combined diagram of process, host-to-host, internet, and network interface layer protocols.

Figure 1.32 shows a combined diagram of various TCP/IP protocols. You can see that the TCP/IP suite (Internet suite of protocols) is more than just two protocols. Note that these are just a few examples of the protocols running at each layer of the TCP/IP communications architecture.

The Big Picture

How does all of this fit together? We have four layers of protocols. We have specifications (RFCs) which give the details of how these protocols function and interact.

TCP/IP Protocol Numbering Scheme

Figure 1.32 shows the combination of the four layers of the TCP/IP protocol stack. Now let's look at a similar figure (Figure 1.33 on page 41) with some additional information. Shown in this figure is the "numbering scheme" of the TCP/IP protocol stack. The numbers are compiled in a clearinghouse document known as the Assigned Numbers RFC (RFC 1700) [Reynolds1994].

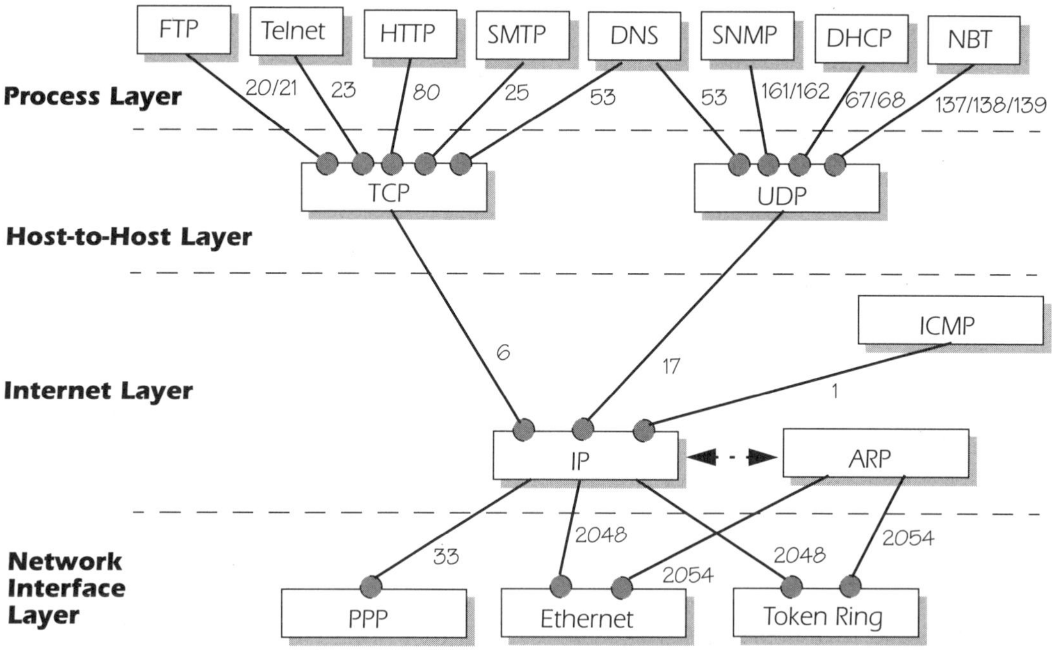

Figure 1.33 Protocol numbers are used at every layer interface. (All numbers are in decimal.)

NSAP: interface between a transport layer protocol and a network layer protocol.

Just what are all of these numbers? At each layer there are different names. In OSI terminology each number is called a *Service Access Point (SAP)* address. Figure 1.34 also shows the numbering scheme, yet adds SAP annotations, as well as TCP/IP terms for the SAPs. That framework would call the binding through which network layer protocols access the link layer protocols, such as Ethernet, a Link Service Access Point (LSAP). An access point for associating a transport protocol with a network protocol would be a **Network Service Access Point (NSAP)**. Similarly, the application or session services would access transport protocols via a **Transport Service Access Point (TSAP)**. But remember, the TCP/IP protocols don't really follow the OSI model, so we have specific terminology for each layer.

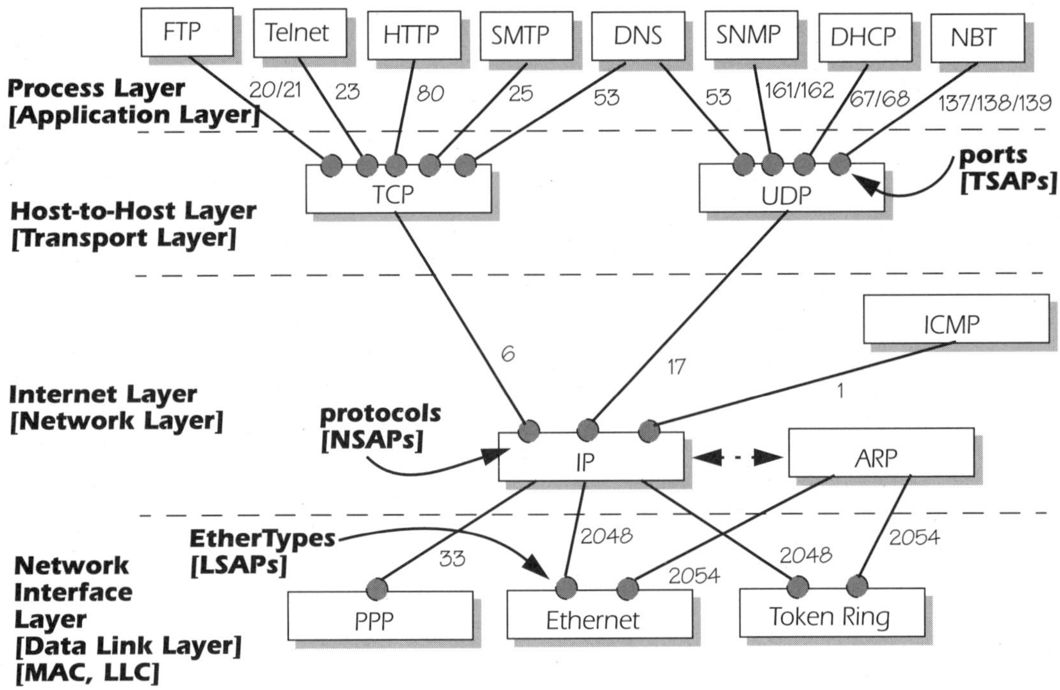

Figure 1.34 Correlations between OSI and TCP/IP layer and access terms.

TSAP: interface between session layer protocol and a transport layer protocol.

The network interface layer protocols pass information up to the internet layer protocols such as IP and ARP by use of certain frame type information and protocol type fields in the network interface frame headers. For instance, with PPP, a value in hex of 0021 (33 decimal) in the protocol type field specifies that the data contained in the frame should be passed as an incoming datagram to IP. Similarly, DIX Ethernet uses a protocol type field value of hex 0800 (2048 decimal) to indicate IP, and hex 0806 (2054 decimal) to indicate ARP messages. Many other media use the same values that Ethernet uses (called EtherType in RFC 1700), often in a SNAP header which is carried in an LLC header. See the particular RFC for the media type you are interested in for details. There may be many protocols running over any given media represented by a network interface. There may also be multiple network interface layer protocols all carrying various internet layer protocols.

The Internet Protocol (IP) itself can carry several protocols, which are identified by the protocol field in the IP header. A list of some of the numbers used in the protocol field are listed in Table 1.3. A complete list is found in RFC 1700. For example, the value of 6 is used for TCP, while UDP is identified with 17, and ICMP is 1.

Table 1.3
A few of the IP protocol type values.

Protocol	Decimal	Hex.	Description
EGP	8	8	Exterior Gateway Protocol
ICMP	1	1	Internet Control Message Protocol
IGMP	2	2	Internet Group Management Protocol
IGRP	88	58	Internet Gateway Routing Protocol
OSPF	89	59	Open Shortest Path First
TCP	6	6	Transmission Control Protocol
UDP	17	11	User Datagram Protocol

UDP and TCP can carry many process layer protocols. Each of the process layer protocols are identified with port numbers, as shown in Table 1.4.

Table 1.4
Sample port numbers used by UDP and TCP.

Protocol	Decimal	Transport	Description
BootP	67	UDP	BOOTstrap Protocol (server)
	68	UDP	BOOTstrap Protocol (client)
DHCP	67	UDP	Dynamic Host Configuration Protocol (server)
	68	UDP	Dynamic Host Configuration Protocol (client)
DNS	53	UDP/TCP	Domain Name System
FTP	21	TCP	File Transfer Protocol (server side of control)
	20	TCP	File Transfer Protocol (server side of data)
HTTP	80	TCP/UDP	HyperText Transfer Protocol (server)
NetBT	138	UDP	NetBIOS datagram service
NetBT	139	TCP	NetBIOS session service
SMTP	25	TCP	Simple Mail Transfer Protocol (server)
SNMP	161	UDP	Simple Network Management Protocol (server a.k.a. agent)
	162	UDP	SNMP (trap manager)
Telnet	23	TCP	Teletype Network protocol
TFTP	69	UDP	Trivial File Transfer Protocol
WINS	137	UDP	Windows Internet Name Service

The identification of the string of protocols used up and down the stack is encoded one layer at a time by the specific protocol used at each layer.

Data Encapsulation

Each layer in the TCP/IP stack is associated with one or more protocols. Each one of those protocols in responsible for providing certain functionality. In order for the protocols to provide this functionality, each protocol will precede the information from the next higher layer with a header. Let's consider an example of an IP datagram sent over Ethernet.

The Ethernet header, as we have seen, is 14 octets in length. The CRC found at the end of the frame is also processed by the Ethernet device driver. If we're running 802.3 Ethernet then we will be running LLC and SNAP as well.

The IP header is commonly 20 octets in length. In a few instances, the IP header may have "options" included in the header, which would bring the header length up to 60 octets. IP passes this datagram down to the interface driver, which adds on the SNAP and LLC headers.

The LLC then passes this frame (LLC and SNAP headers prepended to the IP datagram) down to the MAC sublayer which we said is implemented as 802.3. The MAC gets the LLC frame and builds an 802.3 frame from it by prepending an 802.3 header (the trailer will be added upon transmission) to the 802.2 frame. The MAC layer adds the length of the LLC frame, its source address, and the target address which IP had passed down through LLC, as shown in Figure 1.35.

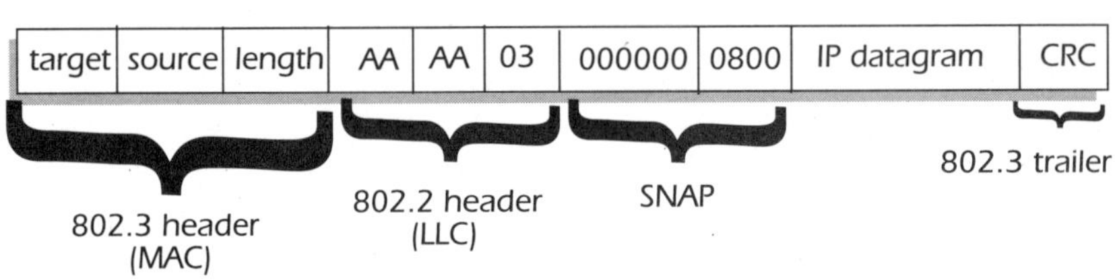

Figure 1.35 IP encapsulation within SNAP, 802.2, and 802.3. (Numbers shown in hex.)

Continue this trend up further and suppose that IP gets its information from UDP which is being used by a process layer protocol. Each piece of software adds its own header information as we pass the message down the stack.

Figure 1.36 shows an example of a process layer protocol passing data down to UDP, which encapsulates this data with a UDP header. Then UDP passes the data down to IP which encapsulates the whole thing (UDP and process information) with an IP header. The network interface layer components (LLC and MAC here) further encapsulate the message.

Figure 1.36 Example of encapsulation of application layer data.

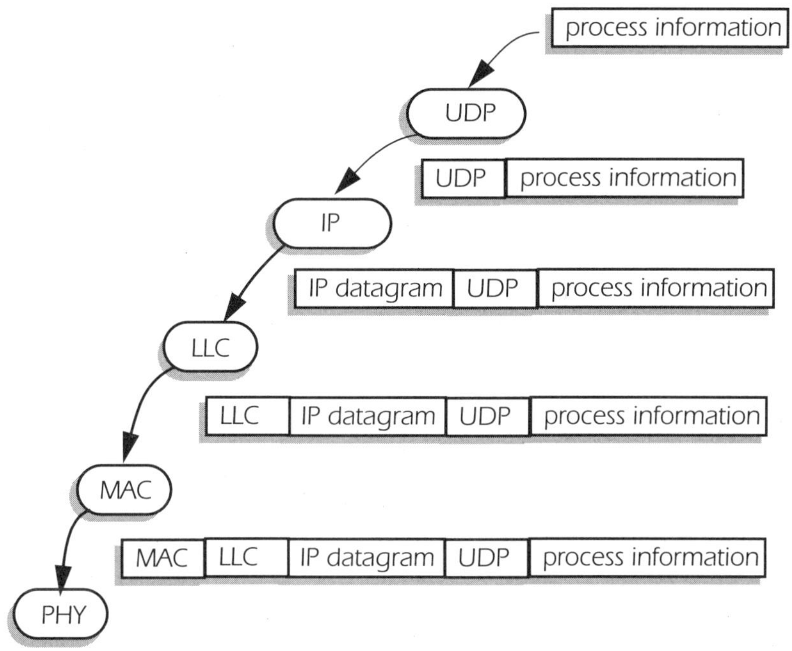

This process works for any protocol running over IP, and in general, we could have either UDP, TCP, or ICMP running over IP. Consider these three as options in what IP can carry and we have Figure 1.37. These are shown with Ethernet II rather than 802.3 so that we don't need to be concerned with LLC and SNAP.

Figure 1.37 Encapsulation of various protocols within IP and then Ethernet II.

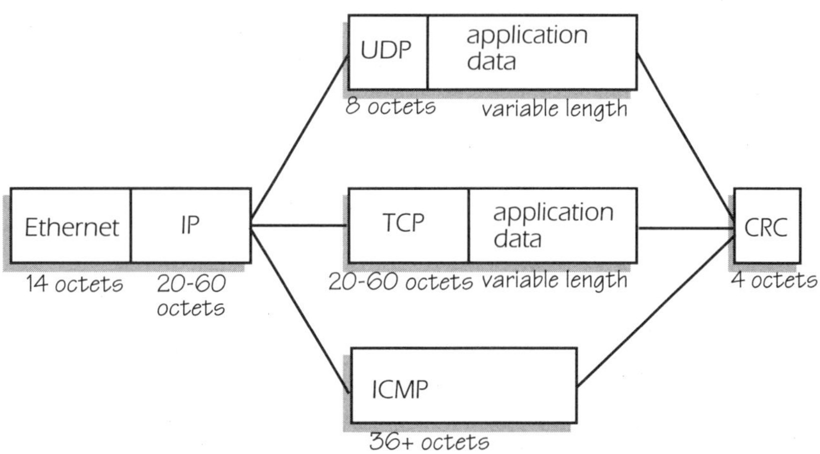

The UDP header is 8 octets in length. Following the UDP header will be data from one of the applications that use UDP: DNS, SNMP, DHCP, NBT, others.

The TCP header is commonly 20 octets in length. When TCP options are exchanged, the header length will be 24 octets.[17] Following the TCP header will be data from one of the applications that use TCP: Telnet, FTP, SMTP, HTTP, others.

The decapsulation procedure follows the same logic in reverse. The protocol types which were added during the encapsulation down the stack are used to determine what piece of software should receive the information during decapsulation.

Politics of the Internet

If the Internet is not the product of one company, who makes the decisions of what it is and how it evolves?

Request for Comments (RFC)

RFCs: documents that describe and define the Internet protocol suite.

The TCP/IP suite is a set of open standards, meaning that the specifications for how to implement these protocols are publicly available. Each one of these specifications is numbered and is given a title. The standards are based on documents called **Request for Comments (RFC)**. The RFCs are descriptions of the Internet, its use, specification of its protocols and management information. Many of the RFCs are "standards track" RFCs, which means that they are the official protocol standards for the TCP/IP stack.

RFCs can be obtained from various places on the Internet. Locations include ds.internic.net, nic.ddn.mil, nis.nsf.net, ftp.isi.edu, and ietf.org. Use

17. With options, the length could be 24 or more octets of TCP header.

anonymous FTP to connect to these sites to download the RFCs. The documents can be searched online at http://ds.internic.net/rfc.

A few of the RFCs for the protocols which have been mentioned in this chapter are shown in Table 1.5.

Table 1.5 RFC numbers for various TCP/IP protocol-related documents.

Acronym	Protocol	RFC Number	RFC Date
ARP	Address Resolution	826	11/1/1982
DHCP	Dynamic Host Configuration	1541	10/27/1993
DNS	Domain Name System	1034, 1035	11/1/1987
FTP	File Transfer	959	10/1/1985
ICMP	Internet Control Message	792	09/1/1981
IP	Internet	791	09/1/1981
NBT	NetBIOS over TCP	1001, 1002	03/1/1987
TCP	Transmission Control	793	09/1/1981
Telnet	Teletype Network service	854	05/1/1983
UDP	User Datagram	768	08/28/1980

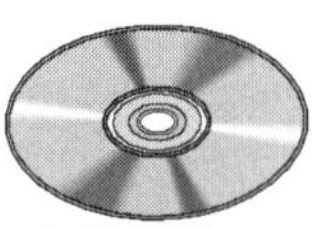

rfc-index.txt

The document rfc-index.txt is a complete list of all of the RFCs, including title, author, date published, number of pages, and format. There are over two thousand RFCs, and only a small percentage of these are actually Internet standards. New RFCs are constantly being published by the RFC editors, who review draft documents written by users, vendors, researchers, or just about anyone else with something to say about the growth and development of the Internet. A copy of the index and the RFCs in Table 1.5 are on the CD.

Administration of the Internet

The organization that is ultimately in control of the Internet is the Internet Architecture Board (IAB), formerly known as the Internet Activities Board. The IAB is a body of the Internet Society (Figure 1.38). The IAB acts as a liaison to outside organizations such as the U.S. Federal Networking Council, and standards organizations such as the ISO/IEC/JTC1, ITU-T, and the ATM Forum. The IAB delegates many of its functions to other organizations.

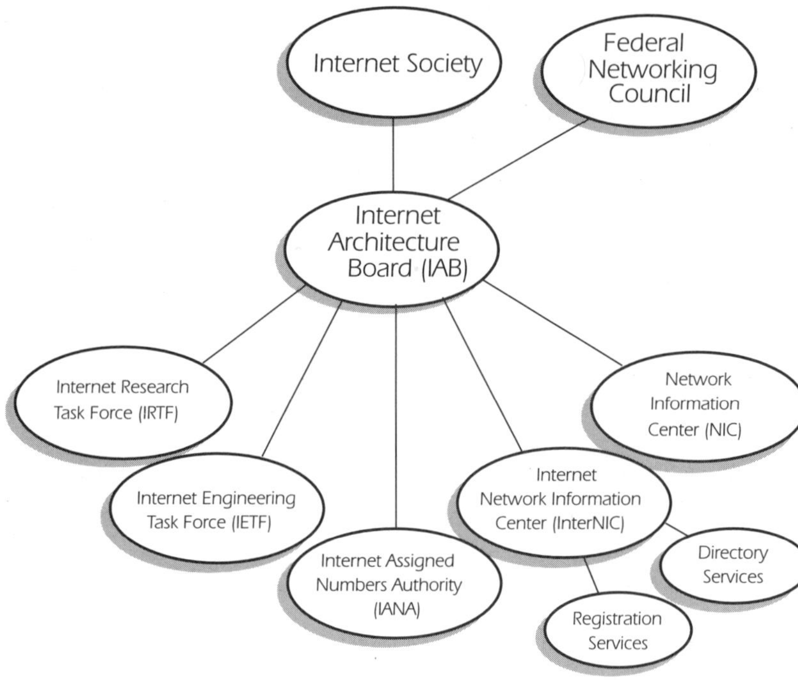

Figure 1.38 Organizational structure of the Internet authorities.

There are two task forces which are a part of the IAB: the Internet Engineering Task Force (IETF) and the Internet Research Task Force (IRTF)[18]. These organizations handle the RFC documents and the research that goes on with respect to the Internet.

The organization which deals with the assignment of numbering and parameters of the Internet protocol suite is the Internet Assigned Numbers Authority (IANA).

Two organizations that your organization may deal with are the Network Information Center (NIC) and the Internet Network Information Center (InterNIC). The NIC deals with the administration of the U. S. military side of the Internet (Milnet) whereas the InterNIC manages the commercial Internet. The assignment of network numbers, domain names, and autonomous functions on the Internet are handled by the InterNIC.

---

18. There is actually a steering group for each of these task forces. The Internet Engineering Steering Group (IESG) and Internet Research Steering Group (IRSG) actually make up the IAB. The IETF and IRTF carry out the day-to-day business of progressing the Internet.

The InterNIC delegates the assignment of certain subdomains within some of the top-level domains[19] to other organizations, including the NIC, the IANA, and Network Information Centers outside of the United States. In fact, the InterNIC has two functions which are handled by separate organizations. The registration services of the InterNIC are handled by Network Solutions, Inc. (NSI) whereas the directory and database services are handled by AT&T.

The roots of the Internet actually started around 1967 and started to take shape in 1969. You can see from some of the dates of the RFCs in Table 1.5 that a few of the key aspects of the Internet are the same today as they have been the same since the mid 1970s and early 1980s. For a history of the Internet, please refer to [Comer1995] or [Hafner1996].

High-Level Addressing

It is not convenient to use physical addresses at all levels in the stack. Higher-level addressing must be introduced for the internetwork layer to be free to utilize various network access layer media.

IP Addresses

Communication using a TCP/IP stack requires each **Network Interface Card (NIC)**[20] to be assigned an IP address as shown in Figure 1.39. IP addresses are 4 octets in length, and are commonly shown in *dotted-decimal* notation.[21]

19. For information on domains, refer to the chapters on DNS.
20. Yes, this book contains the same acronym for the two different objects. NIC refers to a Network Interface Card, as well as the Network Information Center.
21. The dotted decimal notation used for IP addresses is also referred to as dotted-quad notation. IPv6 addresses are written in colon-hex notation.

These IP addresses must be unique in order for machines to communicate. These IP addresses are ultimately assigned by the Network Information Center (NIC) or InterNIC. Each organization will be assigned addresses to use if that organization will be connecting to the Internet. If your organization will not be connecting to the Internet, but just maintaining an "intranet," you can choose your own network identifier.

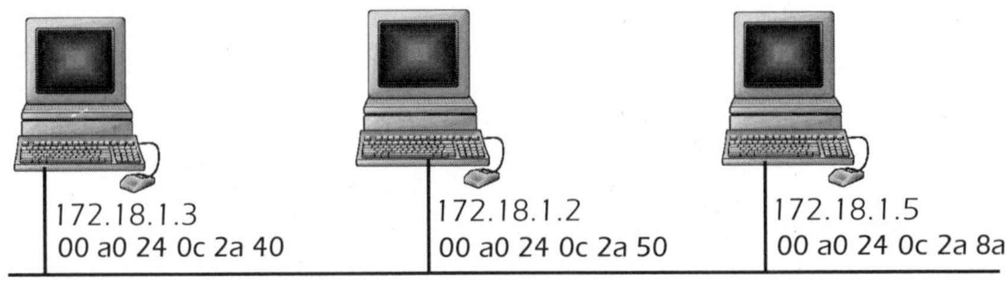

Figure 1.39 Logical (IP) addresses are assigned to each physical (Ethernet) address.

If your organization is large, you may want to try to register an official address. Renumbering a network later will be costly and time-consuming.

Another possibility is to have your own internal numbering scheme, and a firewall which connects to the Internet. If the firewall includes a proxy server, your internal users may use whatever services on the Internet that the proxy server supports. In this kind of scenario, your proxy server, firewall, and Internet router (typically between one and three devices) would have registered IP addresses. The remainder of your hosts could be numbered in any way that the router and firewall will support. For further information on this, refer to the chapter on Proxy Server.

IP addresses are discussed in detail in the next chapter.

Summary

Here's a summary of the items which have been addressed in this chapter.

- TCP/IP is the name which describes the Internet suite of protocols.

- There are four layers in the TCP/IP model:
  - Process
  - Host-to-host
  - Internet
  - Network interface
- Process layer protocols are used by network applications to provide services directly or indirectly to users.
- TCP and UDP are host-to-host protocols which provide two different types of service to the process layer protocols.
  - TCP provides a connection-oriented, reliable transport
  - UDP gives an unacknowledged, connectionless datagram service
- IP itself provides a network layer unacknowledged, connectionless datagram service between machines. UDP and TCP are built on this to provide their services to multiple applications or users.
- Other internet layer protocols such as ARP and ICMP help IP.
- The Internet Society is the main interface for the public to the affairs of the Internet.
- The IETF is the organization which provides guidelines and standards for the Internet community.
- There is a grand numbering scheme which describes the interconnections of the various protocols in the TCP/IP stack.
- High-level addressing frees us from having to remember and configure media-specific hardware addresses.

Further Reading

Here is information about various books and magazines in which to look for further information on the subject.

[Black1993] Black, Uyless, *Computer Networks: Protocols, Standards, and Interfaces, Second Edition*, 1993, Prentice-Hall

[Carl-Mitchell1993] Carl-Mitchell, Smoot, Quarterman, John S., *Practical Internetworking with TCP/IP and UNIX*, 1993, Addison-Wesley

[Comer1995] Comer, Douglas E., *Internetworking with TCP/IP Vol I: Principles, Protocols, and Architecture, Third Edition*, 1995, Prentice-Hall

[Feit1997] Feit, Dr. Sidnie, *TCP/IP Architecture, Protocols, and Implementation/2e*, 1997, McGraw-Hill

[Goralski1995] Goralski, Walter J., *Introduction to ATM Networking*, 1995, McGraw-Hill

[Hafner1996] Hafner, Katie, Matthew Lyon, *Where Wizards Stay Up Late: The Origins of the Internet*, 1996, Simon & Schuster

[Huitema1996] Huitema, Christian, *IPv6: The New Internet Protocol*, 1996, Prentice Hall

[Miller1993] Miller, Mark A., *Troubleshooting TCP/IP: Analyzing the Protocols of the Internet*, 1993, M&T Books

[Postel1981c] Postel, J., *Transmission Control Protocol*, 1981, IETF RFC 793

[Reynolds1994] Reynolds, J., Postel, J., *ASSIGNED NUMBERS*, 1994, IETF RFC 1700

[Romkey1988] Romkey, J., *Nonstandard for Transmission of IP Datagrams over Serial Lines: SLIP*, 1988, IETF RFC 1055

[Simoneau1997] Simoneau, Paul, *Hands-On TCP/IP*, 1997, McGraw-Hill

[Stevens1994] Stevens, W. Richard, *TCP/IP Illustrated, Volume 1: The Protocols*, 1994, Addison-Wesley

[Stevens1990] Stevens, W. Richard, *UNIX Network Programming*, 1990, Prentice-Hall

[Tannembaum1989] Tannenbaum, Andrew S., *Computer Networks, /2e*, 1989, Prentice-Hall

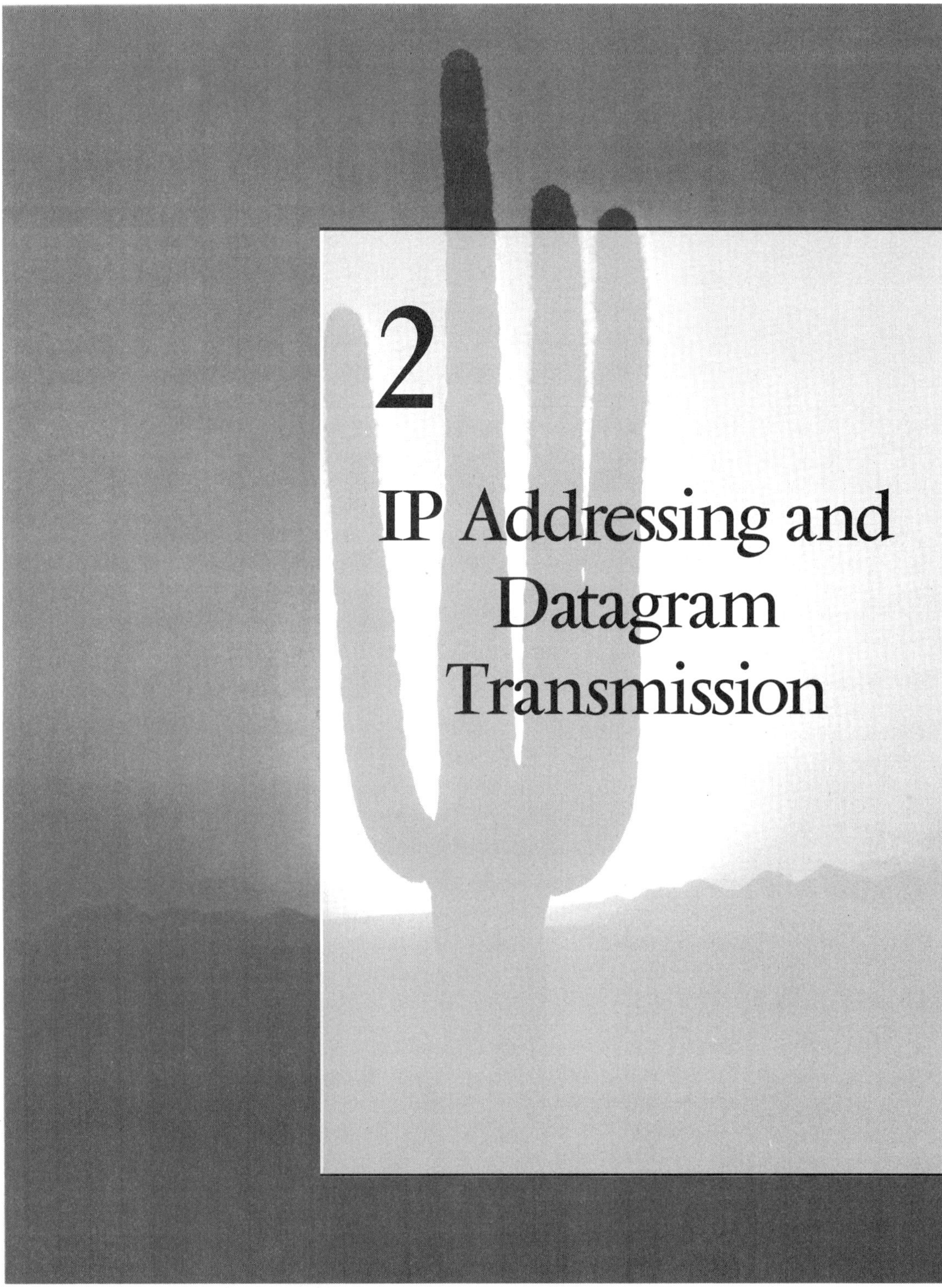

2

IP Addressing and Datagram Transmission

This chapter is about Internet Protocol (IP) addressing. We will define the classes of IP networks, introduce the rules of IP addresses, distinguish between "local" and "remote" destinations, and finally, describe the relationship between IP addresses and hardware addresses.

Why Do We Have IP Addresses, and What Do We Use Them For?

The Internet Protocol (IP) hides the details of various communications media and medium access methods from the actual services provided over the network. IP provides a common access method for internetworks from a small internet of two communicating machines to the global Internet.

IP passes datagrams through the networks from one point to another. How do we specify the source and target machines within the network? If we used physical communication port numbers and hardware addresses directly, we'd need some way of translating all possible types of addresses (within gateways) between the networks. IP still deals with the issues of translating between different kinds of hardware addresses, but in a layered and distributed fashion.

Common Numbering

IP addresses provide a common numbering scheme for interfacing to the network regardless of the type of transmission media you're using. Rather than using the physical addresses related to each media type, logical addresses are assigned.

For instance, rather than using a collection of Ethernet addresses, you may assign logical addresses which are easier for you to remember. One benefit of this technique is that if you change NICs or change network types completely, you don't have to change the addresses you use to identify devices in your network.

Whole networks may be labelled with a common prefix. For instance, the pair of numbers 172.18 could be used as a prefix to identify your network.

Labeling Each Interface

Do we label each machine in the network with an IP address? Not exactly, although it sometimes appears that way. We assign IP addresses to each interface to the network. If each machine has only one network interface, we may think of the IP address as a station identifier. However, devices which have more than one network interface, such as routers and some servers, may have more than one IP address. Consider this analogy. If a building has a driveway on each of two different streets, wouldn't it be useful to have two street addresses so that you could get to the building either way? Devices with two or more addresses can be reached in two different ways.

We don't assign IP addresses directly to a physical interface to the network, but to a logical interface to the network. Recall that the network interface layer performs the functions described by the physical and data link layers of the OSI model. The network interface software can be used to create one or more logical access points to each physical network interface. Implementations which support more than one logical access point to a physical interface may then have more than one IP address assigned to the physical interface.

Binding Addresses to an Interface

How are addresses bound to an interface? The IP software on each machine supports a list of interfaces over which it may communicate. Each interface in the list is maintained with an "interface binding" in IP.

An interface binding consists of several pieces of information, including:

- an IP address
- a subnetwork mask
- the broadcast address
- the maximum reassembly size
- the protocol type for IP
- the interface type
- the interface identifier
- the maximum transmission unit (MTU)

In the example in Figure 2.1, IP has bound the address 26.0.0.1 to a logical instance of the Ethernet driver. IP then uses this logical address, the IP address, for communications. The Ethernet address of the corresponding Network Interface Card (NIC) is not used directly by clients of IP. When IP needs to communicate via that interface, it will inevitably use the Ethernet address indirectly, by using the IP address to hardware address mapping. The section titled "Obtaining Hardware Addresses" on page 72 describes how IP uses the Ethernet address yet hides it from IP clients.

Figure 2.1
IP may bind an IP address to a network interface driver.

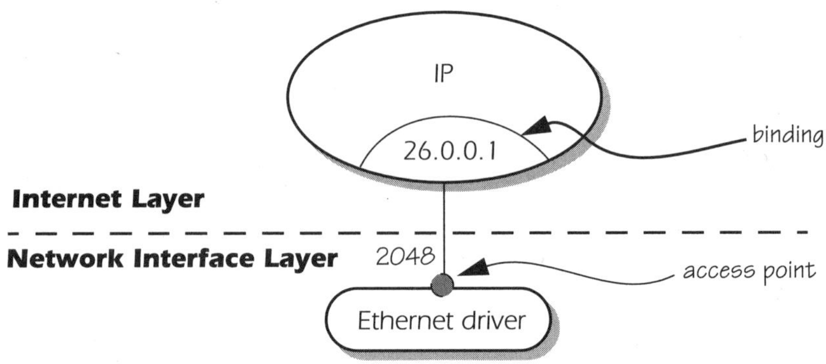

Example of Bound Addresses

Each machine interfaces to the network by performing similar bindings. For three machines on an Ethernet, we would assign an IP address to each ones' network interface. Consider the machines in Figure 2.2.

Because each machine has only one IP address, it's tempting to say that "iguana's IP address" is 172.18.64.2. Strictly speaking, the IP address 172.18.64.2 is bound to the Ethernet interface that iguana happens to be using. This distinction isn't important when there is only one network interface per machine.

Figure 2.2
Three devices with IP addresses bound to their Ethernet interfaces.

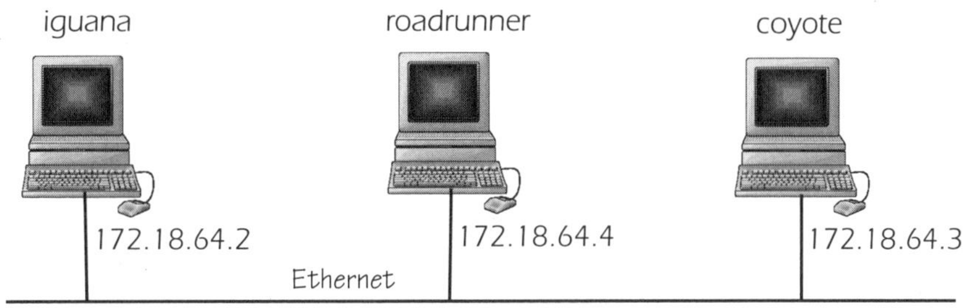

Using Bound IP Addresses to Communicate

If the machine called iguana wants to use IP to talk with coyote, the IP addresses would be used. (We haven't yet talked about how machines would be given names — that's a higher layer issue.) A datagram would be sent from 172.18.64.2 to 172.18.64.3. When iguana's IP attempts to send the datagram, it goes through several steps which may be summarized as follows.

IP will select the appropriate network interface to use to reach coyote. The choices are the loopback interface or the Ethernet interface. The obvious choice is the Ethernet interface (see Figure 2.2) which has the address 172.18.64.2 bound to it. (How IP determines that this is the obvious choice should be clear by the end of the book.) IP then places the source and target IP addresses in the datagram header. Next, IP determines the Ethernet address of coyote's 172.18.64.3 interface. Finally, IP passes the datagram to the Ethernet driver with the target Ethernet address.

The detailed steps are described in "Sending IP Datagrams" on page 66.

Multiple Interfaces

Each network device may have a number of network interfaces. For instance, a network device may have eight Ethernet interfaces. Another network device may have network interfaces of various types, such as an Ethernet interface, an FDDI interface, an AAL5 over ATM interface, and a PPP over ISDN interface.

How does IP handle this kind of arrangement? Several interfaces can function at the same time under IP by having multiple bindings. Each binding independently provides IP with an interface to a network. Figure 2.3 shows IP using one binding per network interface.

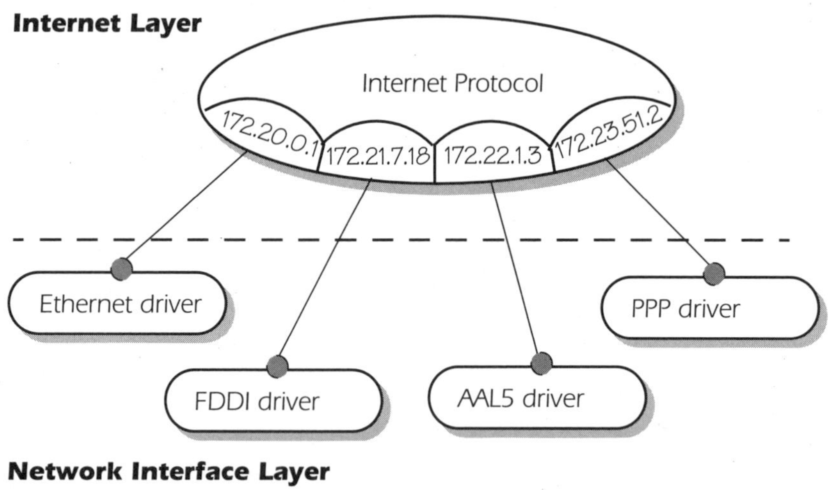

Figure 2.3 IP is using one binding per network interface in this example.

Anatomy of an IP Address

There is a scheme to how IP addresses are assigned and written. This section shows the whys and the wherefores.

Writing Out IP Address Values

All IP addresses are written in the same way. All IP addresses are thirty-two bit values,[1] but rather than writing out a string of thirty-two ones and zeroes, we instead write IP addresses in "dotted decimal" notation. See Figure 2.4 for an example of how to write an IP address using this notation. Occasionally it is useful to write them in binary.

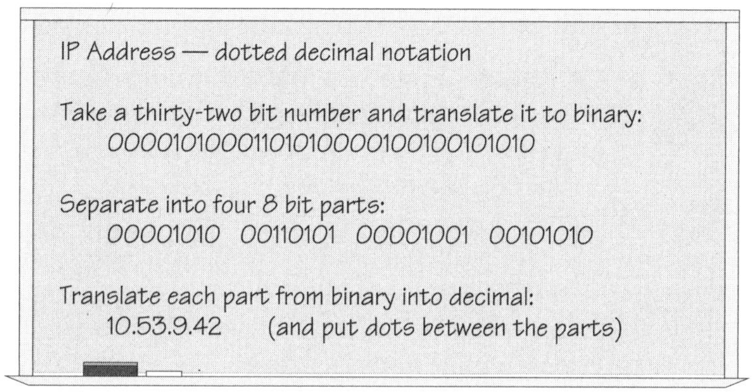

Figure 2.4 How to write an IP address in dotted decimal notation.

Why don't we just use a regular 32-bit unsigned integer notation for IP addresses? Because addresses such as 171,247,914 and 2,886,877,186 and 3,221,225,473 just don't make the structure of IP addresses apparent to us. The corresponding dotted-decimal addresses, 10.53.9.42, 172.18.64.2, and 192.0.0.1 are more easily interpreted. Not only is the four-part number easier for most people to remember, but it also aids in interpreting the type ("class") of address we are dealing with.

Some special IP addresses are reserved for particular uses. The very first IP address, 0.0.0.0, identifies the network of networks. It is used in some cases as the unspecified address. The Host Requirements RFC (RFC1122) states that the address 0.0.0.0 specifies *this* host on *this* network, thus is actually an address meaning the machine itself.

Just as with Ethernet addresses, there are several varieties of IP addresses:

- **network address** — identifies a whole network.

---

1. IP version 4 (the current version) addresses are 32-bits. IP version 6 addresses are slightly larger, weighing in at 128 bits.

- **unicast address** — assigned to a single interface within a network.
- **multicast address** — associated with a group of interfaces in a network.
- **broadcast address** — specifies transmission to all interfaces within a network.

general broadcast address: used to send IP datagram to everyone on the local network: 255.255.255.255

The final IP address, 255.255.255.255 is used to specify the **general broadcast address**. Routers will not pass datagrams destined for this address, thus it is in practice a local area broadcast.

Unicast addresses are picked according to certain rules. Multicast addresses are allocated from a certain range of IP addresses according to group management rules. See the following section which describes the classes of networks for more detail.

Now that we've seen how to write IP addresses, let's look at how to interpret them.

Classes of Networks

If we could use all thirty-two bits of an IP address to identify a network interface number, we could have 4,294,967,296 interfaces in the Internet. We'll call the number 4,294,967,296 (approximately four billion) the size of the IP address space. Not all of these addresses may be assigned to network interfaces, however.

Internet Protocol addresses are arranged in a hierarchical manner. A certain amount of the thirty-two bits is used to identify a network number. The remainder of the thirty-two bits is usually used to identify an interface within that network.

There are five classes of IP addresses shown in Table 2.1. The first three classes: A, B, and C are used to identify addresses in various sized networks. Thus there are three classes of IP networks, yet in common practice many people say that there are three classes of IP addresses. Class D is used for multicast addresses, and class E is experimental addresses.

Table 2.1
Using the first octet of an IP address to determine the class

Leading Bits	Decimal Value of First Octet	Class of Address	Percentage of Address Space
0	0-127	A	50%
10	128-191	B	25%
110	192-223	C	12.5%
1110	224-239	D	6.25%
1111	240-255	E	6.25%

Each of the three classes of networks (A, B, C) divides the thirty-two bits into two parts to allow you to have a certain number of interfaces (or hosts) per network. The first few bits of the IP address are used to indicate the *class of the address.* Conveniently, because we usually write IP addresses in dotted decimal form, it is useful to equate the bit prefix for each class with a range of decimal values for the first octet of the address.

According to Table 2.1, an IP address of 26.0.0.1 would be a part of a class A network, because 26 is within the range 0 to 127.

loopback network:
the last network of each class, used to talk to yourself or test the IP stack.

The last network of each class is reserved as a **loopback network**. For example, if an IP address begins with 127, then the address represents a local loopback address. Similarly, the class B network 191.255.0.0 and the class C network 223.255.255.0 are also reserved for loopback use. The addresses 127.0.0.2, 191.255.0.1, and 223.255.255.111 are possible loopback addresses.

An address within one of the loopback networks will be bound to the loopback network interface. Typically the address 127.0.0.1 is bound to the loopback interface (Figure 2.5), which is the default on NT. None of the other addresses in that loopback network are assigned[2]. IP datagrams sent to that address will not be transmitted onto a physical network — they will be looped back up to IP by the loopback driver. These packets are never transmitted on the physical transmission media.

2. Although only one address in the loopback network is assigned to the loopback interface, a route may be established which sends many (or all) other addresses in the loopback network to that one interface. In the chapters on routing, we'll discuss other routes which use the loopback interface.

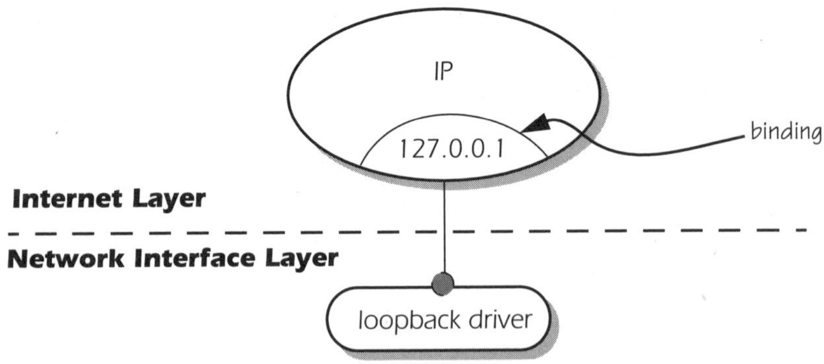

Figure 2.5 Address 127.0.0.1 bound to the loopback interface driver.

A loopback interface is often used when one process on a machine needs to communicate with another process on that same machine using IP. Thus if you are at one with your computer, you use a loopback address to talk with yourself.

Network Identifiers

There are two parts to an IP address: the *network portion* and the *interface portion.* For addresses to be used on the Internet, the network portion is ultimately assigned by the InterNIC: The InterNIC assigns network numbers, these numbers being the prefix for all of an organizations' IP addresses.[3] The network portion of an IP address cannot be changed by the organization it is assigned to (assuming this organization is using these addresses to connect to the Internet.)

While the network portion of the address is assigned by the InterNIC, the interface portion is *locally-administered* — meaning that you can assign values as you determine necessary. Each class of IP address has a specific number of assigned and locally-administered bits.

Each IP network address class is shown in Table 2.2 with the thirty-two address bits divided into network and locally-administered fields. For each class, the binary representation for addresses of that class is shown,

3. Unless you are a network provider or a very large organization, you would not usually get a network address directly from the InterNIC. An Internet Service Provider (ISP) would either assign you a network number or a single address. Small organizations and individuals usually don't even get a fixed assignment, but simply get to borrow an address for a time.

written as the most significant octet (MSO), next most significant octet (NMSO), next least significant octet (NLSO), and least significant octet (LSO).

Table 2.2
Network bits vs. locally-administered bits

Class	Binary Representation MSO	NMSO	NLSO	LSO	Number of Possible Networks
A	0NNNNNNN	LLLLLLLL	LLLLLLLL	LLLLLLLL	126
B	10NNNNNN	NNNNNNNN	LLLLLLLL	LLLLLLLL	16,382
C	110NNNNN	NNNNNNNN	NNNNNNNN	LLLLLLLL	2,097,150

Each bit of the address may be interpreted according to the legend in Table 2.3.

Table 2.3
Legend of IP address bit use.

Digit	Description
0	this bit must explicitly be a zero for this class
1	this bit must explicitly be a one for this class
N	network identifier bits (assigned by InterNIC)
L	locally-administered bits (your organization assigns)

Also shown in Table 2.2 is a calculation of the number of networks which may be represented by each class. For example, for class A there are seven network identifier (N) bits, giving us 2^7, or 128 combinations of which two are reserved, which leaves us with 126 possible class A networks.[4] Table 2.4 shows the number of network interface bits and locally-administered bits for each address class.[5]

Table 2.4
The number of bits for each IP network class.

Class	Network Field Length	Length of Locally-Administered Field
A	8	24
B	16	16
C	24	8

The dividing line between the network portion and the locally-administered portion represents a trade-off between the number of networks

4. Further, if we discount the non-routable network 10, there are only 125 assigned class A addresses.

5. Note that the network field lengths are shown in Table 2.4 are 8, 16, and 24 yet due to the prefixes as shown in Table 2.2, the actual lengths are 7, 14, and 21. The sum of the prefix and network bits is shown in Table 2.4 for simplicity.

and the number of interfaces per network. For the most efficient use of this class structure, only very large networked organizations would get a class A network address. We'll see in the next chapter that another dividing line will be created in the locally-administered field— the line dividing the interface portion from the subnetwork portion.

IP Networks and Broadcast Addresses

network address: refers to the network but not to a specific interface in that network.

network broadcast: used as a target address to send to all machines in the network.

If the locally-administered field is all zeros (binary), then what is represented is a general **network address** (e.g. 172.18.0.0).

If the locally-administered field is all ones (binary), then that represents a **broadcast to that network** (e.g. 172.18.255.255).

If there are all binary ones in both the network and locally-administered field, that represents a *general IP broadcast*. This is written as 255.255.255.255.

If we draw the IP address space for a given network graphically, we can see some of the identifiers which are commonly used. This also helps to draw out your allocated addresses. See Figure 2.6 for an example.

Figure 2.6
The first and last addresses in a network are reserved. The rest are assignable as unicast addresses.

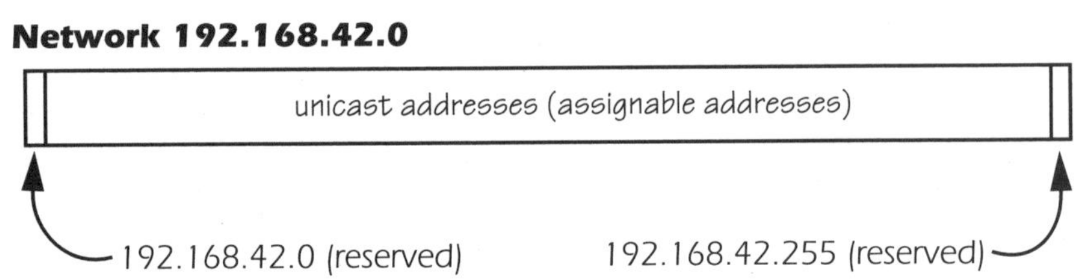

The first IP address within a network identifies the network itself. For example, the class A network 10 is identified as 10.0.0.0. Similarly, the class C network 199.201.203 is identified as 199.201.203.0. The last address within a network is used to identify a broadcast within that network. Table 2.5 shows some examples of this.

Table 2.5
Example network and broadcast IP addresses.

Class	Example Network Address	Broadcast Address for that Network
A	26.0.0.0	26.255.255.255
B	128.1.0.0	128.1.255.255
C	192.1.1.0	192.1.1.255

All of the addresses in between the network address and the network broadcast address are usable as unicast addresses within the network. These are called the assignable addresses because they may be assigned to network interfaces.

Multicast IP Addresses

Class D IP addresses are used to specify multicast targets. The Internet Group Management Protocol (IGMP) is used to convey group information between potential group members. A machine is a member of an IP multicast group if there is one or more software applications on that machine that are currently registered as a member of that group. Some examples of multicast addresses are shown in Table 2.6.

Table 2.6
Example multicast addresses.

Protocol	Multicast Address	Description
RIPv2	224.0.0.9	All RIPv2 routers
OSPF	224.0.0.5	All OSPF routers
OSPF	224.0.0.6	Designated routers
general	224.0.0.1	All systems on this subnet

Routers must be configured to pass multicast datagrams from network to network. A router will forward multicast datagrams to a network if one or more machines in the network are members of the group specified in the multicast target address.

The multicast addresses 224.0.0.0 through 224.0.0.255 are non-routable. They are used for administrative functions.

A machine does not need to be a member of a multicast group in order to send messages to the members of the group.

Non-routable Networks

non-routable network: an IP network that is to be used internal to an organization (i.e. private), not for access to the Internet.

There are some IP network numbers which are reserved for use inside of an organization. In other words, you cannot allow traffic with these IP addresses out onto the Internet. They are often called **non-routable networks** for this reason. These effectively allow private network addressing to be established which isn't used for accessing the Internet.[6]

These non-routable networks are specified in RFC 1597[7], and are shown in Table 2.7.

Table 2.7 Non-routable (private) networks.

Class	Number of Networks	Network Numbers
A	1	10.0.0.0
B	16	172.16.0.0 - 172.31.0.0
C	256	192.168.0.0 - 192.168.255.0

Due to the shortage of official IP network numbers, you may find it useful to use one or more of these network numbers in your organization. Without special gateways, however, none of your machines that are assigned addresses from these networks would be able to communicate with the Internet (and vice versa). We'll discuss such gateways in the chapter on proxy servers.

Sending IP Datagrams

Recall that IP datagrams must be encapsulated in a lower-layer protocol before being transmitted on the network. The destination IP address has already been determined. But what hardware address is to be used in the lower layer header when transmitting the datagram? For instance, if IP is

6. Non-routable networks may not be used for access to the Internet unless you have a proxy (see Chapter 12, "Internet Access Using Proxy Server")
7. [Rekhter1996] RFC 1597 "Address Allocation for Private Internets"

running over Ethernet, how does IP determine the proper Ethernet target address to use when encapsulating the datagram into an Ethernet frame? This will be determined by the Address Resolution Protocol (ARP).

Local vs. Remote Destinations

When sending a datagram, IP has two choices. Either the destination is on the local network, or it is on a remote network. Figure 2.7 shows that the destination IP address is used to determine if the destination is local or remote.

Figure 2.7 Flowchart for determining if a destination is local or remote.

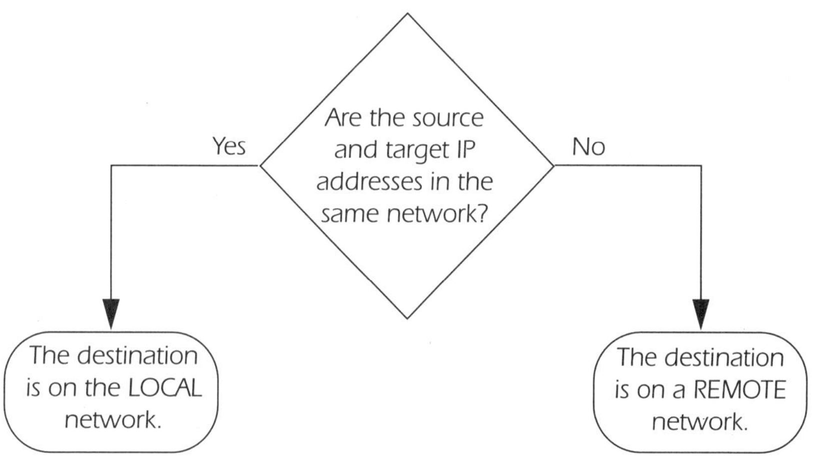

If the destination is a local address, IP needs to:

1. obtain the destination's hardware address.
2. send the datagram to that address.

default router: the IP address of the router that a machine uses when it doesn't know where else to send a datagram.

If the destination is a remote address, IP needs to:

1. obtain the IP address of a router (usually locally configured — called the default router).
2. obtain the hardware address of that router.
3. send the datagram to that address.

Each machine will usually have a **default router** (also called default gateway) configured to use as a next hop toward the destination.

Let's examine each of these procedures in more detail.

Sending IP Datagrams to Local Destinations

When IP receives a datagram to be transmitted, it follows a decision process. IP first checks to see if the source and target IP addresses are on the same network (and subnet as we'll see later). If they are, the destination is a local destination, as shown in Figure 2.8.

Figure 2.8
Direct transmission on a link.

If the target machine is on the local network, the hardware address of the target is obtained, and then the datagram is sent directly to the destination. See "Obtaining Hardware Addresses" on page 72 for a description of how IP determines the target hardware address. The hardware address must be obtained in order to send the IP datagram — recall that the IP datagram is encapsulated in a network interface layer frame (e.g. Ethernet), such as that in Figure 2.9.

Figure 2.9
Two layers of addressing, with MAC destination unknown.

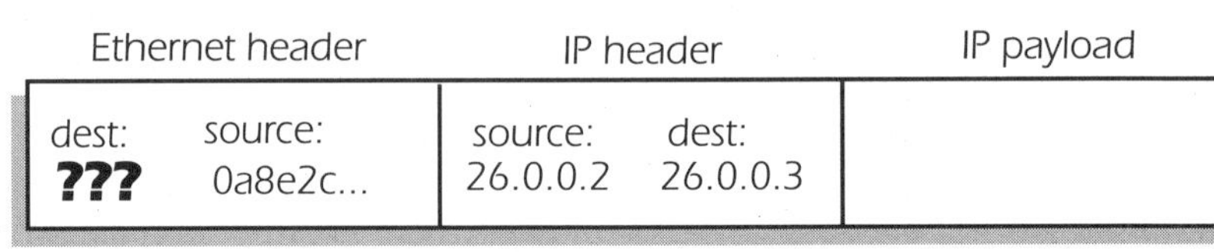

The binding of the source IP address to a network interface is used to determine the physical address of the source.

Once the target hardware address has been determined, the frame may be completed as shown in Figure 2.10, and the frame is sent on the wire.

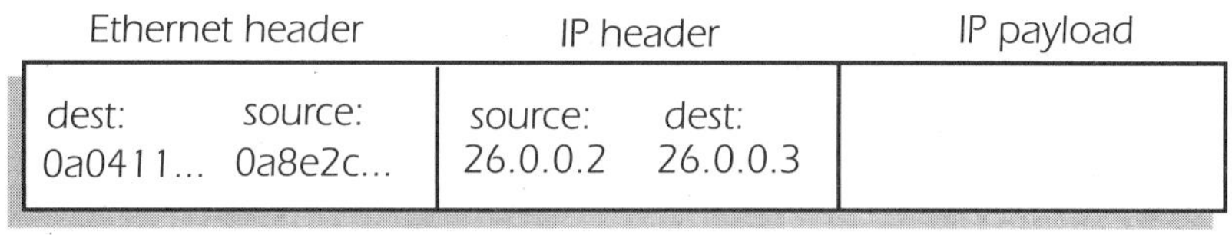

Figure 2.10 The target MAC address is filled in before the frame is sent.

Sending IP Datagrams to Remote Destinations

If IP determines that the source and target addresses are not on the same network, the destination must be a remote destination. This datagram should be sent to the source machine's default router. The router will take that datagram and forward it to the next appropriate machine.

Let's say that iguana is trying to send a datagram to saguaro. Figure 2.11 shows that their respective IP addresses are 26.0.0.2 and 34.0.0.9. Table 2.1 on page 61 shows us that these are both class A addresses. How much of these two addresses do we have to compare to see if they're on the same network? Table 2.4 on page 63 shows that for class A addresses, the network field is the first octet, so we compare the first octet of each address. Because the network numbers 26 and 34 are not the same, we know that 26.0.0.2 and 34.0.0.9 are on different networks. Therefore 34.0.0.9 is a remote transmission from 26.0.0.2. IP goes through a similar method to determine this.

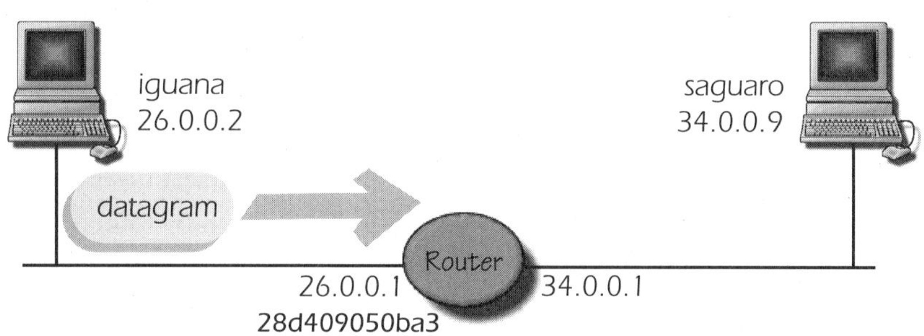

Figure 2.11 Transmission to a remote destination goes through a router.

hop-by-hop transmission: sending a datagram from one machine to the next until it reaches its destination.

Once IP knows that it's dealing with a remote destination, it tries to determine where it can send the datagram to be forwarded toward the remote destination. That is where a router comes in. IP sends the datagram to a router, whose job is to determine where to send it next. This is called **hop-by-hop transmission**.

Assume that iguana's IP software has been configured to use the default router with an IP address of 26.0.0.1. The datagram will be sent to 26.0.0.1. This IP address was selected because it is the address bound to the nearest interface of the nearest router. The default router must be on the same IP network as the sending machine, although it may be physically connected through repeaters, bridges, and switches. Iguana's IP software now has to determine the hardware address which corresponds to the IP address 26.0.0.1. Once it has done this, the datagram can be sent.

Figure 2.12 shows a rendering of the frame sent from iguana's 26.0.0.2 interface to the router's 26.0.0.1 interface. Notice that the IP destination address is 34.0.0.9, not 26.0.0.1! Thus, the IP destination is the eventual destination, not the address of the next hop router. The hardware address however (e.g. 28d409050ba3) is the Ethernet address of the 26.0.0.1 interface of the router.

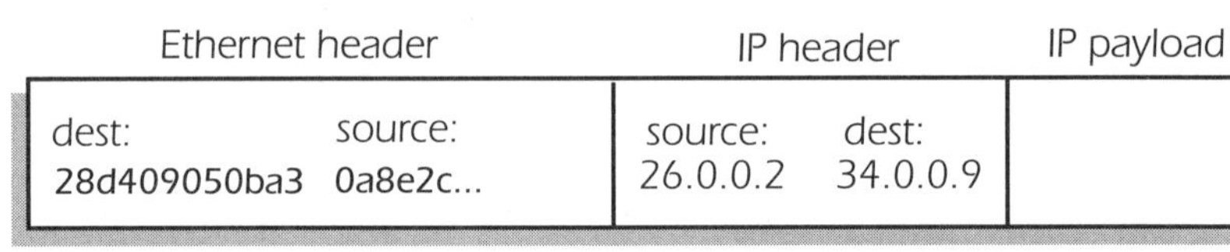

Figure 2.12 The destination IP address is on another network.

What does the router do with this frame once it receives it? It looks at the protocol type, which identifies IP, and passes it to its IP software. The router's IP looks at the target address and realizes that this datagram is not destined for the router itself, but to 34.0.0.9! The router must forward this datagram on toward that destination. The router's IP knows that it can get to network 34.0.0.0 out its interface 34.0.0.1. We'll discuss the details of how IP can know this sort of thing in the chapter "NT Server as an IP Router" on page 245. Until then, just trust us — it knows.

The router forwards the datagram from its 34.0.0.1 interface to 34.0.0.9. It goes through the exact same procedure that IP always goes through. The source and destination IP addresses are now on the same network (34.0.0.0). So the router may perform a local transmission on the second network. It looks up the hardware address of saguaro's 34.0.0.9 interface and encapsulates the datagram in an Ethernet frame to that address.

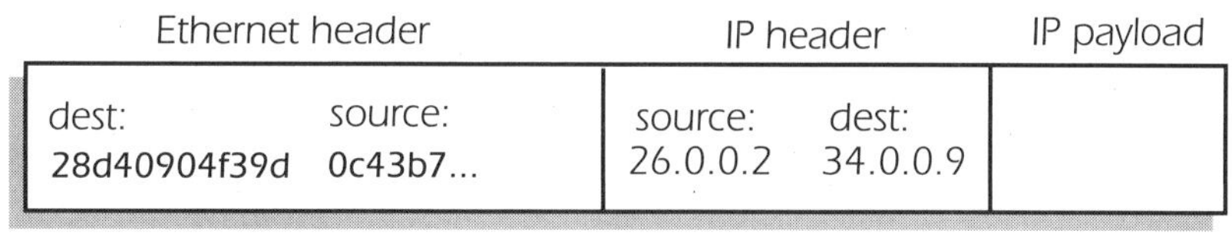

Figure 2.13
The router forwards the datagram to its destination.

Figure 2.13 shows this Ethernet frame which carries the forwarded datagram. Note that the IP addresses have not been touched. The IP source is still iguana's 26.0.0.2 interface; the destination is still saguaro's 34.0.0.9 interface. The Ethernet addresses of course must reflect the actual network interface transmission details. The source Ethernet address is that of the router's 34.0.0.1 interface. The target Ethernet address is that of saguaro's 34.0.0.9 interface in Figure 2.14.

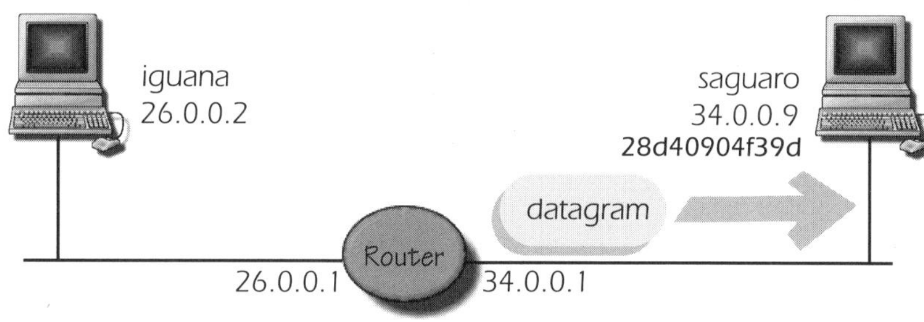

Figure 2.14
The router forwards the datagram locally to its destination.

When saguaro's IP software receives this, it sees that the target IP address matches its own and thus doesn't need to be forwarded, but rather delivered up to the proper host-to-host layer protocol.

The whole end-to-end process involves three steps as shown in the ladder diagram in Figure 2.15.

1. Iguana sends the datagram across the first hop — to the router's near interface.
2. The router forwards this datagram to its far interface.
3. The router sends the datagram to saguaro.

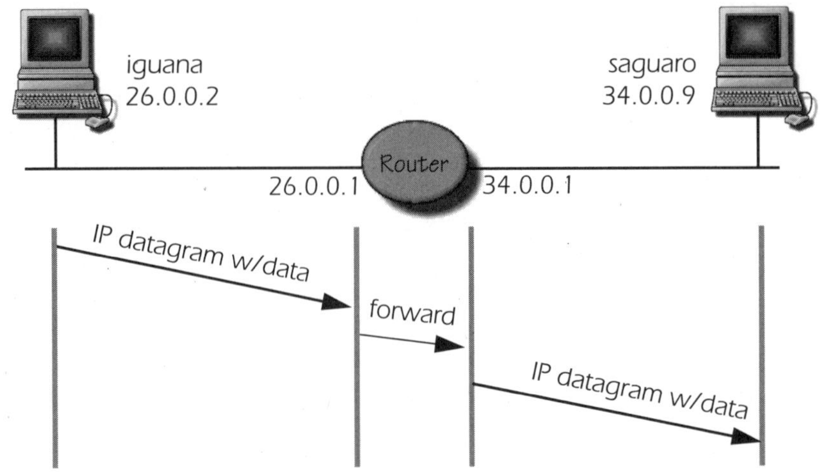

Figure 2.15 Remote transmission in this example involves sending a datagram to a router, and the router sending the datagram to the destination.

TTL: a parameter in an IP datagram which limits the number of hops the datagram may take on its trip to its destination.

This datagram relay technique may be repeated for destinations which are more remote than in this example. The procedure is simply repeated as often as necessary, or at least, until the **time to live (TTL)** of the datagram. Additional details of the routing process are covered in the routing chapter.

Obtaining Hardware Addresses

We discussed that IP uses the network interface layer (e.g. hardware) to send information. IP passes a frame down to a network interface and needs to specify the target hardware address. If IP is sending to a local destination, it needs the hardware address which corresponds to the IP address of that destination. If IP is instead sending to a remote destination, it needs the hardware address of the near interface of the first router, which is a local destination. By selecting a local router when sending to a remote destination, IP always reduces the need for a hardware address to a local problem.

In the section on "Sending IP Datagrams to Remote Destinations" on page 69, it was mentioned that a default router may be used. The default router is specified as a configuration parameter which is discussed in

Chapter 5 "Installing and Configuring TCP/IP on NT" and Chapter 15 "DHCP". How a machine gains knowledge of other routers is discussed in the chapters on routing.

So how does IP find the target hardware address? When this local destination is across a dedicated (non-shared) point-to-point link, IP doesn't actually need a hardware address; it may simply send across the link. For other media, such as shared access networks, IP has to query other machines on the shared link to see if they have the destination IP address bound to their network interface. The protocol used to obtain hardware addresses is called the *Address Resolution Protocol (ARP).* ARP is one of IP's close collaborators in the Internet layer.

What does IP know about the machine whose hardware address it wants?

- It knows the IP address of that machine.
- It knows the target machine is a local destination out its selected network interface.

To obtain the hardware address associated with the target IP address, the machine sends out an *ARP request* datagram. This request is a broadcast, using the broadcast hardware address. Every machine on the local network which is running ARP software hears the request, but only the target machine, which has a binding for the requested IP address, responds to the request as shown in Figure 2.16. The target machine, when it receives this datagram, will reply with its hardware address by sending back an *ARP reply* datagram.

Figure 2.16 Requesting a resolution for an IP address to a hardware (MAC) address.

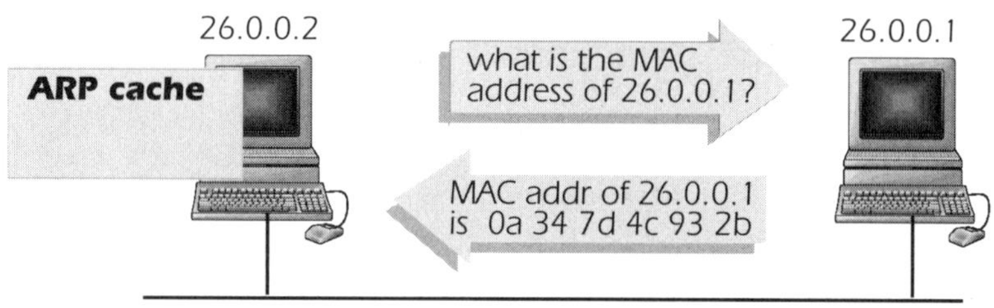

ARP cache: temporary storage found on any IP machine that contains IP to hardware address mappings.

This newly learned hardware address is then stored in the local machine in a safe place in memory called the **ARP cache**. The ARP cache contains a list of local IP addresses and their associated hardware addresses.

Once the hardware address of the target is found, the IP datagram can be put into a network interface (e.g. Ethernet) frame and then transmitted on the network.

The ARP Cache

The ARP cache resides on every machine running a TCP/IP stack. Found in this cache is a listing of IP addresses and their associated hardware addresses. There are both static and dynamic entries in this table.

Dynamic entries are inserted by normal operation of the ARP protocol[8] itself from the ARP reply datagrams. These entries have a maximum time to live (TTL) in the cache. Note that this TTL is *not* related to the IP TTL header field. The TTL for each entry is represented in seconds. When the time to live has expired for an entry, it is removed from the cache. The default ARP cache TTL for Windows NT is two minutes. Many UNIX systems have ARP cache TTLs as long as fifteen or twenty minutes.

Static entries are created by the use of the ***arp*** command at the NT command prompt. The ***arp*** command only has an effect on the local machine's ARP cache. Static entries remain in the cache until the machine is restarted. Possible options to ***arp*** are shown in Table 2.8.

Table 2.8
Windows NT ARP command options.

Option	Description
-d	Delete a particular entry.
-a	Display all entries.
-a <inet addr>	Display entries for the specified IP address.
-a -N <if addr>	Display entries for the specified interface.
-s	Add a static entry to the ARP cache.

The ***arp*** command may be used to look at the current machine's ARP cache. To display all entries, use the ***-a*** option as shown in Figure 2.18.

ARP cache life: number of seconds of inactivity that a learned entry will remain in the cache.

You will only see dynamic entries in the ARP cache for machines that the current machine has sent datagrams to "recently" (within the ARP cache TTL—also called **ARP cache life**). The ***arp*** command doesn't show the remaining time for the entries, but the entries may simply not be in the table the next time you run the command. You will not see address translations for remote machines (such as those on the far side of a router) because the current machine is not actually sending datagram directly to them, but to the router instead.

8. Yes, saying ARP protocol is like saying PIN number or LAN network.

An ARP Cache Example

Consider the network in Figure 2.17 with three subnets.[9] Let's look at the ARP cache of a couple of the machines in this network.

Figure 2.17 This network of three subnets is used for an example of two ARP caches.

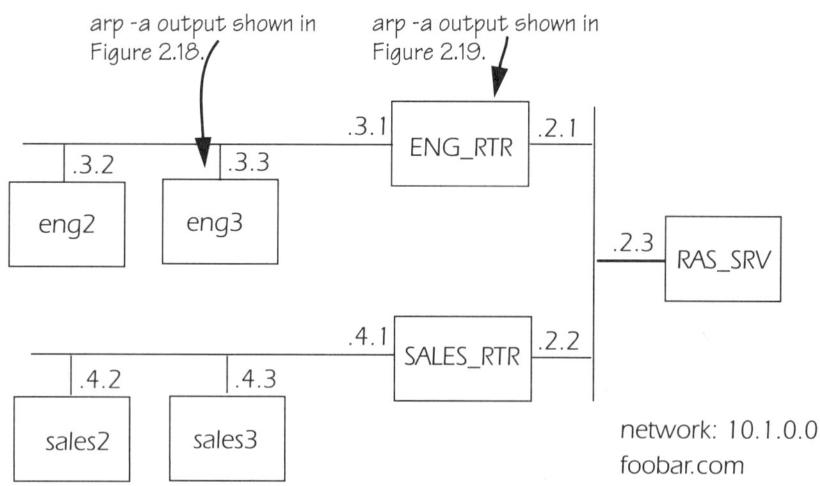

Figure 2.18 shows ***arp -a*** command output executed on eng3 (10.1.3.3). Eng3 has been communicating with ENG_RTR (10.1.3.1) and eng2 (10.1.3.2) via it's Ethernet interface (#2), and so there is an entry in its ARP cache for each of these other machines. Each ARP cache entry includes the IP address and the physical address. No ARP cache entries exist for interface #1 which is a loopback interface.

Figure 2.18 Windows NT ***arp*** command shows IP to MAC address mappings found in the ARP cache.

```
cmd
C:\WINNT>arp -a

Interface: 10.1.3.3 on Interface 2
  Internet Address      Physical Address      Type
  10.1.3.1              00-a0-24-a9-1c-1b     dynamic
  10.1.3.2              00-a0-24-65-aa-40     dynamic

C:\WINNT>_
```

Figure 2.19 shows ***arp -a*** command output executed on ENG_RTR (10.1.3.1). Note that the ARP cache here is shown as two separate tables. There is a

9. Subnets are covered in detail in the next chapter: IP Subnetting.

separate ARP cache per interface. ENG_RTR has sent datagrams to both eng2 and eng3 via its 10.1.3.1 interface, and to SALES_RTR and RAS_SRV by way of its 10.1.2.1 interface.

Figure 2.19
Each network interface has a separate ARP cache.

```
cmd

C:\WINNT>arp -a

Interface: 10.1.3.1 on Interface 3
  Internet Address      Physical Address      Type
  10.1.3.2              00-a0-24-65-aa-40     dynamic
  10.1.3.3              00-a0-24-a6-8d-e9     dynamic

Interface: 10.1.2.1 on Interface 4
  Internet Address      Physical Address      Type
  10.1.2.2              00-80-c7-7c-dc-96     dynamic
  10.1.2.3              00-a0-24-a9-1c-26     dynamic

C:\WINNT>_
```

ARP Cache Registry Values

Some parameters are stored on each Windows NT machine which affect the behavior of ARP. Administration of these parameters are discussed in the section on "Where TCP/IP Parameters are Stored in NT" on page 195 in the "Installing and Configuring TCP/IP on NT" chapter.

ARP maintains a cache of recently used entries for a certain lifetime, measured in seconds. If an ARP entry does not specify a lifetime, a default value is used. The ArpCacheLife registry parameter[10] specifies this default lifetime (Table 2.9).

Table 2.9
Arp Cache Life registry parameter.

Hive:	HKEY_LOCAL_MACHINE
Key:	\System\CurrentControlSet\Services\Tcplp\Parameters
Name:	ArpCacheLife
Type:	REG_DWORD
Value:	120 (default: 120 seconds = 2 minutes)

10. ArpCacheLife and ArpCacheSize do not initially appear in the registry in NT 4.0 — they must be added to the registry, setting the values as appropriate.

The ARP cache can hold a finite number of entries. The ArpCacheSize parameter defines the maximum number of entries in the ARP cache (Table 2.10).

Table 2.10
Arp Cache Size registry parameter.

Hive:	HKEY_LOCAL_MACHINE
Key:	\System\CurrentControlSet\Services\Tcpip\Parameters
Name:	ArpCacheSize
Type:	REG_DWORD
Value:	62 (default)

Broadcast Packets

Recall that a bridge is a device that operates at layer 2 of the OSI stack, while a router operates at layer 3 of the OSI stack. Therefore, bridges will send Ethernet broadcasts through to the other segments, but routers will prevent this. In Figure 2.20, an Ethernet broadcast from iguana will be stopped at the router. Therefore all ARP requests, which are hardware broadcasts, will also be stopped at the router.

Figure 2.20
Broadcasts are often stopped at routers and not forwarded.

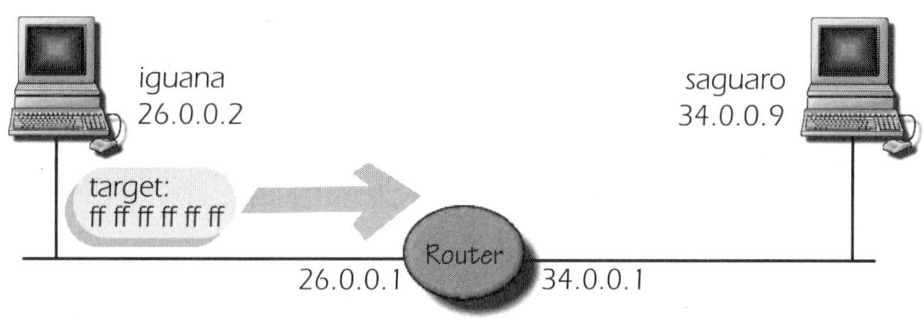

Note that in terms of IP broadcasts, a router can be configured to forward or drop these IP broadcast packets. If you are using DHCP in your network and you have only one DHCP server, you would want to configure the router to pass DHCP broadcasts.

Using ARP in a Routed Network

IP datagrams contain the IP addresses of the source and target machines. However, the source and the target may not be attached to the same LAN — the target address may be a remote destination. In this case, the transmission media is responsible for getting the datagram from one machine to the next, with routers forwarding it on, until ultimately the datagram reaches its destination. The network interface layer header on each link will contain the hardware address of the next "hop".

Figure 2.21 shows an example of this. The sending machine, iguana, determines that the source and target machines are in different networks, and so the datagram must be sent to the default gateway. Iguana is configured with the IP address of the default gateway, but not the hardware address. The hardware address is needed in order to encapsulate the IP datagram in an Ethernet frame.

Figure 2.21
An ARP exchange may be required for each hop.

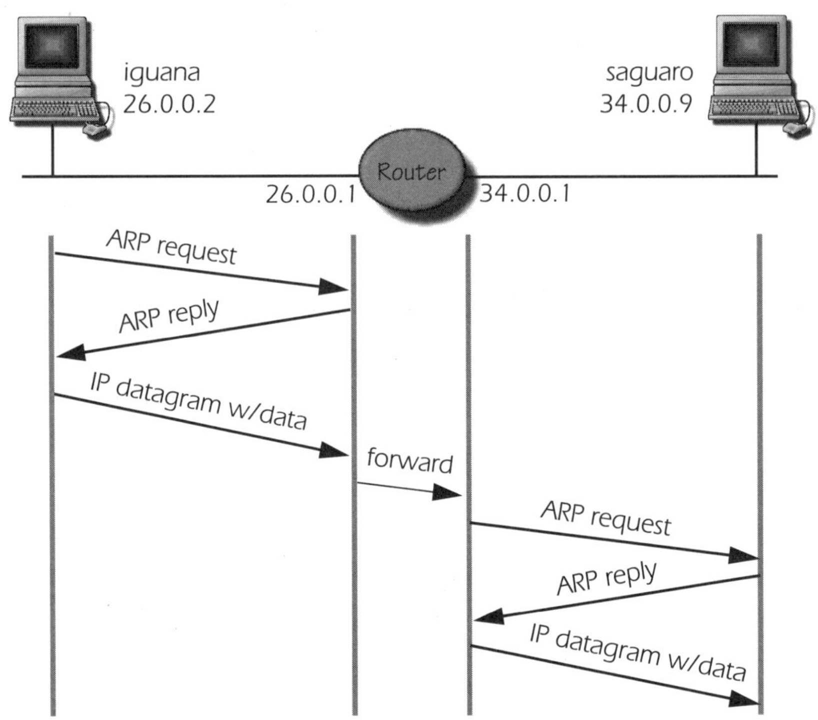

Iguana checks its ARP cache to see if it has a matching entry. Let's assume that it does not. Therefore iguana will broadcast an ARP request, asking for the router's hardware address. The router will reply, and then *iguana* can update its ARP cache and send the IP datagram to the router.

Those steps are repeated at the router. When the router receives the IP datagram, it determines if the destination is local or remote: in the example above, it is a local address from the router. Therefore, the router will check its ARP cache for the address of the target: *saguaro*. Assuming that the router hasn't send any datagrams to *saguaro* recently, there will be no entry in the router's ARP cache. The router will then broadcast an ARP request for the target, *saguaro*. *Saguaro* will reply with its hardware address. Then the router can update its ARP cache and transmit the original IP datagram to the final destination, *saguaro*.

IP Header Fields

If you are interested in the detailed operation of IP, this section will help you. IP header fields are explained in detail in this section. Figure 2.22 shows the format of an IP datagram transmitted on an DIX Ethernet network.

Figure 2.22
The IP header follows a network interface layer (e.g. Ethernet) header.

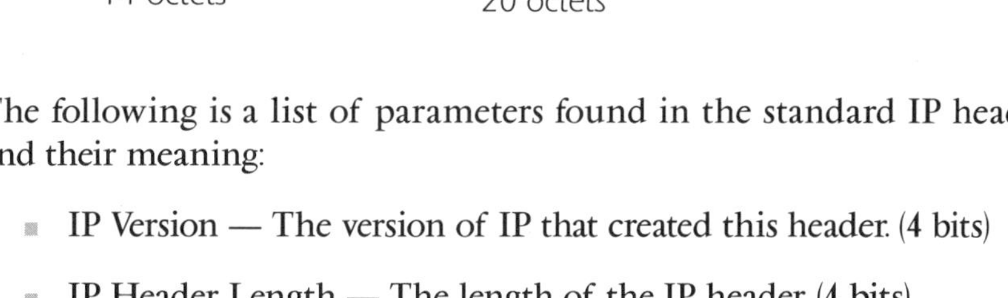

The following is a list of parameters found in the standard IP header, and their meaning:

- IP Version — The version of IP that created this header. (4 bits)
- IP Header Length — The length of the IP header. (4 bits)
- Precedence — Gives some datagrams special handling. (3 bits)

- TOS bits — The type of service requested for this datagram (5 bits)
- Total IP Length — Length of the datagram: payload and header. (16 bits)
- Datagram ID — Pseudo unique identifier. (16 bits)
- Fragmentation — Used when the datagram is fragmented. (16 bits)
- TTL — Time to Live for the datagram. (8 bits)
- Protocol — The protocol that IP is carrying as payload. (8 bits)
- Checksum — IP header checksum. Doesn't cover payload. (16 bits)
- Source IP address (32 bits)
- Destination IP address (32 bits)

These fields are laid out into a compact format which takes five words. Each word in this case is thirty-two bits. Figure 2.23 shows the layout of a standard IP header.

Figure 2.23
Standard IP header layout — five 32-bit words.

bits 0-3	bits 4-7	bits 8-10	bits 11-15	bits 16-19	bits 20-23	bits 24-27	bits 28-31
Vers.	IHL	Prc	TOS	total IP length			
datagram ID number				fragmentation			
time to live		protocol		checksum			
source address							
target address							

Beyond the *standard IP header*, there may also be several options. If included, the options area may be from 1-10 words in length. Rather than counting in this specialized thirty-two bit word format, we usually say that the options area may be 4 to 40 octets long in increments of 4 octets.

Here is a description of the various standard fields in detail. We'll go through the fields in sequence, essentially nibble by nibble and byte by byte.

IP Version Number

The first four bits (nibble) of an IP header form the *IP version number.* The current version of IP is version 4. It has been used since around 1981.Version 6 is just starting to gain popularity. The header contents described here are all about version 4. Version 6 is only the same in the first nibble[11] of the IP header.

IP Header Length

The IP header length measures the number of 32-bit words that are used for the IP header. We can think of each 32-bit word as a chunk of four adjacent octets[12]. The standard IP header takes up five words, or 20 octets. Therefore the minimum legal value in the *IP header length (IHL)* field is 5. An example of this is shown in Figure 2.24. A value greater than five indicates that there are some additional four-octet chunks allocated for use by options. An IHL of 6 specifies 4 options octets, IHL=7 gives room for 8 options octets, and so forth up to IHL=15 which gives us space for 40 options octets. The IHL value is encoded in four bits and packed into the least significant bits of the same octet as the IP version number.

Therefore, with a standard IP version 4 header, which has IHL=5, we have the hex value of 45 in the first header octet.

Figure 2.24
Example value for first IP header octet. (hex=45)

Version				Header length			
0	1	0	0	0	1	0	1

11. A nibble (a.k.a. nybble) is four bits, or half of an 8-bit byte. Traditionally, various byte sizes have been used, however in recent days the popularity of the assumption that bytes are always 8 bits seems to have prevailed, thus making bytes equivalent to octets in most circles. The term octet is still preferred by some people because it is more precisely and explicitly an eight-bit thing. Two nibbles make an octet. It just doesn't have the same ring to it as "a nybble is a half of a byte."
12. Four octets is also referred to as four bytes, longword or word.

Precedence

The next field may be used to specify the *precedence* of the datagram. Most traffic in the Internet is considered "routine" precedence. There are several other levels of precedence which are listed in Table 2.11.

Table 2.11
IP precedence field values.

Precedence	Description
000	Routine Precedence
001	Priority
010	Immediate
011	Flash
100	Flash Override
101	CRTIC/ECP (Emergency Control Procedures)
110	Internetwork Control
111	National Network Control

The precedence values with higher numbers than routine (all others) are considered as reserved for use by military applications[13]. Remember that IP was designed for the U. S. Department of Defense network. Just as the Interstate highway system was designed to transport military troops, so the ARPAnet (and now Internet and MILnet) was designed to handle transport of military information. But when it's not needed for those purposes, we can drive on it (i.e. use it for our routine purposes).

Some implementations of IP are not intended to handle any values other than routine precedence. Routers which do recognize higher precedences will drop datagrams with such values.

13. Some (non military by the way) implementations of OSPF have been known to use the Internetwork Control (110) precedence.

Type of Service

There are five bits allocated to specify a special *type of service (TOS)* for the IP datagram. One of these bits is reserved for future use. The other four may be set mutually exclusively to indicate one of four special types of service. If none of these bits is set, then no special type of service is indicated, also called the "normal" type of service.

- Reserved (16).
- Cost (8) — select a low monetary cost link or circuit for this datagram.
- Reliability (4) — select a high reliability link or circuit for this datagram.
- Throughput (2) — select a high throughput link or circuit for this datagram.
- Delay (1) — select a low delay link or circuit for this datagram.

The precedence and type of service fields are combined into one octet, often called the type of service or TOS octet (Table 2.12). The value of routine and normal data is written in hex as 00.

Table 2.12
Precedence and type of service combined in one octet

Precedence			Type of Service				
0	0	0	X	C	R	T	D

Total IP Length

This field indicates the *total IP length* of the datagram including the header. If this datagram is a fragment[14] of a larger original datagram, the length indicates only how much information is specified in this fragment.

14. Fragmentation is used to break up big IP datagrams into manageable pieces, and is discussed on page 87.

The total IP length field is encoded as a 16-bit unsigned number. This value specifies the number of octets in the "total" IP datagram including the header and upper layer data. So theoretically this length could be between 0 and 65,535. But the minimum length of an IP datagram would be the header alone, so the minimum length is 20.

What if you want to know the size of the payload, or upper layer data that IP is carrying? Take the value of the total IP length field and subtract the number of octets in the header. For instance, with an IP header length of 5 words (20 octets) and a total IP length of 52 octets, we simply subtract the header length from the total length. The result will be 32 octets of data carried in this datagram.

Datagram Identifier

The datagram identifier uniquely (within a certain period of time) identifies a datagram from a particular source. This value is used in association with the fragmentation information described next. The value is assigned even when there is no fragmentation so that it can be used for diagnostic and troubleshooting purposes.

This value is incremented for each datagram sent by IP, thus it will wrap past 65,535 back to zero for every 65,536 datagrams sent.

Fragmentation Fields

The sixteen bits following the datagram identifier are used to encode four fields:

- reserved — one bit
- *don't fragment indicator (DF)* — one bit
- *fragment status (S)* — one bit
- *fragment offset* — thirteen bits

Normal datagrams are not fragmented. The values of DF, S, and the fragment offset would all be zeros, making the whole sixteen bit value zero (the reserved bit should always be zero). When there is fragmentation, you will see non-zero values in either or both of the status and fragment offset fields, such as that shown in Table 2.13. The status field is equal to one, and the fragment offset has a value of 185.

Table 2.13 A typical value for the fragment field in a fragmented datagram.

X	DF	S	Fragment Offset												
0	0	1	0	0	0	0	0	1	0	1	1	1	0	0	1

The fragmentation procedure is discussed on page 88.

Time to Live

The *Time To Live (TTL)* field is specified as the maximum number of seconds this datagram may be allowed to travel through the network toward its destination. Actually it was the number of seconds that routers along the way could hold on to the datagram, as it doesn't account for transmission latency, data link queueing, or bridging. In practice however, most routers decrement this value by one, thus it is essentially a maximum hop count.

Protocol

The upper layer *protocol* carried by IP is specified here. ICMP has a value of 1. TCP has a value of 6, and UDP has a value of 17, usually written in hex as 11. There are about 100 of the 256 possible values for this field assigned to various protocols; ICMP, TCP, and UDP are the ones most commonly used in IP networks. You may refer to the Assigned Numbers RFC [RFC1700] for a detailed list of IP protocol numbers. A few of the protocols you may encounter with Windows NT are listed in Table 2.14.

Table 2.14 Some common protocol types carried by IP.

Protocol	Number	Description
ICMP	1	Internet Control Message Protocol
TCP	6	Transmission Control Protocol
BGP	8	Border Gateway Protocol (not supported)
UDP	17	User Datagram Protocol
GRE	47	Generic Routing Encapsulation
OSPF	89	Open Shortest Path First

Checksum

The checksum field is used as an *IP header checksum* — it provides an integrity check for the header only and not the payload of the datagram. For each datagram which is to be transmitted, the sender calculates a sum of the header contents and stores the sum in the header so that the receiver may check the stored value against its own calculation. The calculation is a one's complement sum (i.e. bitwise exclusive or) of 16-bit chunks of the header, then as a final step, the result is inverted (i.e. one's complement) prior to being stored in the header. Because some of the media over which IP may be carried may not have checksums or CRCs, IP performs this function. Note that IP performs this function regardless of underlying checks or integrity.

If IP receives a datagram that holds a checksum value which doesn't match the sum of the datagram header contents, the datagram is simply (and silently) discarded. This prevents corrupted data from being accepted by IP.[15]

15. The checksum calculation used in IP doesn't absolutely prevent all possible corruption from passing the check, but it checks within an acceptable margin.

Source IP Address

The fourth word of an IP header specifies the *source IP address*. This indicates from whence the datagram came.

When IP sends a datagram, the source IP address is specified so that replies may be sent by the recipient's host-to-host or process layer protocols. The source IP address may also be used by upper layer protocols on the recipient as a part of a connection identifier (e.g. TCP).

Target IP Address

The fifth word of an IP header specifies the *target IP address*. This indicates where the datagram is intended to go.

Transmitting "Big" Datagrams

Each network interface used with IP has a maximum transmission unit (MTU) parameter — the number of octets in the largest datagram which may be sent over that network interface. Ethernet and PPP both have MTUs of 1500 octets. An MTU is typically related to the frame size used by an interface. If no MTU is specified by a network interface driver, IP assumes a *default MTU* of 576 octets.

fragmentation: the process of taking an IP datagram and chopping it up so it will fit into a network interface layer frame.

The total IP length field is 16 bits long, conceptually allowing IP datagrams as long as 65,535 octets in length (including the header). There may be implementation restrictions in the programming interface. One of the features of IP is that it allows you to transmit arbitrarily long datagrams (within its 64K limit) regardless of the underlying transmission media being used. When a datagram fits within the MTU size of the interface it is being transmitted on, the datagram is simply encapsulated in a frame by the network interface driver. However, when the datagram size is larger than the MTU size, IP uses **fragmentation**. In order to receive fragmented datagrams, IP's receive procedure uses a technique called **reassembly**.

Fragmentation

reassembly: the process of recognizing a fragmented datagram and stitching the pieces back together into a whole datagram.

The process of fragmentation is used when IP is transmitting a datagram which is too long to fit into the network interface. When fragmenting a datagram, IP performs the following steps:

1. Notes the size of the IP header on the current datagram.
2. Subtracts this size from the MTU for the interface.[16]
3. Chops the payload being carried by this IP datagram into chunks the size of the MTU minus header size.
4. Puts a copy of the original IP header on each chunk.
5. Writes a unique code in the fragmentation fields of each chunk's IP header.
6. Computes the total IP length and checksum fields as appropriate for each fragment as though they had originally been independent datagrams.

Here are the rules for how IP writes the unique codes in the fragmentation fields.

- The *fragment status* is written as a zero for the last fragment of a datagram, and set to one for all other fragments to indicate that there are more fragments to come.
- The *fragment offset* is the distance in octets after the first octet of the original datagram to the first octet in this fragment. Because the fragment offset field is only 13 bits and the datagram size is 16 bits, this number needs to actually be written in the datagram assuming a factor of eight octets.[17]

For example, with a 1500 octet MTU and a standard IP header (20 octets) we may chop the payload into 1480 octet chunks. By assuming the factor

16. Then round down to the nearest multiple of eight octets.

17. Sixteen minus thirteen is three. We're three bits short in the fragment offset, so to make up for it we assume a multiple of $2^3 = 8$.

of eight, we divide 1480 by 8, giving 185. The values in the fragment offset would be multiples of 185, for instance: 0, 185, 370, 555, 740, 925, etc. in successive fragments. Each fragment but the last would have a total IP length of 1500 octets, and the fragment status would be set to one. The final fragment would have a fragment status of zero and a total IP length big enough to carry the remainder of the payload plus IP header.

Reassembly

Only the final (i.e. target) destination may reassemble a datagram. When any datagram with a non-zero fragment offset or fragment status of one is received, the receiver notes that this datagram is a fragment of a larger whole and therefore begins the reassembly process. Here's the process we'd use if we were IP:

1. See if we already have received any other fragments for this same datagram (same source IP address and datagram identifier). If so, correlate the fragments (go to step 4).
2. Note that we've got a part of this datagram, labelling the note with the source IP address and datagram identifier.
3. Start a timer for the maximum time we'll wait for all fragments of this datagram.
4. Check to see if we've got the whole datagram. This involves stitching together the fragments based on their offsets and sizes. Once we've received all adjacent pieces from offset zero through the fragment with the fragment status of zero, we've got the whole datagram reassembled. Clear the timer and deliver the datagram to the upper-layer protocol as though it had actually been transmitted in one piece.

While fragmentation and reassembly provide a useful service as a part of IP's functionality, the cost in processing time and resources adds to the end to end delay for datagram delivery.

Ding! What happens when the reassembly timer expires before all of the fragments of a datagram have been received? All of the fragments which had been received are discarded. Then the receiver forgets about that datagram, thus the datagram is lost. Before this occurs, an ICMP time exceeded error message is send to the source of the fragments which had been received. If any fragments arrive later, they are treated as a new datagram, and will be later discarded when the timer expires again.

Internet Control Message Protocol (ICMP)

There are two reasons that IP occasionally sends some administrative messages:

- exceptions
- diagnostics / configuration

For both of these administrative tasks, IP uses the *Internet Control Message Protocol (ICMP)*. There are actually several types of ICMP messages which may be categorized into those two general areas. Each ICMP message begins with a common header, followed by information specific to the message type.

The ICMP message header is 32-bits long and specifies three fields as shown in Figure 2.25. The *type* field is simply a number identifying which kind of ICMP message this is. The *code* further qualifies the variety of the message relative to the type. A few of the ICMP message types are described on the next few pages.

Figure 2.25
ICMP message header.

bits 0-3	bits 4-7	bits 8-11	bits 12-15	bits 16-19	bits 20-23	bits 24-27	bits 28-31
Type		Code		Checksum			

The checksum is calculated over the whole ICMP message using the same method as the IP header checksum (page 86).

ICMP messages are carried by IP with a protocol number of one. Yet IP uses ICMP to report diagnostics and exceptions. This is a good example of a symbiotic relationship between protocols.

Destination Unreachable Exception

If for some reason IP cannot deliver a datagram to its intended target, IP may request that ICMP send a message back to the source of the original datagram indicating this exception. ICMP simply reports exceptions or error conditions, but does not attempt to correct them or attempt to determine their cause. ICMP is an informant, not an investigator or jury.

Actually, ICMP isn't used solely by IP. For instance, a target destination may be reachable with IP, but no process is listening on the UDP or TCP port specified in a host-to-host header. It would be up to UDP or TCP to request that ICMP send a destination unreachable message.[18]

There are several reasons that a destination may be unreachable. The different reasons are specified in the code field of the ICMP message header.

Additionally, a copy of the failed IP header and the first eight octets of the upper layer protocol are placed in the ICMP message as shown in Figure 2.26. The type value for destination unreachable messages is 3. Table 2.15 lists the meanings for some destination unreachable code values:

Figure 2.26
ICMP exception message (e.g. destination unreachable or time exceeded).

bits 0-3	bits 4-7	bits 8-11	bits 12-15	bits 16-19	bits 20-23	bits 24-27	bits 28-31
Type		Code		Checksum			
reserved							
failed IP header							
first eight octets of upper layer							

18. TCP actually sends an ACK,RST segment back to the origin when no process is listening at the port. UDP does indeed call upon ICMP to send a destination unreachable.

Table 2.15 Destination unreachable codes.

Description	Code
network unreachable	0
host unreachable	1
protocol unreachable	2
port unreachable	3
don't fragment bit (prevents fragmentation)	4
source route failed	5
destination network unknown	6
destination host unknown	7
source host isolated	8
network administratively unreachable	9
host administratively unreachable	10
network unreachable with specified type of service	11
host unreachable with specified type of service	12
communication administratively prohibited	13
host precedence violation	14
precedence cut-off in effect	15

Time Exceeded Exception

Like the destination unreachable message type, the ICMP time exceeded message type indicates a failure to communicate. The type value for time exceeded messages is 11. There are two varieties of time exceeded message, as shown in Table 2.16. Both use the exception message format like the destination unreachable.

Table 2.16 Time exceeded codes.

Description	Code
time to live exceeded	0
fragmentation reassembly timer expired	1

Diagnostic Echo Service

Besides the exception types of ICMP messages, there are request/reply messages which may be used for configuration or diagnostic purposes. The most common of these diagnostic messages is the echo service The echo request/reply service is used by the diagnostic command ***ping***.

An *echo request* may be sent from one machine to another. The ICMP software on the target will send an *echo reply* back to the source of the echo request. The data carried in the echo request will be echoed back in the echo reply. The type for an echo request is 8, and a type of 0 is used for echo reply messages. The code is 0 for these requests and replies. The message format is shown in Figure 2.27.

Figure 2.27 ICMP diagnostic message (e.g. echo request/reply).

bits 0-3	bits 4-7	bits 8-11	bits 12-15	bits 16-19	bits 20-23	bits 24-27	bits 28-31
Type		Code		Checksum			
Identifier				Sequence Number			
variable length data							

Summary

Here's a summary of the items which have been addressed in this chapter.

- IP addresses provide a common numbering scheme regardless of the type of underlying data link being used.
- Each interface in the network is assigned an IP address.

- Machines may be multihomed simply by having interfaces to more than one network. Routers can forward data between their multiple interfaces.
- IP addresses are written in dotted decimal notation, which helps show the structure of the address, such as the class.
- The header on each IP datagram contains fields which may modify the delivery of datagrams.
- Datagrams may be sent directly to machines on the same network. In order to send datagrams to a machine on another network, the datagram must first go to a router with an interface on the local network.
- To actually transmit a datagram over an interface, IP must first obtain a data link layer (e.g. MAC) address of the immediate target, which will be either the local destination or a local interface on a router.
- ICMP messages are used for exceptions and diagnostics.

Further Reading

Here is information about various books and magazines in which to look for further information on the subject.

[Black1993] Black, Uyless, *Computer Networks: Protocols, Standards, and Interfaces, Second Edition*, 1993, Prentice-Hall

[Comer1995] Comer, Douglas E., *Internetworking with TCP/IP Vol I: Principles, Protocols, and Architecture, Third Edition*, 1995, Prentice-Hall, Inc.

[Feit1997] Feit, Dr. Sidnie, *TCP/IP Architecture, Protocols, and Implementation/2e*, 1997 McGraw-Hill

[Rekhter1996] Rekhter, Y., et al, *Address Allocation for Private Internets*, 1996, IETF RFC 1918

[Simoneau1997] Simoneau, Paul, *Hands-On TCP/IP,* 1997, McGraw-Hill

[Stallings1991] Stallings, William, *Data and Computer Communications, Third Edition,* 1991, Macmillan

[Stevens1994] Stevens, W. Richard, *TCP/IP Illustrated, Volume 1: The Protocols,* 1994, Addison Wesley

[Tanenbaum1989] Tanenbaum, Andrew S., *Computer Networks, Second Edition,* 1989, Prentice-Hall

3 IP Subnetting

Dividing IP networks into smaller, more manageable sections is possible when using subnetting. Subnetting allows you to partition the network into several smaller subnetworks, thereby localizing traffic and increasing network efficiency. Subnetting concepts, rules, and subnet masks will be discussed in this chapter, building upon the concepts in the previous chapter.

How Big Can a Network Be?

How many machines can you effectively have on a network? Several factors must be assessed in order to answer this question. Some of these factors are as follows:

- channel assignment or arbitration on the media
- bursty or continuous data
- variance in traffic from node to node
- quality of service required at peak busy times
- transmission delay
- network protocol characteristics

The combinations of these factors lead to a large number of possibilities. There are guidelines that can be used to determine a practical number. In addition, simulation and network monitoring may be used to arrive empirically at numbers for a particular network.

subnet: a portion of an IP network.

The practical size of a network depends on the media used. One study showed that around 25-30 nodes on an Ethernet segment was a practical upper limit. As routers became popular to connect various segments, the desire to partition a network according to a planned numbering scheme increased. Class A, B, or C networks may have roughly 16 million, 65 thousand, or 250 nodes respectively. With only between a dozen and a hundred nodes per network in practice, it made sense to partition a network into several smaller **subnetworks** (or simply **subnets**), so that the larger network address space is not wasted.

Subnets and Routing

With no subnetting, two hosts attached to the same network segment can communicate directly only if they have matching network identifiers. For example, in Figure 3.1, A and B can communicate directly. However neither A nor B can communicate with C because they have different network identifiers than C.

Figure 3.1 Hosts with different network IDs cannot communicate without the assistance of a router.

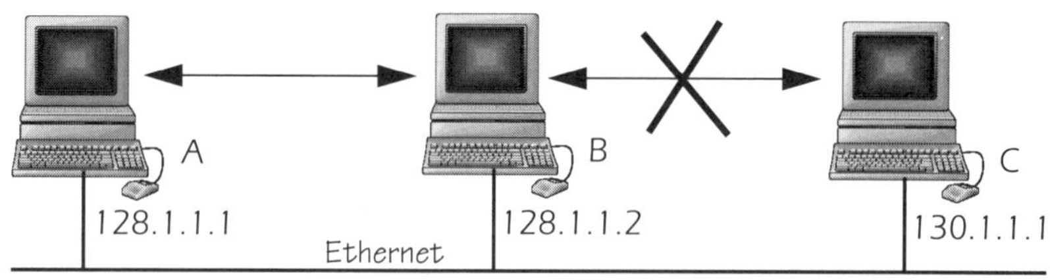

Although A, B, and C are on the same cable, they need a router to communicate.

The same is true of hosts on the same cable, but configured to be on different subnets. In order for machines on different subnets to talk to each other, a router must be involved, and send the datagram from one subnet to the other subnet.

subnet mask: a value used to partition an IP address into three parts: network portion, subnet portion, and interface portion.

In Figure 3.2, a datagram is arriving from the Internet to the organization's gateway (router). Routers make routing decisions based upon a datagram's target IP address and their routing tables. We'll discuss routing tables in the "NT Server as an IP Router" chapter. For now, assume that the router knows to pick its 190.1.20.254 interface. The router then uses that interface address, the associated **subnet mask**,[1] and the target IP address to see if it can send locally out that interface, or if it must send remotely to another router through that interface. All of these pieces of information (IP address and subnet mask from the interface, and the datagram's target address) must be used together in order for the router to do its job.

1. The subnet mask is a parameter of each network interface binding. Subnet masks are described in detail in "Step 5: Convince IP to Use the Subnet Field" on page 112.

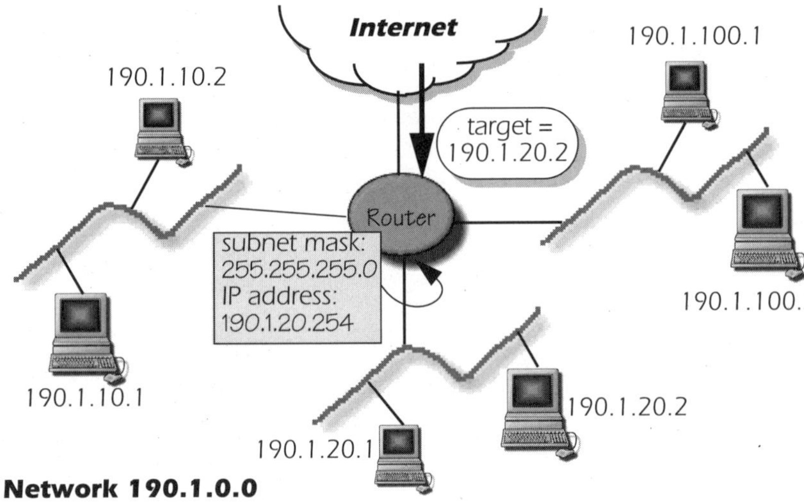

Figure 3.2
The router will use its subnet mask, interface address, and the datagram's target address to see that it can send locally on the bottom LAN.

In this chapter, we'll describe subnetting in several sections:

- Subnetting Basics
- Subnetting Example
- Subnet Details
- Calculating the Number of Subnets and Hosts
- Rules of Subnetting
- Address Utilization
- Calculating Subnetted IP Addresses

Subnetting Basics

subnetting: dividing up a network into smaller, more manageable pieces (subnets).

To ease administrative tasks, an additional level of addressing can be introduced in the network, called **subnetting**. With subnetting you divide your network into several "subnetworks" (or *subnets*) and divide your host machines among the subnets.

Address Space

Recall that with a thirty-two bit IP address, there are roughly four billion possible addresses. This is referred to as the total IP address space. This overall space is divided up into three[2] kinds of networks: 128 class A networks with 16,777,216 addresses in each, 16,384 class B networks with 65,536 addresses each, and 2,097,152 class C networks with 256 addresses each. Some restrictions may apply.

The network address space that you have to work with depends on the class of network address that you have. The network address space is dependent on the size of the locally administered field. Figure 3.3 shows the total IP address space as the rectangle on the left. Three example networks (one of each class) are shown on the right so that you can see the relative sizes (not exactly to scale).

Figure 3.3
The IP address space is divided up into various size networks of three different classes. A sample network of each class is shown.

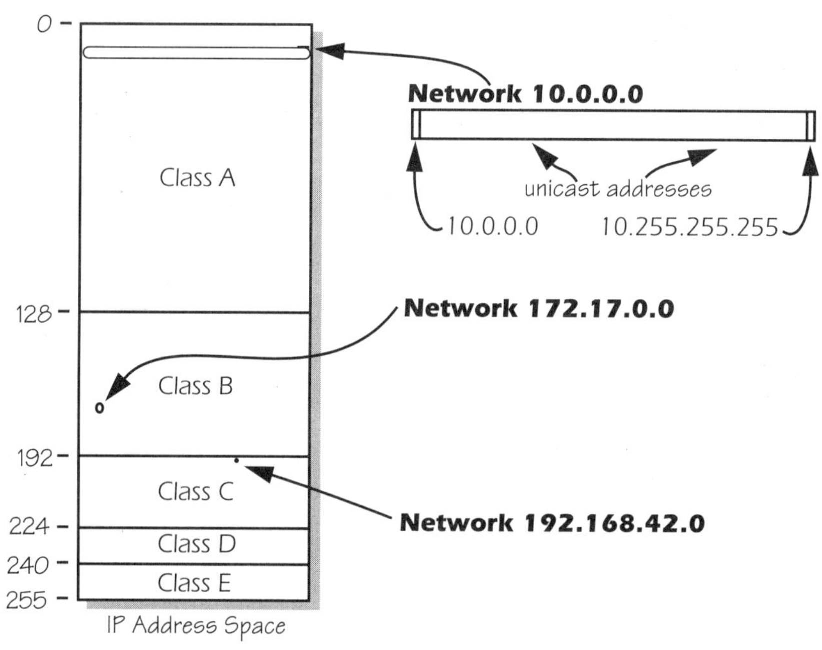

If your organization has a class A network assignment (or you've decided to use the non-routable network 10.0.0.0 internally), you have a fraction of

2. Recall that of the five class of IP addresses, three are used to specify networks.

this space— approximately 16 million addresses. If you don't use all of those addresses, the remainder goes to waste— no other organization can use them. Therefore if organizations have a class A network address yet aren't using a significant percentage of their network address space, there is a tremendous amount of wasted addresses in the global IP addressing scheme.

Also, if you have your network devices spread among multiple locations, all connected to a single physical (or bridged) link, you would not be able to route traffic among the locations! This is because IP uses the network number to make its decisions about routing between networks. If you only have one network number, IP cannot differentiate between the physical locations.

Five—Step Procedure for Subnetting

The solution to this problem is to subnet your network. Assign to each physically grouped (or logically grouped) set of machines a subnet value that is unique within your network addressing scheme. In particular, you should: apply the *five steps of subnetting*:

1. Decide how you want to logically divide your network according to bandwidth, security, cable length, and other parameters.
2. Divide up the network address space into smaller pieces based on your plan.
3. Partition your locally administered field into subnet number and interface number fields accordingly.
4. Assign IP addresses to your machines based on the network, subnet, and interface numbers.
5. Convince IP in each of these machines to base its routing on the subnet number field and not just the network number field.

This is an overview of how to implement subnetting in your network. We'll now look at an example of how these steps can be applied.

Subnetting Example

This example will illustrate the need for subnetting at a small company. We'll walk through the five steps of subnetting for this example, introducing the essential concepts of subnetting.

In the following section, we'll point out further details of subnetting to round out your knowledge of subnetting.

Step 1: Plan Logical Network Divisions

Let's start with the most important step of subnetting. We want to step back and look at what we're trying to interconnect. Consider the small fictitious network shown in Figure 3.4 for this example.

Figure 3.4
Three small networks (and another network) connected with a router.

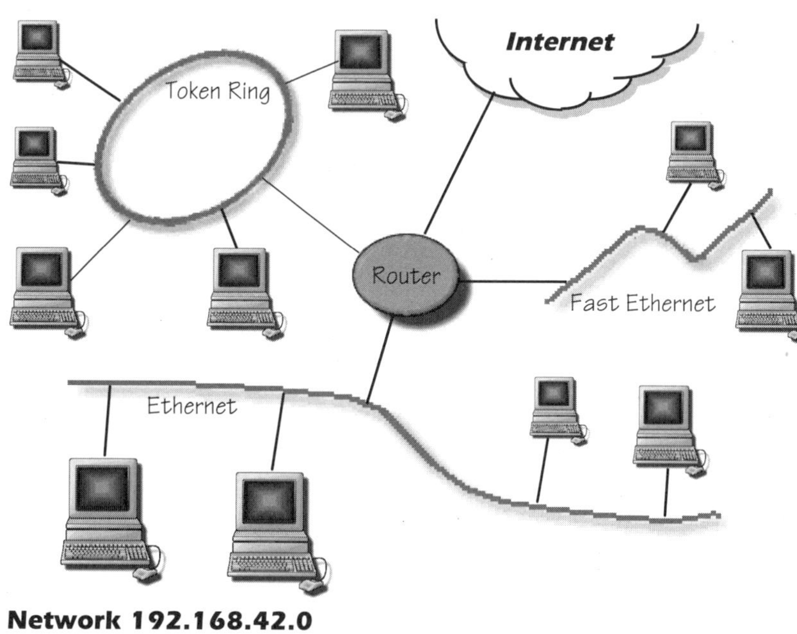

Figure 3.4 shows that network 192.168.42.0 has the following components:

- Eleven host computers.
- One router.
- Three local area networks.
- One wide area link to [an access provider to] the Internet.
- One network number: 192.168.42.0.

This setup is used by a company which makes a product called zizzies. A consultant visited this company to set up a web server for them, and registered the domain name xyzzy.com for them. The consultant walked out when the company claimed that their domain name was misspelled,[3] so now it's up to you to figure out how to finish interconnecting the networks that they have.

Zizzi has five computers which live in their manufacturing area, and are connected by a token ring network. These computers have been running another protocol stack, but Zizzi wants to run TCP/IP on them now.

There are four computers in the product development area. They have been running TCP/IP in this network for over ten years. Since they haven't been connected to the outside world except by something called UUCP, they've been using an IP network number of 192.0.0.0 internally. That will change now.

In the recent past, someone at Zizzi took a machine off the token ring and put it on a fast Ethernet segment. Then they took another machine off development's Ethernet and put it onto the fast Ethernet. These two machines are used as servers.

Now they've gotten a router to replace the old translating bridge that they had been using. They want to connect to the Internet so that they can sell zizzies on the Web.

Zizzi should associate one subnet with each physical network so that the router can handle communication between all of the networks. They should have four logical networks (subnets) — three for the internal networks, and one for the network interface to their Internet access provider.

3. Word-of-mouth contracts are a many-splendored thing.

Step 2: Divide Network Address Space into Subnets

Now that Zizzi knows that they want four subnets, the next step is to divide the network address space that they're using.

Figure 3.5 shows the network address space for network 192.168.42.0 if we're not doing subnetting. You need to assign groups of IP addresses to each subnet. Recall that the class of the network specifies where the dividing line is drawn in the IP address between the network and locally administered portions. The network number 192.168.42.0 is a class C address, therefore there are eight locally administrable bits, giving them a network address space of 256 IP addresses. We'll steal some of these eight bits to identify subnets, which we'll explain in detail in step three.

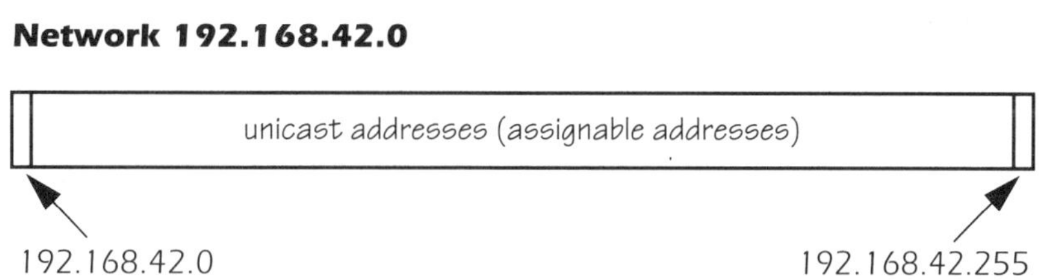

Figure 3.5 The first and last addresses in a network are reserved. The rest are assignable as unicast addresses.

Let's take the first step toward dividing this 256 address space into subnets. Figure 3.6 shows the network when we divide Zizzi's address space in half. This looks like it would allow us to have two subnets, however this wouldn't be enough for Zizzi.

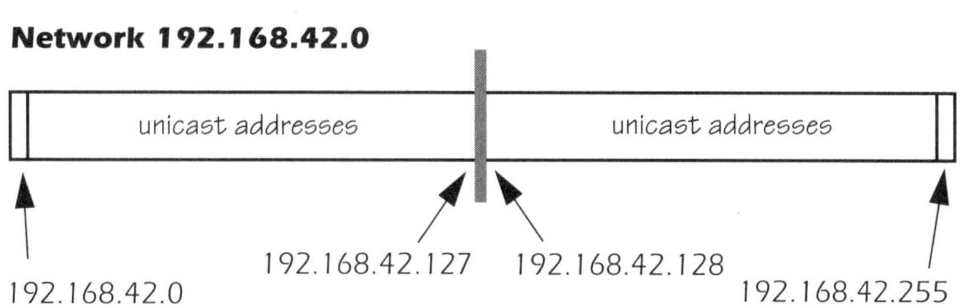

Figure 3.6 Dividing a class C network in half gives us two groups of 128 addresses.

They want four subnets, so let's divide Zizzi's address space into four pieces and see what happens. Figure 3.7 shows an address space split into four pieces. Hmm, nothing happens[4]. In other words, there is a technical reason that this won't work for Zizzi. Let's explain why.

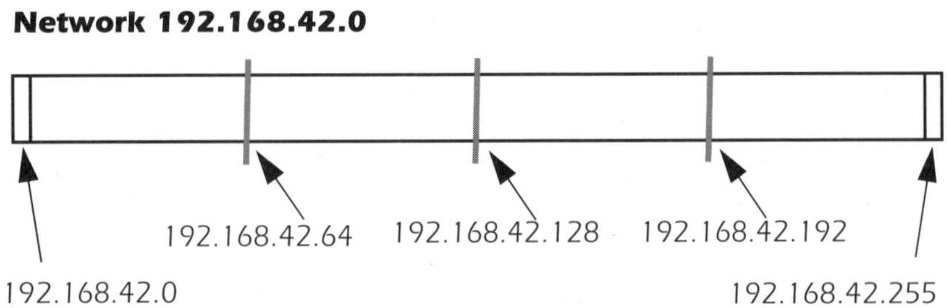

Figure 3.7 Dividing a class C network in quarters gives us four groups of 64 addresses.

There are some rules of subnetting which we haven't yet explained. The first of these is shown in Figure 3.8.

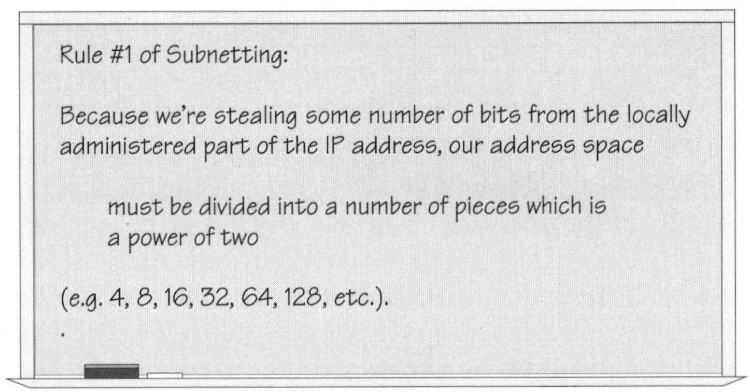

Figure 3.8 Rule #1 of subnetting.

Dividing the address space into four pieces is allowed, because $4 = 2^2$. However rule two of subnetting (see Figure 3.9) prevents us from using all four pieces.

This means that dividing the address space into four pieces won't meet Zizzi's needs because two of these pieces can't be used as subnets. We must divide the address space by the next higher power of two: $2^3 = 8$. The first and last pieces are reserved, leaving us with six usable subnets. This meets our needs. Figure 3.10 shows the network address space divided into eight pieces.

4. "Nothing happens" is the response that the magic word "Xyzzy" yields in a classic computer game when you haven't put all of the pieces of the mystery together yet.

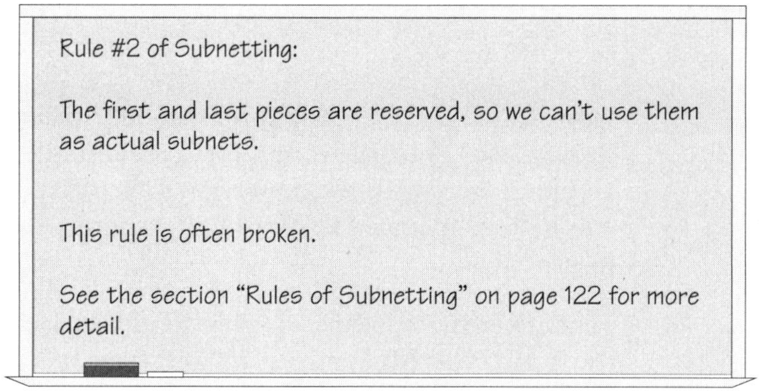

Figure 3.9 Rule #2 of subnetting.

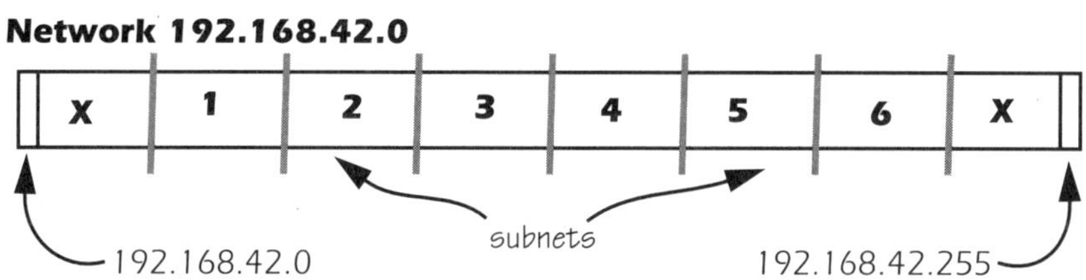

Figure 3.10 After dividing the network address space into eight pieces, we are left with room for six subnets.

With 256 addresses in the network, and eight evenly sized subnets, we have 256/8 = 32 addresses in each subnet. Our address space covers addresses 192.168.42.0 through 192.168.42.255. Let's take the locally administered field of the address (the fourth octet in this case), and assign multiples of 32. These values will be the low end of each subnet. We can add one less than the subnet size, 32-1 = 31, to the low end to get the high end address of each subnet. Table 3.1 shows the subrange of addresses assigned to each subnet. Note that the "high end" addresses are actually reserved, as will be explained later. In the use column, we've selected each of Zizzi's subnets we want each range to cover.

Table 3.1 Break the address space into subnets and assign a use for each one.

Number	Low End	High End	Use
0	192.168.42.0	192.168.42.31	reserved
1	192.168.42.32	192.168.42.63	link to Zizzi's access provider
2	192.168.42.64	192.168.42.95	manufacturing's token ring
3	192.168.42.96	192.168.42.127	unassigned
4	192.168.42.128	192.168.42.159	fast Ethernet w/servers
5	192.168.42.160	192.168.42.191	unassigned
6	192.168.42.192	192.168.42.223	development's Ethernet
7	192.168.42.224	192.168.42.255	reserved

Step 3: Partition Locally Administered Field

How do we address these eight different pieces of the network? We've seen in Table 3.1 that we can just take multiples of our subnet size (32) and prefix this with the network number. That works fine, but computer and network people like to think in binary, so let's look at how this done in binary.

Remember that it takes three bits to identify the eight ($2^3 = 8$) pieces that the network is broken into. If you don't believe this, take three coins, keep them in order and figure out all of the combinations of heads and tails.

We need to borrow three bits from the locally administered field and declare them as *subnet bits*. Remember that Zizzi has a class C address, so there are eight locally administered bits. When we take away three for the subnet field, we are left with five *interface bits*. We'll use these groups of bits as places to assign various numbers when we compose an IP address, thus we'll refer to them as the *subnet field* and *interface field*.

In Zizzi's network, we have three subnet bits and five interface bits, so the subnet field is three bits wide and the interface field is five bits wide.

Figure 3.11 shows a 32 bit IP address broken down into three fields:

- network field
- subnet field
- interface field[5]

Figure 3.11
Three fields for an IP address.

network field	subnet field	interface field
1 1 0 0 0 0 0 0 1 0 1 0 1 0 0 0 0 0 1 0 1 0 1 0	s s s	i i i i i

Note that we've written the binary value for Zizzi's network number 192.168.42.0 in the network field, and noted "s" in the subnet bits, and "i" in the interface bits.

5. The interface field is also called the host field.

Step 4: Assign IP Addresses to Each Interface

Using the subnet field, shown in Figure 3.11, we can have eight values. The values 000 and 111 are reserved. Referring back to Figure 3.4 we have the three internal networks. Let's make the following assignments:

- 100 — the fast Ethernet with the servers.
- 010 — manufacturing's token ring.
- 110 — development's Ethernet.
- 001 — the link to Zizzi's access provider.

These are the subnet numbers we'll use in this network. Note that in Table 3.1 we assigned some ranges of addresses to each of these networks. Here's how the numbers correspond. First, look at the link to Zizzi's access provider. The subnet number we've written here is 001 in binary, which is one in decimal. Multiply this number by the size of each subnet (32), and the result is 32. We can repeat this process with the other numbers.

In Table 3.2 we have these calculations. We employed a method of multiplying by 32 to illustrate a point. Consider Zizzi's subnet number for their fast Ethernet network, written in binary as 100, or 4 in decimal. Multiplying by 32 should be the same as "shifting left" by five bits, or suffixing the number with five zero bits. Indeed, 10000000 binary is 128 decimal. This is why, as shown back in Table 3.1, the low end of subnet number 4 is 192.168.42.128. Furthermore, we can multiply by 32 and add 31 by suffixing the 100 with five ones, giving 10011111 or 159 decimal. Sure enough, the high end of subnet 4 is 192.168.42.159.

Table 3.2 Convert binary subnet numbers to an octet of our IP address (subnet identifier).

Subnet number	Decimal equivalent	Subnet # with five "0"s appended	Decimal equivalent	Subnet # with five "1"s appended	Decimal equivalent
100	4	10000000	128	10011111	159
010	2	01000000	64	01011111	95
110	6	11000000	192	11011111	223
001	1	00100000	32	00111111	63

Now to the task at hand: assigning an IP address to each of the network interfaces in this network. First, look at the fast Ethernet with the servers. in Figure 3.12.

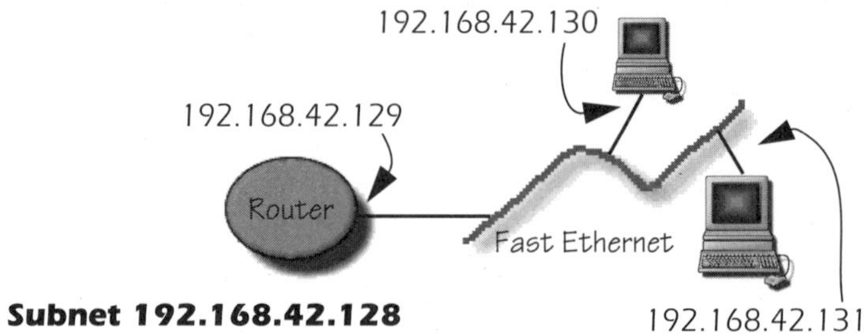

Figure 3.12
A fast Ethernet with two servers and a router.

We've assigned the subnet number 192.168.42.128 to this network. There are three interfaces to this network, one each on three different machines. Let's look at the address space for this subnet.

Figure 3.13 shows the address space for subnet 192.168.42.128 as a subset of the address space for network 192.168.42.0 which we sliced up. As with whole networks, the first and last addresses in each subnet are reserved for use as *subnet address* and *subnet broadcast address* respectively.[6] Thus the subnet identifier for subnet number 4 on network 192.168.42.0 is 192.168.42.128. The subnet broadcast address is 192.168.42.159.

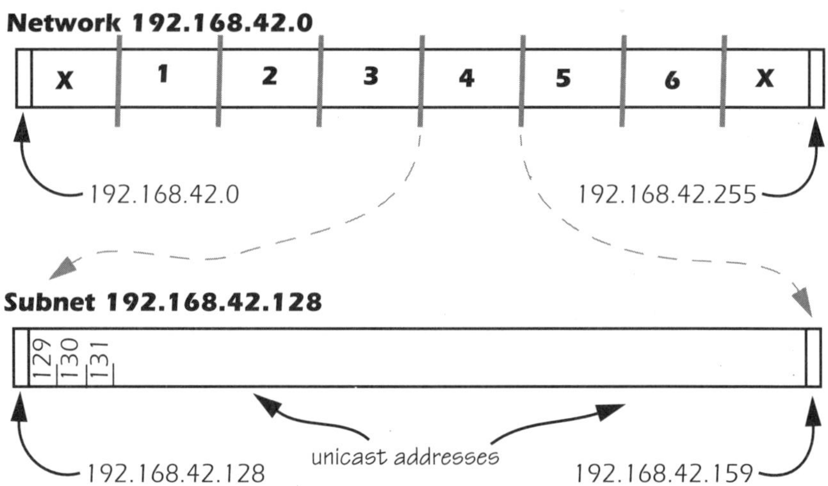

Figure 3.13
The first and last addresses in a subnet are reserved. The rest are assignable as unicast addresses.

The first unicast address in this subnet is 192.168.42.129, which we will assign this to the router, as Figure 3.12 shows. The next two addresses, 192.168.42.130 and 192.168.42.131, can be assigned to the servers.

6. Refer to page 122 for a definition of subnet address and subnet broadcast address.

We can follow the same technique for the manufacturing token ring (Figure 3.14), using subnet identifier 192.168.42.64. Again the router can get the first unicast address, 192.168.42.65, just so it's easier to remember the address of the router. The workstations may be assigned addresses 192.168.42.66 - 192.168.42.70.

Figure 3.14
This token ring has five workstations and a router.

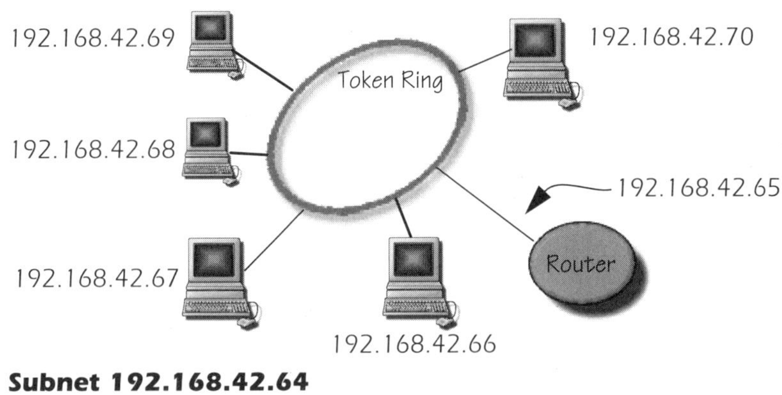

Next the addresses on development's Ethernet (Figure 3.15) may be assigned. This is subnet 192.168.42.192. Yet again (consistency is a wonderful thing), the router gets the first unicast address, 192.168.42.193, on its interface to this Ethernet. The workstations here will get addresses 192.168.42.194 - 192.168.42.197.

Figure 3.15
An Ethernet with four workstations and a router.

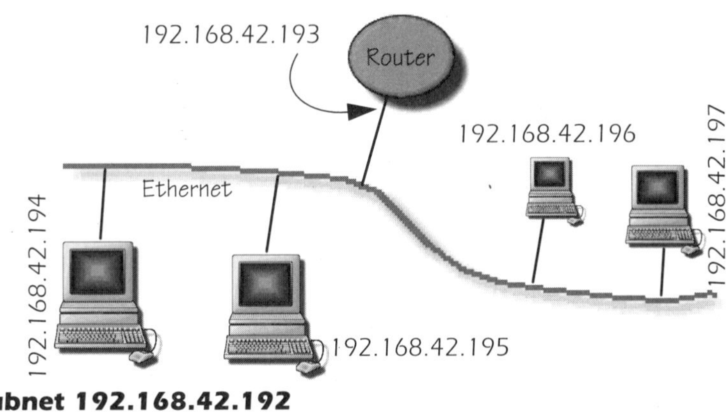

Lastly, there is the connection out to Zizzi's Internet access provider (Figure 3.16). For some kinds of point-to-point interfaces, no addresses are assigned. Let's assume that we want to assign IP addresses to the network interfaces at either end of the link. We've allocated subnet identifier 192.168.42.32 for this little two interface network. Zizzi's router can be assigned the first interface address from that network, 196.168.42.33. Zizzi's network administrator will ask their Internet access provider to use 196.168.42.34 on the router at the other end of the link.

Figure 3.16
This point-to-point network has two interfaces; one on the router shown and the other on the Internet access provider's router.

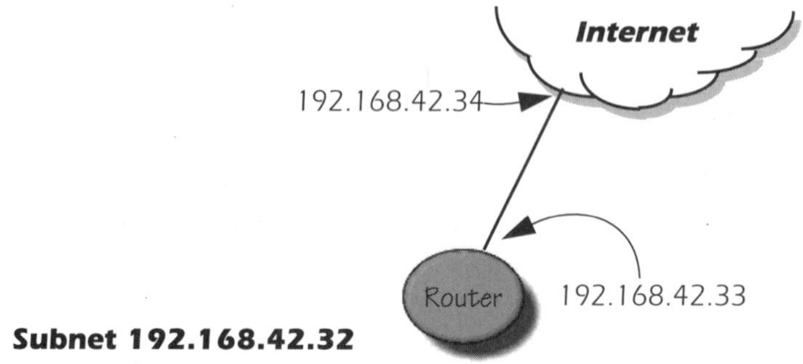

Step 5: Convince IP to Use the Subnet Field

Now that each of the interfaces in this network has been assigned an IP address, we should be able to configure each of these machines to use these addresses on the correct interfaces and it all just works, right?

Not yet.

default subnet mask: a subnet mask which covers the network field for a given class of IP address.

Normally for a class C network address like 192.168.42.0, IP will only look at the network field to make local/remote routing decisions. We must request that IP use both the network and subnet fields together for these decisions. This pertains to the IP software on each machine with an interface in this network.

Now we return to a concept which was introduced on page 99. A **subnet mask** is used by IP to determine how to partition a target IP address for proper routing with subnets. There is a **default subnet mask**, which is used when we are not doing subnetting. More detail on default subnet masks is given on page 117.

Recall that for each datagram that IP sends, it compares the source[7] and target addresses to determine whether the datagram may be sent locally or must be forwarded to a router toward its remote destination. The default subnet mask, as shown in Figure 3.17 tells IP how much of the source and target address it should look at when comparing.

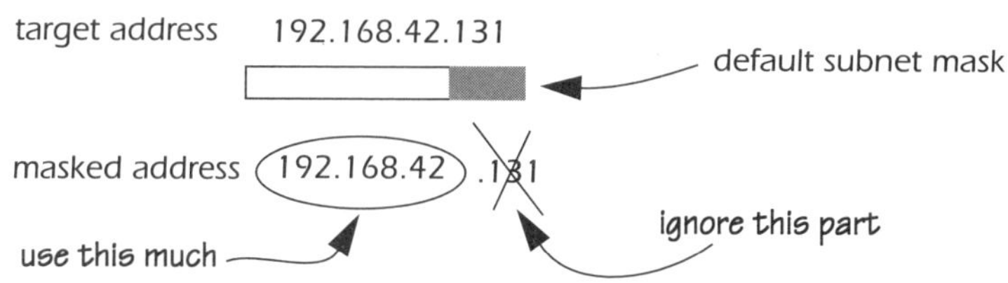

Figure 3.17 A subnet mask instructs IP how much of a target address to look at.

Of course, to see what value we should use for the subnet mask in Zizzi's network, it will be easier to explain if we use binary. The subnet mask is a thirty-two bit value — as big as an IP address itself is. This mask should contain a one in whatever bit positions we want IP to consider as significant for the network/subnet part of an address. There should be zeros in all other bit positions, so that those bits in the interface field are not included in the local/remote transmission decision. Figure 3.11 shows the breakdown of our 32 address bits into the network, subnet, and interface fields. In Figure 3.18 we see the subnet mask for Zizzi's network with all ones in the network and subnet fields and all zeros in the interface field.

Figure 3.18 The subnet mask has ones in the network and subnet fields and zeros in the interface field.

network field																								subnet			interface				
1	1	1	1	1	1	1	1	1	1	1	1	1	1	1	1	1	1	1	1	1	1	1	1	1	1	1	0	0	0	0	0

Subnet masks written like this are difficult to remember and error prone for configuration, copying, and checking with colleagues over the phone. Rather than writing subnet masks in binary, we write them in the same dotted decimal notation that is used for IP addresses.

For a class C network address, such as 192.168.42.0, the default subnet mask would be 255.255.255.0. For Zizzi's mask, as shown in Figure 3.18, we can translate it from binary to dotted decimal notation, as shown in Figure 3.19, which gives us 255.255.255.224.

7. Actually, IP compares the target address with the IP address bound to the interface that it's transmitting through. We'll address this issue when we discuss routing.

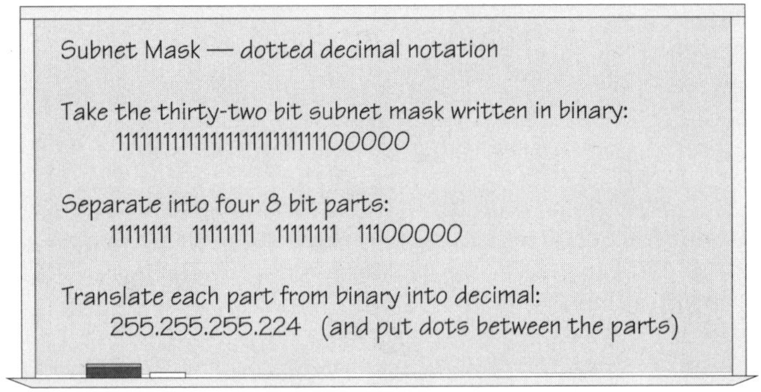

Figure 3.19 How to write a subnet mask in dotted decimal notation.

When each machine's IP software is configured with the correct IP address, the subnet mask parameter should also be set to 255.255.255.224. That will convince each of Zizzi's machines to use the network and subnet fields for local/remote determination. Note that the IP address and subnet mask are parameters on the binding of each network interface which IP uses, not on the whole machine. This means that we will configure four separate IP address/subnet mask pairs on the router.

Although not yet popular in Windows NT, you may see another format for writing the combination of a network number and a subnet mask. Recent practice[8] is to write a network number followed by a slash and the number of one bits in the subnet mask. For example, using Zizzi's network number of 192.168.42.0 and the subnet mask 255.255.255.224 (which has 27 ones and five zeros), this form would be written as 192.168.42.0/27.

Example Conclusion

In configuring an example network for Zizzi, we've walked through some steps which can be used to set up a subnetting scheme. All that would be left for their network is to actually configure their network interfaces. We'll cover the details of how to configure Windows NT machines in the "Installing and Configuring TCP/IP on NT" chapter.

8. The use of the "network slash mask" notation evolved out of the now common practice of having all of the subnet bits adjacent (and then all of the interface bits) as is discussed in this book. The rise of classless inter-domain routing (CIDR) has also contributed.

Subnet Details

Although we've touched on the main topics of subnetting in the Subnetting Example section, there is more to see. Much of the details which didn't apply to Zizzi's network are presented now. This should help you to be able to apply your subnetting knowledge to a broader range of situations, because not all networks are like Zizzi's.

In Figure 3.20, a datagram is arriving from the Internet to the organization's gateway (router). Recall that routers make routing decisions based upon a datagram's target IP address and their routing tables. The router uses the interface address, the associated subnet mask, and the target IP address together in order to determine where to send the datagram

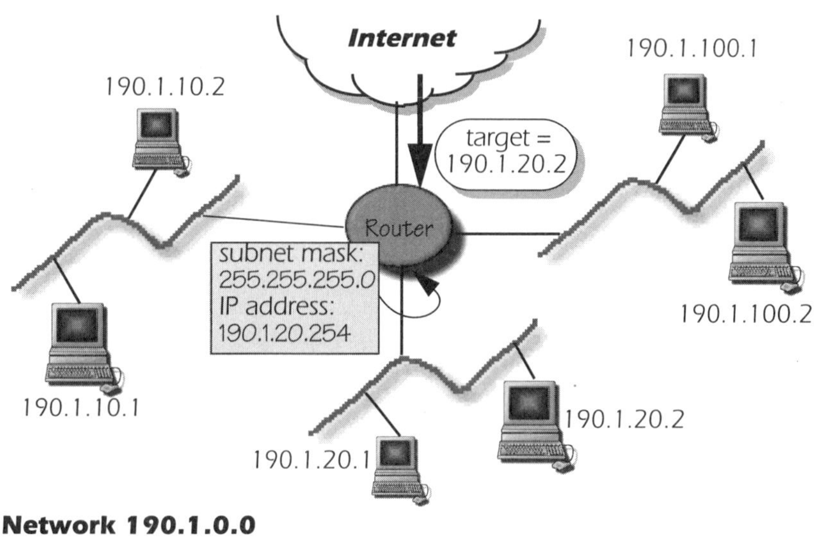

Figure 3.20 The router will use its subnet mask, interface address, and the datagram's target address to see that it can send locally on the bottom LAN.

constant width subnetting: use of the same subnet mask (thus the same width) throughout the network.

The subnet mask tells IP which bits of an IP address to consider as network/subnet and which to treat as interface bits. Effectively, the mask partitions the locally administered portion of an address into subnet and interface (a.k.a. host) fields. Thus the combination of the class of a network and a subnet mask divide the address into the network, subnet, and interface fields.

variable width subnetting: use of subnet masks of different widths in various subnets within a network.

Currently, the most common form of subnetting is **constant width subnetting**. With this form, the same subnet mask (i.e. constant width) must be assigned throughout the network. Another form which is gaining popularity allows various sizes for the subnet field in different areas of the network. This is called **variable width subnetting**.

Subnet masks are written in the same dotted decimal form as IP addresses. To illustrate many of the subnet mask calculations, we'll use binary notation.

Interpreting the Subnet Mask

The example in Figure 3.21 shows how to interpret the subnet mask.[9] The host (interface) address is 190.1.20.2 and the subnet mask is 255.255.255.0.

Figure 3.21
Using the network class and subnet mask to parse the IP address. Four steps are shown here.

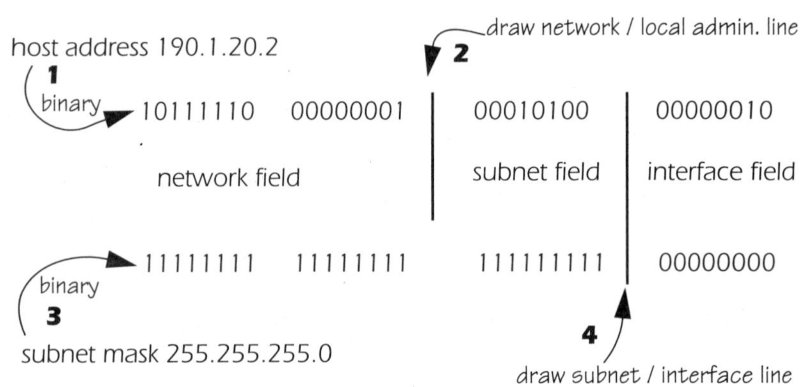

The subnet mask is used to determine the fields of the host address. In this example, the fields are:

- network field (first 2 octets)
- subnet field (3rd octet)
- interface field (4th octet)

9. In step four of Figure 3.21 "draw subnet / interface line," a bitwise logical AND operation is emulated, which is used to divide the address using the subnet mask.

Because the host address 190.1.20.2 begins with 190 decimal we know that it is a class B address. From the "IP Addressing and Datagram Transmission" chapter, we know that a class B address has 16 bits of network field.

The remaining 16 bits of the class B address are locally administered. In this example the subnet mask is not the default for class B (255.255.0.0), but is instead 255.255.255.0. The difference from the default subnet mask for class B is that the bits in the third octet are all ones. This difference divides the locally administered part of the IP address into the subnet field and the interface field. The additional ones in our subnet mask are in the third octet so the third byte of the IP address specifies the subnet number. The remaining 8 bits are zero in the subnet mask so the fourth octet of the IP address is the interface field.

Default Subnet Mask

When a *default subnet mask* is used, there is *no subnetting* in that particular network. The appropriate default subnet mask depends on the class of network.

Note that the IP address 190.1.20.2 (as shown in Figure 3.22) is a class B address. The default subnet mask for class B is 255.255.0.0. Because the subnet mask used is the default subnet mask, there is no subnet field — the remaining 16 bits are all part of the interface field.

Figure 3.22
With as many bits in the subnet mask as the class there is no subnetting.

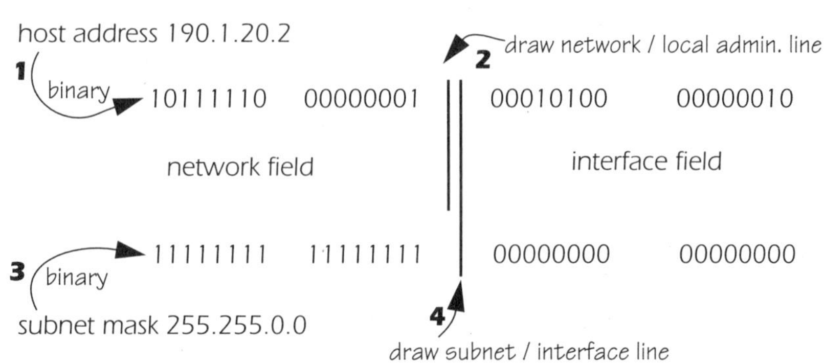

Table 3.3 shows the default subnet masks for classes A, B, and C. Note that each of these masks covers just the network field and none of the locally administered field.

Table 3.3
The classes of address trade off more network identifier bits for host bits.

Class	Length of network field	Length of locally administered field	Default subnet mask
A	8 bits	24 bits	255.0.0.0
B	16 bits	16 bits	255.255.0.0
C	24 bits	8 bits	255.255.255.0

Another Subnet Example

The example in Figure 3.23 uses a 3 bit subnet field. The subnet field is the three bits after the network field, which is 000. This leaves the remainder: **10100 00000010** as the value of the interface field.

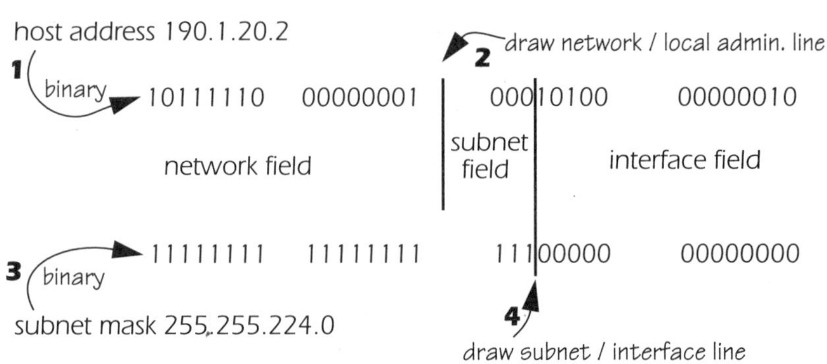

Figure 3.23
Three bits with ones beyond the network field.

Remember that the bits in the subnet mask which are beyond the length of the network field are used to determine the division of the locally administered address into the subnet field and the interface field. Those bits of the subnet mask beyond the network field which are ones are a part of the subnet mask. The one bits in the subnet mask specify those bits in the IP address to be used in determining the value of the subnet field. The zero bits in the subnet mask specify those bits in the IP address to be used for the interface field.

Note that a subnet field with all zeros in a subnet address is not recommended in the specifications, and shouldn't be used as a subnet.

Calculating the Number of Subnets and Hosts

In the previous example, there were 3 bits in the subnet field, and 13 bits in the interface field. Exactly how many subnets can we have with 3 bits in the subnet field? There are two ways that we can answer that question.

The first method to calculate the number of subnets possible is by using the following formula:

$$\text{number of possible subnets} = 2^n - 2$$

Where n is the number of bits in the subnet field. For the previous example, there were three bits in the subnet field. Therefore, the number of possible subnets would be 6.

The second method to determine the number of subnets possible is by using the charts in which someone else has done the calculations for you. We've included charts for class A, B, and C in the following sections. There are only a finite number of valid subnet masks, and all of those possibilities are shown in the tables. For each possible subnet mask, the above formula was used to calculate the number of subnets, as well as the maximum number of hosts per subnet.

To calculate the maximum number of hosts per subnet, the same formula as above can be used:

$$\text{maximum number of hosts per subnet} = 2^n - 2$$

where n is the number of bits in the host field.

Class C Subnetting Table

Class C networks allow administrators to control only eight bits of their IP addresses. If you wish to subnet a class C network, Table 3.4 shows the possibilities.

Notice that using one subnet bit is not allowed. This is because with one subnet bit we would be able to identify two values, yet both are reserved!

Table 3.4
Class C subnetting table.

# Subnet Bits	# Subnets	# Host Bits	# Hosts/ Subnet	Subnet Mask
0	0	8	254	255.255.255.0
2	2	6	62	255.255.255.192
3	6	5	30	255.255.255.224
4	14	4	14	255.255.255.240
5	30	3	6	255.255.255.248
6	62	2	2	255.255.255.252

Similarly, we cannot specify seven subnet bits with a class C network, because we would then have only one bit left for the interface (or host) field, and both values are reserved for that field as well. ($2^1 - 2 = 0$)

Class B Subnetting Table

When using a class B network address, the system administrator can control the last 16 bits of IP addresses in that network. Let's look at the possibilities of how the administrator can partition these bits into the subnet and interface fields (Table 3.5).

Table 3.5
Class B subnet table.

# Subnet Bits	# Subnets	# Host Bits	# Hosts/ Subnet	Subnet Mask
0	0	16	65534	255.255.0.0
2	2	14	16382	255.255.192.0
3	6	13	8190	255.255.224.0
4	14	12	4094	255.255.240.0
5	30	11	2046	255.255.248.0
6	62	10	1022	255.255.252.0
7	126	9	510	255.255.254.0
8	254	8	254	255.255.255.0
9	510	7	126	255.255.255.128
10	1022	6	62	255.255.255.192
11	2046	5	30	255.255.255.224
12	4094	4	14	255.255.255.240
13	8190	3	6	255.255.255.248
14	16382	2	2	255.255.255.252

Class A Subnetting Table

Let's say that you're lucky enough to have a class A network address. How would you subnet it? In the same way as for a class B or C. You have more bits that you can manage, thus you have more possibilities for subnetting. Table 3.6 shows the various combinations.

Table 3.6
Class A subnet table.

# Subnet Bits	# Subnets	# Host Bits	# Hosts/ Subnet	Subnet Mask
0	0	24	a lot!	255.0.0.0
2	2	22	4194302	255.192.0.0
3	6	21	2097150	255.224.0.0
4	14	20	1048574	255.240.0.0
5	30	19	524286	255.248.0.0
6	62	18	262142	255.252.0.0
7	126	17	131070	255.254.0.0
8	254	16	65534	255.255.0.0
9	510	15	32766	255.255.128.0
10	1022	14	16382	255.255.192.0
11	2046	13	8190	255.255.224.0
12	4094	12	4094	255.255.240.0
13	8190	11	2046	255.255.248.0
14	16382	10	1022	255.255.252.0
15	32766	9	510	255.255.254.0
16	65534	8	254	255.255.255.0
17	131070	7	126	255.255.255.128
18	262142	6	62	255.255.255.192
19	524286	5	30	255.255.255.224
20	1048574	4	14	255.255.255.240
21	2097150	3	6	255.255.255.248
22	4194302	2	2	255.255.255.252

Notice that with no subnetting, you have 16,777,214 possible interfaces (host) in the network — that's a lot! Again, use of one, 23, or 24 subnet bits isn't allowed because we wouldn't have enough room to actually specify subnet and host identifiers.

Rules of Subnetting

There are specific restrictions on the values of the fields in an IP address, shown in Figure 3.24. Recall from the previous chapter the following:

- If the locally administered field in an IP address is all zeros (binary), then what is represented is a *network address*[10]. Example of a network address: 128.85.0.0.
- If the locally administered field in an IP address is all ones (binary), then that represents a *broadcast to that network*. Example of a broadcast to the network: 128.85.255.255.

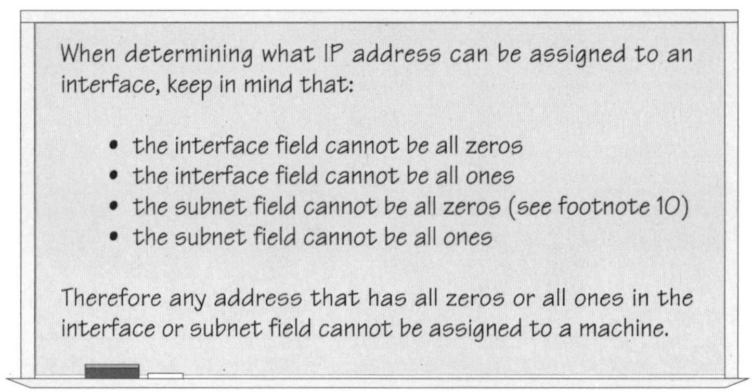

Figure 3.24
Rules for subnet and host field values.

If the locally administered field is divided into two fields, the above must still apply. Additionally, we can apply the concepts of a network address and a network broadcast to subnets:

subnet address: an IP address with the interface field set to all binary zeros. Used when describing the subnet.

- In a subnetted network, if the interface field in an IP address is all zeros (binary), then what is represented is a **subnet address**. Example of a subnetwork address: 128.85.10.0, assuming the subnet mask 255.255.255.0.

10. In Figure 3.24 we state that the subnet field cannot be all zeros so that the subnet address is not ambiguous with the network address. The exception to this rule is that some vendors, such as Novell and Cisco, allow use of subnet zero.

- In a subnetted network, if the interface field in an IP address is all ones (binary), then that represents a *broadcast to that subnet.* Example of a broadcast to the subnet: 128.85.10.255.

The host requirements RFC[11] explains that the interpretation of all zeros and all ones in these fields correspond to the concepts of "*this*" and "*all*," respectively.

With these definitions, an address with all ones in the subnet field means all subnets. For example, with a subnet mask of 255.255.255.0, the IP address 128.85.255.42 specifies interface 42 on all subnets in the 128.85.0.0 network. Using the "all" concept in the interface field, 128.85.188.255 specifies all interfaces on subnet 188 in network 128.85.0.0. The "all" notation also means that 255.255.72.65 specifies interface 65 on subnet 72 in all networks. These notations may be combined so that 255.255.255.255 is all interfaces on all subnets on all networks, but this happens to be otherwise defined as a "limited" broadcast to the local network or subnet. Clearly, none of the three fields, network, subnet, or interface, are allowed to be all ones in an address assigned to any interface in the network.

subnet broadcast address: an IP address with the interface field set to all binary ones. Used when broadcasting to the subnet.

In addition, the "this" definition means that (assuming the same subnet mask) 128.85.188.0 specifies "this" interface on network 128.85, subnet 188. Also, 128.85.0.42 identifies interface 42 on this subnet in network 128.85.0.0. Similarly the address 0.0.0.0 specifies this interface. In other references, 0.0.0.0 is identified as the *unspecified* host.

Address Utilization

We can look at the restrictions imposed by the rules of addressing in another way. Even if we didn't have these meanings of "this" and "all" within the subnet field, but only within the interface field, would we still have to reserve the first and last potential subnets?

11. [Braden1989] (RFC1122) Requirements for Internet Hosts.

Recall that in Figure 3.13 on page 110 we noted that first and last potential subnets were reserved. Figure 3.25 shows a similar picture in that a network is sliced up into several pieces.

Figure 3.25
The first and last potential subnets are invalid because an address in each is ambiguous. An address in the whole network has the same meaning.

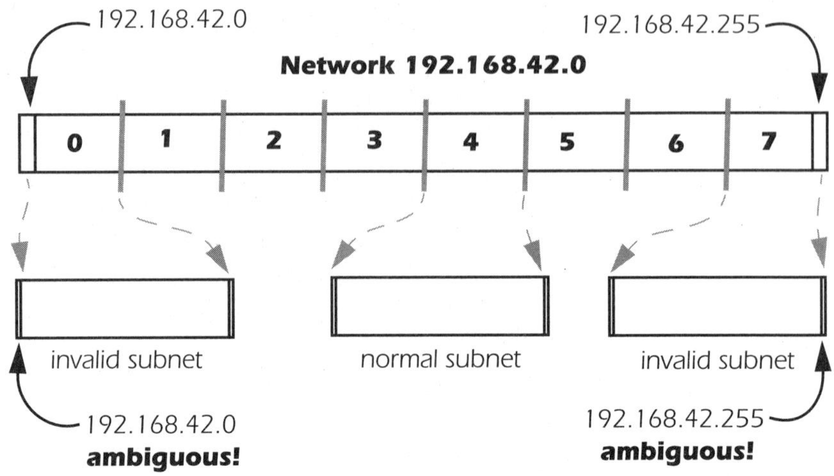

Here the first potential subnet has a subnet address of 192.168.42.0, which is the same as the address for the whole network. This duplicate meaning would potentially cause confusion and failure of operation when using certain routing information protocols. The first potential subnet, such as the one numbered zero here, may therefore not be used. The subnet numbered with a one in the diagram is the first usable subnet.

In the middle of the diagram, we've expanded the view of one of the usable subnets, number four. This subnet has a unique address for a subnet identifier and another unique address for a subnet broadcast address.

The last potential subnet, number seven in the diagram, has a subnet broadcast address which is the same as the network broadcast address. This ambiguity would mean that we wouldn't be able to uniquely use both kinds of broadcast with a conflict. So that all subnets are created equally, this subnet is disallowed. The last usable subnet is the one just before that; in this example, number six is the last subnet.

By reserving the first and last potential subnets from use, the meaning of the network address and network broadcast address are preserved.

Lost Addresses

Reserving the first and last potential subnets in any network does not come without a cost. The addresses which we would otherwise be able to use in these potential subnets are *lost*, in that they cannot be assigned to a network interface. See Figure 3.26.

Additionally, we cannot assign an interface address from the first and last addresses in each subnet because they are reserved as the subnet address and subnet broadcast address respectively.

Within each class of network, there are a certain number of addresses which can be assigned to network interfaces. The network and broadcast addresses are reserved outside of the unicast space and thus cannot be bound to an interface. When you subnet, you lose a certain number of addresses to the reserved addresses for each subnet.

Because the interface field values of all ones and all zeros are not unicast addresses, these are in essence "lost" for each subnet. Two addresses are lost for each subnet. Additionally, the subnet field values of all zeros and all ones are also reserved. This means that you also lose all of the interfaces which could possibly be identified by subnets potentially numbered with subnet identifiers of all zeros and all ones.

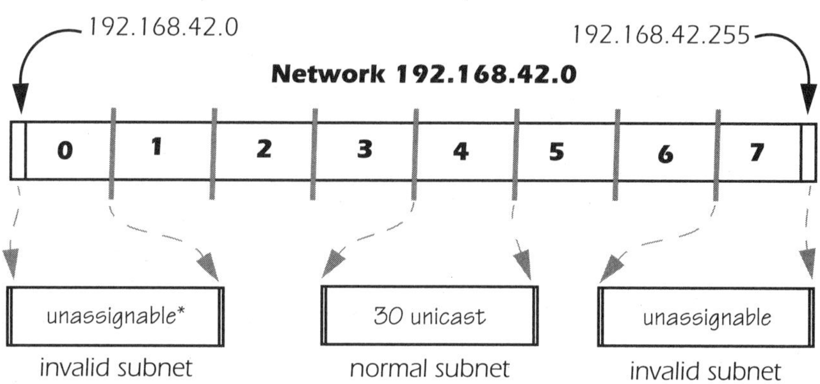

Figure 3.26
All of the addresses in the first and last potential subnets are unassignable (i.e. lost). Additionally, The first and last addresses within each subnet are also reserved.

Maximum Number of Addresses

Mathematically then[12], for *m* subnet bits and *n* interface bits, we have an unachievable maximum of 2^m x 2^n, or $2^{(m+n)}$ interfaces which is the same theoretical number of interfaces without subnetting. Even without subnetting, we lose two addresses — one for the network address and the second for the broadcast addresses. Consider that with no subnetting we have m=0, and 2^0 is 1, so the formula still works. Let's expand the formula for the actual addresses available without subnetting from 2^n -2 to be 2^m 2^n -2 which still works because m=0.

Effective Number of Addresses

Then let's consider that we lose two addresses for each subnet. This is 2 x 2^m which is also written as 2^{m+1}. This value is subtracted from the 2^{m+n}. This too is consistent with the form for no subnetting, where m=0, thus m+1=1, and 2^1 is simply 2. Note that this subtracts out a network and broadcast address from every actual subnet of the 2^m-2 including the two "impossible" subnets — the all zeros and all ones subnets. Then we're left to subtract out all of the interfaces from the all zeros and all ones subnets. The number of interface addresses per subnet is 2^n-2, and we have two impossible subnets, so we subtract out 2 x (2^n - 2). We subtract the two addresses out from the number of interface addresses because we've already accounted for these when we counted the network and broadcast addresses per subnet. The term 2 x (2^n - 2) is equivalent to 2^{n+1} - 4.

Taken all together, we have 2^{m+n} - 2^{m+1} - (2^{n+1} - 4). This is equivalent to (2^m-2)(2^n-2), which is the number of subnets times the number of interfaces per subnet. From the longer form, we can easily see the number of interfaces lost. The number of interfaces lost is 2^{m+1}+2^{n+1}-4. Let's look at the result of this for some typical subnet sizes. This appears to break down

12. By the way, you've just hopped on the "Math Train." No, we won't ask for a ticket, because we're not discussing Kerberos here.

for the no subnetting case, because although the two interfaces must be subtracted, all of these addresses are not broken out.

Notice that these equations, and therefore the examples in Table 3.7, show symmetry of m and n. Essentially then, we have a balancing act of subnets to interfaces where the optimal utilization of the address space, with respect to least interfaces lost, is at the middle — an even balance between subnet and interfaces.

Table 3.7
Number of interfaces for various subnet sizes for class C.

subnet bits (m)	# subnets (2^m-2)	# host bits (n)	# hosts (2^n-2)	# interfaces (2^m-2) (2^n-2)	usable percent
0	0	8	254	254	99%
2	2	6	62	124	48%
3	6	5	30	180	70%
4	14	4	14	196	76%
5	30	3	6	180	70%
6	62	2	2	124	48%

For class C, this is 4 and 4 bits. For class B, 8 and 8, and for class A networks, the even division is 12 and 12 bits.

Class C Subnetting Example

The subnet mask 255.255.255.192, when associated with a class C address, results in a 2-bit subnet field, as shown in Figure 3.27. How many subnets can there be with 2 bits in the subnet field? This can be calculated using the formula 2^n - 2, where n is the number of subnet bits:

- 2^2 - 2 = 2 subnets.

How many interfaces (hosts) can be put in each subnet? That value can also be calculated using the formula, with 6 as the number of host bits:

- 2^6 - 2 = 62 interfaces per subnet.

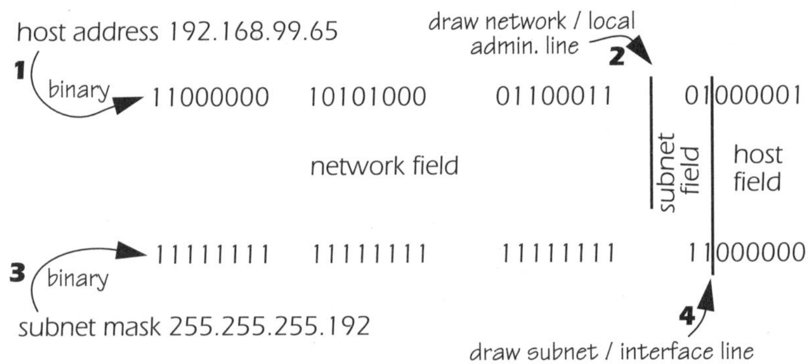

Figure 3.27
A two-bit subnet field with a class C network.

Calculating Subnetted IP Addresses

We are now tasked with calculating the range of IP addresses found in each subnet.

The subnet mask 255.255.255.192, when associated with a class C address, results in a 2-bit subnet field. What are the possible values in a 2 bit field? Flip two coins in order and keep track of the combinations. They are:

- 00 (heads, heads)
- 01 (heads, tails)
- 10 (tails, heads)
- 11 (tails, tails)

However, all zeros and all ones are not allowed in the subnet field. Therefore, there are 2 possible subnets: subnet 01 and subnet 10.

Step-by-Step Address Calculation

A sequence of seven steps may be used to calculate an address within a subnet. We'll walk through an example of how to calculate the IP address based on the network address and subnet mask. This process of assigning an IP address is partly the reverse of the process in interpreting (or parsing) an IP address. As with address interpretation, we must first determine the field boundaries. Here are the first two steps.

1. Convert the network number into binary.
2. Based on the class of the network address, draw the boundary between the network and locally administered fields.

These are shown in Figure 3.28. The network address of 192.168.99.0 is converted into binary, and the class of the address (C) is used to determine where to draw the dividing line between the network field and the locally administered field.

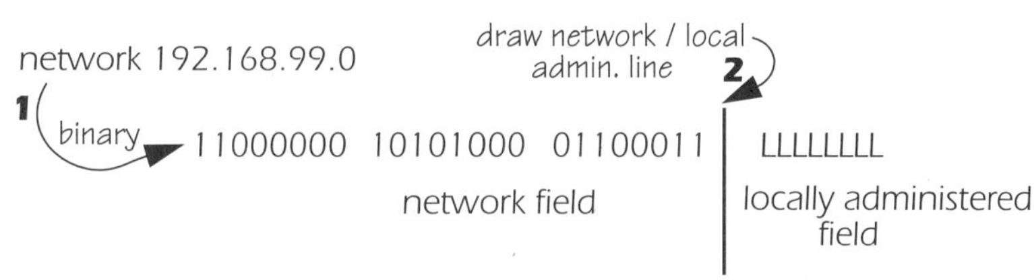

Figure 3.28 The address class determines where the network field ends.

Figure 3.29 continues with the procedure as follows:

3. Convert the subnet mask into binary. Write this number below (or above in this case) the binary rendition of the network number.
4. Note the change of ones to zeros in the subnet mask and draw a line which delineates the subnet and interface fields.

The subnet mask of 255.255.255.192 is written in binary and then a line is drawn between the ones and zeros. In this case, there are two bits with ones beyond the network field, thus the locally administered field is divided into the two bit subnet field and the six bit interface field as shown in Figure 3.29.

Now that we know the field boundaries, we may assign addresses by selecting a subnet number and an interface number. We'll discuss some guidelines for picking numbers shortly.

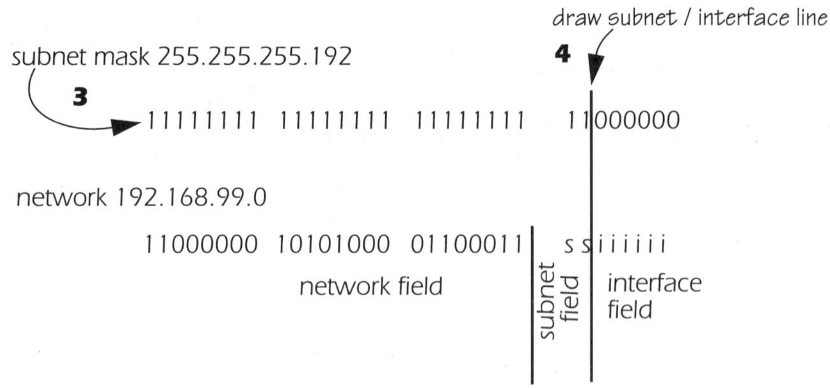

Figure 3.29
The two bits in a class C address show the field boundaries.

The last steps are: (see Figure 3.30)

5. Take the subnet and interface numbers and write them in the appropriate fields. The subnet number is written between the lines you've drawn.
6. Translate the network field into dotted decimal form.
7. Convert the combination of the subnet field and interface field into dotted decimal form, and combine with the converted network field. You now have an IP address.

In this example, we picked the first subnet number 01 and the first host (or interface) number 000001, as shown in Figure 3.30. This gives us 01000001 which in decimal is 65. We combine this with the network number and get an IP address of 192.168.99.65. This is the IP address to be assigned to the first host in the first subnet in this network.

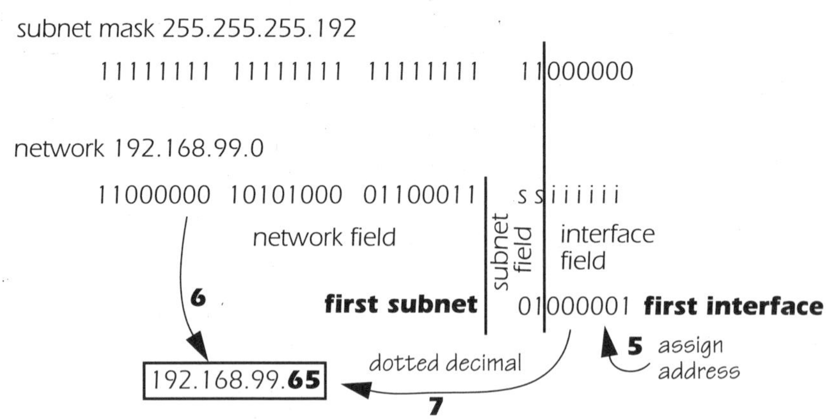

Figure 3.30
The first host (i.e. interface) in the first subnet is 192.168.99.65.

Applying the Procedure for the Whole Network

The results of this and similar calculations for some other examples in this network are show in Table 3.8.

Table 3.8 Some example IP address assignments.

Description	Subnet	Interface	IP Address
first subnet, first interface	01	000001	192.168.99.65
first subnet, second interface	01	000010	192.168.99.66
first subnet, third interface	01	000011	192.168.99.67
first subnet, last interface	01	111110	192.168.99.126
second subnet, first interface	10	000001	192.168.99.129
second subnet, 17th interface	10	010001	192.168.99.145
second subnet, last interface	10	111110	192.168.99.190
second subnet, broadcast	10	111111	192.168.99.191

Using this technique, we can now calculate the range of valid host IP addresses. Starting first with subnet 01, and the remainder of the bits in the last octet being the interface field bits, we now have the last octet to be:

- 01 00 00 01 = 65 decimal

Combine this with the network address of 192.168.99, and we get the first valid IP address in the first subnet to be 192.168.99.65.

The last host in the first subnet would have the following binary value in octet four of the IP address:

- 01 11 11 10 = 126 decimal

Therefore the last valid IP address in the first subnet is 192.168.99.126. The range 192.168.99.65 to 192.168.99.126 can be assigned to interfaces in the first subnet.

There is a quick method to determine the subnet address and the subnet broadcast address. If you already know the range of valid IP addresses for that subnet, then the following holds true:

- subnet address = one below the range of valid IP addresses for subnet.
- subnet broadcast address = one above the range of valid IP addresses for that subnet.

Take a moment and calculate the following values for our example network 192.168.99.0. Don't look at the bottom of the page — that's where the answers are.[13]

- subnet address of the first subnet.
- subnet broadcast address of the first subnet.
- range of IP addresses for the second subnet.

Comparing Subnet Fields

Recall that if the source and target IP address are not in the same network or subnet, the packet is sent to the router for forwarding. The subnet mask is used in conjunction with the IP addresses to determine if the two are in the same subnet.

IP software usually performs this check with a simple masking calculation[14] using the subnet mask to see if the target address and the transmitting interface address are on the same network and subnet.

In human terms however we may use a different approach. For diagnostic purposes, if you have to check if a datagram should go through a router, you may find the following method useful.

1. Are the source and target addresses on the same network?

Imagine yourself in the real world going through this same kind of process. If you'd like to pay a visit to a friend, it may be useful to ask yourself: Is my friend in the same city as I am? If so then you need to ask another question to determine how you should make the trip. If you are in different cities, you may want to concentrate on getting to the airport.

With respect to IP, we may look at the class of the source and target addresses and determine how many octets to compare in decimal. If the class isn't equal, or if these octets (the network field) are not equal, the

13. The first subnet address is 192.168.99.64, and that subnet's broadcast address is 192.168.99.127. The range of (unicast) IP addresses for the second subnet is 192.168.99.129 through 192.168.99.190, which gives us 62 addresses in that subnet.

14. A bitwise "and" calculation, such as "if((datagram.target & if.mask) == (if.address & if.mask))", is often used. Actually the second term is usually precalculated.

datagram should go to a router. If the network addresses are the same, ask another question.

2. Are the source and target addresses in the same subnet?

Back in the real world, you're trying to get to your friend and you know you're in the right city. Are you in the same neighborhood (or street)? If so, you'll probably want to walk down the street. If you're not in the same neighborhood, you'll have to find the closest major intersection which gets you closer to your friend's neighborhood.

So what does this mean for IP? Compare the subnet numbers in the source and target address. We need the subnet mask to know how many bits of the addresses to look at. Convert the IP addresses into binary. (Actually you only need to convert the part beyond the network number.) Draw a line after the number of subnet bits. Compare the subnet fields.

Figure 3.31
How to tell if two addresses are in the same subnet.

source: 192.168.42.68 target: 192.168.42.131

Are the source and target IP address in the same network?

Yes, they are both in network 192.168.42

Are the source and target IP addresses in the same subnet?
Convert the IP addresses and subnet mask to binary to compare.

subnet mask: 255.255.255.224

source binary:	11000000 . 10101000 . 00101010 .	010	00100
binary mask:	11111111 . 11111111 . 11111111 .	111	00000
target binary:	11000000 . 10101000 . 00101010 .	100	00011

In this case, the source and target are not in the same subnet
(subnet 010 ≠ subnet 100)

In the example shown in Figure 3.31, the source and target addresses are in the same network. Compare the subnet fields to determine if they are in the same subnet. The subnet field is between the two vertical lines: it contains a binary 010 in the source address, and a binary 100 in the target address. Is subnet 010 = subnet 100? The answer is no, and so the source and target are *NOT* in the same subnet, therefore IP will have to send this datagram to the router for forwarding.

Summary

Here's a summary of the items which have been addressed in this chapter.

- Many characteristics of networks make it desirable to partition them physically and logically into subnets.
- With subnetting, you take the address space of the network and subdivide it into smaller pieces. Addresses are then assigned from each subnet space.
- In order to partition the address space, you assign some of the locally administered bits of your IP network address to be used as a subnet field and the remainder are used as the interface field.
- A subnet mask is assigned to specify which bits are network/ subnet bits and which are interface bits.
- Some addresses are lost when you subnet due to reserved subnet identifiers. Additionally, in each subnet the subnet identifier and subnet broadcast addresses are also reserved.

Further Reading

Here is information about various books and magazines in which to look for further information on the subject.

[Braden1989] Braden, R., *Requirements for Internet Hosts — Communication Layers,* 1989, IETF RFC 1122

[Comer1995] Comer, Douglas E., *Internetworking with TCP/IP Vol I: Principles, Protocols, and Architecture, Third Edition,* 1995, Prentice-Hall, Inc.

[Feit1997] Feit, Dr. Sidnie, *TCP/IP Architecture, Protocols, and Implementation/2e,* 1997 McGraw-Hill

[Mogul1985] Mogul, J., Postel, J., *Internet Standard Subnetting Procedure,* 1985, IETF RFC 950

[Romkey1988] Romkey, J., *Nonstandard for transmission of IP datagrams over serial lines: SLIP,* 1988, IETF RFC 1055

[Simoneau1997] Simoneau, Paul, *Hands-On TCP/IP,* 1997, McGraw-Hill

4

Windows NT Networking — Under the Hood

Before we jump right into the procedures for installing TCP/IP software in Windows NT, let's step back and look at how Microsoft has implemented TCP/IP in Windows NT. This chapter examines the differences between the Windows NT networking stack and those stacks implemented in other TCP/IP environments.

Warning

Much of the details in this chapter involve what goes on under the hood in Windows NT Networking. The introductory part may be all you need to understand to perform installation. However, many technical bulletins and articles may assume that you are aware of the details in the remainder of this chapter. Programmers will find the details here useful, however this chapter is not intended as a programming reference.[1]

NT Networking Overview

Windows NT itself has a mixed heritage,[2] and the networking aspects are definitely no exception. Some of the features are reminiscent of the VAX/VMS background of its developers, while others show common heritage to UNIX[3] and MacOS networking implementations. There is quite a bit of non-TCP/IP related networking in NT; these components are largely derived from OS/2 and LAN Manager.

With this mixed background and a refocus of Microsoft on real-world networking, it is essential that Windows NT have a well-defined design of its networking features. Windows NT networking is defined in terms of several interfaces:

- User Interface
- Application Interface
- Kernel Interface

1. [Sinha1996] is an example reference you may use for further programming details specific to Windows NT networking.
2. [Custer1993] addresses many of the design aspects of Windows NT's mixed heritage
3. [Stevens1990] discusses many of the aspects of TCP/IP APIs which also can be applied to Windows NT.

- Transport Driver Interface (TDI)
- Network Device Interface Specification (NDIS)
- Hardware Interface

We can look at the functions between these interfaces as though the interfaces divide the functions into layers, as shown in Figure 4.1. These layers don't quite equate to the layers of a network protocol stack implementation, but they'll at least give us a related perspective. Looking at the NT networking stack as a layered model should aid understanding of the functions between the interfaces.

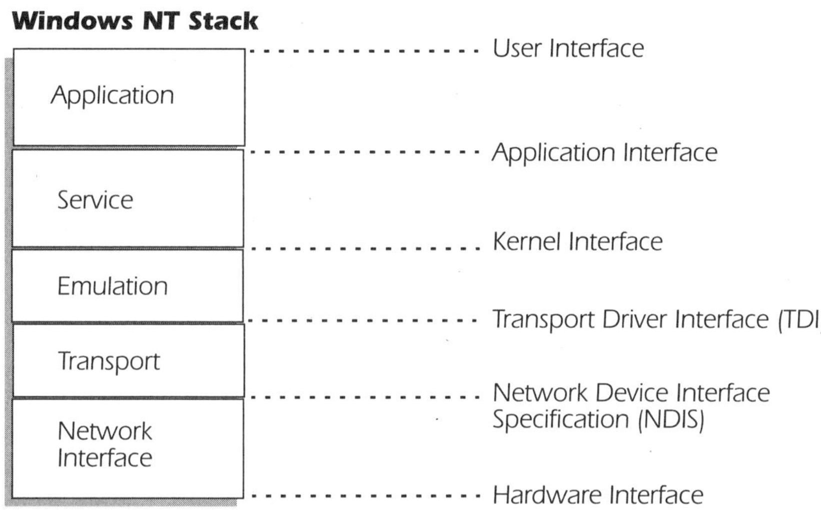

Figure 4.1 The interfaces of the Windows NT networking stack divide the functions into layers.

From an interface-centric view, if you were sitting above a particular interface looking down, you'd see the functions which are made available by a layer to the upper layer. Now we'll look at each of these layers in turn, from the top down. Figure 4.2 shows the big picture of the NT Networking stack. This diagram will be discussed in detail layer by layer in the remainder of this chapter.

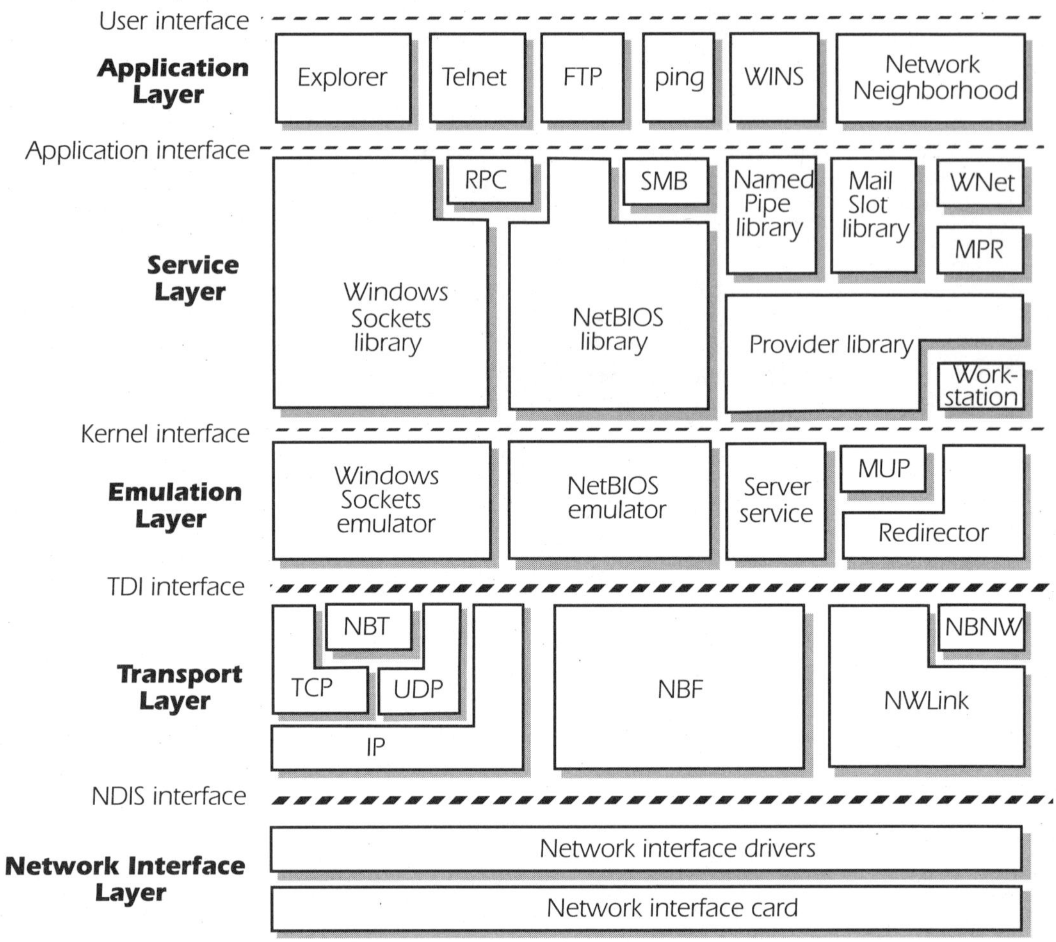

Figure 4.2 Windows NT Networking Stack

Application Layer

The application layer provides functions between the user interface and the application interface.

User Interface

Indeed, the user interface is that which we sit above (conceptually) most often when we use a computer. The user interfaces we have for networking are those which the network applications offer to us. Here are just of few brief examples: (see also Figure 4.3)

- Network Neighborhood — Windows NT offers a file manager, or "Exploreresque" view of the resources available on computers in your network. Shared drives which have been mounted on your computer are accessed (from the application point of view) the same way that local drives are. The accesses go through the normal I/O subsystem. The I/O library accesses the kernel I/O services, which utilize MUP (described in the Emulation Layer section) to access the network resources.
- Telnet — gives you a teletype-like interface to the command line or textual menus of remote computers. Because the Telnet application on Windows NT is derived from the Berkeley UNIX version, it is implemented using the socket library. Telnet uses a TCP socket connection.
- Ping — shows you statistics of diagnostic message passing in your network. Again, ***ping*** uses the socket library to allocate a raw socket so that it may initiate ICMP echo request messages directly over IP.
- FTP — allows you to transfer files between computers. FTP uses the socket library. FTP uses a TCP socket connection per session as well as an additional socket connection for each file transferred.

- WINS — the Windows Internet Name Service is an application which provides a service in the network. It fulfills the functions of the NetBIOS Name Service (NBNS) as described in RFCs 1001 and 1002. The Windows sockets library is used.

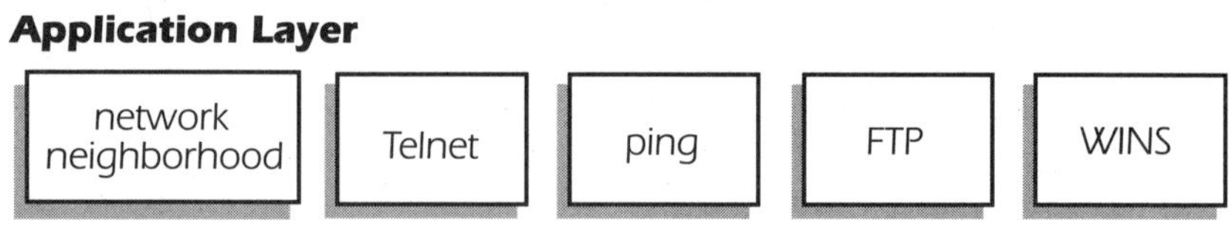

Figure 4.3 The Application Layer provides functions between the user interface and the application interface.

Again, this is just a handful of the networking applications available on Windows NT. Each of these applications needs to communicate its networking needs to the operating system. This is done by making calls to the service layer.

Service Layer

There are a number of services which are considered intrinsic in the operation of NT computers. These services fall between the application interface and kernel interface, in the service layer.

Application Interface

If you are an application programmer, you have numerous network communications paradigms by which you may construct application programs. Usually your access to these various facilities are called *Application Programming Interfaces* (APIs). Related APIs are often collected into libraries.

static binding: when a process gets its own copy of library functions.

dynamic binding: when a process uses a library function in tandem with other processes.

Applications refer to APIs in libraries by one of two general methods. **Static binding** or linking is the process by which an application gets its own personal copy of the library functions. **Dynamic binding** allows each application to simply refer to the library's copy of the function when it needs to, allowing several applications (and instances of the same application) to share the library. Shared libraries are also called dynamically linked (or loaded) libraries (DLLs).

Because many of the services of this layer are implemented in libraries, this could also be called the library layer. Here are some of the network APIs which may be used in Windows NT. These are also shown in Figure 4.4.

- Windows sockets library — allows direct use of the socket interface.
- Remote Procedure Call (RPC) — supports distributed applications.
- NetBIOS library — a programming interface for the network basic input/output (I/O) system (NetBIOS) services.
- Server Message Block (SMB) — provides some predefined services.
- named pipe library — moves information through a connection between applications running on computers in the network.
- mail slot library — allows you to exchange messages without a connection.
- Windows 32-bit networking (WNet) — this networking interface is a part of the Windows 32-bit APIs.
- general input/output method — you can use the traditional I/O calls.

The following sections go into more detail for each of these interfaces. Again, these are programming interfaces. Even if you are not a programmer, it may be useful to know the interface which your application programs use for interoperability reasons.

These various interfaces were developed over the years by several organizations as networking was evolving in minicomputer and microcomputer environments. Many different APIs have been added to

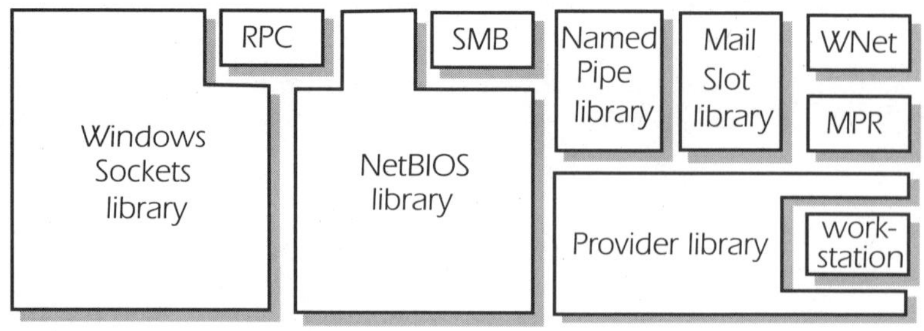

Figure 4.4
The Service Layer provides functions between the application interface and the kernel interface.

Windows NT so that it may support network-oriented software which was developed in these various environments over the years.

Windows Sockets Library

The Windows Sockets library allows direct use of the socket interface derived from the one developed for the Berkeley distributed UNIX networking. Network applications based on the socket libraries have been developed on UNIX systems since the early-mid 1980s. Many commercial products, shareware, and freeware are based on the socket API.

Applications which were written for UNIX environments may be moved to Windows NT by recompiling (and perhaps slightly modifying) the source code. Many applications have been written directly for the Windows Sockets (winsock) API since the late 1980s.

We mentioned in the TCP/IP Architecture chapter that socket addresses are the combination of a network address and an access point address, for example an IP address and a port number. Both the UNIX and Windows varieties of the socket interface support a number of other network addressing schemes, for instance XNS, NetBIOS, IPX, OSI, and local socket addresses. Let's look at how sockets are used to communicate between two processes on different computers — programmers using the socket API must think of communications in terms of sockets.

Step 1 — Requesting a socket descriptor. You have just stepped into the world of sockets. Imagine that you're a human resource; actually you're an application process. You arrive at a new office building, and naturally talk to the human resources manager, Harriet, and say that you're here to do some work. Harriet asks if you have to talk with anyone outside of the building to do this job. You say yes, and she hands you a badge with your picture and a bizarre looking number on it, then tells you that have to use this badge for all of your communications with someone on the outside. She also tells you that if you need to communicate with more than one other person at a time, you will need an additional badge — you'd ask her for another one.

socket descriptor: a combination of numbers used when referring to a socket.

You noticed that Harriet pulled the badge out a basket labeled **socket descriptors** — great, you have a socket descriptor! What do you do with it? She senses your bewilderment and says to go RTFM! "What?" you say. "Right there," she points — "Facilities Manager. You have to go talk to her now." As you turn around, you notice some writing on the badge, shown in Figure 4.5.

Figure 4.5 A socket descriptor (or badge).

A voice in your head explains this. You have a communications socket descriptor, in fact number 319,764 in this building to be exact. (The number itself isn't meaningful but is a reference number for the managers you'll be dealing with in this building.) There are several kinds of socket descriptors, but because you didn't ask for a specific kind, you got a typical one.

address family: a style of address which may be used for a suite of protocols.

The first component in a socket descriptor is the **address family.** The address family describes the structure of the *socket address.* For instance, because TCP and UDP are members of the Internet family of protocols, they share a common address format called AF_INET which consists of an IP address and port number pair. Other address families, such as IPX and NetBIOS families have different address formats (Table 4.1).

Table 4.1 Common socket address families for Windows NT.

Address Family	Description
AF_INET	Internet family of protocols
AF_IPX	Novell IPX family of protocols
AF_NETBIOS	NetBIOS family

There are a few different types of sockets. An application can pick the type that meets its needs, such as connection orientation and reliable or sequenced service. Windows NT supports the two most common of the *socket types* (Table 4.2).

Table 4.2
Socket types.

Socket type	Description
SOCK_STREAM	Connection oriented (stream) socket.
SOCK_DGRAM	Connectionless (datagram) socket.

The combination of address family and socket type may imply the protocol which is to be used. With AF_INET, the two socket types SOCK_STREAM and SOCK_DGRAM currently imply TCP and UDP respectively since they are the protocols which fit the type of socket. Socket descriptors may explicitly select a protocol rather than depending on the implied matching. Because your socket descriptor in our example specifies the {AF_INET, SOCK_STREAM} combination, you can use TCP.

Step 2 — Binding an address to the socket descriptor. You amble down the hall to the facilities manager, Ms. Binda, and ask her for an available office. She asks to see your badge; you hand her your socket descriptor, and she asks if you need a certain office number or if a random number would be fine. "What difference does it make?" you ask. "Do you want people to be able to find you in a well-known place, or are you going to be initiating a conversation with someone else?" is the reply. Let's assume that you'll be initiating a connection to someone else. When you tell Ms. Binda this, she stamps some information on your badge and hands it back to you, saying "You may use office number 1026 on the east side of the building." After you stand in silence for a moment, she adds "Make sure that you use the east side because that where the carrier pigeons (tcps) are; there's also a 1026 on the west side but that's for UDP." You wander toward the elevator which she's pointing at, as you notice what she'd stamped on the badge (Figure 4.6).

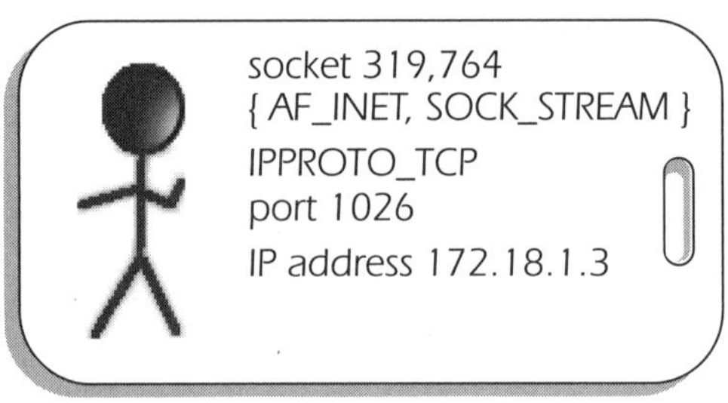

Figure 4.6
The socket address (combination of port and IP address) is bound to the socket descriptor.

The fact that TCP will be the protocol used is noted with the keyword IPPROTO_TCP. The port number 1026 is associated with this socket. The IP address 172.18.1.3, which is the address above the front door of this building is also associated with this socket. So it appears that Ms. Binda has *bound* a socket address to your socket descriptor; now you're armed, dangerous, and ready to communicate with someone using TCP.

Step 3 — Initiate a connection. After dashing up the stairs, pausing at the sign which says Udipee WEST and Teecipee EAST, and taking the east hallway, you end up at office number 1026, and knock on the door. The top half of the door swings open and Joe Teecipee asks "May I help you?"

"I'd like to set up a connection," you mumble. "A connection, huh. OK, I'll need to see some ID," Mr. Teecipee says, adding "and a business card for whom you want to call." You hand over your socket descriptor and a card you got with your friend's address on it (Figure 4.7). "Nope, this won't do," Joe replies, "you need real addresses; these are names. Go check with Et Si services to get a real port number, and talk with the DNS department to get an actual IP address. Then come back and ask me about a connection." You wander away, wondering which to do first.

Figure 4.7 The business card of whomever you want to contact. Remember, you and "whomever" are application processes.

Indeed, to communicate with someone using UDP or TCP you need a socket address which is made up of a port number and IP address. Actually there's even another step that you need to take before you go to the places that Joe Teecipee mentioned; you need to visit the parsing office and have them break this URL into pieces for you. Once you've done this, you'll have the *service name* http, and the *domain name* foobar.com. Next you have to realize that when saying "Et Si services," Joe wasn't referring you to a French and Spanish translation service. He was referring to an office in the basement that can look up the service name http in a file called /etc/services[4] and tell you an actual port number for http. Either before or after that trip, you'll visit the DNS department[5] to resolve that domain name into an IP address. We'll go into more detail about DNS in a later chapter.

You get back to office 1026 in the east hallway, hand Joe your badge, the rewritten business card shown in Figure 4.8, and say "Connect me, please."

Figure 4.8
The actual socket address specifies a port number and IP address because it's an AF_INET family address.

socket address for http://foobar.com

port 80

IP address 192.168.4.17

(note, this is an AF_INET address)

Joe Teecipee bursts into a flurry of running around the office doing things, without saying a word back to you yet. Here's what he's doing.

- sees nothing useful on chalk board, so erases it.
- copies down your socket descriptor number.
- copies down the address you're calling.
- measures the right hand window and writes down the size.
- clears off both window sills (yes, there are two windows in the room).
- (a bunch of other steps that you don't see: i.e. beyond the scope of this discussion).
- copies down a bunch of numbers and codes from the white-board and the word SYN (in blue) onto a segment of paper from a long reel.

4. In Windows NT the services file isn't simply in a top-level etc folder but beneath your install path for NT, such as \WINNT40\system32\drivers\etc\services.

5. In small buildings, there may not be a DNS department, but instead a single desk with a person who can look up names in the /etc/hosts file. Similarly, on really small networks you could use the hosts file rather than DNS. In Windows NT, the hosts files will be at a path like \WINNT40\System32\drivers\etc\hosts.

- opens both windows.
- a pigeon flies in and carries the note out the window.

Refer to the brief description of TCP back in the TCP/IP Architecture chapter if you want to know what happens after this. From the socket perspective however, all we need to know is what happens next. Joe hands you back your ID, says "It is done," and hands you a little instruction card which says how to send and receive information using this connection. Your connection has been established.

Step 4 — Receive information. You have to check back at the door to office 1026 where Joe can give you any information that has arrived for you. You just have to show your badge and give him a tray on which to put the information. If you want, you can wait at the office for information to come in. Alternately, you can ask to be paged when information has arrived.

Step 5 — Send information. When you want to send information over the connection, you put the information on a tray and hand it with your badge to Joe at office 1026.

Step 6 — Close the connection. Once all of your communications over this connection is concluded, you close down the connection. You may turn in your badge to Joe at room 1026. After he's shut down the connection, he'll return the badge to Harriet. Alternately, you could return the badge to Harriet and she'll tell Joe up in 1026 to perform his shutdown procedure.

The process at the other side of a connection has to perform some other steps such as listening for connection requests and accepting them, but the basics are the same as we've seen here. That's really all there is to sockets; the details of how TCP and UDP handle the actual messaging is beyond the scope of this chapter.

As you can see, the application process needs to know quite a bit about communicating in order to use the socket API. The volume of existing applications and the familiarity which programmers have with the socket API makes this the interface of choice for many new applications. Yet direct use of this API forces programmers to think in terms of individual connections and the details thereof. It is sometimes useful to provide a more abstract interface.

Remote Procedure Call (RPC)

RPC: invoking (or calling upon) the services of a procedure, method, or function which may be on another machine.

Sun Microsystems developed a technique for distributing software procedures amongst networked computers;[6] they named this service **remote procedure call (RPC)**. The Open Group's Distributed Computing Environment (DCE) evolved RPC from slightly different roots into the form which was adopted by Microsoft for Windows NT.

The remote procedure call library hides the details of networking to provide a service which allows running software distributed across computers throughout the network. With a socket interface for instance, the details of networking might be embedded within various parts of the application; yet with RPC those details are localized. Programmers must utilize special techniques when writing applications which use remote procedure calls. This involves splitting the procedure into two parts, one with the procedure interface specification, and the other with the implementation details, as shown in Figure 4.9.

Figure 4.9 The programmer of procedure X implements it in two separate pieces so that it may be used with RPC.

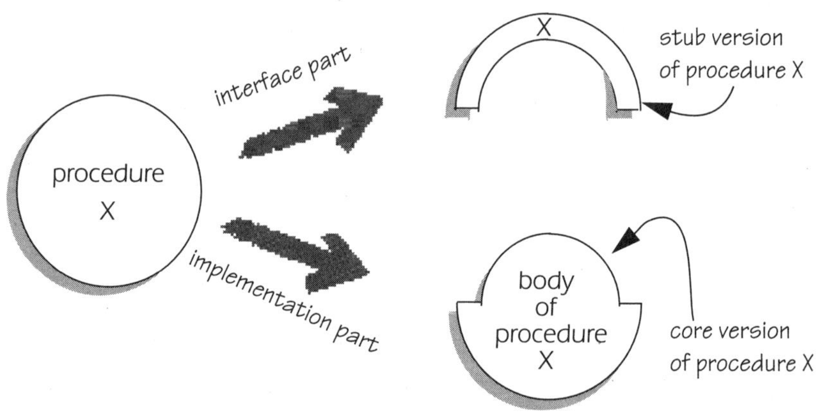

A number of procedures would be assembled into a library to be placed on a computer which is "remote" from the main part of the application.

6. Xerox's Courier RPC system predates both Sun's ONC RPC and Apollo's NCA RPC on which the DCE RPC is based.

The main part of the application still retains the interface parts (a.k.a. stub functions) of the procedures. Therefore the main part "has no idea" that some portions of the application may be running on other computers.

How does the interface part communicate with the implementation part? Each part uses the services of the RPC run-time library (Figure 4.10), which is simply standardized software which hides the communications (e.g. socket programming) details by setting up whatever associations or connections are required. This means that the different parts of the application are now tied only to use of RPC rather than to a specific protocol and message scheme.

Figure 4.10
The two parts of the procedure are adapted to the RPC run-time library.

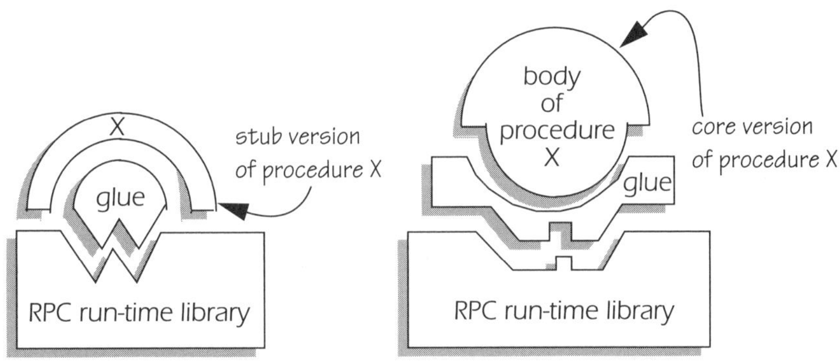

Part of the application may be run on a remote computer system (or systems), off-loading processing and perhaps accessing a database, remote sensor array, remote controls, etc. See Figure 4.11 f an example of this. This is a very powerful abstraction of networking. If we have a remote procedure call service, then why are so many specific high-layer network protocols still developed? People are conditioned to create a new solution for each (supposedly) new problem.

Figure 4.11
Implementation parts of three procedures may be moved to three machines separate from the machine that the interface parts run on.

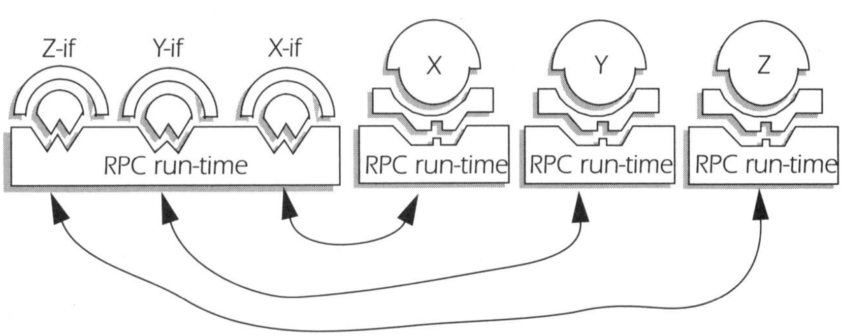

NetBIOS Library

Microsoft's Disk Operating System (DOS) interfaced with firmware built into personal computers. This firmware is called the basic input/output subsystem (BIOS). When networking capabilities were to be added to PCs, an additional programming interface for the network basic input/output system (NetBIOS) services was developed.

The NetBIOS Application Programming Interface (API) was used by IBM in 1985 to create the NetBIOS Enhanced User Interface protocol (NetBEUI). Microsoft used the NetBEUI protocol in various products including LAN manager, MS-Net, and Windows for Workgroups. NetBEUI was designed as a small, efficient protocol for use on LANs of 20 to 200 machines.

Microsoft Windows products today use a modified version of the original NetBEUI. Many PC applications were developed using the NetBIOS API, which has been carried over to Windows NT for compatibility.

Like the socket API, NetBIOS provides support for datagram and connection-oriented (session) services, however there is no support for a variety of address families, and the details of the control block aren't hidden as well as the socket API. However, the main functional difference between the socket and NetBIOS APIs lies in the following design philosophies:

- The NetBIOS API was designed to interconnect small LANs of microcomputers.
- The socket interface was designed for building multiprotocol network services on multiplatform systems over local and wide area networks.

These different design goals have lead to different classes of technology. NetBIOS does not scale well to today's networks, however we will see that applications using the NetBIOS API may be run over tunnels across TCP/IP or IPX networks.

Windows NT networking is rooted in Microsoft networking which is based on NetBIOS. The basic functionality of NetBIOS is broken into four main categories:

- General functions
- Name service functions

- Datagram functions
- Session functions

General. NetBIOS provides commands to interact with the network interfaces which it uses. In NetBIOS terminology, NICs are called adapters or network adapter cards.

NetBIOS computer name: a name associated with a computer that is used by NetBIOS applications (not the same thing as a host name).

Name service. NetBIOS uses **computer names** to identify each machine in the network in much the same way that IP uses IP addresses. The NetBIOS name service (NBNS) handles this association of computer names and adapter addresses in two ways.

In the view of the programmer using the NetBIOS API, the NBNS commands deal with configuring unique names and group names to a computer, thus they provide a function similar to the interface binding functions of IP. However, these names are assigned to computer, not individual adapters because NetBIOS was designed for a single LAN, not an internetwork.

From the network communication view, the NBNS translates between these names and adapter addresses for the same reasons that IP uses ARP to translate between IP addresses and MAC addresses. In fact, commands to delete names from the NetBIOS name table (like an ARP cache) and to find if a name is in use are provided in the API.

Datagram. Just as the socket API provides support for datagram services, we see a datagram service provided by NetBIOS. There are functions for sending and receiving datagrams to specific computers in the network, addressed by computer name. Also provided are functions for sending and receiving broadcast datagrams. In this sense, the NetBIOS datagram service is similar to the socket datagram service.

Session. The NetBIOS session services provide a connection-oriented service like that provided for the stream variety of socket which we discussed during our brief introduction to socket services. The NetBIOS session service, however, provides a very different style of information flow than the stream socket interface — the messages passed over the network are in one-to-one correspondence with the messages through the programming interface. In other words, this session service is message oriented rather than stream oriented. In order to provide for transfer of messages longer than 65,535 octets, some implementations of NetBIOS provide a *chain send* command which may be used to send messages up to 131,071 octets long.

Based on the early definitions of NetBIOS, the API and transport protocols were coupled. Yet with Windows NT, the two are considered to be separate, giving us NetBIOS as the API and the NetBEUI Frame (NBF) protocol as the transport-layer protocol.

Server Message Block (SMB)

As networking of PCs became more popular, it became evident that users wanted services to be provided over the network. NetBIOS provides only basic datagram and session facilities which are the building blocks for services; yet NetBIOS was deficient as a whole solution. NetBIOS was used as a foundation for a set of services, much like predefined (or canned) remote procedures, to perform file access, print spooling, and messaging. A message format called a *Server Message Block* (SMB) is used to implement these services; in fact, SMB is referred to in three ways:

- as a message format;
- as a set of services;
- as a protocol.

CIFS:
a technology for sharing files across an IP network.

Personal computers were developed as a type of microcomputer which was used by one person. Minicomputers and mainframes on the other hand were designed to be used, or shared, by many users. In order for PCs to be useful in the business world (and really in the personal world as well), they needed to be able to duplicate all of the advantages of pooled or shared resources from their bigger cousins. Microsoft and Intel first defined SMB in the late 1980s to support *sharing* files and printers between PCs, thus from that time they are no longer merely *personal* computers. The X/Open standards group later published SMB as an actual standard, and recently several organizations have started the standardization process of the **Common Internet File System (CIFS)** which is based on SMB. Another similar technology was developed by Sun Microsystems in the mid 1980s, based on their RPC, called the *Network File System* (NFS) for sharing files between UNIX systems.

browsing: the process of obtaining a list of available resources on the network.

Implementations of both SMB and NFS are available for most operating systems. There are several versions of SMB, from the *Core Protocol* of the PC Network Program 1.0 through LAN Manager to NT LAN Manager. Windows NT utilizes substantial additions to the core protocol. The most marked of these additions are messages used to look around the network and query computers to determine what resources are available for sharing — a process called **browsing**.

Integral in the design of SMB and the sharing capability that it provides are the *roles* of client and server. A machine which publishes (i.e. shares) information is acting as an *information server*. Other machines which subscribe (i.e. share) to the published information are called *clients*.

Many other networking schemes have been using client/server technologies for decades, however the power of technologies such as NFS and SMB lies in the element of granularity of access. The Internet's File Transfer Protocol (FTP), circa 1971,[7] provides access to individual files but transfers a file as a unit. NFS and SMB provide random access to files on an octet-wise[8] basis, as though the files were on a local storage device such as a hard disk.

Effective positioning of SMB within the protocol stack is crucial to its power of delivering transparent sharing. Thus SMB is used not only as an API, but also as the protocol which the Microsoft networking redirector uses to communicate between the workstation and server services. These services are described in later sections.

Note that in order to use SMB to communicate with computers which don't run Windows NT or LAN Manager, there must be SMB software on those other machines. Many packages are available, such as samba for UNIX and VMS, and DAVE for MacOS.

---

7. RFC114 is dated 1971, and has gone through many changes to the current standard, RFC959 which is dated 1985.
8. Actually file access is essentially on a block by block basis, yet the operating system using these services provides the octet-wise access.

Named Pipe Library

Take a used paper towel roll (a rolled up menu or any tube will do) and set a salt shaker at one end and a pepper shaker at the other end. If the salt wants to talk with the pepper, it can talk through the pipe between them. UNIX systems utilized pipes to talk between applications; in fact a number of applications may be strung (or piped) together by a series of pipes. In other words, if the salt wants to talk with the pepper, and the pepper talks with the ketchup and the ketchup talks with the mustard, we have gossipy applications by using pipes. This is one form of modular programming.

named pipe: mechanism for communicating between two processes which may be on different machines.

If the mustard thinks that someone may want to talk with it, it could establish an endpoint for a pipe and assign a well known name to the free end. Another application could open this **named pipe** to communicate with the mustard. Named pipes were added to many versions of UNIX as an extension to the traditional[9] negotiated pipes.

Named pipes provide a connection-oriented mode of communication between applications which may be on different machines in the network. The sending application simply writes to the pipe as it would write to a sequential file or teletype. The receiving application reads information coming out of the pipe just as it would read from a sequential file or teletype. Thus once a named pipe is set up, the details of networking are hidden from the applications using the pipe.

OS/2 provided a similar named pipe facility. The Windows NT named pipe API is derived from the OS/2 named pipe API; these calls allow you to establish and communicate through a connection between applications running on computers in the network.

9. Traditional pipes are created by a couple of added steps to the process fork/exec tango.

Mail Slot Library

mail slot: a connectionless endpoint for communication which supports a datagram service.

Some applications don't need the commitment of a connection oriented service, but prefer a connectionless or datagram service. This kind of service is similar to postcard or newspaper delivery, thus is called a **mail slot** API.

Derived from the OS/2 mail slot API, these calls allow you to exchange messages without a connection. The mail slot service provides a datagram service similar to that provided by UDP. Analogously, mail slots are to named pipes what UDP endpoints are to TCP connections.

Windows 32-bit Networking (WNet)

This networking interface is a part of the Windows 32-bit APIs. The functions of the Windows 32-bit Networking (*WNet*) interface are supported by a library called the *Multi-Provider Router* (MPR). This is not a router in the networking sense, but rather the operating system sense. The MPR dispatches (i.e. "routes") processing to a *provider library* which provides the requested service.

Windows NT comes with a default provider library supporting MS-Net. Other provider libraries are available; for instance, Banyan offers a provider library for VINES support. Once an appropriate provider library has been selected, processing is performed by the library to service the request.

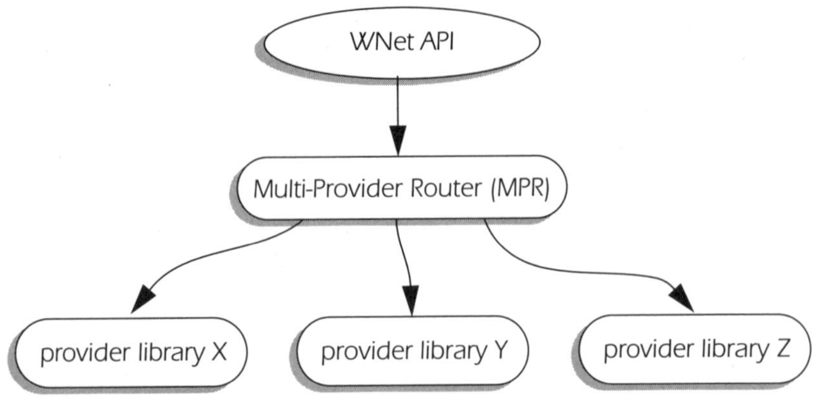

Figure 4.12
The multi-provider router (MPR) dispatches calls to the workstation service which uses the designated provider library.

The MPR is like a taxi dispatcher who selects a driver who can meet the needs of the client and sends the driver out onto the streets; the designated provider library may service the request as it wishes. Unlike a taxi driver, typically a provider library will not complete the service alone, so let's consider another analogy in order to look deeper into this process.

You walk into a restaurant and are greeted by a host who selects a table and wait-person for your group. The host chose the table and wait-person based upon your party's size and atmosphere requirements. Although your wait-person may be your interface to the restaurant services from this point, they do not work alone. Just as it is common for a wait-person to call upon the services of a chef or bartender in order to meet your needs, a provider library typically utilizes a redirector to handle the technical details of your request. A *redirector* is a kernel service which redirects, by way of translation, operations from the originating computer to a remote computer. We'll discuss redirectors in more detail in the emulation layer section.

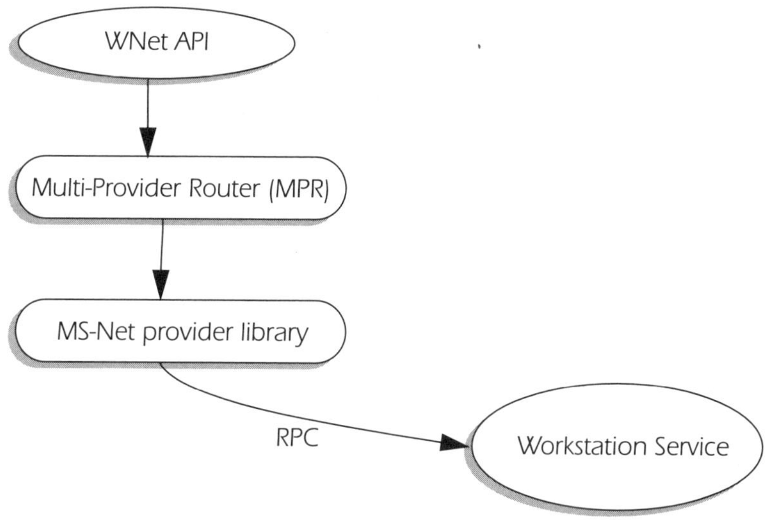

Figure 4.13
The MS-Net provider library calls (via RPC) upon the services of the Workstation service to handle the request.

For the MS-Net provider library, Microsoft doesn't pass control directly to the redirector, but instead calls (via RPC) another process called the *workstation service*, which in turn accesses the MS-Net redirector.

The workstation service runs as a separate task (or process) from those applications making requests of it. Typically the applications making use of the workstation service are clients using a service on another machine; thus they are workstation oriented. This doesn't mean that the workstation service only runs on Windows NT Workstation — it also runs on Windows NT Server. It is the role that the workstation service provides, that of a proxy for the client, that lends to its name.

General Input/Output Method

Finally, you can use the traditional Windows I/O calls, and rely on the kernel to translate these into networking accesses to the appropriate redirector.

Emulation Layer

Between the service and transport layers lie some Windows NT kernel functions which translate calls into the transport driver interface. In essence, these functions emulate separate network stacks, decoupling the APIs from the details of the transport software, thereby achieving independence for the APIs from a particular transport driver.

Kernel Interface

As a systems programmer who writes library software for application programmers, you may interface your library directly to the networking services provided by the Windows NT kernel.

- Windows sockets emulator — the kernel counterpart of the socket library.
- NetBIOS emulator — the kernel counterpart of the NetBIOS library.
- I/O services — I/O services which use the Multiple UNC Provider.
- Redirector — a direct link into a redirector may be available to you.

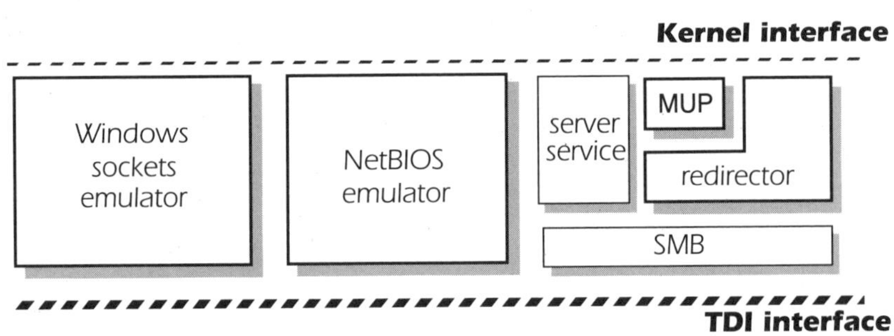

Figure 4.14 Emulation Layer.

Windows Sockets Emulator

The kernel counterpart of the socket library is called the Windows Sockets emulator. This emulator translates operations from the socket paradigm to operations over the TDI interface. Recall that the socket library supports various protocols, such as TCP/IP, IPX, and NetBEUI thus the Windows Sockets emulator handles the details of selecting an appropriate transport driver.

NetBIOS Emulator

The kernel counterpart of the NetBIOS library is called the NetBIOS emulator. This emulator translates NetBIOS calls into TDI accesses.

Server Service

The functional complement to the workstation service is the *server service*. The server service makes resources available for access to the workstation services of other machines. The default server service which comes with Windows NT supports MS-Net networking compatibility, thus it communicates with the redirectors supporting the workstation service using the SMB protocol. Because the resources which are usually accessed across the network are file system resources (e.g. files, named pipes, mail slots), the server service is implemented as a file system driver for efficiency.

I/O Services

UNC: a naming scheme for resources which may be shared in a network. (e.g. \\saguaro\pub\yyz)

URL: used to refer to resources on the Internet, or any IP network. (e.g. http://q/z)

A **Universal Naming Convention (UNC)** may be used to identify services in the system, which is similar in concept to an Internet **Uniform Resource Locator (URL)**. The Andrew File System (AFS) was developed at CMU as an alternative to Sun's Network File System (NFS) for allowing file systems on one computer system to be used on another. The notation used in AFS derived the use of the leading slash ("/") for the root of a file tree in UNIX systems, using a double slash ("//") as the "root of roots" and the top level was a machine name. Similarly, the URL notation for the World-Wide Web uses the double slash before an Internet domain name. The UNC notation of a double backward slash ("\\"), derived from LAN Manager, provides a similar meaning for names such as \\saguaro\ntserver\stuff.

I/O services may use the *Multiple UNC Provider* (MUP) multiplexor to dispatch your calls to one of many possible redirectors. If you're using the general I/O methods, the kernel I/O services will be called upon to process your requests. The processing of MUP is remarkably similar to that provided outside the kernel level by MPR. The trade-offs of each of the two methods are similar to any user thread (library) vs. kernel driver trade-off.

Redirector

A direct link into a redirector may be available to you. This is most often used by the provider libraries.

MUP also makes calls to the redirectors. A redirector is essentially a kernel module that translates and forwards service calls to another machine.

Figure 4.15 shows that MPR and MUP effectively accomplish the same overall goal — choosing among several redirectors. The MPR selects the appropriate provider library, which accesses the appropriate redirector (perhaps through a process such as the workstation service). Alternately, when an application is using the normal I/O library rather than the MPR, the I/O library will call upon the services of the MUP. The MUP chooses the appropriate redirector and accesses it directly.

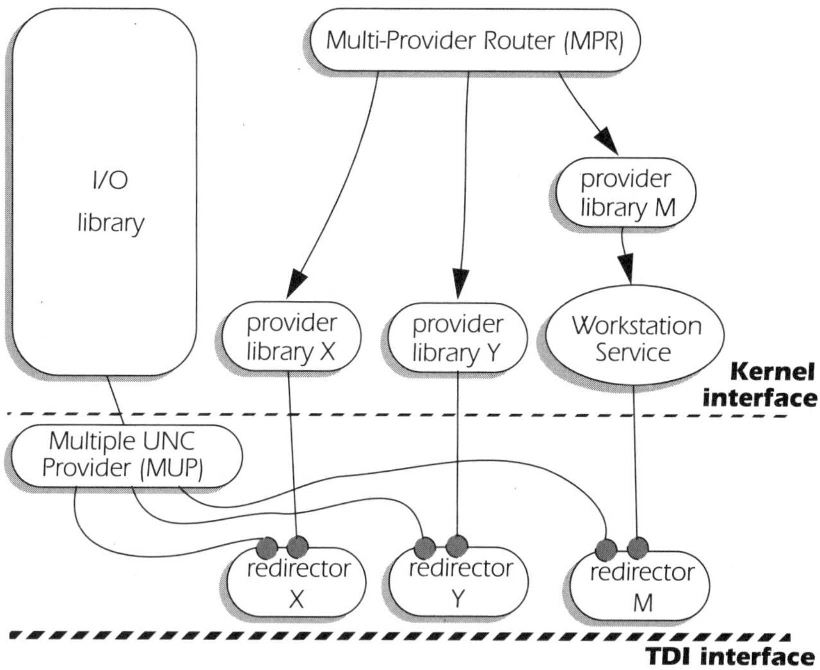

Figure 4.15 The provider libraries call their respective redirectors (perhaps on behalf of a process like the workstation service) while the MUP provides an interface to the redirectors for I/O service.

The redirectors access the appropriate transport layer entity via TDI, but each redirector is implemented as a file system driver in Windows NT, so they translate file system I/O requests into network messages for the TDI.

We noted that the socket and NetBIOS software at this layer emulates the traditional software accesses into TDI calls. Each redirector is actually emulating a file system by using network resources, using traditional network messaging protocols. The NetWare redirector translates I/O requests into NetWare messages, while the Microsoft networking redirector translates I/O requests into SMB messages.

Transport Layer

Although the functions beneath the emulation layer are not strictly all transport entities in the traditional sense, that's about the best general name by which we can refer to them.

Transport Driver Interface (TDI)

If you're working on an optional redirector, or enhancing the Windows sockets emulator, your kernel driver needs to access the resources of one or more transport drivers for network access. Perhaps you just want to know what the existing redirectors are dealing with.

The Transport Driver Interface (TDI) provides a well-defined means of accessing transport layer protocols without being bound to a specific driver. This gives emulation layer programmers flexibility to create generic software which could use any of the following choices which meet the needs of their emulator.

- Transmission Control Protocol (TCP) — this protocol is used world-wide in the global Internet, in corporate LANs, WANs, and VLANs.
- User Datagram Protocol (UDP) — this protocol is used in many services for which the connection-oriented and retransmission behavior natures of TCP are not well-suited.
- NetBIOS over TCP/IP (NBT) — this transport entity allows PC networks to be tunneled through UDP and TCP (therefore IP) networks.
- raw IP Interface — there occasionally comes a time when you don't want the features of TCP or UDP but want to access an IP network. Use the raw interface. Some diagnostic programs such as ***ping*** use this interface.
- NetBIOS Frame (NBF) — the protocol aspect of the NetBIOS Enhanced User Interface (NetBEUI).
- NetWare Link (NWLink) — implements IPX and SPX protocols for support of and interoperability with Novell NetWare networks.
- NetBIOS over IPX (NBNWLink) — similar to NBT in that it can tunnel NetBIOS accesses over IPX networks. This is also called NBNW.

Figure 4.16
The transport layer.

There could be other transport drivers installed, such as:

- DECnet — from Digital Equipment Corporation (DEC).
- AppleTalk — from Apple Computer.
- VINES — from Banyan.

Others may be available from third party developers. Older version of Windows NT had few transport drivers written to use TDI and NDIS, so Microsoft had to provide support for a popular UNIX network programming model, called STREAMS,[10] in order to provide a system which could be networked. Most operating systems vendors (e.g. Sun, Apple, IBM, HP) support STREAMS as a standard cross-platform driver interface, thus a NIC or protocol vendor could write a STREAMS driver once for UNIX, MacOS, and Windows NT. Now that there are transport drivers available which support TDI and NDIS directly, Microsoft has shifted its reliance on STREAMS interfaces and implemented its own version of the TCP/IP suite using native TDI and NDIS access. The *STREAMS Environment* still exists in Windows NT, and may be useful when you find NIC drivers in STREAMS format but not TDI and NDIS.

10. STREAMS was developed in a prototype version on top of a 4.1 BSD UNIX foundation, and was first productized in UNIX System V revision 3. It provides for development of any character-oriented driver, for networking, terminal, or printer support. STREAMS supports a common interface for all layers, such as transport, network, and data link drivers, and is far more flexible than TDI and NDIS for multi-vendor environments and tunneling.

Transmission Control Protocol (TCP)

The Transmission Control Protocol (TCP) is the protocol associated with most information services of the Internet and modern corporate networks. TCP was described in the "TCP/IP Architecture" chapter.

Typically this TDI driver would be accessed through the Windows Sockets emulator when an application uses the socket library with an AF_INET address family and SOCK_STREAM type sockets.

TCP is also used indirectly by NBT for NetBIOS session services. NetBIOS session services are created by NetBIOS emulator requests, Windows Sockets emulator requests for AF_NETBIOS with SOCK_STREAM sockets, or a redirector such as the MS-Net redirector which wants a NetBIOS compatible transport.

User Datagram Protocol (UDP)

The User Datagram Protocol (UDP) provides the same sort of port addressability for applications as TCP does. UDP however lacks the connection-orientation and reliability based on retransmissions and acknowledgments. Therefore, UDP is often used for administrative rather than user information services.

The Windows Sockets emulator requests the services of UDP when an application uses the socket library with an AF_INET address family and SOCK_DGRAM type sockets.

The NetBIOS datagram services may use UDP in much the same way that TCP is used by the NetBIOS session services. Usually these requests would come from the NetBIOS emulator, however they could also be generated from Windows Sockets emulator requests for AF_NETBIOS with SOCK_DGRAM sockets.

NetBIOS over TCP/IP (NBT)

NetBIOS over TCP/IP is often called NBT or NetBT. Recall that NetBEUI is a non-routable protocol; tunneling (e.g. over IP) was necessary to extend Microsoft networking beyond a single LAN[11]. This transport entity was defined in 1987 in RFCs 1001 and 1002 to allow PC networks to be tunneled through UDP and TCP (therefore IP) networks. This transport may thus be used to connect NetBEUI networks at different sites. Note that NBT can provide three services: session service, datagram service, and name service, just as NBF can[12].

The session services are run over TCP port 139, the datagram services over UDP port 138, and the name service is run over UDP port 137.

Raw IP Interface

raw socket: the method an application can use to talk to IP directly.

Some applications may want to use the Internet Protocol (IP) directly., without UDP or TCP. Two examples are ***ping*** and ***tracert***. This kind of access with a socket interface is called a **raw socket**.

Access to a raw IP interface may be restricted to privileged users due to the potential for a malicious programmer to write software which acts nearly like TCP or another protocol.

11. An alternative to tunneling NetBEUI over routable network protocols, such as IP, is to create a virtual LAN (VLAN) or emulated LAN (ELAN) for NetBEUI computers using technology such as the ATM Forum's LANE.
12. The positioning of NetBT underneath TDI was taken from [Microsoft1996] "Core Protocol Stack Components"

NetBEUI Frame (NBF)

The protocol aspect of the NetBIOS Enhanced User Interface (NetBEUI) is called the *NetBEUI Frame* (NBF) protocol, which is used to transport NetBIOS information directly without tunneling. It is therefore restricted to transport within the semantic confines of the NetBIOS model — within one small (typically unrouted) network.

This protocol provides compatibility with existing LANs that use NetBEUI.

NetWare Link (NWLink)

Microsoft's NetWare Link (NWLink) protocol implements a version of Novell's Internetwork Packet eXchange (IPX) and Sequenced Packet eXchange (SPX) protocols for support of and interoperability with Novell NetWare networks.

NWLink may be used to support applications using the socket library with AF_IPX family addresses. Sockets of type SOCK_DGRAM would use IPX, whereas SOCK_STREAM sockets would use SPX.

NetBIOS over IPX (NBNWLink)

NetBIOS may also be run over NWLink — this is called NBNWLink or NBNW. This is similar to NBT in that it can be used to tunnel NetBIOS, but in contrast, NBNW uses IPX and SPX rather than UDP and TCP. This is useful for tunneling NetBIOS over IPX networks.

Network Interface Layer

Windows NT's network interface layer is roughly equivalent to an implementation of the network interface layer which runs under the Internet Protocol.

Network Device Interface Specification (NDIS)

The Network Device Interface Specification (NDIS) provides a well-defined way for transport drivers to access network interface layer drivers. It is generic so that it may support IP, NBF, and other transport/network protocols.

Let's say that you're writing a new transport protocol and need to have it access various network media. You'd write the transport software so that it invokes NDIS facilities which handle the media access for you. Some media supported with NDIS drivers currently are:

- Ethernet
- Token Ring
- FDDI (Fiber Distributed Data Interface)
- ATM (Asynchronous Transfer Mode)
- PPP (Point to Point Protocol)

If you are a system administrator installing a new type of NIC into one or your machines, you would want to make sure that the vendor (or a third party) provides NDIS compatible driver software for the NIC. Alternately, if you are dealing with STREAMS drivers you will want to enable the STREAMS environment in Windows NT.

Summary

Here's a summary of the items which have been addressed in this chapter.

- There are six interfaces[13] in Windows NT Networking:
    - User Interface
    - Application Programming Interface (API)
    - Kernel Interface
    - Transport Driver Interface (TDI)
    - Network Device Interface Specification (NDIS)
    - Hardware Interface (not discussed)
- We may consider these interfaces as slicing the Windows NT Networking scheme into a stack of five layers. This means that we don't count the user and the hardware as layers because they are not a part of Windows NT.
    - Application Layer
    - Service Layer (a.k.a. library layer)
    - Emulation Layer
    - Transport Layer
    - Network Interface Layer
- Windows NT implements NetBIOS, the NetBEUI Frame (NBF) protocol, and Server Message Block (SMB) messages for compatibility with previous Microsoft and IBM networking schemes.
- Windows NT implements NWLink for Novell SPX/IPX support, STREAMS for driver compatibility, and TCP/IP for standards-based networking.
- NetBIOS over TCP (NBT, a.k.a. NetBT) and NetBIOS over NWLink (NBNW) are supported for communicating with NetBIOS (and SMB over NetBIOS) messages to non-NBF machines.
- Native transport drivers are accessed with TDI, and native network interface drivers are accessed using NDIS.

---

13. There is actually also a provider interface, which would give us seven.

Further Reading

Here is information about various books and magazines in which to look for further information on the subject.

[Black1993] Black, Uyless, *Computer Networks: Protocols, Standards, and Interfaces, Second Edition*, 1993, Prentice-Hall

[Braden1989] Braden, R., *Requirements for Internet Hosts — Communication Layers*, 1989, IETF RFC 1122

[Comer1995] Comer, Douglas E., *Internetworking With TCP/IP Vol I: Principles, Protocols, and Architecture, Third Edition*, 1995, Prentice-Hall, Inc.

[Custer1993] Custer, Helen, *Inside Windows NT*, 1993, Microsoft Press

[Feit1997] Feit, Dr. Sidnie, *TCP/IP Architecture, Protocols, and Implementation/2e*, 1997 McGraw-Hill

[Goralski1995] Goralski, Walter J., *Introduction to ATM Networking*, 1995, McGraw-Hill

[Microsoft1996] Microsoft, *Microsoft Windows NT Server Networking Guide*, 1996 Microsoft Press

[Mogul1985] Mogul, J., Postel, J., *Internet Standard Subnetting Procedure*, 1985, IETF RFC 950

[Robertson1997] Robertson, Wayne, Koop, Edward, *Windows 95 and NT Networking: A Guide for Professionals*, 1997, McGraw-Hill

[Romkey1988] Romkey, J., *Nonstandard for Transmission of IP Datagrams over Serial Lines: SLIP*, 1988, IETF RFC 1055

[Sharpe1996] Sharpe, Richard, *Just what is SMB?, V1.0*, 1996, http://samba.anu.edu.au/cifs/docs/what-is-smb.html

[Sinha1996] Sinha, Alok K., *Network Programming in Windows NT*, 1996, Addison-Wesley

[Stallings1991] Stallings, William, *Data and Computer Communications, Third Edition*, 1991, Macmillan

[Stevens1990] Stevens, W. Richard, *UNIX Network Programming*, 1990, Prentice-Hall

[Tanenbaum1989] Tanenbaum, Andrew S., *Computer Networks, Second Edition*, 1989, Prentice-Hall

5

Installing and Configuring TCP/IP on NT

In this chapter, we'll present not only the installation of TCP/IP on Windows NT, but will also introduce methods for troubleshooting the installation and basic operation of TCP/IP.

Installation Overview

Before delving deep into the procedure for installing and configuring TCP/IP software in Windows NT, let's step back and assess what we'll be doing.

Installing TCP/IP

During a typical Windows NT software installation, you are presented with a collection of check boxes representing the installation options. Normally, the TCP/IP software check box has been marked by default. If this box was unchecked during installation, TCP/IP is not installed. We'll walk through the installation process in this chapter.

Configuring TCP/IP

After installing TCP/IP, certain parameters must be configured on that machine before the protocol can be used. The first and most important parameter that must be configured is a unique IP address. This IP address would use the network number that was assigned to an organization. If this organization is connected to the Internet, the address must be unique throughout the whole Internet; otherwise it must be unique within the organization. The second most important parameter to be configured is the subnet mask. Those are the only two parameters which must be configured, as shown in Figure 5.1.

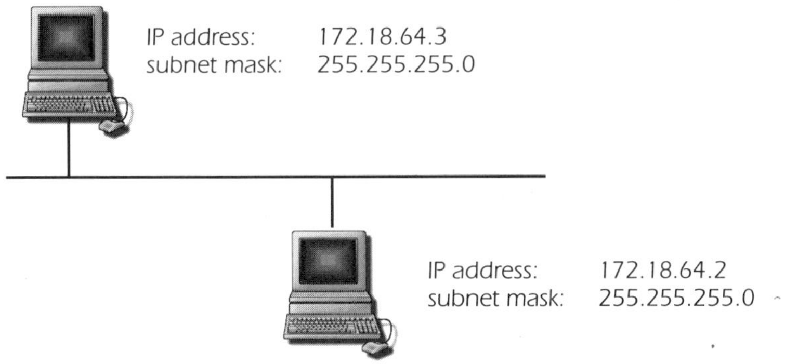

Figure 5.1
The IP address and subnet mask must be configured for each host.

Another parameter which is commonly required is the default router IP address. The default router IP address is configured so that your computer can communicate beyond its local area (Figure 5.2). Other parameters may be configured as appropriate for that network (for example, name server IP address).

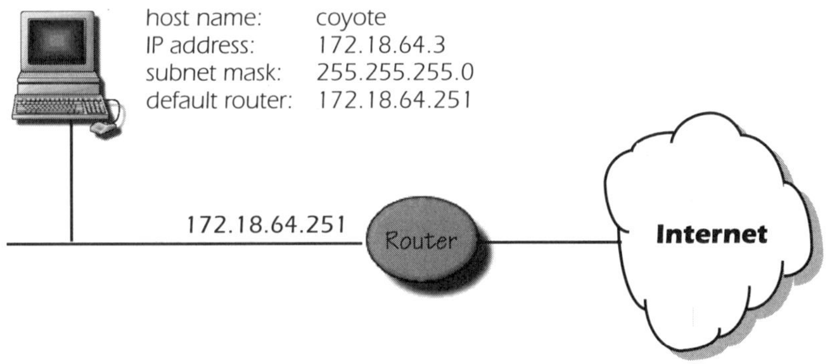

Figure 5.2
The default router address must be configured to allow internetworking.

If you enter these parameters at the machine itself, and the parameters are not changed on the fly by some application, the information is static, thus it is a static configuration. Servers should be configured with static addresses; however, workstations and mobile devices may have their configuration information updated dynamically. This sort of dynamic configuration is supported by protocol called the Dynamic Host Configuration Protocol (DHCP).[1] You may wish to use dynamic configuration to simplify the configuration management of each of your workstations.

1. Refer to Chapter 15, DHCP.

Testing TCP/IP

After we've gone through the configuration steps, we'll show you some quick methods for testing the TCP/IP installation. By using these steps, you'll be testing not only for proper installation of the TCP/IP software, but also of the network interface and connection to the network. Taking a little time after each installation to sanity check the software can save you a lot of troubleshooting time later.

Example Network

Beginning now, and continuing through the rest of the chapters, we'll be building a network for the company foobar.com. The beginnings of this network is shown in Figure 5.3. In this chapter, we'll be installing and configuring TCP/IP on the computer called eng3.

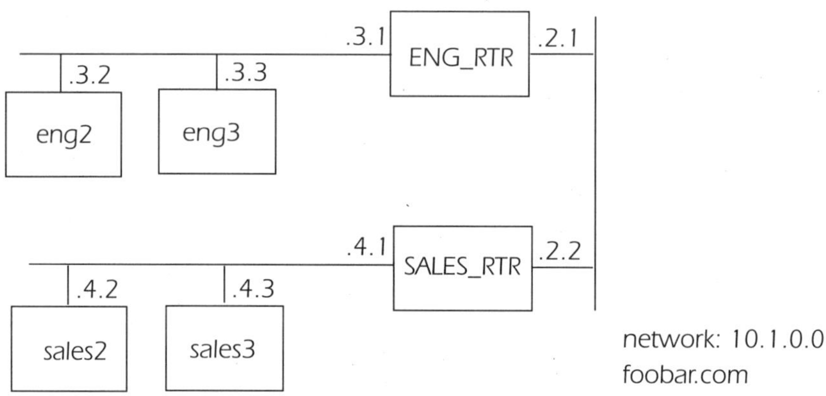

Figure 5.3 The beginnings of the network foobar.com. This network will be referenced throughout the book.

The network number we're using is a class A non-routable (i.e. private) network 10.0.0.0. We've chosen the network number 10.1.0.0 to be used throughout the organization, with the third byte representing the subnet number.

With a class A address, the network field is eight bits wide. Our subnet field will be 16 bits, and the interface field is eight bits. This is shown in Figure 5.4.

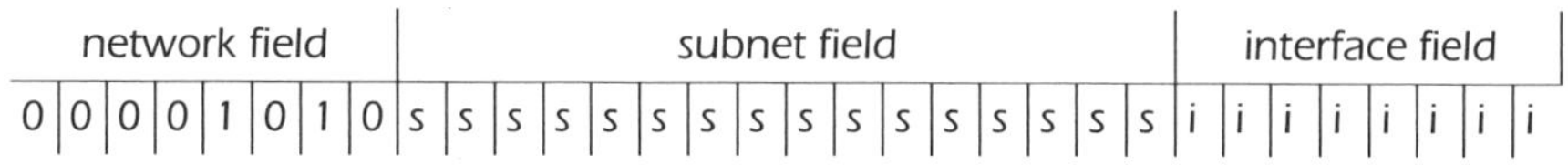

Figure 5.4
Three fields for an IP address.

We'll focus in on the engineering subnet. The engineering router, ENG_RTR, has an interface on this network with the address 10.1.3.1. The configuration parameters for eng3 are shown in Figure 5.5.

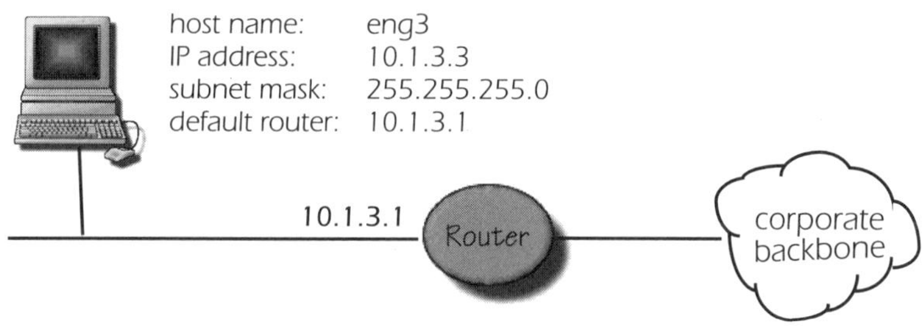

Figure 5.5
Eng3 configuration parameters.

Installing TCP/IP

To install the TCP/IP software on a computer, you need the Windows NT source files from the NT installation CD. Note that only a user in the Administrator group has the ability to modify the network settings (found in the *Network Control Panel* application.)

Network Control Panel

The *Network Control Panel* is the main control screen for all the network settings in Windows NT (Figure 5.6). From this screen you can add, configure, update and remove software and adapter drivers.

To obtain this screen, press *Start* in the task bar and select *Settings*, then *Control Panel*. From the *Control Panel* window, open *Network*. A shortcut is to select *Network Neighborhood* (on your desktop) and right-click. Select *Properties* at the bottom of the pop-up menu to bring up the *Network Control Panel*.

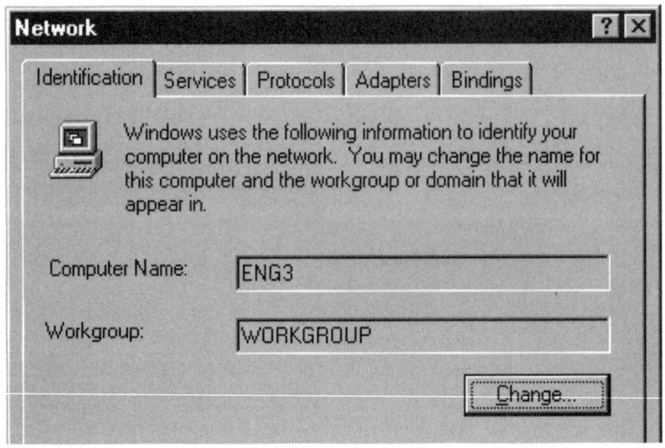

Figure 5.6
Network control panel showing the Identification tab.

The *Network Control Panel* has five tabs. Each tab provides you with control over various kinds of network configuration information for this computer. These tabs are used to view and configure all of the networking software running under Windows NT, not only TCP/IP.

After opening the *Network Control Panel*, pull the *Identification tab*. On this pane you should see the Microsoft computer name, as well as the workgroup or domain of the machine. These parameters are not used directly by the TCP/IP software, but by NetBEUI and related software such as WINS.

TCP/IP Installation

The *Network Control Panel*'s *Protocols tab* lists the network protocols currently installed on the computer. In Figure 5.7 we see that only the NetBEUI protocol is already installed on this computer.

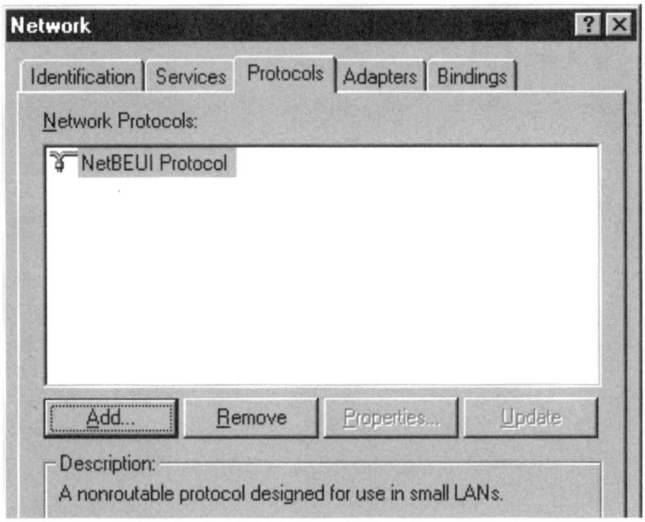

Figure 5.7 Currently installed protocols.

Pressing the *Add* button will bring up a screen listing all the possible protocols that can be installed (Figure 5.8).

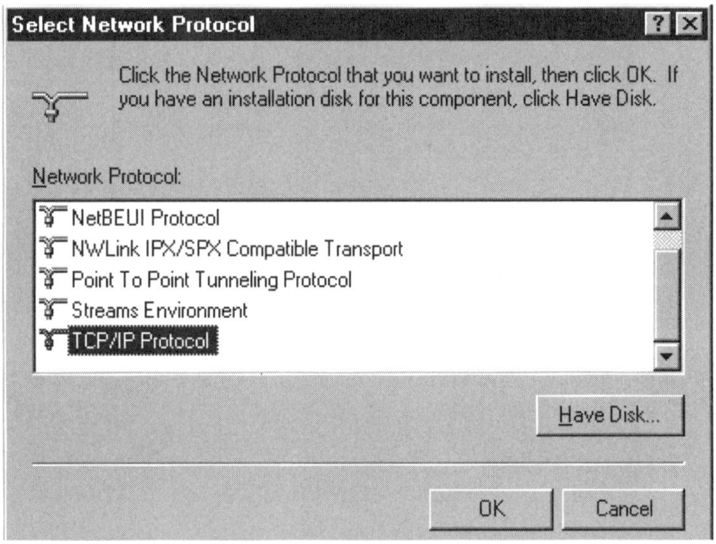

Figure 5.8 Select the TCP/IP protocol.

The term "TCP/IP Protocol" is used to represent the suite of core TCP and IP related protocols. Once that option is chosen, you will be prompted for the location of the installation files. Enter the path of the software distribution on your computer. For instance, if you are installing from a CD-ROM (drive E:) on an Intel '386 derived computer, your path may be E:\i386 or something similar. The installer will copy files from the source and then install them in their proper places.

Configuring TCP/IP

Once the installation has completed, the installer automatically brings up the TCP/IP configuration panel.

TCP/IP Configuration Dialog

The *Microsoft TCP/IP Properties* dialog provides you with the ability to configure typical TCP/IP client information. This screen has several tabs, each tab configuring different TCP/IP properties (Figure 5.9).

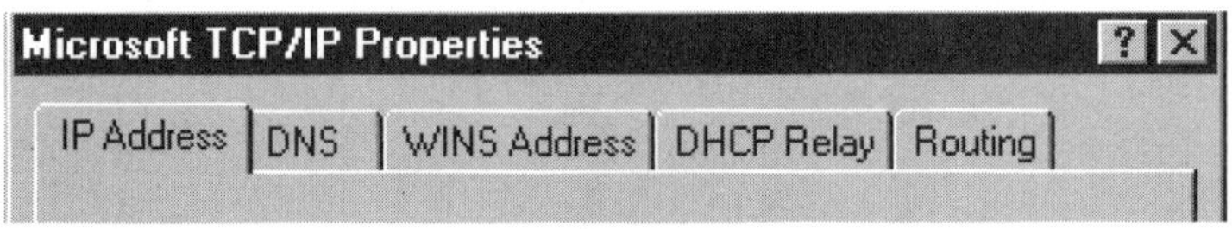

Figure 5.9 Configuration tabs for TCP/IP

We'll talk about each of these screens in the next few pages. For many of the screens, you should refer to future chapters for more detail, as described in Table 5.1.

Table 5.1 Refer to these other chapters for further configuration information.

Topic	Chapter
What is DNS?	11, "Domain Name Resolution"
How do I install DNS?	11, "Domain Name Resolution"
How can NT be a router?	7, "NT Server as an IP Router"
Can NT be a "real" router?	8, "Using Steelhead as a RIPv2 Router"
Do I need DHCP and how do I install it?	15, "DHCP"
How does DHCP really work?	15, "DHCP"
Why would I want WINS?	16, "NetBIOS Name Resolution"
How do I install WINS?	16, "NetBIOS Name Resolution"

IP Address Configuration

The IP address configuration pane is used to enter the basic information required for TCP/IP connectivity. This screen is shown in Figure 5.10.

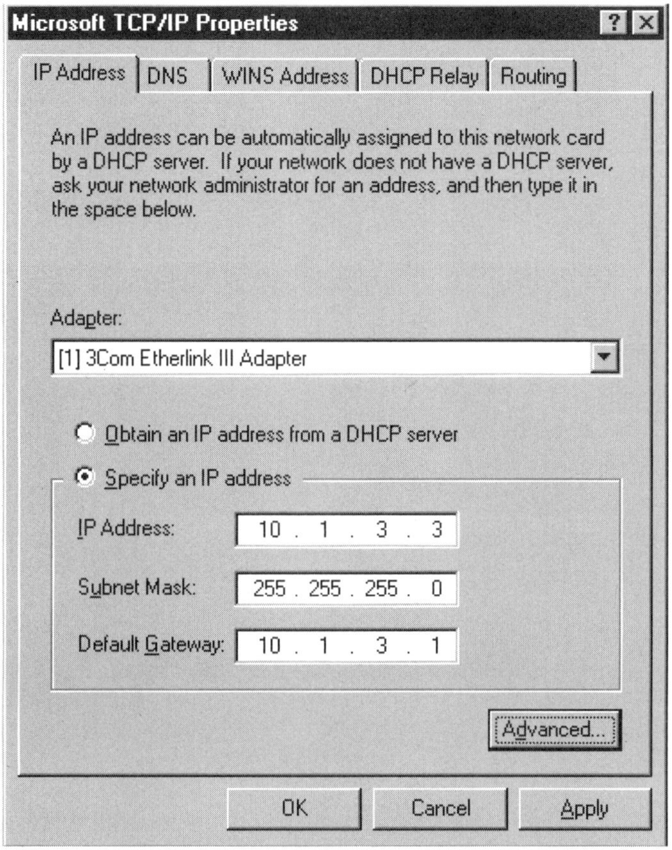

Figure 5.10 IP address information for eng3 has been entered here.

So how do you know what values to enter? As the instructions on the pane indicate, if you are installing a workstation or server in a network which someone else administers, then you should ask what values to use. If you are the network administrator, you must choose values for these parameters.[2] For our example, we've entered the information for eng3 (see Figure 5.5) into the screen shown in Figure 5.10.

2. Refer to the chapters on IP addressing and IP subnetting for further information

If the *Obtain an IP address from a DHCP server* radio button is pressed, the IP Address, Subnet Mask, and Default Gateway fields will be grayed out — DHCP will assign these parameters to the computer. If the *Specify an IP address* button is instead pressed, you may enter the IP address, subnet mask, and default gateway for this computer.

Note the option menu for the adapter in the middle of the IP address pane. If you have more than one adapter (NIC) installed, select each adapter from this menu and configure them each in turn. For further details about this procedure, refer chapter 7, NT as an IP Router.

Note that in the lower-right corner of the IP address pane there is an *Advanced* button. Pressing the *Advanced* button opens the *Advanced IP Addressing* configuration dialog, as shown in Figure 5.11.

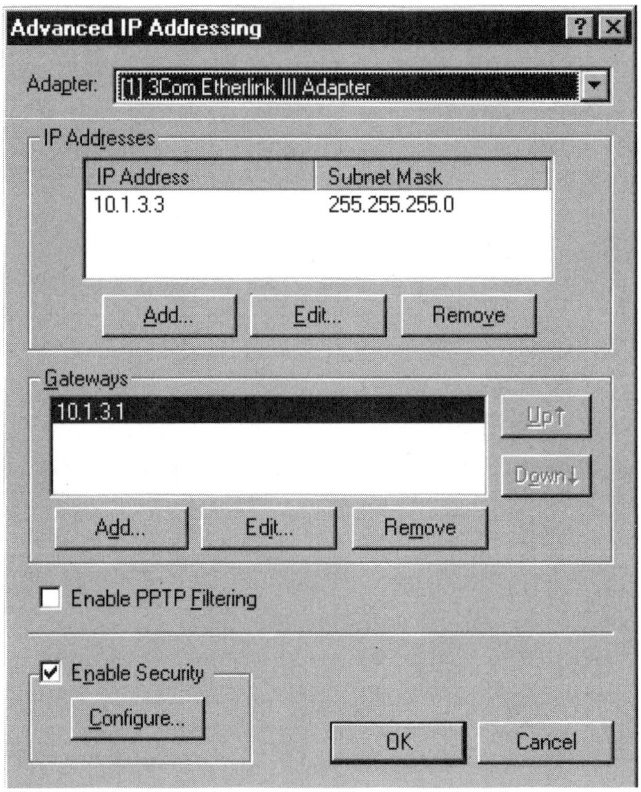

Figure 5.11 Advanced IP Addressing screen.

Each of the sections of the *Advanced IP Addressing* screen are discussed in the next few pages.

Multiple IP Addresses per NIC

You may wish to add multiple unicast IP addresses if a computer is supposed to function as a server on several subnets. Another use would be if the machine is a "virtual host" (i.e. for a web site). NT can support up to 256 IP addresses per NIC.

Suppose you have two subnets on the same cable. You need a server on each subnet, one at 172.19.6.1 and the other at 172.19.7.1. However, you only have one server. You would configure the one NIC on that server to respond to both 172.19.6.1 and 172.19.7.1, and things will work properly.

For an example of multiple IP addresses on one NIC, refer to chapter 14 for the discussion on IIS.

Multiple Gateways

dead gateway detection: the process of detecting that a router has gone down, such that another router can be used to forward traffic.

Normally, IP supports one default gateway. Within IP itself, because it is not an acknowledged service, there is no way to determine if a gateway is down. RFC 816 specifies a way to reselect gateways based on TCP status information. The features of this RFC have been implemented in the Windows NT TCP/IP software as a feature called **dead gateway detection**.

If you enter more than one gateway, the first gateway will be IP's default gateway. If the dead gateway detector determines that gateway is having problems, the next gateway in the list will be selected as the IP default gateway. This process continues for failed gateways until the list of addresses you supply is exhausted.

To enable dead gateway detection, set the registry parameter *EnableDeadGWDetect* to a value of 1 (true). The location and type of *EnableDeadGWDetect* are shown in Table 5.2. This registry value does not exist in the registry upon initial installation of NT- the key will need to be added. Refer to the end of this chapter for a discussion on editing the registry.

Table 5.2 EnableDeadGW Detect registry parameter.

Hive:	HKEY_LOCAL_MACHINE
Key:	\System\CurrentControlSet\Services\Tcplp\Parameters
Name:	EnableDeadGWDetect
Type:	REG_DWORD
Value:	0 (false) or 1 (true)

PPTP Filtering

The Point-to-Point Tunneling Protocol (PPTP) is used to send data securely over internetworks, such as the Internet. If the PPTP protocol is installed on this machine, PPTP filtering can be enabled. PPTP filtering will prohibit the receiving of any packets that are not associated with the PPTP protocol.

To enable PPTP filtering, check the box *Enable PPTP Filtering* on the *Advanced IP Addressing* screen (Figure 5.12).

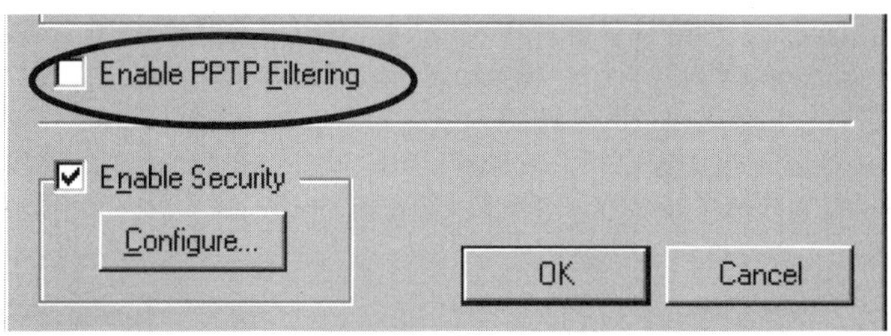

Figure 5.12 Bottom part of the Advanced IP Addressing screen.

For more information on PPTP, refer to chapter 10.

TCP/IP Security Configuration

You can filter incoming packets to this machine by checking the box *Enable Security* found at the bottom of the *Advanced IP Addressing* screen (Figure 5.13). Once the box is checked, bring up the *TCP/IP Security* screen by clicking *Configure*.

Figure 5.13 Bottom part of Advanced IP Addressing screen.

Recall that during our discussion of the Windows NT transport layer (chapter 4) we noted that there are three transport protocol interfaces: UDP, TCP, and the raw IP interface. Figure 5.14 depicts the incoming packet filtering that Windows NT may perform.

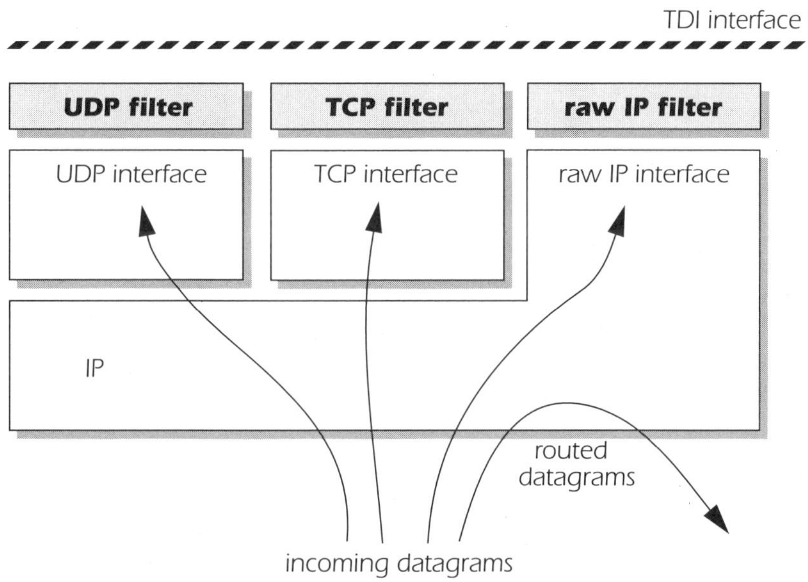

Figure 5.14 Each of the "transport" protocols, UDP, TCP, and raw IP have their own filtering. Note the position of the raw IP filter — neither UDP nor TCP messages are subject to it. Also, datagrams routed through this machine are not affected by any of these filters.

There is an independent filter for each of the transport protocols. These filters apply only to datagrams (or segments) that are to be delivered to the upper layer protocols. Datagrams which are routed through this machine are not affected. Due to the placement of the raw IP filter (beside, not below UDP and TCP), UDP and TCP messages are not affected by the raw IP filter.

The *TCP/IP Security* screen (Figure 5.15) is used to enable incoming packet filtering on the host itself. Note that there are three independent filter specifications, one per transport protocol. You can either allow or disallow certain packets from being processed by this machine. Filtering is based upon port number, or in the case of "raw" IP, by IP protocol number.

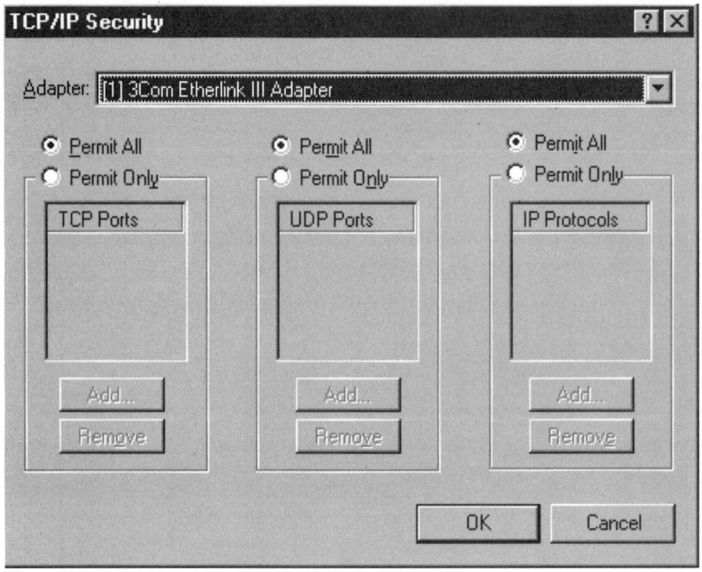

Figure 5.15
TCP/IP Security configuration.

Recall that port numbers are essentially numbers associated with particular applications. A list of the of the possible TCP and UDP ports is found in the directory%systemroot%\system32\drivers\etc in the file called SERVICES. You can select from this list the application port numbers that you want to allow or disallow from entering this machine. Enter these port numbers in the appropriate TCP Ports or UDP Ports column.

How does the TCP port filtering work? Recall from Chapter 1, TCP/IP Architecture, that the very first packet sent to start a TCP session is a SYN packet. This SYN packet is destined for a particular application, identified by the destination port number in the TCP header. TCP can filter those initial connection attempts, only allowing packets through that are destined for particular port numbers. For connections to ports that are not allowed, a TCP reset packet is returned to the sender.

The list of port numbers in the UDP ports column are the port numbers of packets that will be sent through UDP to the appropriate application.

The list found under the IP Protocols column specifies the IP protocols for which incoming datagrams will be accepted by the Raw IP transport[3] (used to provide raw sockets). It does not control packets sent to other transports (such as TCP or UDP).

---

3. For information on the raw IP transport, refer to Chapter 4, page 167. For a list of IP Protocols, refer to RFC1700.

DNS Tab

Figure 5.16 shows the next configuration screen— *DNS tab*. This screen is used only if you will be using DNS to resolve names to IP addresses. All the client parameters relating to DNS are entered on this screen. This screen is from our example network, foobar.com, for the machine eng3.

Figure 5.16
DNS configuration with the domain name specified.

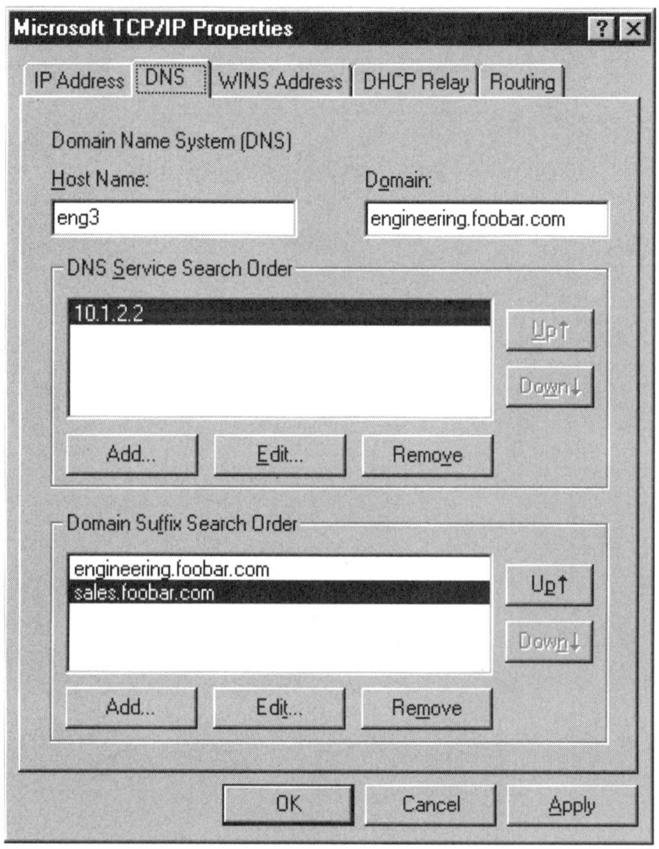

The hostname is the high-level alias for the primary IP address of this computer. The hostname is NOT the same thing as the NetBIOS computer name (see Figure 5.6), although they are commonly set to the same value.

In order for this machine to be a DNS client, it must be configured with a DNS server's IP address, so that it can send name queries to that machine. Refer to Chapter 11, "Domain Name Resolution," for a detailed discussion of DNS and this configuration screen.

WINS Address Tab

If you are using Microsoft networking features such as file sharing and print serving in your TCP/IP network, you may find a use for the Windows Internet Name Service (WINS). The client configuration dialog as shown in Figure 5.17 allows you to enter primary and secondary WINS server addresses.

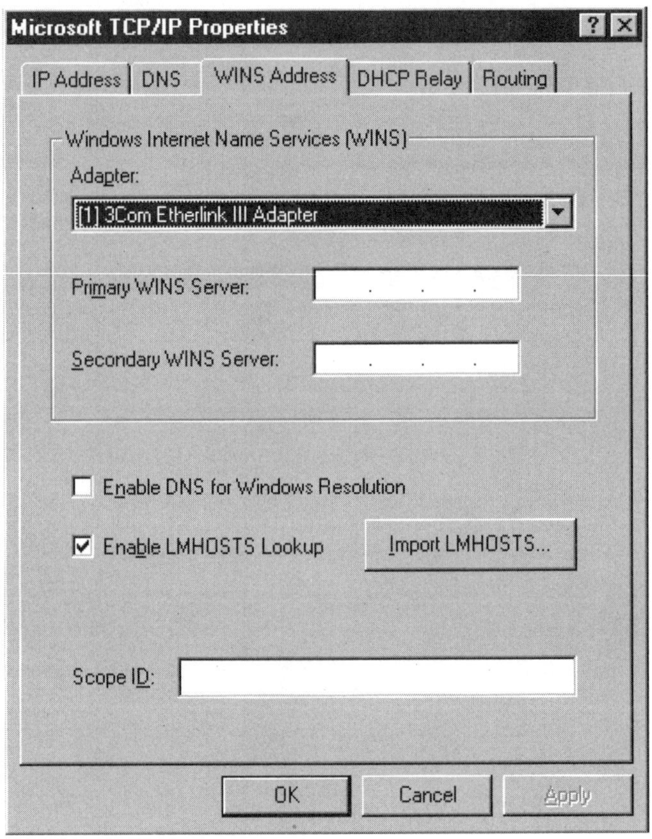

Figure 5.17 The addresses of primary and secondary WINS servers may be entered in this dialog.

Refer to the "NetBIOS Name Resolution" chapter, chapter 16, for a detailed discussion of WINS.

DHCP Relay Tab

If you decide to use the automatic configuration facilities of the Dynamic Host Configuration Protocol (DHCP) in a large network, you may want to have some machines relay DHCP messages from one network/subnet to another.

Figure 5.18
Parameters for setting up DHCP relaying may be established in this dialog.

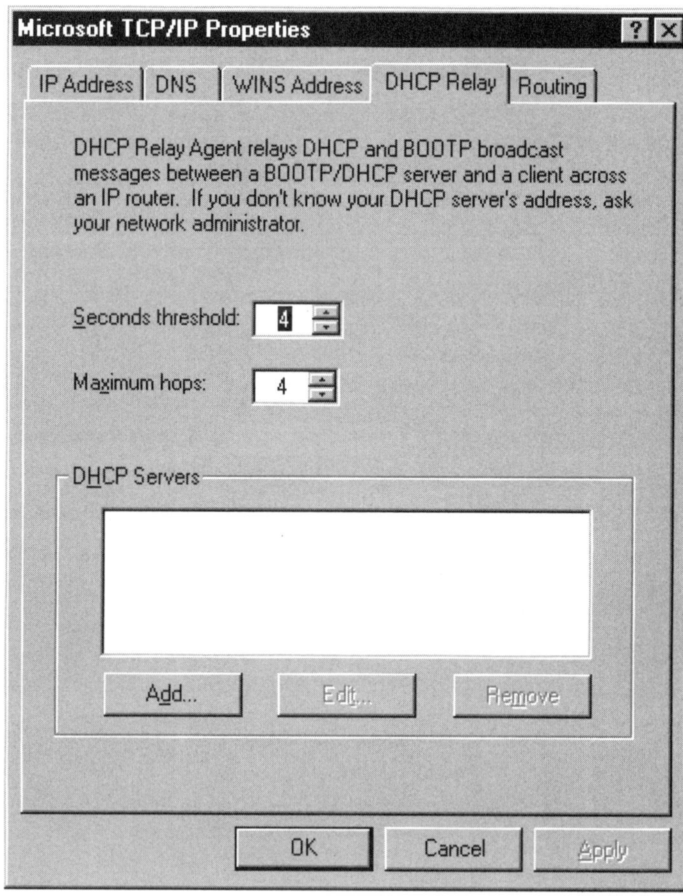

The dialog shown in Figure 5.18 allows you to configure the parameters associated with this relay function. Refer to the DHCP chapter (chapter 15) for a further discussion on this screen.

Routing Tab

Windows NT may be used as a simple IP router. This requires that the IP software in Windows NT be configured to allow forwarding between its network interfaces.

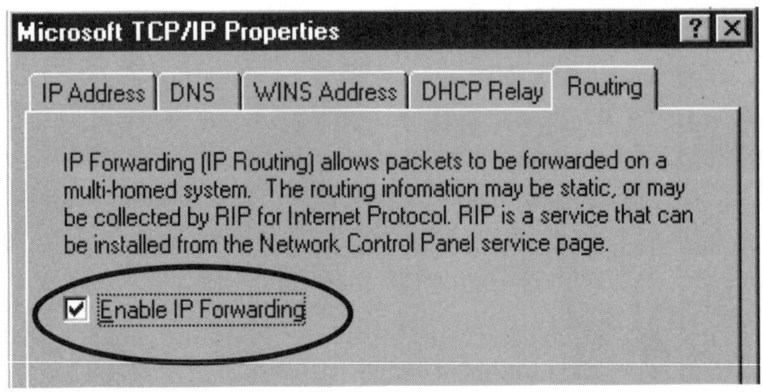

Figure 5.19 Windows NT server may function as a simple IP router after forwarding is enabled with this dialog.

Figure 5.19 shows the dialog which allows you to enable IP forwarding to turn Windows NT into a router. Further details of routing are discussed in chapter 7, "NT Server as an IP Router". If you are considering using NT as a router, you should also read chapter 8, "Using Steelhead as a RIPv2 Router".

Testing the Installation

There are two commands which will be used to test the configuration of TCP/IP: ***ipconfig*** and ***ping***.

The command ***ipconfig*** will show the configuration of TCP/IP on that machine. If you do not give any command-line options, ***ipconfig*** will tell you the configured IP address, subnet mask and default gateway of the current machine. An example of this is shown at the top of the window in Figure 5.20.

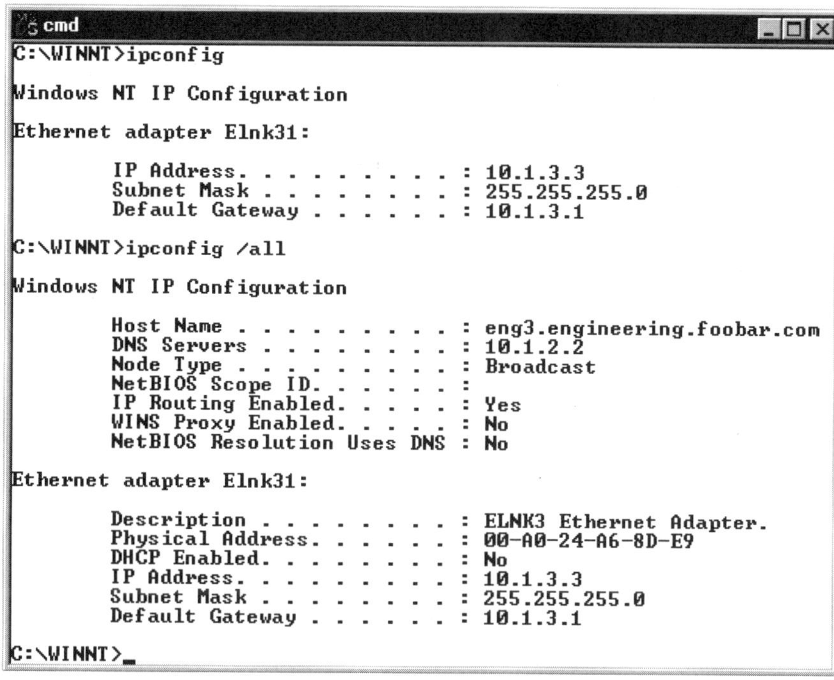

Figure 5.20
The ipconfig command may be used to view the current configuration.

When troubleshooting, make sure that the address shown matches what you input during the installation. Note that a default gateway should be specified, otherwise the machine will not be able to communicate with hosts not directly attached to its local segment.

You may want more information than ***ipconfig*** divulges by default. There is an option to list all of the information that the command can give you. The ***/all*** option for ***ipconfig*** lists more of the configured TCP/IP parameters, shown at the bottom of Figure 5.20.

If the device has multiple NICs installed, or is a Remote Access Server, additional interfaces will appear in the output of ***ipconfig***. Figure 5.21 shows that there are two NICs installed in that machine, and that machine has the Remote Access Service installed, operating as both a RAS client and RAS server.

```
command prompt

C:\WINNT>ipconfig

Windows NT IP Configuration

Ethernet adapter CE2XPS2:

        IP Address. . . . . . . . . : 10.1.9.1
        Subnet Mask . . . . . . . . : 255.255.255.0
        Default Gateway . . . . . . :

Ethernet adapter Elnk31:

        IP Address. . . . . . . . . : 10.1.8.1
        Subnet Mask . . . . . . . . : 255.255.255.0
        Default Gateway . . . . . . :

PPP adapter NdisWan8:

        IP Address. . . . . . . . . : 10.1.2.66
        Subnet Mask . . . . . . . . : 255.0.0.0
        Default Gateway . . . . . . : 10.1.2.66

PPP adapter NdisWan7:

        IP Address. . . . . . . . . : 198.211.92.140
        Subnet Mask . . . . . . . . : 255.255.255.0
        Default Gateway . . . . . . : 198.211.92.140

C:\WINNT>
```

Figure 5.21 Multiple interfaces as shown by ipconfig.

Wntipcfg

The program ***wntipcfg.exe*** is installed with the NT Resource Kit. This program gives the same information as ***ipconfig***, but displays it in a graphical window.[4] Figure 5.22 shows the initial screen of ***wntipcfg***.

4. Wntipcfg has the same look and feel as the Windows 95 program, winipcfg.exe.

Figure 5.22
Output of wntipcfg.exe.

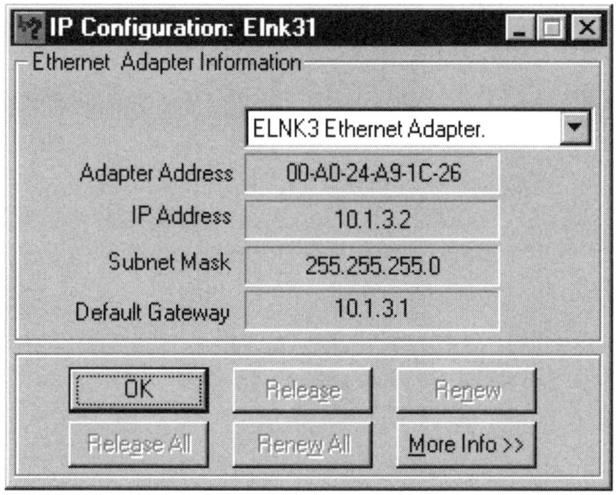

Additional information can be displayed by pressing the *More Info* button at the bottom of the screen, which will give you information similar to the output of ***ipconfig /all***. Also, if this machine is a DHCP client, the currently assigned IP address can be renewed or released using the buttons on this screen.

Ping

The ***ping*** command may be used to test connectivity to a host. ***Ping*** uses the ICMP echo service. An ICMP echo request message is sent to the target specified on the command line. The target echoes back a reply which the ***ping*** command receives and reports to the user. NT by default sends four ICMP echo request messages to the target, expecting four replies. An example of ping output is shown in Figure 5.23.

```
C:\WINNT>ipconfig

Windows NT IP Configuration

Ethernet adapter Elnk31:

        IP Address. . . . . . . . . : 10.1.3.3
        Subnet Mask . . . . . . . . : 255.255.255.0
        Default Gateway . . . . . . : 10.1.3.1

C:\WINNT>ping 10.1.3.1

Pinging 10.1.3.1 with 32 bytes of data:

Reply from 10.1.3.1: bytes=32 time<10ms TTL=255
Reply from 10.1.3.1: bytes=32 time<10ms TTL=255
Reply from 10.1.3.1: bytes=32 time<10ms TTL=255
Reply from 10.1.3.1: bytes=32 time<10ms TTL=255

C:\WINNT>_
```

Figure 5.23 Ping of another machine on the same subnet.

The following steps can be used in the order listed to troubleshoot connectivity problems:

- Test that TCP/IP is installed by testing a ***ping*** to the loopback address 127.0.0.1. This tests that you have IP installed correctly- it does not test connectivity with the network.
- A logical next step would be to test local connectivity through the NIC driver to itself by running ***ping*** with the IP address that you've assigned to the NIC (e.g. 10.1.3.3). We'll see however in the chapter on "NT Server as an IP Router" that the ***ping*** messages would actually be sent over the loopback interface. This may still be a useful test to confirm that the address was entered correctly.
- ***Ping*** a machine on the same segment to assure that the media and NICs are properly connected and TCP/IP is configured for local communication.
- ***Ping*** the default router. Figure 5.23 shows an example of where we pinged the near interface of ENG_RTR at 10.1.3.1.
- ***Ping*** a machine on the other side of the router to test default gateway and router configuration.

Recall that by default, four echo requests are sent by NT's ***ping***, and in our example, we received four replies. Figure 5.24 is a ladder diagram which shows the ICMP echo request/reply packet exchange.

Figure 5.24
Ping packet exchange.

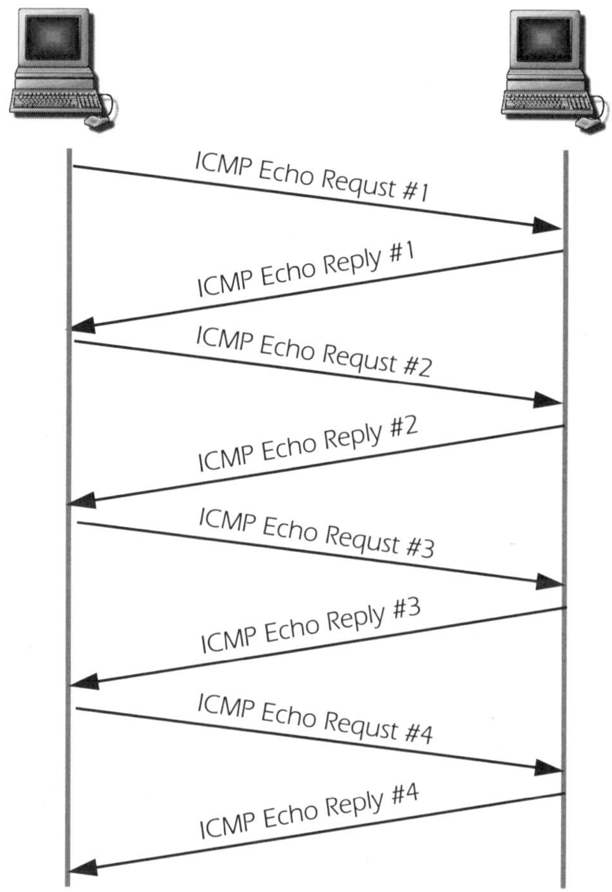

Where TCP/IP Parameters are Stored in NT

The Windows NT *registry* is a collection of most of the configuration parameters for the operating system and its applications. This database can be modified by a system administrator using various tools. Two registry editing programs that are installed with NT 4.0 are ***regedt32.exe*** and ***regedit.exe***. You'll find that ***regedt32*** has more capabilities, except in one area: ***regedit*** has better search capabilities. The main window of the program ***regedit*** is shown in Figure 5.25.

Warning

Most of the settings found in the registry can, and should, be modified by the appropriate control panel or user interface. Before modifying the registry, make a backup of it. Modifying the registry directly can cause problems if you make a mistake, so be careful!

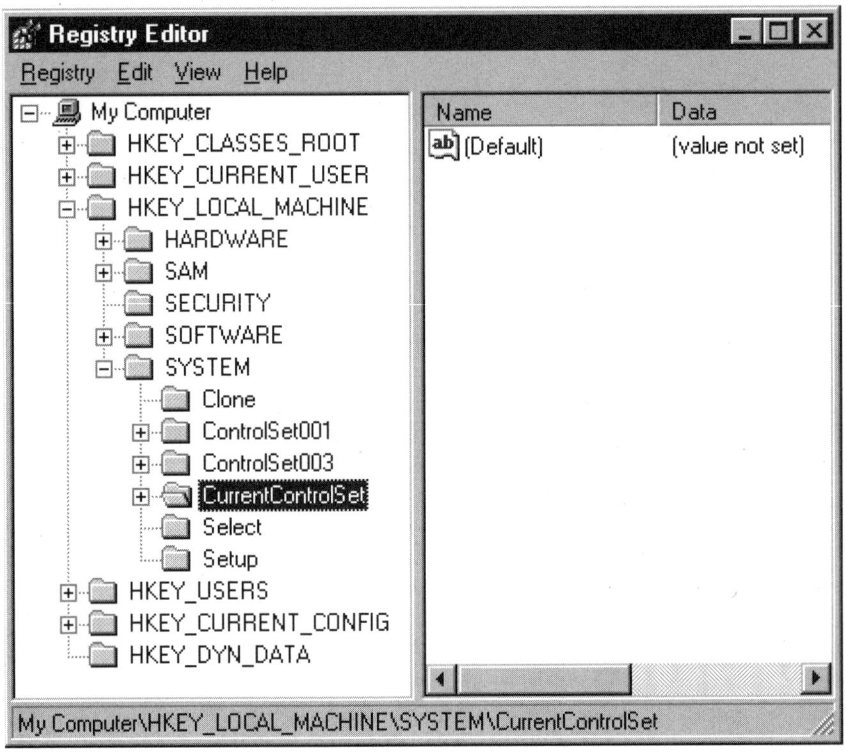

Figure 5.25 Registry editor application open to the HKey_Local_Machine\System\CurrentControlSet key.

Many of the configuration parameters for the TCP/IP stack in NT are found in the following registry location:

HKey_Local_Machine\System\CurrentControlSet\Services\Tcpip

The other location that contains TCP/IP specific values is:

HKey_Local_Machine\System\CurrentControlSet\Services*NIC*

where NIC is the name of the network interface card as assigned by NT. (This name is shown as the device name in the output of the NT command ***ipconfig***.)

Traversing the Registry Tree

Registry parameters listed in this book will be shown in tables formatted like Table 5.3 and Table 5.4. Recall from the "IP Addressing and Datagram Transmission" chapter that we discussed two registry parameters, *ArpCacheLife* and *ArpCacheSize*.

The Address Resolution Protocol (ARP) maintains a cache of recently used entries. Entries in this cache are maintained for a certain lifetime, measured in seconds. If an ARP entry does not specify a lifetime, a default value is used. The *ArpCacheLife* registry parameter (Table 5.3) specifies this default lifetime.

Table 5.3
ArpCacheLife registry parameter.

Hive:	HKEY_LOCAL_MACHINE
Key:	\System\CurrentControlSet\Services\Tcplp\Parameters
Name:	ArpCacheLife
Type:	REG_DWORD
Value:	120 (default)

The ARP cache can hold a finite number of entries. The *ArpCacheSize* parameter defines the maximum number of entries in the ARP cache (Table 5.4).

Table 5.4
ArpCacheSize registry parameter.

Hive:	HKEY_LOCAL_MACHINE
Key:	\System\CurrentControlSet\Services\Tcplp\Parameters
Name:	ArpCacheSize
Type:	REG_DWORD
Value:	62 (default)

Let's try to find these two parameters in the registry. Starting from the point shown in Figure 5.25, at the *CurrentControlSet*, follow the key portion of these parameters. Open up *CurrentControlSet* and then *Services*. Next, select *Tcpip* and you should see something like that shown in Figure 5.26.

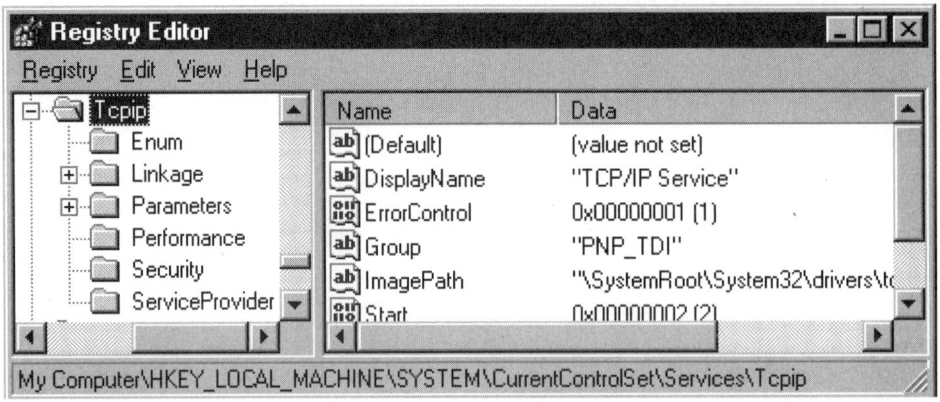

Figure 5.26 The Tcpip key selected in the registry editor has many subkeys and values.

We can see from the keys specified in Table 5.3 and Table 5.4 that from this point, the *Parameters* key should be where we find the actual parameter values. Opening up the *Parameters* key yields a display like that in Figure 5.27. The parameters are shown in the right-hand pane of the window.

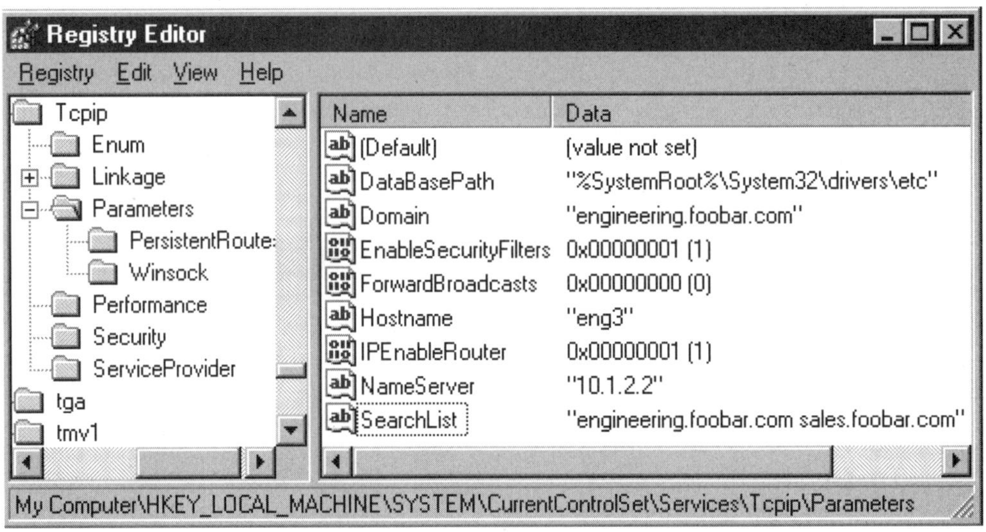

Figure 5.27 TCP/IP parameters are shown here.

Look through the list of parameters. Several of the configuration parameters which were just entered for TCP/IP are shown here, including the *Hostname* and *IPEnableRouter* parameters.

Notice the *ArpCacheLife* and *ArpCacheSize* parameters are not shown. The default values for many parameters are hard-coded directly into the Windows NT software. When a parameter is to be altered from its default value, the parameter must be added to the registry. The Windows NT software will check for the existence of a particular registry value before using the default value.

Adding Registry Parameters using Regedit.exe

The *ArpCacheLife* and *ArpCacheSize* parameters weren't in the registry, thus we know that their default values are being used by NT.

First, let's add the *ArpCacheLife* parameter to the registry. Figure 5.28 shows the first step toward adding a registry parameter. Note that Table 5.3 identified that the type of this parameter is REG_DWORD, which is a double-word (32-bit number).

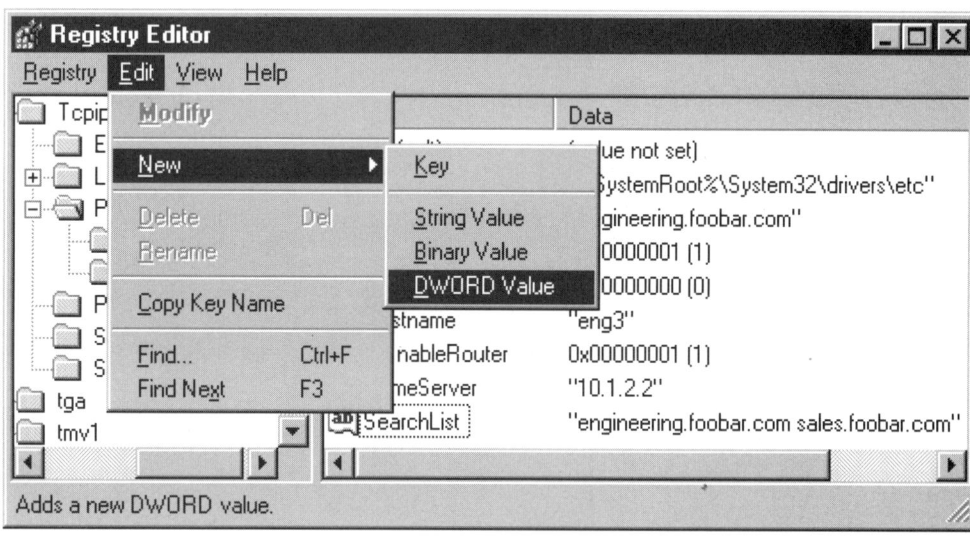

Figure 5.28 Use the edit menu to add a new value to the set of TCP/IP parameters.

Adding a new double-word parameter to the registry creates an entry such as "New Value #1" shown in Figure 5.29. Enter the name *ArpCache-Life* and press the enter key to name the parameter.

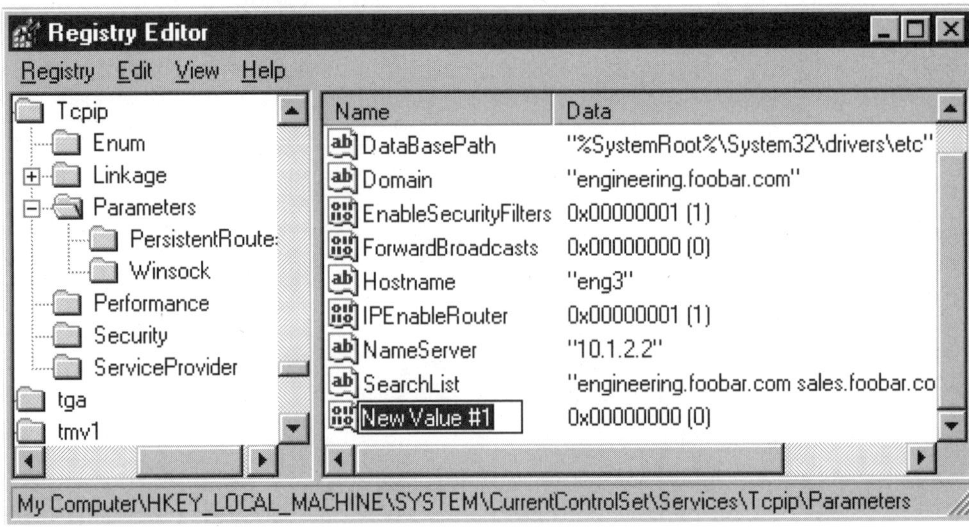

Figure 5.29 A name must be entered for the new value.

Double-click on a parameter to edit its value. As Figure 5.30 shows, the value for the parameter may be entered in either hexadecimal or decimal format. We've selected decimal and entered the value of 120. Since 120 seconds is the default value for this parameter, there will be no difference in the way ARP behaves.

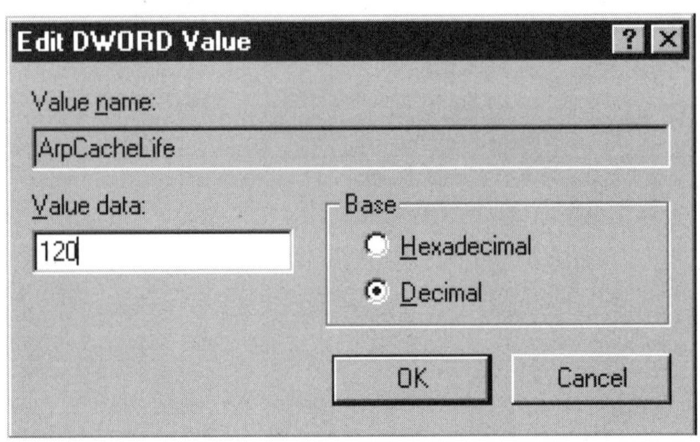

Figure 5.30 A value of 120 seconds (two minutes) is entered for the ArpCacheLife parameter.

We've repeated the steps of adding and naming the parameter for the *ArpCacheSize*, then double-clicking gives the same kind of dialog to edit the value, in which we entered a decimal value of 62 as shown in Figure 5.31.

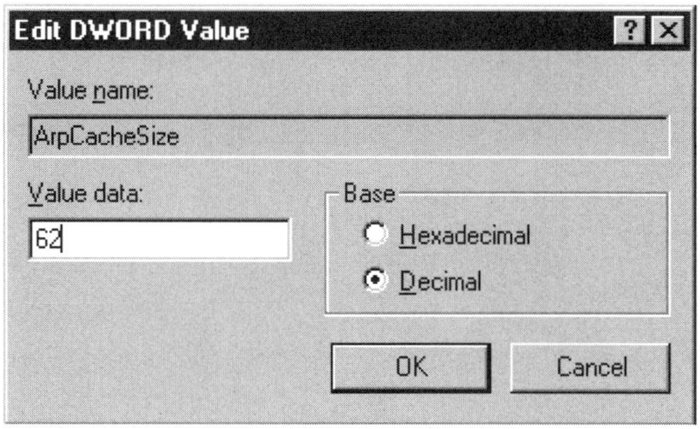

Figure 5.31 A value of 62 entries is entered for the ArpCacheSize parameter.

After parameters are added, use *View->Refresh* to refresh the display. The two new parameters are shown in the display in Figure 5.32.

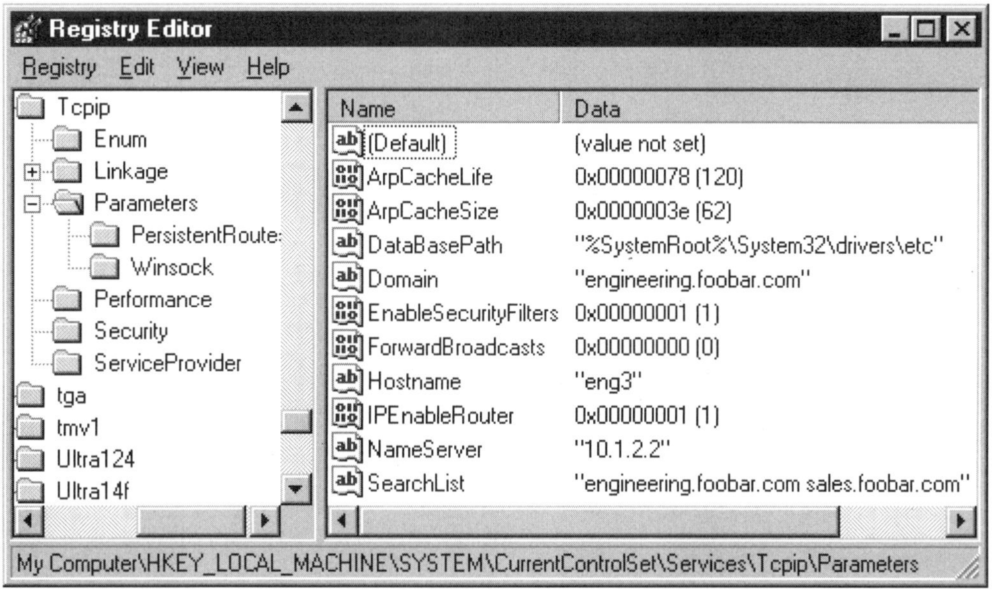

Figure 5.32 The ArpCacheLife and ArpCacheSize parameters are shown in the list.

Summary

Here's a summary of the items which have been addressed in this chapter.

- To use TCP/IP, each workstation, server, or router must have this software installed and configured. Steps for installing TCP/IP software in Windows NT are discussed.
- The basics of configuring IP include assigning an IP address, subnet mask, and default gateway (router) address to be used for each network interface. An example of this configuration is shown.
- In order to use domain names (rather than IP addresses) to refer to other machines, you may set up a DNS server and configure each machine to be a DNS client. While DNS server configuration is covered in later chapters, this chapter provides steps to configure DNS clients.
- The Windows NT TCP/IP implementation can be configured to restrict incoming traffic by use of filters. Two different types of filters are discussed.
    - PPTP filtering may be enabled to discard any incoming traffic which is not received on a PPTP interface.
    - Transport protocol filters allow configuration of specific protocols (by port or protocol number) which are to be received or discarded by a machine.
- Basic IP routing may be enabled on NT. When necessary, an NT machine may also be configured to act as a DHCP relay agent. WINS name resolution may also be enabled. See Table 5.1 for more information about these.
- Commands such as ***ipconfig***, ***wntipcfg***, and ***ping*** may be used to test the installation and configuration of the TCP/IP software.
- Certain configuration parameters may be adjusted by using a registry editor. Examples of a few of these parameters is discussed.

Further Reading

Here is information about various books and magazines in which to look for further information on the subject.

[MSPress1997] Microsoft Press, *Microsoft Windows NT Resource Kit,* 1997, Microsoft Press

[Thomas1997] Thomas, Steven, *Back Office Registry Professional Reference,* 1997, McGraw-Hill

Part Two

The Details

6

Examining Network Traffic Using Network Monitor

Setting up and maintaining any network can be a complex effort if you don't have a clear view of what the actual traffic in the network consists of. We'll now look at how to monitor activity on your network.

- Why do we want to monitor traffic?
- What does it help us understand in later chapters?

These questions are answered in the summary of this chapter (page 242).

Protocol analyzer: a tool used to capture and analyze network traffic.

Protocol analyzers are software tools which look at raw network traffic data from a network and help us to understand it. Some protocol analyzers simply display statistics of the volume of the network traffic. Other protocol analyzers provide detailed decoding of each frame or packet from the network.

Many such tools exist and are available as freeware, shareware, or fully supported products from several vendors. Microsoft has such a tool, which they call *Network Monitor.*

Microsoft Network Monitor

Network Monitor ("netmon") is a protocol analyzer that is part of the *Systems Management Server* (SMS) software package from Microsoft. This tool is very useful in troubleshooting network problems. It has many of the typical protocol analyzer features, such as: packet capture and decode, filtering of packets based on address or protocol type, and statistical summaries of network traffic. Network Monitor can be installed on any NT machine for you to use for troubleshooting.

Network Monitor installation files can also be found on the NT Server 4.0 CD. However, this version of Network Monitor is only able to capture and decode packets addressed to the machine it is running on. For a fully-functional version, use the one from SMS.

Note

Note that the Network Monitor application is not included on the CD with this book. You must obtain Network Monitor from an SMS installation CD. An alternative is to use the Network Monitor application that is located on the NT Server 4.0 CD.

One feature of Network Monitor is that it can be running at the same time as other network applications. This is an advantage over other protocol analyzer software that requires complete control of the NIC.

In terms of network security, this program is a tool that is only supposed to be used to troubleshoot network problems. Since this program can capture all packets being sent on the LAN, the possibility that any user can use this tool to capture packets with sensitive data is a serious security problem. To deal with this issue, a feature has been added to allow you to scan the network and locate any machines running this program.

Statistics Dialog

The main dialog of Network Monitor (Figure 6.1) displays various statistics about the local network. Statistics include:

- percent network utilization
- frames / sec
- bytes / sec
- broadcasts / sec
- multicasts / sec
- number of packets sent to or from certain MAC addresses
- summary for each MAC address of how many frames it has sent or received, how many bytes it has sent or received, and the number of broadcasts or multicasts it has sent

Once a capture has begun, these statistics are updated in real-time. When a capture has stopped, the contents of the packets can be viewed, using the *Capture -> Display Captured Data* menu option.

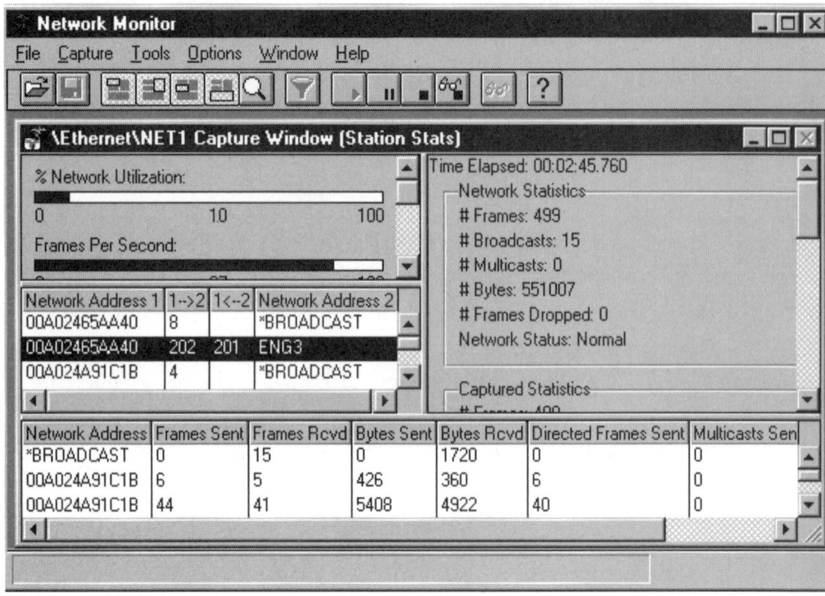

Figure 6.1
Network Monitor Statistics dialog

Example Capture: Ping Packets

Figure 6.2 is a network diagram used to create the a network monitor capture that will be discussed in detail in the next few pages. In particular, the capture is of packets sent between ENG2 (10.1.3.2) and ENG3 (10.1.3.3).

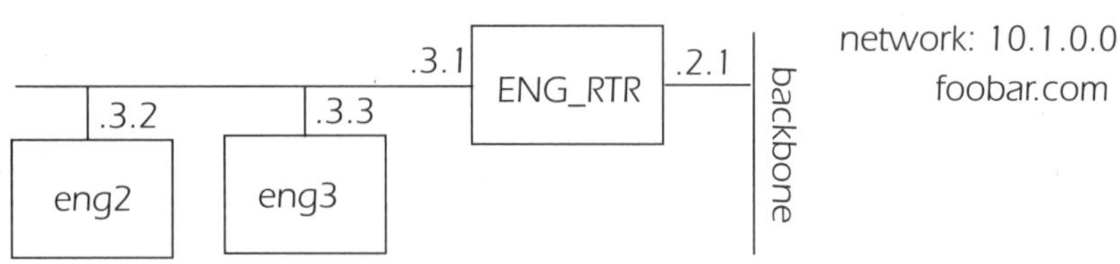

Figure 6.2
The engineering subnet was used to create the following network monitor captures.

In testing this network, we issued a ***ping*** command from ENG2 as shown in Figure 6.3. Note that we're running Network Monitor on ENG3 so the packet captures we see are from that perspective. Recall that the *ping* command generates ICMP *echo request* messages. When the ICMP software on ENG3 receives an echo request, it will respond with an *echo reply* message back to ENG2.

Figure 6.3 Network Monitor is run on a machine on the network, but it doesn't have to be one involved in the communication being monitored.

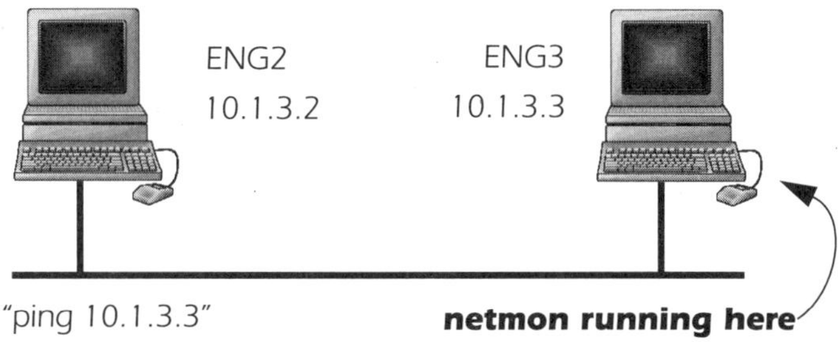

Figure 6.4 is an example of the summary pane of the capture view dialog for a capture. The captured packets are stored on the CD found in the back of this book. Throughout the book, we will refer to certain packet captures as examples. If you'd like to examine the packet captures in more detail, install Network Monitor on your machine, and then load the appropriate capture file.

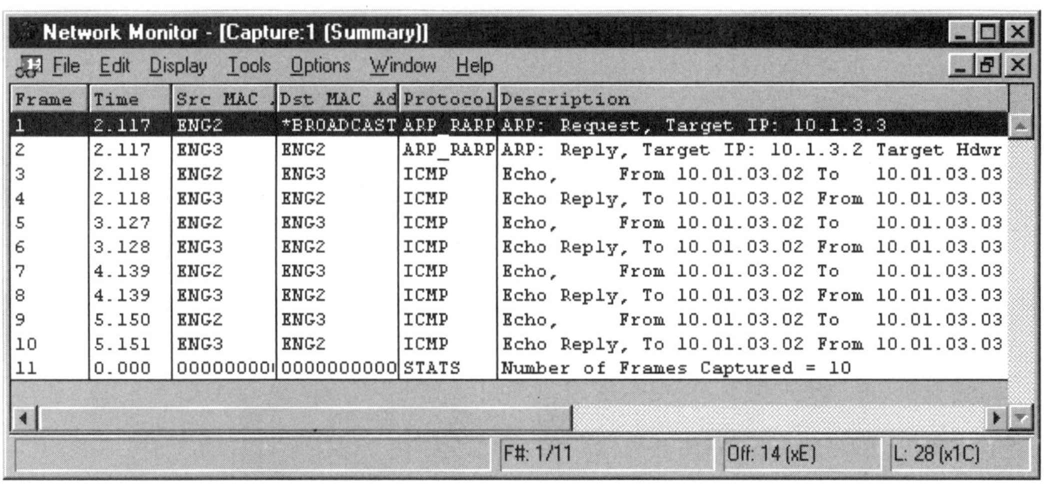

Network Monitor - [Capture:1 (Summary)]

File Edit Display Tools Options Window Help

Frame	Time	Src MAC	Dst MAC Ad	Protocol	Description
1	2.117	ENG2	*BROADCAST	ARP_RARP	ARP: Request, Target IP: 10.1.3.3
2	2.117	ENG3	ENG2	ARP_RARP	ARP: Reply, Target IP: 10.1.3.2 Target Hdwr
3	2.118	ENG2	ENG3	ICMP	Echo, From 10.01.03.02 To 10.01.03.03
4	2.118	ENG3	ENG2	ICMP	Echo Reply, To 10.01.03.02 From 10.01.03.03
5	3.127	ENG2	ENG3	ICMP	Echo, From 10.01.03.02 To 10.01.03.03
6	3.128	ENG3	ENG2	ICMP	Echo Reply, To 10.01.03.02 From 10.01.03.03
7	4.139	ENG2	ENG3	ICMP	Echo, From 10.01.03.02 To 10.01.03.03
8	4.139	ENG3	ENG2	ICMP	Echo Reply, To 10.01.03.02 From 10.01.03.03
9	5.150	ENG2	ENG3	ICMP	Echo, From 10.01.03.02 To 10.01.03.03
10	5.151	ENG3	ENG2	ICMP	Echo Reply, To 10.01.03.02 From 10.01.03.03
11	0.000	000000000	0000000000	STATS	Number of Frames Captured = 10

F#: 1/11 Off: 14 (xE) L: 28 (x1C)

Figure 6.4 Packet capture of a Ping session.

netmon1.cap

For this example, the name of the capture file is netmon1.cap. You can load this capture file using the *File->Open* menu item. But make sure to load the address database as well, called netmon_ch.adr. Refer to "Loading the Address Database" on page 220 to see how to load the address database. If the database was loaded successfully, the *Src MAC Addr* and *Dest MAC Addr* columns on your screen will match Figure 6.4.

Figure 6.4 shows captured packets that occurred when ENG2 pinged ENG3. It lists in chronological order the packets that it has received. Each packet (frame) is numbered sequentially, and a time stamp is shown for each packet (the number of seconds that have passed from the start of the capture).

The next two columns show the source and destination MAC addresses for each packet. If Network Monitor learned the NetBIOS computer name for that machine, it is shown in the MAC address column.

The protocol column lists the protocol that is found in that particular packet. The example packets above show that two ARP packets were captured, and then eight ICMP packets.

The description column gives more details as to the contents of the packet.

Three additional columns, not shown above, are Source Other Address, Destination Other Address, and Type Other Address. Notice that shown above is only the MAC address or NetBIOS name. If the packet contains IP addresses or IPX addresses, those will be listed in the last 3 columns.

Network Monitor Packet Decode

Double-clicking on any of the packets will bring up the *Capture Detail* pane, as shown in Figure 6.5.

The *Capture View* (or *Capture Detail*) dialog consists of three panes:

- summary pane (top)
- detail pane (middle)
- hex pane (bottom)

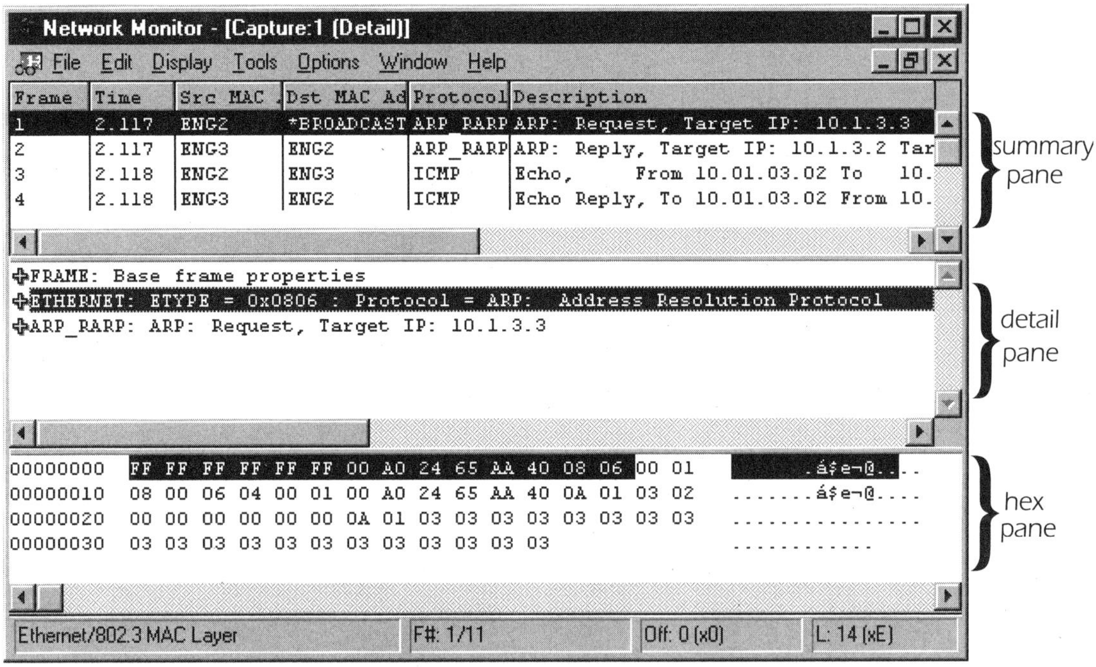

Figure 6.5 Network monitor packet decode.

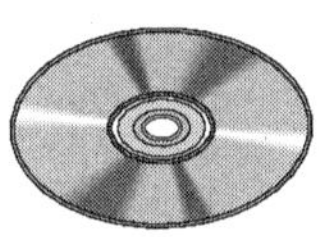

netmon1.cap

In the summary pane, one packet will be highlighted — that will be the packet that is decoded in the middle and bottom part of the dialog.

In the detail pane, a decode of the packet contents is shown. Each encapsulated protocol will have an entry, with a plus sign (+) or minus sign (-) to the left of it. The plus sign signifies that there is more detail to that header, and clicking on that line will expand that header so that you can see the contents.

The bottom pane shows the hex data found in the packet. Part of this data may be highlighted — if it is, the highlighted part corresponds to the highlighted header in the detail pane.

ARP Request Packet

Before the echo request may be sent over the network, a physical address must be determined for the destination machine. As we saw in the IP Addressing chapter, the Address Resolution Protocol (ARP) is used to perform this translation. The machine wanting to send the IP datagram (in this case, carrying the ICMP echo request) issues an ARP request.

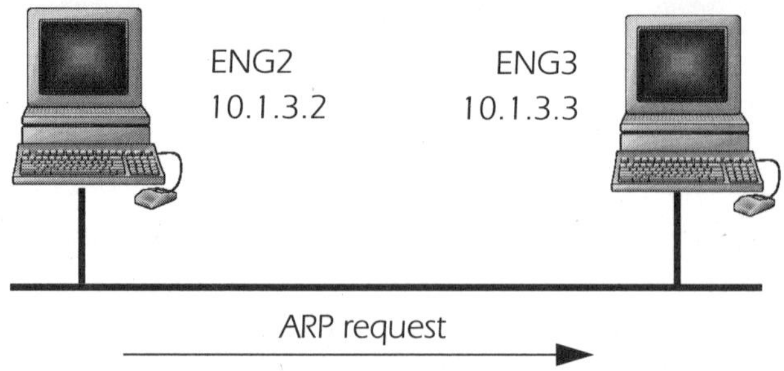

Figure 6.6 Before sending an IP datagram, the machine obtains the destination hardware address by sending an ARP request.

netmon1.cap

In Figure 6.6, ENG2 has an IP packet for ENG3. ENG2 checks its ARP cache, and finds it doesn't have the hardware address for ENG3. Therefore ENG2 broadcasts an ARP request on the wire. As shown in Figure 6.7, the target hardware address of the Ethernet packet is a broadcast. The protocol type field (ETYPE) is 0x0806, which translates to the protocol ARP.

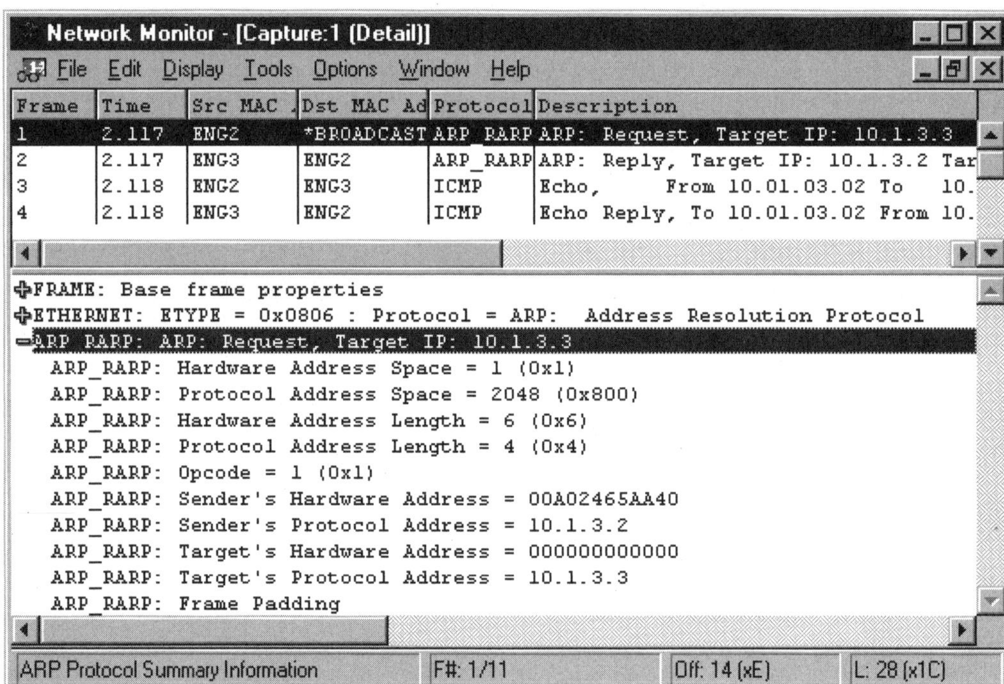

Figure 6.7 ARP request packet decode.

The ARP request is looking for the hardware address of IP address 10.1.3.3, listed in the target protocol address field. The sender of the ARP request has an IP address of 10.1.3.2, with a hardware address of 00a02465aa40. The "opcode" in the ARP packet tells us that this packet is a request (opcode =1). The other fields in the ARP packet are used to calculate the byte placement of the addresses within the packet.

ARP Reply Packet

All machines on the Ethernet which carries the ARP request will see the request. Normally only the machine which is using the IP address in the ARP request will respond. As shown in Figure 6.8, the ARP response message is sent back to the originator of the ARP request containing the physical address of the responder.

Figure 6.8
ARP response sent back to originator of request.

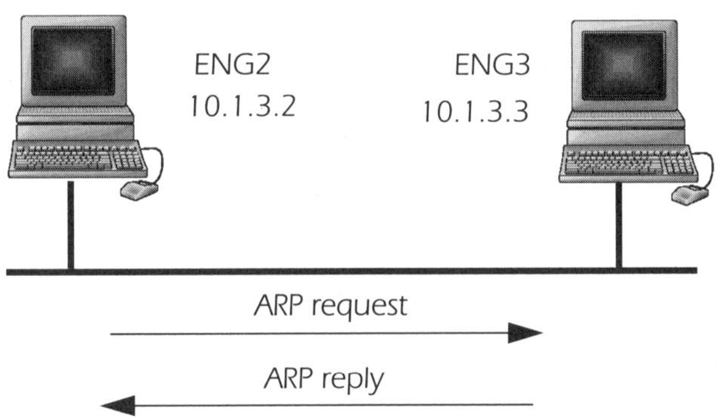

As seen from the packet decode in Figure 6.9, the ARP reply is an Ethernet unicast, from ENG3 to ENG2. Notice the ARP reply contents are very similar to the request. Differences include:

- both the source and target hardware address fields are filled in
- the opcode = 2 (reply)

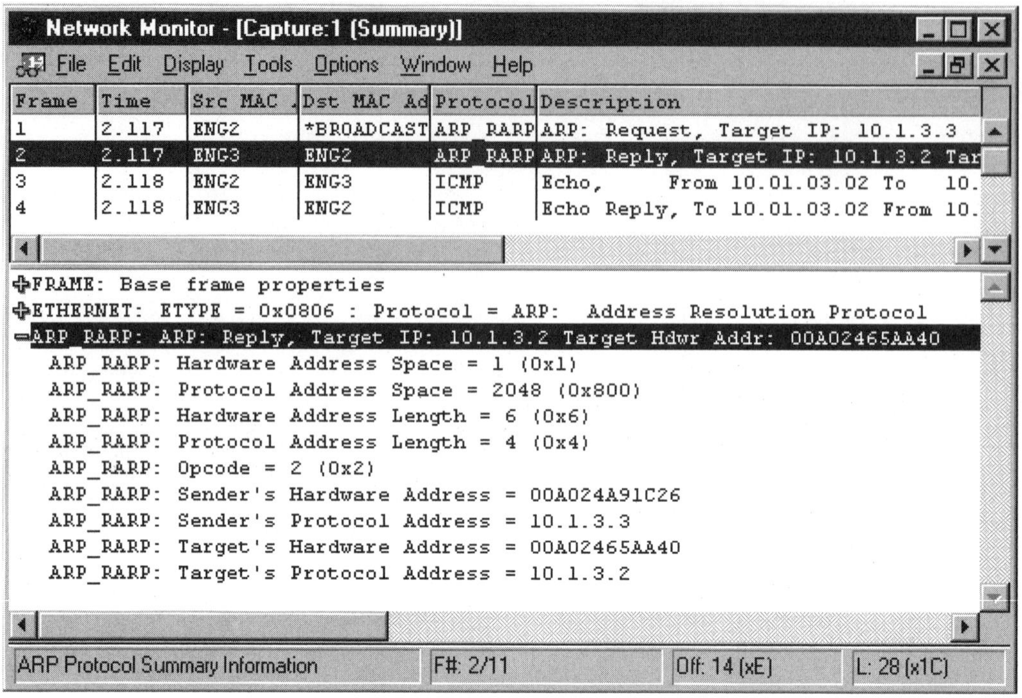

Figure 6.9 ARP reply packet decode.

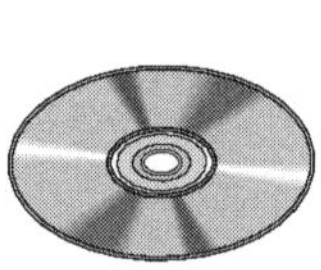
netmon1.cap

Once the machine which originated the ARP request receives and processes this ARP reply, it knows the physical address of the destination for the echo request. Note that the answer is in the source hardware address field of the ARP reply.

ICMP Echo Request Packet

Now that IP has an address translation for the target IP address, the datagram may be sent. Since the application is ping, the datagram will be an ICMP echo request. Figure 6.10 shows the IP packet, and ICMP echo request, being sent from ENG2 to ENG3.

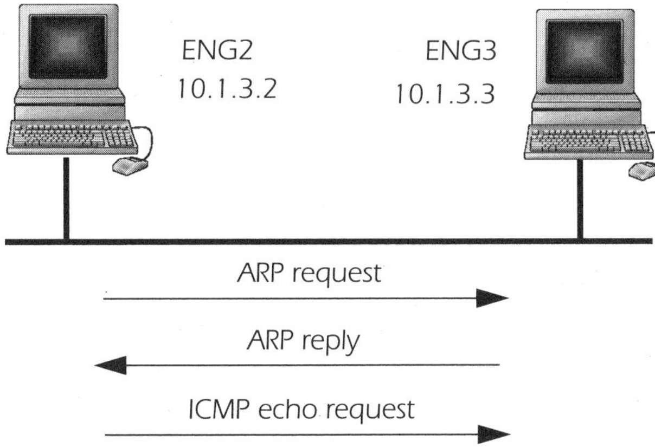

Figure 6.10 The echo request datagram is sent.

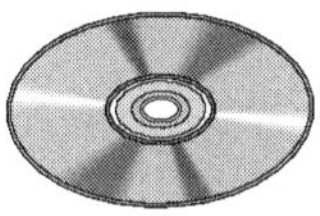

netmon1.cap

The packet decode of the ICMP echo request is shown in Figure 6.11. Notice the layers of encapsulation: Ethernet is carrying IP (protocol type 0800), and IP is carrying ICMP. The echo request packet will contain data that is to be echoed by the target.

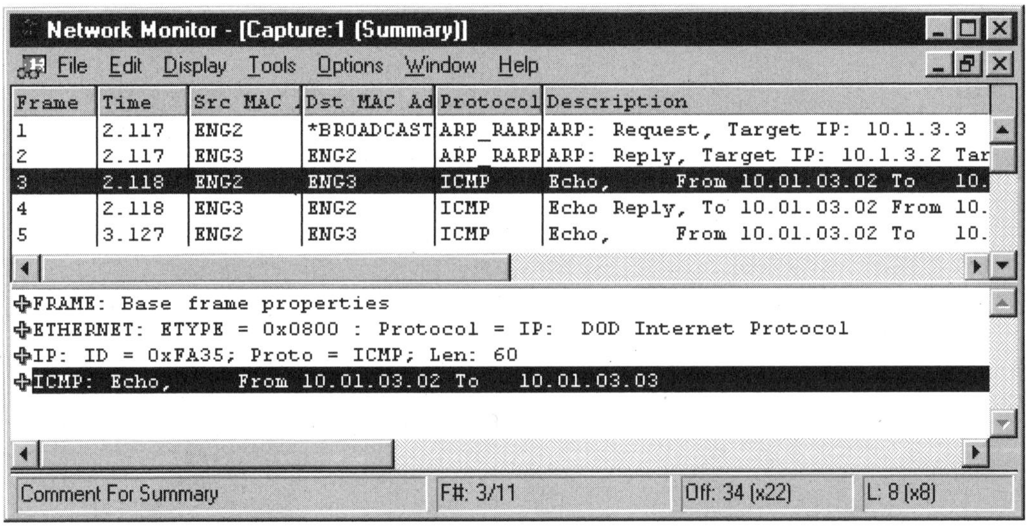

Figure 6.11 Echo request.

The reply to the echo request would be the next packet in the packet capture. This packet is sent with a unicast target address; it is sent directly to the querying machine (ENG2). The ICMP echo reply is not shown here, can be viewed using Network Monitor and loading the file netmon1.cap.

Address Database

The address database contains addresses that Network Monitor has learned by monitoring traffic, as well as addresses that have been manually entered. This database is used so that user-friendly names (rather than MAC or network addresses) may be displayed by Network Monitor. This allows you to focus more on the details of the traffic you're analyzing rather than the addresses used.

The address database is viewed using the *Display -> Addresses* menu. An example *Address Database* dialog is shown in Figure 6.12.

Figure 6.12
Viewing the address database on ENG3

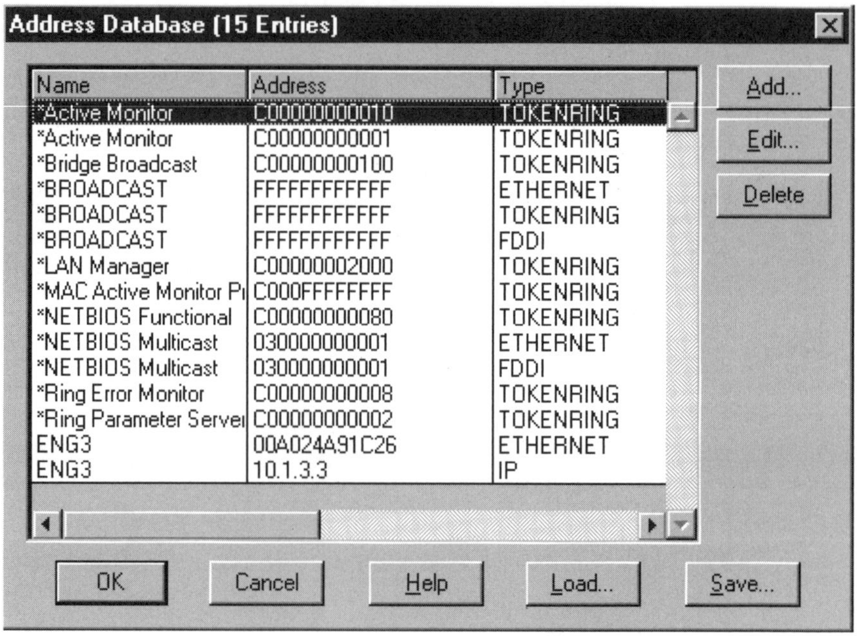

Note that the bit order within each octet of Token Ring addresses is the reverse of those in Ethernet and FDDI. This is why the NetBIOS multicast address appears as 030000000001 in the address table for Ether and FDDI, but as C00000000080 for Token Ring.

Addresses can be manually added/modified using the *Add* or *Edit* buttons. An itemized list of some of the types of addresses that can be added is shown in Figure 6.13.

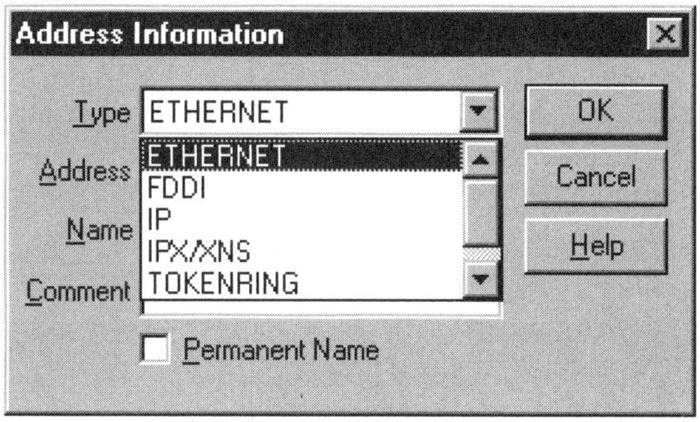

Figure 6.13 An itemized list for the address type parameter shows the names of the address types supported by Network Monitor.

Once you have selected the appropriate address type, you may enter the value of the address. Figure 6.14 shows an example Ethernet address being added, for ENG2. You may also enter a comment for further information regarding the use of the machine identified.

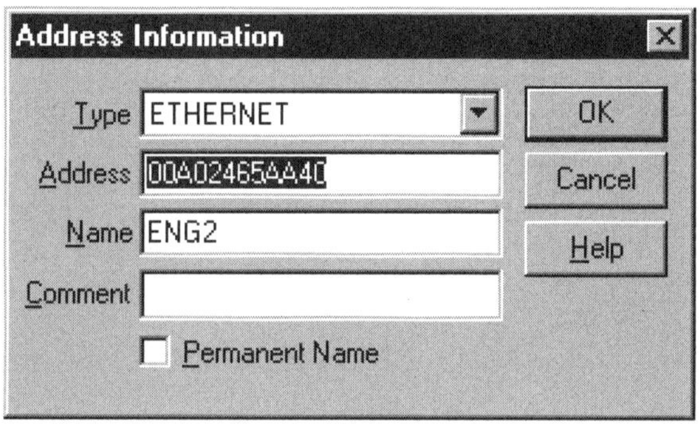

Figure 6.14 An address and name pair may be entered to be used as a shorthand in Network Monitor.

The address database can be saved to a file, and later can be loaded to interpret the MAC addresses. Address database files end with an ".adr" suffix, and by default will be saved in the same directory as the Network Monitor executable, netmon.exe. The default address database, default.adr, is loaded upon startup of Network Monitor.

Loading the Address Database

To load a new address database, use the *Load...* button in the *Address Database* dialog shown at the bottom of Figure 6.12. Figure 6.15 shows the resulting dialog.

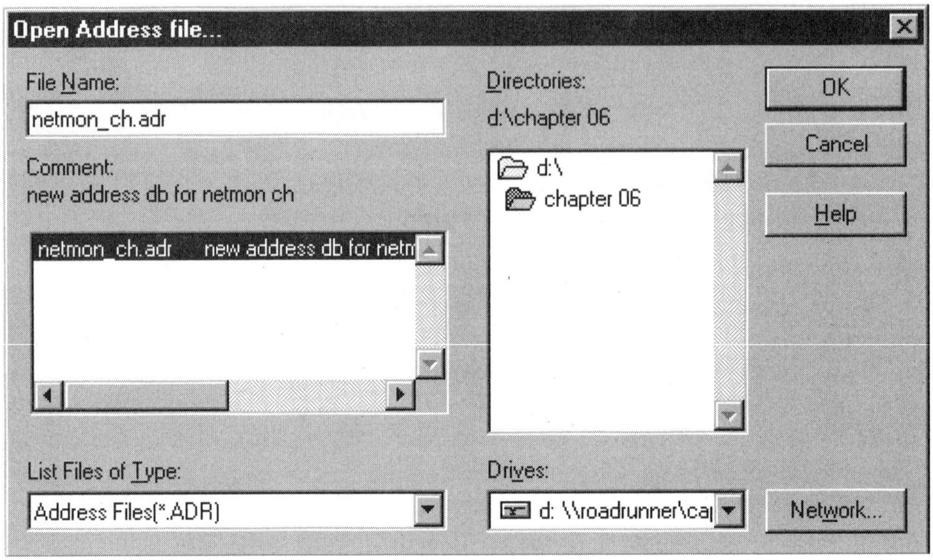

Figure 6.15 Address files may be loaded into Network Monitor with this dialog.

From the *Open Address file* screen, you can load Network Monitor address files. For the example captures for this chapter, the address file name is netmon_ch.adr, and is found on the CD in the chapter 6 directory.

Configuring Passwords and Assigning Network Card Descriptions

After Network Monitor is installed, a new control panel application is available: Monitoring Agent. When this control panel is started, the *Configure Network Monitoring Agent* dialog appears (Figure 6.16).

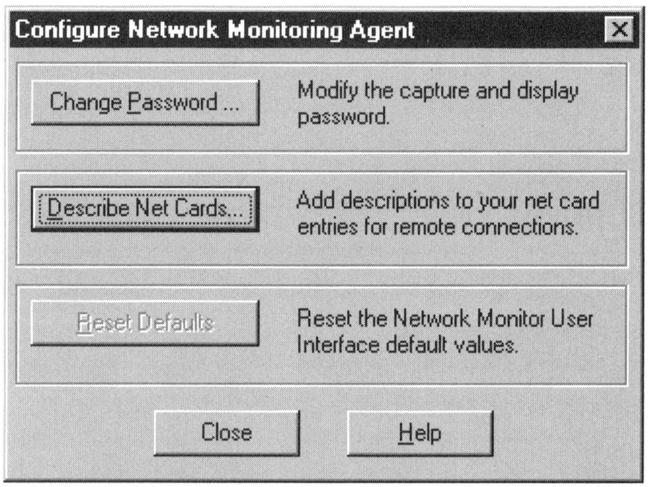

Figure 6.16 The Network Monitor Agent may be configured with this dialog to set up remote monitoring capability.

You can configure the passwords for the agent such that users cannot capture and/or display data. Clicking on the *Change Password* button shown in Figure 6.16 will result in the *Network Monitoring Password Change* dialog as shown in Figure 6.17.

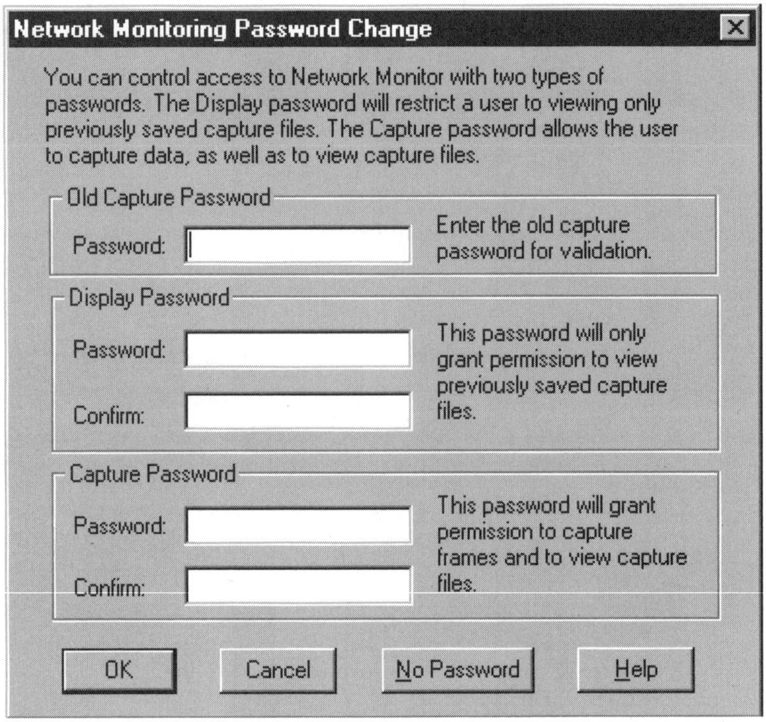

Figure 6.17 This dialog provides the ability to configure password protection of network monitoring.

You can also assign a description to each of the network cards. This becomes handy when there is more than one NIC installed in the machine. This is also handy when connecting to this agent from a remote machine. Figure 6.18 is from ENG_RTR, which has two NICs installed— one on subnet 10.1.2.0, and the other on subnet 10.1.3.0. Notice that *Edit Description* button was used for both network cards, and an appropriate description was assigned to each card.

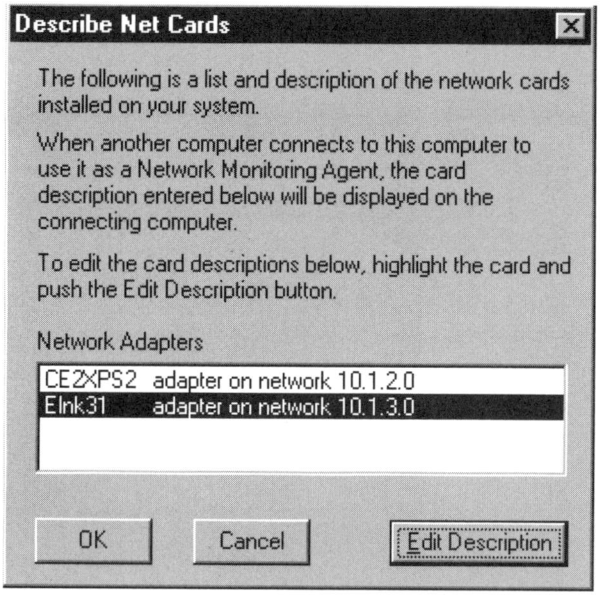

Figure 6.18 The actual names of the NICs on one machine are not always memorable. From this dialog, you may edit descriptions for each NIC according to function.

Filtering Packets that Are Displayed

Once you have captured packets from your LAN in Network Monitor, you can display a subset of the captured packets using a display filter. Filtering is allowed on the following areas:

- address
- protocol type
- protocol property

Notice that when Network Monitor's capture window (the one with the statistics, e.g. Figure 6.1) is in front, control and configuration of capture operations may be performed using the *Capture* menu. Once packets have been captured, and the window with the Summary, Detail, and Hex for that capture is in front, the *Capture* menu is replaced with the *Edit* and *Display* menus (refer back to Figure 6.5 or Figure 6.11 for examples).

After packets have been captured, under the *Display* menu, select *Filter*, and the dialog shown in Figure 6.19 will appear.

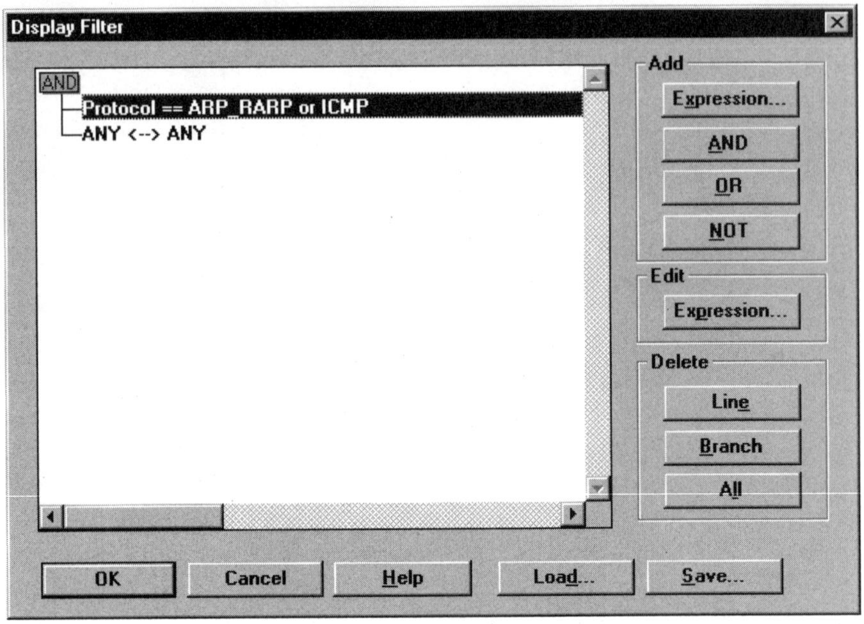

Figure 6.19
Viewing the current display filters.

The display filters in effect in Figure 6.19 are shown in two lines, and are combined by a logical AND. The first expression line is selecting the protocol to be displayed to only be ARP_RARP protocol or ICMP protocol. Packets containing any other protocol type will not be displayed. The second expression line represents the source and target packet addresses. In this case, ANY <-> ANY means that a packet from any host to any host will be displayed. This example illustrates two of the methods of filtering: by address and by protocol type.

Additional expressions can be added to this list, using a logical AND, OR, or NOT. Sub-branches can be created as well, to create an expression tree. The display filter can be saved to disk, and loaded later, to save valuable troubleshooting time.

Filtering by Address

Double-clicking on the expression ANY <-> ANY will bring up the *Expression* dialog, shown in Figure 6.20, with the *Address tab* selected. Potential source and target addresses will be listed on both sides of the dialog. Select one or both stations whose addresses you want to filter on. In addition, select whether station 1 is the source (using the arrow pointing to the right) or if direction doesn't matter (the arrow pointing in both directions.)

Figure 6.20
Filtering by address.

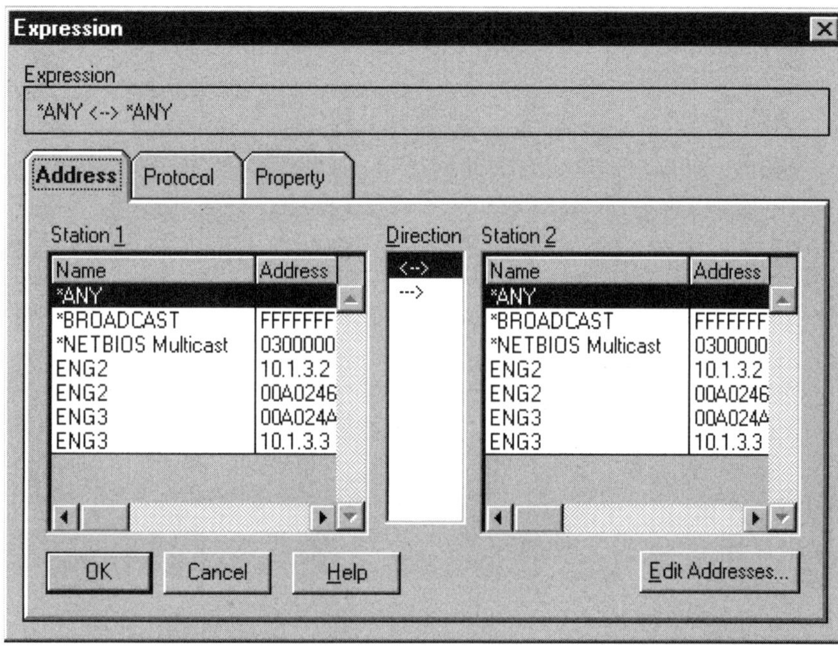

Clicking on the *Edit Addresses* button will bring up the *Address Database* dialog, as we saw back in Figure 6.12.

Filtering by Protocol Type

In some cases, you may not want to see all of the traffic between two machines, but know a protocol type which you could focus in on. This may be useful even when you haven't selected specific machines (by address).

Selecting the *Protocol tab* in the *Expression* dialog will result in the dialog shown in Figure 6.21.

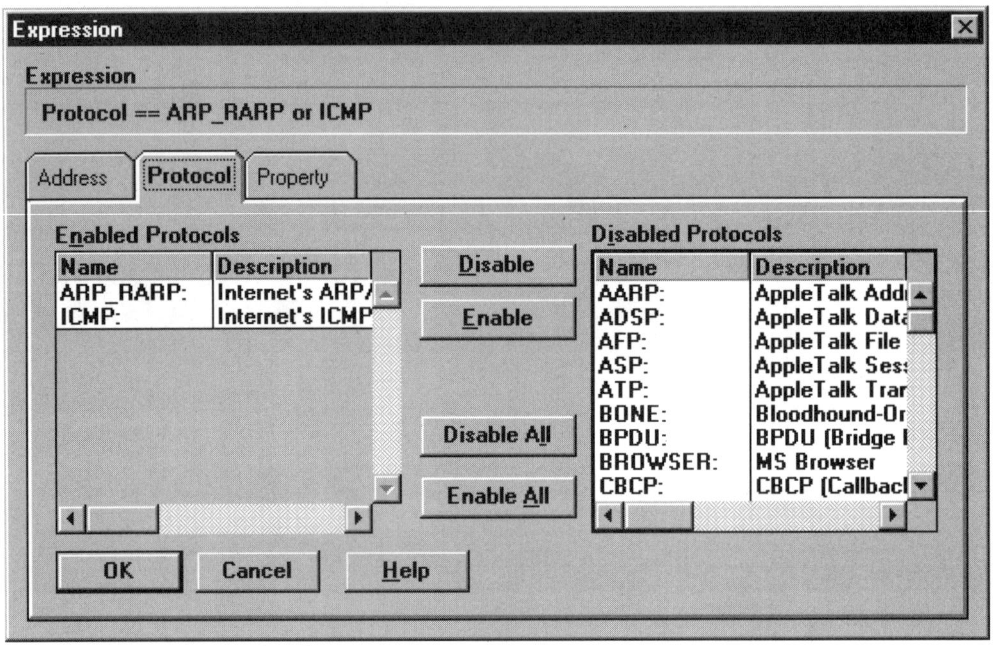

Figure 6.21 Filtering by protocol type.

Use this dialog to select protocols to filter. Figure 6.21 shows that only ARP/RARP and ICMP traffic will be displayed for this example. The filter allows either of these protocols to be displayed, but filters out the other protocol types.

Filtering by Protocol Property

Sometimes even all of the traffic for a specific protocol may even be too much to read through to find a problem in your network. You may be more specific by selecting a property of a specific protocol. In other words, you may filter to see messages only if a specific parameter in a message for a specific protocol has a certain value.

Selecting the *Property* tab on the *Expression* dialog will result in the dialog shown in Figure 6.22. A list of protocol properties appears on the left side of the dialog. Select from the list the protocol you are interested in, and double-click to view properties of that protocol that can be used to filter.

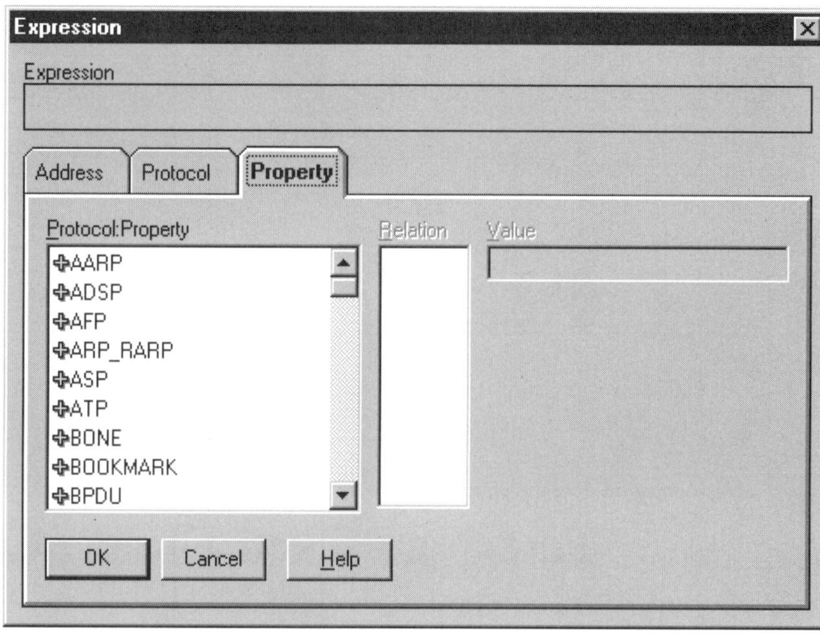

Figure 6.22
Selecting protocol properties to filter.

For example, suppose you want to view only FTP packets that contain the FTP command USER. Select FTP from the Protocol:Property list, and expand its properties to view the dialog shown in Figure 6.23.

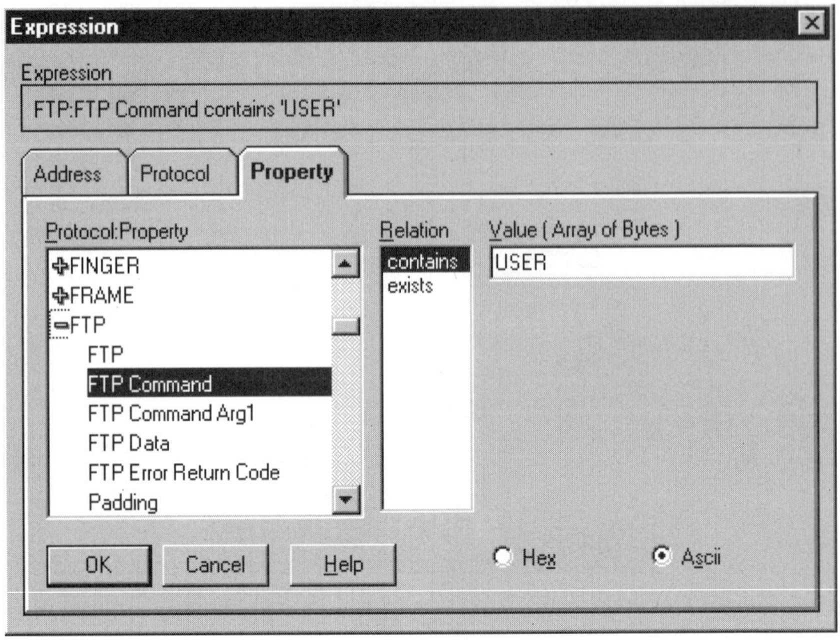

Figure 6.23
Once a protocol is selected, its properties may be displayed

In Figure 6.23, the FTP property "FTP Command" is selected. Also selected is the type of the value field (either hex or ASCII). Then, the expected value of "USER" was entered. When this filter is applied, only FTP packets containing the FTP command USER will be displayed.

Filtering Packets During Capture

There may be situations when you want to reduce not only the number of packets displayed, but also the number of packets which are captured. Network Monitor provides a second kind of filter, like the display filters, which are called capture filters because the filtering is performed during the capture process. When Network Monitor's main window (statistics) is in front, the *Capture* menu is present. The *Capture Filter* dialog (Figure 6.24) is obtained from the menu item *Capture-> Filter.* Note that you can create and edit capture filters when you are not currently capturing.

Figure 6.24
An example capture filter.

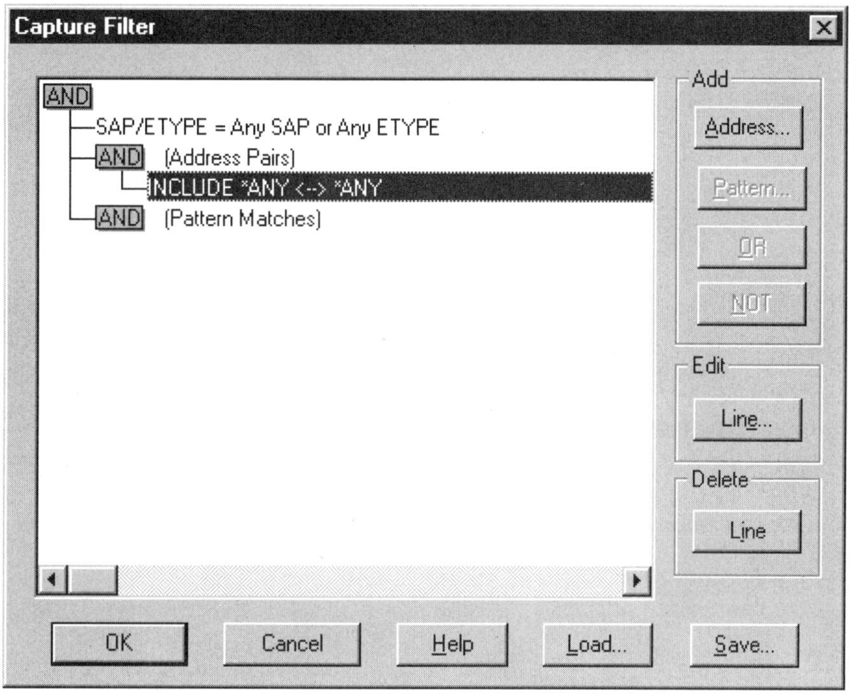

There are three components in the capture filter:

- SAP/ETYPE
- address pairs
- pattern matches

When you select the address pair line, the *Add Address* button is enabled as shown in the figure, yet when the pattern matches line is selected the *Add Pattern* button is enabled instead.

Each of the three components in the capture filter are discussed on the next few pages.

Filtering on SAP/ETYPE During Capture

The first parameter in the capture filter is a Service Access Point (SAP) or Ethernet Type (ETYPE) as specified in the data link headers.[1] Double-click on that line in the filter to edit it. The dialog *Capture Filter SAPs and ETYPEs* will appear (Figure 6.25).

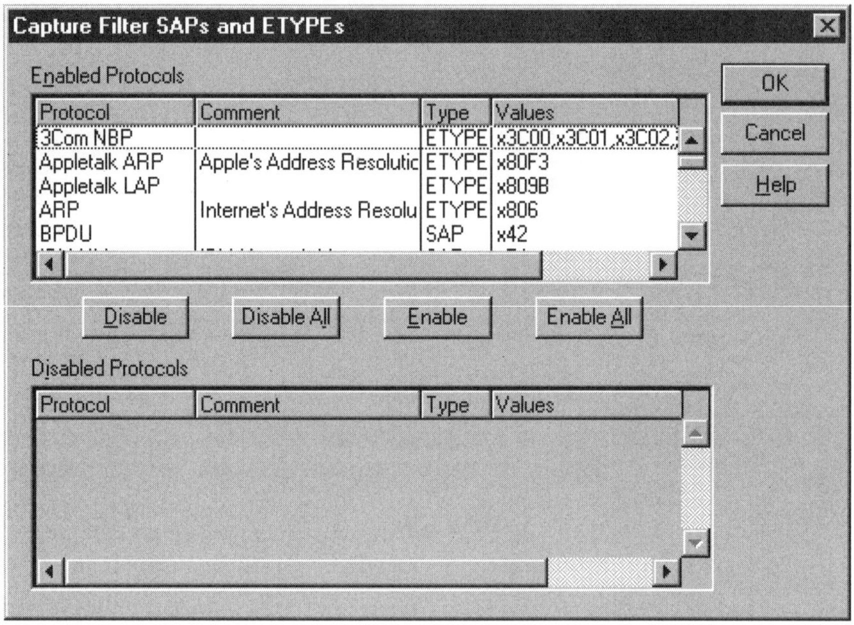

Figure 6.25
A protocol type (SAP or ETYPE) may be specified for a capture filter

For instance, if you select *Disable All,* then double-click ARP, then IP (thus enabling them) and select *OK,* you will have SAP/ETYPE = ARP or IP in the capture filter.

Note that the filtering with SAP/ETYPE discrimination is more simplistic than the display filter protocol filtering. Therefore the filter computation may be performed quicker while capturing.

1. The SAP is specified in the 802.2 LLC header, whereas the ETYPE is specified in either the protocol type field of an Ethernet II header or the protocol field of a SNAP header which has an organizationally unique identifier (OUI) value of 000000. Refer to the TCP/IP Architecture chapter for more detail.

Filtering on Addresses During Capture

Setting up filtering of addresses for capture filters is similar to the setup for display filters. The differences, as shown in Figure 6.26, are that you may include or exclude addresses for capture filters, and you have three direction choices rather than just two.

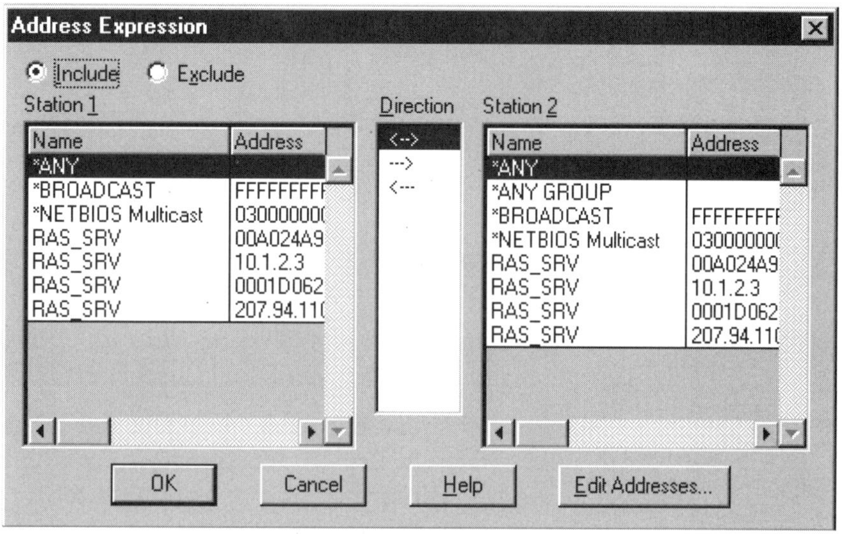

Figure 6.26 Combinations of addresses may be included or excluded from the filter.

Up to four address pairs may be specified in a capture filter. Note that when multiple address patterns are specified, the exclude statements are evaluated with precedence over the include statements. Therefore care must be taken so that general exclude statements don't inadvertently mask the effects of more specific include statements.

Filtering on Pattern Matches During Capture

Capture filters may have a useful feature which isn't precisely present with display filters. Arbitrary patterns may be compared against each packet. With display filters, you had the Protocol and Property options which were a canned form of the same concept.

Arbitrary patterns of octets may be specified in hexadecimal or ASCII notation using the pattern matching dialog as shown in Figure 6.27.

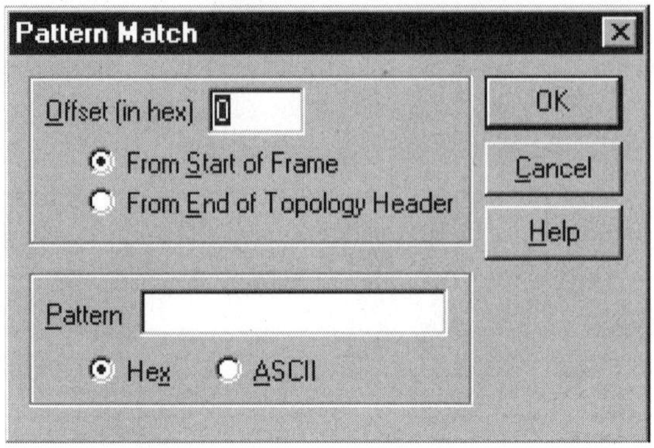

Figure 6.27
A pattern of octets may be specified at any point within a frame using either hex or ASCII notation.

If you wanted to check for a protocol type of 0800 (IP) with Ethernet II framing, you could enter an offset of 0C, and a pattern of 0800.

To check for an IP version 4 header with no options (once you know that you have an IP header) you could check at offset 0E for a pattern of 45.

Note that some frame, packet, datagram, and message sizes may vary so it may be useful to use known fixed offsets whenever possible to avoid ambiguity/misinterpretation of a filter pattern. The specification of an offset from the end of a topology header rather than the start of a frame may be useful for this purpose.

Loading Capture Filters

Once you've changed many of the filter settings, you may want to save the settings for later using the *Save...* button at the bottom of the *Capture Filter* dialog (e.g. Figure 6.24). When you want to reload the settings into another Network Monitor session, you may use the *Load...* button in the *Capture Filter* dialog. Figure 6.28 shows the *Load Capture Filter* dialog.

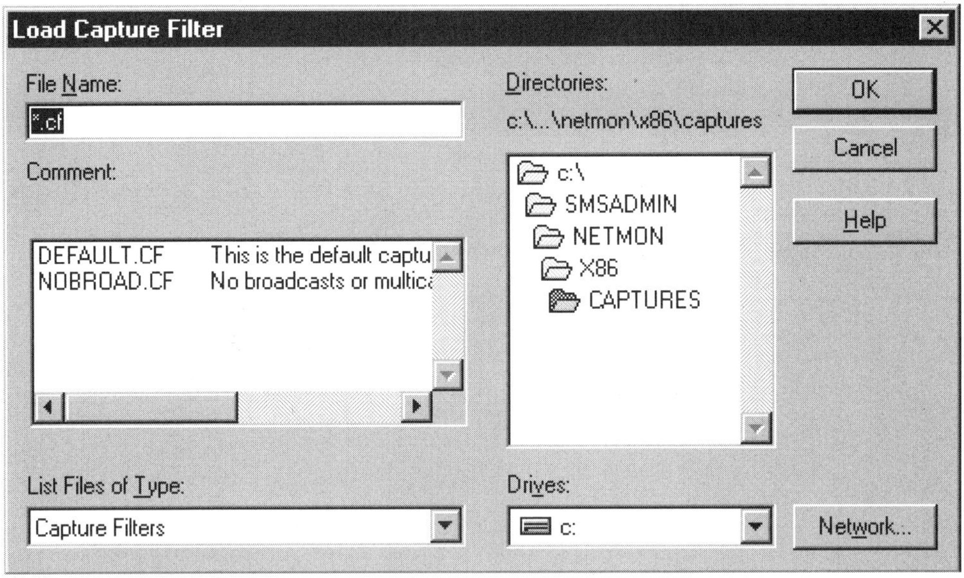

Figure 6.28 The load capture filter dialog may be used to restore a capture filter configuration.

The default suffix for capture filter save files is ".cf". The predefined entries, default.cf and nobroad.cf are shown in Figure 6.28.

Selecting the Network to Monitor

Network Monitor can be used to monitor any of the following:

- any NIC installed in the local machine
- any dial-up connection to the local machine
- any NIC installed in a remote machine

Let's examine each of these choices.

Selecting the NIC to Monitor

From the *Capture* pull down menu, the *Networks* option brings up the dialog in Figure 6.29, *Select Capture Network*.

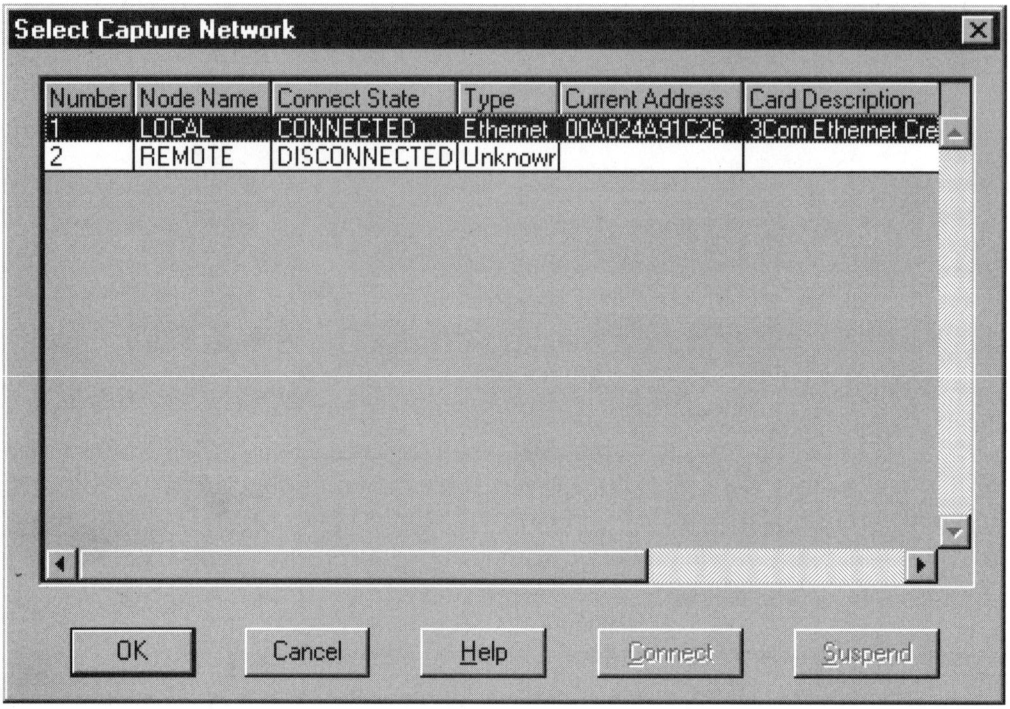

Figure 6.29 Selecting a NIC to monitor.

In this example, there is one NIC installed in this machine, called network #1. It is a locally-attached NIC, with a MAC address of 00a024a91c26. The description column shows that it is a 3Com Ethernet card. The entry for network #2, which is currently disconnected, can be used to connect to a remote network monitor agent, and monitor the packets on a remote network.

Monitoring a Dialup Connection

Suppose you have a machine that is connected to both a LAN, as well as a modem (Figure 6.30). It is possible to monitor both of the interfaces using Network Monitor, although you can't do both at the same time.

Figure 6.30 Network monitor operates on multiple interfaces

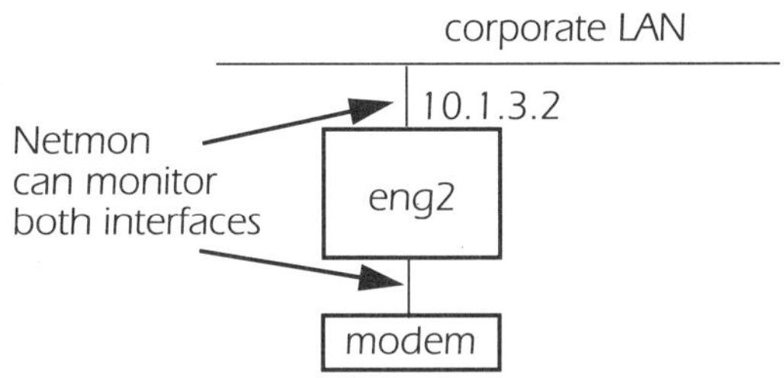

The *Select Capture Network* dialog for machine ENG2 is shown in Figure 6.31. ENG2 has both a modem and Ethernet card installed..

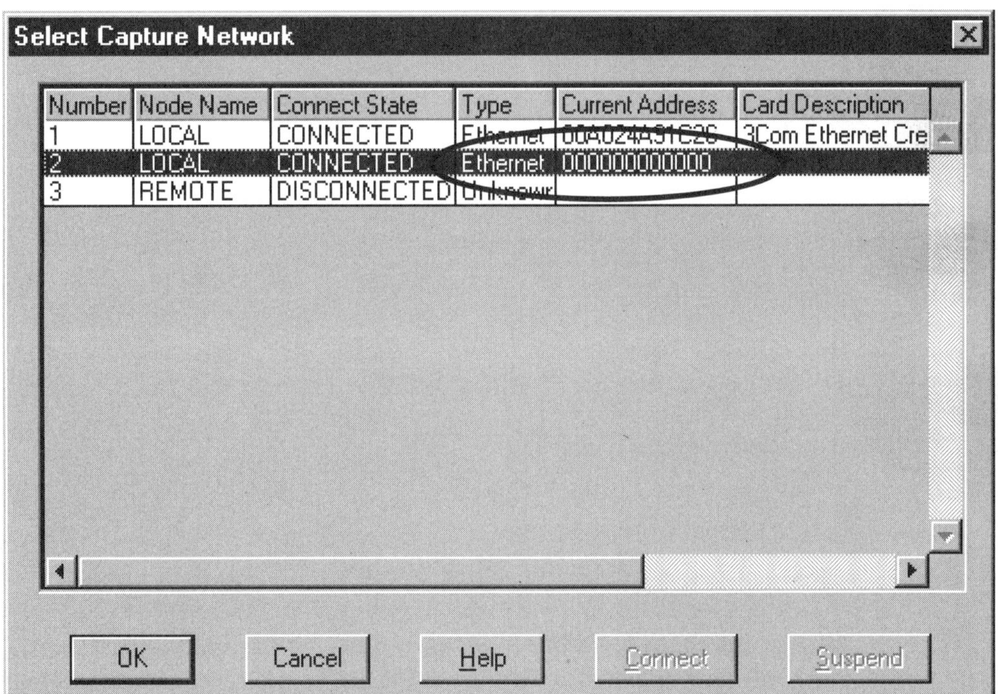

Figure 6.31 Network Monitor can be used to monitor a modem connection by selecting the "Ethernet" interface with address of all zeros.

Notice that there are 3 networks listed: the local Ethernet card as network #1, network #2 labeled as Ethernet with a MAC address of all zeros, and network #3 being a remote network.

Note

Network #2, the one that is labeled as Ethernet, but with no MAC address, is actually the modem interface! If you select this network as the network to be monitored, you will be able to capture all the packets that are sent between your machine, and the machine at the other end of the dial-up connection.

Monitoring a Remote Network

For the following example, the goal is to monitor network 10.1.2.0 from machine ENG2. Therefore we will use the network monitor agent on ENG_RTR to remotely monitor the other network. Figure 6.32 shows what we want to accomplish.

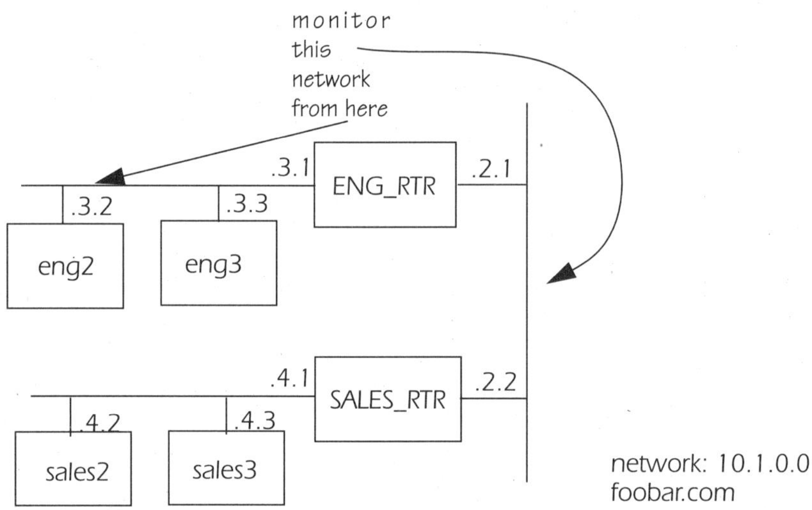

Figure 6.32
A remote network can be monitored using Netmon.

In order to use a remote machine to capture packets, that machine must have the Network Monitor Agent service started. It can be started manually, or automatically from boot, using the *Services Control Panel,* shown in Figure 6.33. You can also start the agent by using the command ***net start nmagent.*** If the Network Monitor Agent service is not started, the remote machine running Network Monitor (as a client) will not be able to connect.

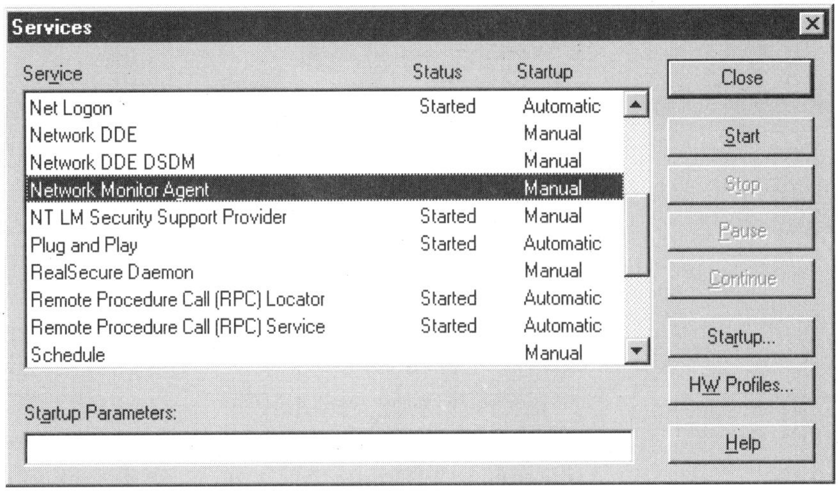

Figure 6.33 Start the Network Monitor Agent Service using the Services Control Panel on the remote machine.

Once the network monitor agent is started on the remote machine (ENG_RTR in the example), it can be used remotely to capture packets from Network Monitor as a client (ENG2 in the example).

To begin the connection to a remote agent (e.g. ENG_RTR), bring up the *Select Capture Network* dialog (Figure 6.34) on the client (e.g. ENG2). Select the REMOTE network, and click on *Connect*. The *Connect to Network Monitoring Agent* dialog appears (Figure 6.35).

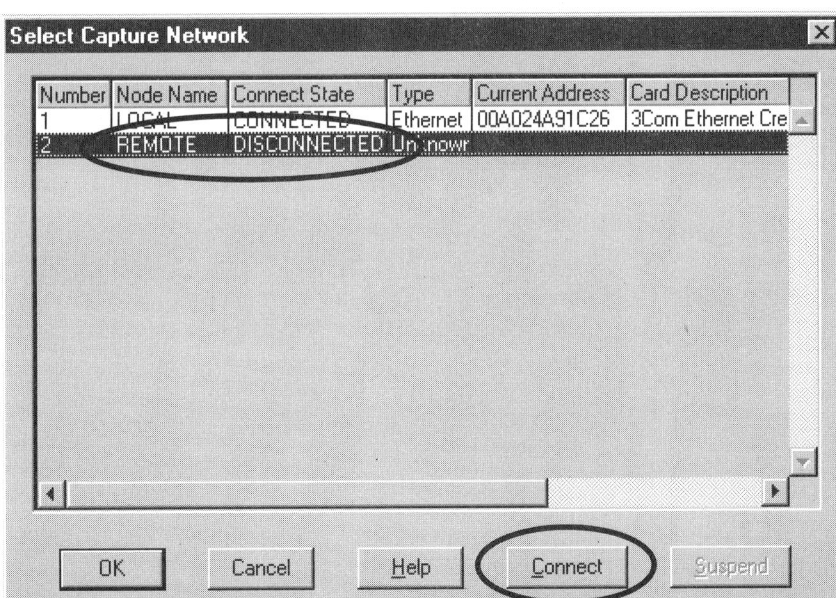

Figure 6.34 Click on Connect to bring up the Connect to Monitoring Agent dialog.

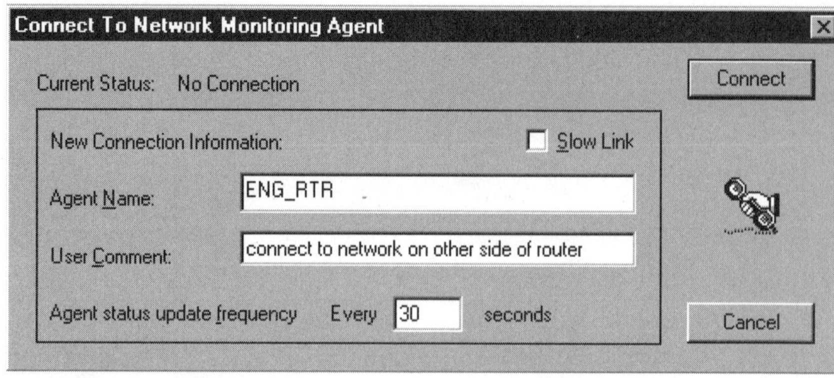

Figure 6.35 Connecting to a remote monitoring agent.

Figure 6.35 shows a snapshot of the *Connect To Network Monitoring Agent* dialog on ENG2 when ENG2 was attempting to connect to ENG_RTR. The name (not IP address) of the remote agent is entered (ENG_RTR). Note that you cannot use an IP address to connect, it must be a name that is resolvable to an IP address (using WINS, LMHOSTS).[2] Set the agent status update frequency to a large number to lessen the performance hit on your local network.

When you click on connect, the name is resolved to an IP address. Next, a connection is established using your local username and password. If your local account does not has administrative privileges on the remote machine, you will NOT be able to connect (Figure 6.36).

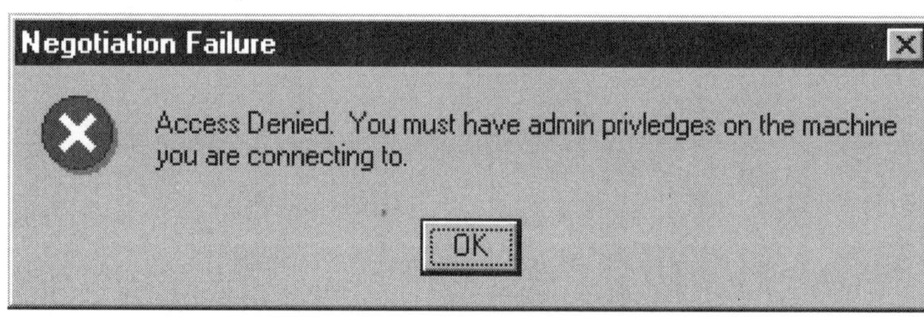

Figure 6.36 Use of a remote monitoring agent requires administrator privileges.

Once it is determined that your account has administrator privileges, the *Select Agent Network Card* dialog appears (Figure 6.37).

2. Refer to the NetBIOS Name Resolution chapter for information on WINS and LMHOSTS.

Figure 6.37 Choosing a NIC to use on the remote machine.

From the list of available network cards on the remote machine, select the network you want to monitor. (Recall from earlier that you need to set the card description on the remote machine to something appropriate.). In this example, network 10.1.2.0 is chosen. Now the user can proceed to run network monitor to capture and filter packets from that remote network.

One caveat: you are greatly increasing the traffic on your local LAN by using this remote monitoring method. If possible, it is recommended that you only monitor locally (i.e. don't use network monitor agents) to prevent network congestion. In other words, only use network monitor agents when absolutely necessary.

TCPIP.INI Configuration File

The file TCPIP.INI is found in the PARSERS directory of the Network Monitor installation. It contains a list of port and protocol numbers that is use by NetMon to decode the packets. Figure 6.38 shows an example of this file.

Note

Note: In order for Netmon to decipher port 1723 packets as PPTP, the last line under [TCP_HandoffSet] needed to be modified from its original value of 5678. This is true as of the current version of Network Monitor (v4.00.350).

Figure 6.38
The TCPIP.INI file contains a list of protocol numbers and their names.

```
[IP_HandoffSet]
  1    = ICMP
  2    = IGMP
  6    = TCP
  17   = UDP
  47   = GRE
  89   = OSPF

; tcp handoff data for NBT
; 1000 is NS
; 1001 is SS
; 1002 is DS

[TCP_HandoffSet]
  20   = FTP
  21   = FTP
  23   = TELNET
  25   = SMTP
  53   = DNS
  79   = FINGER
  80   = HTTP
  102  = ISO
  111  = RPC
  119  = NNTP
  137  = NBT, 1000
  138  = NBT, 1002
  139  = NBT, 1001
  389  = LDAP
  1024 = NBT, 1001
  1047 = NBT, 1001
  1362 = TDS
  1433 = TDS
  1723 = PPTP

[UDP_HandoffSet]
  53   = DNS
  67   = DHCP
  68   = DHCP
  111  = RPC
  161  = SNMP
  162  = SNMP
  137  = NBT, 1000
  138  = NBT, 1002
  139  = NBT, 1001
  520  = RIP
  2049 = RPC

[UDP_TO_DNS]
;  If a UDP to NBT frame has a source of DNS and a destination of NBT
;  The formatting should be DNS, not NBT, ie, no double byte encoding.
BASE_HANDOFF_ON_SRC_PORT=1

[RPC_HandoffSet]
  2049   = NFS
```

Why Monitor?

Imagine that you are asked to diagnose the efficiency of a jet engine without being allowed to look at fuel consumption or the amount of heat generated by the engine. Or perhaps you've got a grain bin in your barn, and you notice grain scattered outside of the bin every morning. Is it rabbits? Rats? Where are they coming from?

In management of communication networks, you may need to measure efficiency, troubleshoot packet loss or high end-to-end delay. You need tools and measurement techniques for network management. Network monitoring can act as a periscope into a sea of network traffic, or as microscope into the complex culture of connections between your machines.

Network Monitor performs two kinds of monitoring.

- Statistics of overall traffic on a network may be used to determine network utilization, overall packet counts, per station counts, and session counts.
- Packets may be captured for detailed analysis.

For performance management or accounting, the statistics are often a good measurement tool. Packet capture is usually useful for diagnosing specific faults or tuning of performance of your networks. Proper filtering of captured information is essential to practical monitoring.

With routers, servers, and other network equipment which speak many protocols, how do you know if new hardware or software from one vendor, or new traffic from a user has affected your network? Do all of the pieces of equipment speak the protocols in the same way? Which ones comply with standards? You can use a protocol analyzer to answer these questions.

Traffic monitoring is useful because it provides a perspective into the operation of your network.

Using Network Monitor Throughout This Book

As an educational tool, use of network monitoring tools provides a tangible view into what's really happening under the hood.

Throughout the remainder of this book, several protocols and services based on those protocols are discussed. Packet captures are used to clearly explain what does, can, or should happen with these protocols. Several packet captures are included not only in descriptions in the text, but also on the accompanying CD with this book. These captures may be examined in detail for understanding of the examples beyond what we've described in the following pages.

Summary

Here's a summary of the items which have been addressed in this chapter.

- Protocol analyzers are tools which may be used to monitor traffic in networks. Two of the most common features of protocol analyzers are statistical analysis, packet capture, and packet decode.
- Various features of Network Monitor were discussed, including basic packet capture and decode, viewing and modifying the address database, and filtering packets.
- An example of Network Monitor packet captures was shown to display ICMP messages.
- Network Monitor can also captures packets across a serial (e.g. modem) interface. It can also capture packets on a remote LAN.

Further Reading

Here is information about various books and magazines in which to look for further information on the subject.

[Comer1995] Comer, Douglas E., *Internetworking with TCP/IP Vol I: Principles, Protocols, and Architecture, Third Edition,* 1995, Prentice-Hall, Inc.

[Miller1993] Miller, Mark A., *Troubleshooting TCP/IP: Analyzing the Protocols of the Internet,* 1993, M&T Books

[Stevens1994] Stevens, W. Richard, *TCP/IP Illustrated, Volume 1: The Protocols,* 1994, Addison-Wesley

7

NT Server as an IP Router

We briefly introduced IP routing in the chapter on IP Subnetting, but delayed the details of how routing is performed in Windows NT. This chapter continues with further details of IP routing and addresses the steps needed for Windows NT to be a part of your enterprise routing solution.

Windows NT Server has some routing capabilities, and Microsoft's Routing and Remote Access Service (RRAS, a.k.a. Steelhead) extends the capabilities so that NT is capable of performing the functions of a low-end router. This means that Windows NT may be used in lieu of an entry-level router for small workgroups and small offices.

Why Do We Route?

Routing is performed so that we can optimize the path taken by information travelling from one point to another in a network. In fact, the need is even more fundamental — routing is necessary to interconnect networks.

router: a device that forwards packets from one network to another

Bridging and switching allow interconnection of data links to form a network. The glue that ties together several networks (into an internetwork) is a routing function. Datagrams are taken from one network to another by this routing function. A network device which primarily performs this routing function is called a **router**.

Bridges and switches restrict collision domains to individual data links. Routers do this as well, yet also restrict the broadcast domain.

Communication Between Hosts on Different Networks

With no subnetting (for class B, a mask of 255.255.0.0), two hosts attached to the same network segment can communicate directly only if they have matching network identifiers. In Figure 7.1, X and Y can communicate directly. However neither X nor Y can communicate with Z because they have different network identifiers than Z.

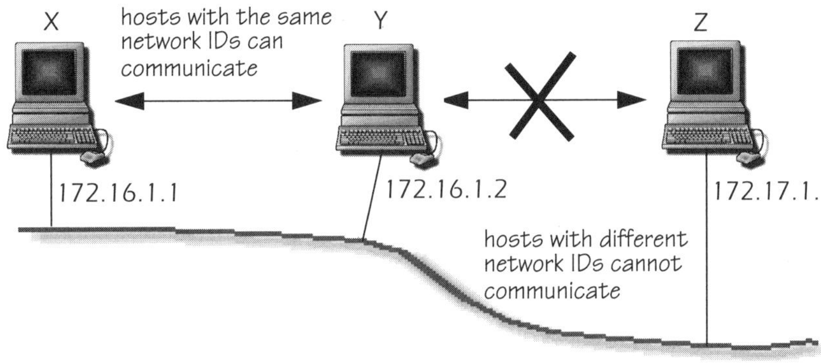

Figure 7.1 IP allows hosts on the same logical network/subnet to communicate directly.

The network address of X and Y is 172.16.0.0, and Z's network address is 172.17.0.0. The logical addresses assigned to each network interface for use with IP force a grouping and division of devices into networks. Even though X, Y, and Z are on the same cable, they need a router to communicate.

Communication Between Hosts on Different Subnets

The same logical division of IP networks applies to subnets as well. With a subnet mask of 255.255.255.0, node W in Figure 7.2 is in a different subnet than X and Y. Therefore X and Y can communicate with one another (same network ID and subnet) but neither X nor Y can talk to W.

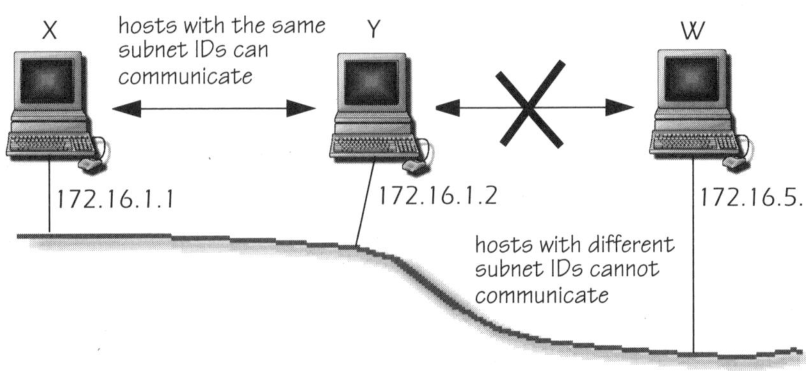

Figure 7.2 Hosts on the same subnet may communicate directly.

Again, even though X, Y, and W are on the same cable, they need a router to communicate. The router could be any other machine on the same cable which has an interface on each subnet.

Figure 7.3 shows a router added into the scenario and now X and Y may communicate with W via the router. Having multiple subnets on the same physical wire, however, is not recommended.

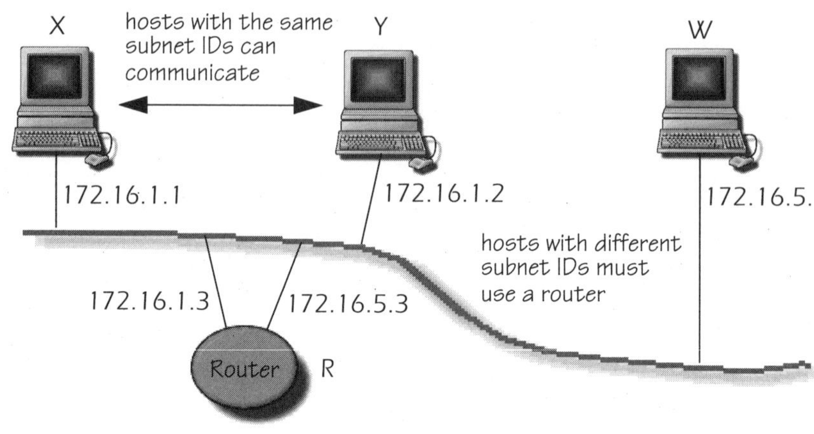

Figure 7.3 Hosts on different subnets must use a router to communicate.

Simple IP Routing Example

Let's examine the steps it would take to send a packet from machine X to machine W in Figure 7.3. The steps are as follows:

1. X realizes that W is on a different subnet by applying[1] the subnet mask 255.255.255.0 to its own address and to W's and comparing the results — 172.16.1.0 is not equal to 172.16.5.0.
2. X decides that it must send this datagram via the router R. The router's near interface, 172.16.1.3 is on the same subnet as X's 172.16.1.1 interface.
3. X figures out how to send the datagram to the router. X's 172.16.1.1 interface is on an Ethernet, thus X resolves the router's 172.16.1.3 address into a MAC address via ARP.

1. A bitwise logical AND operation is used to apply a subnet mask to an IP address. Each bit position in the result of this operation is a one if and only if that bit position holds a one in both the mask and the address to be masked.

4. X sends the datagram to the router using an Ethernet unicast transmission.
5. The router R looks at the datagram and realizes that it doesn't have a network interface with the address 172.16.5.1. Hence, this datagram must be either dropped or forwarded. Luckily for X and W, IP forwarding is enabled on R.
6. R determines which interface it should forward the datagram through, and selects the 172.16.5.3 interface.
7. R uses ARP to resolve 172.16.5.1 into a MAC address.
8. R sends (i.e. forwards) the datagram using an Ethernet unicast transmission.
9. W receives the datagram and notices that the target address is its own, so passes the datagram to the appropriate upper layer protocol as specified by X.

To summarize, the following mechanisms are used to route an IP datagram:

- transmission of IP over a data link (e.g. Ethernet);
- address resolution (e.g. ARP);
- forwarding a datagram on toward its destination;
- determination of the next hop along a route toward a datagram's destination (e.g. by X and R);
- selecting the interface to the next (or final) hop.

Broadcast Datagrams

One advantage of routers is that they block data link layer broadcasts, therefore broadcast traffic will be localized to one segment. As seen in Figure 7.4, an Ethernet broadcast from coyote will be stopped at the router.

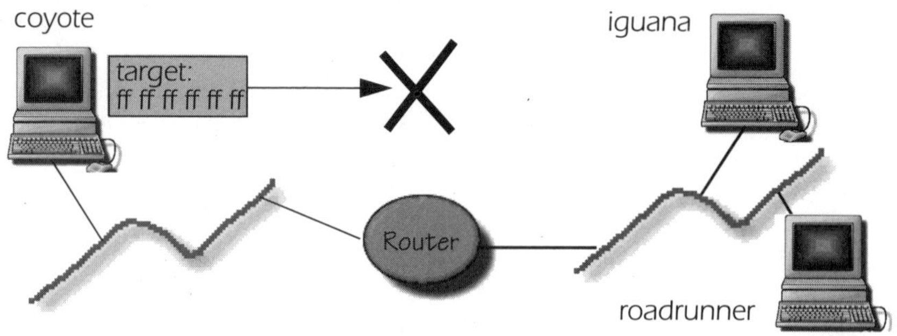

Figure 7.4
Routers may block link-layer broadcasts.

A router may be configured to either forward or drop IP broadcast datagrams. In some cases, such as with DHCP packets, you would want the router to forward the broadcasts. DHCP packets are sent as a broadcast, and if you only have one DHCP server, but multiple subnets, you must configure the router to pass the DHCP broadcast packets. Refer to Chapter 15, DHCP, for more details on this scenario.

Routing Process

routing table: list of reachable networks and the interfaces to use to reach those networks.

The router in Figure 7.5 has interfaces to three networks. That router's **routing table** contains a list of networks that can be reached and the interface through which the router should send datagrams to each network.

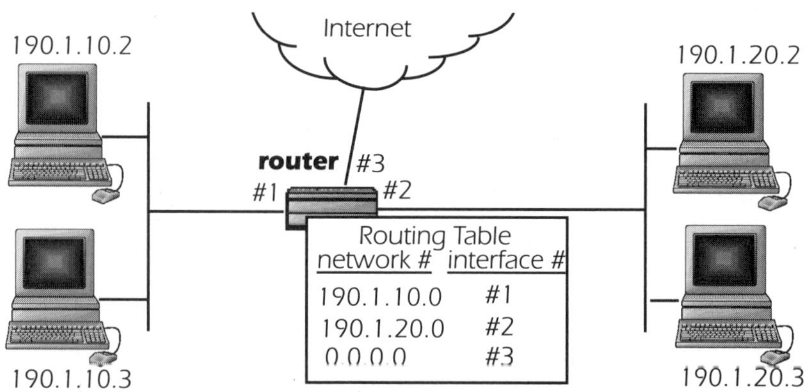

Figure 7.5
The routing table enables the IP software on the router to forward datagrams to the right interface/network

The following is the IP routing process:

- When a host wants to transmit an IP datagram to another network, the default router configured for that host is used as the destination to send the datagram.
- The routing table on the router is consulted for a path to that network, and the datagram is sent out the appropriate interface.
- If the destination network is not listed in the routing table, the router will forward the datagram to its default router address, if one is configured. In the above table, the default router is specified by 0.0.0.0. If no default router is configured, then the router sends an error message back to the source of the datagram.

multihomed: a machine with more than one IP address binding.

The term **multihomed** is used to describe a machine with two or more IP addresses. Actually, to be more precise, a machine with two or more NICs is called **physically multihomed** since it is physically attached to two separate networks. If there is more than one IP address assigned to a single NIC, it is called **logically multihomed**. Both terms are generalized as multihomed.

Updating Routing Tables using Routing Protocols

How are these routing tables updated? There are two possibilities:

static routing: routing tables are updated manually.

- Someone manually configures the table when the router is installed and makes changes later when needed. This is called **static routing**: the routing tables have to be updated manually. Simplistic routers are only capable of static routing. You may also want to use static routing for security reasons.[2]

routing protocol: a protocol used between routing devices to exchange routing information.

- The router itself exchanges information with other routers using a **routing protocol**. Updating tables using a routing protocol is called **dynamic routing**. Dynamic routing requires much less configuration by a network administrator and is

2. If you use RIP in as your routing protocol, it is possible for a hacker to perform a denial of service attack by attaching a purposely misconfigured RIP router to your network. Refer to page 316 for a further discussion.

therefore a better choice for large internetworks. Routing changes are propagated to other routers and networks via routing protocols.

dynamic routing: routing tables are updated with routing protocols.

Some routing protocols are effective within an organization, thus they are called **interior routing protocols**. Example interior routing protocols are:

interior routing protocol: routing protocol used internal to an organization.

- Routing Information Protocol (RIP) version 1 — A simple routing protocol which only measures the number of hops to a specific network. This is an example of a distance vector protocol.
- Open Shortest Path First (OSPF) — A complicated routing protocol which takes into consideration many other factors, such as network topology and link state.
- Interior Gateway Routing Protocol (IGRP) — IGRP and Enhanced IGRP (EIGRP) are protocols developed by Cisco Systems that improve upon RIP, but do not include all of the features (yet) of OSPF. IGRP is a distance vector (i.e. hop count) protocol like RIP. EIGRP handles type of service information.
- RIPv2 — An enhancement of RIP which also provides some but not all of the features of OSPF. Like the older RIP, RIPv2 is a distance vector protocol. RIPv2 can be more efficient because it uses a multicast address for advertisements. It also passes subnet mask and route tag information to support variable width subnetting.

exterior routing protocol: routing protocol used external to an organization, i.e. on the Internet backbone.

Other routing protocols provide routing information on how to get from one organization to the next, and are therefore called **exterior routing protocols**. Examples of exterior routing protocols are:

- Exterior Gateway Protocol (EGP) — This is a basic routing protocol for use across the exterior interface of an organization. Routers at the edge of an organization are often called gateways.
- Border Gateway Protocol (BGP) — The use of BGP has surpassed EGP as the exterior routing protocol of choice. BGP is commonly used on the Internet backbone.

Enabling IP Routing

NT can be configured to forward IP datagrams between multiple interfaces. This is configured using the "Enable IP Routing" check box on the *Routing tab* in the *TCP/IP Properties screen* from the *Network Control Panel*. (See Figure 7.6.)

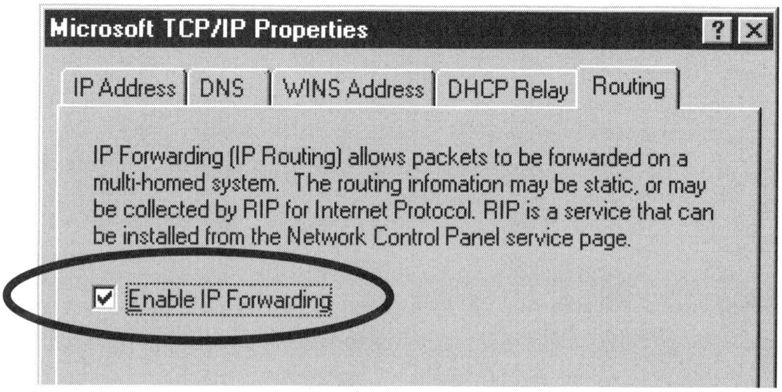

Figure 7.6 Windows NT will forward IP datagrams if this box is checked.

After IP forwarding is enabled, you will need to determine how its routing tables will be updated. If you choose the static method, you must configure the routing table at this time. If you choose the dynamic method, you must install a routing protocol— namely, RIP version 1. Both of these methods are discussed on the next few pages.

Static IP Routing

The multihomed NT server in Figure 7.7 has interfaces to two networks. The routing table contains a list of networks that can be reached and the interface through which the router should send datagrams to each network.

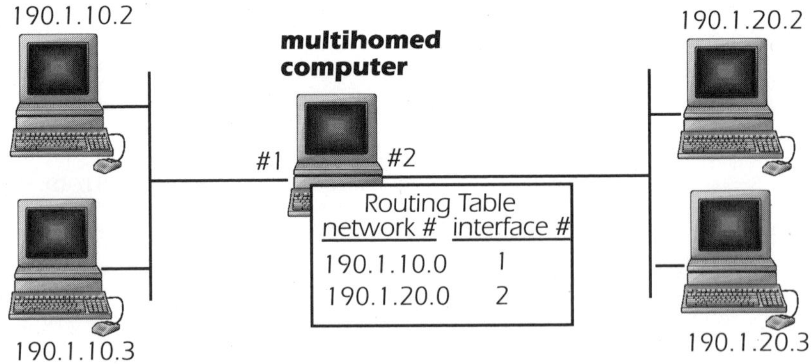

Figure 7.7 A multihomed computer may serve as a router if IP forwarding is enabled.

This and other static routers can only communicate to the networks they were informed about using manual manipulation of the routing table. In order to perform multi-hop routing, each static router must be configured with entries for all networks on the internetwork. Therefore, using static routes exclusively limits your internetworking to a fairly small scale. Static routes could be used in special cases on corporate or Internet routers that are running a routing protocol.

The command to use to manually configure the routing table on an NT router is the ***route*** command.

Manipulating the Routing Table Using the Route Command

The ***route*** command is used to view and modify the routing table. There are various options, as shown in Table 7.1.

Table 7.1 Windows NT route command options.

Option	Description
add <destination> [MASK <netmask>] [<gateway>] [METRIC <metric>]	Adds a route.
-p add <destination> [MASK <netmask>] [<gateway>] [METRIC <metric>]	Adds a persistent route.
delete <network> <gateway>	Deletes a route.
change <network> <gateway>	Modifies a route.
print	Displays the routing table.
-p print	Shows the persistent routes.
-f	Removes all gateway entries.

persistent route: a route that is not removed upon reboot of NT.

A route that remains in the NT routing table after reboot is called a **persistent route.** Note that routes added using the ***route*** command are removed upon reboot, except when using the -p (persistent) option.

If configuring a network mask, the word "mask" must appear on the command line preceding the subnet mask. The same is true of the word "metric"- "metric" must precede the metric value. (Refer to "Interpreting the Routing Table" on page 256 for a discussion of metric.) The words "mask" and "metric" are not case-sensitive.

It is possible to use network names instead of network numbers as one of the arguments. A list of network names and their associated addresses is found in the file:

```
%systemroot%\system32\drivers\etc\networks
```

Example Network with Static Routes

Figure 7.8 represents the current network configuration of foobar.com. It contains three subnets: the backbone, engineering subnet, and sales subnet.

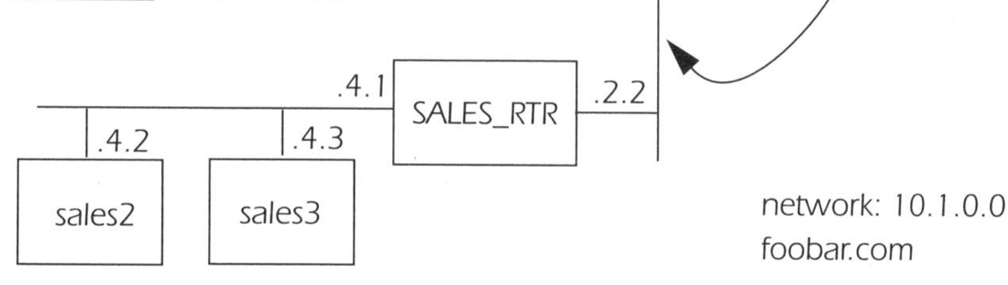

Figure 7.8
Static routes may be used to tell the routers how to get traffic between the departmental subnets.

In order for routers ENG_RTR and SALES_RTR to route properly between the subnets, IP routing had to be enabled on those two machines. The following commands were issued to enable this:

<u>on ENG_RTR:</u>

route -p add 10.1.4.0 mask 255.255.255.0 10.1.2.2 metric 2

<u>on SALES_RTR:</u>

route -p add 10.1.3.0 mask 255.255.255.0 10.1.2.1 metric 2

The issued commands are shown in the screen captures in Figure 7.14 on page 260 and Figure 7.15 on page 260.

Interpreting the Routing Table

metric: a value used in determining the route to use when forwarding packets.

Even a single homed TCP/IP host has to make routing decisions. These routing decisions are controlled by the routing table. The routing table commonly contains a list of the networks that can be reached, how they can be reached, and a metric of how many hops it takes to get to that network. In general, a routing **metric** is some value used to prefer one route over another when the network addresses are equal.

hop count: number of intermediate nodes a datagram must pass through to reach its destination network.

The specific use of **hop count** as the metric is used by simple routing protocols such as RIP.

Figure 7.9 shows the routing table for an NT machine with a single NIC.

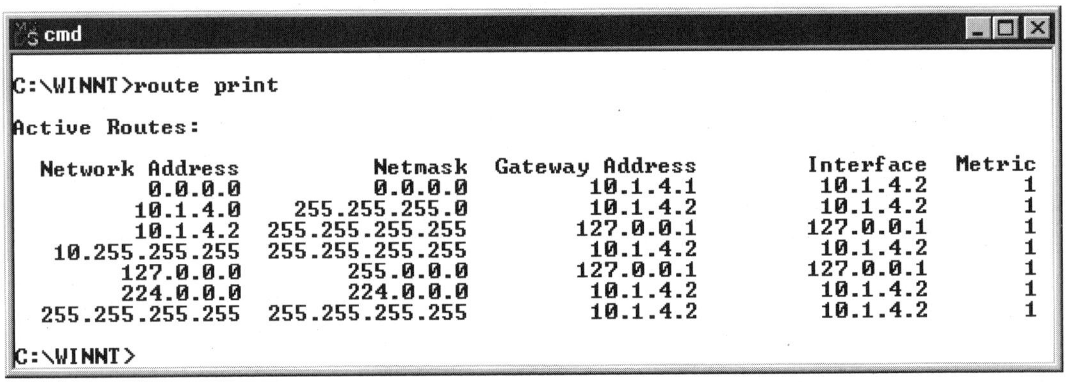

```
cmd

C:\WINNT>route print

Active Routes:

  Network Address          Netmask  Gateway Address        Interface  Metric
          0.0.0.0          0.0.0.0         10.1.4.1         10.1.4.2       1
         10.1.4.0    255.255.255.0         10.1.4.2         10.1.4.2       1
         10.1.4.2  255.255.255.255        127.0.0.1        127.0.0.1       1
  10.255.255.255   255.255.255.255         10.1.4.2         10.1.4.2       1
        127.0.0.0        255.0.0.0        127.0.0.1        127.0.0.1       1
        224.0.0.0        224.0.0.0         10.1.4.2         10.1.4.2       1
  255.255.255.255  255.255.255.255         10.1.4.2         10.1.4.2       1

C:\WINNT>
```

Figure 7.9 Displaying routing table on SALES2

The network address column in Figure 7.9 can be interpreted as shown in Table 7.2.

Table 7.2 Analysis of the routing table from Figure 7.9 for the SALES2 machine.

Address	Description
0.0.0.0	The default gateway for the interface specified. In the example, for interface 10.1.4.2, the datagram should be sent to 10.1.4.1.
127.0.0.0	Local loopback. Datagrams are sent to the loopback interface.
10.1.4.0	Subnet address. Communications with any other interface on this network goes out interface 10.1.4.2 which is in subnet 10.1.4.0.
10.1.4.2	Local IP address. Datagrams sent to this address will be sent to address 127.0.0.1 (the loopback address) rather than actually going to the Ethernet driver.
10.255.255.255	Network broadcast address. Datagrams to be sent to everyone on network 10.0.0.0 will be sent to this address
224.0.0.0	IP multicast address.
255.255.255.255	general IP broadcast address.

The interface column in Figure 7.9 shows that there are two network interfaces on the SALES2 machine: 10.1.4.2 and 127.0.0.1. The address 10.1.4.2 is bound to the Ethernet interface, and the address 127.0.0.1 is bound to the loopback interface as shown in Figure 7.10.

Figure 7.10 The machine SALES2 has IP addresses bound to two network interfaces, an Ethernet interface and a loopback interface.

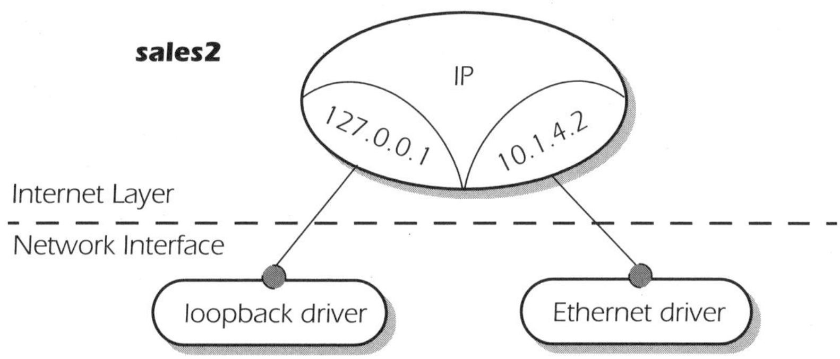

Each row in the routing table uses one of these two interfaces. Note that the routing table specifies that traffic to either 127.0.0.1 or 10.1.4.2 is sent out the 127.0.0.1 interface, and is thus looped back to IP. All other traffic is sent out interface 10.1.4.2.

One entry in the table is worth noting again- the entry for the default gateway, identified by network address 0.0.0.0. Recall that the default gateway is the packet destination when IP doesn't know where else to send the packet. The interface used to send these packets is still 10.1.4.2. However, the packet destination is of the router, 10.1.4.1. This router will hopefully know where to send the packets that SALES2 "doesn't know" where to send.

Routing Tables for Multihomed Machines

Now that we've seen a routing table for a single homed machine, let's look at some routing tables for the routers in this network. Before any static routes are added to these machines, the routing tables are essentially as though these machines were simply multihomed machines.

Figure 7.11 shows the routing tables for the routers before the ***route add*** command is issued.

```
cmd

C:\WINNT>route print

Active Routes:

  Network Address          Netmask  Gateway Address       Interface  Metric
         10.1.2.0    255.255.255.0         10.1.2.1        10.1.2.1       1
         10.1.2.1  255.255.255.255        127.0.0.1       127.0.0.1       1
         10.1.3.0    255.255.255.0         10.1.3.1        10.1.3.1       1
         10.1.3.1  255.255.255.255        127.0.0.1       127.0.0.1       1
   10.255.255.255  255.255.255.255         10.1.2.1        10.1.2.1       1
        127.0.0.0        255.0.0.0        127.0.0.1       127.0.0.1       1
        224.0.0.0        224.0.0.0         10.1.2.1        10.1.2.1       1
  255.255.255.255  255.255.255.255         10.1.2.1        10.1.2.1       1

C:\WINNT>
```

Figure 7.11 Routing table on ENG_RTR before any static routes are added.

The interface column in the routing table shows that three network interfaces are being used on ENG_RTR, as depicted in Figure 7.12. Note that communication to destinations (see network address column) 10.1.2.1, 10.1.3.1, and 127.0.0.0 all are routed to use the loopback (127.0.0.1) interface. The corresponding network masks are used to determine how precise of a match of the network address with the target IP address is required.

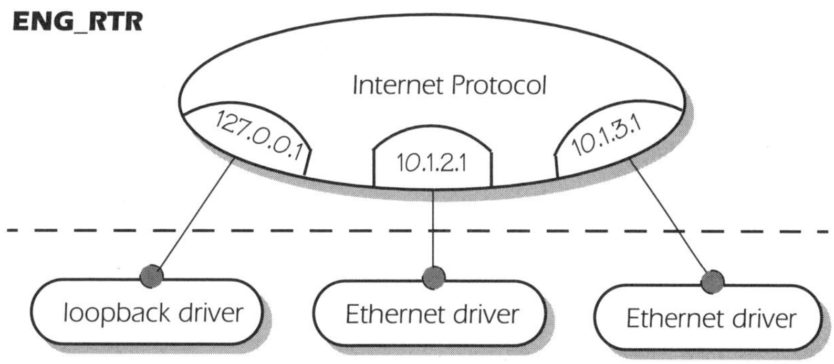

Figure 7.12 ENG_RTR has IP addresses bound to three network interfaces, two Ethernet interfaces and a loopback interface.

Similarly, Figure 7.13 shows the routing table for SALES_RTR which has interfaces 10.1.2.2 and 10.1.4.1.

```
command prompt

C:\WINNT>route print

Active Routes:

  Network Address          Netmask  Gateway Address        Interface  Metric
         10.1.2.0    255.255.255.0         10.1.2.2         10.1.2.2       1
         10.1.2.2  255.255.255.255        127.0.0.1        127.0.0.1       1
         10.1.4.0    255.255.255.0         10.1.4.1         10.1.4.1       1
         10.1.4.1  255.255.255.255        127.0.0.1        127.0.0.1       1
   10.255.255.255  255.255.255.255         10.1.2.2         10.1.2.2       1
        127.0.0.0        255.0.0.0        127.0.0.1        127.0.0.1       1
        224.0.0.0        224.0.0.0         10.1.2.2         10.1.2.2       1
  255.255.255.255  255.255.255.255         10.1.2.2         10.1.2.2       1

C:\WINNT>_
```

Figure 7.13 Routing table on SALES_RTR before any static routes are added.

The routing table entries which we have shown for ENG_RTR and SALES_RTR are established when the IP addresses are bound to the network interfaces. The bindings and the routing entries are distinct mappings in IP, yet they work together so that IP may do its job.

Routing Tables with Static Routes Added

In order for the routers to know how to route to networks which are not directly connected, the routers must be told about other routes — one method of instructing the routers is by setting up static routes.

Figure 7.14 illustrates the use of the ***route -p*** command to add a persistent route so that ENG_RTR knows how to route datagrams to the sales subnet 10.1.4.0. We've specified a metric of two to indicate that the sales subnet is two hops away. Datagrams are sent to the SALES_RTR via the backbone subnet and then forwarded on to the destination on the sales subnet.

```
cmd

C:\WINNT>route -p add 10.1.4.0 mask 255.255.255.0 10.1.2.2 metric 2

C:\WINNT>route print

Active Routes:

  Network Address          Netmask  Gateway Address        Interface  Metric
         10.1.2.0    255.255.255.0         10.1.2.1         10.1.2.1       1
         10.1.2.1  255.255.255.255        127.0.0.1        127.0.0.1       1
         10.1.3.0    255.255.255.0         10.1.3.1         10.1.3.1       1
         10.1.3.1  255.255.255.255        127.0.0.1        127.0.0.1       1
         10.1.4.0    255.255.255.0         10.1.2.2         10.1.2.1       2
   10.255.255.255  255.255.255.255         10.1.2.1         10.1.2.1       1
        127.0.0.0        255.0.0.0        127.0.0.1        127.0.0.1       1
        224.0.0.0        224.0.0.0         10.1.2.1         10.1.2.1       1
  255.255.255.255  255.255.255.255         10.1.2.1         10.1.2.1       1

C:\WINNT>
```

Figure 7.14 ENG_RTR now has a static route to get to the sales subnet.

A corresponding static route is added to SALES_RTR so that it may forward datagrams to ENG_RTR for delivery to the engineering subnet. The command and resulting routing table of ENG_RTR is shown in Figure 7.15.

```
command prompt

C:\WINNT>route -p add 10.1.3.0 mask 255.255.255.0 10.1.2.1 metric 2

C:\WINNT>route print

Active Routes:

  Network Address          Netmask  Gateway Address        Interface  Metric
         10.1.2.0    255.255.255.0         10.1.2.2         10.1.2.2       1
         10.1.2.2  255.255.255.255        127.0.0.1        127.0.0.1       1
         10.1.3.0    255.255.255.0         10.1.2.1         10.1.2.2       2
         10.1.4.0    255.255.255.0         10.1.4.1         10.1.4.1       1
         10.1.4.1  255.255.255.255        127.0.0.1        127.0.0.1       1
   10.255.255.255  255.255.255.255         10.1.2.2         10.1.2.2       1
        127.0.0.0        255.0.0.0        127.0.0.1        127.0.0.1       1
        224.0.0.0        224.0.0.0         10.1.2.2         10.1.2.2       1
  255.255.255.255  255.255.255.255         10.1.2.2         10.1.2.2       1

C:\WINNT>_
```

Figure 7.15 SALES_RTR now has a static route to get to the engineering subnet.

At this point, both routers are correctly configured to route between the two subnets. This can be tested using the ***ping*** command, to ping from machines on one subnet to machines on the other subnet.

Note that routes are for one direction only. For bidirectional communication between two machines, there must be a route in each direction.

Persistent Routes

The static routes added in Figure 7.14 (for ENG_RTR) and Figure 7.15 (for SALES_RTR) were added using the -p option to the ***route*** command. This makes these routes persistent. Recall a persistent route is one which will not be forgotten when the machine is rebooted.

There was no indication in the ***route print*** command output that these routes were persistent. As with the ***route add*** command, the -p option may be used with the ***route print*** command to specify persistent routes.

Note that in the examples (Figure 7.16 shows ENG_RTR and Figure 7.17 shows SALES_RTR) the normal output of active routes is shown and then the persistent routes are shown.

```
cmd

C:\WINNT>route -p print

Active Routes:

  Network Address          Netmask  Gateway Address        Interface  Metric
         10.1.2.0    255.255.255.0         10.1.2.1         10.1.2.1       1
         10.1.2.1  255.255.255.255        127.0.0.1        127.0.0.1       1
         10.1.3.0    255.255.255.0         10.1.3.1         10.1.3.1       1
         10.1.3.1  255.255.255.255        127.0.0.1        127.0.0.1       1
         10.1.4.0    255.255.255.0         10.1.2.2         10.1.2.1       2
   10.255.255.255  255.255.255.255         10.1.2.1         10.1.2.1       1
        127.0.0.0        255.0.0.0        127.0.0.1        127.0.0.1       1
        224.0.0.0        224.0.0.0         10.1.2.1         10.1.2.1       1
  255.255.255.255  255.255.255.255         10.1.2.1         10.1.2.1       1

Persistent Routes:

  Network Address          Netmask  Gateway Address  Metric
         10.1.4.0    255.255.255.0         10.1.2.2       2

C:\WINNT>
```

Figure 7.16 Persistent routing information shown for ENG_RTR.

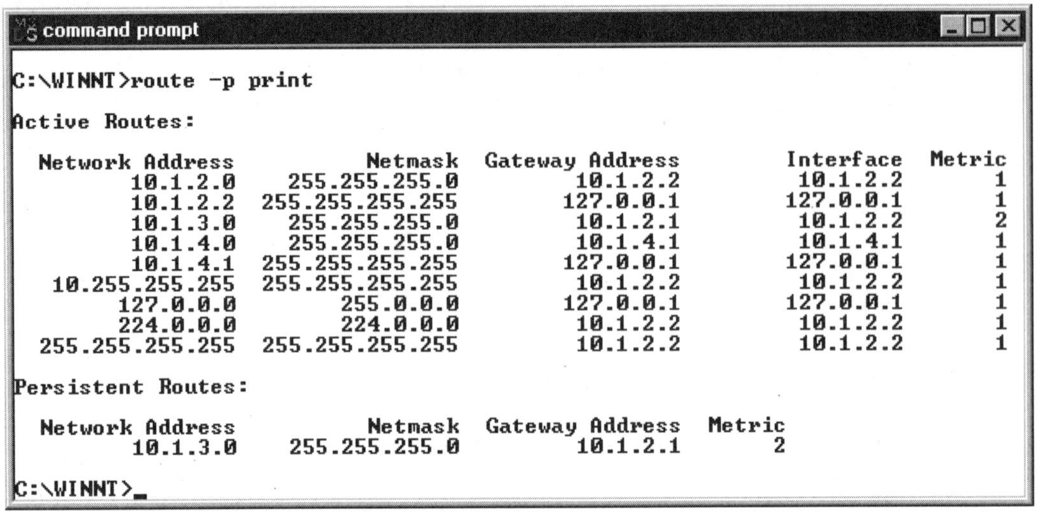

```
command prompt

C:\WINNT>route -p print

Active Routes:

  Network Address          Netmask  Gateway Address        Interface  Metric
         10.1.2.0    255.255.255.0         10.1.2.2         10.1.2.2       1
         10.1.2.2  255.255.255.255        127.0.0.1        127.0.0.1       1
         10.1.3.0    255.255.255.0         10.1.2.1         10.1.2.2       2
         10.1.4.0    255.255.255.0         10.1.4.1         10.1.4.1       1
         10.1.4.1  255.255.255.255        127.0.0.1        127.0.0.1       1
   10.255.255.255  255.255.255.255         10.1.2.2         10.1.2.2       1
        127.0.0.0        255.0.0.0        127.0.0.1        127.0.0.1       1
        224.0.0.0        224.0.0.0         10.1.2.2         10.1.2.2       1
  255.255.255.255  255.255.255.255         10.1.2.2         10.1.2.2       1

Persistent Routes:

  Network Address          Netmask  Gateway Address  Metric
         10.1.3.0    255.255.255.0         10.1.2.1       2

C:\WINNT>_
```

Figure 7.17 Persistent routing information shown for SALES_RTR.

Review of IP Communication

Now that the details of routing tables have been addressed, let's review the flow of IP communications with an example of how this information is used. The current network diagram is shown in Figure 7.18.

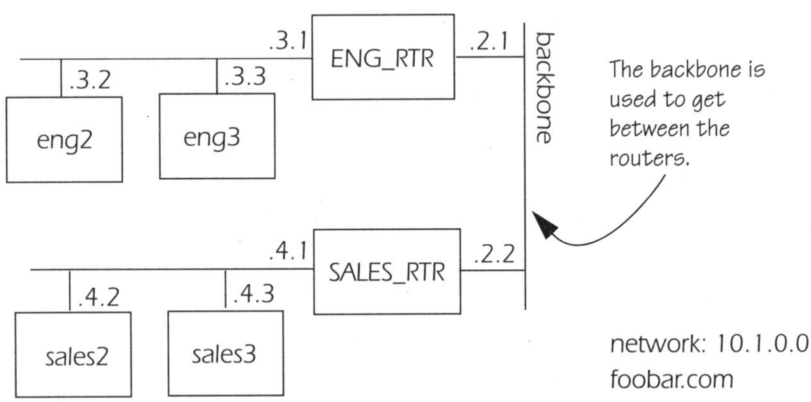

Figure 7.18 Current network diagram.

Assume that SALES2 wants to send a datagram to ENG3. The source IP address in the datagram will be 10.1.4.2 and the target IP address will be 10.1.3.3. The routing table for SALES2 is shown in Figure 7.19.

```
cmd

C:\WINNT>route print

Active Routes:

  Network Address          Netmask  Gateway Address        Interface  Metric
          0.0.0.0          0.0.0.0         10.1.4.1         10.1.4.2       1
         10.1.4.0    255.255.255.0         10.1.4.2         10.1.4.2       1
         10.1.4.2  255.255.255.255        127.0.0.1        127.0.0.1       1
   10.255.255.255  255.255.255.255         10.1.4.2         10.1.4.2       1
        127.0.0.0        255.0.0.0        127.0.0.1        127.0.0.1       1
        224.0.0.0        224.0.0.0         10.1.4.2         10.1.4.2       1
  255.255.255.255  255.255.255.255         10.1.4.2         10.1.4.2       1

C:\WINNT>
```

Figure 7.19 SALES2 routing table.

The IP software on SALES2 looks in its routing table for a route matching the target address 10.1.3.3. Network address 0.0.0.0 is the only matching route, so the datagram will be sent out the 10.1.4.2 interface to 10.1.4.1. ARP will be used to obtain the hardware address of 10.1.4.1. Then the packet is sent to SALES_RTR (hop #1).

When SALES_RTR's IP receives this datagram it will notice that the target IP address is not its own, and will attempt to forward it. IP looks for a route matching 10.1.3.3 in the routing table, and finds 10.1.3.0 which matches because of the 255.255.255.0 mask used. SALES_RTR then forwards this datagram out interface 10.1.2.2 to 10.1.2.1 (ENG_RTR). Once again ARP is used to obtain the hardware address of ENG_RTR's NIC on the backbone. Then the packet is sent to ENG_RTR (hop #2).

When ENG_RTR's IP receives this datagram it will notice that the target IP address is not it's own, and will attempt to forward it. IP looks for a route matching 10.1.3.3 in the routing table and finds 10.1.3.0. ENG_RTR then forwards this datagram out interface 10.1.3.1 to 10.1.3.3. ARP is used to obtain the hardware address of ENG3. Then the packet is sent to ENG3 (hop #3).

When ENG3 receives this datagram, it will see that the target address matches its own and deliver it to the appropriate upper layer protocol.

The end-to-end trip was three hops.

RIP Operation

The Routing Information Protocol (RIP) is used to exchange routing table information between routers. This allows us to automate the process of learning routes between routers so that we may not have to add static routes. Thus RIP is an example of a dynamic routing. The routing isn't actually performed any differently with dynamic routing than with static routing— what is different is the way in which routes in the routing tables are updated.

Consider the network in Figure 7.20. If we were to set up static routes in the routers for this network, we'd want to do the following:

- Tell router A how to send to subnets 30 and 40.
- Tell router B how to send to subnets 10 and 40.
- Tell router C how to send to subnets 10 and 20.

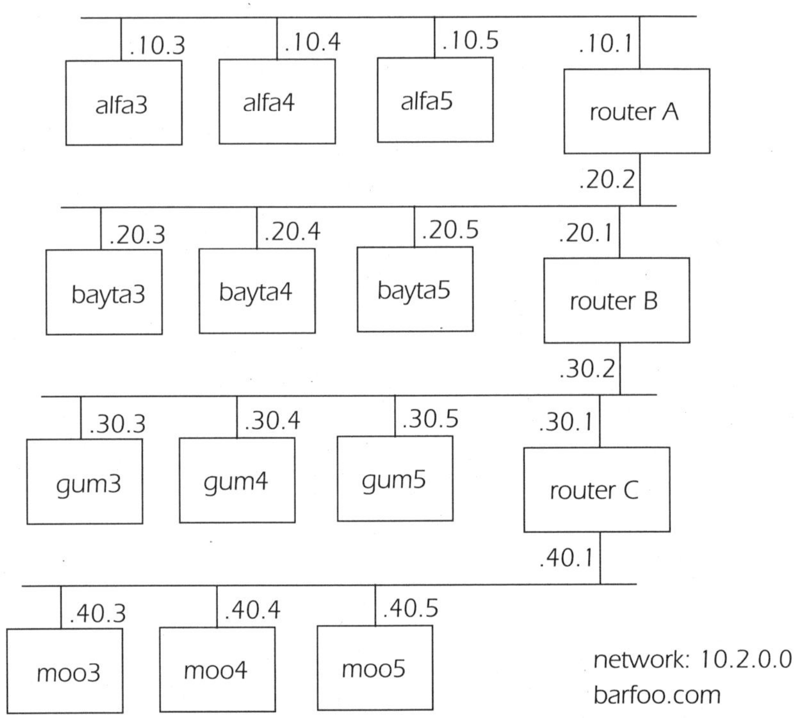

Figure 7.20
Four subnets are connected by three routers.

A routing protocol can update the routing tables for us, and make our lives as system administrators much simpler. If we install RIP on each router, the routers could tell the others about the networks they know about. Figure 7.21 illustrates a simpler view of the network. We'll use Figure 7.21 as the basis for our discussion of RIP.

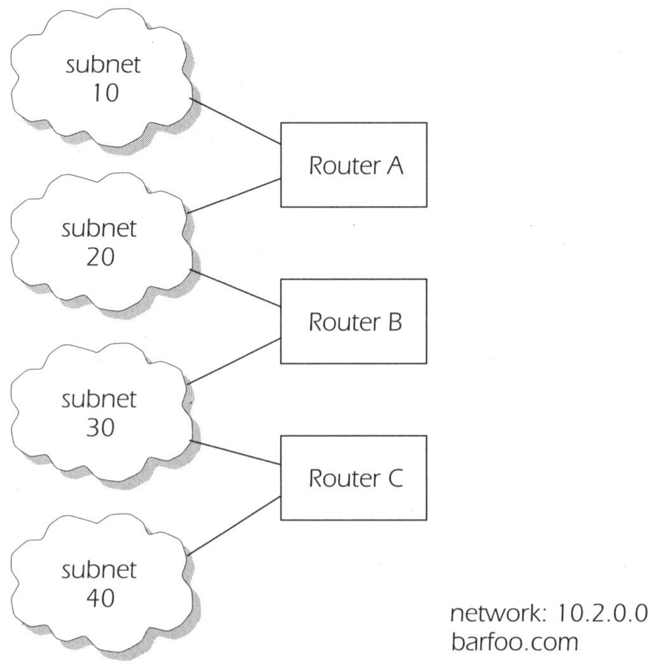

Figure 7.21
The simplified view of the network allows us to focus on the RIP messages which will be exchanged by the routers.

What Do the Routers Know Initially?

Here we have three routers which know only about the routes to their directly connected networks. In the next several figures, we'll see how these routers update their routing tables through exchanges of routing information using RIP.

Figure 7.22 shows the initial configuration of the routing tables upon powerup. Each router only knows about the networks it is directly attached to. So router A only knows about subnets 10 and 20, B only knows about subnets 20 and 30, and router C only knows about subnets 30 and 40. Each of those subnets has a metric (hop count) of one. A hop count of one implies that the router is directly connected to that subnet.

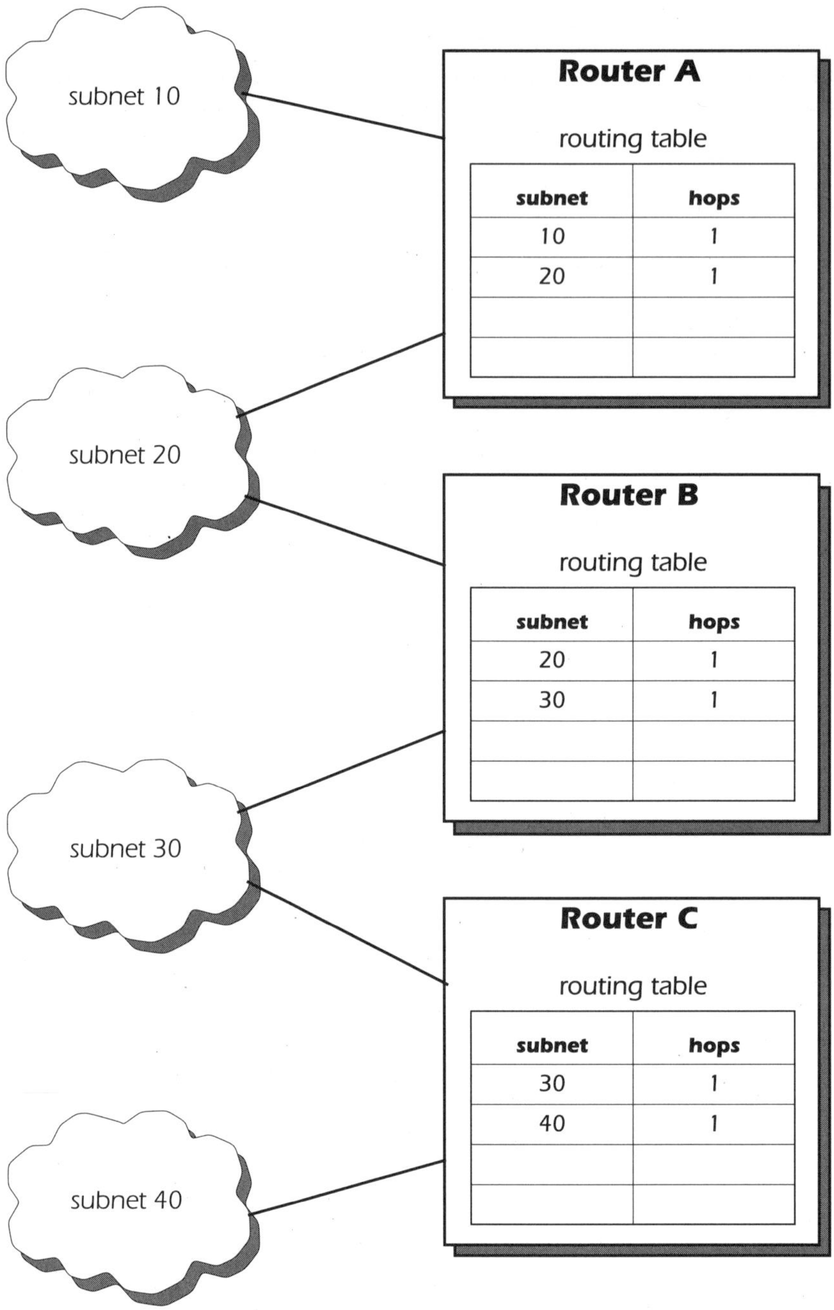

Figure 7.22 Initial routing tables — before any networks have been learned.

First RIP Message

Let's assume that router A is the first to send a RIP message. (Note that all machines running RIP will send RIP messages every 30 seconds). The RIP message from router A lists the networks that it can reach on its other interfaces and the number of hops to each of those networks.

Recall that RIP is found at the application layer of the TCP/IP stack, and it uses UDP port 520. The RIP message is sent as a broadcast in subnets 10 and 20 (Figure 7.23). Router B will receive the message sent on subnet 20. The action that router B will perform is shown in the next step.

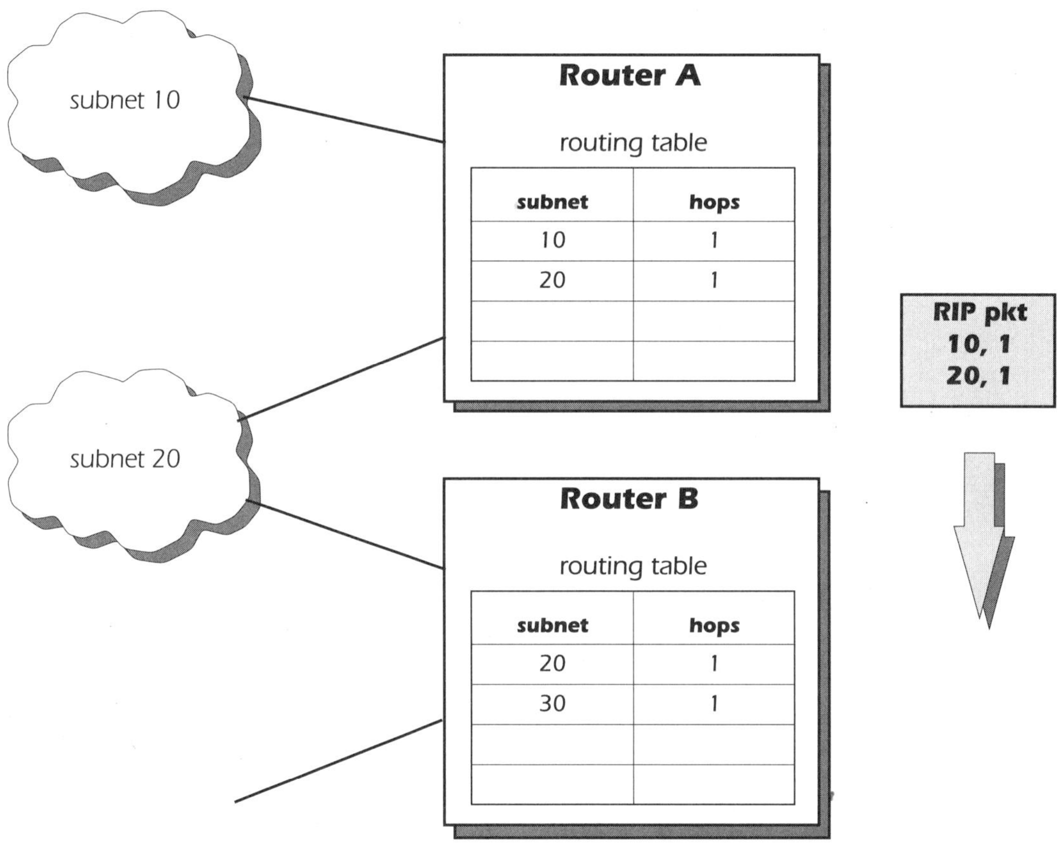

Figure 7.23 Time = 10 seconds from boot. Router A sends RIP message as shown.

Router B Updates Routing Table

When router B receives the first RIP message from router A, it updates its own routing table as necessary (Figure 7.24). In particular, any new networks that are advertised will be added to the table. Also, if there are any networks advertised with a lower hop count than in the current routing table, that entry will be replaced by the new one.

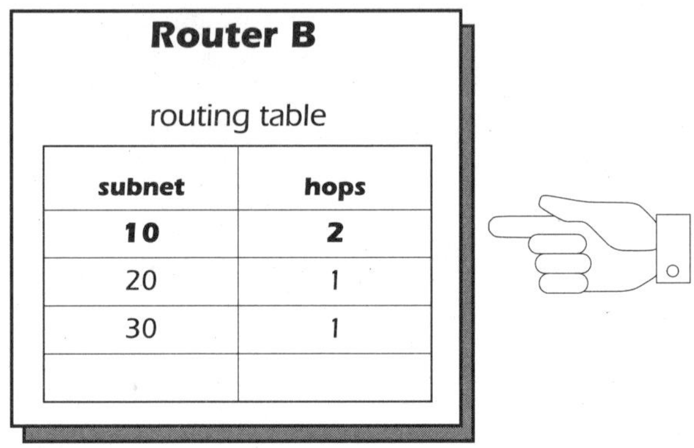

Figure 7.24 Router B receives RIP message and changes its routing table.

One thing we can conclude from this is that routes in the routing table that have a hop count greater than 1 are typically routes that have been learned from a routing protocol. (This generalization assumes that no static routes with a metric greater than 1 were added to that routing table.)

Another RIP Exchange

A few seconds later, assume that router B sends a RIP message. One message will be sent to subnet 20, another will be sent to subnet 30 (Figure 7.25). Routers A and C will process these messages (described next).

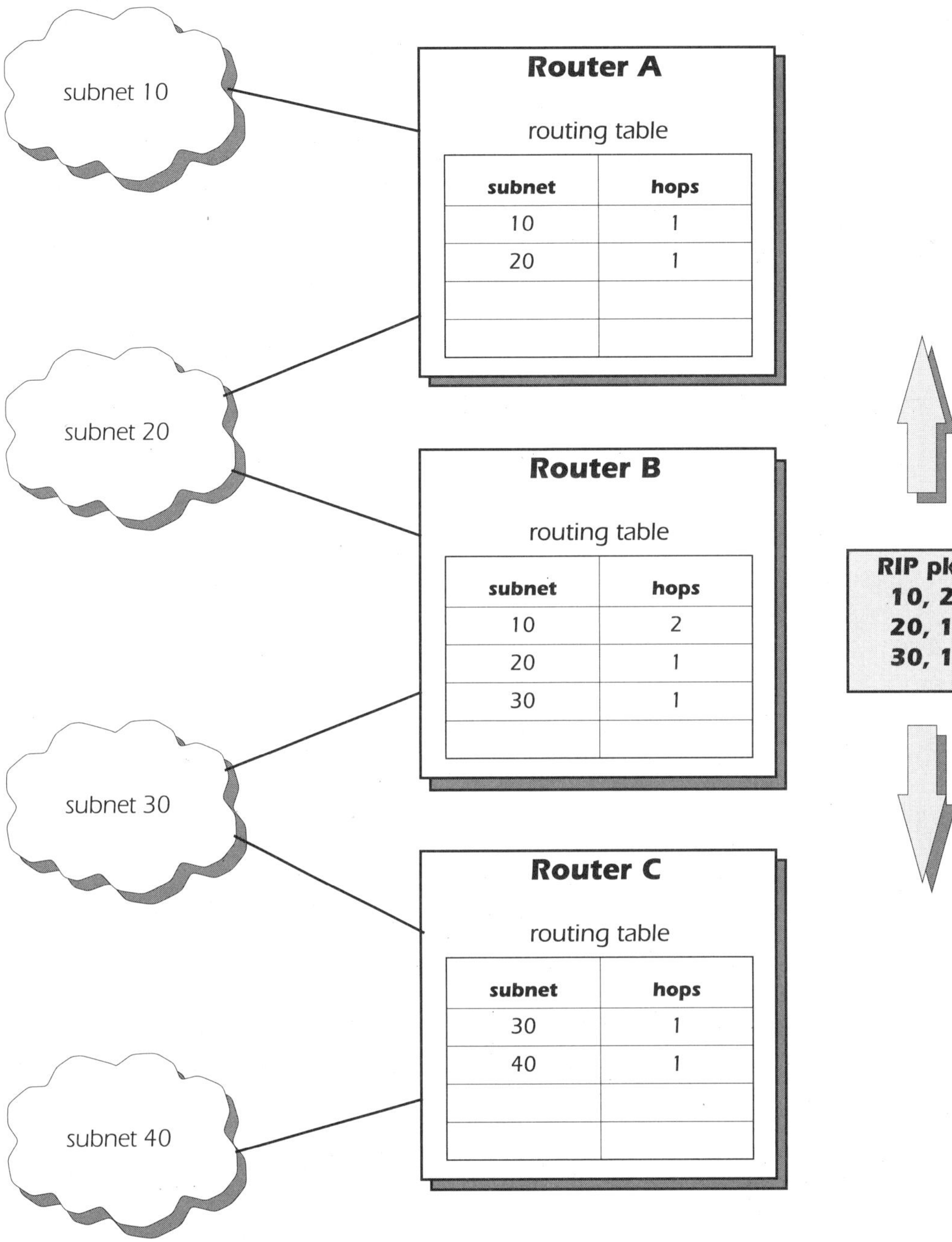

Figure 7.25 Time = 15 seconds. Router B sends RIP message as shown.

Routers A and C Update Tables

When routers A and C each receive the RIP message from router B, they will update their routing tables, as shown in Figure 7.26. New entries are added to both router A and C's tables.

Figure 7.26
Routers A and C update their routing tables.

Router A

routing table

subnet	hops
10	1
20	1
30	**2**

Router C

routing table

subnet	hops
10	**3**
20	**2**
30	1
40	1

Yet Another Routing Exchange

A few seconds later, router C sends a RIP message to all of its neighbors — router B. Notice that the RIP message contains entries for all subnets in this network (Figure 7.27).

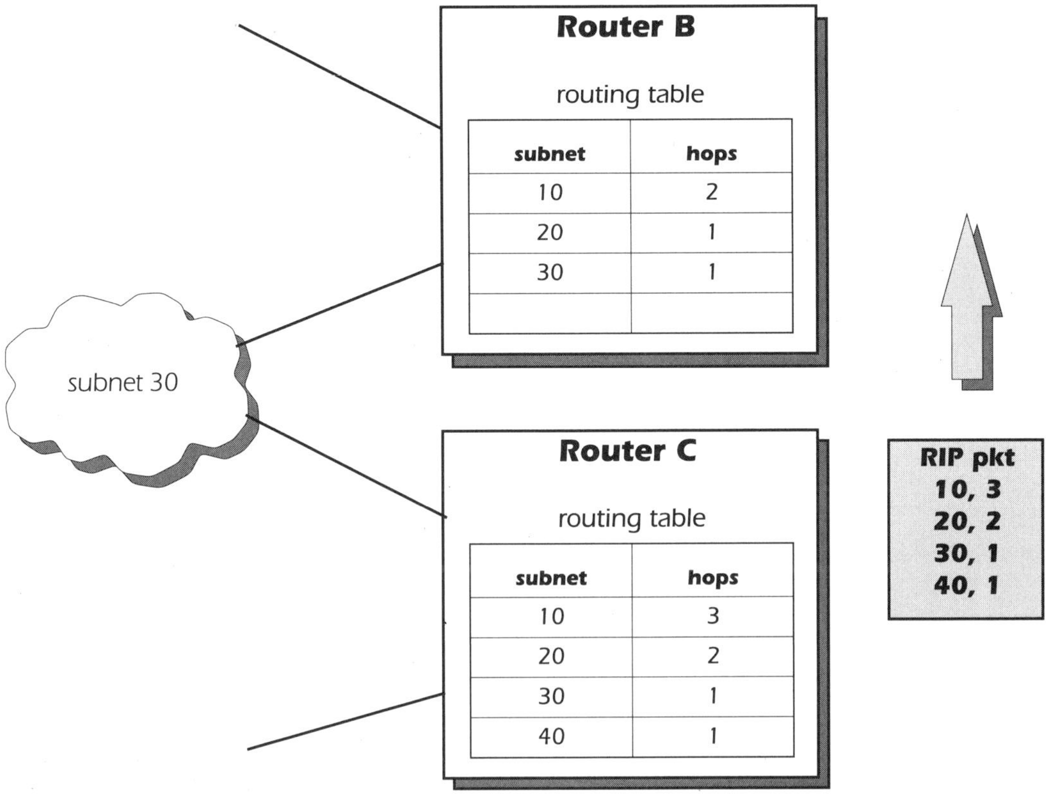

Figure 7.27 Time = 25 seconds. Router C sends RIP message as shown.

Router B Updates Its Table (Again)

When router B gets the update from router C, it will update the entry for subnet 40 (Figure 7.28).

Figure 7.28
Router B updates its routing table again.

Router B

routing table

subnet	hops
10	2
20	1
30	1
40	**2**

Next, router B will tell routers A and C about all of its routes. Router C already knows all of this information so it will ignore the updated information. Router A doesn't yet know a route to subnet 40, so it uses B's advertisement and update its routing table so that subnet 40 is known as being three hops away. The resulting routing table for router A is shown in Figure 7.29.

Figure 7.29
Router A updates its routing table again after getting an update from router B.

Router A

routing table

subnet	hops
10	1
20	1
30	2
40	**3**

It takes some time for updates to trickle through the network based on RIP's periodic updates. Eventually, the routing knowledge in a steady-state network converges to a consistent and coherent view.

What Do RIP Version 1 Messages Look Like?

As we've seen in the first RIP message on the backbone (Figure 7.38), there may be more than one route advertised per RIP message. Let's look in a little more detail at the layout of RIP messages.

RIP sends broadcast messages from UDP port 520 to UDP port 520. These messages are sent out every interface of the machine. Each RIP message begins with a RIP header, as shown in Figure 7.30.

Figure 7.30
RIP message header.

bits 0-3	bits 4-7	bits 8-11	bits 12-15	bits 16-19	bits 20-23	bits 24-27	bits 28-31
Command		Version		Reserved			

The RIP message header is 32-bits long and specifies two fields. The first field is the first octet of the header and holds a command code. The command code specifies if the message is a request (1) or response (2). Most RIP messages are actually unsolicited responses. The next field is the version number, transmitted as an octet. RIP version 1 is described here. The remaining 16 bits of the 32-bit header are reserved.[3]

These response messages may carry up to 25 advertisements. If a router has more than 25 routes to advertise, it may send multiple RIP response messages, each with up to 25 routes. Each route advertisement is five 32-bit words in length, as shown in Figure 7.31.

Figure 7.31
RIP advertisement layout.

bits 0-3	bits 4-7	bits 8-11	bits 12-15	bits 16-19	bits 20-23	bits 24-27	bits 28-31
Family				Reserved			
Address							
Metric							

Each advertisement specifies one route. The following information is included:

3. RIP messages are laid out with 32-bit alignment for ease of processing.

- the address family of the network route being advertised.
- the network address of the route.
- a weighting metric associated with the route.

The *address family* is specified because RIP was designed to be able to advertise routes for many different protocols. IP is address family 2.

Next comes the *network address* which is an IP subnet or network address that is being advertised. IP addresses, which are 32-bits long, only take up the first third of the address field. Ninety-six bits are used for the address to accommodate a fixed width field for all address families supported.

The *metric* specifies a weight for the route, which is specifies a hop count to the network for most uses of RIP. This value may be between one and fifteen in normal advertisements. The value of sixteen is used to specify an infinite hop count, thus an unreachable network. The metric is supposed to be set to 1 for directly connected networks.

Note that the netmask associated with the route is not a part of the advertisement, thus when using RIP, all of the routes advertised must have a consistent mask. In other words, constant-width subnet masking is required for a network which uses RIP.

What does a whole RIP message look like? Recall that in the example in Figure 7.38 there were two routes advertised. Figure 7.32 shows the message format for a RIP message with the header and two advertisements. Again, there may be up to 25 advertisements per message.

Figure 7.32
Example of RIP header with two advertisements.

bits 0-3	bits 4-7	bits 8-11	bits 12-15	bits 16-19	bits 20-23	bits 24-27	bits 28-31
Command		Version		Reserved			
Family #1				Reserved			
Address #1							
Metric #1							
Family #2				Reserved			
Address #2							
Metric #2							

Does RIP Always Advertise All Known Routes?

As a generally rule, RIP traditionally is considered to be a rather chatty protocol — it normally would tell everything it knows to anyone who would listen. More specifically, in the normal mode of operation, RIP:

- advertises all known routes, perhaps in more than one message.
- broadcasts unsolicited responses out all interfaces.
- sends unsolicited responses every thirty seconds.

split horizon: route advertisements received on a particular interface will not be sent back out that interface.

Two use features incorporated into many current RIP implementations (including NT) are *split horizon* and *poison reverse*. The goal of both of these features is to hasten the rate at which the routers learn of changes in the network, as well as to prevent routing loops.

When the **split horizon** feature is implemented, RIP will not advertise a route out the same interface from which it learned that particular route. This is intended to prevent routing loops.

poison reverse: route advertisements received on a particular interface are sent out the same interface received, but with a metric of 16.

An even stronger method of avoiding routing loops is the feature called **poison reverse**. In poison reverse, RIP will advertise a route back toward the neighbor from which it came, but with an infinite (16) hop count as the metric.[4]

What does IP do when it receives such an advertisement? There are three cases.

1. If the receiving RIP doesn't know about the route, it will treat the advertisement as though its neighbor had said "I don't know how to get to this network." As this is no better than the receiving RIP router's lack of knowledge, the advertisement is ignored.
2. When RIP knows about the route, yet the gateway address in the routing table doesn't match the advertising router's address, the route is ignored. This is the case for SALES_RTR in the previous example. This is the intention of poison reverse.
3. When RIP knows about the route, and the gateway address does match that of the advertising router, the route will be updated to a metric of 16, regardless of the previous metric.

4. If you can't wait to see an example of poison reverse, flip ahead to the packet capture on page 281.

convergence of routing tables: a state when all the routing tables have stabilized after a routing change has occurred.

A related routing concept is **convergence of the routing tables**. Convergence has occurred when all routers in the network have an up-to-date routing table. When a router or link goes down, RIP routers will propagate that information across the network, until all the routers know about that change.

How Does RIP Construct a Route from an Advertisement?

RIP uses the information in advertisements to construct routing table entries. Consider the different pieces of information in an advertisement, and those in a routing table entry.

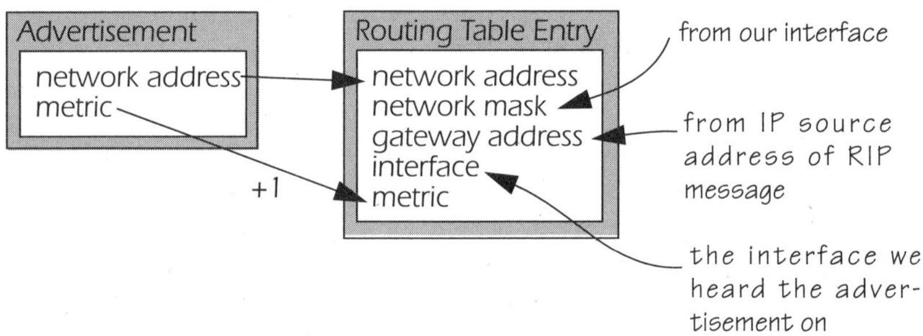

Figure 7.33 Correlation between routing table entry and advertisement.

As shown in Figure 7.33, the elements of a routing table entry are derived from several sources. The router obtains information from the message itself and the interface it was received on, as shown in Table 7.3.

Table 7.3 How routing table entries are derived from RIP messages.

Source	Routing table parameter
network address field in the RIP message	network address
netmask of receiving interface	netmask
source IP address of RIP message	gateway address
IP address of receiving interface	interface
calculated from metric field in RIP message	metric

When an advertisement is received, RIP knows that the metric specified is the hop count used by whomever sent the advertisement. Because that advertiser is one hop away from the receiver, the effective hop count for the receiver is one greater than the metric value in the advertisement.

RIP checks to see if there is already a routing table entry with the same network address as the advertisement. If there is already an entry, RIP will compare the current metric in the routing table entry with the effective (i.e. +1) metric of the advertisement. If the advertisement's effective metric is not better than the one in the current routing table entry, the advertisement is ignored. Otherwise (i.e. the advertisement is a better route toward the destination network) the routing table entry is updated with the information from the advertisement.

If the effective metric advertised is greater than or equal to 16, the network is considered unreachable via the advertised route.

Installing RIP Version 1

RIP version 1 (RIPv1) for IP is installed from the *Network Control Panel -> Services tab*. Pressing the *Add* button results in the screen shown in Figure 7.34. RIP installation does not prompt the user for any configuration— after the machine is rebooted, RIP will be running.

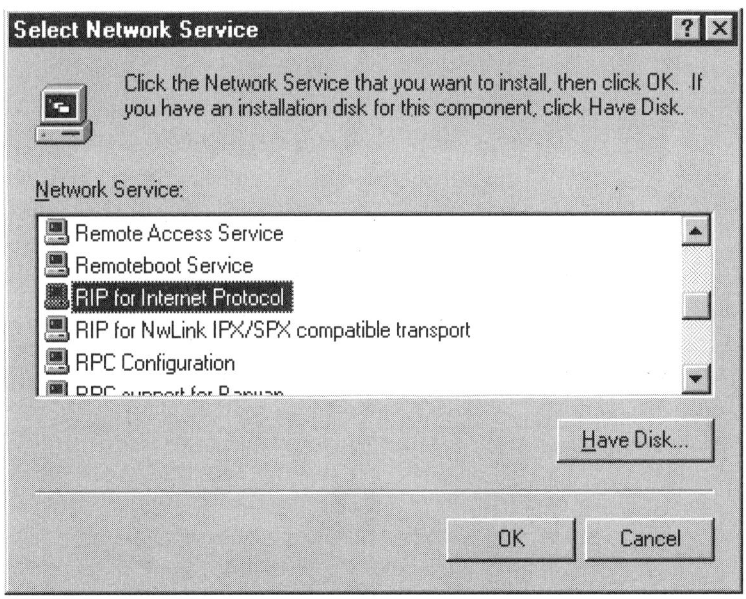

Figure 7.34 Install RIPv1 using this screen.

If you find that after you install RIP, your routing table is not being updated, or no RIP messages are being sent by the NT router, you need to check the RIP registry values. Certain RIP registry parameters may have different defaults, depending on the number of NIC cards installed in the machine. If you install RIP in a machine with only one NIC, and then install a second NIC, the RIP registry parameters will likely be set wrong.

RIP Registry Entries

RIP commonly generates unsolicited response messages to keep its neighbors up to date. These responses are sent periodically (see *UpdateFrequency* below). When the *SilentRip* registry parameter is set to one, RIP will not generate these periodic messages (Table 7.4). However, RIP in silent mode will listen to RIP broadcasts and update its routing table.

Table 7.4
SilentRip registry parameter.

Hive:	HKEY_LOCAL_MACHINE
Key:	\System\CurrentControlSet\Services\IpRip\Parameters
Name:	SilentRip
Type:	REG_DWORD
Value:	0 (not silent), or 1 (silent)

The default value for *SilentRip* is one (silent) if the machine is single homed but the default is zero (not silent) if the machine is multihomed.

The *UpdateFrequency* parameter controls the period by which the unsolicited response messages are sent (Table 7.5). For instance, a value of 30 specifies these messages will be sent every thirty seconds.

Table 7.5
UpdateFrequency registry parameter.

Hive:	HKEY_LOCAL_MACHINE
Key:	\System\CurrentControlSet\Services\IpRip\Parameters
Name:	UpdateFrequency
Type:	REG_DWORD
Value:	30 (default)

While the default is 30 seconds, typical values which may be useful are between 15 seconds and 24 hours (86,400 seconds).

RIP may periodically write diagnostic information to the system log. The *LoggingLevel* parameter specifies a logging level as a threshold — the minimum level for entries to be written into the system log (Table 7.6).

Table 7.6
LoggingLevel registry parameter.

Hive:	HKEY_LOCAL_MACHINE
Key:	\System\CurrentControlSet\Services\IpRip\Parameters
Name:	LoggingLevel
Type:	REG_DWORD
Value:	0 (no logging) 1 (error messages) (default) 2 (warning messages) 3 (errors, warnings, and informational messages)

RIP Version 1 Packet Captures

After RIP v1 was installed on both routers, Network Monitor was used to capture packets in three locations on the network. The capture files shown in the next few pages are stored on the CD with the filenames specified in Figure 7.35.

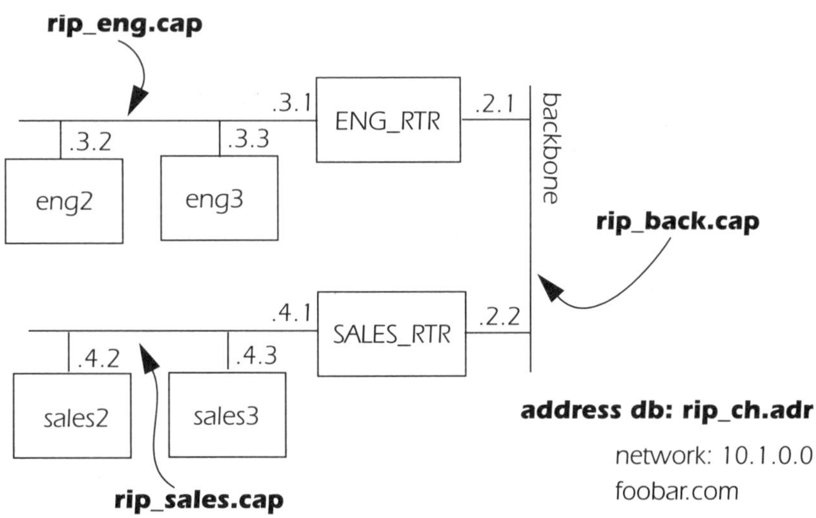

Figure 7.35
RIP messages for each subnet have been captured and saved on the CD. An address database has also been saved.

Before we look at the packets, let's look at the router's routing tables after RIP was made operational. Figure 7.36 and Figure 7.37 show the routing tables on the routers after RIP messages have been exchanged.

```
cmd

C:\WINNT>route print

Active Routes:

  Network Address          Netmask  Gateway Address        Interface  Metric
         10.1.2.0    255.255.255.0         10.1.2.1         10.1.2.1       1
         10.1.2.1  255.255.255.255        127.0.0.1        127.0.0.1       1
         10.1.3.0    255.255.255.0         10.1.3.1         10.1.3.1       1
         10.1.3.1  255.255.255.255        127.0.0.1        127.0.0.1       1
         10.1.4.0    255.255.255.0         10.1.2.2         10.1.2.1       3
   10.255.255.255  255.255.255.255         10.1.2.1         10.1.2.1       1
        127.0.0.0        255.0.0.0        127.0.0.1        127.0.0.1       1
        224.0.0.0        224.0.0.0         10.1.3.1         10.1.3.1       1
        224.0.0.0        224.0.0.0         10.1.2.1         10.1.2.1       1
  255.255.255.255  255.255.255.255         10.1.2.1         10.1.2.1       1

C:\WINNT>
```

Figure 7.36 ENG_RTR after RIP updates.

```
command prompt

C:\WINNT>
C:\WINNT>route print

Active Routes:

  Network Address          Netmask  Gateway Address        Interface  Metric
         10.1.2.0    255.255.255.0         10.1.2.2         10.1.2.2       1
         10.1.2.2  255.255.255.255        127.0.0.1        127.0.0.1       1
         10.1.3.0    255.255.255.0         10.1.2.1         10.1.2.2       3
         10.1.4.0    255.255.255.0         10.1.4.1         10.1.4.1       1
         10.1.4.1  255.255.255.255        127.0.0.1        127.0.0.1       1
   10.255.255.255  255.255.255.255         10.1.2.2         10.1.2.2       1
        127.0.0.0        255.0.0.0        127.0.0.1        127.0.0.1       1
        224.0.0.0        224.0.0.0         10.1.4.1         10.1.4.1       1
        224.0.0.0        224.0.0.0         10.1.2.2         10.1.2.2       1
  255.255.255.255  255.255.255.255         10.1.2.2         10.1.2.2       1

C:\WINNT>
```

Figure 7.37 SALES_RTR after RIP updates.

Notice that both routing tables contain routes to the other network, as expected. But what is not expected is the metric of 3! What happened here? It turns out that nothing has gone wrong, that a metric of 3 is what should be expected with NT 4.0. We'll have to look at the packets to see why.

RIP Message from ENG_RTR onto Backbone

rip_back.cap
frame #1

The first packet capture to examine is rip_back.cap. This capture was taken on the foobar.com backbone. During the minute and a half time period that Network Monitor was capturing, six RIP messages were sent— three from ENG_RTR, three from SALES_RTR. Figure 7.38 shows the contents of a RIP message sent from ENG_RTR. It contains information on two networks: 10.1.3.0 and 10.1.4.0.

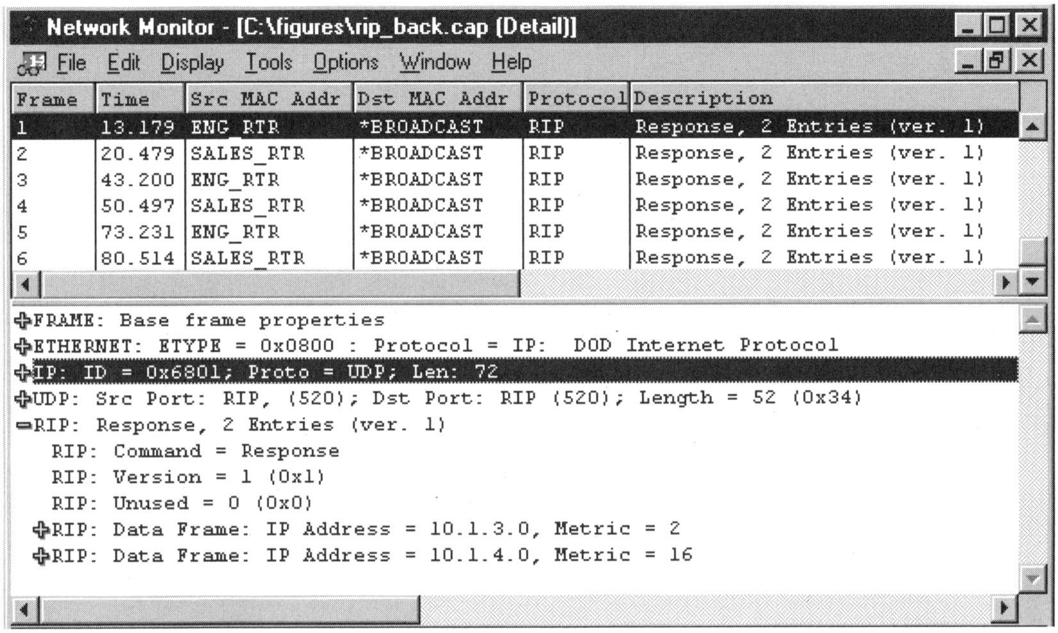

Figure 7.38 The first RIP message on the backbone subnet.

The first network is network 10.1.3.0 with a metric of 2 as shown in Figure 7.38. But recall from the network diagram that ENG_RTR is directly attached to network 10.1.3.0. *What is occurring is that the NT router is adding a metric of 1 to the actual hop count of 1 in the outbound message.*

WARNING

Why is NT saying a directly-attached network is 2 hops away? We do not know the reason, other than saying it is a design flaw with NT RIP. Be careful of this, as when you integrate NT RIP routers with other RIP routers, your routing tables may not contain the shortest paths to get to networks.

The second network listed in the packet capture is 10.1.4.0, which is the sales subnet. The hop count shown is sixteen (16) which represents an infinite distance in RIP. Thus this entry states that "do not send packets destined to 10.1.4.0 to me, as I won't forward them." This is an example of poison reverse.

RIP Message from SALES_RTR onto Backbone

rip_back.cap
frame #2

The second RIP message on the backbone is broadcast from SALES_RTR, and looks similar to the other RIP message (Figure 7.36). The network that SALES_RTR is directly attached to, 10.1.4.0, has a hop count of 2, which is expected. Packets for the engineering subnet 10.1.3.0 should not be sent to this router, as is indicated by the hop count of 16.

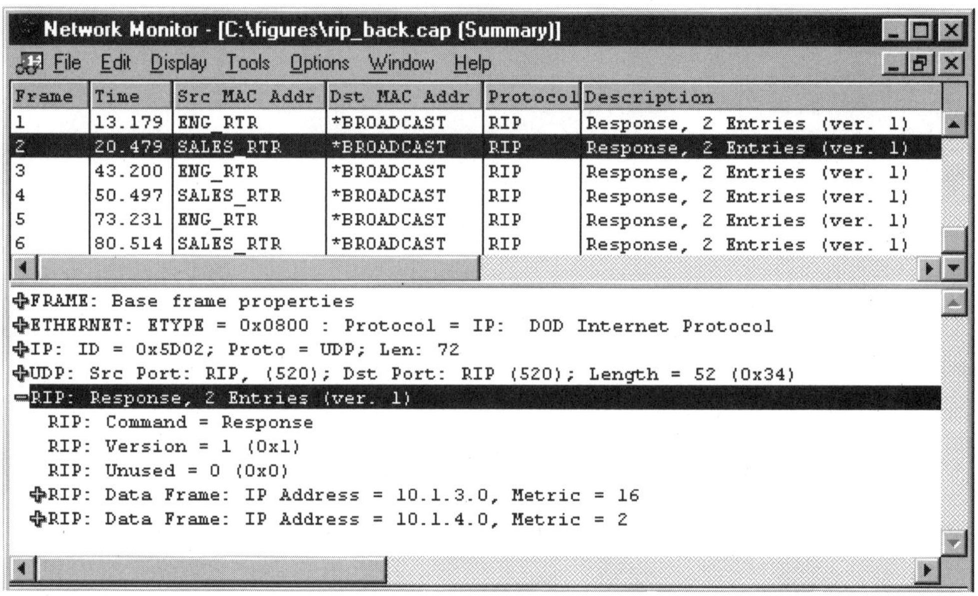

Figure 7.39 The second RIP message on the backbone subnet.

Some disadvantages of RIP version 1 can be seen in the trace above:

- Packets are sent to the IP broadcast address 255.255.255.255.
- Packets are sent every 30 seconds.

Broadcasting the RIP messages causes unnecessary processing on each of the TCP/IP hosts on each of the networks receiving these broadcasts. More specifically, each machine attached to this LAN will receive the broadcast, and identify it as an IP datagram. The IP software will identify the datagram as a UDP datagram, and UDP will notice that (if there is no RIP software on that machine) there is no one listening on port 520, so the datagram will then be discarded. A lot of work is performed on each machine in order to ignore these messages.

The normal advertisement interval is thirty seconds. This is demonstrated with frames 1, 3, and 5 from ENG_RTR and frames 2, 4, and 6 from SALES_RTR in Figure 7.39. RIP will broadcast one or more messages out each interface at this interval even if no routing information has changed since the last update.

RIP Message from ENG_RTR onto Subnet 10.1.3.0

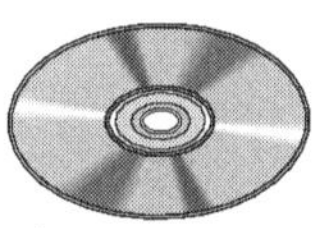

rip_eng.cap

ENG_RTR sends RIP messages out its other interface onto the engineering subnet. Figure 7.40 shows the one of these RIP messages. Now that we know that a value of 2 means that network is directly attached to the NT router, we see that network 10.1.2.0 is directly attached.

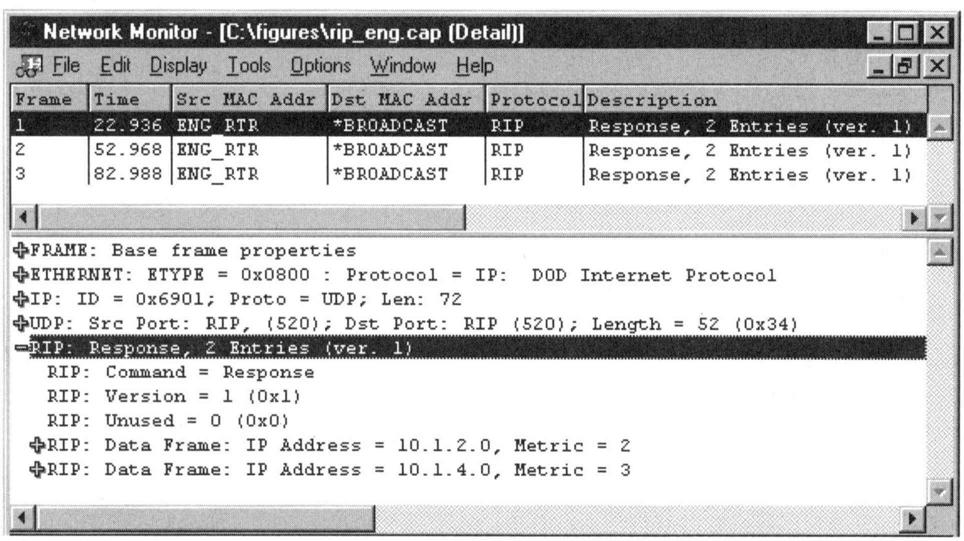

Figure 7.40 A RIP message sent on the engineering subnet.

RIP Message from SALES_RTR onto Subnet 10.1.4.0

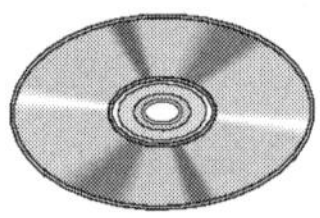

rip_sales.cap

The SALES_RTR also sends RIP advertisements onto the sales subnet, 10.1.4.0, as shown in Figure 7.41. Note that the values in the time column are not exactly thirty seconds, but somewhat greater. This behavior is seen in some implementations of RIP due to either clock drift in RIP's time base, and/or failure of RIP to reset the timer until after it is done with its processing for an advertisement.

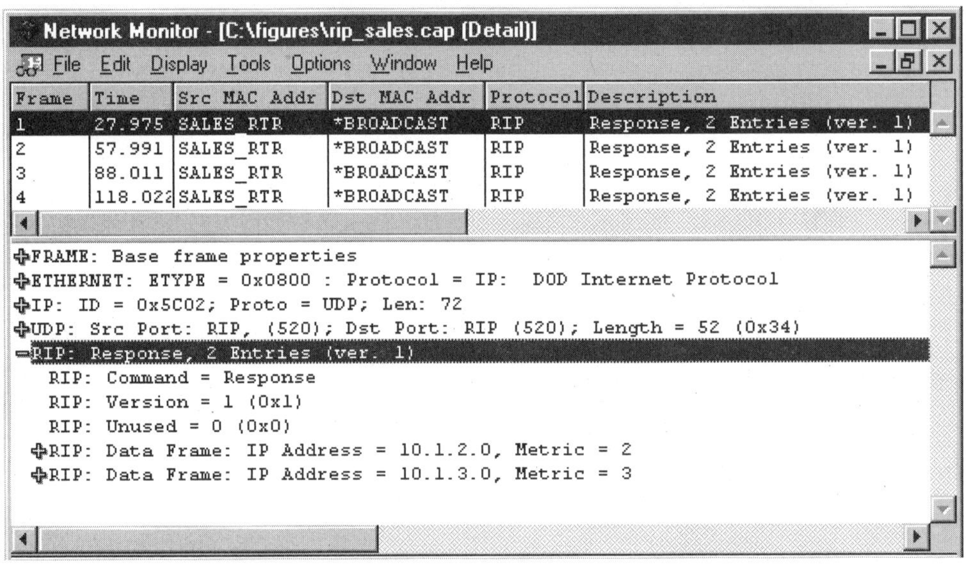

Figure 7.41 A RIP message sent on the sales subnet.

The first entry is for network 10.1.2.0 and tells us that SALES_RTR is directly attached to that network.

Testing Routes

The ***tracert*** command can be used to diagnose problems with routing. It reports the route taken by a datagram to a specific destination.

For this example, examine the network shown in Figure 7.42. ***Tracert*** was issued on ENG3 to the machine SALES2.

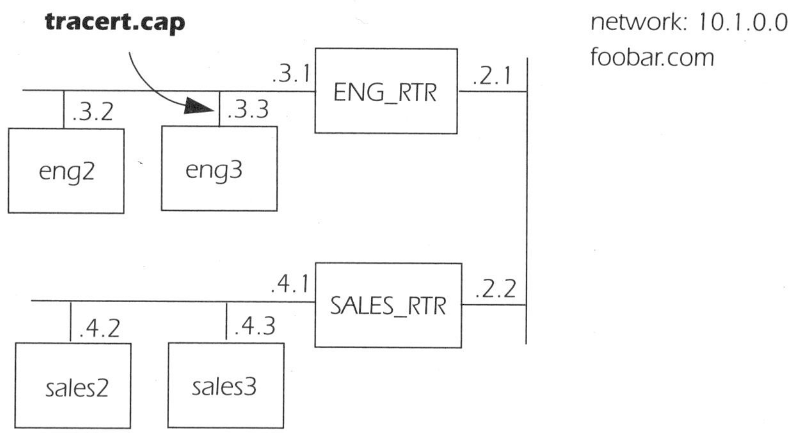

Figure 7.42 The tracert command allows testing of the routes in this network.

The result of the tracert command is shown in Figure 7.43. The first column of output specifies the hop number. The next three columns are the round-trip times in milliseconds for three attempts to reach the next destination (router). An asterisk (*) in any of the time columns means that the attempt timed out. The fourth column is the hostname and IP address of the responding system.

Figure 7.43 Example tracert command from ENG3 to SALES2.

```
command prompt

C:\WINNT>tracert 10.1.4.2

Tracing route to SALES2 [10.1.4.2]
over a maximum of 30 hops:

  1    <10 ms   <10 ms   <10 ms  ENG_RTR [10.1.3.1]
  2    <10 ms   <10 ms   <10 ms  SALES_RTR [10.1.2.2]
  3    <10 ms    10 ms   <10 ms  SALES2 [10.1.4.2]

Trace complete.

C:\WINNT>_
```

Notice that ***tracert***, by default, resolved names to IP addresses. Therefore, the command takes longer to complete than if no resolution were performed.

A quick reply from ***tracert*** can be had when using the ***-d*** option, "do not resolve addresses to hostnames". When the name resolutions aren't performed, the command responds much faster. The following was executed on ENG3.

Figure 7.44
Tracert -d doesn't obtain hostnames for the IP addresses.

```
command prompt

C:\WINNT>tracert -d 10.1.4.2

Tracing route to 10.1.4.2 over a maximum of 30 hops

  1    <10 ms   <10 ms    <10 ms   10.1.3.1
  2    <10 ms   <10 ms    <10 ms   10.1.2.2
  3    <10 ms    10 ms    <10 ms   10.1.4.2

Trace complete.

C:\WINNT>
```

Tracert Operation

Tracert is implemented by setting the TTL field in the IP datagram to successively incrementing values (beginning with 1), such that each router in the path will send back an error message (TTL expired).

As shown in Figure 7.44, the first hop gets to the near interface of ENG_RTR (10.1.3.1), the second hop to the near interface of SALES_RTR (10.1.2.2), and the third and final hop to SALES2 (10.1.4.2).

tracert.cap

The resulting Network Monitor capture is shown in Figure 7.45, again monitoring from ENG3. You can bring up this capture in network monitor by loading the file tracert.cap, as well as the address database rip_ch.adr.

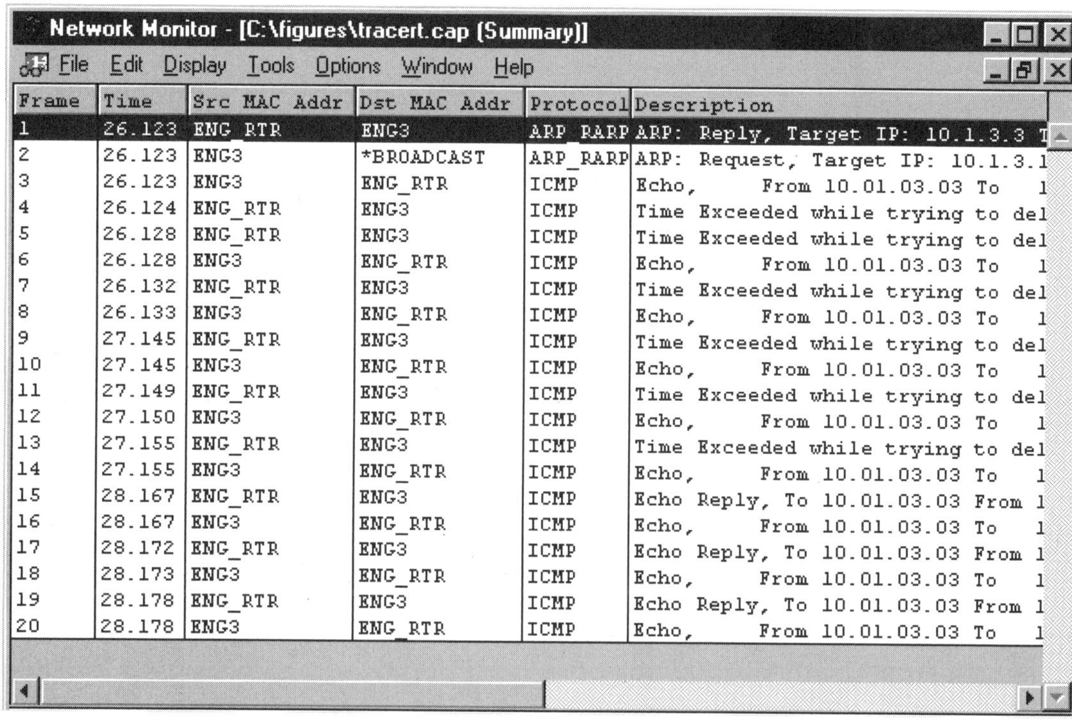

Network Monitor - [C:\figures\tracert.cap (Summary)]

File Edit Display Tools Options Window Help

Frame	Time	Src MAC Addr	Dst MAC Addr	Protocol	Description
1	26.123	ENG_RTR	ENG3	ARP_RARP	ARP: Reply, Target IP: 10.1.3.3 T
2	26.123	ENG3	*BROADCAST	ARP_RARP	ARP: Request, Target IP: 10.1.3.1
3	26.123	ENG3	ENG_RTR	ICMP	Echo, From 10.01.03.03 To 1
4	26.124	ENG_RTR	ENG3	ICMP	Time Exceeded while trying to del
5	26.128	ENG_RTR	ENG3	ICMP	Time Exceeded while trying to del
6	26.128	ENG3	ENG_RTR	ICMP	Echo, From 10.01.03.03 To 1
7	26.132	ENG_RTR	ENG3	ICMP	Time Exceeded while trying to del
8	26.133	ENG3	ENG_RTR	ICMP	Echo, From 10.01.03.03 To 1
9	27.145	ENG_RTR	ENG3	ICMP	Time Exceeded while trying to del
10	27.145	ENG3	ENG_RTR	ICMP	Echo, From 10.01.03.03 To 1
11	27.149	ENG_RTR	ENG3	ICMP	Time Exceeded while trying to del
12	27.150	ENG3	ENG_RTR	ICMP	Echo, From 10.01.03.03 To 1
13	27.155	ENG_RTR	ENG3	ICMP	Time Exceeded while trying to del
14	27.155	ENG3	ENG_RTR	ICMP	Echo, From 10.01.03.03 To 1
15	28.167	ENG_RTR	ENG3	ICMP	Echo Reply, To 10.01.03.03 From 1
16	28.167	ENG3	ENG_RTR	ICMP	Echo, From 10.01.03.03 To 1
17	28.172	ENG_RTR	ENG3	ICMP	Echo Reply, To 10.01.03.03 From 1
18	28.173	ENG3	ENG_RTR	ICMP	Echo, From 10.01.03.03 To 1
19	28.178	ENG_RTR	ENG3	ICMP	Echo Reply, To 10.01.03.03 From 1
20	28.178	ENG3	ENG_RTR	ICMP	Echo, From 10.01.03.03 To 1

Figure 7.45 Network Monitor trace of the tracert -d from Figure 7.44.

WARNING

The sequence of messages shown in Figure 7.45 for this example appear to be out of order, with the response to a given request sometimes coming before the request itself. Actually, this a problem which you'll often see with Network Monitor. The cause is that the real-time clock on most PCs used by Windows NT does not give Network Monitor accurate precision for timing millisecond operations. Additionally, the point at which Network Monitor actually monitors the transmit and receive paths does not lend well to achieving time transparency.

Let's walk through the capture to illustrate the operation of ***tracert***. Figure 7.46 shows a simplified ladder diagram of the frames from Figure 7.45.

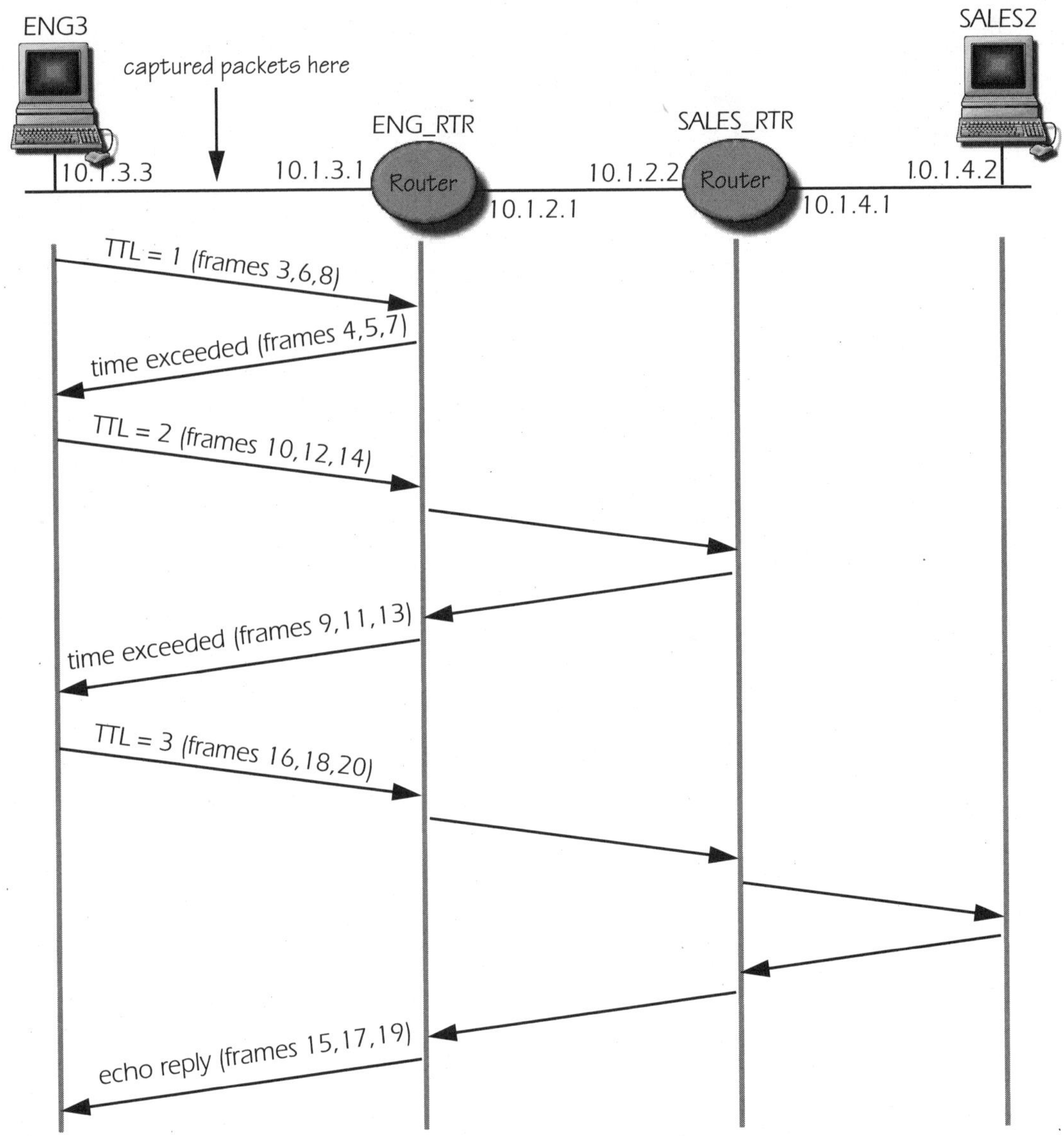

Figure 7.46 Ladder diagram of tracert operation corresponding to packets shown in Figure 7.45.

Note the following when relating Figure 7.46 back to the packet capture in Figure 7.45.

- The frames in the packet capture appear to be out of order. This is due to the fact that the capture was performed on ENG3, which is one of the participants in the exchange. Recall that Network Monitor does not handle minute timing deltas correctly.

- Only the frames between ENG3 and ENG_RTR are captured, which is normal for protocol analysis. In order to see what occurs between ENG_RTR and SALES_RTR, a capture would need to be performed on that subnet. The same is true of the packets between SALES_RTR and SALES2.

- Although there are two interfaces on each router, only one vertical line is shown to represent either router, so that the diagram is easier to read.

- The ARP request/reply in frames 2 and 1 are not shown in the ladder diagram. Also, ARPs which may have occurred between the routers and with SALES2 are not shown.

- Three attempts are made by ***tracert*** with each TTL setting, which will be discussed shortly. In the ladder diagram, only one instance is depicted.

The ladder diagram shows that ***tracert*** proceeds like this:

1. ENG3 makes an attempt to contact the target (ENG2) by addressing an ICMP echo request (like those used by ***ping***), with the TTL in the IP header set to 1 (frame 3).
2. When ENG_RTR receives this datagram, it sees that it should forward it on, yet to do so it must decrement the TTL, which hits zero. Therefore, ENG_RTR sends back an ICMP time exceeded message (frame 4). When ***tracert*** receives this error, it notes the source address and determines that ENG_RTR is the first hop along the route.

   These first two steps are repeated two more times (frames 6,5 and then again in frames 8,7). This is normal for ***tracert***, so that path variations may be noted. In this example, there are no variations.
3. Having detected the first hop, ***tracert*** goes one step further. Another echo request is sent toward ENG2, this time with a TTL of 2 (frame 10). ENG_RTR will decrement the TTL to 1 and forward this packet to SALES_RTR.
4. SALES_RTR receives this packet and decrements the TTL to 0. SALES_RTR sends back an ICMP time exceeded message to the originator of the failed packet (frame 9). ***Tracert*** determines that SALES_RTR is the second hop to get to the destination.

   Steps 3 and 4 are repeated two more times (frames 12,11 and then again in frames 14,13).

5. Having determined the first two hops, but still not reaching the target, ***tracert*** sends another echo request toward SALES2 with a TTL of 3 (frame 16). ENG_RTR and SALES_RTR send this on, each decrementing the TTL (to 2 and 1 respectively).
6. When SALES2 receives the ICMP echo request, its IP software delivers this to ICMP which satisfies the request. SALES2 sends an echo reply back toward ENG3. SALES_RTR forwards this to ENG_RTR, which forwards it to ENG3 (frame 15). This successful reply is noted by ***tracert***.

   The test is repeated two more times (frames 18,17 then frames 20,19).

Both ***ping*** and ***tracert*** may be used to test the ability of your routers to route packets correctly, however ***tracert*** supplies more detailed information.

Summary

Here's a summary of the items which have been addressed in this chapter.

- Routing is performed such that the path that a packet travels may be optimized.
- Routing tables contain information as to the network that can be reached and the best way to reach those networks.
- The best way to update routing tables is using a routing protocol, as static routes require substantial maintenance.
- The ***route*** command may be used to view the routing table on an NT box acting as a router. The command can also be used to display the routing table on an NT client.
- RIP is a distance vector protocol that is used to disseminate routing information between RIP routers.
- ***Tracert*** is a testing utility used to determine the path that a packet will take to a particular destination.

Further Reading

Here is information about various books and magazines in which to look for further information on the subject.

[Comer1995] Comer, Douglas E., *Internetworking with TCP/IP Vol I: Principles, Protocols, and Architecture, Third Edition*, 1995, Prentice-Hall, Inc.

[Hedrick1988] Hedrick, C., *Routing Information Protocol,* 1988, IETF RFC 1058

[Huitema1995] Huitema, Christian, *Routing in the Internet,* 1995, Prentice Hall

[Perlman1992] Perlman, Radia, *Interconnections: Bridges and Routers,* 1992, Addison Wesley

[Stevens1994] Stevens, W. Richard, *TCP/IP Illustrated, Volume 1: The Protocols,* 1994, Addison-Wesley

8

Using Steelhead as a RIPv2 Router

The previous chapter covered the basics of routing using Windows NT and focused on the Routing Information Protocol (RIP) version 1. In this chapter, a more advanced routing protocol, RIP version 2, is discussed, as implemented in Steelhead.

RRAS: The NT service that performs routing. Also known as Steelhead.

Steelhead was Microsoft's code name for NT's new routing capabilities and user interface. The official name for Steelhead is **Routing and Remote Access Service (RRAS)**. As we saw in the previous chapter, NT Server 4.0 has limited IP routing capability. Steelhead extends the capabilities to perform many of the functions found in a low-end hardware router. Consequently, NT may become a low-cost alternative to purchasing a dedicated piece of routing hardware.

Why Was It Called "Steelhead"?

Traditionally, Microsoft Windows was a desktop operating system. Recently, NT Server is becoming more viable as a server or computer room operating system. With the advent of the Routing and Remote Access Service (RRAS) software, which had been code-named Steelhead, Microsoft may be pushing Windows NT into the wiring closet with switches and routers. In fact, Windows NT may be running your switches and routers. It intends to be the intelligence in your hardware.

RRAS performs functions normally associated with a hardware router. Hardware is often made of steel. It is from these concepts that the term Steelhead was derived.

Hardware Routing

Normally, a waveform arrives at your network interface card (NIC) and the hardware/firmware in the NIC converts this signal into a bunch of bits. The bits are then organized into frames. The frames are usually then sent up to some software in the bridge/switch/router/computer and interpreted. It's not just one piece of software that processes the frames—

in a router there are often several pieces of software involved, such as a NIC driver, an NDIS wrapper, some glue code, and eventually a network protocol such as IP.

Let's stop at this point and tell you that software is slow.

Continuing with the example, the IP software looks at the datagram and decides where this datagram should go next. It selects an interface and sends the datagram through NDIS to the NIC driver software. This software sends the datagram to the NIC. The software/firmware/hardware on the NIC sends this datagram out toward the next router where all of this happens again.

The new routing architecture for Windows NT can short-circuit the above process. NICs are being developed that have the capability to support a small routing table in them. The NT operating system kernel, which normally manages all of the NIC driver, NDIS, and IP functions could delegate a part of the overall routing table to each of these new intelligent NICs. The NICs may now detect datagrams which their routing tables indicate should go to each other, and forward them across the system bus without being slowed down by the CPU or operating system software. In this case, this is an operating system that knows how to negotiate and when to get out of the way. This is hardware routing in Windows NT with Steelhead.

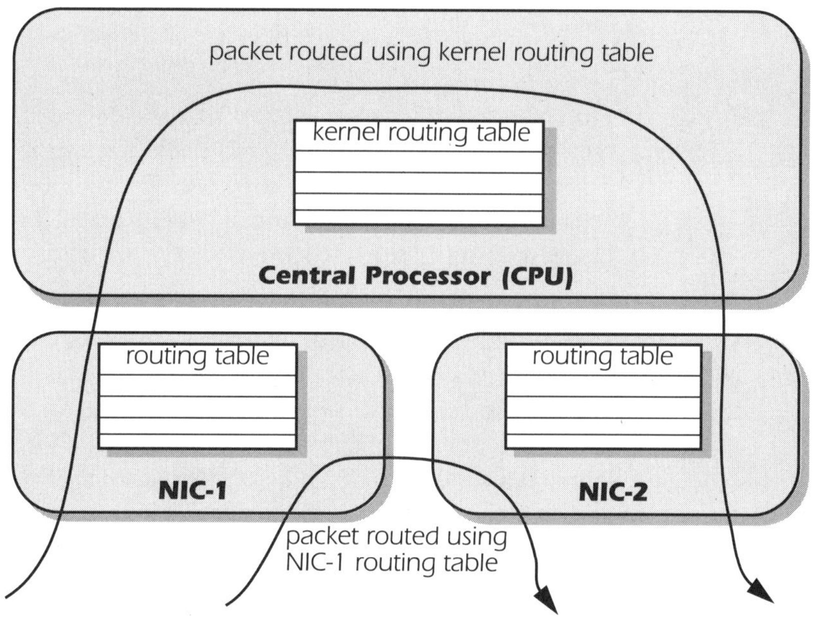

Figure 8.1
The routing table is split into multiple tables. The NICs here each have a routing table, and the kernel has a routing table.

But it gets even better. The system bus could also become a bottleneck. To fix this problem, more than one port could be supported on a NIC. Steelhead is designed so that NICs may use their routing tables to forward between their own ports, thus not requiring packets to be sent on the system bus.

Figure 8.2
Each NIC may have more than one physical port (e.g. Ethernet port).

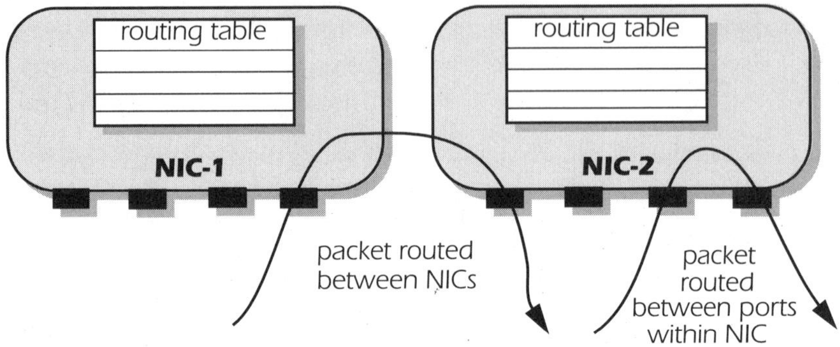

By using Steelhead, a vendor can build a router with one architecture and vary the cost of different models by plugging in more complex NICs without needing to change the software.

Kernel Routing Table

In the previous chapter, we saw that the NT ***route*** command can be used to view the current routing table. We'll see shortly that the RRAS Manager menu item *View IP Routing Table* may be used to show the routes currently known by Steelhead. Steelhead also adds yet another way to view routing tables — the ***kernrout*** command.

Kernrout displays the routing table in a format somewhat closer to how the actual table exists in the NT kernel than what the ***route*** command shows. ***Kernrout*** is used to manage the "kernel portion" of the routing table. The hardware portions of the routing table reside in the NICs. Since we are running with "unintelligent" NICs, the complete routing table is in the kernel. Therefore, the ***kernrout*** output contains the same information as the ***route*** output.

Figure 8.3 shows an example output of the ***kernrout print*** command. This command was executed on ENG_RTR, and so it will contain the same entries as shown Figure 7.36 back in Chapter 7.

```
cmd

C:\WINNT>kernrout print

IP STACK ROUTE TABLE
--------------------

Destination          Mask                 NextHop           I/f   Metric   Protocol
===================================================================================
10.1.2.0             255.255.255.0        10.1.2.1          2       1         2
10.1.2.1             255.255.255.255      127.0.0.1         1       1         2
10.1.3.0             255.255.255.0        10.1.3.1          3       1         2
10.1.3.1             255.255.255.255      127.0.0.1         1       1         2
10.1.4.0             255.255.255.0        10.1.2.2          2       3         8
10.255.255.255       255.255.255.255      10.1.2.1          2       1         2
127.0.0.0            255.0.0.0            127.0.0.1         1       1         2
224.0.0.0            224.0.0.0            10.1.2.1          2       1         2
224.0.0.0            224.0.0.0            10.1.3.1          3       1         2
255.255.255.255      255.255.255.255      10.1.2.1          2       1         2
===================================================================================
```

Figure 8.3 The routing table on ENG_RTR.

Notice that there are both host routes and subnet routes in this table. For instance, the route to destination 10.1.3.1 is explicit for all 32 bits because the mask specifies all 32 bits, thus it is called a host route. On the other hand, the route to destination 10.1.3.0 doesn't identify just one host, but with the mask of 24 bits on and eight bits off (255.255.255.0), it specifies a subnet.

The first host route (10.1.2.1) is for the IP address bound to one of the Ethernet interfaces (interface 2) of the router, but the route specifies to send to interface 1 (the loopback interface). Similarly, the route to 10.1.3.1 (interface 3) uses the loopback interface as well, thus it is another address bound to this machine.

Another interesting aspect of this routing table is that there are two entries to the 224.0.0.0 network, which is a class D address (i.e. multicast). One of the routes is for the first Ethernet interface (2), and the second route is for the second Ethernet interface (3). This means that multicast addresses will be sent out both of those interfaces.

The right-most column in Figure 8.3 lists the protocol associated with this route. This is not the same as the protocol shown in the RRAS Manager routing table display (Figure 8.29). For ***kernrout***, we have the value 2, which identifies the address family for IP.

Notice that the interface (I/f) column of the ***kernrout*** output is displayed as a number rather than an IP address bound to the interface. Table 8.1 describes each interface for this example:

Table 8.1
Kernrout Interface numbers and associated interface.

Interface index	Interface description
1	loopback interface (address 127.0.0.1)
2	the first Ethernet interface (address 10.1.2.1)
3	the second Ethernet interface (address 10.1.3.1)

At first glance, it may be a difficult task to associate interface numbers with the actual interface. But to make this task simpler, remember two things:

- The loopback interface is always interface #1.
- The interface number of 2 and above directly corresponds to the order which interfaces are listed in the output of ***ipconfig***. The first interface listed in the output of ***ipconfig*** is interface number 2, the next is interface number 3, and so on.[1]

The options to ***kernrout*** are shown in Table 8.2.

Table 8.2
Windows NT kernrout command options.

Option	Description
add <destination> <mask> <NextHop> <interface #> <metric>	Adds a route.
delete <destination> <mask> <NextHop> <Interface #>	Deletes a route.
exists <destination> [mask]	Checks to see if a route to that destination exists in the routing table. If a mask is given, checks for existence of destination and mask combination.
print	Displays the routing table.

1. The interface numbers also coincide with the interface index used by SNMP

IP Routing Protocols Supported by RRAS

RRAS supports the following protocols for dynamically updating routing tables within a network:

- RIP versions 1 and 2
- OSPF

Version 1 of RIP was discussed in the previous chapter. Although RIPv1 is popular, it places an excessive load on a network for the amount of work it does.

Version 2 of RIP *(RIPv2)* improves on RIP by allowing the administrator to reduce the amount of traffic generated by configuring the announcement timer. Further, RIPv2 provides additional information in its messages for updating the routing tables while retaining message compatibility with the older RIP.

The *Open* version of the *Shortest Path First (OSPF)* routing algorithm goes even further than RIPv2 at improving the benefit per cost ratio of dynamic routing table updates. OSPF operation is beyond the scope of this book. For a good reference on OSPF, refer to [Huitema1995].

RIPv2 Improvements Upon RIPv1

RIPv2 improves upon RIPv1 in many ways. The following is a list of the features of RIPv2.

- RIPv2 extends the format of RIPv1 messages in a compatible way so that RIPv1 and RIPv2 may interoperate.
- Unsolicited RIPv2 messages are sent every 30 seconds by default, but is configurable.
- RIPv2 may send its unsolicited messages by broadcast, or by multicast (uses the multicast address 224.0.0.9).

- Messages may be sent in unicast fashion to a list of neighbors.
- The lifetime of routes learned by RIP will expire after a configurable amount of time.
- RIPv2 messages may contain a password, which could be used by the receiving router to authenticate the sender. This is only slightly more secure than RIPv1, as is discussed on page 316.
- RIPv2 messages can be sent to and accepted from only a select list of routers.
- Both RIPv2 and RIPv1 can be configured to use split horizon and poison reverse to quicken routing table convergence time.
- RIPv2 passes subnet mask information, so it supports variable width subnet masking.

RIPv2 messages are sent to and from UDP port 520 (the same as RIPv1).

RIPv2 Operation

The basic operation of RIPv2 is similar to the operation of RIPv1, however there are a few differences. In this section, we'll examine the format of the RIPv2 messages, and explain how RIP builds its routing table from RIP advertisements.

What Do RIPv2 Messages Look Like?

As we've seen in the previous chapter, there may be more than one route advertised per RIP message. The message format used in RIPv2 is an extension of that used in RIPv1. Let's look in a little more detail at the layout of RIPv2 messages.

Each RIPv2 message begins with a RIPv2 header, as shown in Figure 8.4.

Figure 8.4
RIPv2 message header.

bits 0-3	bits 4-7	bits 8-11	bits 12-15	bits 16-19	bits 20-23	bits 24-27	bits 28-31
Command		Version		Routing Domain			

The RIP message header is 32-bits long and specifies three fields. The first field is the first octet of the header and holds a command code. The command code specifies if the message is a request (1) or response (2). Most RIP messages are actually unsolicited responses. The next field is the version number, transmitted as an octet. RIP version 2 is described here. The remaining 16 bits of the 32-bit header represent the *routing domain.* In RIPv1, the two octets now occupied by the routing domain field were reserved as zeros, thus for compatibility, the default value for the routing domain is zero.

Response messages may carry up to 25 route advertisements in RIPv1[2]. The same is true in RIPv2 except when the advertisements are authenticated. The authentication header, shown in Figure 8.5, is the same size as a route advertisement, thus 24 authenticated advertisements may be carried in a single RIPv2 message.

Figure 8.5
RIPv2 authentication header.

bits 0-3	bits 4-7	bits 8-11	bits 12-15	bits 16-19	bits 20-23	bits 24-27	bits 28-31
Authentication Mark				Authentication Type			
Password (16 octets)							

The *authentication mark* has a value of FFFF (hex) which differentiates the authentication from a router advertisement. Next is the *authentication type,* which currently must have a value of 1 to indicate *password authentication.* The remainder of the authentication header (16 octets) is a left-aligned null padded clear-text *password.* The function of the authentication header is discussed in the interface configuration section.

2. Each route advertisement is 20 octets, thus the length of the maximum group of advertisements (25) is 500. Including the RIP header (4 octets) this totals 504 octets. With a UDP header (8 octets) we're up to 512 octets. This is a nice round number which fits in the default MTU IP datagram.

If a router has more than the full complement of routes to advertise, it may send multiple RIP response messages, each with up to the full complement of routes. Each route advertisement is five 32-bit words in length, as shown in Figure 8.6.

Figure 8.6
RIPv2 advertisement layout.

bits 0-3	bits 4-7	bits 8-11	bits 12-15	bits 16-19	bits 20-23	bits 24-27	bits 28-31
Family				Route Tag			
Address							
Subnet Mask							
Next Hop Address							
Metric							

Each advertisement specifies one route. The following information is included:

- the address family of the network route being advertised
- the route tag
- the network address of the route
- the subnet mask for that route
- the next hop address for the route
- a weighting metric associated with the route

The *address family* is specified because RIP was designed to be able to advertise routes for many different protocols. IP is address family 2.

route tag: used to identify the router the advertised network is physically attached to.

The second field is a *route tag*, which way be used to indicate the way in which the route was learned. For instance, a router speaking RIPv2, BGP, and OSPF with different networks may tag routes learned from each kind of protocol or area with a different number.

Next comes the *network address* which is an IP subnet or network address which is being advertised.

The *subnet mask* associated with the network address is specified in RIPv2 advertisements so that the constant-width subnet masking restriction associated with RIPv1 is lifted. In other words, RIPv2 supports use of variable-width subnet masking.

RIPv2 also includes a *next-hop address* in its advertisements. This allows proxy reporting of routing information. An address of 0.0.0.0 in this field uses the default behavior of RIPv1. In this case, RIPv2 uses the source IP address of the advertisement as the next hop address.

The *metric* specifies a weight for the route, which specifies a hop count to the network for most uses of RIP. This value may be between one and fifteen in normal advertisements. The value of sixteen is used to specify an infinite hop count, thus an unreachable network. The metric is supposed to have a value of 1 for directly connected networks.

What does a whole RIPv2 message look like? Recall that in the example in the previous chapter with RIPv1, there were two routes advertised. Figure 8.7 shows the message format for a RIPv2 message with the header and two advertisements.

Figure 8.7
Example of RIPv2 header with two advertisements.

bits 0-3	bits 4-7	bits 8-11	bits 12-15	bits 16-19	bits 20-23	bits 24-27	bits 28-31
Command		Version		Routing Domain			
Family #1				Route Tag #1			
Address #1							
Subnet Mask #1							
Next Hop Address #1							
Metric #1							
Family #2				Route Tag #2			
Address #2							
Subnet Mask #2							
Next Hop Address #2							
Metric #2							

How Does RIPv2 Construct a Route From an Advertisement?

Like RIPv1, RIPv2 also uses the information in advertisements to construct routing table entries. Consider the different pieces of information in an advertisement, and those in a routing table entry.

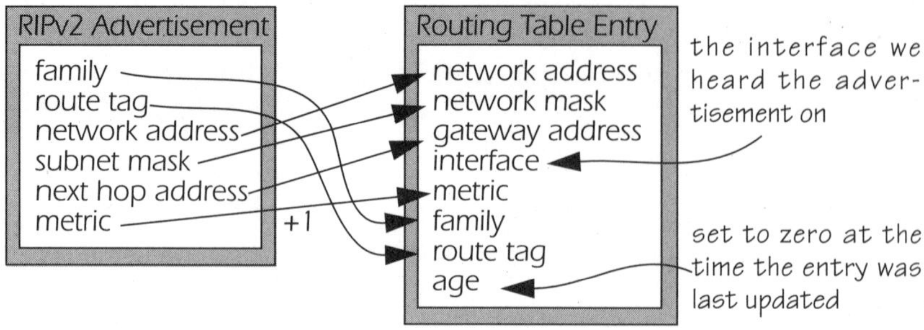

Figure 8.8 Correlation between routing table entry and a RIPv2 advertisement.

The elements of a routing table entry are derived from several sources. The sources are shown graphically in Figure 8.8, and in table form in Table 8.3.

Table 8.3 How routing table entries are derived from RIPv2 messages.

Source	Routing table parameter
network address field in the RIP message	network address
netmask field in the RIP message	netmask
next host field in the RIP message, or if that is 0.0.0.0, from the source IP address of RIP message	gateway address
IP address of receiving interface	interface
calculated from metric field in RIP message	metric
address family field in the RIP message	family
route tag field in the RIP message	route tag
set to zero when this entry is initially learned or whenever it is updated (used for expiration timeout)	age

When an advertisement is received, RIPv2 knows that the metric specified is the hop count used by whomever sent the advertisement. Because that advertiser is one hop away from the receiver, the effective hop count for the receiver is one greater than the metric value in the advertisement.

RIPv2 checks to see if there is already a routing table entry with the same network address as the advertisement. If there is already an entry, RIPv2 will compare the current metric in the routing table entry with the effective (i.e. +1) metric of the advertisement. If the advertisement's effective metric is not better than the one in the current routing table entry, the advertisement is ignored. Otherwise the routing table entry is updated with the information from the advertisement.

If the effective metric advertised is greater than or equal to 16, the network is considered unreachable via the advertised route.

Installing RRAS

Obtain the file mpri386.exe[3] from either the Microsoft web site or an RRAS distribution CD. Executing it will uncompress its contents to a directory you specify, as shown in Figure 8.9.

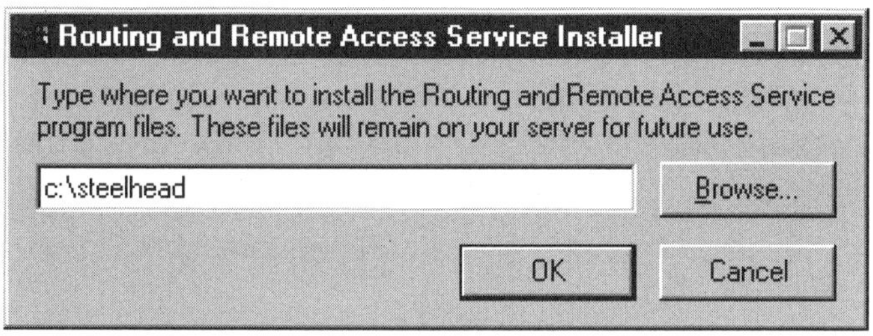

Figure 8.9 Specify where you want Steelhead installed.

Once the files are expanded into the directory you specified, you can proceed with the installation or abort, as shown in Figure 8.10.

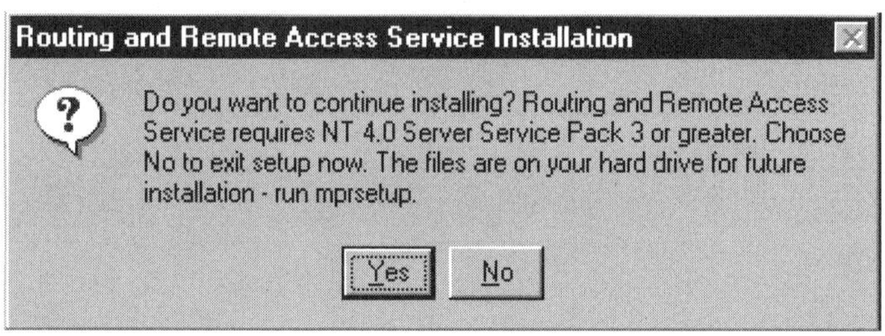

Figure 8.10 Once the files have been uncompressed, you may defer installation.

If you quit at this point, you may begin installation again by using the command ***mprsetup.exe <dirname>*** where dirname is the directory where the files were uncompressed.

3. Note that with respect to RRAS, the name mpri386 refers to the Multiple Protocol Router (MPR) for the Intel 386 (et al) platform. Microsoft also uses the acronym MPR to specify the Multiple Provider Router as described in the Windows NT Networking chapter. The two are very different things.

The RRAS installer checks to see if there are conflicting services installed on this computer. A dialog such as that shown in Figure 8.11 displays a list of the conflicting services — those which perform similar functions to RRAS. Those services must be removed before installing RRAS.

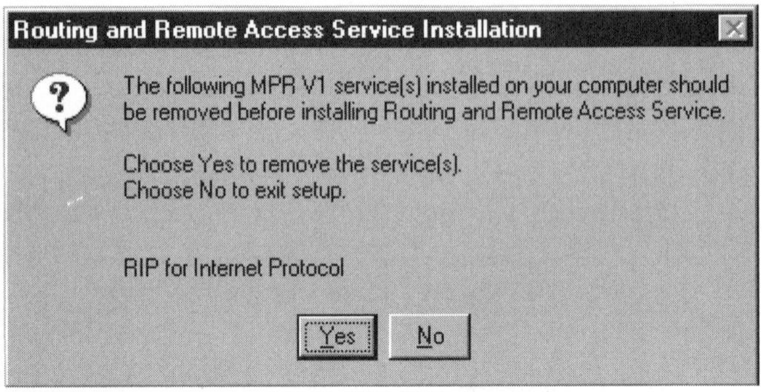

Figure 8.11 RRAS installation may automatically remove conflicting services, yet it first asks for your confirmation.

RRAS installation allows you to choose the components to install (Figure 8.12). The LAN routing option includes the ability to run RIP.

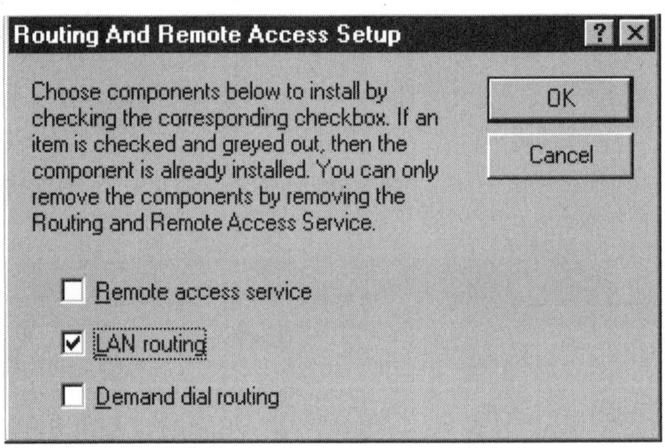

Figure 8.12 RRAS can be installed in three pieces: RAS, LAN routing, and Demand dial routing.

RRAS Manager

RRAS Manager is started from *Programs -> Admin Tools -> Routing and RAS Admin.* Figure 8.13 shows the main screen for the RRAS Manager.

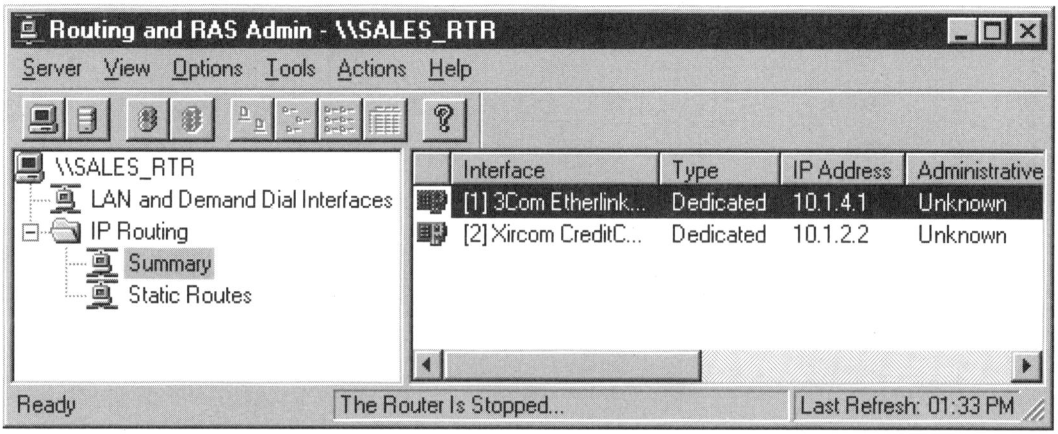

Figure 8.13 RRAS Manager is used to control and configure the router.

Notice that under the IP routing summary, we have two NICs installed, a 3Com Ethernet card, and a Xircom Ethernet card. This is a screen from the SALES_RTR, which has interfaces on the sales subnet (10.1.4.0) and the company backbone (10.1.2.0).

Installing and Configuring RIPv2

Once RRAS is installed, you can select which routing protocols you want to operate on the router interfaces. Of the three IP routing protocols available, you should choose the protocol that is compatible with the other routers. If the other routers are using OSPF, install OSPF on your NT router. If the other routers are using RIPv1, install and use the protocol called "RIPv2", but configure it to only send and receive RIPv1 messages. The remainder of this chapter will discuss how to configure Steelhead's RIP to operate for both RIPv1 and RIPv2 packet formats.

The following steps are used to install and configure RIPv2.

1. Install RIPv2 software.
2. Configure RIPv2 parameters.
3. Select the interfaces to use RIPv2.
4. Start the router.

Installing RIP

RIP is installed using RRAS Manager. A new protocol is added using the menu item *Actions->Select Routing Protocol.* The *Select Routing Protocol* dialog (Figure 8.14) gives a list of routing protocols that can be installed. Installing the RIP software only requires selecting *RIP version2 for Internet Protocol* from the list and pressing ok.

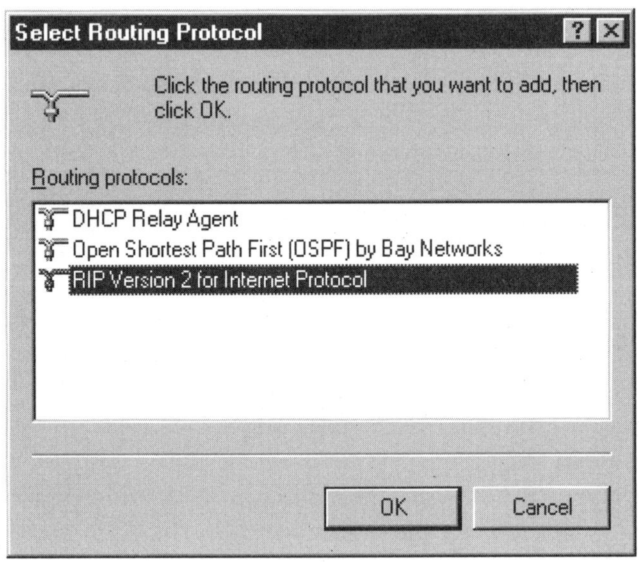

Figure 8.14
Select the routing protocol to install.

Configuring RIP

Once the RIP software is installed, it must be configured. The configuration dialog presents itself once the installation of RIP is complete. If you want to reconfigure RIP later, simply select *RIP for Internet Protocol* under *IP Routing* in RRAS Manager and use the pop-up menu (e.g. right-click) to select *Configure RIP*.

The *General tab* of the *RIP for Internet Protocol Configuration* dialog is shown in Figure 8.15.

Figure 8.15 The general configuration for RIPv2 is shown here.

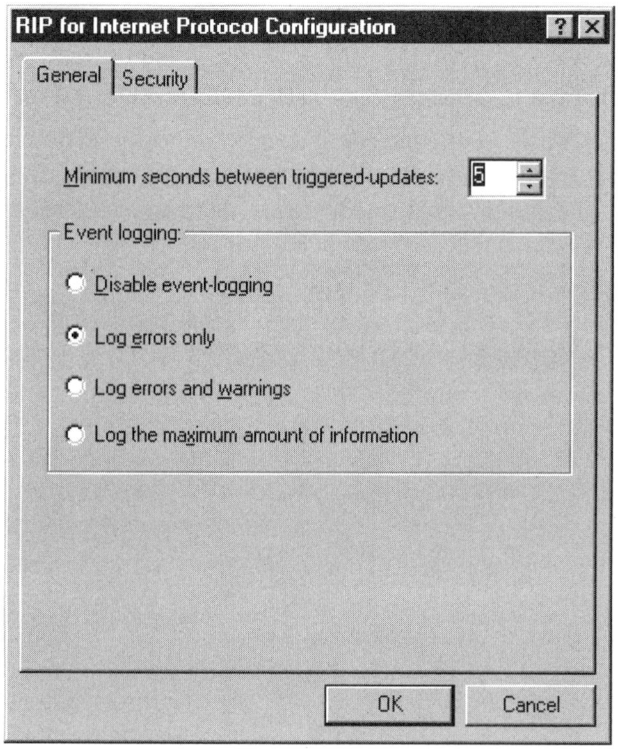

triggered update: a routing protocol message sent as a result of a change in the network configuration.

One of the goals of a routing protocol is to inform other routers when there is a change in the network configuration. This change could be caused by a failed router or a failed link. When a failure does occur, a feature called **triggered update** will cause RIP to send the "bad news" nearly immediately rather than waiting for the next scheduled update. This improves convergence time.

There could be a problem, however, if a router's interface oscillates between states of "up" and "down." In that case, multiple triggered updates would be sent, creating a tidal wave of updates as the information is sent from one router to the next. In order to temper RIP's desire to act quickly, there is a mandatory minimum delay between *any two* triggered updates. Figure 8.15 shows a the triggered update delay is set to a minimum time interval of five seconds, which is recommended.

During operation, RIP may detect many events which it thinks are worth reporting. The degree of event logging which RIPv2 will write to the system log files is configurable to four levels (Figure 8.15.) The default level is to log errors only.

RIPv2 Security Configuration

The screen used to configure this security is shown in Figure 8.16. The default behavior is to process all advertisements received.

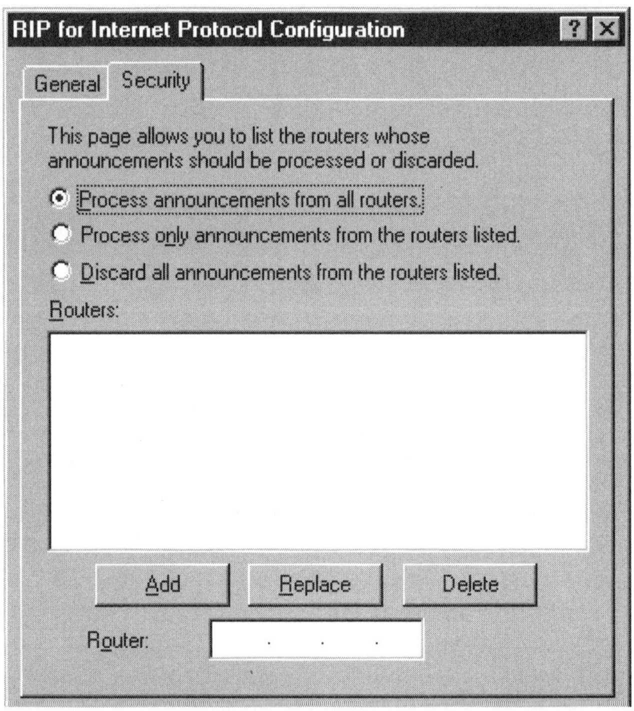

Figure 8.16
RIPv2 has several security features which you may configure here.

Optionally, you may supply a list of IP addresses of routers from which RIPv2 will accept advertisements. RIPv2 messages from all other routers will be ignored. Simply enter an IP address in the entry box toward the bottom of the dialog and press the *Add* button. Repeat this process with the IP address of each additional router from which this one should accept advertisements. Select the *Process only announcements from the routers listed* option.

Alternately, by selecting the *Discard all announcements from the routers listed* option, RIPv2 will instead use the list of routers you supply to specifically ignore messages from those routers, but accept messages from all other routers.

There are several ways in which these two options could be used together in a collection of routers. Two ways discussed below are:

- misconfigured router sending bogus information
- shared network between separately managed organizations

Consider what happens when a hacker (or berserk router) generates RIP messages advertising cheap (e.g. hop count metric = 1) routes to all of your sensitive networks, such as your finance, human resources, and engineering departments. Normally, the RIP software in the departmental routers would accept these advertisements and change their routing tables to send all traffic to the new cheap "router." That machine could either simply absorb all of the information, or forward it to other routers.

Using this security screen, you may restrict the advertisements to which RIPv2 will pay attention and thus use to update its routing tables. This allows you to deter problems which may be caused by such simple attacks (or accidents).

Routing Domains

routing domain: a group of routers that all share routing information

The second way the screen in Figure 8.16 can be used is to create separate **routing domains**. With separate routing domains, routing information is not distributed outside the domain.

Consider an example where five routers are connected to a common backbone (Figure 8.17). The common backbone is shared by two separate organizations, yet the routing information is not shared. The organization operating routers A and C has a separate routing domain (called the "left routing domain") than the organization operating routers B and D ("right routing domain").

The routers are configured as follows:

- Routers B and D are set up to *only process advertisements from each other.*
- Routers A and C are set up to i*gnore advertisements from routers B and D.*

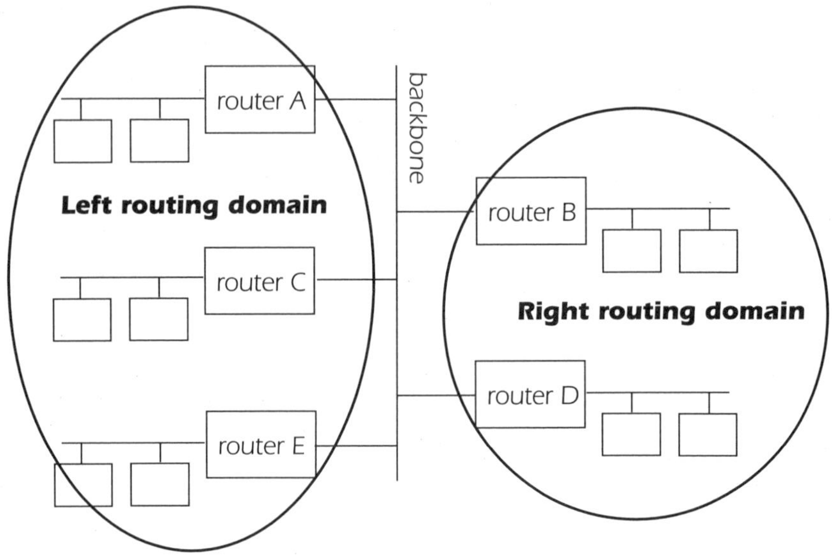

Figure 8.17 The router security options could be used to create distinct routing domains.

Now assume that the organization operating A and C adds another router E. Router E could be configured with either kind of restriction to keep the routing domains separate. But consider the following:

- If E is set up to *only process advertisements from A and C,* when another router is added to the left routing domain, further configuration will be required.
- If E is set up to *explicitly ignore advertisements from B and D,* when another router is added to the right routing domain, further configuration is still required.

Therefore, there is no correct answer for which method to choose. You must determine which routing domain is less likely to expand, and select the configuration option appropriately.

Interface Configuration

After RIPv2 is installed, there are no interfaces initially configured, as shown in Figure 8.18, thus it is effectively inactive.

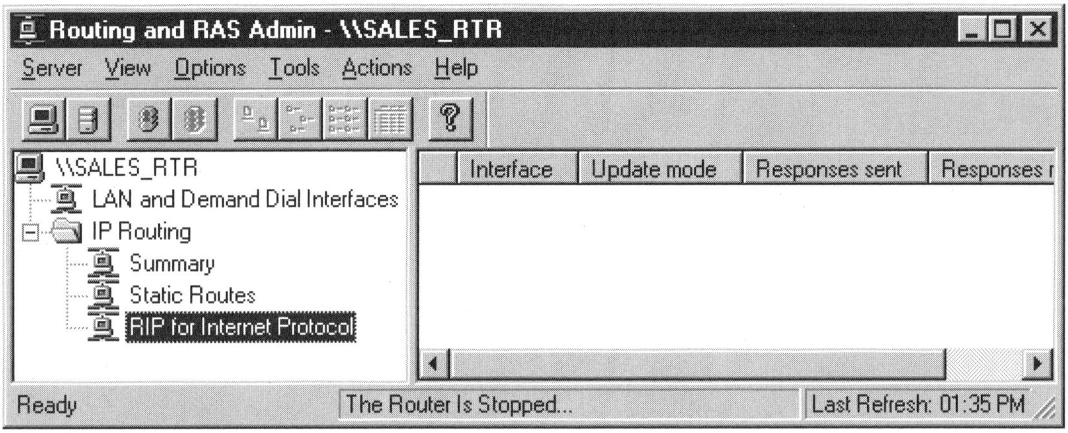

Figure 8.18 RIPv2 has not yet been configured to use any interfaces.

You need to select the interfaces that will use RIPv2. Right-click on *RIP for Internet Protocol,* and select *Add Interface* from the pop-up menu. The *Select Interface for RIP Version 2 for Internet Protocol* dialog will appear (Figure 8.19.) After adding the interface, properties of that interface will need to be configured.

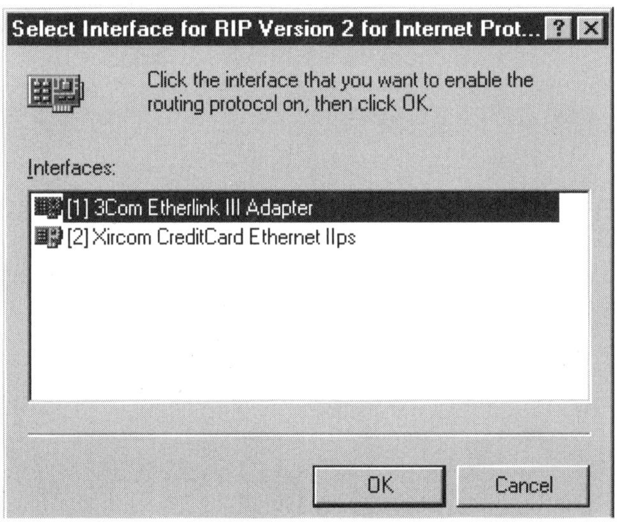

Figure 8.19 RIPv2 will be enabled on each interface you configure.

Interface Properties

Each interface used by RIPv2 may have independent configuration properties. The *RIP Configuration - Interface* screen will be used to configure each interface for RIP-specific parameters. The four areas of configuration are represented by the 4 tabs at the top of the screen, as shown in Figure 8.20.

Figure 8.20 Four configuration areas for RIP properties.

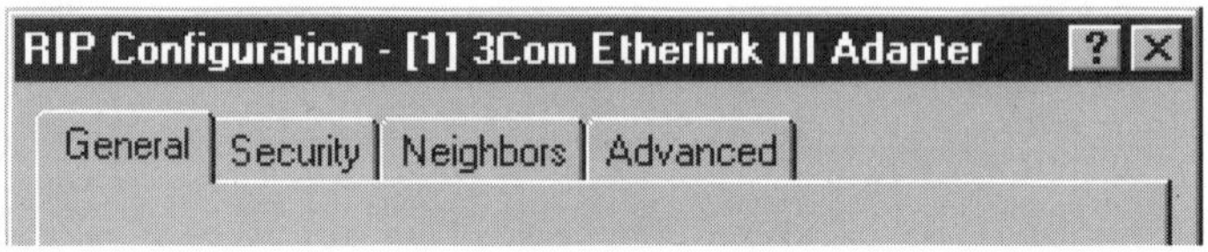

Each of these areas will be discussed in the next few pages.

RIP Interface: General Tab

The *General tab* shown in Figure 8.21 allows customization of the RIP messages used on this particular interface.

- The *operation mode* of the interface may be set to the RIPv1 behavior of *periodic update mode*, and is selected as the default for LAN interfaces. Alternately, *auto-static update*[4] mode may be selected. This mode ignores unsolicited routing advertisements and does not generate advertisements. It will however issue a RIPv2 routing request message and use the response to establish a static route. This mode is the default for demand-dial interfaces.

4. The selection of auto-static mode is not the same as selecting silent RIP (outgoing) and the ignore incoming packets options

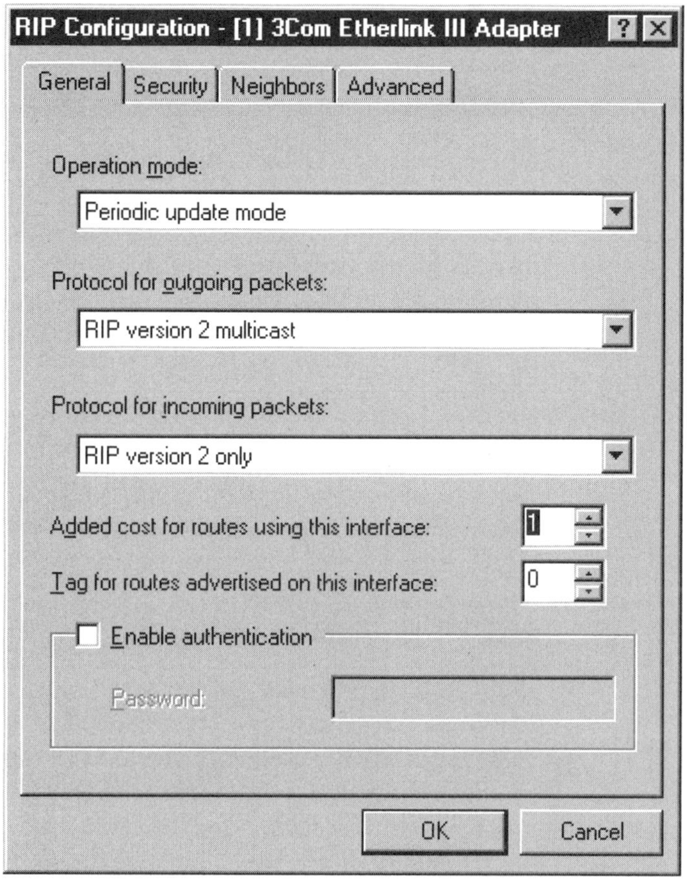

Figure 8.21 The general interface configuration options are selected here.

- The possible choices for *protocol for outgoing packets* are:
    - *Silent RIP*— Disables RIP operation on this interface.
    - *RIPv1 broadcast* — RIP message in the version 1 packet format, sent as an IP broadcast. Use this option if you have RIPv1 routers in your network.
    - *RIPv2 broadcast* — RIP message in the version 2 packet format, sent as a broadcast.
    - *RIPv2 multicast*— Use of the multicast option will reduce the amount of processing on other non-router machines in the same network. The disadvantage is that RIPv1-only routers will not receive these messages because they do not subscribe to the 224.0.0.9 multicast group. This option should only be used in a network of all RIPv2 routers.

- The *protocol for incoming packets* may be selected. By default, RIPv1 and RIPv2 messages will be processed. Alternate selections may be made to accept only one version or the other. The fourth option is to *ignore incoming packets*.
- During normal RIP operation, the metric used specifies the number of hops to a destination using this route. Each router which uses a route necessarily adds one to the metric, and if that route is then forwarded in another advertisement, that already incremented value is advertised. A distance of 16 hops is considered an infinite (i.e. unreachable) distance. This restricts RIP to the ability to advertise routes of 15 hops.

  The *added cost for routes using this interface* parameter allows you to break this whole philosophy, yet may be used in small networks to add a carefully crafted facsimile of *route cost*. The value of this parameter is added to routes received on this interface before entering them into the routing table. The default for this parameter is 1. Larger values may be specified to synthetically force RIPv2 to favor other lower hop-count (now faux cost) routes.
- RIPv2 advertisements specify a **route tag** with each route. A route tag is used to identify the router the advertised network is physically attached to. Therefore if you are using route tags, all routers within a routing domain should have a unique route tag. By default, the value is zero, but the *tag for routes advertised on this interface* parameter allows other values to be specified.
- RIPv2 may perform authentication. When the *enable authentication* parameter is checked, the *password*[5] supplied (up to 16 characters) will be published in all RIPv2 advertisement messages out this interface. Also, each RIPv2 message received on this interface must contain this password in order to be processed.

  For example, if three routers A, B, and C as shown in Figure 8.22 are configured to use RIPv2 with authentication, then the passwords must match for each interface pair.

---

5. The password is not encrypted! Thus RIPv2 is only slightly more secure than v1. If someone has connected a RIP router (or something that pretends it is) to your network, they are probably able to connect a protocol analyzer and see your RIPv2 password. In other words, this password may only protect against accidental, not intentional, attacks.

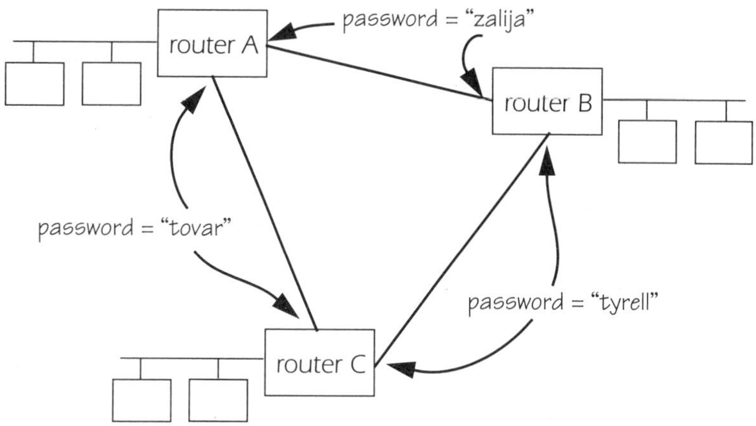

Figure 8.22 The interface authentication password is configured per interface but must match at both ends.

RIP Interface: Security Tab

The *Security tab* is shown in Figure 8.23. The box at the very top of the window has two options that have independent configuration parameters. The first selection displays and allows you to control security applied *when accepting routes* on this interface. The second selection allows configuration of rules applied *when announcing routes* out this interface.

For either direction, you specify one of the following router actions:

- Process all routes.
- Process only advertisements for routes which match the list of address ranges.
- Process all advertisements except for routes which match the list of address ranges.

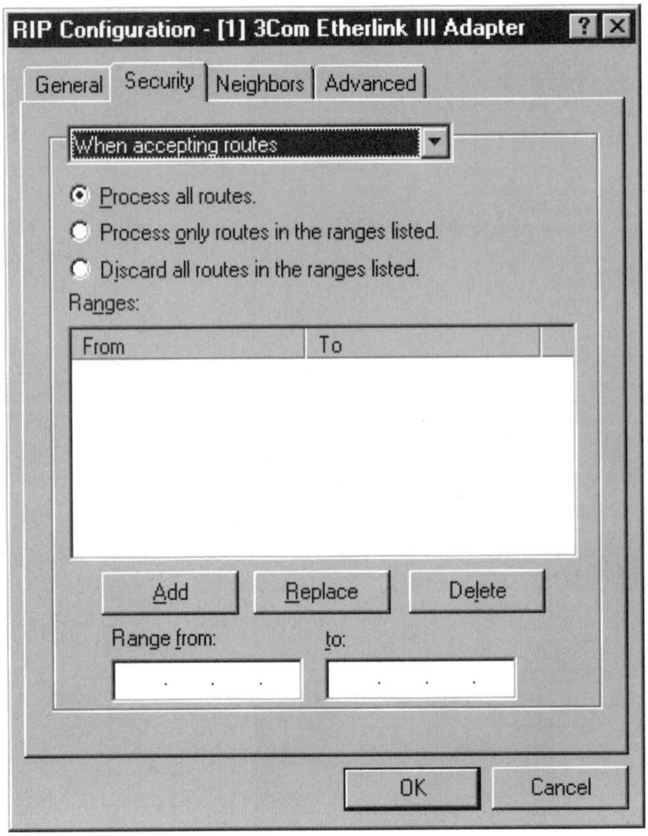

Figure 8.23 The security properties for this interface may be configured here.

RIP Interface: Neighbors Tab

neighbor: a router that RIP information is exchanged with.

With RIPv1, advertisements are sent in unsolicited response messages as broadcasts. RIPv2 allows these messages to be sent to the RIPv2 multicast address (224.0.0.9). The *Neighbors tab* (Figure 8.24) allows greater control as to which routers will receive the RIP messages.

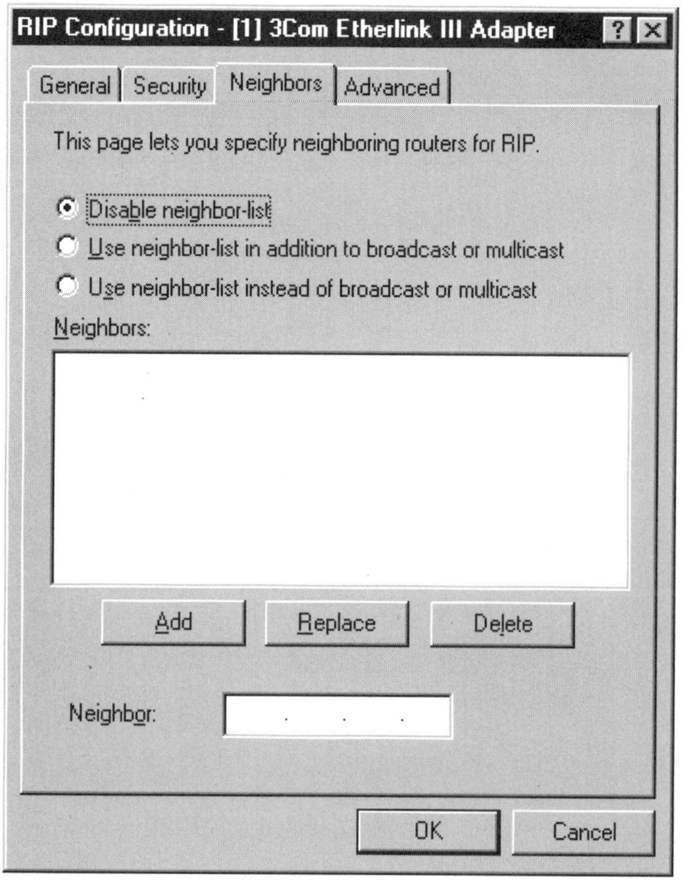

Figure 8.24
RIPv2 may use a list of neighbors in addition to or rather than broadcasts.

This is especially useful when some of your routers don't support filtering based on the source of the advertisement as Steelhead does (refer back to Figure 8.16). It is also useful when the routers which should be advertised to are either:

- Not on a broadcast network.
- Not on the same segment.

Through this configuration dialog you may establish a list of neighbors which may be advertised out this interface. The three styles of neighbor advertisements are as follows:

- Don't use the list of neighbors. Simply send via broadcast or multicast as otherwise configured.

- Use the list of neighbors for sending unicast advertisements as well as the normal broadcast/multicast advertisements for greater coverage.
- Restrict advertisements sent out this interface to only be unicast communication to the neighbors in the list.

The IP addresses of the neighbors are specified by entering them one by one in the box toward the bottom of the dialog and using the *Add* button for each.

This sort of list may be useful when non-RIP routers are involved in a network. For example, see Figure 8.25.

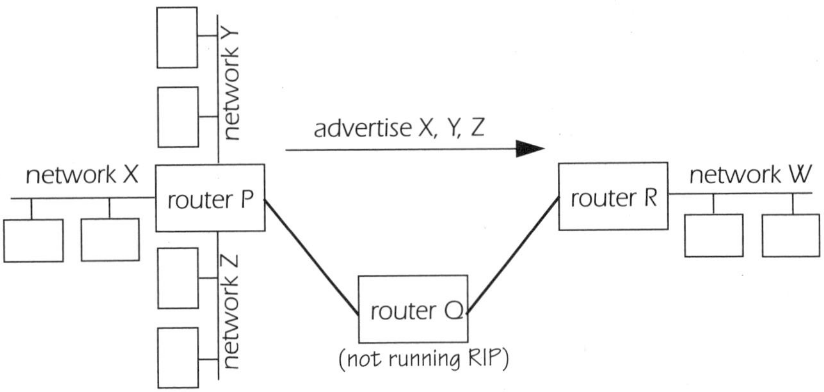

Figure 8.25
The neighbor list may be used to allow advertisements to traverse a non-RIP router.

Assume that router Q is fast but not all that intelligent — it doesn't run RIPv2[6]. It has static routes, which means low (i.e. none) overhead in communicating routing information, and that's sometimes a good idea for security reasons as well. Routers P and R are running Steelhead.

So that routers P and R don't have to follow the least common denominator and be configured with static routes, they may use neighbor lists. For instance, we could configure router P with a neighbor list to send advertisements to router R. Because Q would block broadcasts and would not accept and re-advertise RIP messages, we need to send the advertisements through it using a unicast address as the destination IP address.

6. Actually, some people would say that router Q not running RIPv2 is a sign of its intelligence. :-)

RIP Interface: Advanced Tab

There are several additional parameters in the *Advanced tab* of the *RIP Configuration* dialog as shown in Figure 8.26.

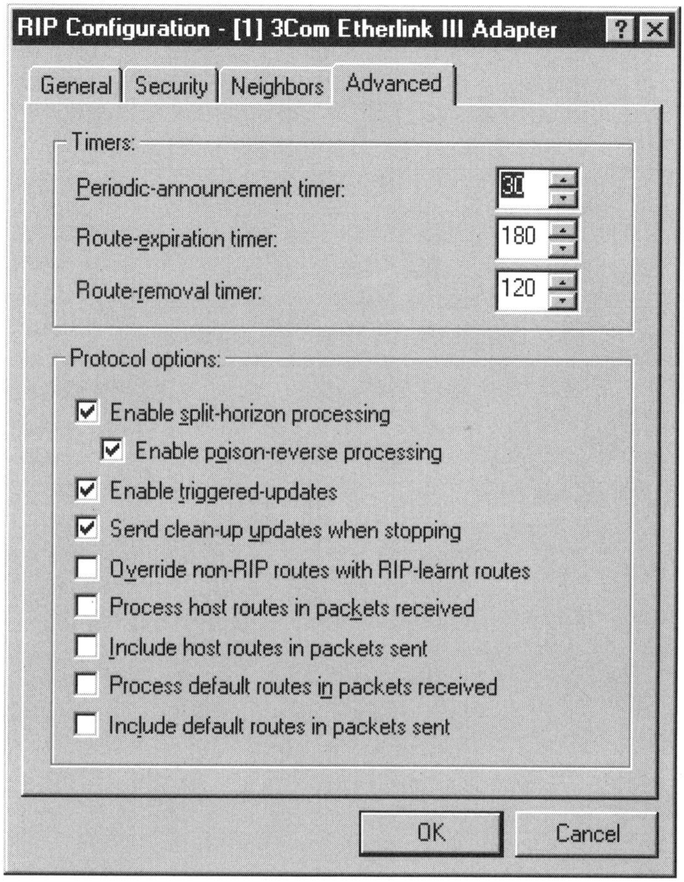

Figure 8.26
There a multiple RIP parameters that are set using Advanced tab of RIP interface configuration.

First, there are three timers which allow you to tune the operation of RIPv2.

- The *periodic announcement timer* parameter allows modification of the default 30-second unsolicited response interval. This parameter may be set from 15 to 86,400 seconds (1 day).

route expiration: when a learned route has not been refreshed by the advertising router after a certain amount of time.

- The *route expiration timer* parameter may be used to control the length of time that RIPv2 will allow a learned route to remain active in the routing table. This value may be set from 15 to 259,200 seconds (3 days). The default is 180 seconds (3 minutes).
- Once a route has expired, it may be marked as invalid but still exist in the routing table. The *route removal timer* may be configured independently of the route expiration timer parameter. After a router becomes expired, it takes a certain amount of time (route removal timer) before it is removed from the table. The default is 120 seconds.

Configuration of several *protocol options* is also available in this dialog:

- The options to *enable split-horizon processing* and to *enable poison-reverse processing* are used to control the behavior of these features as described in the section "Does RIP Always Advertise All Routes?" in the previous chapter.
- The parameter to *enable triggered updates* turns the feature by that name on or off as necessary. Triggered updates were described in the general RIPv2 configuration.
- If you ever shut down the router software, it may send RIPv2 advertisements with an infinite hop-count as the metric to instruct other routers to not use these routes. The parameter *clean-up updates when stopping* controls this behavior.
- Normally, routes which are not established in the routing table by RIP (e.g. static routes) will not be touched by RIP even when an advertisement received by RIP has a better metric. The parameter *override non-RIP routes with RIP-learnt routes* reverses this behavior.

host route: a route to a specific IP address (host). Contrast with network or subnet route.

- Host routes and default routes are not normally advertised nor processed on receipt. The parameters *process host routes in packets received,* and *include host routes in packets sent* reverse these behaviors for host routes. Similarly, the parameters *process default routes in packets received* and *include default routes in packets sent* reverse the behavior for default routes.

Starting the Router

Now that RIP is installed and the interfaces are configured, the router must be started. The status of the router is shown in the center of the bottom of the RRAS manager window (Figure 8.27).

To start the router, press the green stoplight icon in the icon bar. To stop the router press the red stoplight icon.

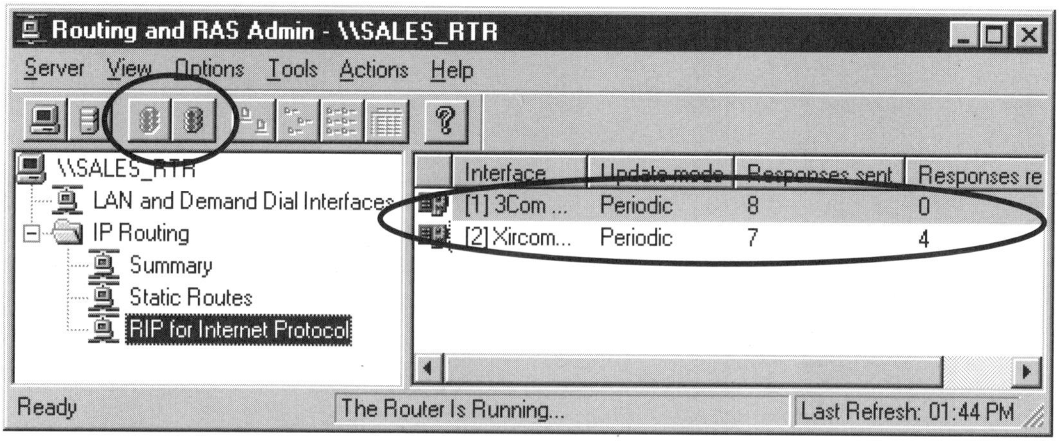

Figure 8.27 The router status is shown here.

One method to determine if RIP is operating properly is to view the RIP status, as shown in Figure 8.27. The responses sent and responses received columns will show increasing numbers if RIP is operating properly. (F5 can be used to refresh the screen, or auto refresh can be configured in the *Options* menu.)

Another way to determine if things are operating normally is to view the routing table. To view the routing table, highlight *Static Routes*, right click, and select *View IP routing table* as depicted in Figure 8.28.

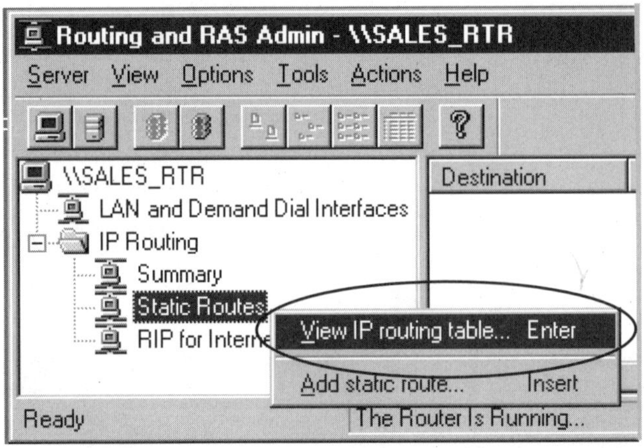

Figure 8.28 Use this pop-up menu item from the Static Routes item to view the routing table.

The routing table for SALES_RTR is shown Figure 8.29. Notice that it appears very similar to the routing table in the previous chapter.

IP routing table

Destination	Network mask	Gateway	Interface	Metric	Protocol
10.1.2.0	255.255.255.0	10.1.2.2	[2] Xircom CreditC...	1	Local
10.1.2.2	255.255.255.255	127.0.0.1	Internal Loopback ...	1	Local
10.1.3.0	255.255.255.0	10.1.2.1	[2] Xircom CreditC...	3	RIP
10.1.4.0	255.255.255.0	10.1.4.1	[1] 3Com Etherlink ...	1	Local
10.1.4.1	255.255.255.255	127.0.0.1	Internal Loopback ...	1	Local
10.255.255.255	255.255.255.255	10.1.2.2	[2] Xircom CreditC...	1	Local
10.255.255.255	255.255.255.255	10.1.4.1	[1] 3Com Etherlink ...	1	Local
127.0.0.0	255.0.0.0	127.0.0.1	Internal Loopback ...	1	Local
224.0.0.0	224.0.0.0	10.1.2.2	[2] Xircom CreditC...	1	Local
224.0.0.0	224.0.0.0	10.1.4.1	[1] 3Com Etherlink ...	1	Local
255.255.255.255	255.255.255.255	10.1.2.2	[2] Xircom CreditC...	1	Local
255.255.255.255	255.255.255.255	10.1.4.1	[1] 3Com Etherlink ...	1	Local

Ready

Figure 8.29 The routing table for SALES_RTR is displayed via RRAS Manager.

The columns shown in Figure 8.29 will be the same columns as shown in the ***route*** command output, with one exception. The last column, Protocol, lists the routing protocol that was used to obtain the associated network entry. In this example, one route was learned by RIP, for network 10.1.3.0.

RIP Version 2 Packet Captures

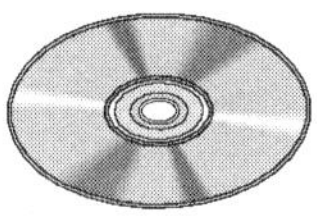

As was done in the previous chapter for RIPv1, these capture files and address database are stored on the CD with the names specified in Figure 8.30. Because this is the same network layout, the address database is the same.

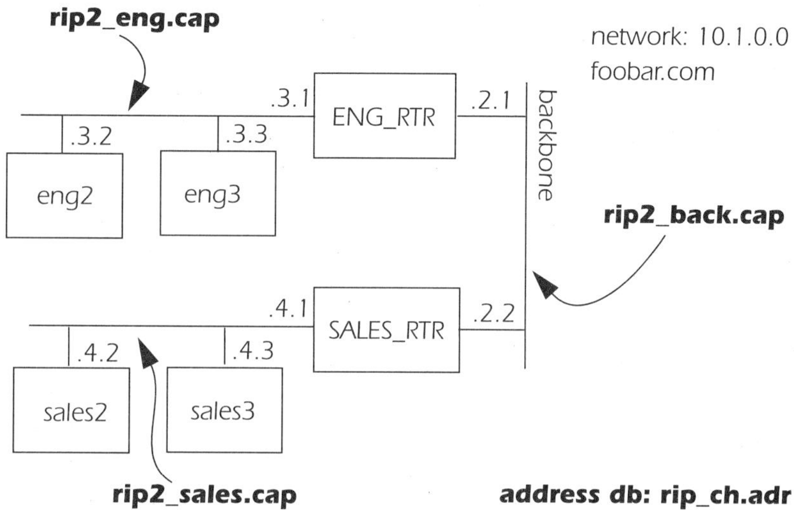

Figure 8.30
RIPv2 messages for each subnet have been captured and saved on the CD. An address database has also been saved.

But before we look at the packets, lets look at the router's routing tables after RIPv2 was made operational.

Refer back to the routing tables shown previously in this chapter:

- ENG_RTR — see Figure 8.3 on page 297.
- SALES_RTR — see Figure 8.29 on page 324.

RIPv2 Message from ENG_RTR onto Subnet 10.1.3.0

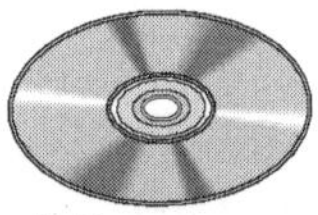

rip2_eng.cap

First, let's look at a RIPv2 message sent by ENG_RTR onto the engineering subnet as shown in Figure 8.31. The capture file rip2_eng.cap is highlighted in the figure. Also noteworthy is the IP destination address, 224.0.0.9, which is the RIPv2 multicast group address.

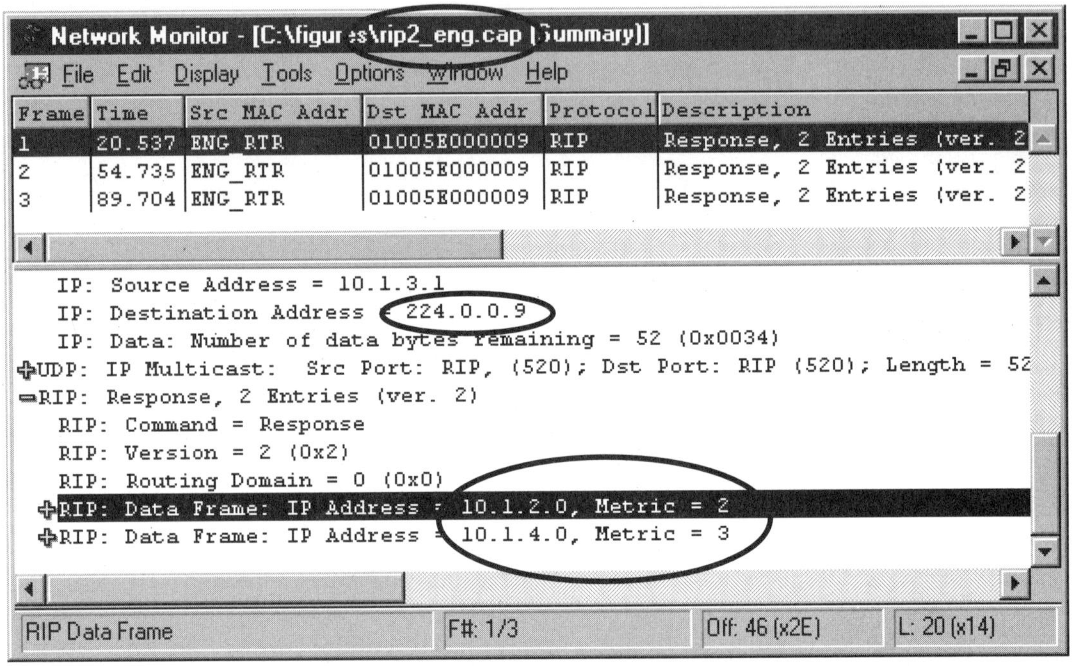

Figure 8.31 A RIPv2 message sent on the engineering subnet.

The two routes advertised are for 10.1.2.0 (backbone subnet) with a metric of 2 and to 10.1.4.0 (sales subnet) with a metric of 3. The metrics listed in the routing table in Figure 8.3 were 1 and 3, respectively. Intuitively, according to the specification for RIP, the backbone is one hop away, and the sales subnet is two hops away, and they should be advertised that way. This anomaly may cause problems with some network engineers, and with some network management software which assumes correct implementation.

RIPv2 Message from SALES_RTR onto Subnet 10.1.4.0

rip2_sales.cap

Next, we'll look at the RIPv2 message from the SALES_RTR onto the sales subnet shown in Figure 8.32. Note that this message is sent as a multicast to 224.0.0.9. The first route advertised is to the backbone 10.1.2.0 in 2 hops, while Figure 8.29 showed it being one hop from this router as we would expect. The second advertisement is for a route to the engineering subnet 10.1.3.0. The metric to the engineering subnet is 3 hops, which is the same as the number in the routing table in Figure 8.29. However, we would expect both values to be 2 — the number of hops to the engineering subnet.

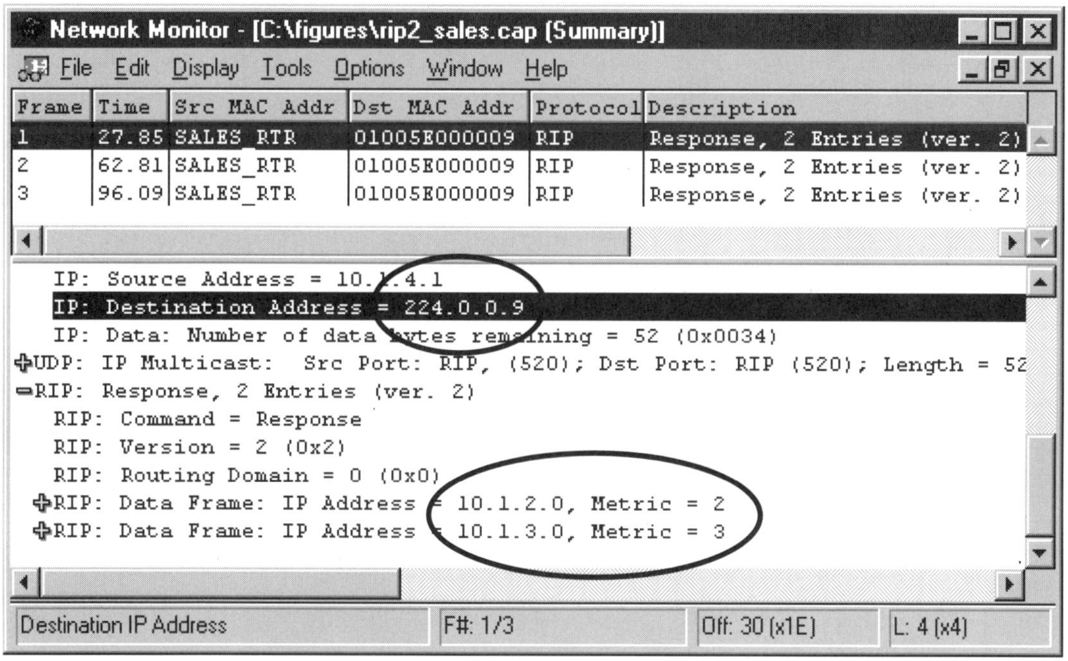

Figure 8.32 A RIPv2 message sent on the sales subnet.

RIPv2 Message from ENG_RTR onto Backbone

rip2_back.cap
frame #1

Each router sends RIPv2 messages onto the backbone subnet. The first message we'll look at is shown in Figure 8.33 from the ENG_RTR. The first advertisement is for the engineering subnet with a metric of two, although the routing table and our intuition tell us it should be one. The second advertisement is a poison reverse of the route to the sales subnet 10.1.4.0 which ENG_RTR has in its table with cost 3, yet advertises at 16.

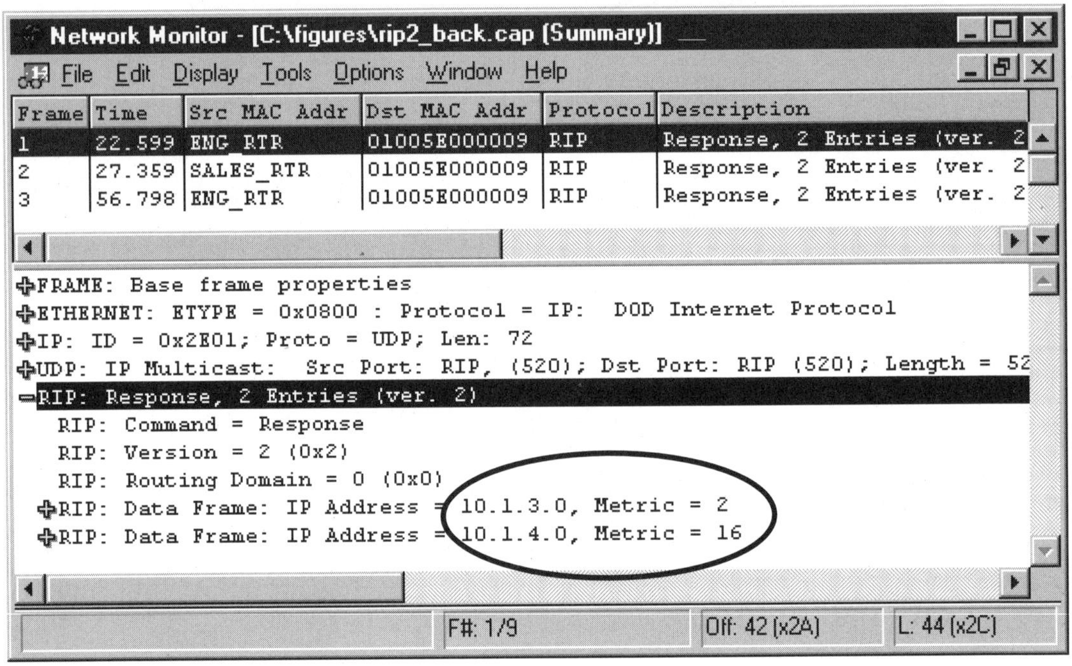

Figure 8.33 The first RIPv2 message on the backbone subnet.

RIPv2 Message from SALES_RTR onto Backbone

rip2_back.cap
frame #2

The second message we'll look at on the backbone is from SALES_RTR with two advertisements as shown in Figure 8.34. The route to the engineering subnet is poisoned with a metric of 16. The route to the sales subnet has a metric of two as we have come to expect but not condone.

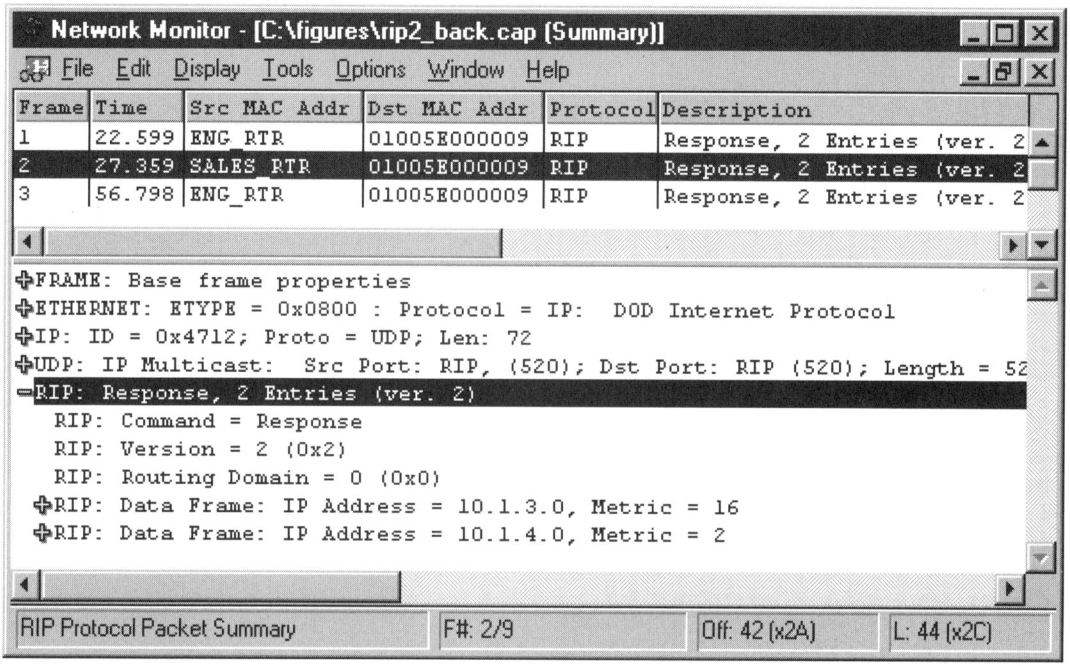

Figure 8.34 The second RIPv2 message on the backbone subnet.

Summary

Here's a summary of the items which have been addressed in this chapter.

- The Routing and Remote Access Service (a.k.a Steelhead) provides additional routing capabilities beyond the standard NT 4.0 capabilities, including support for RIPv2.
- RIPv2 improves upon RIPv1 in various ways, including use of a multicast destination, use of triggered updates, and selectively processing or distributing RIP messages.
- The design of Steelhead is such that NT can potentially be used as the operating system found in hardware routers.
- The ***kernrout*** command is used to view the "kernel portion" of the routing table.
- RIPv2 packet structure allows for usage of more fields than the RIPv1 packet structure.
- An example packet capture was shown that illustrated poison reverse in action.

Further Reading

Here is information about various books and magazines in which to look for further information on the subject.

[Baker1997] Baker, F., Atkinson, R., *RIP-2 MD5 Authentication,* 1997, IETF RFC 2082

[Comer1995] Comer, Douglas E., *Internetworking with TCP/IP Vol I: Principles, Protocols, and Architecture, Third Edition*, 1995, Prentice-Hall, Inc.

[Halpern1996] Halpern, J., Bradner, S., *RIPv1 Applicability Statement for Historic Status,* 1996, IETF RFC 1923

[Hedrick1988] Hedrick, C., *Routing Information Protocol,* 1988, IETF RFC 1058

[Huitema1995] Huitema, Christian, *Routing in the Internet,* 1995, Prentice Hall

[Malkin1994] Malkin, G., *RIP Version 2 — Carrying Additional Information,* 1994, IETF RFC 1723

[Malkin1994b] Malkin, G., *RIP Version 2 — Protocol Applicability Statement,* 1994, IETF RFC 1722

[Malkin1994c] Malkin, G., Baker, F., *RIP Version 2 — MIB Extension,* 1994, IETF RFC 1724

[Meyer1997] Meyer, G., Sherry, S., *Triggered Extensions to RIP to Support Demand Circuits,* 1997, IETF RFC 2091

[Perlman1992] Perlman, Radia, *Interconnections: Bridges and Routers,* 1992, Addison Wesley

[Sherry1997] Sherry, S., Meyer, G., *Protocol Analysis for Triggered RIP,* 1997, IETF RFC 2092

[Stevens1994] Stevens, W. Richard, *TCP/IP Illustrated, Volume 1: The Protocols,* 1994, Addison-Wesley

9

Remotely Accessing the Corporate Network

Remote access to resources at another location is an essential part of networking. There are several reasons for wanting remote access, and several techniques of accomplishing this access. In this chapter we'll look at how Microsoft's *Remote Access Service (RAS)* may be used to provide remote access.

We'll examine three scenarios for remote access and look at technologies used by RAS to satisfy each set of requirements. Two of the technologies used are:

- the *Point-to-Point Protocol (PPP)* used to provide network access.
- the *Point-to-Point Tunneling Protocol (PPTP)* which provides a means of implementing *Virtual Private Networks (VPNs)* over networks such as the Internet.

Options for Remotely Accessing the Corporate Network

There are several options that may be used to remotely access a corporate network.

1. Private, direct dialup access to the corporate network.
   - RAS client uses telephone network to connect to a RAS server at the corporate network.
2. Encrypted (private) access to corporate network using Internet.
   - Use PPTP to connect a remote NT or Windows 95 client (e.g. laptop) to the corporate network.
   - Use PPTP to connect a remote office NT server to the corporate network.

These methods have similar characteristics. There will be an *access point* to the corporate network, as shown in Figure 9.1, to which the *remote client* (individual or network) connects.

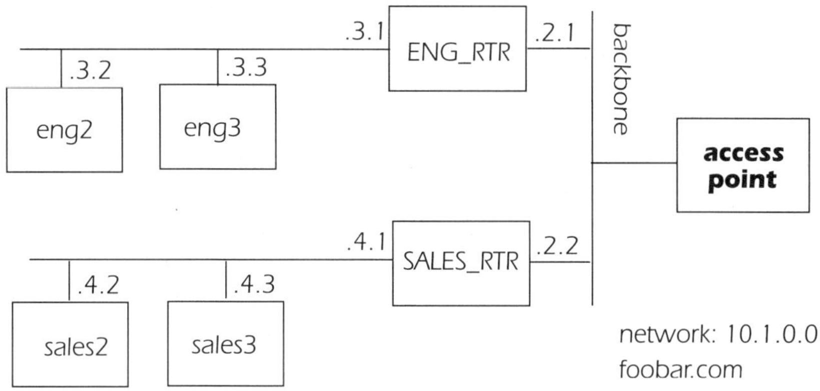

Figure 9.1 A example of a corporate network to which we want to provide remote access.

Let's look at the details of each of these remote access options, and identify differences in the access point and remote client.

Private Direct-Dial Access to a Corporate Network

The first option for remote access provides private, direct dialup access to the corporate network. In this scenario, a RAS client uses the *Public Switched Telephone Network* (PSTN) to connect to a RAS server in the corporate network, as shown in Figure 9.2

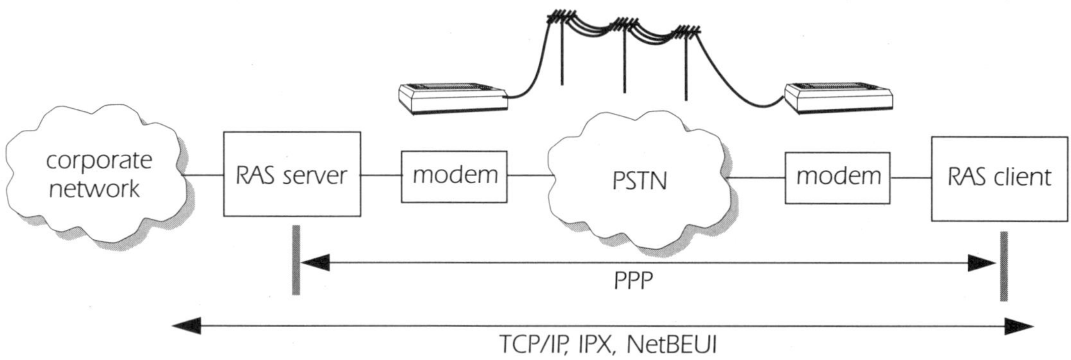

Figure 9.2 Private, direct dialup access to a corporate network.

This method requires that the Remote Access Service be installed on both the client and the server. Point-to-Point Protocol will be used over the dialup connection to transmit any or all of the following protocols: IPX, NetBEUI and TCP/IP.

There are a few disadvantages to using this method, listed below.

- This scenario opens a potential security hole — hackers with "war dialers" may be able to break into your corporate network.
- Users must dial the corporate phone number directly — this could incur long distance phone charges.
- Resources are needed to support the load of all simultaneous users at peak usage levels.

For more information, refer to the section "Private Direct-Dial Access to a Corporate Network" on page 348.

Connecting a Single Machine to the Corporate Network Using the Internet

The second option for remote access involves use of the Point-to-Point Tunneling Protocol (PPTP). This option entails encrypted (private) access over the Internet connecting remote Windows machines and the corporate network. An example of this is shown in Figure 9.3

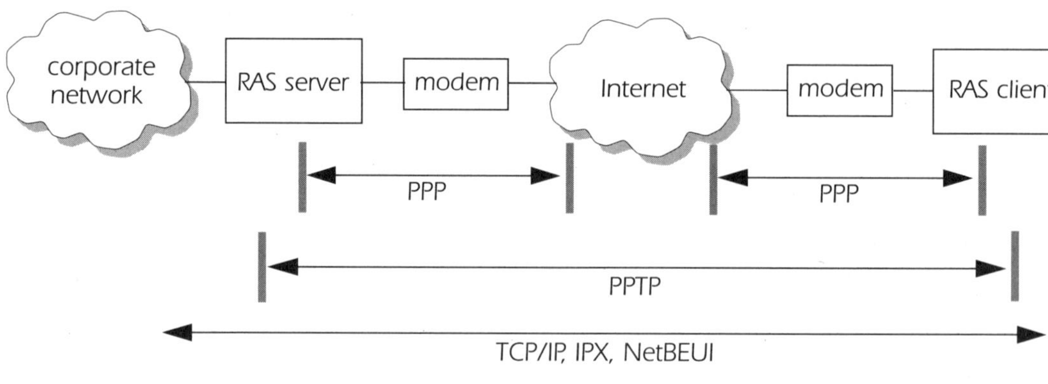

Figure 9.3 Client access tunneled through the Internet to a corporate network.

This method requires that both TCP/IP and PPTP be installed on the client and the server. TCP/IP, IPX and NetBEUI traffic may all be tunneled over this link. However, since the Internet is being used as the intermediate network, long-distance phone charges can be avoided.

The disadvantages to using PPTP include the following:

- Access to the remote network may be slower than with the direct connection scenario due to Internet traffic.
- A security hole also exists in this method. Connecting any private network to the Internet is a security risk. However, you could enable PPTP filtering on the PPTP server, which will prevent non-PPTP traffic from entering the corporate LAN.
- When using PPTP without Steelhead, the only connections that can be made are from client to server. To obtain server-to-server PPTP connections, Steelhead must be installed.

For more information on PPTP, refer to Chapter 10, "Securely Accessing the Corporate Network Using PPTP".

Connecting a Remote Office to the Corporate Network Using the Internet

The third option builds on the second option, in that PPTP is still used. However, in this option a remote office rather than an individual machine is connected to the main office.

To implement this method, both ends of the PPTP connection must have RAS and PPTP installed, as well as Steelhead. Figure 9.4 illustrates this scenario.

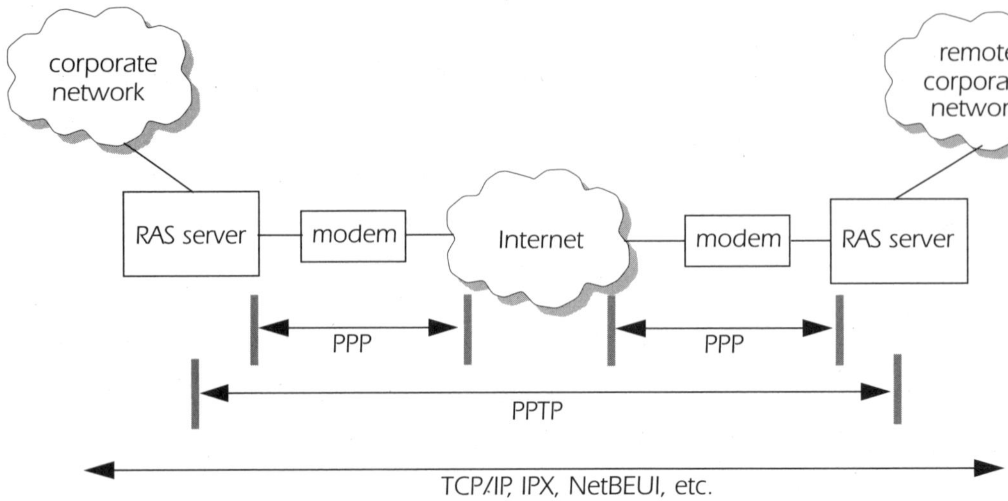

Figure 9.4 Server access tunneled through the Internet to a corporate network.

For more information, refer to Chapter 10, "Securely Accessing the Corporate Network Using PPTP".

PPP Operation

The *Point-to-Point Protocol (PPP)* can take a bit stream, such as that sent over a serial communications link, and turn it into a series of packets for various network layer protocols. PPP is an Internet standard, and is very popular for facilitating remote access to networks.

We can set up a simple network by connecting together the serial ports of two computers and setting up PPP software on each computer to use the serial link as a communications link, as shown in Figure 9.5.

Figure 9.5 Two computers using PPP over a serial link.

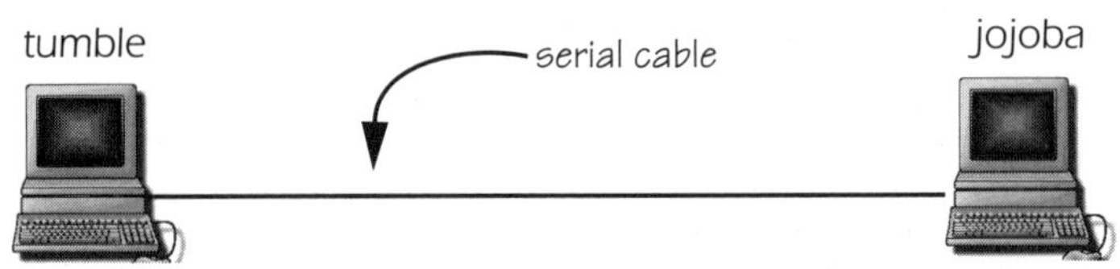

Rather than using a serial cable to connect the computers *directly*, we may alternately introduce a pair of modems or digital access devices and a carrier (e.g. telephone) network in between. Each computer is then *indirectly* connected using a complete serial line.

This kind of set up will work for just about any two computers. More importantly for connecting corporate networks together, PPP may also be run on bridges and routers to provide network interfaces over the wide area.

PPP Framing

One of the functions provided by PPP is the ability to send messages from the station at one end of the link to the station at the other end. But how does PPP make a sequence of bits or octets look like a message? PPP puts boundaries, a beginning and an end, on each message. The main reason why PPP frames each message is to align the message on an octet boundary. The frame format used by PPP is shown in Figure 9.6.

Figure 9.6
PPP frame header layout (ignoring flags).

1 octet	1 octet	2 octets	0-1500 octets	2 octets
Target Address	Control Field	Protocol Type	Payload Data (message)	CRC

Let's take a look at the pieces of a PPP frame. The payload data is variable length, as with Ethernet. The default *Maximum Receive Unit (MRU)* for PPP is specified as 1500 octets of payload. There are six octets of overhead in the frame (i.e. ignoring the flags used for framing).

- The *target address* comes first. It takes up one octet. The normal value is FF (hex) which specifies all machines (usually one) at the other end of the link.

- Next is the *control field*. It also takes up one octet. Typically, this specifies *unnumbered information* with a value of 3.

- Third we have an identifier for the kind of information which PPP is carrying in the message. Because the information is actually a part of a higher-layer (e.g. network) protocol, this field is called a *protocol type*. The protocol type is two octets.

- Then each octet of the message payload is transmitted. There are some special rules which must be followed so that the receiver doesn't confuse the information with framing octets.
- Finally, we have two octets which serve as a *frame check sequence (FCS)*. The value is calculated using a cyclic redundancy check (CRC) formula.

Multiprotocol Data Link

It is a common misconception that only IP can be carried over a PPP link. In fact, multiple network layer protocols can be carried by IP. The *protocol type* field in the PPP packet allows PPP to support multiple protocols simultaneously. A few of the PPP protocol types are shown in Table 9.1.

Table 9.1
PPP protocol types–protocols that can run on top of PPP

Protocol	# (hex)	Description
IP	0021	Internet Protocol
DDP	0029	Datagram Delivery Protocol
IPX	002B	Internetwork Packet Exchange
PPPML	003D	Point-to-Point Protocol – Multilink
IPCP	8021	IP Control Protocol
DDPCP	8029	DDP Control Protocol
IPXCP	802B	IPX Control Protocol
NBFCP	803F	NetBIOS Frame Control Protocol
CCP	80FD	Compression Control Protocol
LCP	C021	Link Control Protocol
PPPPAP	C023	PPP Password Authentication Protocol
LQR	C025	Link Quality Report
CBCP	C029	Call-Back Control Protocol
PPPCHAP	C223	PPP Challenge Handshake Authentication Protocol

Let's say that we have two network protocols, Q and Z, and their associated PPP protocol types. In both computers and the end of a PPP connection, the protocol software for Q and Z would register with PPP so that PPP knows where to send incoming packets (Figure 9.7). In packet transmission, PPP would enter the appropriate protocol number in the protocol number field before sending the packet down the stack. For incoming data, the PPP protocol type field would be used to determine to what protocol PPP should send the packet.

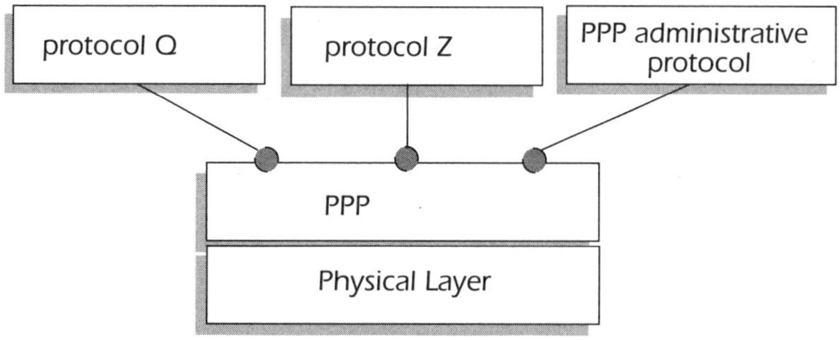

Figure 9.7 The PPP protocol type field allows support of many subscribers to the PPP service, such as the network protocols Q and Z.

PPP Link Phases

Each PPP link goes through several phases of operation. Every link starts in the dead state, and must transition through the establish and authenticate states and into the network state in order to transfer any network layer packets. The various phases of a PPP link are shown in Figure 9.8.

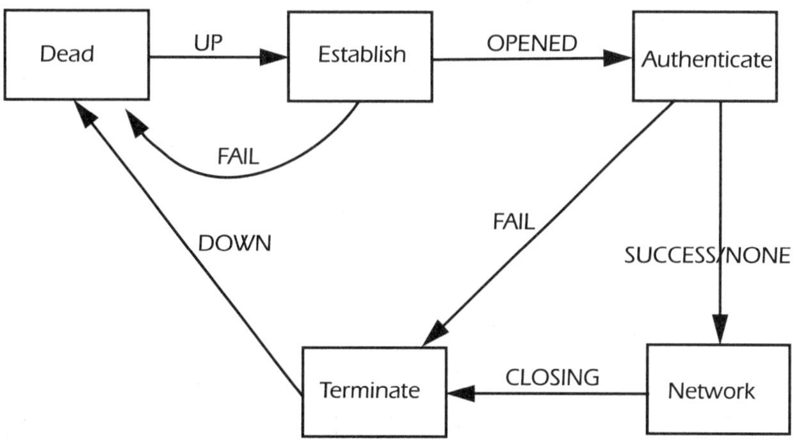

Figure 9.8 Any PPP link goes through several phases.

In particular, let's discuss the phases before the network layer protocol packets (i.e. IP) are exchanged. Those three phases are broken down as:

- phase 1— PPP link establishment phase
- phase 2— authentication phase
- phase 3— network layer protocol establishment phase

After these phases complete, IP packets (as well as NetBEUI and IPX packets) can be sent across the PPP connection.

Phase 1 — PPP Link Establishment

When the data link is needed, PPP determines that an underlying physical transport exists and enters the *establishment phase*.

Several messages are exchanged in PPP frames during the establishment phase in order to set up the data link. This may involve negotiation of data link layer options. This is handled by a part of PPP called the *Link Control Protocol (LCP)*. The LCP comes into play during other phases as well, but is essential to the link establishment phase. In fact, no other types of messages may be exchanged over PPP until the LCP has done its job here and has told PPP to go to the next phase.

LCP is used throughout the connection. It is shown here only in the startup. LCP is also used during connection teardown and failures.

Figure 9.9 shows that LCP is run on top of PPP. The PPP protocol type for LCP is 21 hex.

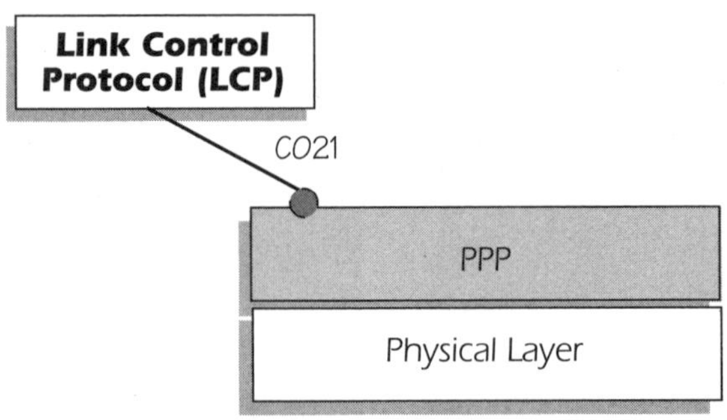

Figure 9.9
PPP notes that physical layer communication is possible and starts building a data link using LCP.

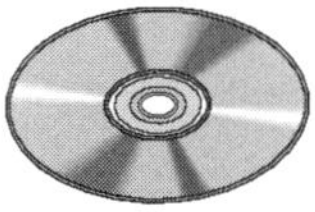

pppstartup.cap

Figure 9.10 shows the Network Monitor capture of this link establishment. The capture file, pppstartup.cap is found on the CD. There is no address database file associated with this capture.

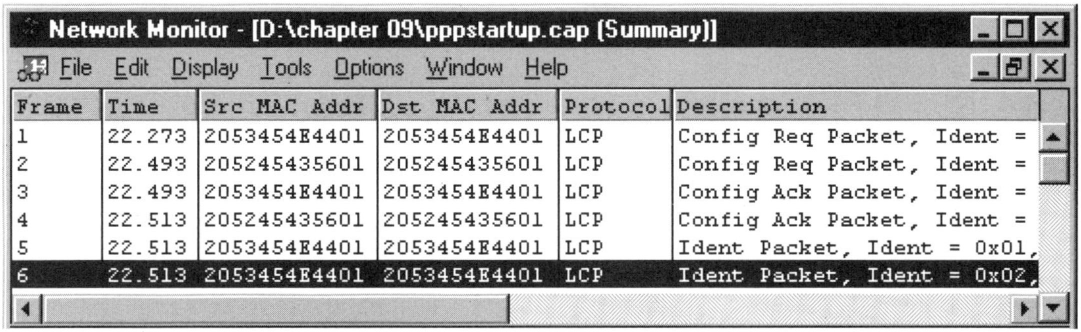

Network Monitor - [D:\chapter 09\pppstartup.cap (Summary)]

File Edit Display Tools Options Window Help

Frame	Time	Src MAC Addr	Dst MAC Addr	Protocol	Description
1	22.273	2053454E4401	2053454E4401	LCP	Config Req Packet, Ident =
2	22.493	205245435601	205245435601	LCP	Config Req Packet, Ident =
3	22.493	2053454E4401	2053454E4401	LCP	Config Ack Packet, Ident =
4	22.513	205245435601	205245435601	LCP	Config Ack Packet, Ident =
5	22.513	2053454E4401	2053454E4401	LCP	Ident Packet, Ident = 0x01,
6	22.513	2053454E4401	2053454E4401	LCP	Ident Packet, Ident = 0x02,

Figure 9.10 PPP Phase 1: link establishment using LCP

After LCP has established the link, the next phase is begun.

Phase 2 — Authentication

Once the link is established, PPP enters the *authentication phase*. It is during this phase that the client is authenticated by the server. There are two methods which may be used for authentication.

- *Password Authentication Protocol (PAP)*
- *Challenge Handshake Authentication Protocol (CHAP)*

The form of authentication used depends on options which were negotiated during the link establishment phase by LCP. Figure 9.11 shows that another protocol has begun to be sent over PPP— the CHAP protocol. The PPP protocol type for PPPCHAP is C223 hex. (Note that LCP is still operational, but at this time sending no packets.)

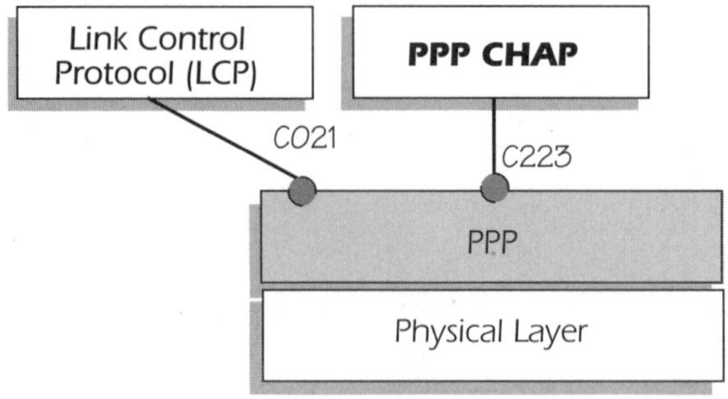

Figure 9.11 Once the link is established, authentication can occur using PPP CHAP

Figure 9.12 shows an example of the CHAP packets that are exchanged during the authentication phase. In this example PPP CHAP challenge/response is used.[1]

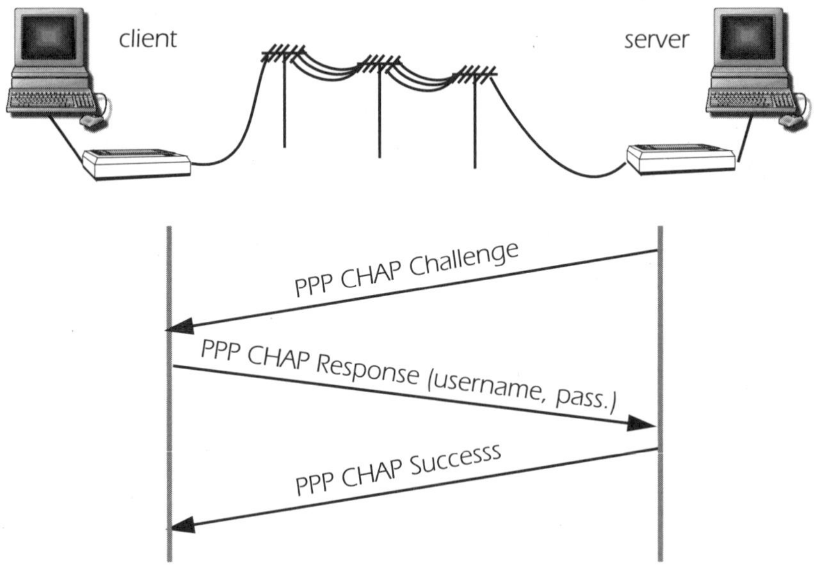

Figure 9.12 Example PPP connection, phase 2—authentication

After a logon request is received, the PPP server issues a PPP CHAP challenge to the client. The client replies with a PPP CHAP response containing identification such as username and password. This information is encoded using the challenge as a key.

1. PPP CHAP challenge/response is a different protocol than NT challenge/response. For information on NT challenge/response, see "NT Challenge Response" on page 548.

Figure 9.13 shows a capture of authentication packets which show the CHAP authentication following the LCP packets from pppstartup.cap which were shown in Figure 9.10.

pppstartup.cap

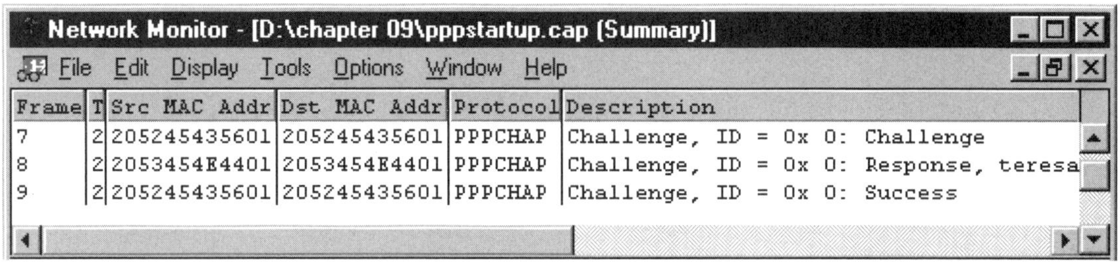

Figure 9.13 PPP Phase 2: authentication

Phase 3 — Network Layer Protocol Link Establishment

Once the link has been successfully authenticated, PPP proceeds to the *network phase*. During this phase, one or more *network control protocols* may communicate over PPP in order to negotiate use of their corresponding network layer protocols over PPP.

A few of the protocols that may used at this stage:

- *Callback Control Protocol (CBCP)* — used to determine if the server should call the client back. Callback is used when the server wishes to confirm the identity of the caller by hanging up and calling back for auditing and/or security purposes.
- *Compression Control Protocol (CCP)* — used to determine the method in which data will be compressed over this link.
- *Internet Protocol Control Protocol (IPCP)* — used to set up an IP connection over the PPP link. IPCP negotiates IP address and MTU information.

Each of these protocols is shown in the ladder diagram in Figure 9.14.

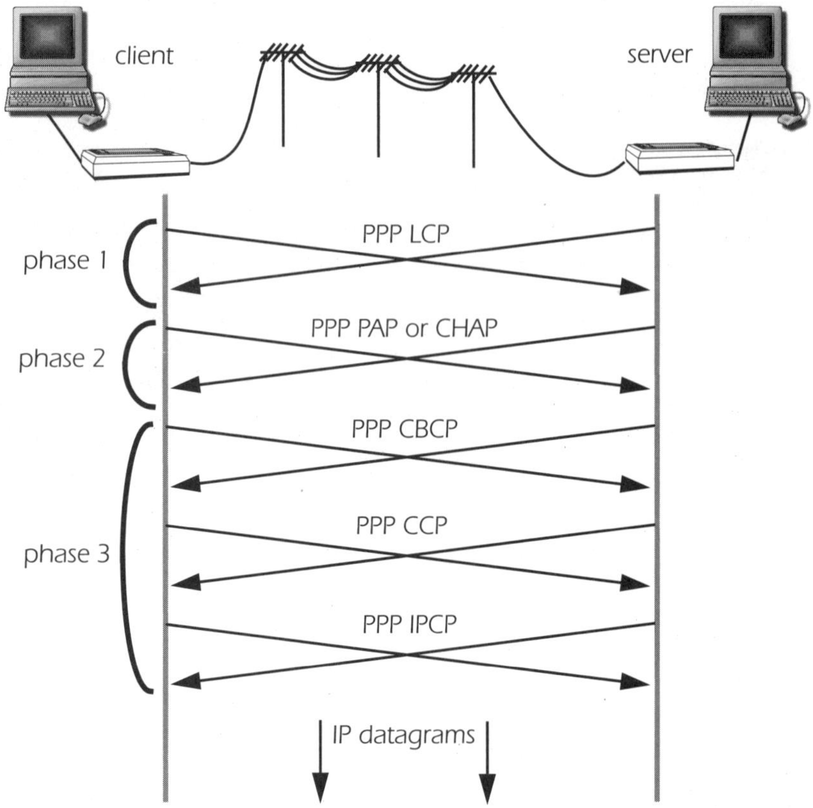

Figure 9.14 Phase 3— network layer protocol link establishment follows phases one and two.

Note that the crossing arrows are used as a short-hand to indicate that messages of the noted type are exchanged, without reference to a specific number or direction of messages.

Continuing with phase three of the example of pppstartup.cap, we'll examine CBCP, CCP, IPCP, and finally IP traffic. Example CBCP packets are shown in Figure 9.15.

Network Monitor - [D:\chapter 09\pppstartup.cap (Summary)]

File Edit Display Tools Options Window Help

Frame	Time	Src MAC Addr	Dst MAC Addr	Protocol	Description
10	23.0	205245435601	205245435601	CBCP	Callback Request, Ident = 0x01
11	23.0	2053454E4401	2053454E4401	CBCP	Callback Response, Ident = 0x01
12	23.1	205245435601	205245435601	CBCP	Callback Acknowledgement, Ident

Figure 9.15 PPP Phase 3: Callback Control Protocol packets.

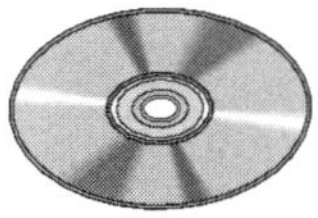

pppstartup.cap

In this example, the packets exchanged during the CBCP sequence did not require a callback to occur. Therefore, phase three continues normally.

A few of the CCP and IPCP packets are shown in Figure 9.16.

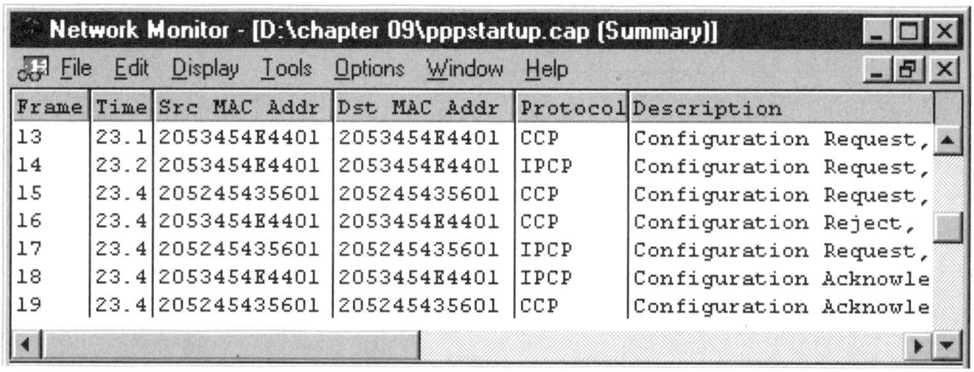

Network Monitor - [D:\chapter 09\pppstartup.cap (Summary)]

File Edit Display Tools Options Window Help

Frame	Time	Src MAC Addr	Dst MAC Addr	Protocol	Description
13	23.1	2053454E4401	2053454E4401	CCP	Configuration Request,
14	23.2	2053454E4401	2053454E4401	IPCP	Configuration Request,
15	23.4	20524543560l	20524543560l	CCP	Configuration Request,
16	23.4	2053454E4401	2053454E4401	CCP	Configuration Reject,
17	23.4	20524543560l	20524543560l	IPCP	Configuration Request,
18	23.4	2053454E4401	2053454E4401	IPCP	Configuration Acknowle
19	23.4	20524543560l	20524543560l	CCP	Configuration Acknowle

Figure 9.16 PPP Phase 3: CCP and IPCP packets are used to establish the network layer protocol.

Once this negotiation is complete, IP has a binding to run over PPP as shown in Figure 9.17.

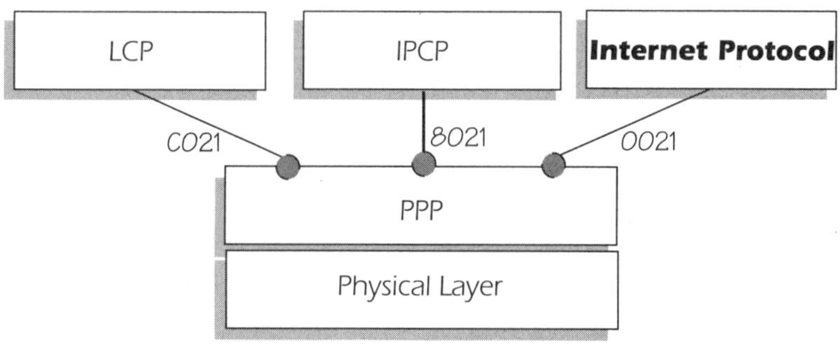

Figure 9.17 IP can be transmitted over the PPP link once IPCP has set up the connection parameters.

Recall that several network layer protocols may configure bindings onto a single PPP interface. Each such protocol may terminate its use of PPP, yet PPP retains the data link even when there are no network protocols bound to it. PPP links must be explicitly terminated using LCP.

When the binding for IP is present, IP datagrams may be sent and received over the PPP interface. Other protocols may be sent over the same PPP link if they are negotiated with their own control protocol.

The end of the CCP packet exchange and the first IP datagrams over the PPP interface are shown in Figure 9.18. These first IP datagrams carry an echo request (frame 36) and a destination unreachable (frame 37).

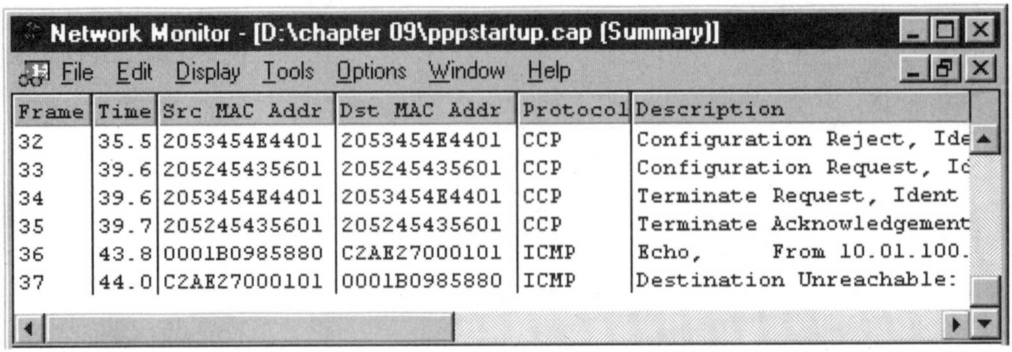

Network Monitor - [D:\chapter 09\pppstartup.cap (Summary)]

File Edit Display Tools Options Window Help

Frame	Time	Src MAC Addr	Dst MAC Addr	Protocol	Description
32	35.5	2053454E4401	2053454E4401	CCP	Configuration Reject, Ide
33	39.6	205245435601	205245435601	CCP	Configuration Request, Id
34	39.6	2053454E4401	2053454E4401	CCP	Terminate Request, Ident
35	39.7	205245435601	205245435601	CCP	Terminate Acknowledgement
36	43.8	0001B0985880	C2AE27000101	ICMP	Echo, From 10.01.100.
37	44.0	C2AE27000101	0001B0985880	ICMP	Destination Unreachable:

Figure 9.18 Network-layer packets (ICMP) can now be transmitted over the connection.

Private Direct-Dial Access to a Corporate Network

The first option for remote access provides private, direct dialup access to the corporate network. In this scenario, a *Remote Access Service (RAS)* client uses the Public Switched Telephone Network (PSTN) to connect to RAS server in the corporate network, as depicted in Figure 9.19.

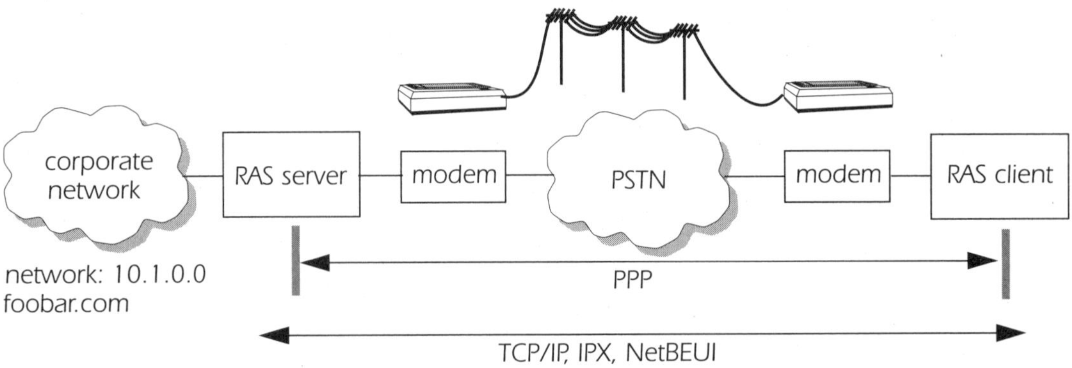

Figure 9.19 Private, direct dialup access to a corporate network.

This technique may be used for dialing into the corporate network from home, while on the road, etc. While we'll describe this in terms of the PSTN, the same method may be applied over ISDN, ATM, or any other service which allows you to establish a physical layer connection which will support PPP.

The corporation runs a RAS server on a Windows NT machine which has the appropriate kind of physical connectivity — in this case that's a modem connected to the PSTN. Because RAS uses PPP for this connection, you may use not only a Windows NT or Windows 95 RAS client, but other clients such as MacOS or UNIX clients running PPP. We'll look at the use of Windows NT as both the client and server.

Any protocol which can run over PPP, such as IP, IPX, NetBEUI may be used with RAS as long as you have support for it on both the client and server.

Who is the RAS Server and Who is the RAS Client?

What is the distinction between the RAS client and RAS server? When you configure the RAS software on a machine, you must specify whether you want to be able to initiate calls, receive calls, or both.

- A *RAS client* may *only initiate* calls.
- A *RAS server* may *send and receive* calls.

The receiver of a RAS call is *supporting* or *providing* for remote access, thus it plays the server role. The initiator of a RAS call is *using* the remote access service, thus it is a client.

Potential Security Problems with Remote Access

Security

One of the disadvantages of RAS is that it opens up a potential security hole into your system. Hackers or crackers may use a technique called *war dialing* to repeatedly attempt to dial into your RAS server until they are successfully authenticated. Hackers may stop there, yet this is usually the starting point for a cracker's work.

Your legitimate users would dial the phone number of the modem line. This may involve long distance charges for your users who do work remotely. Rather than dealing with the reimbursement issues, you may opt for a toll-free number, yet that opens the door to hackers running up your bills even if they don't succeed at breaking in.

Each modem is a single resource for a single user. This means that it is easy for a hacker to cause a denial of service to your intended users — the hacker simply keeps the line busy. Even under perfectly legitimate use, if more than one user at a time requires access, someone gets a busy signal. There are three ways of dealing with this issue.

- Outsource the dial-in access to someone with a modem bank and have one (potentially dedicated) line from this organization to your own.
- Use remote access equipment which is specifically designed to support many users and modem banks.
- Connect a bank of dozens or hundreds of modems (as necessary) to your Windows NT RAS server and invest enough money in the machine to support the load.

The bottom line of all of these issues is that you should carefully develop a remote access plan, perhaps starting with a small trial.

Overview of Installation Steps for NT 4.0 RAS

The following steps will be used to install and configure the *RAS client*.

1. Install and configure RAS service.
2. Create phonebook entry for corporate RAS server.

The following steps will be used to install and configure the *RAS server.*

1. Install and configure RAS service.
2. Allow users dialin access.
3. Configure RAS service to start upon boot.

After both the client and the server have been configured, connection between the two can be tested.

Client Step 1: Install and Configure RAS Service

Open the *Network Control Panel* and select the *Services tab.* Press *Add* to add the Remote Access Service software to your machine. The *Select Network Service* dialog will appear (Figure 9.20).

Figure 9.20
Select the Remote Access Service from this dialog.

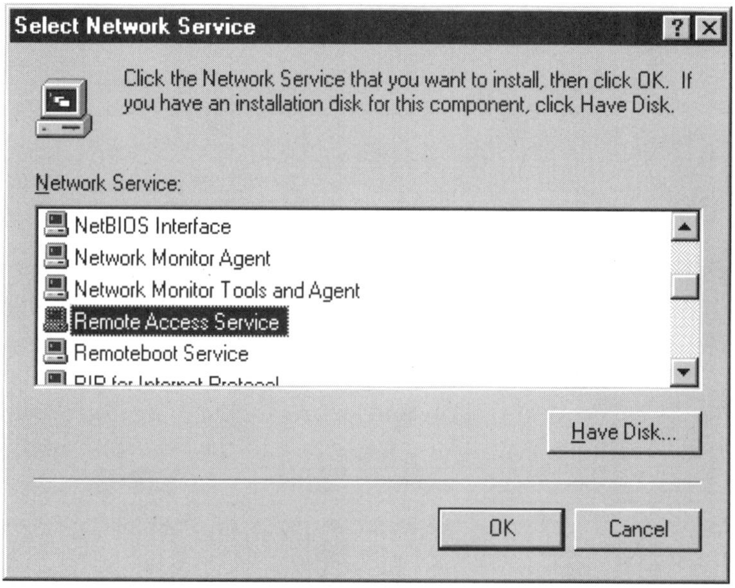

Note that installing the Remote Access Service installs both client and server software to the machine. It is in the configuration where you will specify that this machine is a client.

The first step in the RAS configuration is to add a device to use for the communication link. In our setup, we used the main communications port, COM1, with a standard modem attached, as shown in Figure 9.21.

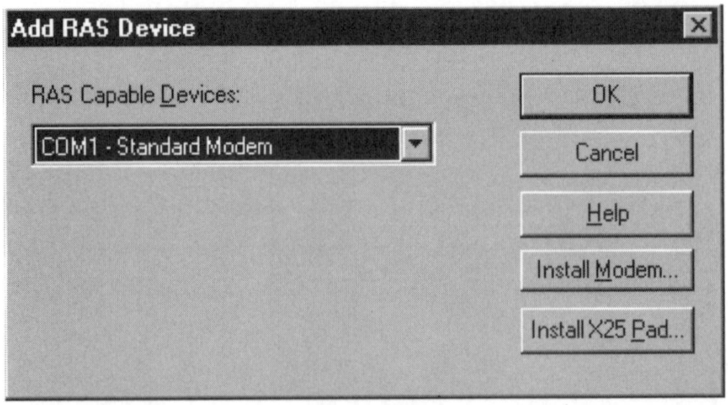

Figure 9.21 Select a device to use for this RAS client. We've selected COM1 for use with a modem.

Next to appear will be the *Remote Access Setup* dialog (Figure 9.22).

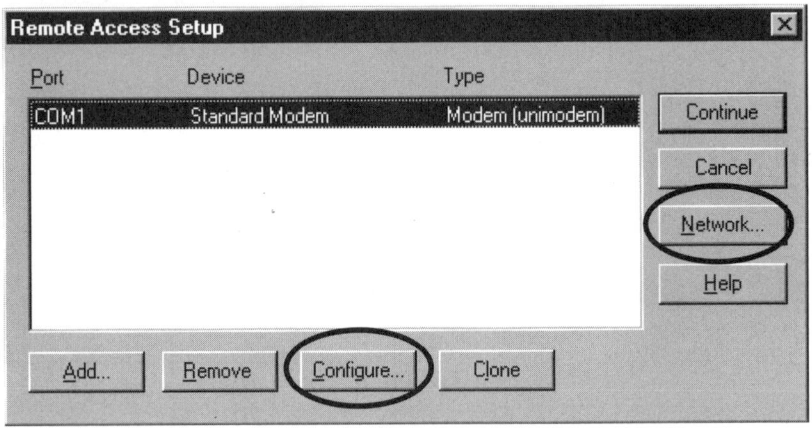

Figure 9.22 The Remote Access Setup dialog is the central point of configuration for RAS.

The two buttons in this dialog which we'll use are *Configure* and *Network*. The *Configure* button allows you to configure general use of the device, and the *Network* button allows you more specific control over what network protocols will be used. First, with the device selected, pressing the *Configure* button will result in the *Configure Port Usage* dialog (Figure 9.23).

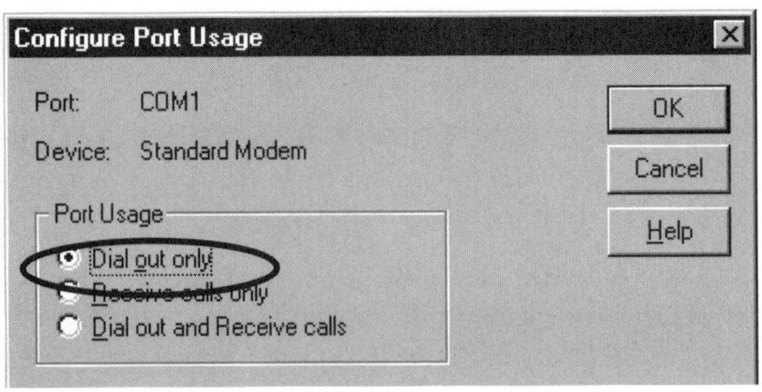

Figure 9.23 Selecting the dial out only option for the port designates this port for use as a RAS client.

Recall that a RAS client will only perform dial out. Select the *Dial out only* option in this dialog to indicate that you're configuring a client.

Now that this machine is configured as a client, we need to configure which protocols it will use on the dial-out connection. From the *Remote Access Setup* dialog in Figure 9.22, pressing the *Network* button yields the *Network Configuration* dialog shown in Figure 9.24.

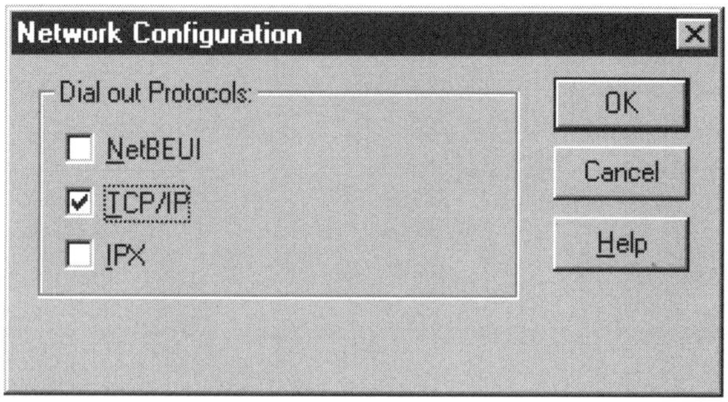

Figure 9.24
Note that because this is a client (i.e. dial-out only) interface, the only Network Configuration options are for dial-out protocols.

Use the *Network Configuration* dialog to select which network protocols you want to allow to be run over the dial-out connection. Now the RAS client software has been configured. You must reboot the machine so that these changes will take effect.

Client Step 2: Create Phonebook Entry for Corporate RAS Server

In order to dial a RAS server, you must configure parameters to be used by the client. You may have configurations on this client for many servers that you wish to connect to. Each configuration is called a *phonebook entry.*

Launch the *Dialup Networking* application from the *Start -> Programs -> Accessories* menu. Once in the application, if you have not previously configured a phonebook entry on this machine, the *New Phonebook Entry Wizard* (Figure 9.25) will automatically be started.

Figure 9.25
The name of the phonebook entry (configuration) may be specified in this dialog.

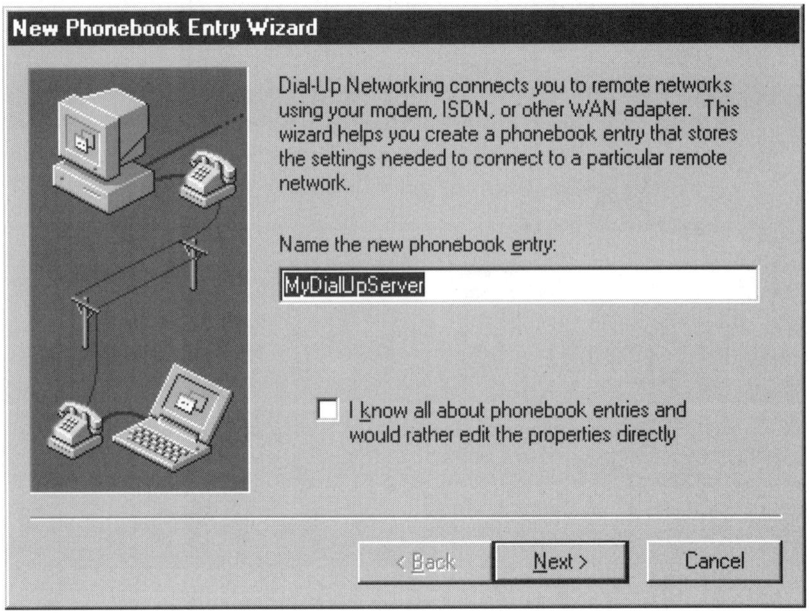

Enter the name of the phonebook entry (i.e. what you want to call the configuration) and press the *Next* button. The *Server* dialog will appear (Figure 9.26)

Figure 9.26
This dialog allows you to describe some of the characteristics of the server that you'll be connecting to.

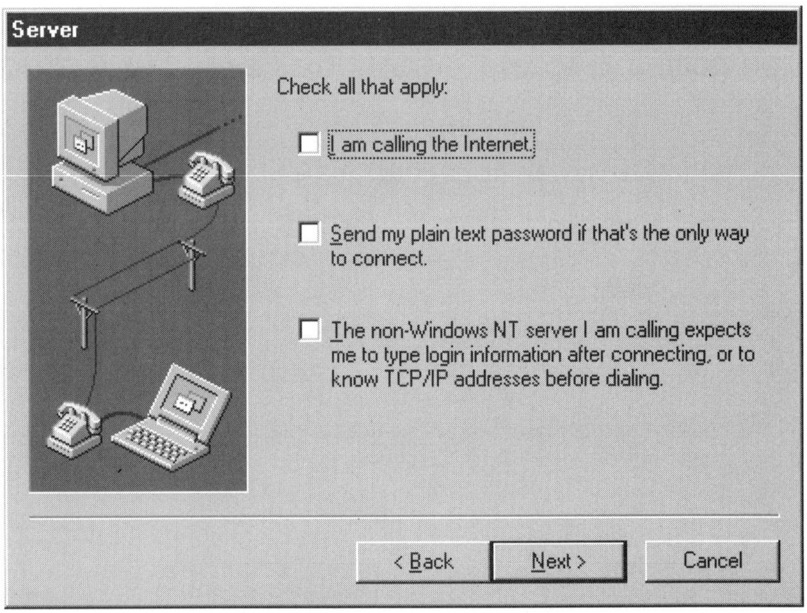

Because we're dialing into a corporate headquarters, we don't need to check any of these boxes. Simply press the *Next* button and the dialog in Figure 9.27 will appear.

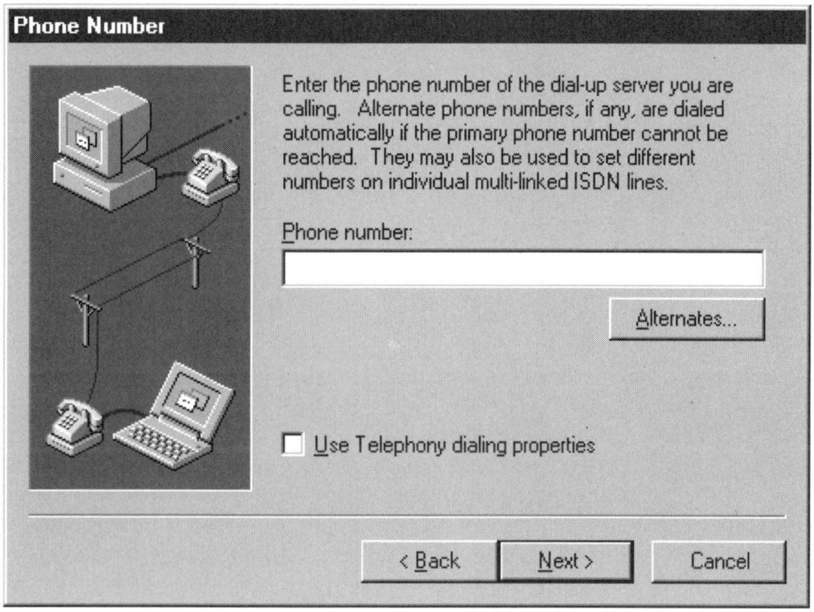

Figure 9.27
Enter the phone number of the RAS server at the corporate headquarters here.

Enter the phone number of the RAS server in this dialog and press the *Next* button. The final screen of the wizard will appear; press the *Finish* button. The new phonebook entry is created.

If you have a RAS server to connect to, you may test your configuration now by pressing the *Dial* button in the *Dialup Networking* application.

Server Step 1: Install and Configure RAS Service

Many of these screens will be similar to the RAS client screens just shown. A few of the screens will have parameters that pertain only to RAS servers. The first few steps will use the exact same screens as is in the client configuration, so they will be summarized here

- Add the Remote Access Service using the *Network Control Panel.* (Figure 9.20)

- Select a device to use for the communication link. (Figure 9.21)
- In the *Remote Access Setup* dialog (Figure 9.22), use *Configure* to bring up the screen shown in Figure 9.28.

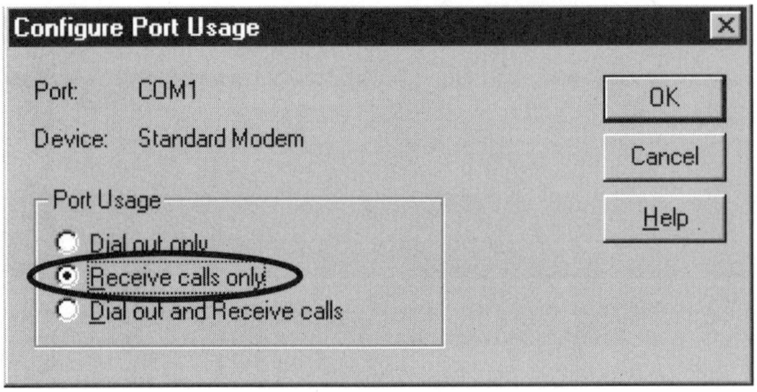

Figure 9.28 The RAS server is configured to receive calls only.

Now we have the distinguishing characteristic in the configuration of the client and server. Recall that for the client you selected *Dial-out only.* Since the server is intended to receive calls, select *Receive calls only* (assuming this server will never dial-out).

Back in the *Remote Access Setup* dialog (Figure 9.22), press the *Network* button. Notice the resulting dialog as shown in Figure 9.29 is different than the *Network Configuration* dialog for the client configuration (Figure 9.24). This is due to the difference in selection of dial-out only versus receive calls only.

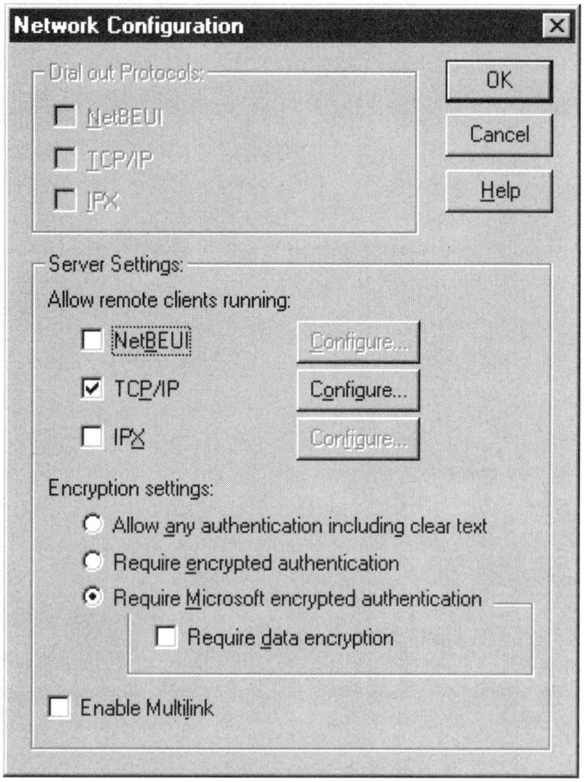

Figure 9.29 Because this is a server (receive only) the dialog has been expanded to include several server settings.

The port usage was set to allow calls to be received only, thus the dial-out options in this dialog are grayed out. There are now several server settings at the bottom of the (much larger) dialog. These options allow selection and configuration of the network protocols which clients may use. Additionally there are a number of selections for encryption of the link.

Because our remote client will be connecting in with TCP/IP, we've checked the *TCP/IP* box. If IPX and/or NetBEUI was also going to be sent over the PPP connection, those boxes would be checked as well. When we press the *Configure* button for TCP/IP, the dialog in Figure 9.30 presents itself.

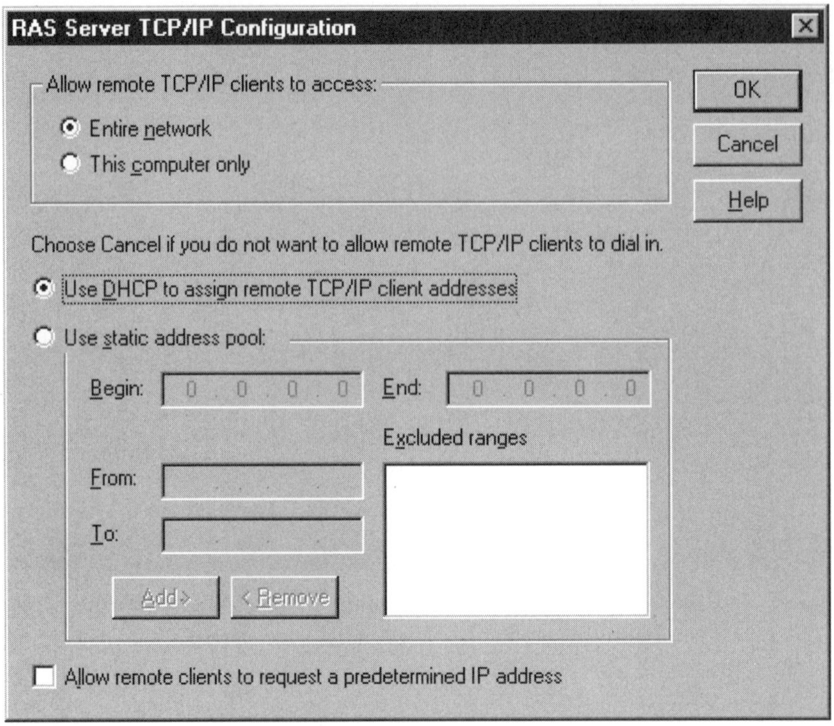

Figure 9.30 The remote client should be able to access the entire network, so we've pushed that radio button here.

The *RAS Server TCP/IP Configuration* dialog allows you to set up the access and addressing for the client. We want our remote clients to have access to the entire company network, thus we've selected the *Entire network* option. If the remote client doesn't have a *fixed* IP address[2], the RAS server may either:

- request a DHCP assigned address on behalf of the client, or
- pick an address from a static pool.

This completes the configuration of the RAS Server service. However, we must now start the service, and allow users to dial-in.

2. Fixed IP addresses are also referred to as static IP addresses, and as in this dialog, predetermined IP addresses.

Server Step 2: Allow Users Dialin Access

In order for a RAS server to be usable, one or more users must be granted permission to dial in.

Start the *User Manager* application. Configure the user properties for the user you wish to grant dial in access by double-clicking on the entry for that user. Press the *Dialin* button as shown in Figure 9.31.

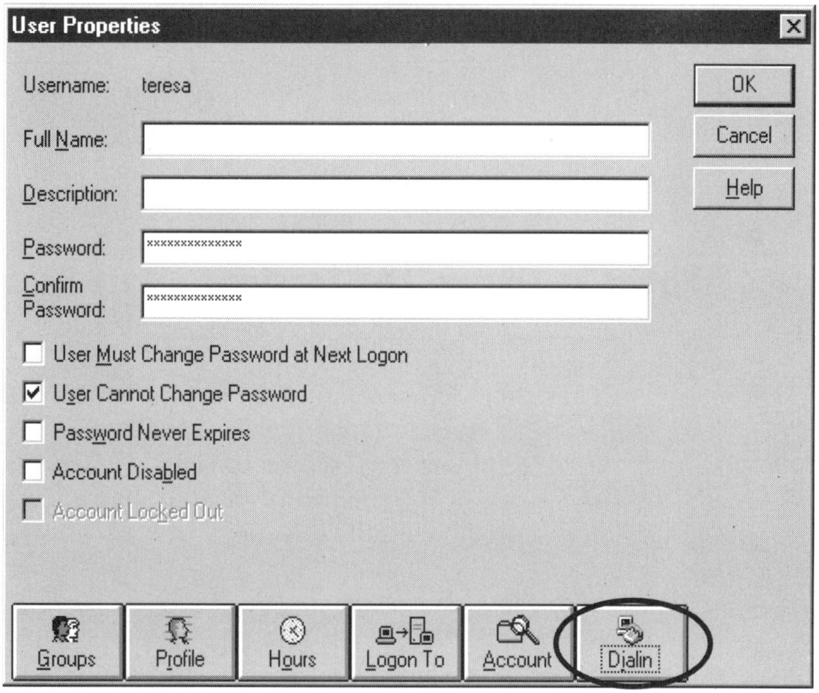

Figure 9.31 Specify the Dialin aspects of the user properties by using this button.

The *Dialin Information* dialog, as shown in Figure 9.32 appears. Check the box for *Grant dialin permission to user.* For security purposes, you may wish to have the RAS server call the user back. If you know the phone number which each user will *always* call from, you could configure a preset phone number for each user. For users who may be on the road, perhaps calling in from a different number each time, you may wish to use the *Set By Caller* option.

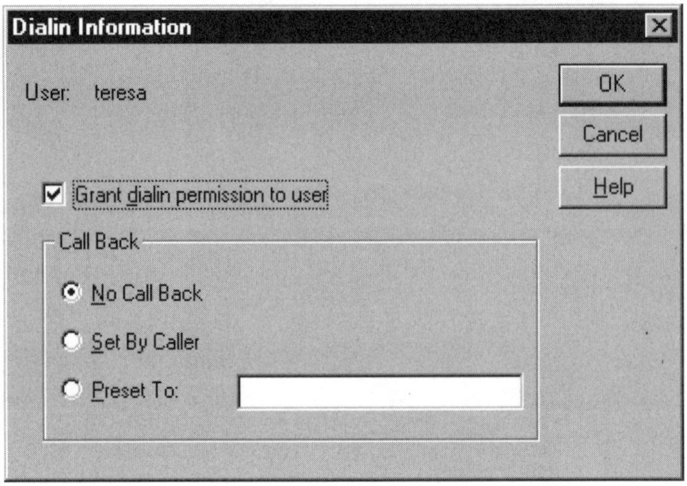

Figure 9.32
There are several call back options which may be selected for each user who has been allowed to connect their RAS client into the server.

Server Step 3: Configure RAS Service to Start Automatically

Now the RAS server must be made effective each time that the server machine restarts. Open the *Services Control Panel* and select the *Remote Access Server* service as shown in Figure 9.33. Press the *Start* button to start the server now. Press the *Startup* button to permanently configure the server to automatically start up.

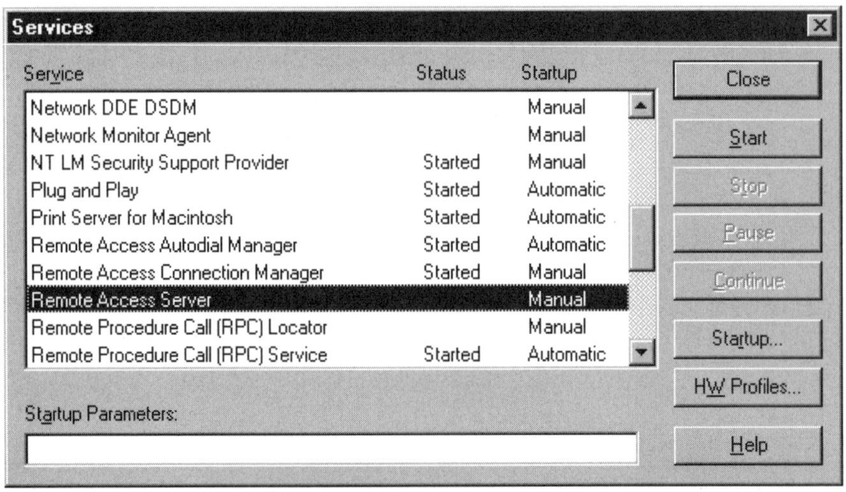

Figure 9.33
Configure automatic startup of the RAS server using the *Startup* button

Testing the RAS Client and Server

To test the configuration of the server and the client, open the *Dialup Networking* application on the client (Figure 9.34). The *Dialup Networking* application is found under *Start->Programs->Accessories* menu.

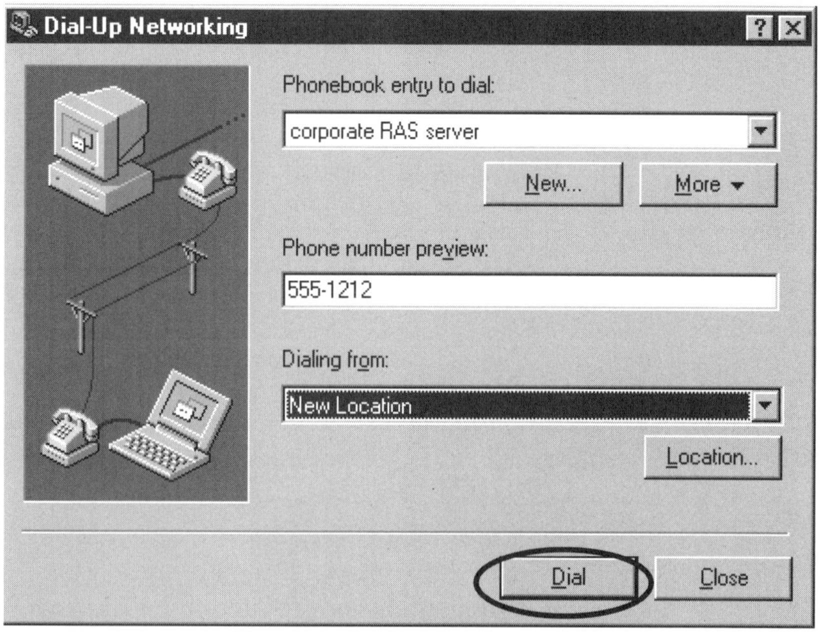

Figure 9.34 Use the Dialup Networking application on the client to dial the RAS server.

Under *phonebook entry to dial,* select the name you assigned to the RAS server. Dial the RAS server— the client should be able to successfully connect. Note that when the server answers the call, a PPP connection will be established.

After the connection has been established, applications like Explorer or Map Network Drive can be accessed and used over the dialup link.

Summary

- Remote access options include directly-dialing the corporate office, or using the Internet to connect the remote use and corporate LAN.
- The Point-to-Point Protocol (PPP) is the protocol used to send data over serial links.
- PPP can carry multiple network-layer protocols, including the most popular one, IP.
- The Remote Access Service is installed on both a client and server computer to allow for dial-in access.

Further Reading

Here is information about various books and magazines in which to look for further information on the subject.

[McGregor1992] McGregor, G., *The PPP Internet Protocol Control Protocol (IPCP)*, 1992, IETF RFC 1332

[Meyer1996] Meyer, G., *The PPP Encryption Control Protocol (ECP)*, 1996, IETF RFC 1968

[Pall1997] Pall, G., *PPP NetBIOS Frames Control Protocol (NBFCP)*, 1997, IETF RFC 2097

[Rand1996] Rand, D., *The PPP Compression Control Protocol*, 1996, IETF RFC 1962

[Simpson1993] Simpson, W., *The PPP Internetworking Packet Exchange Control Protocol (IPXCP)*, 1993, IETF RFC 1552

[Simpson1994] Simpson, W., *The Point-to-Point Protocol (PPP),* 1994, IETF RFC 1661

[Simpson1996] Simpson, W., *PPP Challenge Handshake Authentication Protocol (CHAP),* 1996, IETF RFC 1994

[Simpson1997] Simpson, W., *PPP Vendor Extensions,* 1997, IETF RFC 2153

[Sklower1996] Sklower, K., Meyer, G., *The PPP DES Encryption Protocol (DESE),* 1996, IETF RFC 1969

10

Securely Accessing the Corporate Network Using PPTP

We've seen that the Point-to-Point Protocol (PPP) can be used to connect a client into a corporate network by directly dialing into the company. That method works well for the following scenarios:

- A small number of users are dialing in.
- The users are all dialing locally.

If you have a large number of users, or users in remote locations, RAS may not be the best solution. If users could use the Internet for access to the corporate network, both of those problems would be solved.

However, one of the problems with transmitting data over the Internet is that it is a public network, and data sent over the Internet is by default not encrypted. To fix this potential security hole, various protocols have been created that can be used to securely transmit data over the Internet. One of these protocols is the still-in-the-works standard of IPSEC.[1] Another one of these protocols is the *Point-to-Point Tunneling Protocol (PPTP)*.[2]

This chapter will discuss how to use PPTP to securely connect remote users to the corporate network.

Tunneling and VPNs

Assume that you have two machines which can communicate using an existing (real) network, as shown in Figure 10.1.

1. The IP Security (IPSEC) suite of RFCs (1825-1829) specify a security architecture for the Internet [Atkinson1995b], a framework for authentication and encryption, and required authentication and encryption choices.
2. PPTP was specified as an Internet draft, but has expired. For similar functionality, look to the new Layer Two Tunneling Protocol (L2TP) [Hamzeh1997].

Figure 10.1 Two computers using a real network.

tunnel: a channel which data is sent over. Often the data is a layer 3 protocol encapsulated by another layer 3 protocol.

Next, assume that the users (or administrators) of these two machines don't trust their corporate information to the other users (or operators) of the real network. The users may negotiate some sort of encryption scheme to use for all communications which must be secured across the real network. These users are effectively building a **tunnel** across the real network (Figure 10.2).

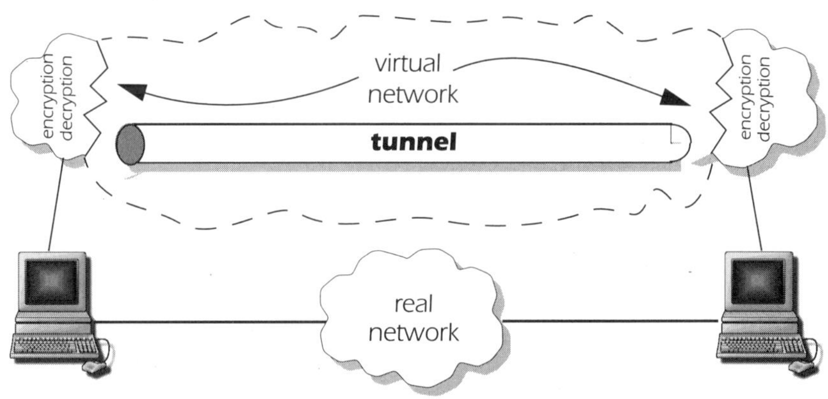

Figure 10.2 Two computers using a virtual network.

VPN: a network which is used like a private network, but uses a public network infrastructure.

This tunnel they have built runs on top of the connection they already use for the real network. Each machine has an interface to their end of the tunnel, thus communication across the tunnel is effectively a point-to-point *virtual network*. Because these machines encrypt and decrypt at either end of the tunnel, it is actually a **Virtual Private Network(VPN)**[3]. The underlying real network may still be used by the machines for any insecure communication.

The distinction between a virtual network and a virtual private network is not often made clear by vendors and service providers. A part of the problem is that there are so many definitions of VPN. These concepts

3. Additionally, if either or both of these machines act as gateways for actual private networks, then the scope of the VPN may encompass the union of both private networks.

have existed for quite some time in telecommunications and networking. In the telephony world, examples of VPNs are private branch exchanges (PBXs) and Centrex-type services. In networking, switching equipment[4] is often implemented with features to segregate users into different groups, which is another type of VPN.

Thus, in the general sense, *VPNs are simply collections of members which share the same physical infrastructure.* Another aspect of this broad definition is that data sent across a VPN is often, but not always, encrypted. In the case of PPTP on NT, the data is encrypted if the "Require Data Encryption" box on either the client or server's configuration dialog is checked.[5]

From a practical standpoint, the word *private* in a virtual network implies privacy of data, and encryption should be a part of the solution. *This chapter will therefore use the more specific definition of VPN which implies encryption.* This chapter will also assume that all PPTP data is being encrypted when sent.

What is a PPTP Tunnel Made of?

PPTP provides a way of creating a point-to-point tunnel by encrypting each payload and encapsulating the result. A PPTP tunnel is created by building on top of existing network interfaces used by IP. Thus any two IP clients with PPTP software may create such a tunnel (Figure 10.3).

4. For example, many Ethernet switches and ATM switches allow either static or dynamic configuration of VPN membership.
5. Refer to Figure 10.28 for an example of this dialog on a PPTP server.

Figure 10.3
PPTP builds a tunnel on top of a pair of regular interfaces.

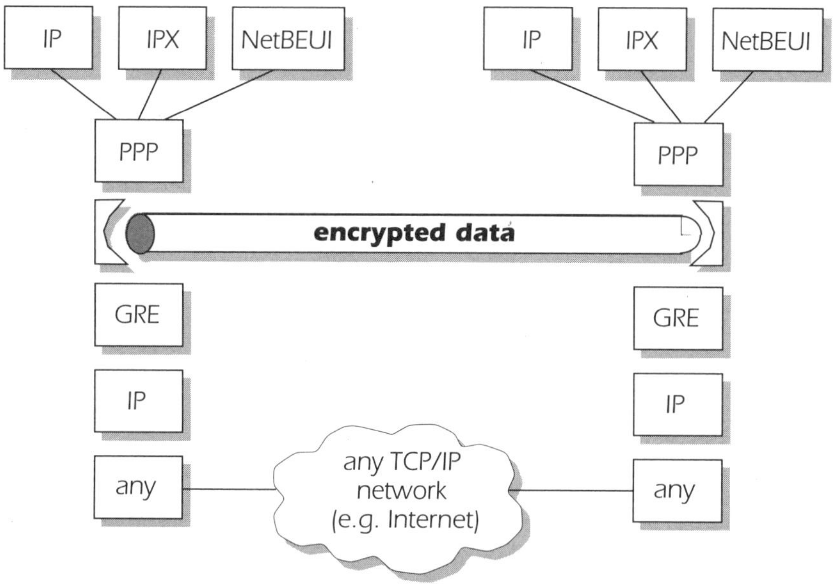

Such a tunnel may therefore be run over a any IP network, whether it be a LAN running all Ethernet interfaces or a pair of heterogeneous subscriber interfaces to the Internet.

This tunnel is constructed with the *Generic Routing Encapsulation (GRE)* protocol being used over IP.[6] The payload for each GRE packet is an encrypted PPP frame. Thus an association between the two machines using GRE with negotiated encryption essentially has a private virtual connection via the tunnel. This connection appears to the clients of GRE to be a PPP link, when in actuality it is a tunnel over a whole IP-based Internet which may or may not have any actual PPP links.

VPN interface: a network interface that when used, will encrypt transmitted packets.

By making the network interface to the tunnel appear as a **VPN interface** with PPP framing, the ability for all of the protocols which normally run over PPP, such as IP, IPX, and NetBEUI, is built-in.

Any frames sent out the VPN interface will be encapsulated in PPP framing, and then passed through the encryption which has been negotiated for the tunnel. The whole PPP frame, header and payload, is encrypted (Figure 10.4).

6. There is a pair of RFCs which describe GRE [Hanks1994] and how it is used with IP [Hanks1994a]. PPTP uses a variant of GRE which is described in the PPTP specification [Hamzeh1997].

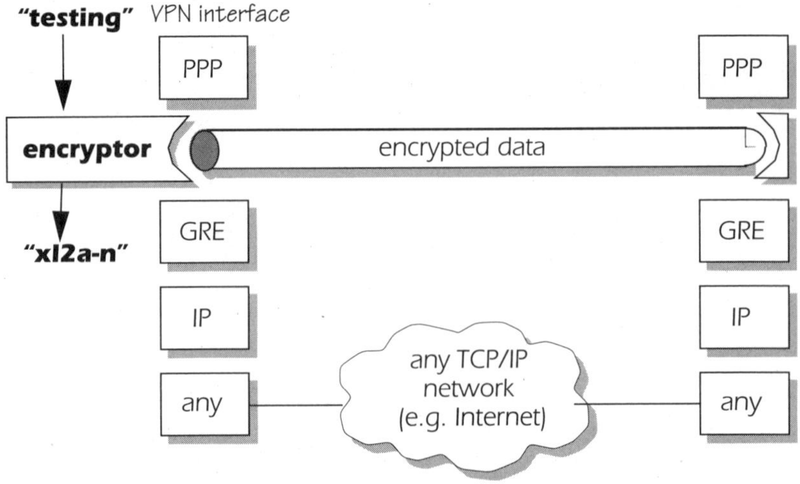

Figure 10.4 PPTP's PPP frames (and their contents) are encrypted prior to transmission. Similarly, decryption occurs on reception.

Similarly, any IP datagrams which are received by the underlying IP with a protocol type specifying GRE (protocol type 47) will be passed to GRE. In turn, GRE will select the proper decryption which has been negotiated for the tunnel and pass the *clear-text*[7] PPP frame to the receive function of the VPN interface.

Figure 10.5 provides an example of an encapsulated telnet message. Assume that you had telneted into a UNIX machine and once there had issued the command "ls /usr/teresa" to list (ls) the files found in the directory /usr/teresa[8]. Let's follow the encapsulation down the stack.

7. The common phrase "clear-text" simply means that the PPP frame and payload are now in normal clearly-encapsulated-binary form.
8. Telnet usually defaults to character-oriented mode, but we've assumed line mode here for simplicity.

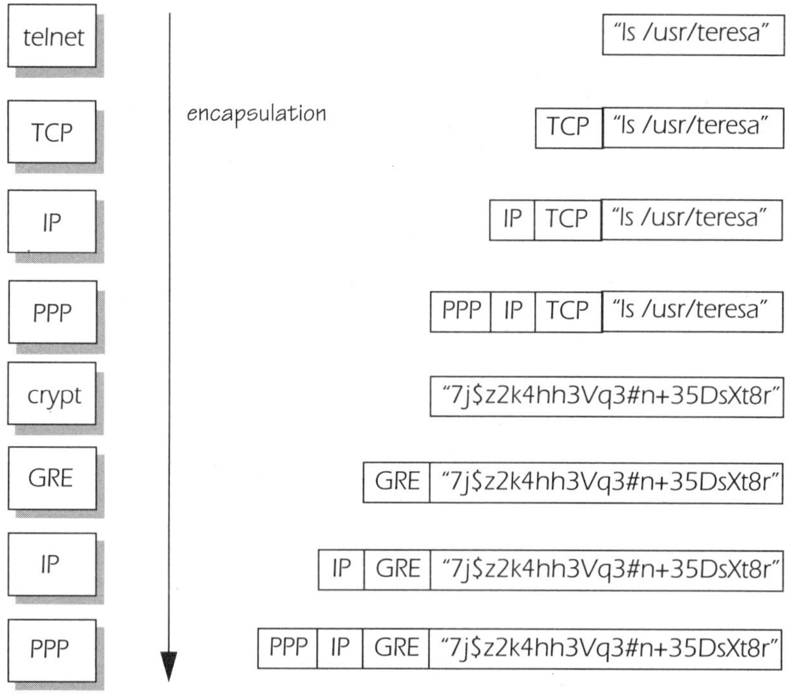

Figure 10.5 PPTP provides a negotiated tunnel interface with encapsulation in PPP, GRE, and IP.

The telnet client passes the command that you've typed down to TCP which adds a TCP header to the segment and passes the result down to IP. Next, IP adds its own header to the TCP and telnet information, forming a datagram. After finding a route and appropriate interface, IP sends the datagram to a network interface that it thinks runs PPP. In fact, this VPN interface does use PPP framing, but then passes the whole frame through an encryption function.

The whole PPP frame is encrypted. The PPP frame includes the following:

- PPP header
- IP header
- TCP header
- Telnet information: "ls /usr/teresa"

This encrypted frame is passed down to GRE which adds its own header (including an encryption key) and passes the result down to IP. As usual, IP adds its own header and after selecting an interface based on its routing information, sends the resulting datagram to the selected interface, which in this case is a PPP interface. Note that in another example, this could have been a FDDI or Ethernet (or any kind) of network interface.

At the other end of this PPP link, the IP datagram gets decapsulated from PPP and routed toward to the next hop toward its target, which is the other end of the tunnel.

Once at the other end of the tunnel, the IP datagram is passed up to GRE to be *detunneled.* In other words, the decapsulation, decryption, and rendering into PPP undoes the *tunneling* done at the other (sending) end.

How Does PPTP Make the Tunnel?

During the discussion of what a PPTP tunnel is made of, you may have noticed that PPTP itself is not a part of the actual tunnel. In reality, PPTP is a negotiator which oversees the construction, maintenance, and destruction of the tunnel.

All of the tunnel administration is performed over a TCP connection to port 1723[9] to a PPTP server. This is called the *control connection,* and the protocol used over this connection is PPTP.

There is a common format for all PPTP messages, which all start with a header as shown in Figure 10.6.

Figure 10.6 PPTP message header.

bits 0-3	bits 4-7	bits 8-11	bits 12-15	bits 16-19	bits 20-23	bits 24-27	bits 28-31
Length				PPTP Message Type			
Magic Cookie							

The *length* field specifies the size in octets of the entire message including the header. The *PPTP message type* will have a value of one to indicate control messages, and the value of two is reserved for future use to indicate management messages. The *magic cookie* must have a value of 1A2B3C4D (hex) according to the specification.

9. In the original specification, the control channel was to use port 5678, but this was later changed to 1723.

A summary of the tunnel establishment signalling messages over the control channel is shown in Figure 10.7.

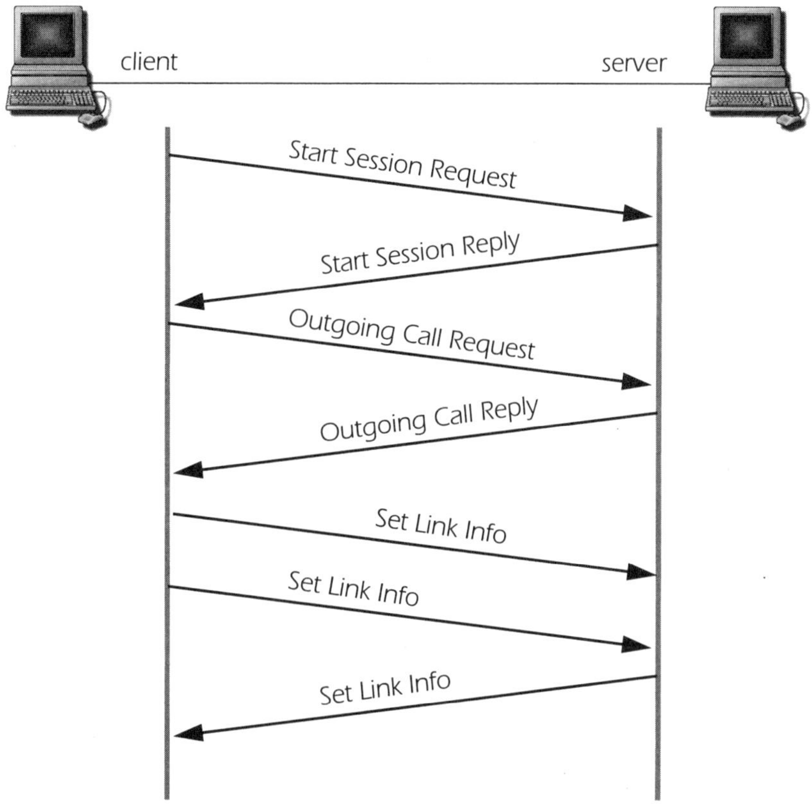

Figure 10.7
The PPTP connection setup is performed on a TCP connection from the client to port 1723 on the PPTP server.

Once a control connection has been established, the client sends the first message, which is called a *Start Session Request*.[10] The format of the Start Session Request is shown in Figure 10.8. Actually, the result code field and error code field are reserved (must be zero) in the Start Session Request.[11]

The server responds with a *Start Session Reply* message to the client. The format is the same as that used for the Start Session Request with the exception of the result and error codes, which are specified in the reply to indicate a successful channel establishment or other condition.

10. In the original specification, the Start Session Request had been called Start Control Connection Request.

11. The control channel may be used to start up more than one tunnel (e.g. session) by going through this sequence once for each tunnel.

Figure 10.8 PPTP message format for Start Session Request and Start Session Reply.

<table>
<tr><td>bits 0-3</td><td>bits 4-7</td><td>bits 8-11</td><td>bits 12-15</td><td>bits 16-19</td><td>bits 20-23</td><td>bits 24-27</td><td>bits 28-31</td></tr>
<tr><td colspan="4">Length</td><td colspan="4">PPTP Message Type</td></tr>
<tr><td colspan="8">Magic Cookie</td></tr>
<tr><td colspan="4">Control Message Type</td><td colspan="4">Reserved</td></tr>
<tr><td colspan="4">Protocol Version</td><td colspan="2">Result Code</td><td colspan="2">Error Code</td></tr>
<tr><td colspan="8">Framing Capabilities</td></tr>
<tr><td colspan="8">Bearer Capabilities</td></tr>
<tr><td colspan="4">Maximum Channels</td><td colspan="4">Firmware Revision</td></tr>
<tr><td colspan="8">...</td></tr>
<tr><td>...</td><td colspan="6">Host Name (64 octets)</td><td>...</td></tr>
<tr><td colspan="8">...</td></tr>
<tr><td colspan="8">...</td></tr>
<tr><td>...</td><td colspan="6">Vendor String (64 octets)</td><td>...</td></tr>
<tr><td colspan="8">...</td></tr>
</table>

Next, the client sends an *Outgoing Call Request* message to the server. Figure 10.9 shows the format of the Outgoing Call Request.

Figure 10.9 PPTP message format for Outgoing Call Request.

<table>
<tr><td>bits 0-3</td><td>bits 4-7</td><td>bits 8-11</td><td>bits 12-15</td><td>bits 16-19</td><td>bits 20-23</td><td>bits 24-27</td><td>bits 28-31</td></tr>
<tr><td colspan="4">Length</td><td colspan="4">PPTP Message Type</td></tr>
<tr><td colspan="8">Magic Cookie</td></tr>
<tr><td colspan="4">Control Message Type</td><td colspan="4">Reserved</td></tr>
<tr><td colspan="4">Call Identifier</td><td colspan="4">Call Serial Number</td></tr>
<tr><td colspan="8">Minimum Data Rate (bps)</td></tr>
<tr><td colspan="8">Maximum Data Rate (bps)</td></tr>
<tr><td colspan="8">Bearer Type</td></tr>
<tr><td colspan="8">Framing Type</td></tr>
<tr><td colspan="4">Receive Window Size</td><td colspan="4">Packet Processing Delay</td></tr>
<tr><td colspan="4">Phone Number Length</td><td colspan="4">Reserved1</td></tr>
<tr><td colspan="8">...</td></tr>
<tr><td>...</td><td colspan="6">Phone Number (64 octets)</td><td>...</td></tr>
<tr><td colspan="8">...</td></tr>
<tr><td colspan="8">...</td></tr>
<tr><td>...</td><td colspan="6">Subaddress (64 octets)</td><td>...</td></tr>
<tr><td colspan="8">...</td></tr>
</table>

The call request specifies a number of parameters, such as the *call identifier.* The call identifier is used to uniquely distinguish the call from others between this client/server pair. The call which PPTP is trying to set up here is the tunnel. This call identifier will be used at both ends of the tunnel to specify tunneling and detunneling information such as the encryption used.

Also, several parameters in the call request specify parameters for the communications channel used by the call. A pair of parameters specify a minimum and maximum data rate requested for the call. In practice, Windows NT usually specifies a range of acceptable data rates from 300 bps to 10 Mbps. The *framing type* requests a synchronous or asynchronous channel, while the *bearer type* requests an analog or digital channel. The *receive window size* identifies the number of packets which may be outstanding in receive processing at any given time.

The *phone number* and *subaddress* parameters specify a number to be dialed to establish the service. Yet for PPTP service in Windows NT, these are usually empty because the IP address of the PPTP server to contact is likely all that is needed to establish the tunnel.

The server will reply to this outgoing call request by sending an *Outgoing Call Reply* message back to the client. The format of the outgoing call reply message is shown in Figure 10.10.

Figure 10.10 PPTP message format for Outgoing Call Reply.

<table>
<tr><td>bits 0-3</td><td>bits 4-7</td><td>bits 8-11</td><td>bits 12-15</td><td>bits 16-19</td><td>bits 20-23</td><td>bits 24-27</td><td>bits 28-31</td></tr>
<tr><td colspan="4">Length</td><td colspan="4">PPTP Message Type</td></tr>
<tr><td colspan="8">Magic Cookie</td></tr>
<tr><td colspan="4">Control Message Type</td><td colspan="4">Reserved</td></tr>
<tr><td colspan="4">Call Identifier</td><td colspan="4">Peer Call Identifier</td></tr>
<tr><td colspan="2">Result Code</td><td colspan="2">Error Code</td><td colspan="4">Cause Code</td></tr>
<tr><td colspan="8">Connect Speed (bps)</td></tr>
<tr><td colspan="4">Receive Window Size</td><td colspan="4">Packet Processing Delay</td></tr>
<tr><td colspan="8">Physical Channel Identifier</td></tr>
</table>

Most of the fields in this reply correspond with the fields in the outgoing call request. Once this message has been processed, the tunnel is effectively set up.

Other PPTP messages will be sent on this control connection throughout the life of the tunnel, to perform such functions as:

- setting sequence information for the link.

- testing the control connection with an echo/reply type heartbeat.
- request/reply messages to clear the call.
- request/reply messages to stop the session.

None of the actual tunneled data is passed on this TCP connection. Only the PPTP messages for negotiating the characteristics needed to establish and maintain the tunnel are sent over the control channel.

pptpsetup.cap

The packet capture of the startup is shown in Figure 10.11, from the file pptpsetup.cap.

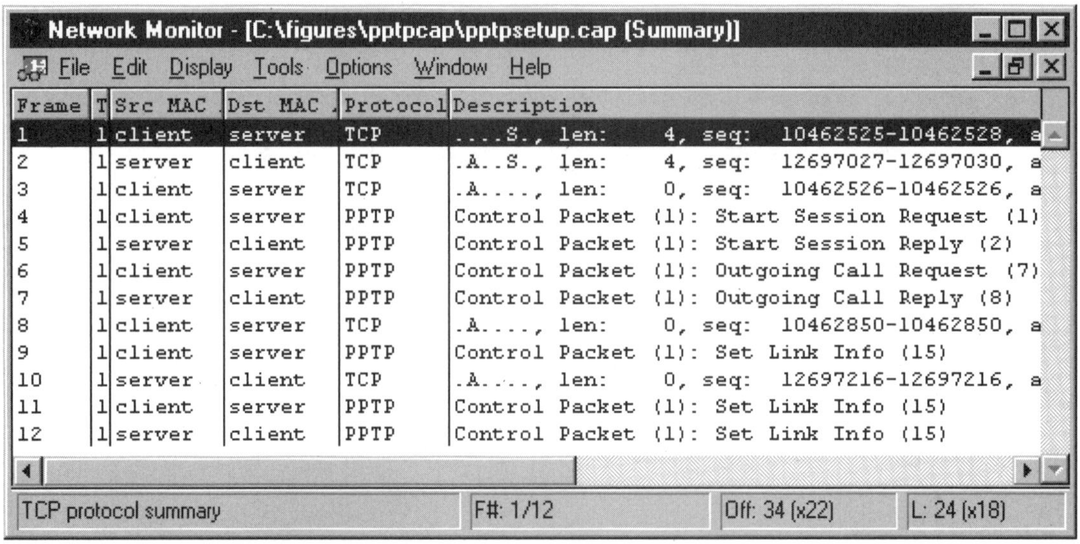

Network Monitor - [C:\figures\pptpcap\pptpsetup.cap (Summary)]

File Edit Display Tools Options Window Help

Frame	T	Src MAC	Dst MAC	Protocol	Description
1	1	client	server	TCP	....S., len: 4, seq: 10462525-10462528, a
2	1	server	client	TCP	.A..S., len: 4, seq: 12697027-12697030, a
3	1	client	server	TCP	.A...., len: 0, seq: 10462526-10462526, a
4	1	client	server	PPTP	Control Packet (1): Start Session Request (1)
5	1	server	client	PPTP	Control Packet (1): Start Session Reply (2)
6	1	client	server	PPTP	Control Packet (1): Outgoing Call Request (7)
7	1	server	client	PPTP	Control Packet (1): Outgoing Call Reply (8)
8	1	client	server	TCP	.A...., len: 0, seq: 10462850-10462850, a
9	1	client	server	PPTP	Control Packet (1): Set Link Info (15)
10	1	server	client	TCP	.A...., len: 0, seq: 12697216-12697216, a
11	1	client	server	PPTP	Control Packet (1): Set Link Info (15)
12	1	server	client	PPTP	Control Packet (1): Set Link Info (15)

TCP protocol summary | F#: 1/12 | Off: 34 (x22) | L: 24 (x18)

Figure 10.11 Packet capture of the PPTP connection setup

Note that in order for Network Monitor to decipher port 1723 packets to be PPTP, the TCPIP.INI file needed to be modified (see the Network Monitor chapter). The incorrect number which Netmon may be using is 5678. If the incorrect number is being used then the PPTP messages will just show up as TCP segments in Netmon.

Details of Tunneling with GRE

Once the tunnel has been negotiated with PPTP, it is used to tunnel PPP frames in each direction between the client and server.

Recall that all of these PPP frames (see Figure 10.4) are encapsulated for transmission over an IP network using the Generic Routing Encapsulation (GRE) technique[12]. PPP thinks that it is running over a physical communications link which simply doesn't require leading and trailing flags or bit stuffing. Effectively, the tunnel negotiated by PPTP uses GRE to make IP and all the underlying network interface and physical technologies look like a piece of virtual wire.

The GRE packet header is shown in Figure 10.12.

Figure 10.12
GRE header format.

<table>
<tr><td>bits 0-3</td><td>bits 4-7</td><td>bits 8-11</td><td>bits 12-15</td><td>bits 16-19</td><td>bits 20-23</td><td>bits 24-27</td><td>bits 28-31</td></tr>
<tr><td colspan="4">Flags</td><td colspan="4">Protocol Type</td></tr>
<tr><td colspan="4">Payload Length</td><td colspan="4">Call Identifier</td></tr>
<tr><td colspan="8">Sequence Number (optional)</td></tr>
<tr><td colspan="8">Acknowledgment Number (optional)</td></tr>
</table>

When the tunnel is established, the PPP software at either end of the tunnel starts the normal PPP link establishment. Thus, the LCP, IPCP, and other negotiations occur as they normally would, as was shown in Figure 9.14 on page 346.

When encryption is desired on the tunnel, it is actually implemented via negotiation by the Compression Control Protocol (CCP) as it would be on a PPP link running over a serial link.

There are several steps in constructing a tunnel which is usable by IP. First there are the PPTP exchanges for negotiating the session and call parameters. (These were shown in Figure 10.7 and Figure 10.11.) Then there are the several phases of PPP related protocols, which may include:

- PPP LCP phase for link establishment[13]
- PPP PAP or PPP CHAP for authentication

12. PPTP actually uses a modified version of GRE than that specified in the IETF RFC. This enhanced GRE uses an acknowledgment number for flow control.

13. Refer to Chapter 9 for a discussion of LCP and CHAP.

- CBCP (Callback Control Protocol)
- CCP (Compression Control Protocol)
- IPCP (IP Control Protocol)

Figure 10.13 shows each of these phases. The arrows going in both directions and crossing each other are meant to imply that packet order is not being shown in this diagram.

Figure 10.13
The construction of a tunnel has several phases involving PPTP and then several PPP related protocols.

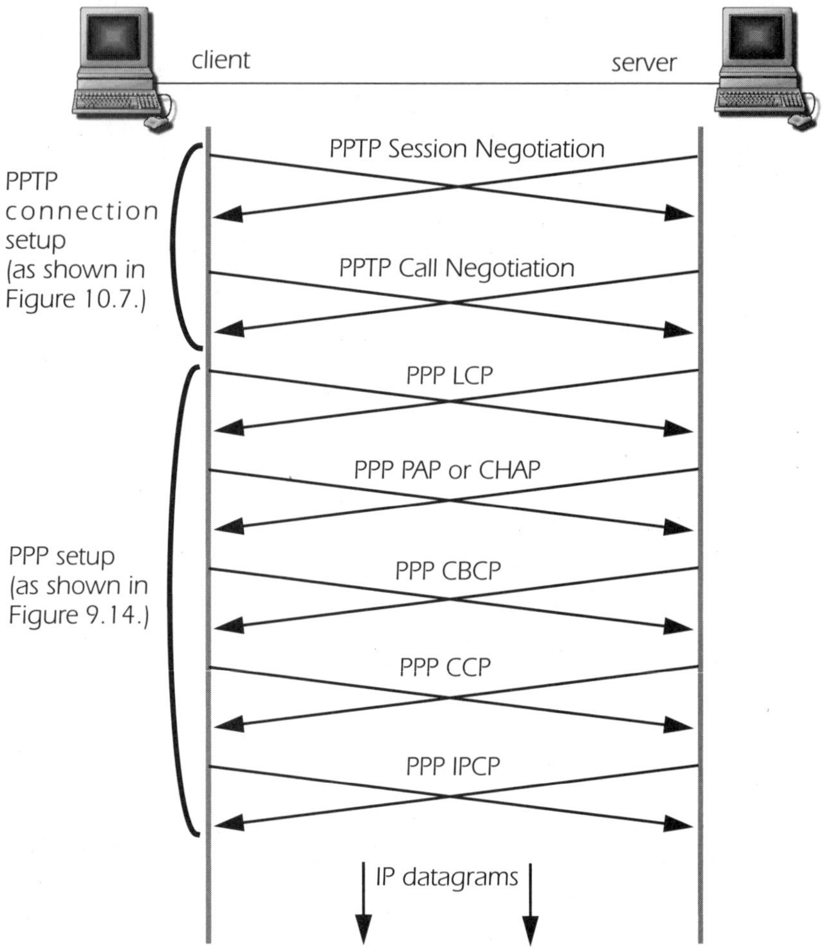

First, the PPTP connection setup (session and call negotiation) occurs. Once the tunnel is established, the normal PPP setup takes place as shown in the lower part of the diagram. As is usual with a PPP connection, following the IPCP exchange, IP datagrams may be passed over the network interface.

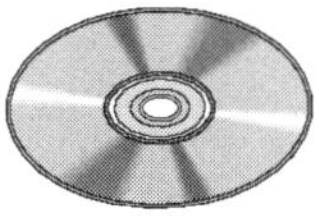

pptptunnel.cap

Figure 10.14 shows a packet capture of the middle phases of the ladder diagram: the LCP, PPP CHAP, and the beginning of the CBCP phase. These packets are found on the CD in the file pptptunnel.cap.

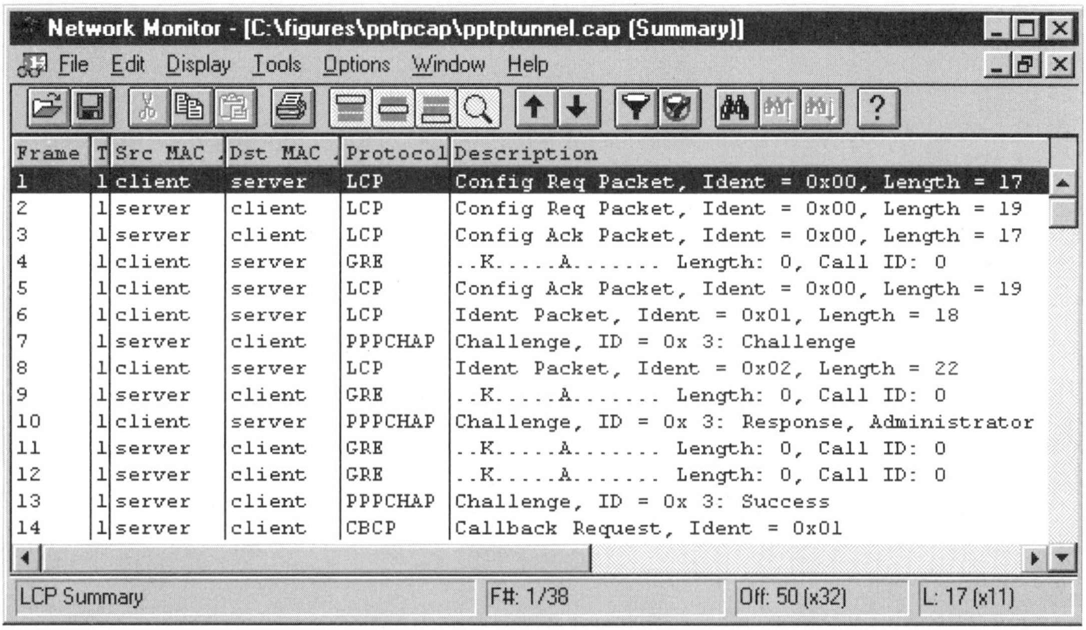

Figure 10.14 Packet decode of LCP and PPPCHAP phases of the tunnel establishment.

Note that for the packet capture in pptptunnel.cap, a filter was configured with protocol = GRE. Due to the role of the machine on which the packet capture was done, there are two packets for every message once the tunnel is created. One of these packets is encrypted and the other is not. We only wanted to see the packets that were encrypted, thus we created a filter with protocol = GRE.

Connecting a Single Machine to the Corporate Network Using the Internet

You can have encrypted (private) access to a corporate network across the Internet using PPTP to connect a remote NT or Windows 95 client (e.g. laptop) to the corporate network. Figure 10.15 shows the intended network configuration for the remote access portion of the foobar.com network.

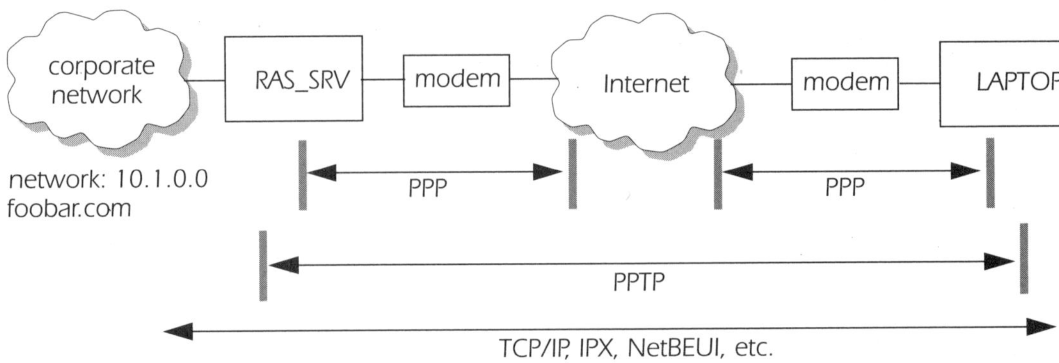

Figure 10.15 Access tunneled through Internet to a corporate network.

Let's assume the Remote Access Service is installed and operational on both the RAS_SRV and LAPTOP. Also required for this configuration is a fixed, valid IP address for the RAS_SRV for it's connection to the Internet. The steps to configure PPTP and establish a PPTP session are as follows:

1. Install PPTP on both client and server machines.
2. On the client, configure dial-out interface to require data encryption (this enables PPTP). On the server, require data encryption on the incoming device.
3. Client dials and connects to the Internet using PPP.

4. Client creates a phonebook entry to dial the RAS_SRV, but using the RAS_SRV's IP address as the "phone number".[14]
5. Client "dials" the server, which sets up the encrypted (PPTP) connection.

The details of installation of a PPTP client and server will be covered in the following sections.

Overview of PPTP Installation and Configuration Steps (NT 4.0)

This procedure assumes that you have already installed, configured, and tested RAS on the client and server as described in the previous chapter. The following steps are to be performed on the machine which is to be the *PPTP client*.

1. Install PPTP protocol.
2. Configure a RAS VPN device.
3. Create a phonebook entry for the PPTP server.

The following steps are to be performed on the machine which is to be the *PPTP server*.

1. Install PPTP protocol.
2. Configure a RAS VPN device.
3. (Optional) Configure the server to only receive and send PPTP packets. This is called PPTP filtering, and the screen used to enable PPTP filtering is shown on page 184.

After both the client and the server have been configured, the connection between the two can be tested.

14. The domain name of the RAS server could also be used, and DNS would be used to resolve the address.

Client Step 1: Install PPTP protocol

These steps assume you already configured the box as a RAS client, as in the previous chapter.

It is important to note that PPTP is a protocol, and so will be installed using *Network Control Panel->Protocols tab* (Figure 10.16). Use of PPTP *alters the RAS service*, as will be made apparent when we revisit the RAS configuration. PPTP depends on RAS in providing its service. Basically, PPTP creates VPN devices for use by RAS.

Selecting *Add* under *Protocols tab* brings up the *Select Network Protocol* dialog (Figure 10.16). Notice that the Point-to-Point Tunneling Protocol selection does not have distinct client and server varieties. Instead, PPTP software can operate either way, but in the configuration process, either client behavior or server behavior is selected.

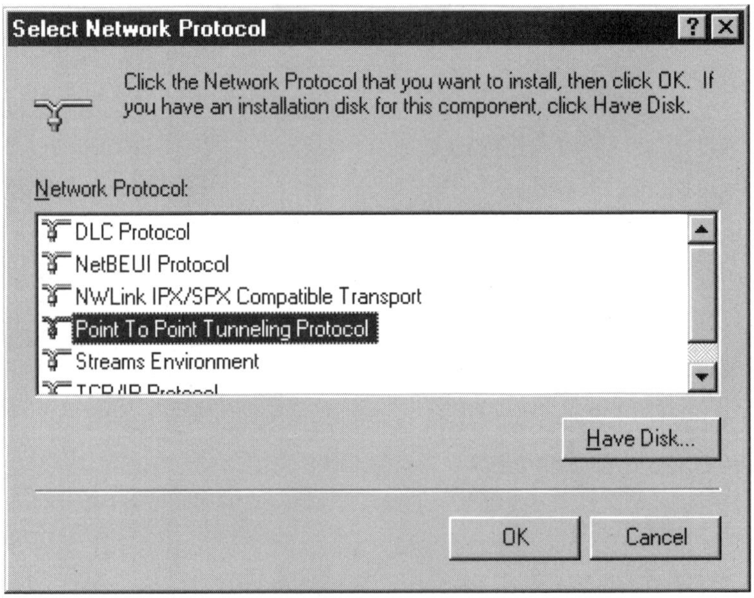

Figure 10.16 Select the Point-to-Point Tunneling Protocol from this dialog.

Once the PPTP files are installed on your machine, you will be prompted to configure PPTP.

Client Step 2: Configure the RAS VPN Device

Recall from the discussion of PPTP that either end of a tunnel is essentially a virtual private network (VPN) interface. The first prompt is for the number of VPNs you wish to use, as shown in Figure 10.17. A PPTP client will usually only need one VPN interface.

Figure 10.17 The PPTP configuration only needs to know how many VPN interfaces you want.

The remainder of the configuration of the PPTP client is effectively Remote Access Service (RAS) configuration of the VPN interface which has been created. The setup procedure will announce this to you as shown in Figure 10.18.

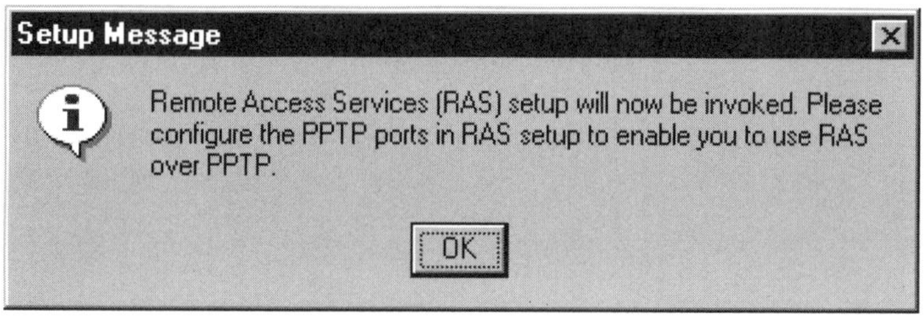

Figure 10.18 Once the number of VPN devices has been specified, you will proceed with RAS configuration.

Because you already have a RAS device on this machine (as added in the prerequisite RAS configuration), you are not automatically prompted to add a device, but instead are presented with the RAS setup dialog as shown in Figure 10.19.

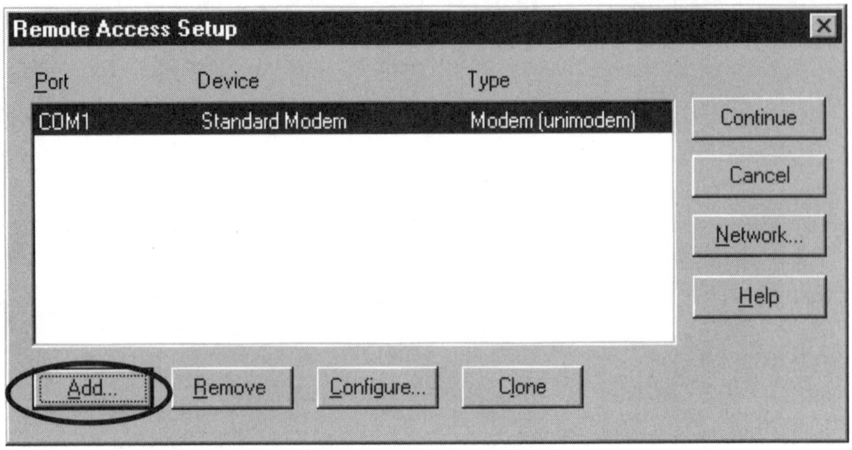

Figure 10.19 Use the Add... button to select a VPN device to use with RAS

Press the *Add* button so that you may instruct RAS to use the VPN device for remote access. The *Add RAS Device* screen like the one shown in Figure 10.20 will appear so that you may select the appropriate VPN device.

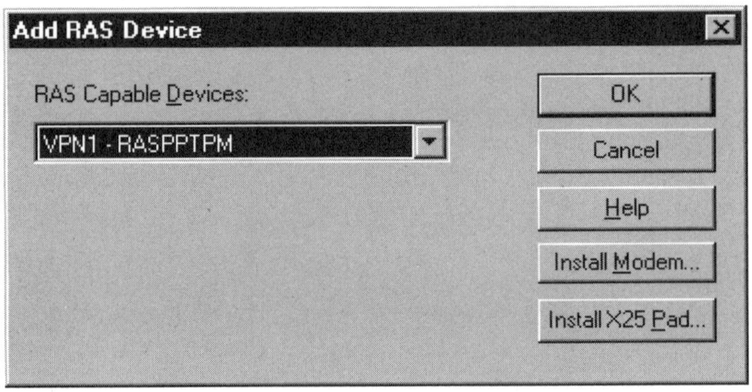

Figure 10.20 Add the VPN device which will be enabled by PPTP.

If you have only one VPN device and it is the only RAS capable device which is not already in use by RAS, it will be selected. If the pop-up menu does not show the proper device, select the one you want to use. Then press the OK button.

Back at the *Remote Access Setup* dialog, as with the simple (non-PPTP) RAS configuration, there are two buttons which we're interested in using here. Make sure that the appropriate VPN device is selected and press the *Configure* button.

The familiar *Configure Port Usage* dialog appears as shown in Figure 10.21. Because this machine is to use the VPN device as a client, select the *Dial out only* option and press OK.

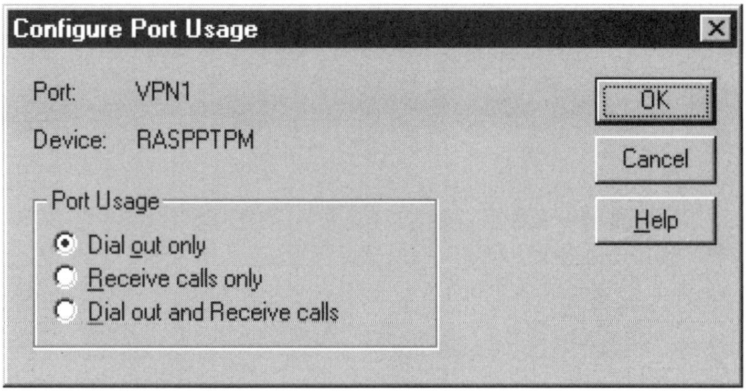

Figure 10.21 Selecting the dial out only option here designates the VPN1 port to be used as a RAS client device.

Back at the *Remote Access Setup* dialog, we want to select the protocols to run over the tunnel. Press the *Network* button to obtain the *Network Configuration* dialog (Figure 10.22). Select TCP/IP as the protocol of choice for this VPN interface.

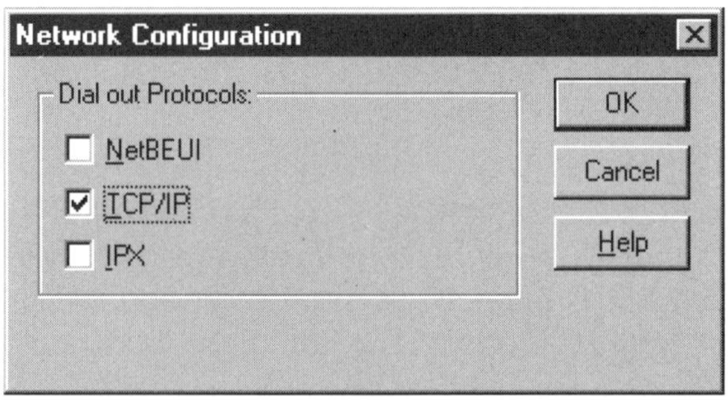

Figure 10.22 Select only TCP/IP for use with the PPTP tunnel.

Let's review the configuration just completed. In the previous chapter a physical interface, COM1, was configured for use with RAS. Now we've added a virtual interface with the PPTP configuration, and then added it to the RAS list of device as shown in Figure 10.23. This device, VPN1, looks like an ordinary communications port to RAS. The PPTP software will establish a tunnel in order to simulate a link through this port.

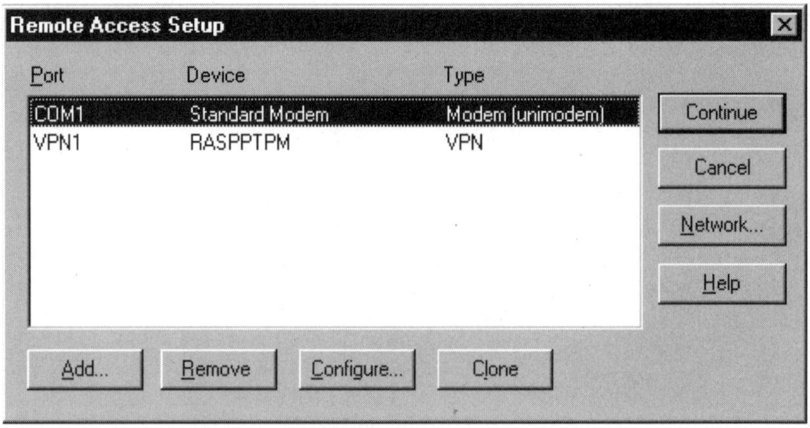

Figure 10.23 A second RAS device is created for encrypted communication.

PPTP client installation is complete. Now a phonebook entry must be made to dial the PPTP server.

Client Step 3: Create a Phonebook Entry for the PPTP Server

Start the *Dialup Networking* application from the *Start -> Programs -> Accessories* menu. Press the *New* button in the *Dialup Networking* dialog to create a new phonebook entry to connect to the PPTP server. As shown in Figure 10.24, we've called the phonebook entry "PPTP connection to HQ."

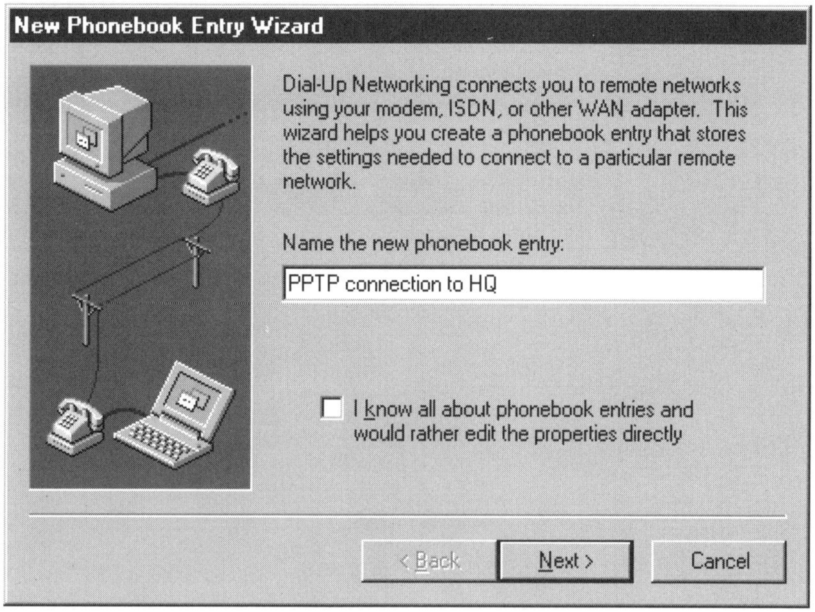

Figure 10.24 Use a descriptive name for the VPN that you're connecting to.

Figure 10.25 shows the dialog you use to select the device to use for the new connection. For the PPTP connection, select the VPN device.

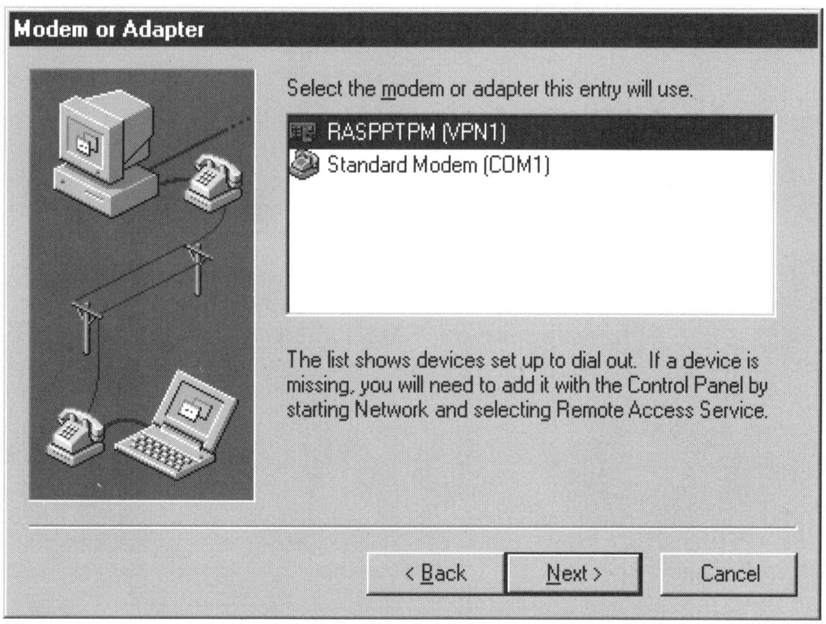

Figure 10.25 Select the VPN device for use with the PPTP connection.

The *Phone Number* dialog as shown in Figure 10.26 appears. Recall that the VPN interface will be set up over an existing IP interface. Therefore there is no phone number to be dialed because we'll be running the VPN device over an IP network rather than a phone network.

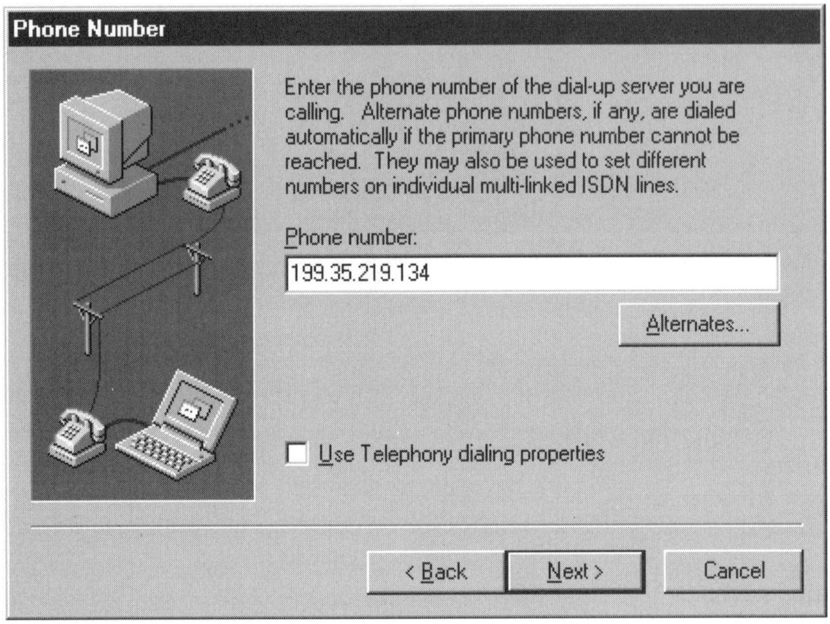

Figure 10.26 Enter the IP address or FQDN of the RAS server you'll be connecting to.

In this dialog you will enter the "phone number" of the PPTP server at headquarters— either an IP address or domain name. The IP address must be a *permanent IP address*, one that is valid on the Internet.[15] This implies that the Internet service at the headquarters is either running over a dedicated line, or a static address has been negotiated for use on an ISDN or modem access line.

In this example, the IP address of the RAS server at the headquarters of foobar.com is 199.35.219.134 as shown in Figure 10.26. Alternately, if a Fully Qualified Domain Name (FQDN) is available for the RAS server from the Internet, then that notation could also be used in this dialog.

When using an FQDN in this dialog, be sure that it may be resolved from the point in the Internet at which the RAS client is connecting in.

15. It is possible to connect server to server using dialup (i.e. randomly assigned) addresses, however, this requires the client's phonebook entry to be modified every time the PPTP server receives a new IP address

If the name you use for the RAS server is only resident in an internal DNS, you must use an IP address.

The new phonebook entry is complete. It should be available in the pop-up menu in the *Dialup Networking* dialog as shown in Figure 10.27.

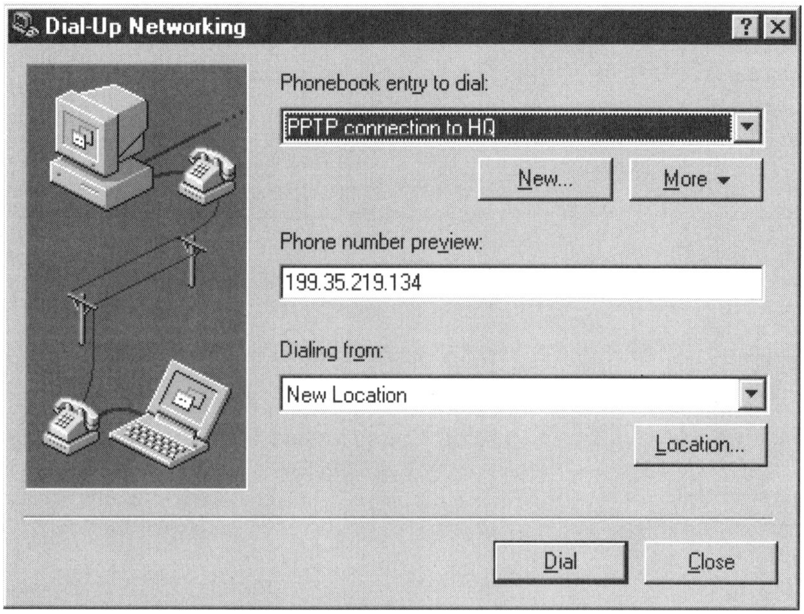

Figure 10.27 The entry for connecting to headquarters via PPTP has been added.

Server Step 1: Install PPTP

These steps assume that you have already configured the machine as a RAS server, as described in the previous chapter. These steps are to be performed on the machine to be used as a PPTP server.

Add the PPTP protocol using the *Protocols tab* of the *Network Control Panel,* as was described in Client Step 1.

Server Step 2: Configure a RAS VPN Device

After the PPTP files are copied to the machine, the *PPTP Configuration* screen appears (Figure 10.28). If there will be only one PPTP client connected in at any given time, then use the value of one here. To support multiple simultaneous VPN clients on this PPTP server, select a larger number. The maximum number of VPNs supported by the Microsoft PPTP software is 256. Size this number according to your needs.

Figure 10.28
On a PPTP server, you may want to have more than one VPN interface.

Next, RAS configuration will begin. As was done with the PPTP client, start the process of adding a VPN to the *Remote Access Setup* dialog, as shown in Figure 10.29, by pressing the *Add* button.

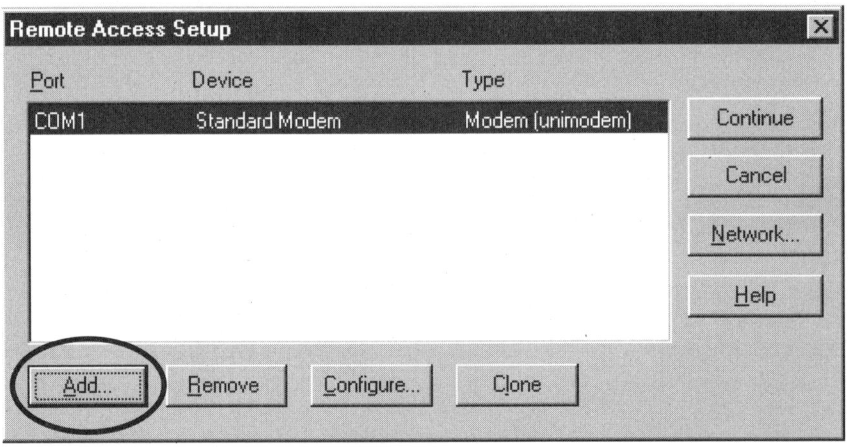

Figure 10.29
You will need to add and configure the VPN devices.

If you've instructed PPTP to add more than one device, then there may be several options in the pop-up menu in Figure 10.30. When you've chosen the appropriate one (all are created equally), press OK.

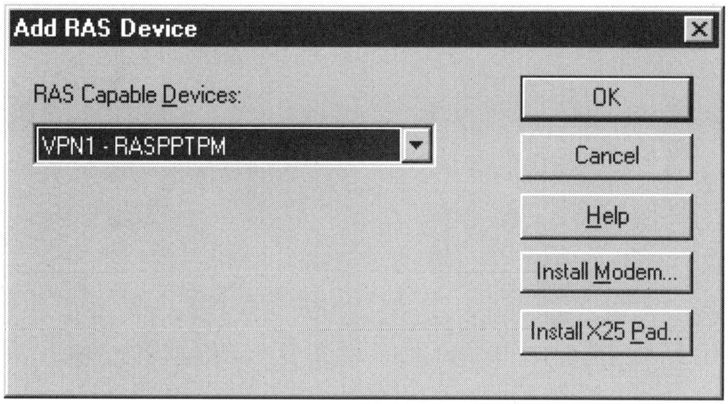

Figure 10.30 For a PPTP server with more than one VPN device, you may select the appropriate one with this dialog.

As usual, we're going to use the *Configure* and *Network* buttons on the *Remote Access Setup* dialog once we've selected the new device which has just been added. The *Configure* button yields the dialog shown in Figure 10.31.

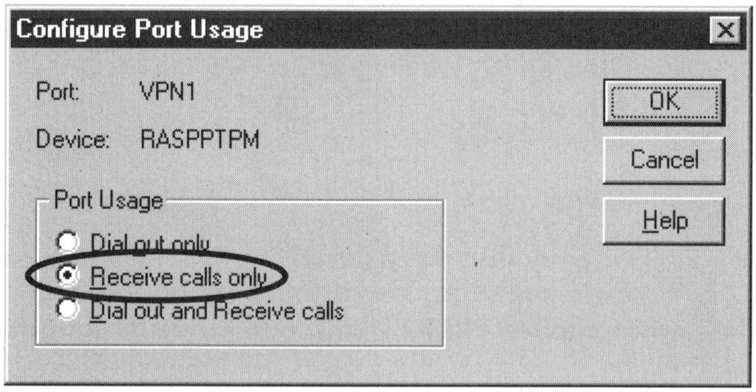

Figure 10.31 PPTP servers should be set to receive calls.

Because this is a PPTP server, we want to select the *Receive calls only* option in this dialog.

If you had selected more than one VPN interface for this PPTP server, add and configure the port usage on all of the remaining interfaces now.

Now we're back at *Remote Access Setup* dialog. Pressing the *Network* button results in the dialog shown in Figure 10.32.

Figure 10.32
Select the Require data encryption option in this dialog to enable the PPTP encryption feature.

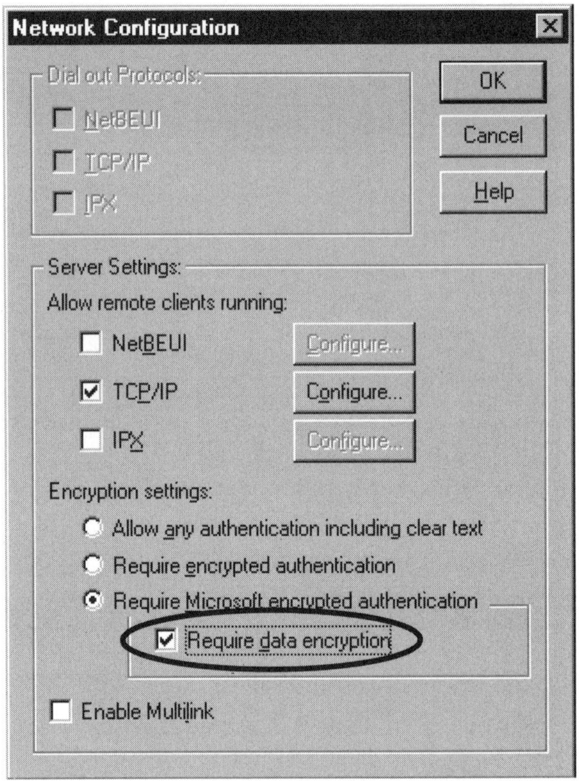

Configure this screen as appropriate for an incoming connection. Checking the box to require data encryption is the method you use to tell the server to use PPTP on this connection.

Note that the *Network Configuration* dialog holds true not just for the COM1 device or the VPN1 device, for both of these devices on this machine! When you set parameters in this dialog, they are being changed for the Remote Access setup in general, not just for one device.

The Remote Access Setup in Figure 10.33 shows both the physical and the virtual interfaces used for remote access.

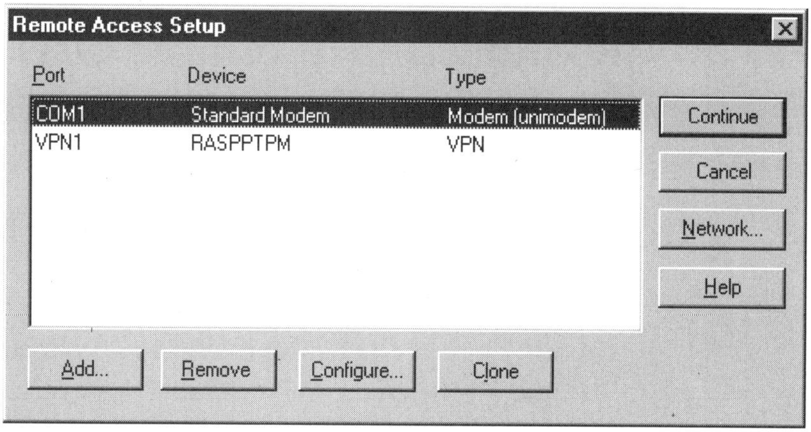

Figure 10.33 The second RAS device is created for encrypted communication.

If you have more than one VPN device on this server, they should all appear in this dialog.

Testing the PPTP Connection

Once both the client and the server are configured, the connection process occurs in two phases:

1. The client dials a local ISP to connect to the Internet.
2. When the Internet connection is in place, the client "dials" the connection to the PPTP RAS server.

At this point, the client will have access to the corporate network, and can be comforted by the fact that all the data sent over the Internet is encrypted. You can confirm this by using Network Monitor to watch the data traversing the modem interface.

Connecting a Remote Office to the Corporate Network Using the Internet

We've seen that RAS may be used with PPTP VPN devices in order to securely connect a single client machine into the corporate headquarters via the Internet.

In this section, we'll examine the details of connecting in a remote office network into the corporate headquarters network by using PPTP and the Routing and Remote Access Service (RRAS). Figure 10.34 shows the scenario which we'll be using in this section.

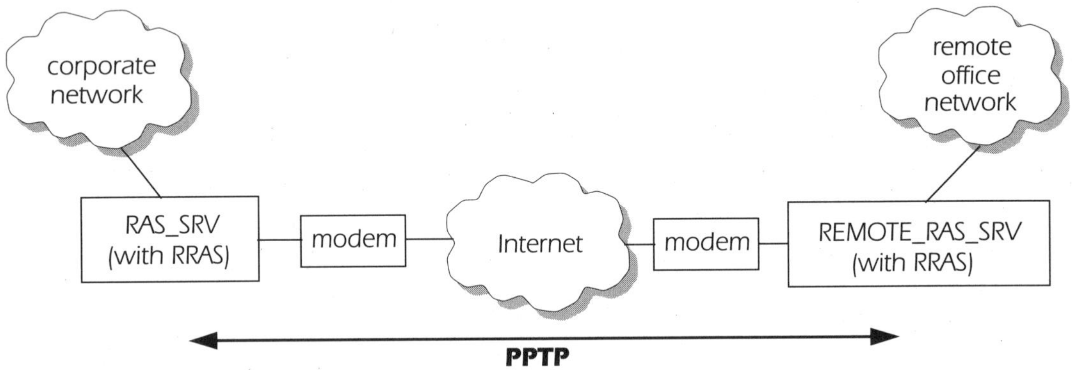

Figure 10.34 The remote office network will be connected into the corporate network using PPTP.

In order to connect more than one machine (e.g. the whole network) from the remote office into the headquarters network, the RAS client must be able to route across its LAN interface(s) and its remote access interface.

While the normal NT 4.0 implementation of PPTP supports client to server access, it does not support server to server calls. RRAS (a.k.a. Steelhead) does support server to server PPTP connections.

The difference from our previous configuration is that Steelhead as well as PPTP is installed on both servers.

Install Steelhead (RRAS) on Both Servers

The "Using Steelhead as a RIPv2 Router" chapter covered the installation and configuration of Steelhead. The chapter "Remotely Accessing the Corporate Network" addressed the traditional RAS installation and configuration. The single machine access scenario earlier in this chapter detailed the configuration of RAS with PPTP. Because you've now seen all of the component details, we won't show each dialog during the installation and configuration processes.

Note: we want to install Steelhead on each of the two servers, so repeat this procedure for each server.

Bring up the *Routing and Remote Access Setup* dialog, as shown in Figure 10.35. Select the *Remote Access Service* and *LAN routing* options as necessary.

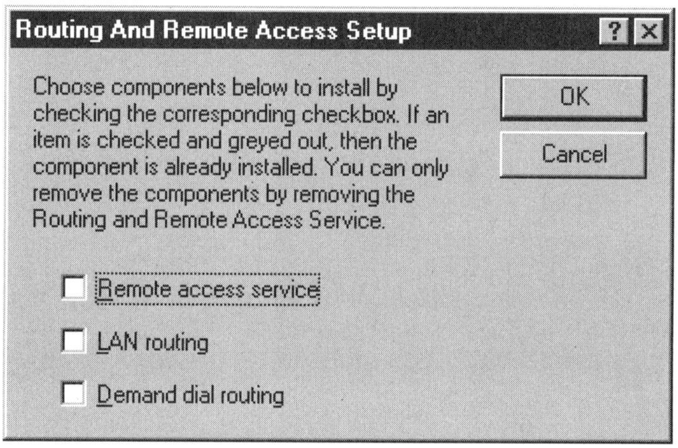

Figure 10.35 Install both the Remote access service and LAN routing aspects of RRAS on both servers.

The primary configuration difference between the RAS server at headquarters and the remote RAS server is found in the *Configure Port Usage* screen (Figure 10.36). Set the port usage for the VPN1 interface on the headquarters server RAS_SRV to receive calls as a RAS server. Configure the server in the remote office, REMOTE_RAS_SRV, to dial out as a RAS client.

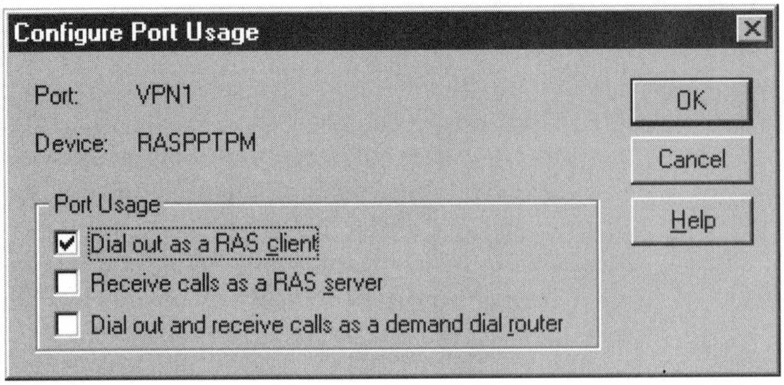

Figure 10.36 The VPN configuration for the remote office is set to only allow dial out.

Installation continues as was described in the previous section. Once Steelhead and PPTP are installed on both RAS servers, the connection can be tested.

Using RRAS Admin to Check the Connection

The *Routing and Remote Access Service Administration* tool (*Routing and RAS Admin*) may be used to monitor and control the connection. Figure 10.37 shows the status on RAS_SRV of a connection from REMOTE_RAS_SRV into the headquarters network.

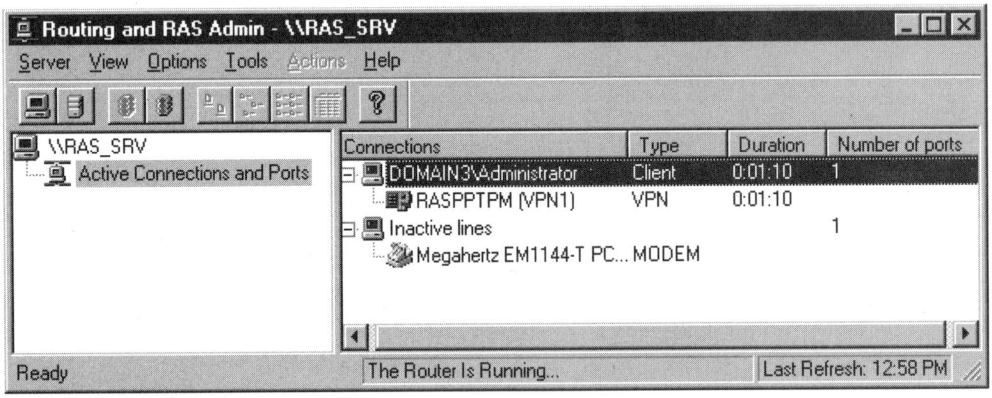

Figure 10.37 RRAS Admin shows a connection from the remote office.

Kernel Routing Tables

Recall from chapter 8 that the ***kernrout*** command displays the contents of the "kernel portion" of the routing table, as opposed to the portion stored in the NICs themselves. But the case of non-sophisticated NICs, the kernel portion and the NIC portion are stored in the same place—the kernel.

The current network configuration is shown in Figure 10.38. A PPTP connection will be established between the remote RAS server and the corporate RAS server.

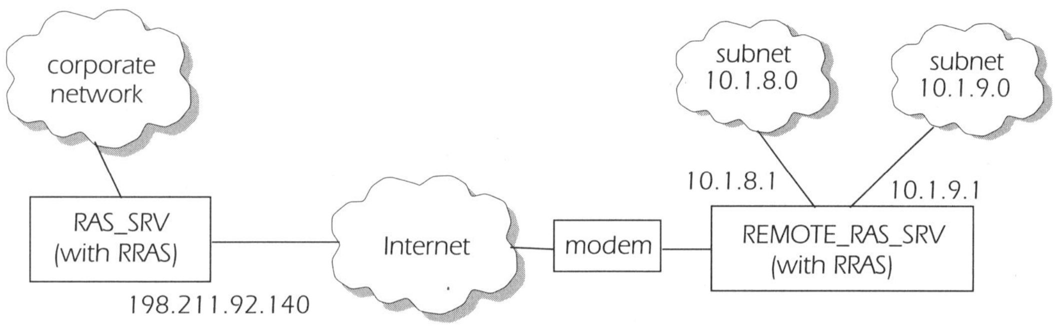

Figure 10.38 The remote office network will be connected into the corporate network.

In this section, we will view the routing table on the remote RAS server in three states:

- before connecting to the Internet
- after connecting to the Internet
- after establishing a PPTP connection to headquarters

By viewing the routing tables, we will gain a better understanding of the process of connecting two offices together over the Internet.

Routes Prior to Dialup Connection

Figure 10.39 shows the output of a ***kernrout*** command run on the REMOTE_RAS_SRV prior to dialing the headquarters.

```
command prompt
C:\WINNT>kernrout print

IP STACK ROUTE TABLE
--------------------

Destination         Mask                NextHop            I/f  Metric  Protocol
================================================================================
10.1.8.0            255.255.255.0       10.1.8.1            3     1        2
10.1.8.1            255.255.255.255     127.0.0.1           1     1        2
10.1.9.0            255.255.255.0       10.1.9.1            2     1        2
10.1.9.1            255.255.255.255     127.0.0.1           1     1        2
10.255.255.255      255.255.255.255     10.1.9.1            2     1        2
127.0.0.0           255.0.0.0           127.0.0.1           1     1        2
224.0.0.0           224.0.0.0           10.1.9.1            2     1        2
224.0.0.0           224.0.0.0           10.1.8.1            3     1        2
255.255.255.255     255.255.255.255     10.1.9.1            2     1        2
================================================================================

C:\WINNT>_
```

Figure 10.39 Kernrout shows the routing table before dialing the headquarters.

Notice the host routes to 10.1.8.1 and 10.1.9.1, both of those interfaces installed in that machine. Recall that interface #1 is the loopback interface. Interface #2 will be the first interface listed in the output of ***ipconfig***, and interface #3 will the next interface listed in ***ipconfig***'s output.

Routes After Dialup Connection

After the REMOTE_RAS_SRV has connected via PPP dialup to the RAS_SRV, we may again use ***kernrout*** to examine the routing table, as shown in Figure 10.40.

```
C:\WINNT>kernrout print

IP STACK ROUTE TABLE
--------------------

Destination        Mask               NextHop          I/f  Metric  Protocol
============================================================================
0.0.0.0            0.0.0.0            198.211.92.140   5      1        2
10.1.8.0           255.255.255.0      10.1.8.1         3      2        2
10.1.8.1           255.255.255.255    127.0.0.1        1      1        2
10.1.9.0           255.255.255.0      10.1.9.1         2      2        2
10.1.9.1           255.255.255.255    127.0.0.1        1      1        2
10.255.255.255     255.255.255.255    10.1.9.1         2      1        2
127.0.0.0          255.0.0.0          127.0.0.1        1      1        2
198.211.92.0       255.255.255.0      198.211.92.140   5      1        2
198.211.92.140     255.255.255.255    127.0.0.1        1      1        2
198.211.92.255     255.255.255.255    198.211.92.140   5      1        2
224.0.0.0          224.0.0.0          198.211.92.140   5      1        2
224.0.0.0          224.0.0.0          10.1.8.1         3      1        2
224.0.0.0          224.0.0.0          10.1.9.1         2      1        2
255.255.255.255    255.255.255.255    10.1.9.1         2      1        2
============================================================================

C:\WINNT>_
```

Figure 10.40 Kernrout shows the routing table after dialing the headquarters.

A new route has been added, to network 198.211.92.0, going out the dial-out interface. The IP address of the dial-out interface is 198.211.92.140, as shown in the routing table, as well as in Figure 10.41. The name of the dial-out interface in use is NdisWan7, and is interface #5.

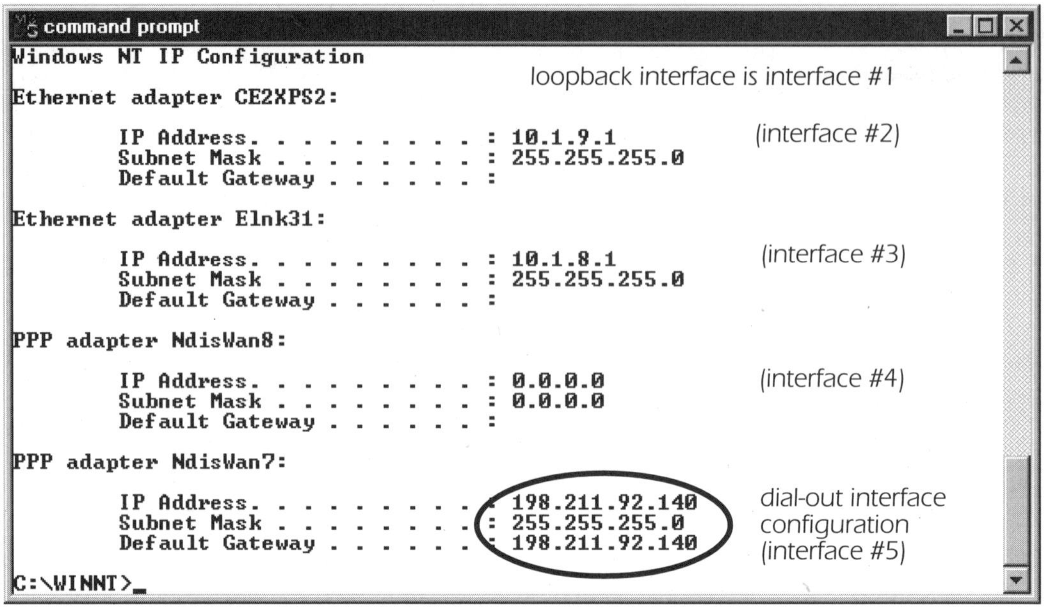

Figure 10.41 Ipconfig shows the interface for access to the Internet.

Note also that the dial-out interface (interface #5) has been used as the default route (destination 0.0.0.0 with mask 0.0.0.0) so that all traffic to a destination not matching any other route will be sent out to the headquarters. This means that we don't have to have explicit entries to get to the networks at headquarters (10.1.2.0, 10.1.3.0, 10.1.4.0) from this router.[16]

There are now three routes to the multicast "network" 224.0.0.0. Any multicasts will be sent out interfaces 2, 3, and 5 — both Ethernets and the WAN link to the corporate headquarters office.

Notice that the metric used to communicate locally on either Ethernet is 2, yet to go across the WAN link, the metric is 1.

16. The subnets at the headquarters are shown in Figure 9.1 on page 335.

Routes After Tunnel Creation

Next we create a tunnel over the Internet to get to the main office. The remote RAS server dials the corporate RAS server and uses PPTP to establish the tunnel. After this has been done, we use ***kernrout*** again to generate the output shown in Figure 10.42.

```
command prompt
C:\WINNT>kernrout print


IP STACK ROUTE TABLE
--------------------

Destination         Mask                NextHop             I/f  Metric  Protocol
==================================================================================
0.0.0.0             0.0.0.0             10.1.2.66           4      1       2
0.0.0.0             0.0.0.0             198.211.92.140      5      2       2
10.0.0.0            255.0.0.0           10.1.2.66           4      1       2
10.1.2.66           255.255.255.255     127.0.0.1           1      1       2
10.1.8.0            255.255.255.0       10.1.2.66           4      1       2
10.1.8.0            255.255.255.0       10.1.8.1            3      2       2
10.1.8.1            255.255.255.255     127.0.0.1           1      1       2
10.1.9.0            255.255.255.0       10.1.2.66           4      1       2
10.1.9.0            255.255.255.0       10.1.9.1            2      2       2
10.1.9.1            255.255.255.255     127.0.0.1           1      1       2
10.255.255.255      255.255.255.255     10.1.9.1            2      1       2
127.0.0.0           255.0.0.0           127.0.0.1           1      1       2
198.211.92.0        255.255.255.0       198.211.92.140      5      2       2
198.211.92.140      255.255.255.255     127.0.0.1           1      1       2
198.211.92.255      255.255.255.255     198.211.92.140      5      1       2
207.93.134.70       255.255.255.255     198.211.92.140      5      1       2
224.0.0.0           224.0.0.0           10.1.9.1            2      1       2
224.0.0.0           224.0.0.0           198.211.92.140      5      1       2
224.0.0.0           224.0.0.0           10.1.2.66           4      1       2
224.0.0.0           224.0.0.0           10.1.8.1            3      1       2
255.255.255.255     255.255.255.255     10.1.9.1            2      1       2
==================================================================================

C:\WINNT>_
```

Figure 10.42 Kernrout shows routes to the headquarters once we're connected.

Again, look down the list and you'll find the new addition, 10.1.2.66, is the address of the VPN interface. This address is also listed in the next hop column with an interface number of 4. Wanting to know the name of this interface, we ran the ***ipconfig*** command again, the output of which is shown in Figure 10.43. We may now call interface 4 by the name NdisWan8.

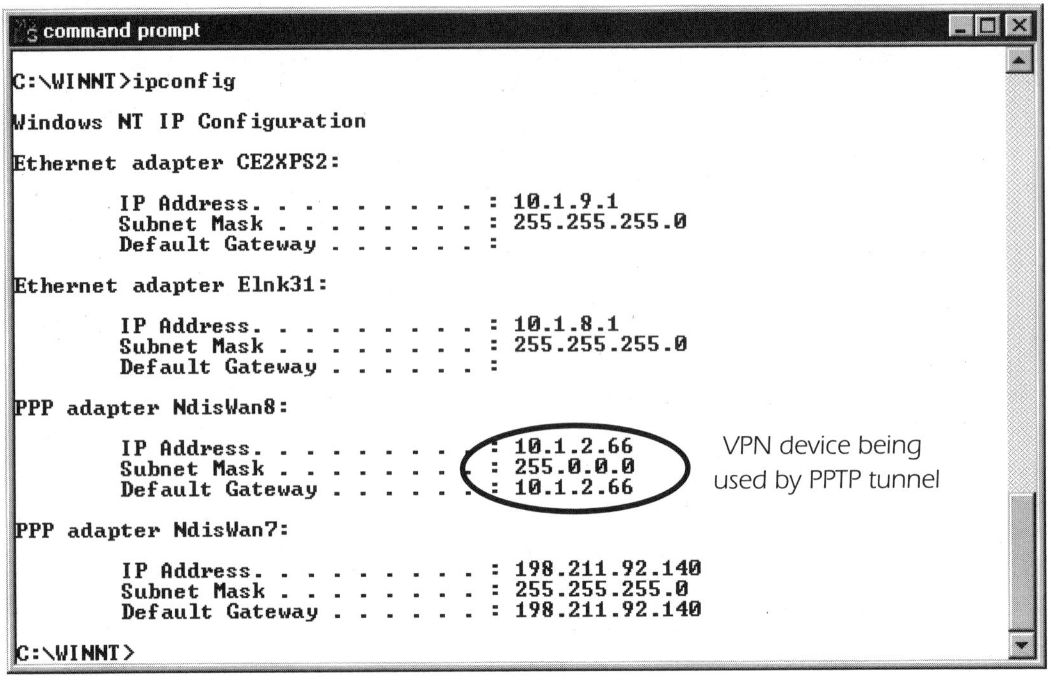

Figure 10.43 The interfaces to the Internet (NdisWan7) and the headquarters (NdisWan8) are shown after we've connected in to the headquarters.

Notice that all of the networks have a route to the WAN and there are now four multicast routes.

Summary

Here's a summary of the items which have been addressed in this chapter.

- Virtual Private Networks (VPNs) may be used to privately communicate between two sites over a public network (e.g. the Internet).
- The Point-to-Point Tunneling Protocol (PPTP) is a technology which allows creation of VPNs. Each VPN interface appears to be a PPP interface to the network protocols.

- Data sent over a VPN connection established with PPTP can be encrypted. The data is also encapsulated by the Generic Routing Encapsulation (GRE).
- PPTP can be implemented using NT 4.0 alone, or NT 4.0 with additional software (Steelhead). With NT 4.0 alone, only PPTP clients can connect to a PPTP server. With the additional software, PPTP servers can connect to other PPTP servers.

Further Reading

Here is information about various books and magazines in which to look for further information on the subject.

[Atkinson1995] Atkinson, R., *IP Authentication Header,* 1995, IETF RFC 1826

[Atkinson1995a] Atkinson, R., *IP Encapsulating Security Payload (ESP),* 1995, IETF RFC 1827

[Atkinson1995b] Atkinson, R., *Security Architecture for the Internet Protocol,* 1995, IETF RFC 1825

[Hamzeh1996] Hamzeh, K., Pall, G., Verthein, W., Taarud, J., Little, W., *Point-to-Point Tunneling Protocol — PPTP,* 1996, Internet Draft <draft-ietf-pppext-pptp-00.txt>

[Hamzeh1997] Hamzeh, K., Kolar, T., Littlewood, M., Pall, G., Taarud, J., *Layer Two Tunneling Protocol "L2TP",* 1997, Internet Draft <draft-ietf-pppext-l2tp-08.txt>

[Hanks1994] Hanks, S., Li, T., Farinacci, D., Traina, P., *Generic Routing Encapsulation (GRE),* 1994, IETF RFC 1701

[Hanks1994a] Hanks, S., Li, T., Farinacci, D., Traina, P., *Generic Routing Encapsulation over IPv4 Networks,* 1994, IETF RFC 1702

[Karn1995] Karn, P., Metzger, P., Simpson, W., *The ESP DES-CBC Transform,* 1995, IETF RFC 1829

[Metzger1995] Metzger, P., Simpson, W., *IP Authentication using Keyed MD5,* 1995, IETF RFC 1828

11

Domain Name Resolution

Use of IP addresses in applications isn't incredibly user-friendly. Domain names and their simpler cousins, hostnames, may be used in applications as short-hand (or descriptive) names instead of IP addresses. As IP still uses IP addresses, any application using domain names must find a resolution of that name into an IP address prior to actual communication.

domain name: user-friendly alias for an IP address that follows a particular naming scheme.

Domain names are the hierarchical user-friendly names like sales2.sales.foobar.com, which may be used in most TCP/IP applications to hide the details of IP addresses

domain name resolution: the process of obtaining an IP address for a computer's domain name.

Domain name resolution is the process of obtaining an IP address for a computer's domain name.

This chapter discusses both Domain Name System (DNS) client and server configuration. The steps needed to bring the Microsoft DNS up and running quickly are described in this chapter. More advanced DNS configuration topics are discussed in Chapter 13, "Advanced DNS Configuration".

WARNING: What we are talking about here are *Internet* domain names. These are NOT the same things as Microsoft domain names. Be careful, as this is a common misconception among people new to domain name resolution.

The Host File

resolver: a piece of software which translates domain names into IP addresses.

Most implementations of TCP/IP have a distinct piece of software which performs the function of resolving domain names to IP addresses— this is called a domain name resolver, or simply a **resolver**.

hostname: simple text names used to refer to computers.

Before domain names were invented, the network consisted of large computers which provided (i.e. hosted) computing services, thus these computers were called hosts. These hosts were identified using simple text names, which are called **hostnames**.

host file: a static file containing IP addresses and the associated names.

When IP data needs to be sent to a particular hostname, the domain name resolver first checks a local file that contains hostnames and IP addresses. This file is called the **host file**. The host file is a simple text file which contains a list of hostnames and their IP addresses. With a host file, you are assigning IP addresses statically. An example host file is shown in Figure 11.1

Figure 11.1
An example host file.

```
# Example host file
192.168.42.193        router_dev
192.168.42.194        xylem
192.168.42.195        zazu
192.168.42.196        zylo
192.168.42.197        zozomo
```

In a host file there is one line per IP address. The first item on each line is the IP address of the host. Following the IP address is one or more hostnames to be associated with that IP address.

On Windows NT this file is called:

%systemroot%\system32\drivers\etc\hosts

The problem with host files is that a copy of the file must exist on each host on which you want the mappings to be used. Thus, maintaining these files can become a hassle, as any changes must be propagated to all hosts.[1]

This high level of maintenance was motivation to create a better method, especially as the number of nodes attached to the Internet increased. A distributed database would be created that extended throughout the Internet. Each organization would maintain their part of the database, and name queries would be sent to the appropriate server. This system, of course, was DNS.

1. The host file could possibly be shared between machines, however the name resolutions in this network are then dependent on the reliability of the file sharing.

Domain Name System (DNS)

It would be very difficult to maintain host files on all the machines in your company, let alone the Internet. To solve this problem, a distributed database was created and is used throughout the Internet to provide name resolution. DNS servers each maintain a part of this database — typically the part that refers only to their own organization.

primary DNS server: a DNS server that contains the master database for a specified domain.

Every company typically has a DNS server which systems at the site may consult for domain name to IP address resolution (Figure 11.2). The DNS server database contains domain name to IP address mappings, among other records. This database contains entries for *every host* within the organization. To make things simpler for system administrators, only one[2] DNS server in the organization will contain all records for that domain, and could be called the "master database". That machine is then called the **primary DNS server**.

Figure 11.2
Three DNS servers, one per domain.

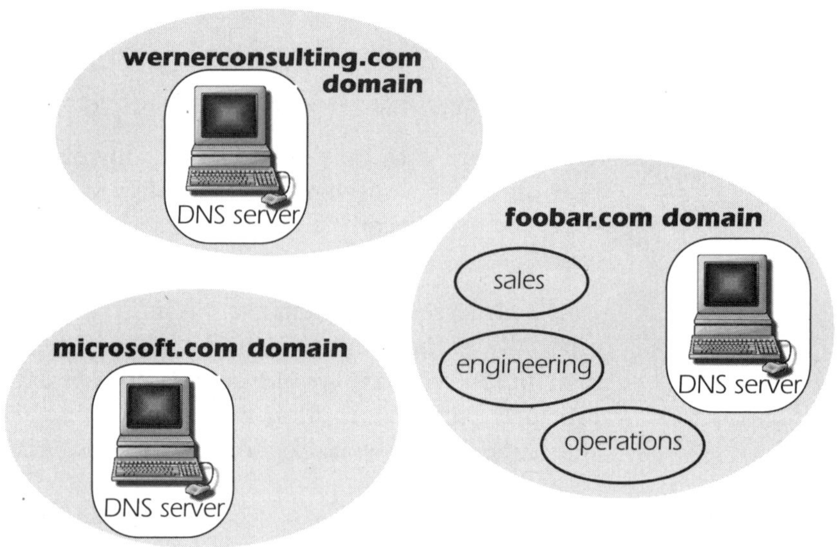

2. It is possible to have several primary servers in an organization. Each server is a primary for a separate subdomain within the organization's domain.

secondary DNS server: DNS server that acts as a backup to one or more primary DNS servers.

Secondary DNS servers contain information copied from other primary DNS servers, or other secondary servers. The information is copied to the secondary servers at regular time periods (discussed in Chapter 13). The secondary servers are the backup servers in case the primary goes down. Secondary servers also reduce the load on the primary. Secondary servers could be used at the remote end of a slow link, such that queries on the remote network are answered locally by the secondary.

authoritative for a domain: a DNS server which is a primary or a secondary for that domain.

The primary DNS server is said to be **authoritative for that domain**. If that server doesn't know the IP address for a name that is supposedly in its domain, that machine effectively does not exist. Secondary servers for a domain are also authoritative for that domain.

Order of Name Resolution Methods

The resolver will use the following methods in the order listed.[3] Once an IP address is obtained, the rest of the methods are skipped.

1. checking the local host file.
2. querying the Domain Name Server.

In the case of Microsoft operating systems, there may be some additional steps, such as:

3. sending a name resolution request to a Windows Internet Name Service (WINS) server (if the resolver is configured as a WINS client).
4. broadcasting a name resolution request on the local LAN.
5. consulting the local LAN Manager host file (LMHOSTS).

Let's consider an example of the resolution process for the machines in Figure 11.3. The DNS client wants to talk to the machine named coyote.wernerconsulting.com. The DNS client's resolver consults the local host file first. In this example, there is no match in that file. The resolver then sends a query to the DNS server. The DNS server obtains the IP

3. The order of the methods used is predefined and not configurable with Windows NT. Some other operating systems allow you to configure the order.

address[4] of the machine coyote.wernerconsulting.com and sends that IP address back to the client's resolver. The client can now initiate a session (e.g. Telnet, FTP, HTTP) to the destination using the IP address.

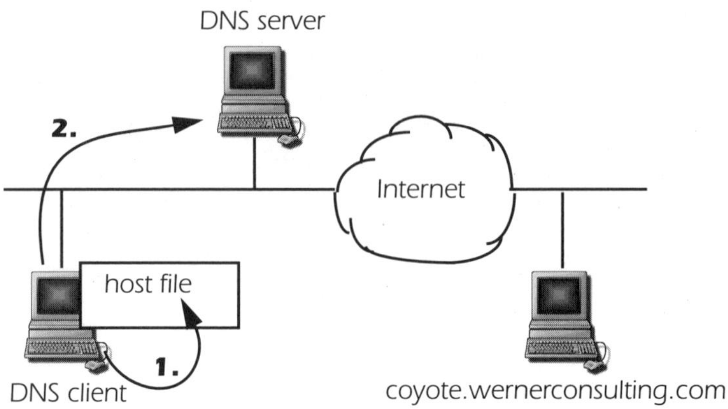

Figure 11.3
Name resolution in action.

Domain Names

A domain name maps to an IP address. This mapping can be done locally through a file or by a remote server. TCP/IP applications must use IP addresses for all IP communication, so they must use a *resolver* to map any domain names into IP addresses.

All of the following refer to the same machine:

domain name:	coyote.wernerconsulting.com
IP address:	172.18.0.1
hardware address:	00 a0 3b 0b 3d f4

4. We will see how the DNS server obtains this IP address in the section "DNS in the Internet" on page 412.

The Domain Name Tree

The hierarchy of domains may be drawn as a tree starting at the top of the tree, called the root. Figure 11.4 shows an example of the domain name tree. The top-level domains are the two-letter ISO-3166 country codes and the traditional organizational domains for the U. S. Within the "us" domain there are domains for each state and three special domains: fed, nsn, and isa. Other countries have their own organizational structures represented as domains. Within each U. S. state there are domains for various state-level organizations as well as a structure for counties and cities. For example, the city government of Phoenix, Arizona has registered the domain "ci.phoenix.az.us" and has a World-Wide Web server with a domain name of www.ci.phoenix.az.us.

Note that domain names are written from leaf to root, such as our example coyote.wernerconsulting.com. The domain which is highest in the tree (e.g. com) will be written at the right-most side of the domain name. Subdomains will be written to the left of a higher-level domain.

Figure 11.4 Example domain name tree, highlighting coyote.wernerconsulting.com.

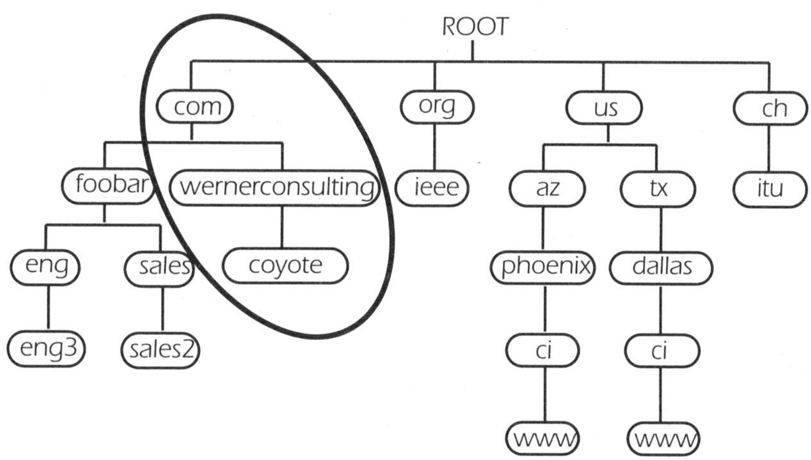

Once you have registered a domain name with the appropriate registration authority[5], you have control over how subdomains are named within that domain. You may create a domain name structure to model your organization's structure, with various divisions, departments, and groups. If your organization is geographically widespread, you may wish

5. The registration authority in the U. S. is the Internet Network Information Center (InterNIC).

to instead arrange domains according to office locations or regions. The subtree which you create is rooted at the domain name your organization has registered.

domain name label: a simple name which identifies one level in the tree.

Figure 11.5 shows that domain names are made up of one or more labels. Each domain name **label** may be up to 63 characters long, and the total domain name may be up to 255 characters. These characters may be a-z, 0-9, and the hyphen "-". A simple hostname is an example of a domain name label. For example, "coyote" is a name of a host in the Werner Training and Consulting, Inc. network, found in the domain wernerconsulting.com. Combine two labels with a dot to build a hierarchical domain name; for example, coyote.wernerconsulting.com.

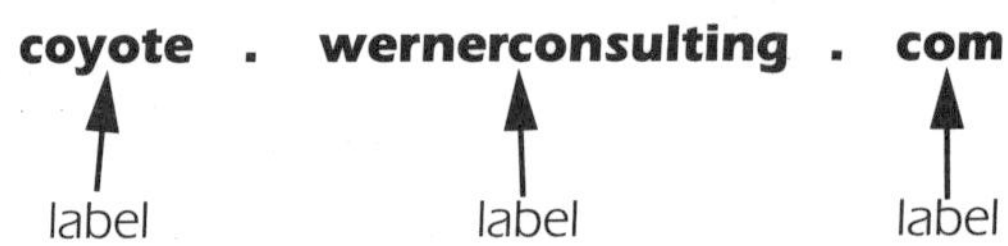

Figure 11.5 Domain names are made up of one or more labels separated by dots.

fully qualified domain name: the complete domain name beginning with a hostname (leaf) and ending with the root domain.

When you have specified the hierarchy of domain name labels from a host up to the top of the domain name hierarchy you have a *Fully Qualified Domain Name* (FQDN). All FQDNs must end with a dot (e.g. "coyote.wernerconsulting.com.").[6] At the top level of the hierarchy are organization domains and geographic domains. In the United States, the organizational domains of com, edu, gov, mil, net, and org are commonly used. Two-letter geographic domains (per country) are more commonly used in the rest of the world (e.g. de, jp, se, uk, etc.) and are quickly gaining popularity in the U. S.

DNS in the Internet

Your local DNS server maintains a database of the domain name to IP address mappings within your company. Machines within your organization may be configured to query this DNS server which will respond with a matching IP address.

6. FQDNs end with a dot because the root is identified by a null label.

Two questions commonly asked about name resolution are:

- How does a machine within your organization obtain the IP address of a machine in an organization across the Internet?
- How does a machine outside of your organization obtain an IP address of a machine in your organization?

Let's look at an example which illustrates how DNS can answer both questions. Figure 11.6 shows several steps[7] for resolving a domain name into an IP address which your web browser may use to access www.microsoft.com.

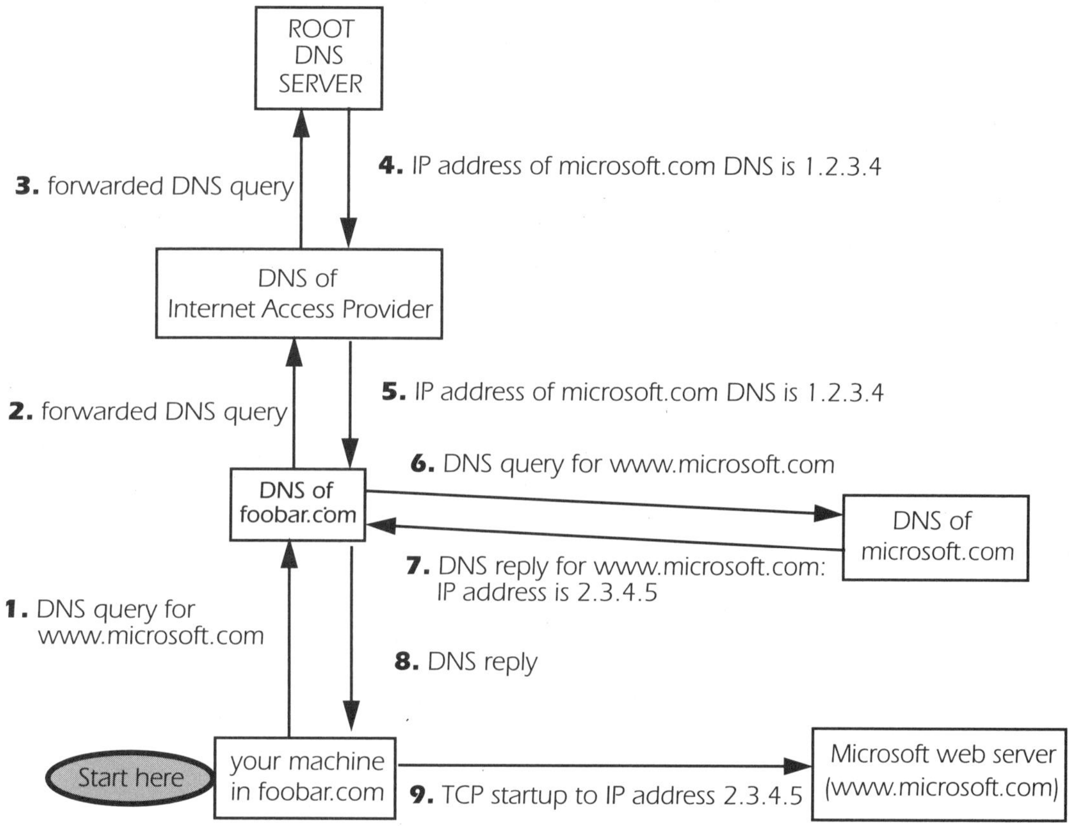

Figure 11.6 Example steps in domain name resolution for www.microsoft.com. Note: IP addresses shown are for example only.

7. These steps focus on DNS; however, this may be a good point to recall that ARPs, bridging, encapsulation, routing, and other such things are going on under the hood for each of the DNS messages.

Start at your machine in the lower left corner of the diagram. From here, we'll walk through nine steps toward accessing the web page.

Your machine (within foobar.com) has been configured to use a specific DNS server within your company.

1. Your machine sends a DNS name query message to foobar.com's DNS server.

   Assume that this DNS server at foobar.com doesn't currently have any entries for www.microsoft.com. This is because it has been configured with only foobar.com information, and hasn't recently gotten information about www.microsoft.com. Luckily, this DNS server has been configured to defer queries that it doesn't know the answer to up to your organization's *Internet Access Provider's (IAP)* DNS server.

2. The DNS at foobar.com forwards the query to the IAP's DNS.

   Let's also assume that the IAP's DNS does not serve www.microsoft.com, nor has another client of this IAP requested DNS information about www.microsoft.com recently. Luck still is on your side, because someone at this IAP has configured their DNS to forward DNS queries for domains ending in .com that it can't resolve up to a *root server.*

3. The IAP's DNS server forward's the query to a root DNS server.

   Assume that this root server knows all of the next-level subdomains of the top-level domain that you're looking for. In other words, in www.microsoft.com, the *top-level domain* is simply .com. If this server knows all next-level subdomains for .com, it knows microsoft.com.

   This root server does not know the full translation for www.microsoft.com; however, it will provide partial information because it knows the address of microsoft.com's DNS server.

4. The root DNS server replies to the IAP's DNS server with the partial reply containing the IP address of microsoft.com's DNS server (e.g. 1.2.3.4).

   The IAP's DNS server may store this translation in a cache for a period of time so that it doesn't have to bother the root server if it is asked again soon.

5. The IAP's DNS server returns the response with the IP address of microsoft.com's DNS server down to foobar.com's DNS server.

The foobar.com DNS server caches this information for a short time so that it doesn't have to query the IAP's DNS any time soon for the same information. It notices that it doesn't have a complete answer to pass back to your computer, yet it does know the IP address of microsoft.com's DNS server.

6. The DNS server at foobar.com forwards the query for www.microsoft.com on to the microsoft.com DNS server at 1.2.3.4.

   The microsoft.com DNS server has a translation for www.microsoft.com, which indicates that the/an IP address of their web server is 2.3.4.5.

7. The microsoft.com DNS server returns a name query response to the foobar.com DNS server indicating that the IP address of www.microsoft.com is 2.3.4.5.

   The foobar.com DNS server may cache this information as well so that it doesn't have to bother microsoft.com's DNS server in the near future.

8. The foobar.com DNS server returns the name query response to your machine, indicating that what you wanted is 2.3.4.5.

   Your machine takes this information and realizes that it has a resolution for the domain name www.microsoft.com into 2.3.4.5.

9. Your web browser may now use this address to set up an HTTP connection to www.microsoft.com by creating a TCP connection to port 80 on IP address 2.3.4.5.

The rest is up to TCP and HTTP. DNS has done its part.

Answers to the two earlier questions should now be at hand.

- You machine finds IP addresses of machines in other organizations through the proper configuration of a hierarchy of DNS servers.
- Machines in other organizations find your IP address by (ultimately) querying the primary DNS server for your organization.

Packet Captures of DNS Queries

The resolver on the DNS client will try to contact the DNS server which has been configured on that client computer. The DNS *Name Query* is passed to the server. As shown in Figure 11.7, the name query packet contains the domain name which the client is trying to resolve. The name query packet is sent to UDP port 53.

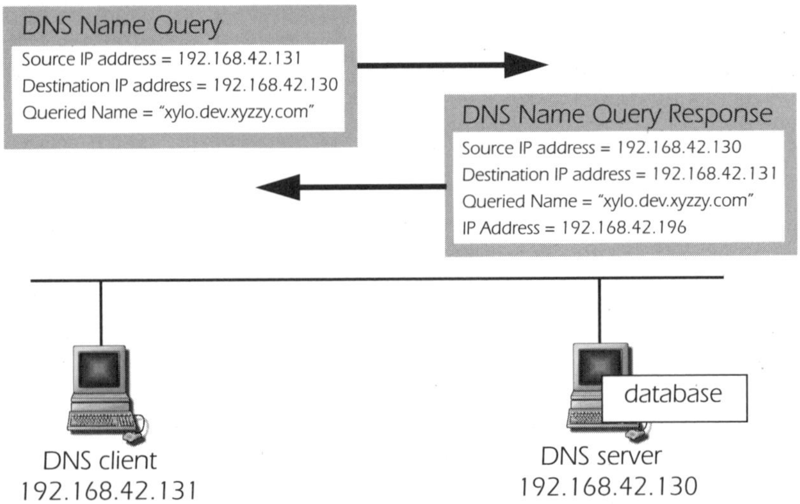

Figure 11.7 The DNS client issues a name query and the server replies with a name query response.

The DNS server receives the name query packet, and if the server has a mapping which matches the name query then a response containing the mapping will be sent back to the requesting resolver. Note that the *Name Query Response*, as shown in the diagram, has the IP address that matches the domain name.

The resolver receives the name query response packet. The resolver will then pass the translation to the application.

When your DNS server has to consult a higher level DNS (root) server it will cache the result for a period of time. That way subsequent requests may be serviced directly without consulting the root server.

Example Name Query/Name Reply Packets

In the example DNS query/response captured on the CD, the machine ENG3 sends a DNS query to the DNS server called PRI_DNS, as shown in Figure 11.8. The machine ENG3 wants to find out the IP address of the machine named sales2.sales.foobar.com. The DNS server checks its database for the IP address of sales2, and sends a reply back to ENG3.

Figure 11.8 ENG3 queries the DNS server to resolve a domain name to an IP address

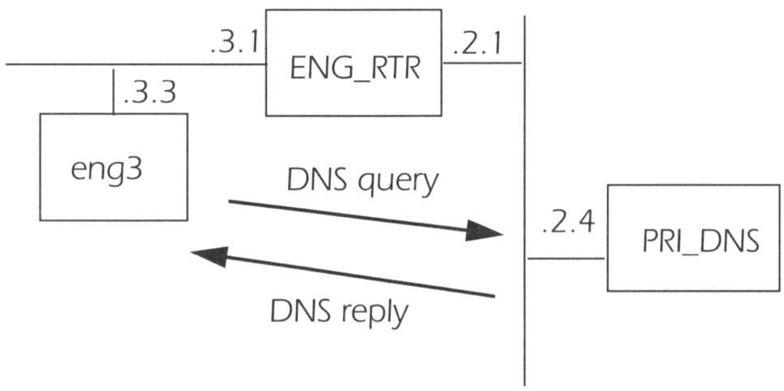

Figure 11.9 shows the contents of the name query packet. The capture file is found on the companion CD, and is called dnsquery1.cap. The address database file for this chapter is called dns_ch.adr. Load the capture and address files at this time to see the contents of the query and the reply packets.

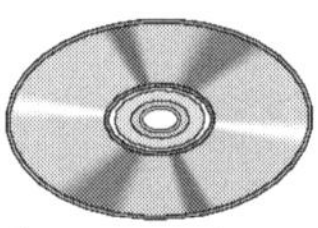

dnsquery1.cap

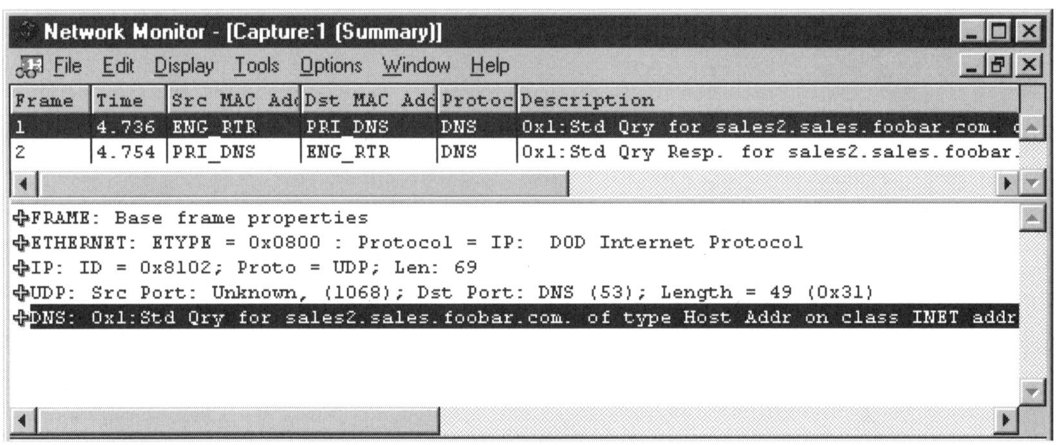

Figure 11.9 DNS Name Query packet

The properties of a name query packet are listed in Table 11.1.

Table 11.1 The properties of a name query packet.

Header	Description
IP	unicast, sent to the IP address of the DNS server
UDP	destination port 53 (DNS server)
DNS	query for the host address (IP address) of sales2.sales.foobar.com.

In response to the name query, the DNS server will respond with a Name Query Response packet, as shown in Figure 11.10.

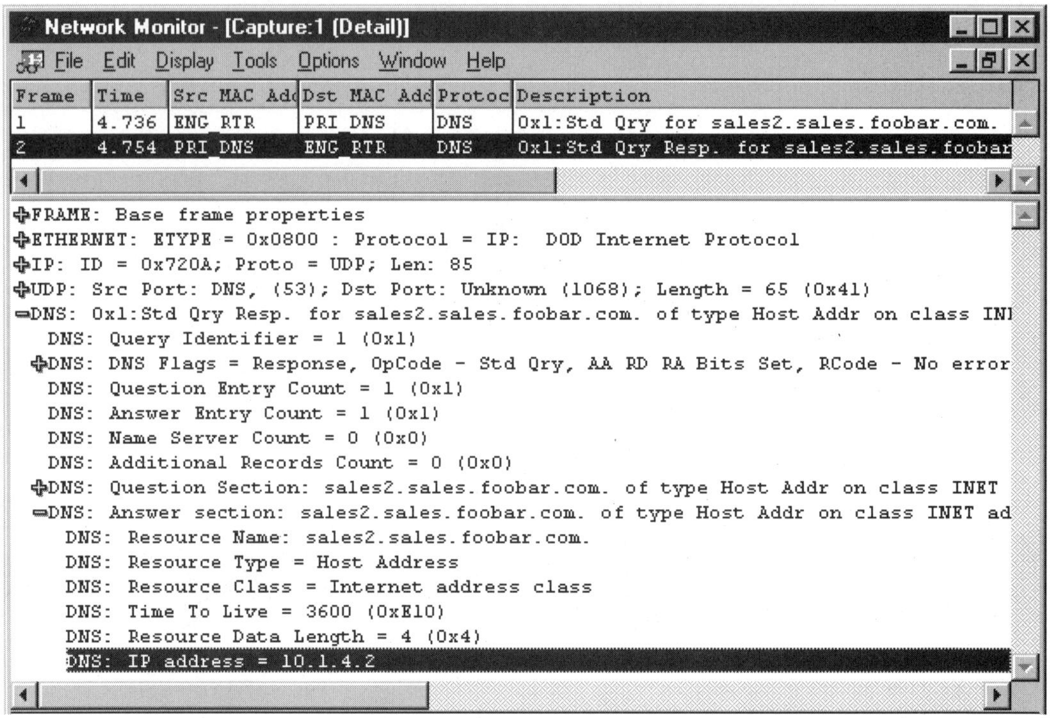

Figure 11.10 DNS Name Query Response packet

The properties of a name query response packet is listed in Table 11.2.

Table 11.2 The properties of a name query response message.

Header	Description
IP	unicast, sent to the IP address of the DNS client
UDP	destination port 53 (DNS server)
DNS	flags: response, AA (authoritative answer) question section: sales2.sales.foobar.com. answer section: 10.1.4.2

Configuring a Client to Use DNS

Configuring an NT client to use DNS is a simple process, using just one screen. The screen is the *DNS tab*, found under *Network Control Panel -> Protocols -> TCP/IP-> Properties*. The screen is shown in Figure 11.11.

Figure 11.11 DNS tab on the Microsoft TCP/IP Properties dialog.

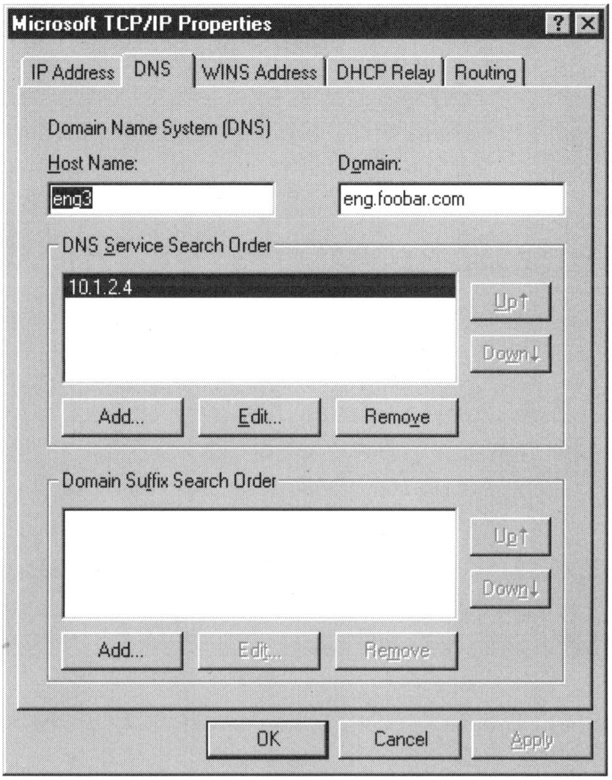

In order to configure the client to send queries to the DNS server, all that is really needed is the IP address of the DNS server. Multiple DNS servers can be queried if configured. The fields in this screen are described in Table 11.3.

Table 11.3
The fields of the DNS client configuration.

Field	Description
Host name	The DNS hostname. Note that this field defaults to the same as the NetBIOS computer name.
Domain	Name of the domain this machine is a member of.
DNS Search Order	Add IP addresses of the DNS servers in your organization. You can enter multiple DNS server IP addresses. If the first DNS server in the list does not reply, the next is tried.
Suffix Search Order	A list of the domain names that will be appended to queried hostnames (suffix search list is discussed in "DNS Domain and Searchlist" on page 439).

Installing Microsoft DNS Service

The most popular implementation of a DNS server is the UNIX *Berkeley Internet Name Domain (BIND)*. BIND has been ported to many platforms[8]. The first DNS server for Windows NT was from a company named FBLI[9], however the *Microsoft DNS Server* is based on BIND version 4.9.3.

The Microsoft DNS Server is installed using the *Network Control Panel -> Services tab*. Pressing the *Add...* button will bring up the dialog shown in Figure 11.12.

8. Refer to http://www.isc.org/ for current information on BIND.
9. Refer to http://www.fbli.com/ for details.

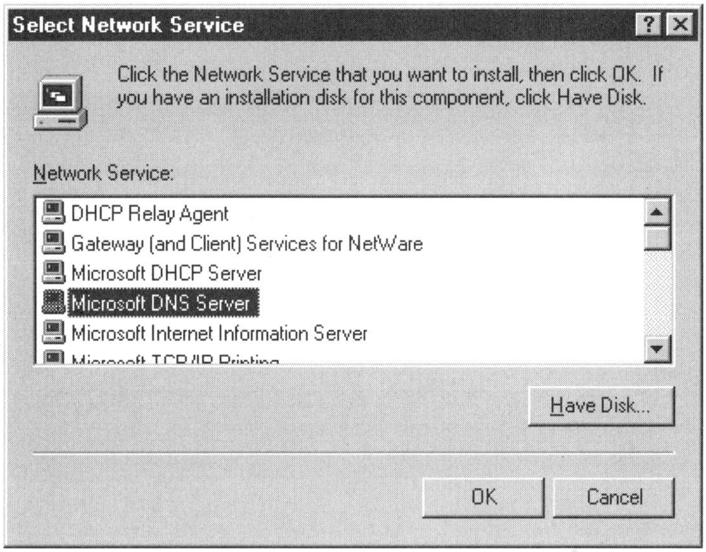

Figure 11.12 *Adding the Microsoft DNS Server service.*

DNS Manager

One advantage of the Microsoft DNS Server is that it may be administered with a graphical interface called DNS Manager. It is found under *Start -> Programs -> Admin Tools.* DNS Manager is used for all configuration changes to the DNS server. The main screen for the DNS Manager is shown in Figure 11.13.

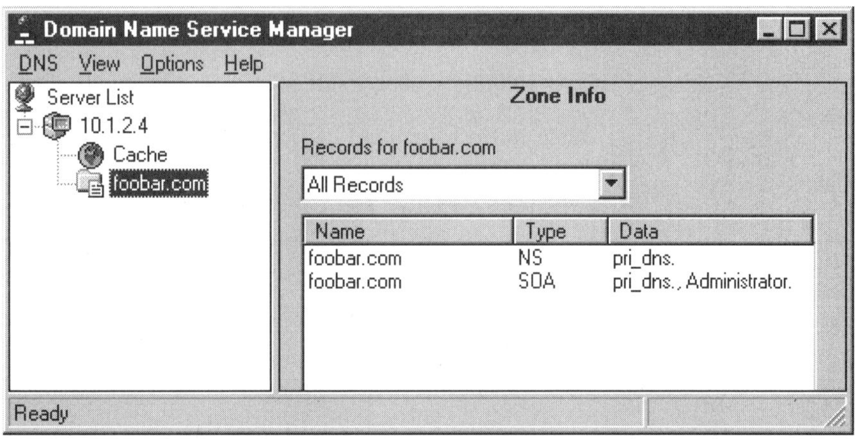

Figure 11.13 DNS Manager is used to configure the DNS Server.

You can use this application not only to administer a DNS Server on your local machine, but also to connect to a remote NT DNS server, as long as your user account is in the administrators group on the remote DNS server. The DNS Manager executable is called ***dnsadmin.exe***. Once the application starts, you can use the menu item *DNS -> New Server* to connect to a remote Microsoft DNS Server[10].

Basic DNS Configuration

Recall that DNS is a distributed database. A DNS server is simply a specific kind of database server which is responsible for a portion of the overall DNS database, and which responds to domain name queries. There needs to be a record in this database for each FQDN to IP address translation.

This section shows the steps to add records for a newly installed DNS server. At the end of this section, the DNS database will be populated with all the domain names and IP addresses of all the machines in the *internal corporate network*. Chapter 13, "Advanced DNS Configuration", discusses addresses connecting the DNS server to the Internet.

The basic configuration topics covered in this chapter are:

- creating the database
- examining database files
- testing with ***nslookup***

These examples assume that this machine is the primary DNS server for the Foobar Company. Therefore, it is authoritative for the domain foobar.com. Figure 11.14 is the current network diagram for foobar.com, and will be used as a guide to add addresses and names to the DNS database.

10. DNS Manager uses RPC to connect to remote servers.

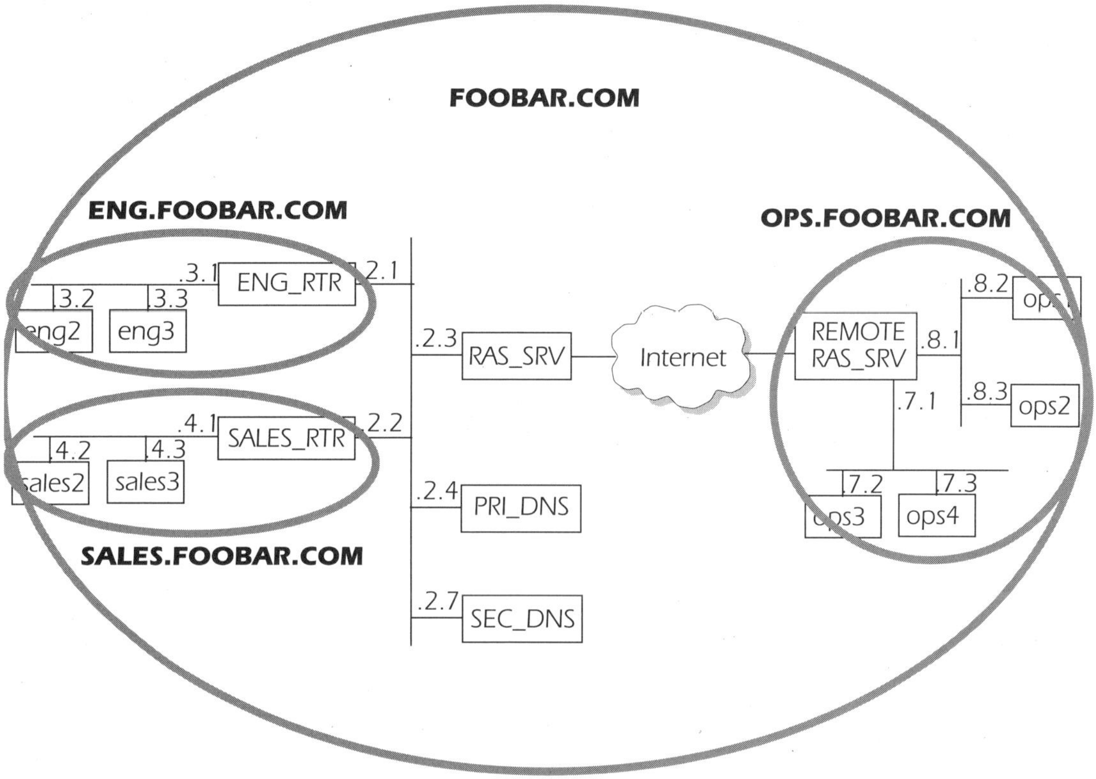

Figure 11.14 Subdomains within foobar.com.

zone: a database that contains information about one or more domains.

A **zone** is a database that contains information about one or more domains. Within each zone, you can create domains, such as engineering.foobar.com and sales.foobar.com. (Often, the terms *zone* and *domain* are used interchangeably.) A new zone can be added using the menu *DNS -> New Zone*. The *Creating new zone* screen appears (Figure 11.15).

Figure 11.15 Selecting zone type.

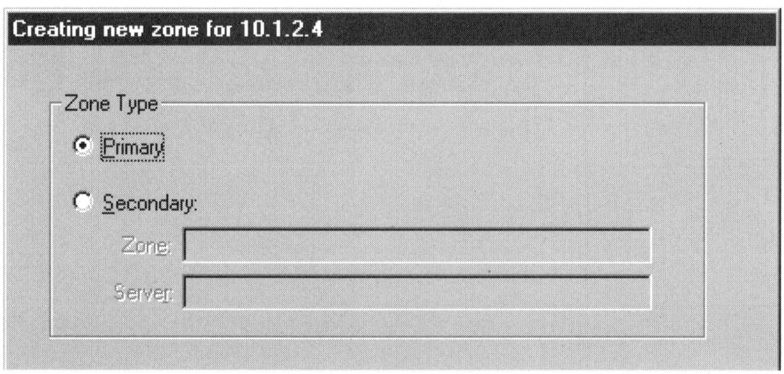

Since we are creating this DNS server from scratch for the foobar.com domain, we select *primary* as the zone type (Figure 11.15). Recall that a primary DNS is the DNS that contains the master database of hostname to IP address mappings. This database is copied to secondary DNS servers.

The next screen that appears is shown in Figure 11.16. The zone name foobar.com is entered, as well as a zone file. The zone file is a file that contains all the records for that zone. The default zone file name is the name of the zone followed by .dns.

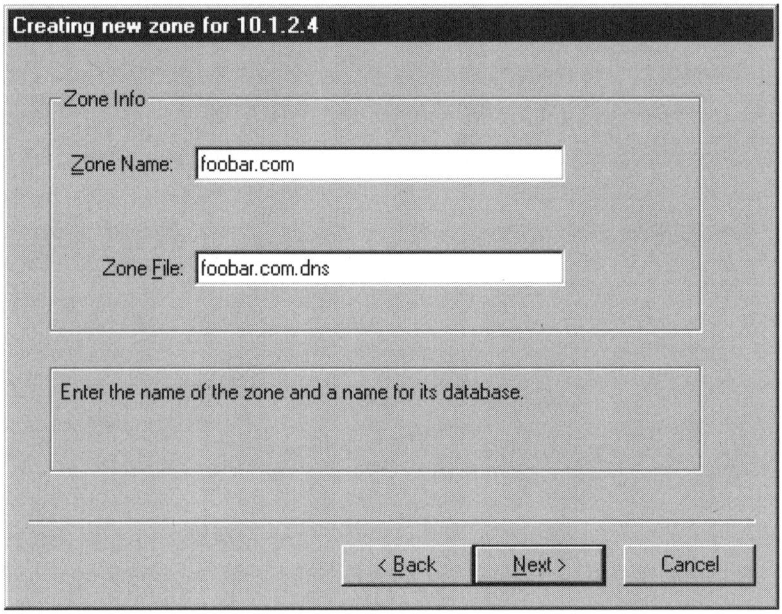

Figure 11.16 Entering the new zone name.

These zone files are located in %systemroot%\system32\dns. A listing of the initial files found in that directory is shown in Figure 11.17

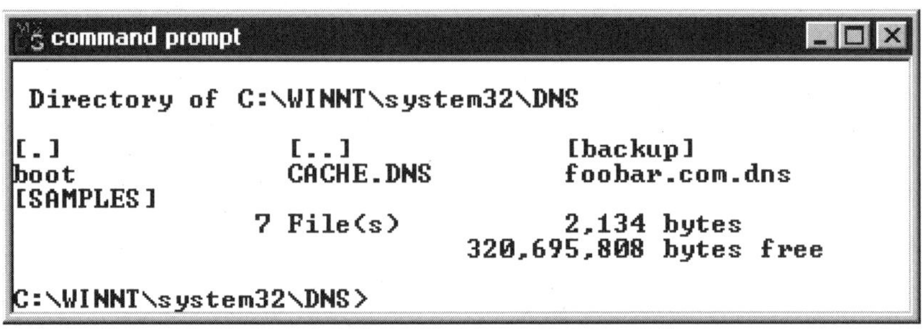

Figure 11.17 The DNS directory contains the zone database files, as well as other DNS configuration files.

Now that the zone is created, it appears in the list of zones in the left pane of the DNS Manager (Figure 11.18). Notice that two records have been created for foobar.com: an NS record and a SOA record. We will see very shortly the meanings of NS and SOA records.

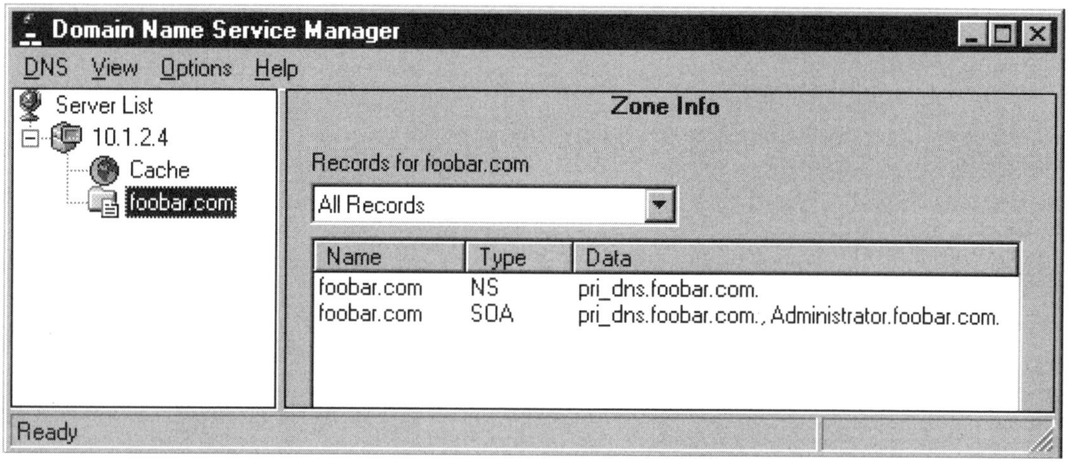

Figure 11.18 Newly-created foobar.com zone contains two records: NS and SOA.

Let's look at the configuration file foobar.com.dns (Figure 11.19) from the DNS directory. The file contains two records as well: an NS record and a SOA record.

```
;   Database file foobar.com.dns for foobar.com zone.
;       Zone version:  11
;

@       IN     SOA     pri_dns.foobar.com.  Administrator.foobar.com.
(
                        1           ; serial number
                        3600        ; refresh
                        600         ; retry
                        86400       ; expire
                        3600      ) ; minimum TTL

;
;   Zone NS records
;
@       IN     NS      pri_dns
;
;   Zone records
```

Figure 11.19 Initial contents of foobar.com.dns. Note that the lines beginning with semicolons are comments.

In fact, these are just two ways of viewing the same records. The file foobar.com.dns, as shown in Figure 11.19, is actually a text file which is part of the zone database. Traditionally, system administrators would edit this sort of file directly to configure their zones on their DNS server. The graphical interface (DNS Manager) is simply a front-end which is designed to make the configuration easier.

DNS Record Types

There are several types of DNS records. Each record type holds a specific kind of information resource in the database. The common name for a record in the database is *resource record*. Some of the basic[11] DNS record types and descriptions are listed in Table 11.4.

Table 11.4
The basic DNS record types.

Record type	Name	Description
NS	Name Server record	Contains the name of the name server. An example is shown in Figure 11.19.
SOA	Start Of Authority record	Contains cache and secondary server exchange configuration parameters. An example is shown in Figure 11.19.
A	Address record	Contains a mapping from domain name to IP address. An example is shown in Figure 11.31 on page 434.
PTR	Pointer record	Contains a mapping from IP address to name. An example is shown in Figure 11.32 on page 435.
CNAME	Canonical Name record	Contains a mapping from a domain name to another domain name (alias).

We will be creating each of these types of records during the configuration process.

11. For details on additional DNS record types, refer to [Albitz1995] or the RFCs.

Adding Domains

Now that the primary zone foobar.com has been added to this DNS server, it is time to add some domains. Actually, because these domains will be added "beneath" the foobar.com domain, they are often called *subdomains*. In Figure 11.14, we have circled the subdomains we want to add: eng, sales, and ops, for the engineering, sales, and operations departments.

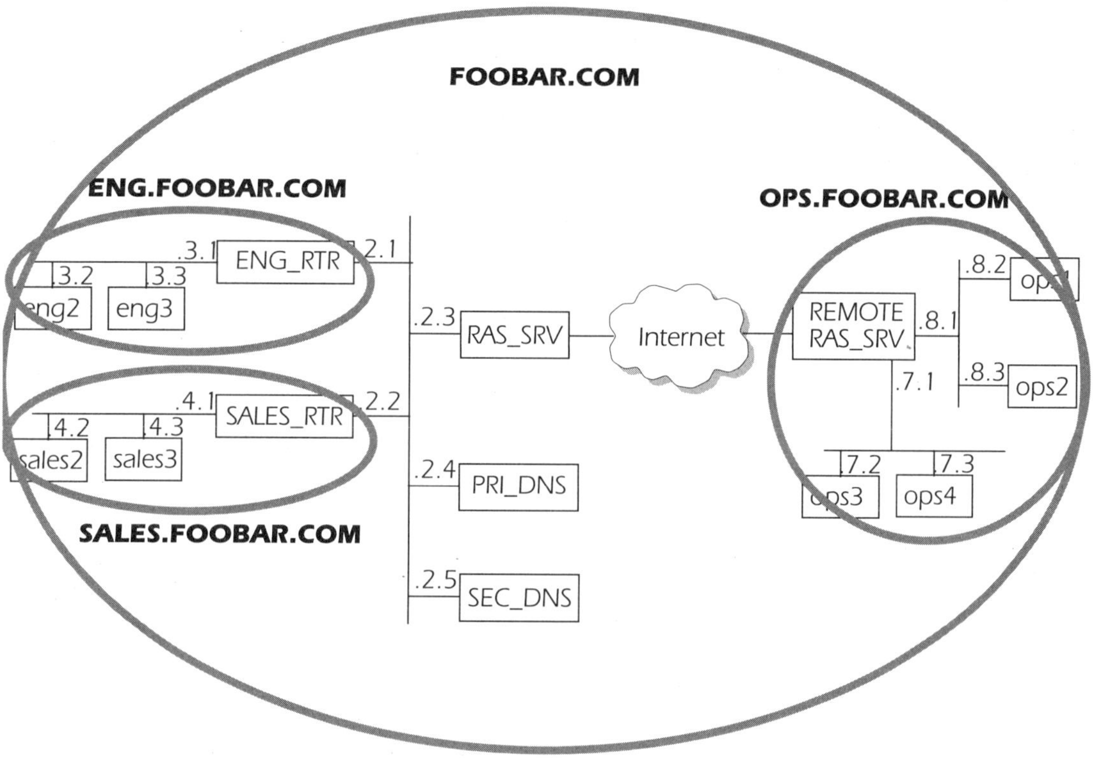

Figure 11.20 Subdomains to add using DNS Manager.

In the DNS Manager, use the *DNS -> New Domain* menu item to add each subdomain[12]. In the screen which appears, you enter the subdomain name. Figure 11.21 shows three subdomains have been added to foobar.com: eng, sales and ops.

12. Make sure that the domain is selected in DNS Manager prior to using the DNS -> Add Domain menu item.

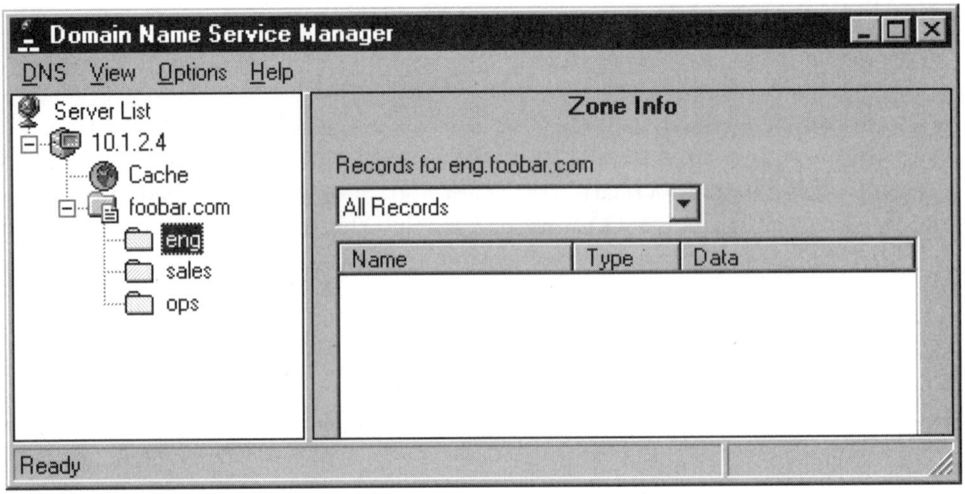

Figure 11.21 The subdomains eng, sales, and ops have been created in foobar.com.

Adding Hosts

Now that the subdomains have been added, we'll add the hosts to each subdomain. Effectively, we want to add an address (A) resource record for each host to the zone database. For each host, select the subdomain to which the host is to be added and use the *DNS -> New Host* menu item.

In the *New Host* dialog, shown in Figure 11.22, enter the hostname and IP address. Make sure to check the box to *Create Associated PTR Record* for this host, then press the *Add Host* button. This creates the PTR record for that host.

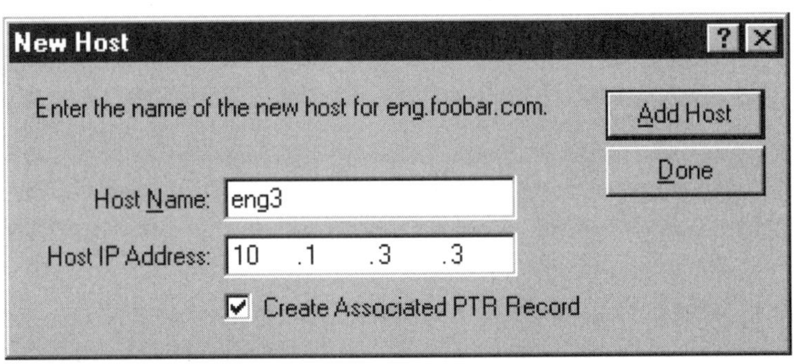

Figure 11.22 Adding a hostname and IP address.

At this point, you may see an error message, as shown in Figure 11.23. Let's investigate its meaning now, and we'll return to adding the hosts shortly.

Figure 11.23 Configuration error message if in-addr.arpa zone has not been created.

Reverse Lookup: in-addr.arpa Domain

reverse lookup: querying a DNS server with an IP address to obtain the associated domain name.

When you have an IP address and would like to know the domain name associated with it, you may request a **reverse lookup**. The in-addr.arpa zone is used to answer "reverse queries." Instead of the question being, "What is the IP address of eng3.eng.foobar.com?", the reverse query would ask, "What is the name of the machine with IP address 10.1.3.3?"

Records to answer reverse queries must be stored under a different subtree than the foobar.com zone: that is in the in-addr.arpa tree. These records are of type PTR (pointer), and as you can guess, contain an IP address and the domain name that it matches.

Let's examine the domain name tree of the Internet (Figure 11.24). The root of the tree is shown at the top. Domain names are categorized top-down, but read and pronounced bottom-up.

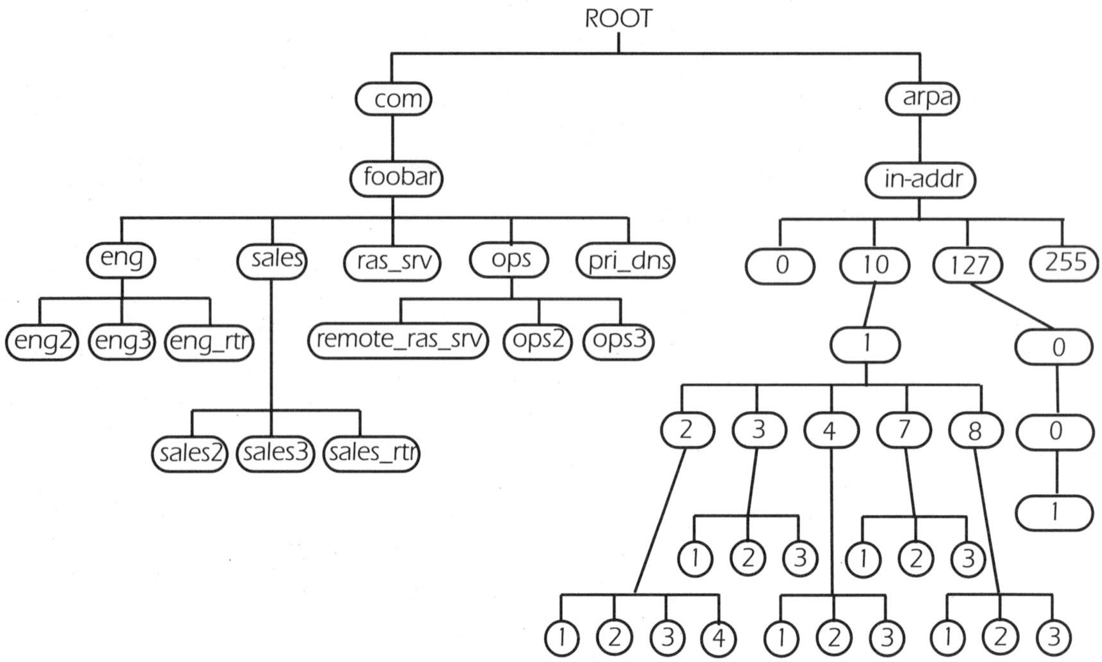

Figure 11.24 Domain tree for the foobar.com and in-addr.arpa zones.

When we write IP addresses in dotted decimal notation, they are most significant/general on the left and least significant (most specific) on the right. In order to use an IP address as a key in the domain name hierarchy, it must be categorized as domain names are: with the most significant part closest to the root (top) and the most specific part closest to the leaf nodes (bottom). This leads to an interesting feature of writing IP addresses— the IP address will appear to be in octet reversed order!

In order to put IP addresses into the domain name tree, they need a branch under which they may be registered. Internet addresses were developed under the auspices of the ARPAnet, thus are registered under the arpa top-level domain with the branch name in-addr. As depicted in Figure 11.24, the IP address 10.1.3.3 would be written as 3.3.1.10.in-addr.arpa. in order to index into the domain name tree.[13]

13. Thankfully, the DNS Manager doesn't require us to manipulate PTR addresses that are shown in this format. DNS Manager shows the IP addresses in the normal dotted-decimal notation.

All of the PTR records for the IP addresses in the example network are stored under the 10.1 branch of the in-addr.arpa tree. PTR records can be created at the same time as A records, assuming the appropriate in-addr.arpa subdomains have already been created.

So upon initial installation of the DNS server, we must create the zone in-addr.arpa. Use the *DNS -> New Zone* command again, and indicate that this is a primary zone. Create the zone named in-addr.arpa, as shown in Figure 11.25.

Figure 11.25 Creating the zone in-addr.arpa

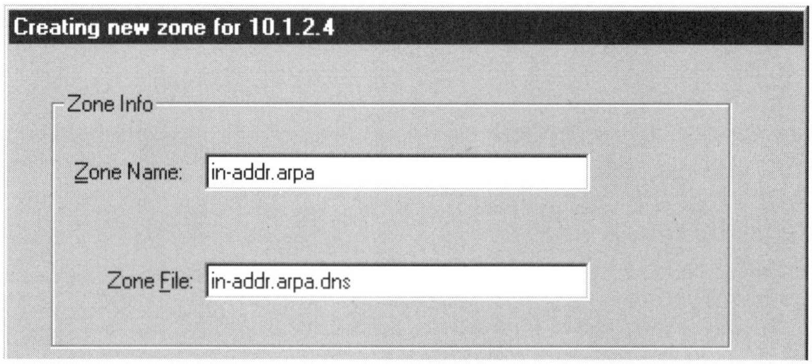

Once you have finished creating the new zone, it will appear in the DNS Manager display as shown in Figure 11.26. Notice that there are several subdomains automatically added to this zone: 0, 127, and 255.

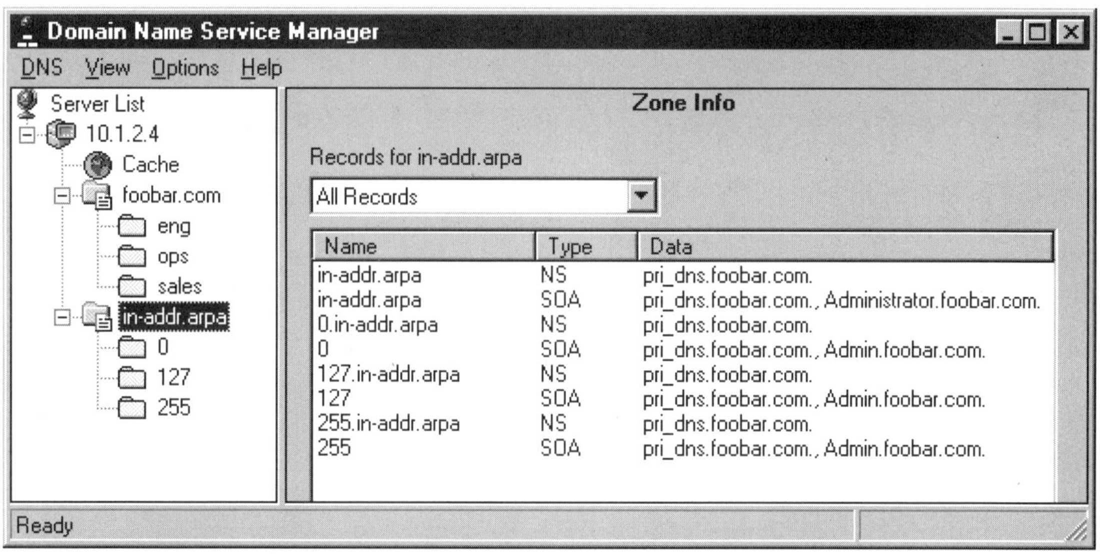

Figure 11.26 Default entries in in-addr.arpa

Adding Hosts Revisited — with PTR Records

When we tried to add our hosts previously, the error message in Figure 11.23 informed us that the associated PTR record could not be created. Now that the in-addr.arpa zone has been added to the server, we'll repeat the procedure again.

Use the *DNS -> Add Host* menu to bring up the dialog shown in Figure 11.27, and check the box to *create associated PTR record.* The hostname and IP address will be used to create both the A and PTR records when *Add Host* is selected.

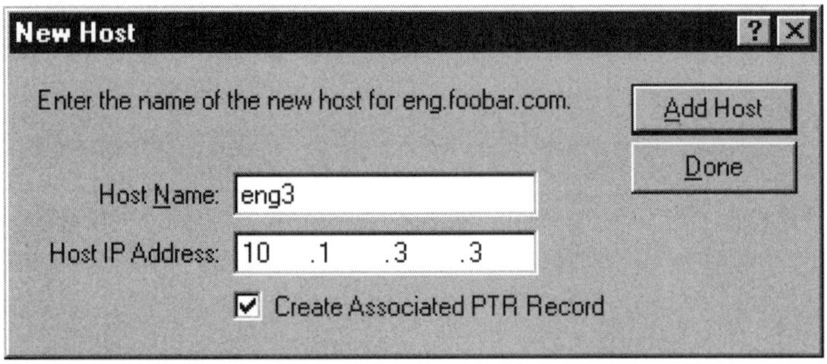

Figure 11.27 Check the box at the bottom of the New Host dialog to create an associated PTR record when the A record is created.

Figure 11.28 shows that the A record for ENG3 was added to the database.

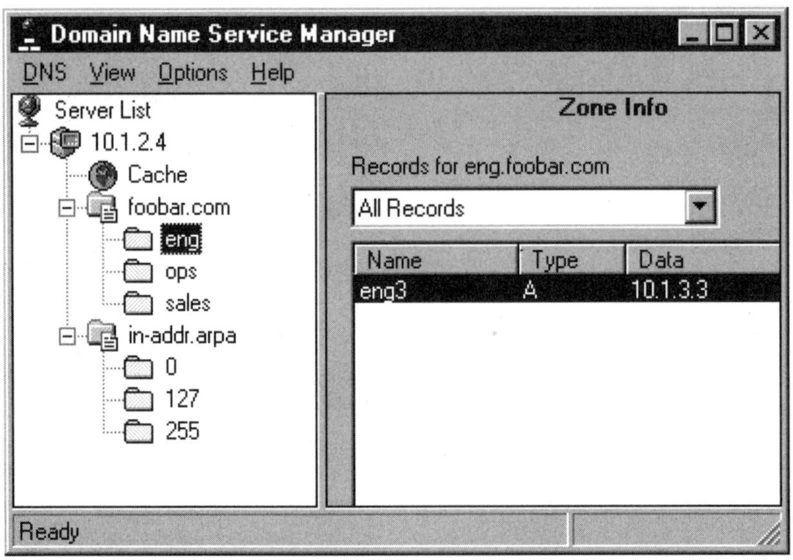

Figure 11.28 An A record was created when a host was added to the database.

The PTR record was also created, as shown in Figure 11.29.

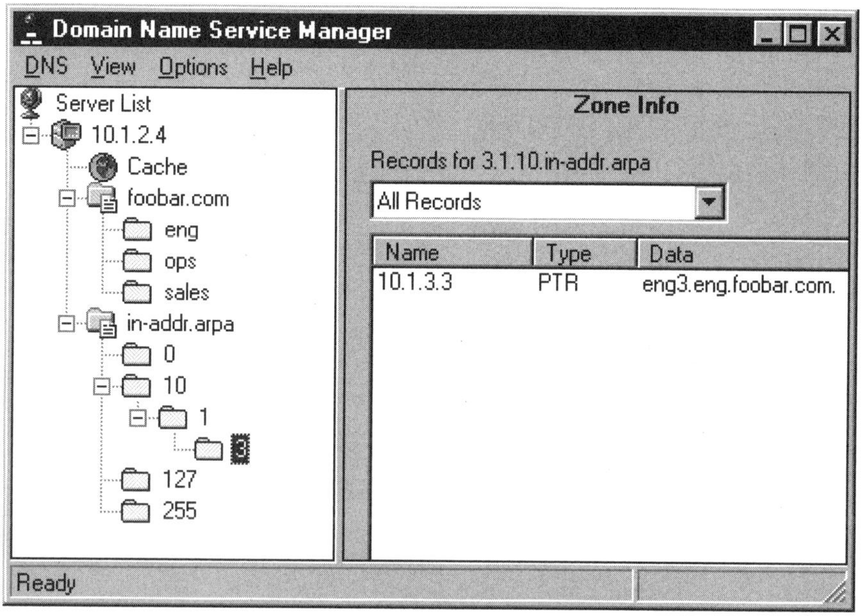

Figure 11.29 The PTR record for ENG3 was created at the same time as the A record

Now we add all the rest of the entries for the network. Make sure that the appropriate subdomain is selected before adding each host. Once all the entries are added, use the *Update Server Data Files* command, as shown in Figure 11.30, to write the records out to the DNS file in the DNS directory.

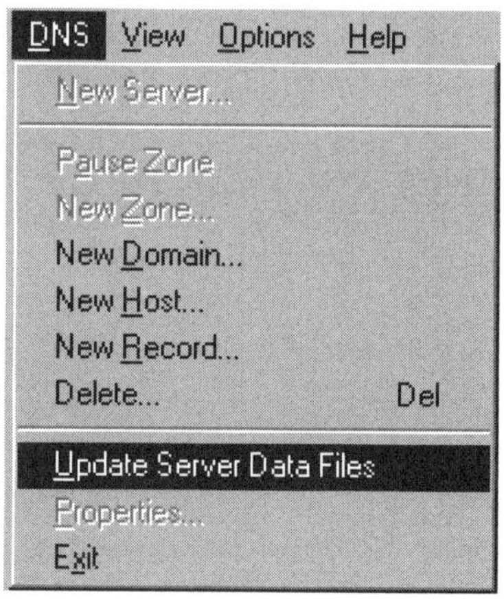

Figure 11.30 Update Server Data Files writes the changes to the DNS files.

Let's look at the foobar.com.dns and in-addr.arpa.dns files to confirm the changes. The foobar.com.dns file now has appended to it a list of zone records, as shown in Figure 11.31.

```
;   Zone records
;

eng2.eng            IN     A       10.1.3.2
eng3.eng            IN     A       10.1.3.3
ops2.ops            IN     A       10.1.8.2
ops3.ops            IN     A       10.1.8.3
sales2.sales        IN     A       10.1.4.2
sales3.sales        IN     A       10.1.4.3
```

Figure 11.31 Address records for foobar.com.dns.

The SOA and NS records are still at the top of the file. They haven't been shown again for the sake of brevity.

Notice that the domain names in the left column are relative names because they are written with no trailing dot. They are relative to the domain name of the zone, which is foobar.com. Hence, the last line, sales3.sales as a relative name could also have been identified with the FQDN sales3.sales.foobar.com., which would be equivalent.

Each line specifies a domain name, followed by the class of the record (IN, or Internet), then the type of resource record (A, or address). Finally, the IP address written in normal dotted quad decimal form appears at the end of the line.

Thus, the DNS Manager has written a standard DNS configuration file for us when we issued the *Update Server Data Files* command. Because the A records are a part of the foobar.com zone, they appear in the foobar.com.dns configuration file.

Similarly, the PTR records are also written out by DNS Manager. The PTR records however are part of the in-addr.arpa zone, thus they are written to the configuration file for that zone.

The in-addr.arpa.dns file begins with the same records (SOA,NS) as the foobar.com.dns file, but ends with the records shown in Figure 11.32.

```
2.3.1.10                IN      PTR     eng2.eng.foobar.com.
3.3.1.10                IN      PTR     eng3.eng.foobar.com.
2.4.1.10                IN      PTR     sales2.sales.foobar.com.
3.4.1.10                IN      PTR     sales3.sales.foobar.com.
2.8.1.10                IN      PTR     ops2.ops.foobar.com.
3.8.1.10                IN      PTR     ops3.ops.foobar.com.
```

Figure 11.32 Pointer records for foobar.com.dns.

Note that the domain names in the left column do not end with dots; they are relative names — relative to the domain name (i.e. origin) of the zone. Thus the last entry, 3.8.1.10, could alternately be written as 3.8.1.10.in-addr.arpa. as a FQDN.

In summary, we've added entries for many of the hosts in this network to the DNS database. Domain name resolvers in the network may now consult the DNS server to obtain the IP addresses which correspond to domain names. These translations are based on the A records. Because we added PTR records as well, the DNS server may also answer reverse queries for which a resolver wants a domain name matching an IP address.

Testing the DNS Server Using Nslookup

Nslookup is a tool that is used to test the DNS server configuration. ***Nslookup*** now comes with the NT 4.0 software, as part of the TCP/IP utilities. In order for ***nslookup*** to work properly, your local machine must be configured to use DNS, as ***nslookup*** uses that configuration information to send queries.

When ***nslookup*** starts up, it uses the local DNS configuration to find out the default DNS server's name and IP address. Figure 11.33 shows the client configuration for ENG3. Notice that the DNS server configured is 10.1.2.4.

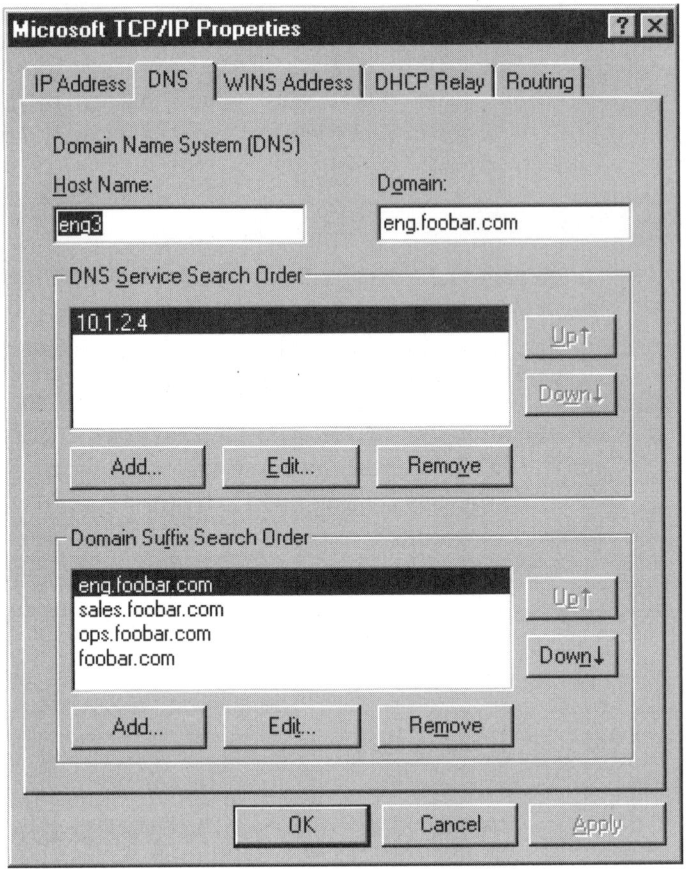

Figure 11.33 The DNS configuration for the client eng3.eng.foobar.com.

Upon startup, ***nslookup*** performs a reverse-name query to find out the name of the DNS server it is configured to use. If the DNS server doesn't contain a PTR record that maps to its own IP address, an error will occur, shown in Figure 11.34.

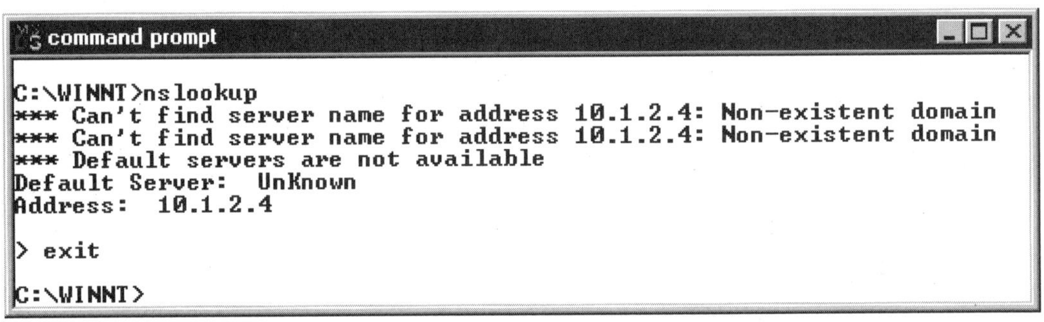

Figure 11.34 Nslookup error– DNS server lacking a PTR record for itself.

To resolve[14] this error, we need to add a PTR record for the DNS server itself. Otherwise, ***nslookup*** will not be able to resolve the IP address to a hostname, as it wants to when it starts up.

Create an entry in the DNS server zone to map its IP address to its FQDN, shown in Figure 11.35.

Figure 11.35
Adding the A and PTR records for the DNS server's name and IP address.

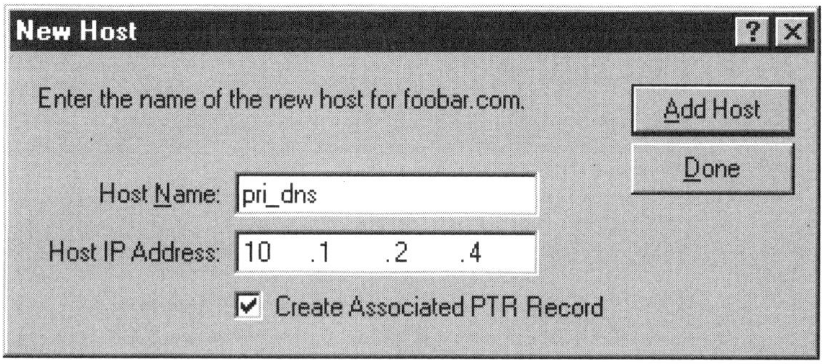

Now that this problem is resolved, the command ***nslookup*** will start properly, and present the user with a prompt of ">". Many commands can be entered at this prompt. If the user-entered text does not match one of the predefined commands, it is assumed that the text is a hostname or IP address that should be resolved to the corresponding information. An example of ***nslookup***, where two DNS host queries are sent to the DNS server, is shown in Figure 11.36.

Figure 11.36
Example use of nslookup to query a DNS server for information

```
command prompt

C:\WINNT>nslookup
Default Server:  pri_dns.foobar.com
Address:  10.1.2.4

> sales2
Server:  pri_dns.foobar.com
Address:  10.1.2.4

Name:    sales2.sales.foobar.com
Address:  10.1.4.2

> bogus
Server:  pri_dns.foobar.com
Address:  10.1.2.4

*** pri_dns.foobar.com can't find bogus: Non-existent domain
> exit

C:\WINNT>
```

14. No pun intended. ;-)

The first query, from eng3, displays the IP address for the host sales2.sales.foobar.com, as returned by the DNS server pri_dns.foobar.com. The second query, for a machine called bogus, resulted in an error, since the machine does not exist in the foobar domain.

Debug Option to Nslookup

The ***-debug*** option to ***nslookup*** will display the contents of the name query reply packets. Each reply packet is displayed between a pair of dashed lines. This option is very useful in troubleshooting name resolution problems.

Recall that when ***nslookup*** starts up, it uses the local DNS configuration to find out the IP address of the default DNS server. ***Nslookup*** then sends a reverse request to the DNS server to find out the hostname of that DNS server. In Figure 11.37, notice that it is querying the IP address 4.2.1.10.in-addr.arpa, and is a lookup for the PTR record. The DNS server did have a PTR record for that query, and so the IP address is resolved to the name pri_dns.foobar.com.

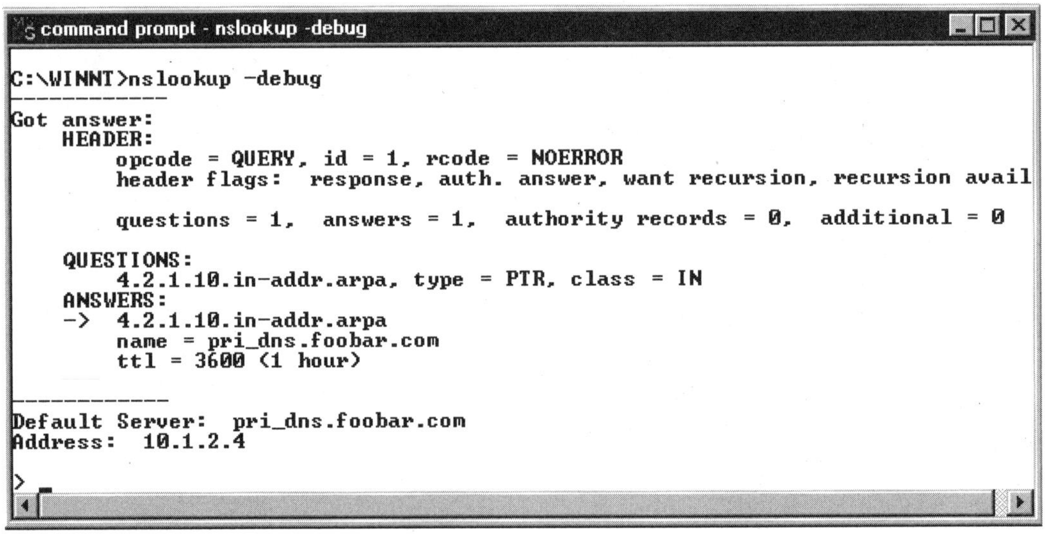

Figure 11.37 The debug option of nslookup displays the contents of the DNS reply packets.

To continue with the debug output, examine Figure 11.38. It shows a name query for eng2.eng.foobar.com. The answer to this query is shown at the bottom of the screen, after the dashed line.

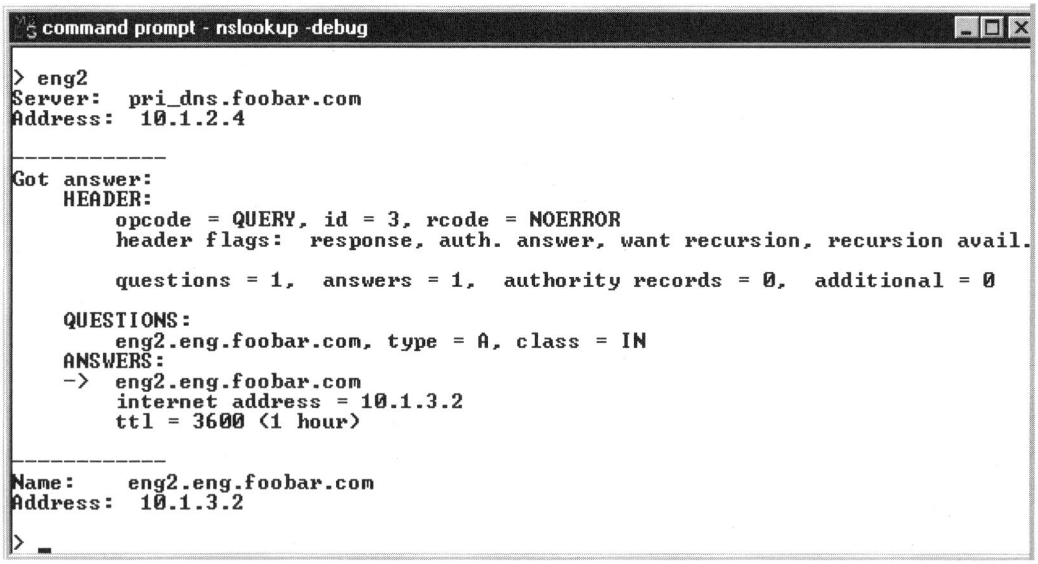

Figure 11.38 Example nslookup -debug output for a name query

Most clients do not cache information retrieved from the DNS server. Therefore the TTL entry shown above is of no consequence to this client. However, if this packet was sent to another DNS server, then that DNS server is instructed to cache this entry for a maximum of one hour.

DNS Domain and Searchlist

Figure 11.33 showed the DNS configuration for eng3, which included a domain suffix search list. This search list is used when sending queries to the DNS server. If the user-specified name is not a FQDN, a suffix will be appended to the name before the query is sent. If most communication is within the first domain or two listed, the user then will not have to enter the full domain name to reach those hosts.

The ***set all*** command to ***nslookup*** shows the current configuration that ***nslookup*** is using to resolve names. As shown in Figure 11.39, the searchlist is displayed (srchlist=...), which matches the configured searchlist shown in Figure 11.33.

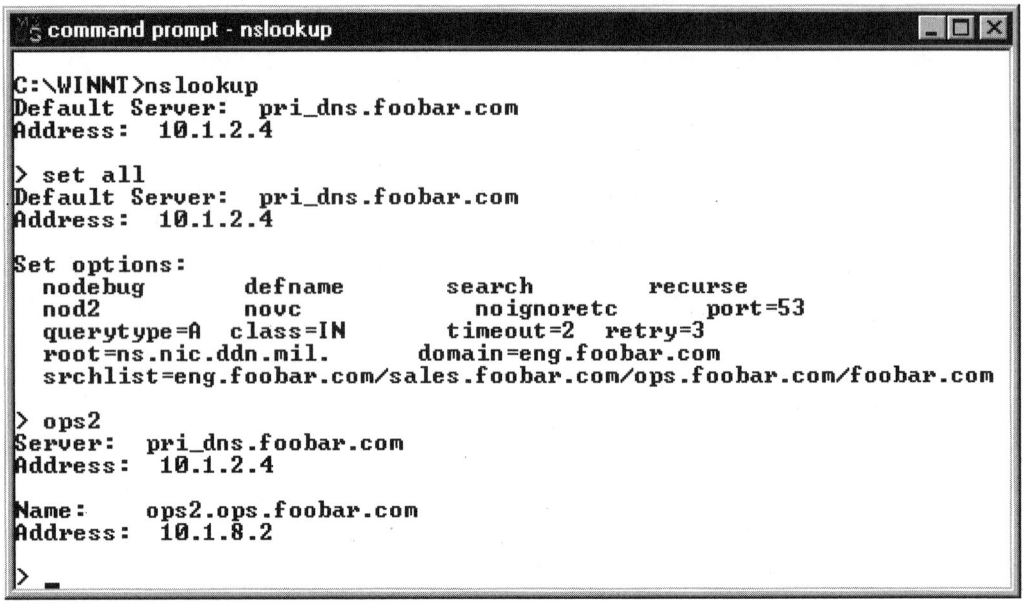

Figure 11.39 Nslookup set all command shows that the searchlist matches the searchlist in the client configuration screen.

The second command issued in Figure 11.39 is a query for the machine ops2. As we'll see shortly, three queries were sent to the DNS server to resolve this name. The queries were for:

- ops2.eng.foobar.com
- ops2.sales.foobar.com
- ops2.ops.foobar.com

Thus each of the suffixes was tried in the specified order until a match was found. Hostnames that do not end in a dot will be appended with each suffix in the order listed. So in the example shown in Figure 11.40, we see the same behavior.

```
command prompt - nslookup -debug
> bogus
Server:  pri_dns.foobar.com
Address:  10.1.2.4

------------
Got answer:
    HEADER:
        opcode = QUERY, id = 3, rcode = NXDOMAIN
        header flags:  response, auth. answer, want recursion, recursion avail.

        questions = 1,  answers = 0,  authority records = 0,  additional = 0

    QUESTIONS:
        bogus.eng.foobar.com, type = A, class = IN

------------
------------
Got answer:
    HEADER:
        opcode = QUERY, id = 4, rcode = NXDOMAIN
        header flags:  response, auth. answer, want recursion, recursion avail.

        questions = 1,  answers = 0,  authority records = 0,  additional = 0

    QUESTIONS:
        bogus.sales.foobar.com, type = A, class = IN

------------
------------
Got answer:
    HEADER:
        opcode = QUERY, id = 5, rcode = NXDOMAIN
        header flags:  response, auth. answer, want recursion, recursion avail.

        questions = 1,  answers = 0,  authority records = 0,  additional = 0

    QUESTIONS:
        bogus.ops.foobar.com, type = A, class = IN

------------
------------
Got answer:
    HEADER:
        opcode = QUERY, id = 6, rcode = NXDOMAIN
        header flags:  response, auth. answer, want recursion, recursion avail.

        questions = 1,  answers = 0,  authority records = 0,  additional = 0

    QUESTIONS:
        bogus.foobar.com, type = A, class = IN

------------
*** pri_dns.foobar.com can't find bogus: Non-existent domain
> _
```

Figure 11.40 Successive queries will be attempted based on entries in the search list until a matching response is returned.

In this example, however, the name we are trying to resolve, bogus, does not exist in any of the domains in the search list. Four attempts are made because there are four entries in the search list.

When the fourth query fails, the resolver has reached the end of the search list, thus it returns a failure indication to the application (in this case, ***nslookup***).

Network Monitor was used to capture the messages in this scenario, as shown in Figure 11.41, and the capture file is stored on the CD as dnsquery2.cap. The address database dns_ch.adr should be used with this capture file.

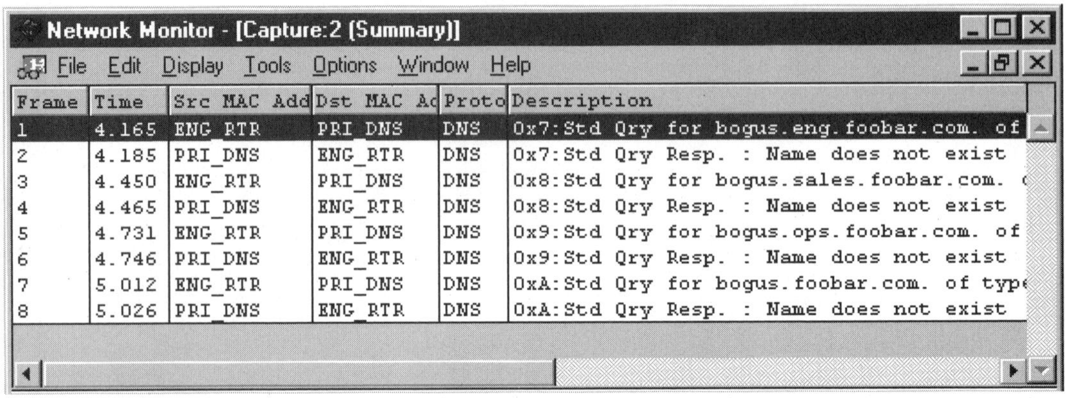

Frame	Time	Src MAC Add	Dst MAC Ad	Proto	Description
1	4.165	ENG_RTR	PRI_DNS	DNS	0x7:Std Qry for bogus.eng.foobar.com. of
2	4.185	PRI_DNS	ENG_RTR	DNS	0x7:Std Qry Resp. : Name does not exist
3	4.450	ENG_RTR	PRI_DNS	DNS	0x8:Std Qry for bogus.sales.foobar.com.
4	4.465	PRI_DNS	ENG_RTR	DNS	0x8:Std Qry Resp. : Name does not exist
5	4.731	ENG_RTR	PRI_DNS	DNS	0x9:Std Qry for bogus.ops.foobar.com. of
6	4.746	PRI_DNS	ENG_RTR	DNS	0x9:Std Qry Resp. : Name does not exist
7	5.012	ENG_RTR	PRI_DNS	DNS	0xA:Std Qry for bogus.foobar.com. of type
8	5.026	PRI_DNS	ENG_RTR	DNS	0xA:Std Qry Resp. : Name does not exist

Figure 11.41 Several query attempts are made with successive suffixes.

These messages may summarized as follows

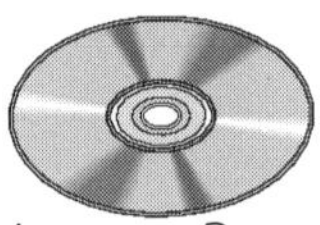

dnsquery2.cap

- frame 1: eng_rtr queries pri_dns for bogus.eng.foobar.com.
- frame 2: pri_dns responds with a "does not exist" message.
- frame 3: eng_rtr queries pri_dns for bogus.sales.foobar.com.
- frame 4: pri_dns responds with a "does not exist" message.
- frame 5: eng_rtr queries pri_dns for bogus.ops.foobar.com.
- frame 6: pri_dns responds with a "does not exist" message.
- frame 7: eng_rtr queries pri_dns for bogus.foobar.com.
- frame 8: pri_dns responds with a "does not exist" message.

After this, ***nslookup*** has run out of entries in the search list, and thus reports the failure to resolve bogus.

Summary

Here's a summary of the items which have been addressed in this chapter.

- The Domain Name System is a database distributed throughout the Internet which contains IP address to domain name mappings. An organization maintains their own part of the database- the part that defines their own hosts and IP addresses.
- Domain name resolution is the process of obtaining an IP address for a particular domain name. The reverse is also possible- obtaining a domain name for a particular IP address.
- Primary DNS servers contain the original name to IP address records. Secondary servers are DNS servers configured to obtain a copy of a primary server's database, and so secondaries can also answer DNS requests.
- Domain names are organized in a hierarchical tree, and are assigned to organizations from an authoritative body. In the U.S., the assigning organization is the InterNIC.
- The Microsoft DNS server can be installed on NT and configured to operate as a fully-functional DNS server.
- The ***nslookup*** command is used to test a DNS server. Among other things, ***nslookup*** sends name queries to DNS servers, and displays the results.
- Records found in the DNS database have various types. A few of the types discussed were A, PTR, CNAME, NS and SOA.

Further Reading

Additional information on DNS may be found in the following references.

[Albitz1994] Albitz, Paul and Lui, Cricket, *DNS and Bind,* 1994, O'Reilly & Associates, Inc.

[Mockapetris1987a] Mockapetris, P.V., *Domain Names — Concepts and Facilities,* 1987, IETF RFC 1034

[Mockapetris1987b] Mockapetris, P.V., *Domain Names — Implementation and Specification,* 1987, IETF RFC 1035

[Mockapetris1989] Mockapetris, P.V., *DNS Encoding of Network Names and Other Types,* 1989, IETF RFC 1101

12

Internet Access Using Proxy Server

Access to the Internet (or other external network) may be supported in many ways, however using an intermediary (a *proxy*) may offer several advantages for your organization. In fact, the same technologies which allow your organization to securely access the Internet may also be used to provide information to the Internet without jeopardizing your unpublished internal information.

Proxies may also be used to support consolidated connections between different sites, or internal to a given site for controlled individual or departmental information access.

This chapter introduces what proxies are and how they may be useful. First we'll discuss HTTP operation, and various Internet access options. Next a detailed discussion will ensue on the topic of firewall and proxy operation. Finally, Microsoft Proxy Server 2.0 features will be discussed, as well as client configuration. And of course, we can't have a chapter without packet captures!

Hypertext Transfer Protocol (HTTP)

The World Wide Web is based on the *HyperText Transfer Protocol (HTTP)* which runs on top of TCP/IP. Many browsers, such as Netscape Navigator, support more than just HTTP since they have FTP, gopher, and email clients built in as well.

Many times you've probably seen names like http://www.w3.org, and recently advertisements are not even including the http prefix! It's that common. But what is HTTP?

HTTP is used to retrieve documents, some of which may be in a *HyperText Markup Language (HTML)* format. This protocol is used by web browsers, web servers, and specialized applications which also use the web as a medium.

HTTP Messages

The basic use of HTTP is to connect a client workstation to a web server. HTTP supports two primary types of messages (Figure 12.1):

- request sent to the server (Get)
- response sent back to the client (Response)

Figure 12.1
HTTP is a request / response protocol used for information retrieval.

A request from an HTTP client to a server specifies that the client wishes to get a resource from the network. The message sent for this request is the word "GET" followed by a space, the Uniform Resource Locator (URL) of the resource, another space, and the version of the protocol, ending with a carriage return and line feed. The following example is from RFC 1945 which describes HTTP/1.0:

```
GET http://www.w3.org/pub/WWW/TheProject.html HTTP/1.0
```

One of HTTP's main uses is for information retrieval— it is essentially a lighter-weight version of FTP. In the instance above, we are retrieving with HTTP/1.0 the file /pub/WWW/TheProject.html. Hopefully the server will respond with the information requested.

Parsing an HTTP Request

A user normally enters the Web location they wish to visit into a browser. The browser translates the location into an HTTP message. Each HTTP message is passed in text form and therefore must be parsed in order to determine the action to be taken. Consider this full request:

```
GET http://www.w3.org/pub/WWW/TheProject.html HTTP/1.0
```

This request may be broken into the pieces shown in Figure 12.2.

Figure 12.2
Parsing an URL.

```
protocol: http

server: www.w3.org

request: GET /pub/WWW/TheProject.html HTTP/1.0
```

Let's look at the steps which our browser might go through:

1. Parse the name into its various parts as shown in Figure 12.2.
2. Resolve the name www.w3.org into an IP address. Let's say for this example that the IP address is 172.16.12.3.
3. Look up the HTTP protocol number. The standard HTTP port is TCP port 80.
4. Establish a TCP connection to port 80 on 172.16.12.3.
5. Send the request GET /pub/WWW/TheProject.html HTTP/1.0 over the connection.
6. Receive the response back from the server.
7. Process and display the results.

So HTTP is a pretty simple protocol— request a file, display the file. Web browsers may perform some additional processing as a part of step 7. For instance, if the document is an HTML document, the browser will scan the HTML document for inline images and send additional requests by repeating steps 1-7 for each image.

HTTP Packet Exchange

HTTP consists of GET requests and the replies to those requests. These packets are sent across a TCP connection, using port 80 on the server side. Figure 12.3 shows the ladder diagram of an HTTP exchange.

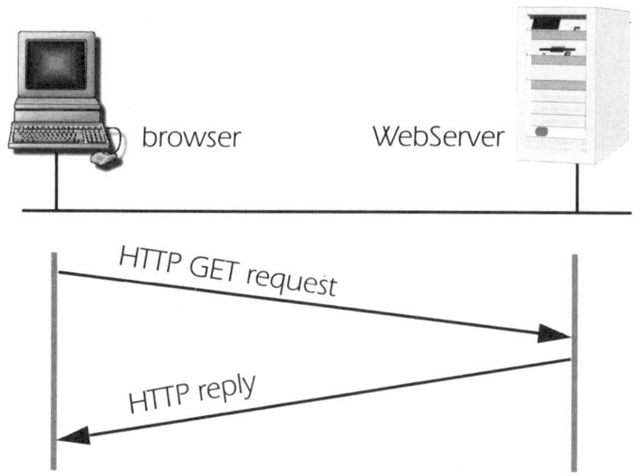

Figure 12.3 Exchange of an HTTP GET request and HTTP reply.

These packets are also shown in the Network Monitor packet capture in Figure 12.4. It shows HTTP packets exchanged between the client named browser, and the server called WebServer. The TCP startup sequence is now shown in this capture.

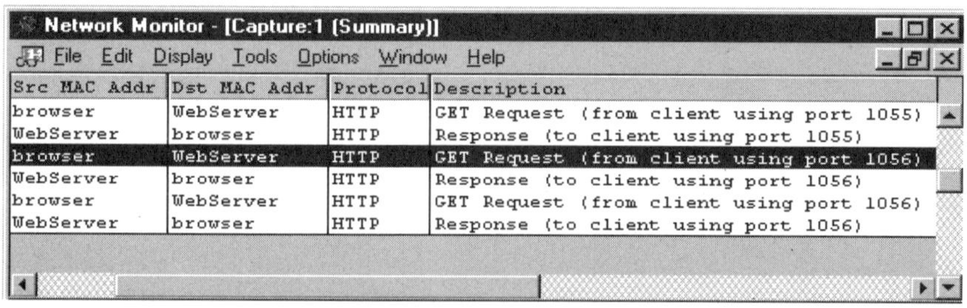

Src MAC Addr	Dst MAC Addr	Protocol	Description
browser	WebServer	HTTP	GET Request (from client using port 1055)
WebServer	browser	HTTP	Response (to client using port 1055)
browser	WebServer	HTTP	GET Request (from client using port 1056)
WebServer	browser	HTTP	Response (to client using port 1056)
browser	WebServer	HTTP	GET Request (from client using port 1056)
WebServer	browser	HTTP	Response (to client using port 1056)

Figure 12.4 A capture of HTTP request and response messages.

In the capture shown in Figure 12.4, the client (browser) sent three separate GET requests, and received from the WebServer three reply packets. Each response received by the client was processed (formatted) and displayed on the user's screen.

This example is just a small portion of a typical HTTP connection. Multiple messages are typically exchanged during normal HTTP communication.

Internet Access Options

There are several methods which may be used to connect a corporate network to the Internet using NT as the connecting machine. The Internet gateway could be just NT Server 4.0, NT Server with Steelhead software installed, or NT Server with Proxy Server software installed. Each of these options is described in the next few pages.

Using NT Server 4.0 to Access the Internet

Windows NT Server 4.0 is able to route IP traffic between network interfaces. There are limited filtering capabilities which may be used. Figure 12.5 shows one method for using NT Server to connect an organization to the Internet.

Figure 12.5
Access to the Internet using basic NT Server routing.

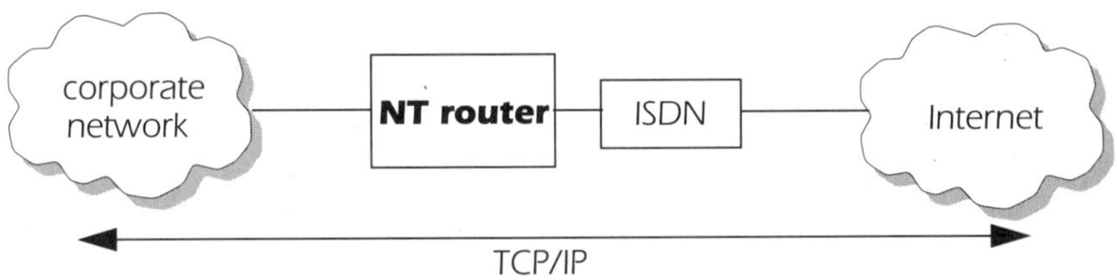

There are several requirements which must be met in order to use NT Server as a router in this way.

- The organization has to have InterNIC[1] registered addresses.
- Access to an Internet Access Provider (IAP), Internet Service Provider (ISP), or Point of Presence (POP) is needed.

1. For corporate registrations in the United States, the InterNIC is the registration organization which assigns Internet addresses. The registration authority for other countries and U.S. military organizations may be different. Unless your organization either provides Internet access or is very large, your registration will probably be handled by a third party, such as an ISP.

- The machine used as an NT router needs to be configured in the following ways:
    - RAS service must be configured as a dial-out client if the connection to the Internet is not a permanent one.
    - IP forwarding must be enabled using the TCP/IP control panel.
    - Packet filtering must be established using the *TCP/IP Security* configuration screen. (See "TCP/IP Security Configuration" on page 184.)
    - RIP messages must not be sent on the external interface.

There are a few substantial disadvantages of this method.

- Little security is offered by simple packet filtering found in NT Server 4.0 itself (i.e. without Steelhead or Proxy).
- InterNIC registered addresses are required for every server and client inside your organization.[2]

The management and security aspects of this scheme are reason enough to consider the next two scenarios instead.

Using Steelhead Router to Access the Internet

Another method for Internet access for an organization is to use a Steelhead router (Figure 12.6) rather than the simpler NT server version.

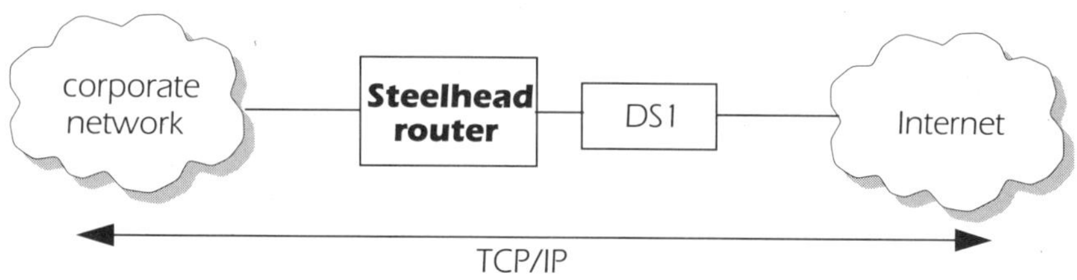

Figure 12.6 Steelhead provides more secure access through improved filtering

2. Even if you can get a large enough block of IP addresses for your organization, the use of clear internal address information traversing the Internet could be a security risk.

The requirements for using Steelhead as a router to the Internet are similar to those for using the traditional routing in NT server:

- Access to an Internet Access Provider (IAP), Internet Service Provider (ISP), or Point of Presence (POP) is needed.
- The machine used as a Steelhead router needs the following:
  - RRAS (Steelhead) must be configured as a dial-out client.
  - Routing must be enabled using the RRAS Manager.
  - Packet filtering must be established using the RRAS Manager.
  - RIP and OSPF messages must not be sent on the external interface.
- Registered IP addresses are still needed for the whole organization in this scenario.

This method of Internet access has some disadvantages as well:

- Registered IP addresses are still needed.
- Although the packet filter capabilities of Steelhead are an improvement on those offered by the plain NT server routing, more access may be allowed than you may want.

Using Proxy Server to Access the Internet

Yet another option for accessing the Internet is by using Microsoft's Proxy Server (Figure 12.7). The details of how proxy servers work will be covered in the next section. Basically, the Proxy Server relays traffic between the Internet and the corporate network, but in a more selective fashion than a Steelhead or NT router does.

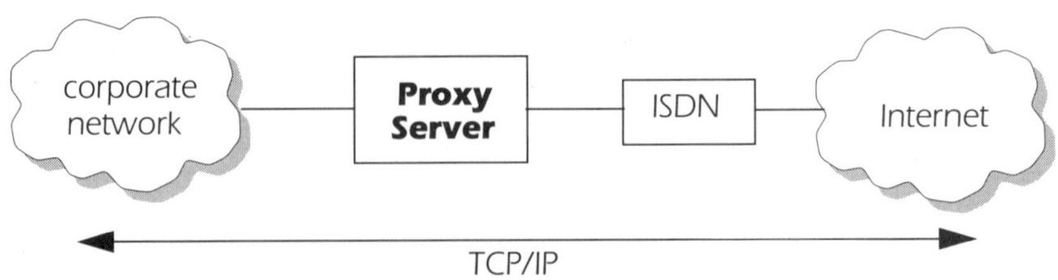

Figure 12.7 Access to the Internet through a proxy server.

The requirements for this scenario include:

- NT Server with Internet Information Server and Proxy Server
- Either packet filtering should be enabled, or the workstation and server service should be disabled on the interface to the Internet.
- Clients must be configured to use proxy access to the server, and in some cases, special software must be installed on each client.

There are a few advantages to choosing this option:

- InterNIC registered addresses are not required for the whole corporate network, only one address for the proxy server's external interface.
- The security offered by Proxy Server is greatly enhanced beyond the level offered by Steelhead.

There will be a disadvantage:

- Proxy client software will likely need to be installed on each client, since Proxy Server 2.0 is not a "non-intrusive" proxy. The details of this will be discussed shortly.

Current Network Diagram

Let's revisit the network used in many of the examples in this book. In order to illustrate the operation of a proxy server, we show a bit more of the network, as diagrammed in Figure 12.8.

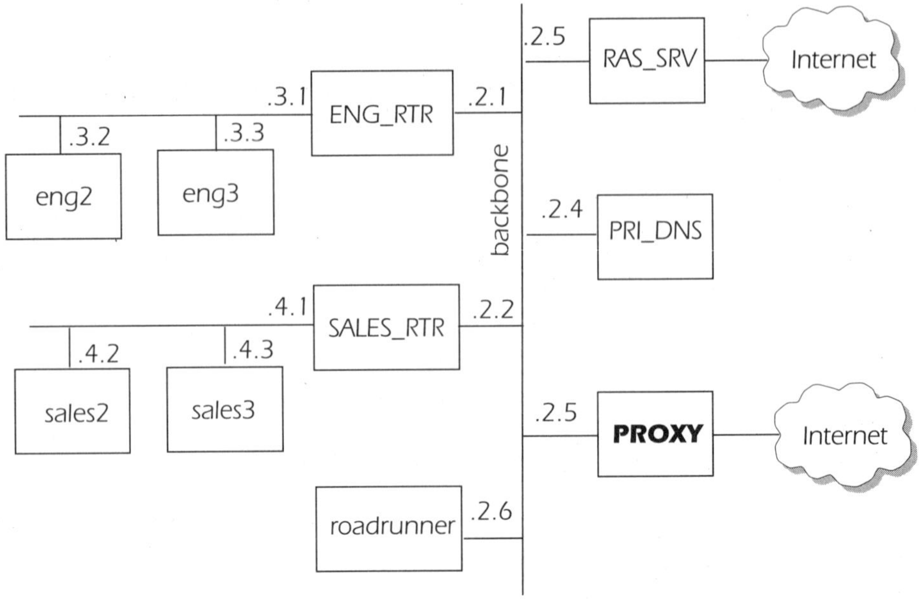

Figure 12.8 Network diagram showing proxy server.

The remote access server (RAS_SRV) toward the top of the diagram is used to interconnect a remote operations office using PPTP (described in chapters 9 and 10).

A new addition, the proxy server (PROXY) also connects to the Internet. Yet rather than being used for tunneled access to a remote office only, this connection is used to support access from any of the internal departments (including remote offices) to resources on the Internet.

How Proxy Servers Work

Although the purpose of networks is to support communication, in some cases we don't want unrestricted communication. Usually the desire for restricting the flow of information has to do with security, finance, and ownership.

Firewalls

firewall: a device used to separate traffic between an internal and external network.

A common method of restricting information flow in a network is to use a **firewall**. Rather than preventing the spread of fire, electronic firewalls are intended to prevent information from spreading beyond a certain boundary. Thus a firewall effectively partitions traffic into the "inside" network and the "outside" network. The inside network is often called an *intranet*, and the outside network may be called an *external net*.

Figure 12.9
A firewall divides a network into internal and external parts.

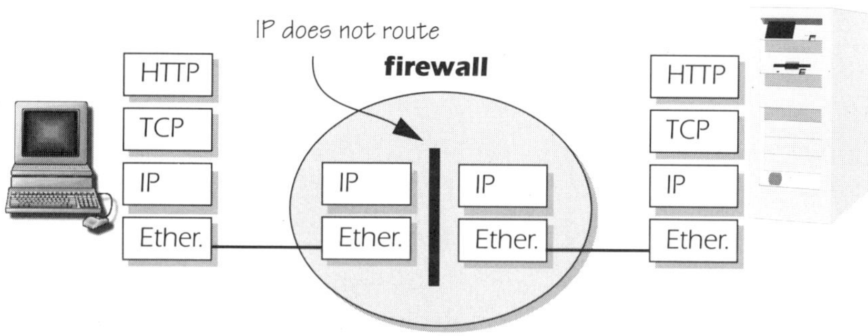

An example of a machine which acts as a firewall is a multihomed host which does not have routing enabled, as shown in Figure 12.9. If no packets pass between the inside and outside networks, this device is called an *absolute firewall*. If some traffic is allowed to go between the inside and outside networks, the device is a *selective firewall*. Absolute firewalls of course have no practical application— just unplug the network cable to the Internet and you have an absolute firewall! What we'll see in practice are selective firewalls.

Filtering Router as a Firewall

One method of creating a selective firewall is to:

1. First build an absolute firewall which lets nothing pass between the internal and external networks.
2. Second, configure explicit permissions which allows selective packets pass through the firewall.

The most common example of this technique is a *filtering router* or *screening router.* A filtering router is shown in Figure 12.10.

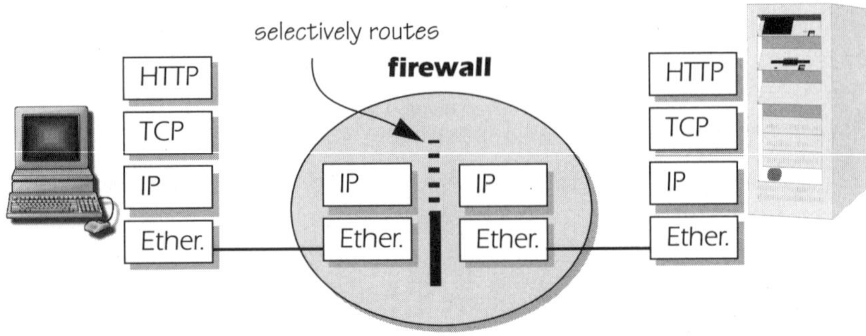

Figure 12.10
A filtering router allows some traffic through.

filtering router: a router which selects which packets are allowed through, and which packets are dropped.

The **filtering router** is configured to permit certain types of datagrams to be routed. Other datagrams will be dropped. This selective permeability of the firewall allows great control over the traffic which is allowed through.

Many hardware routers implement this sort of feature. In fact, some basic filtering is possible with the normal Windows NT Server *Advanced IP Configuration* screen (Figure 5.15 on page 186). Steelhead provides much more advanced filtering specifications.

Consider the example shown in Figure 12.11. The client, roadrunner, sends an HTTP GET request to the web server on the right. The first three segments exchanged are the three-step TCP connection establishment handshake. The router has been configured to allow outbound TCP segments destined to port 80, thus the first segment is allowed to go out to the server.

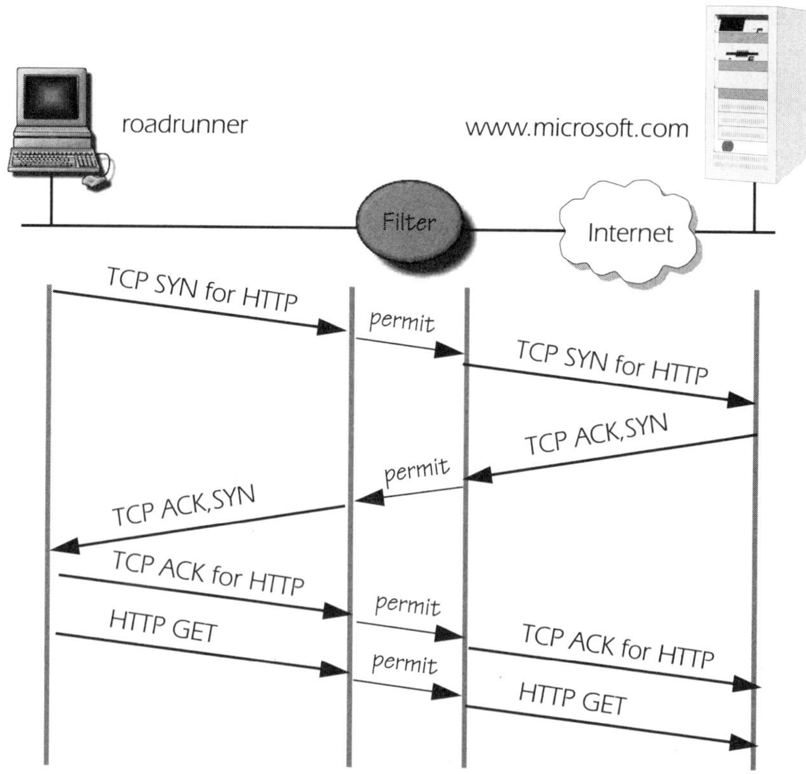

Figure 12.11 Filtering router permits or denies routing of each datagram.

simple filtering routers: routers that filter by simple criteria, such as port number.

stateful inspection: the process of a firewall keeping track of TCP connection states, such that connections in a certain direction can be restricted

The second segment comes back from the web server to the firewall, and the firewall looks at the segment. Should the router allow it to be forwarded, or should it drop it? In **simple filtering routers**, we would have to allow any connections from port 80 in. If the filtering process were more complex, however, the router could make note of the first segment (the original SYN) as it is permitted out. From that point in time, the router could keep track of the *state* of the connection. Then rather than allowing just any TCP segment which comes from port 80 in through the firewall, the selection process can be more discriminating. If the firewall is maintaining the state of the connection, it knows that a SYN has passed outward, and will allow an ACK,SYN to come back in with the inverse socket addresses (IP address, port number). This is called **stateful filtering** or **stateful inspection**, and there are varying degrees in the complexity which may be implemented. What we called simple filtering routers previously are also called **stateless firewalls**.

address translation: the process of mapping internal (non-routable) IP addresses to Inter-NIC-registered addresses. This allows internal machines to communicate with nodes on the Internet.

non-intrusive firewall: a firewall that doesn't require special software on the client or server in order to operate properly.

Another more advanced feature which you may find in some firewalls is **address mapping**, also called **address translation**. Address translation allows you to use private or non-routable network numbers inside your organization. A device that performs address translation will assign a public (i.e. InterNIC registered) address to datagrams sent out of the organization, and map back to the internal address for the response.

The main advantage to address translation is that you only need one InterNIC assigned address! All the machines internal to the organization can have non-routable addresses assigned, yet they all can communicate with nodes on the Internet.

A great advantage of using filtering as a firewall technique is that it may be *transparent*, or *non-intrusive*. With a **non-intrusive firewall**, the client and server don't need any software or configuration changes in order to be used with the firewall.

One of the potential drawbacks of filtering routers is that the configuration requires an understanding of TCP and UDP port numbers, and in some cases, an understanding of TCP connection establishment. Furthermore, an understanding of IP (and sometimes MAC) address usage at your site is often required. Use of filtering routers in a dynamic environment (i.e. where new addresses and new protocols are added frequently) can become even more problematic.

Use of a filtering routers can be very effective when the IP addresses and/or protocols used on either side of the firewall can be controlled.

Proxy Server as a Firewall

Another method of selective firewalling is to:

1. Build an absolute firewall which lets nothing pass between the internal and external networks.
2. Construct an explicit gateway to facilitate selective services to flow between the networks.

In this case, a *gateway-firewall* has been created. Figure 12.12 shows an example of a gateway-firewall.

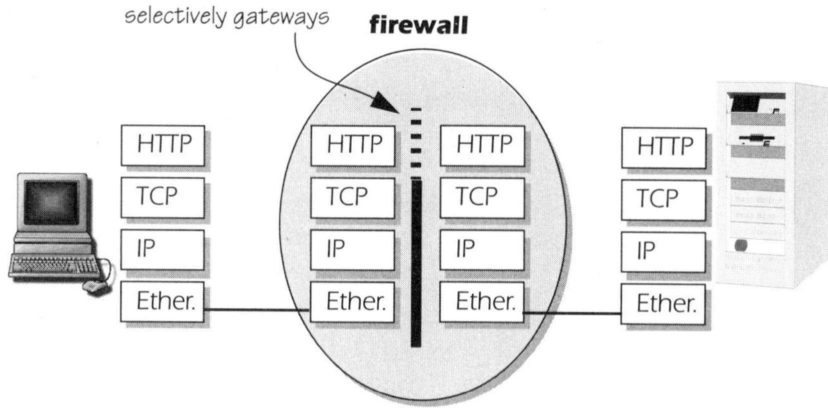

Figure 12.12
A filtering gateway (proxy) allows some traffic through.

gateway-firewall: a firewall which processes packets at levels 4-7 of the OSI stack.

Now end-to-end communication takes on a different meaning. In order to communicate through the gateway, we must talk directly to it, yet tell it that we inevitably want to communicate to someone else. The **gateway-firewall** will consider the request, and if it is acceptable according to its configuration, it will forward (i.e. gateway) the message on toward its destination.

In most forms of this kind of gateway firewall, the forwarded message is sent as though it had come from the gateway itself. Because the gateway carries out the communication on our behalf, it is called a *proxy*, or because many communications are for services, a *proxy server*.

proxy: a device that carries out a request on behalf of someone else.

The **proxy** shown in Figure 12.13 performs two roles. On the one hand, it acts like a server for communication with the client, roadrunner. On the other hand, the proxy acts like a client on behalf of roadrunner (thus it's a proxy) to contact the server at www.wernerconsulting.com. This bivalent identity of the proxy allows for some interesting benefits, which we'll discuss shortly.

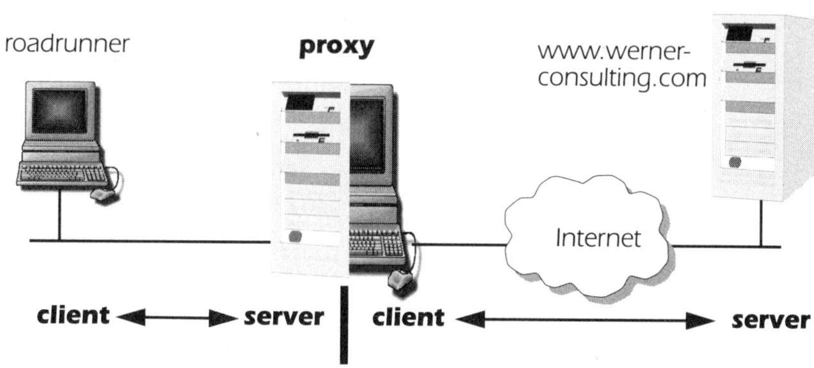

Figure 12.13
The proxy server acts like a server for the actual client, and it acts like a client for the actual server.

The following is another analogy for the operation of a proxy server. Suppose you were visiting another country, and staying in a hotel where the use of the one telephone in the building was severely restricted. In order to place a call, you would tell the front desk clerk that you want to dial number XXX-YYY. The clerk places the call for you, and tells you the other party has answered, and said hello. However, instead of handing you the phone, the clerk asks you what you want to say next, and you tell the clerk. The clerk speaks this message into the phone, and then tells you the other party's reply. The whole conversation goes on like this, until either you or your friend say good-bye to the clerk, who then hangs up the phone.

A proxy server could be considered that clerk who relays your messages between you and your friend. Of course the initial call setup had to be approved, whether it was by the clerk or the proxy.

Example of Proxy Operation

Figure 12.14 shows a proxy server forwarding on an HTTP GET request to an HTTP server. Compare this ladder diagram with the ladder diagram of a filtering router (Figure 12.11). Recall that with the filtering router, end-to-end transfer of datagrams was non-intrusive. With the proxy, the transfer of individual datagrams end-to-end is *intrusive*. The proxy intercepts and interprets each segment. In fact, the proxy doesn't even begin a session with the actual server until after a TCP connection is set up between the client and the proxy server, and the proxy received the HTTP GET request. Thus, the client is indeed connected to the proxy server, but must be made to think that it is connected to the actual server.

Once the proxy server gets the HTTP GET request, it will reformulate the request and set up a connection to the actual server. Once that connection has been established, the proxy will forward the request over that connection to the actual server.

When the actual server replies to the proxy, the proxy must remember which connection the initial request had come in on. The proxy sends the reply back to the original client over that connection.

Figure 12.14
Proxy server forwards on request through an independent connection.

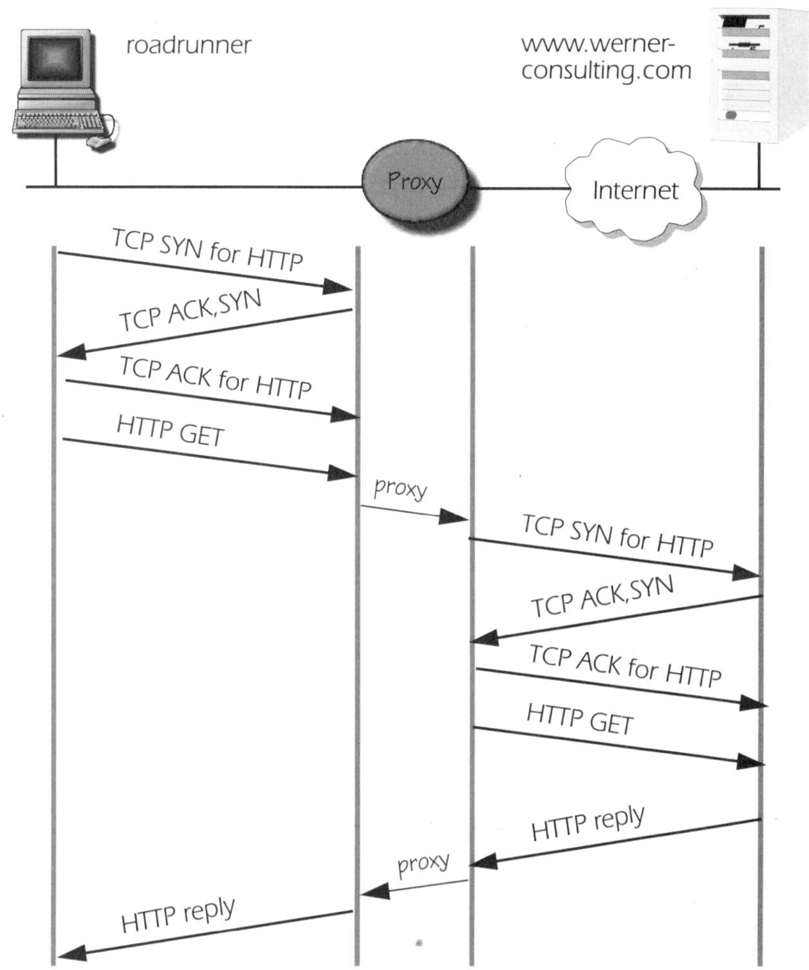

Types of Proxies

As discussed earlier, proxy servers are typically non-transparent to the client. With a *non-transparent proxy,* the client will need to be configured for information about the proxy server, as well as the protocol and/or port numbers for the client to use.

However, it is possible for proxies to operate transparently. This *transparent proxy* would inspect each incoming datagram and decide it should be routed or gatewayed (proxied). Thus the proxy is performing *multi-layer inspection*- examining multiple protocol headers in a packet in order to determine whether to forward, drop, or proxy the packet.

caching proxy: a proxy that caches web pages for a certain period of time.

A **caching proxy** is a proxy that keeps a copy of information previously retrieved. This cache of information (web pages) would be used to answer future requests for the same web page. (The future requests would have to be within a certain time period of when the original web page was cached.) A caching proxy may speed up Internet response time. It may also reduce the load on the proxy to Internet link, such as when that link is a slow-speed connection.

Proxy Side Effects

Recall that the proxy plays two roles: that of a server, and that of a client. Figure 12.15 shows an expanded view of a proxy. This expanded view shows the mapping table, which is used to determine which clients map to which Internet connections. Also shown is the cache, which contains recently-retrieved web pages.

Figure 12.15
Anatomy of a proxy server.

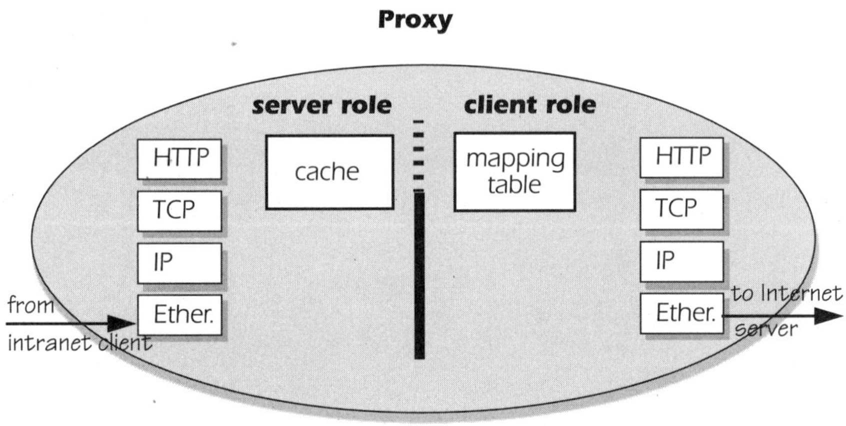

A few of the implications of the proxy design are listed below.

- Since the proxy is acting as a server, it should be able to handle potentially a large number of clients connecting in for proxy service. Also, the proxy must have sufficient resources to handle the load so that it doesn't become a substantial bottleneck.
- For non-transparent proxies, client software or configuration is required for each client.
- For caching proxies, response time may improve, and slow Internet links will not need to be used as often to retrieve frequently-accessed web pages.
- Proxy servers perform address translation, so InterNIC-assigned IP addresses are not required for the intranet machines.
- A proxy usually uses its own external interface address for outside communications. From the outside, this may make all clients look like they are all on the same system.

Hybrid Firewalls

The features of filtering routers and proxies may be combined. Usually this type of implementation is similar to a multi-layer inspection.

Alternately, the services which make up the firewall functions may be divided across several machines. For example, a filtering router may be placed at the outer edge of an organization for their Internet access. Publicly accessible services could be installed on the network on the organization's side of the filter. Then a proxy server could provide access to the organization's users out through this intermediate network to the Internet. An example of this is shown in Figure 12.16.

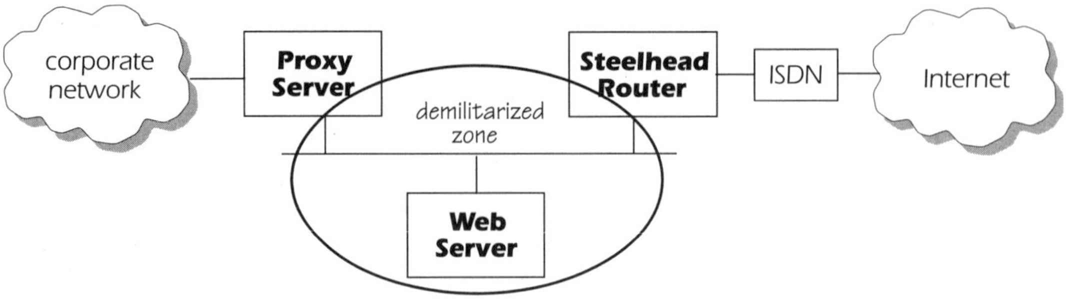

Figure 12.16 A demilitarized zone may be created between firewalls.

demilitarized zone (DMZ): a network that connects an intranet to the Internet, where the interfaces to the internal and external network are firewalls.

The intermediate network is often called a **demilitarized zone (DMZ)**, because the traffic on that network has been filtered, and the services available on that network do not hold any proprietary information.

The access devices at either end of the DMZ may be proxy servers, filtering routers, or other types of firewall devices. There may be DNS servers, web servers, and other resources made available in the DMZ. Some organizations create multiple DMZs with different kinds of access devices at the edges for enhanced security.

Mapping Clients to Servers

How does a proxy server support more than one client simultaneously? The answer to that question lies in another question. How does TCP/IP support more than one application on the same machine?

Consider an ordinary TCP/IP user who is loading email from a post office, scanning news groups on another server, browsing two web pages at a time, downloading the latest stock information, and uploading a new specification to the publications department's server as shown in Figure 12.17. TCP and UDP uses port numbers to address different applications, whether those applications are fulfilling a client, server, or peer role in communications. Each application has a distinct port number. With TCP, connection identifiers consist of a socket-IP address pair, thus the same user could have two distinct instances of an application (e.g. web browser) connected to the same server.

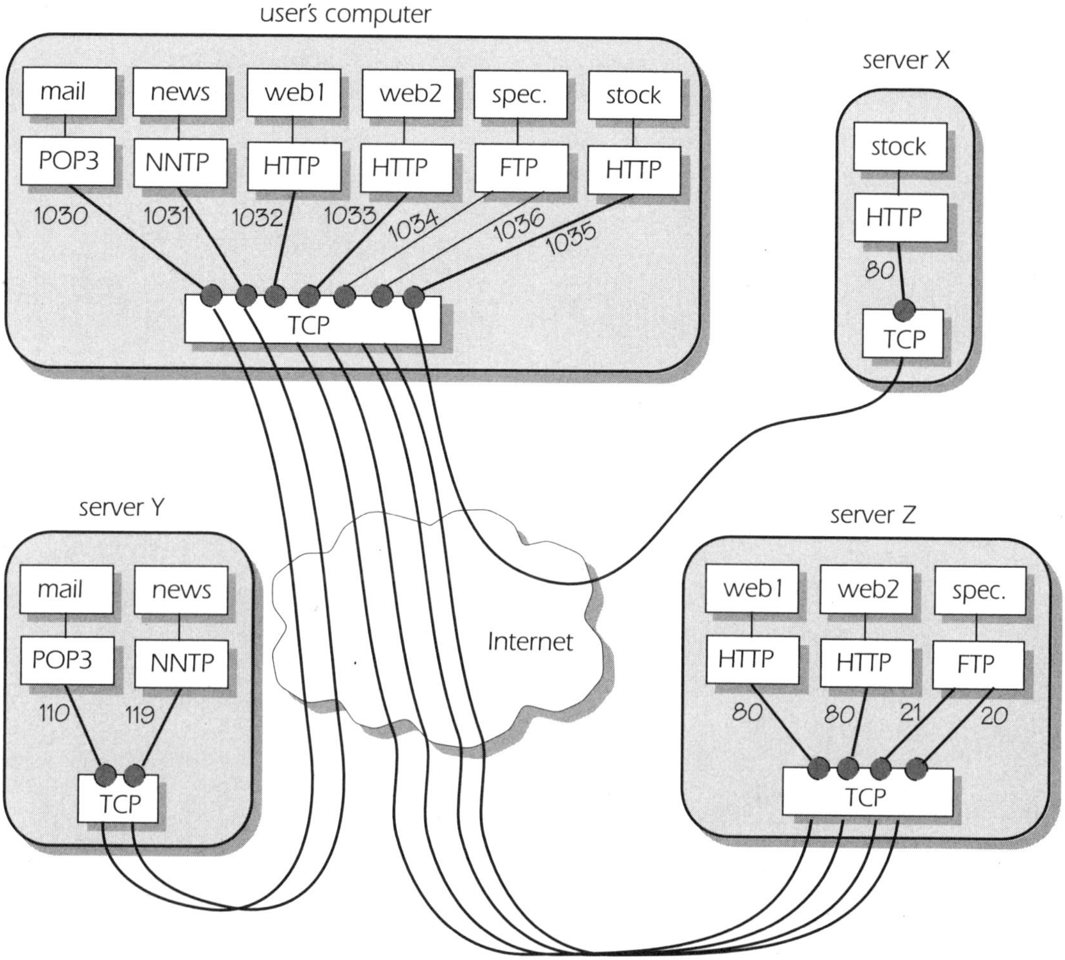

Figure 12.17 One user with connections to three servers.

Now consider a number of users all using a minicomputer. Each client application is assigned a distinct port number. Thus, the requirement for multiple connections from a proxy server to one or many servers is handled by TCP naturally. TCP also by design handles many connections to one device. What is not necessarily built-in to TCP is how the two portions of any end-to-end connection get associated. This is integral to the operation of a proxy.

The proxy server maintains a mapping table of the association between a client connection (e.g. internal) and a connection to the actual server (e.g. external). This is shown in Figure 12.18.

Figure 12.18
The map table helps a proxy keep track of what connections go together.

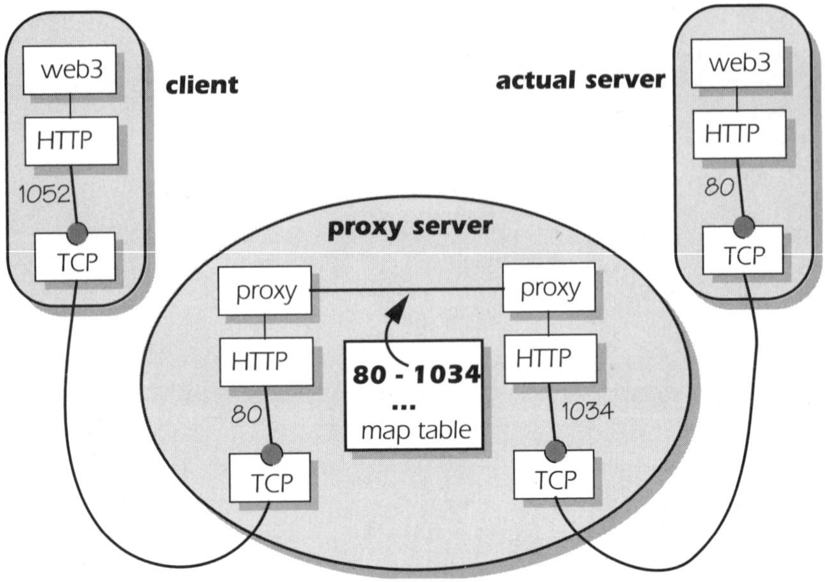

In Figure 12.18, there is a mapping table consisting of one entry with just port numbers. In reality, the mapping table also contains internal IP address as well as other information.

Non-transparent Client Configuration

As discussed earlier, without stateful multi-layer inspection techniques, most proxies are not able to provide transparent access to clients. In other words, the client must be aware that it is connecting to a proxy server. Furthermore, the client must know how to formulate queries specially so that the proxy server knows how to set up the connection to the actual server and associate the two connections with a map table entry.

This means that the normal protocol for information access has to be either augmented or replaced with a proxy server access protocol. In other words, the client applications need to be modified or supplemented so that they can use the proxy. Most web browsers have this sort of proxy access software built in.

This proxy access software for the client (or simply *proxy client software*) may require configuration before it can be used. For instance, consider that you want to send all HTTP requests destined for local servers to be passed directly to those servers, yet all HTTP requests which are addressed to machines across the Internet should be sent to the proxy server using the proxy access protocol. In some cases, the determination of normal access vs. proxy access is based on domain names, while in others it may be based on IP addresses.

local address table (LAT): a table used to determine which IP addresses are on the internal network.

For example, Microsoft Proxy Server includes proxy client software which bases normal vs. proxy access on a **Local Address Table (LAT).** The LAT contains ranges of IP addresses which are considered internal, and thus may be processed normally without proxying.

The LAT is used by both the client and server proxy software. By using the LAT, Microsoft Proxy Server is performing address translation.

Proxy Server 2.0 Services

Microsoft's *Internet Information Server (IIS)* provides HTTP and FTP services to a network. Microsoft's Proxy Server 2.0 extends the features offered by IIS by supporting proxied access through IIS to another network.

A few configuration notes about Proxy Server:

- Because Proxy Server is based on IIS, you must have IIS installed first to run proxy server.
- When Proxy Server is installed, it disables incoming web access via the external interface. However, if you installed the IIS FTP server, that service is still available to Internet clients— beware!
- The Proxy Server is configured to use the DNS as specified in the TCP/IP settings for that machine. The Proxy Server will handle name resolution for the clients.[3]

3. Queries addressed to DNS servers on the Internet are not forwarded by the Proxy Server.

- It is recommended that you disable the server and workstation services from operating on the adapter to the Internet. Also disable NetBIOS on this adapter. (Use the *Network Control Panel-> TCP/IP Properties->Bindings tab* to disable these.)

Figure 12.19 shows the main screen for Internet Service Manager after the Proxy Server has been installed. Notice that the Internet Service Manager shows three additional services:

- Web proxy
- WinSock proxy
- SOCKS proxy

Each of those proxies handles different kinds of Internet requests. They are discussed in the next few pages.

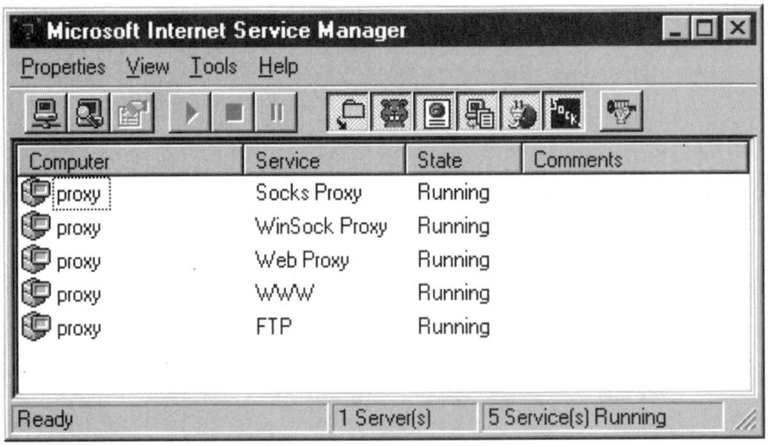

Figure 12.19 Using Internet Service Manager to configure proxy services.

Web Proxy

The World Wide Web, and HTTP, were developed at CERN[4] in 1991. The most common form of web proxying is called a *CERN-proxy*. Microsoft has implemented this in Proxy Server, and it is called *Web Proxy*.

4. Conseil Europeen pour la Recherche Nucleaire

Recall from our discussion of HTTP that a full request for HTTP may be written in the following form:

```
GET http://www.w3.org/pub/WWW/TheProject.html HTTP/1.0
```

If a client wishes to talk to a server directly, it will parse the request into its components as we described earlier. The client would resolve the domain name (www.w3.org) and look up the service type (http), then set up a TCP connection to the resulting IP address and port number. Then the client will communicate with the server using HTTP. The request sent to the server will be the remainder of the request:

```
GET /pub/WWW/TheProject.html HTTP/1.0
```

The protocol will then proceed as expected.

If on the other hand, the client doesn't wish to talk to the actual server directly, but wants to use a proxy, it performs the following steps:

1. Set up a connection to the configured proxy server to port 80.
2. Send the full request, including the complete URL.

This CERN-proxy request may contain service types of HTTP, FTP, and Gopher.

The proxy server will receive this request and parse it into its components. The service may be either HTTP, FTP, or Gopher. Figure 12.20 shows an example of FTP. The proxy resolves the domain name from the URL and sets up a connection to the appropriate port (21 for the FTP control port) at the actual server. In this example, because the actual server is accessed with FTP, a separate control connection (1100 to 21) and data connection (1099 from 20) are required. The proxy server handles the transfer of information between the FTP connection to the actual server and the HTTP connection to the client.

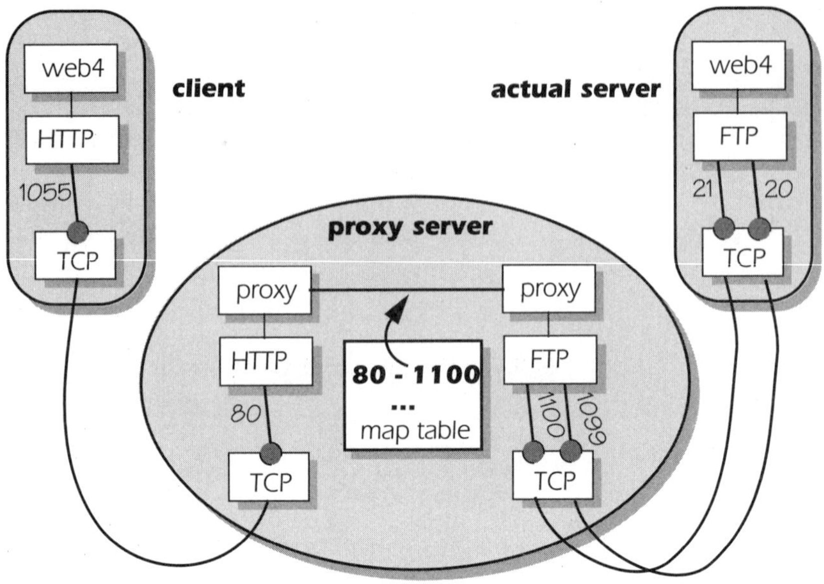

Figure 12.20 CERN-proxy uses HTTP between the client and the proxy server, and the appropriate protocol (HTTP, FTP, Gopher) between the proxy and the actual server.

WinSock Proxy

An alternative to the Web Proxy service is the WinSock Proxy. The WinSock client software replaces the winsock.dll file with a new winsock.dll— one that sends requests to the proxy server.

Rather than setting up a connection to the proxy server, the modified WinSock library on the client sends negotiation and control information over a control channel (UDP port 1745). The client and the proxy server exchange configuration information. This information tells the client which WinSock requests must be forwarded to the proxy server and which may be processed directly (Figure 12.21).

When a client wishes to start a connection, it negotiates over the control channel with the proxy server what port it should use to connect to the proxy. The client then connects to the proxy server at the prescribed random port.

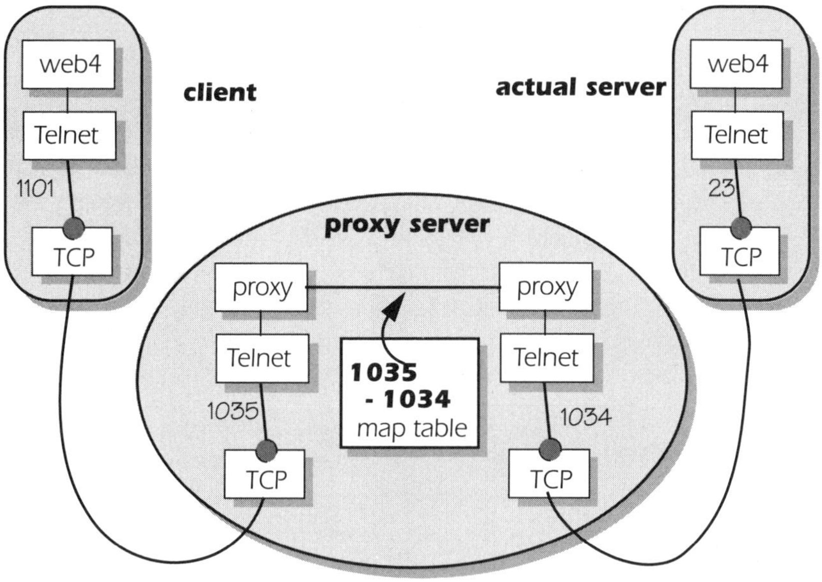

Figure 12.21 WinSock proxy negotiates a random port to use to connect to the proxy server. The proxy server then uses another random port to connect to the actual server at the well known port for the service.

SOCKS Proxy

RFC1928 describes the SOCKS Protocol Version 5, which is another proxy access method. Proxy Server 2.0 implements an earlier version, SOCKS V4. The newer version of SOCKS has been extended to support UDP and negotiation of strong authentication.

Like the other proxy access methods, SOCKS communicates with the proxy server to negotiate options for access. SOCKS uses TCP port 1080.

SOCKS V4 client software is built in to most modern web browsers. Also, many Unix and Macintosh applications can be configured to use the SOCKS proxy.

Client Configuration

Microsoft Proxy Server clients can use one or more methods to communicate with the proxy server. If the clients are NT or Windows 95 machines, they will be Web Proxy and WinSock proxy clients. If the clients are Unix or Macintoshes, they will be Web Proxy clients and possibly SOCKS clients.

Web Proxy Clients

If the clients will only be using a CERN-proxy compliant web browser, the only configuration needed is to tell the browser to use a proxy at a specific IP address. Thus Unix and Macintosh clients running Netscape Navigator can use the proxy to access the web.

Of course, Internet Explorer is CERN-proxy compliant. The configuration screen to use in IE is on the *Internet Explorer Properties* screen, *Connection Tab* (Figure 12.22). If the *Connect through a proxy server* box is checked, this browser will use a proxy server for HTTP, SSL, FTP, and Gopher requests. The proxy server will not be used to connect to the machines listed in the *Exceptions* portion of the screen.

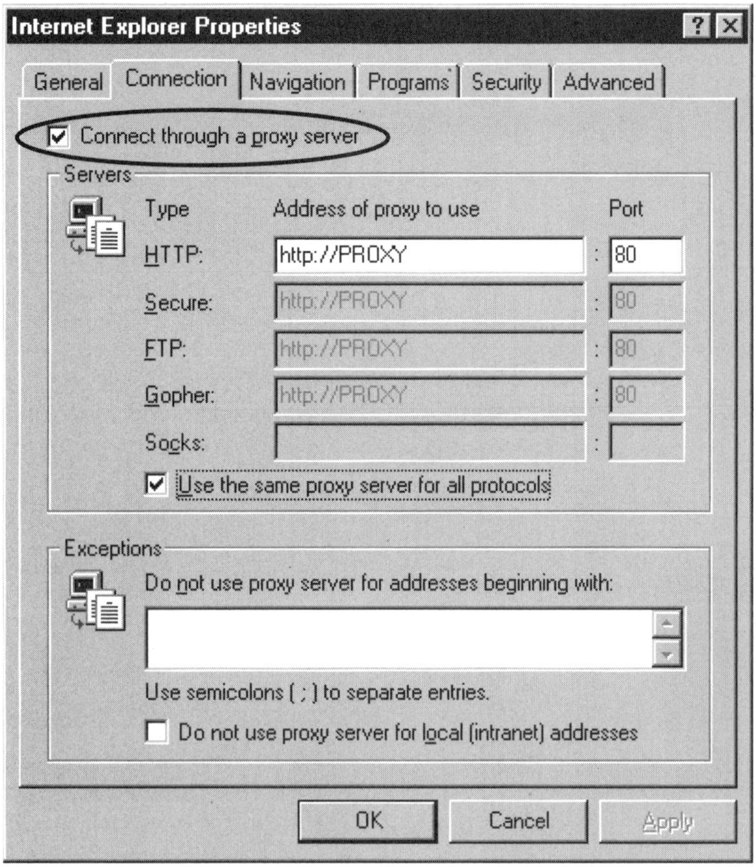

Figure 12.22 Internet Explorer's proxy configuration.

Additional proxy configuration information is found under the *Advanced tab*, under the *Automatic Configuration* subscreen (Figure 12.23). Each time that Internet Explorer starts up, it will load a configuration file from the URL specified in this dialog.

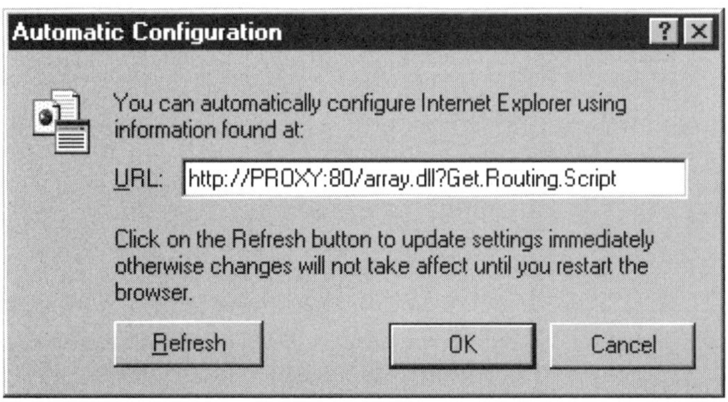

Figure 12.23 The routing script contains instructions for Internet Explorer so that it may decide whether to use proxy for certain addresses.

SOCKS Proxy Clients

As was described, it is possible to use browsers which are CERN-proxy compliant to access the web from Unix and Macintosh machines. However, other networking applications on Unix and Macintosh machines must be configured to use SOCKS to communicate with the Microsoft proxy server.[5] You would need to obtain and install SOCKS-compatible client applications in order for those devices to communicate to the Internet.

There is no reason to obtain SOCKS-compliant applications for NT or Windows 95, as all the software on Microsoft operating systems can use the WinSock proxy with just a simple configuration setup.

WinSock Proxy Clients

In the case of Microsoft operating systems, you do not need to obtain new client applications if you are using the Microsoft Proxy Server. All you need to do is install the WinSock client software.

To configure the client to use the WinSock proxy client software, download and execute the setup program from the proxy server. In Figure 12.24, we show the URL used for our example network.

5. Note that the Microsoft Proxy Server by default denies access to all SOCKS clients. This can be changed using the SOCKS Properties-> Permissions tab, or by modifying the file SOCKS.CFG on the proxy server.

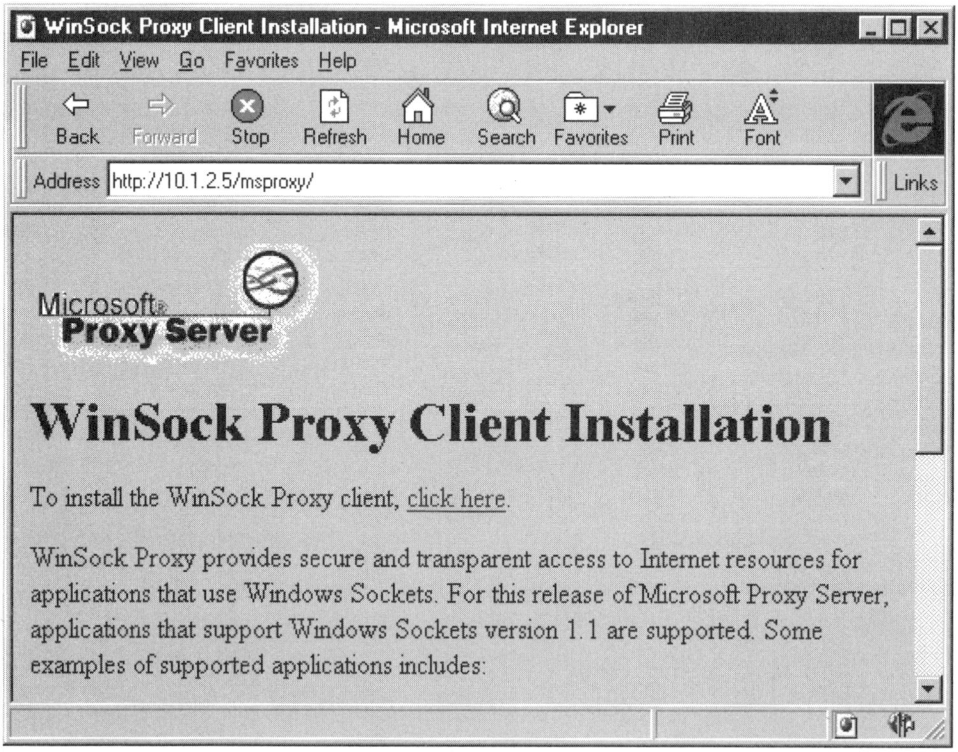

Figure 12.24 Visit the msproxy location on the proxy server to download the client setup.

After the proxy client software is installed there is a new control panel: WSP Client. This control panel may be used to configure the WinSock proxy client software (Figure 12.25).

Figure 12.25 You may disable the WinSock Proxy Client using the WSP Client control panel when you use a different network from this computer.

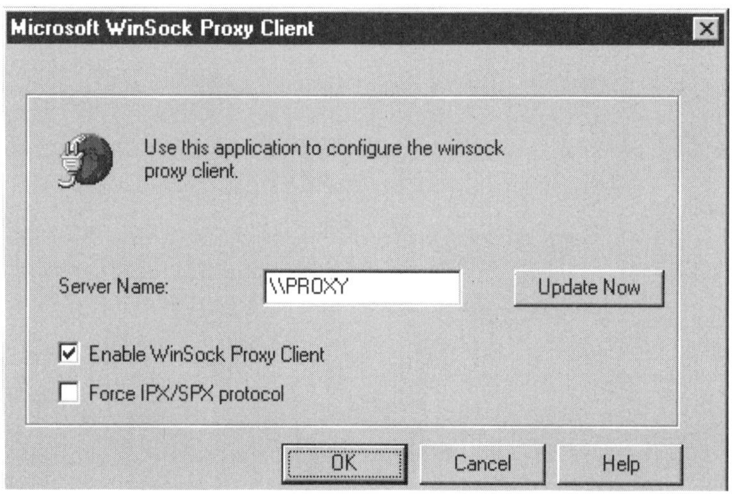

As shown in Figure 12.25, the WSP Client software may be enabled and disabled by using the control panel. When this software is disabled, it is effectively as though you hadn't installed the proxy client software on this machine. This may be useful when you take that computer out of the office environment, and connect to another network (e.g. Internet dial-up) where proxy is not used.

Comparison of Web/SOCKS/WinSock Proxy Protocols

The three possible proxy protocols, CERN proxy protocol, SOCKS protocol, and WinSock proxy (WSP) protocol, are compared in this section. Each of the following three figures shows two TCP/IP stacks— one on the left, one on the right. The first figure shows the CERN proxy protocol.

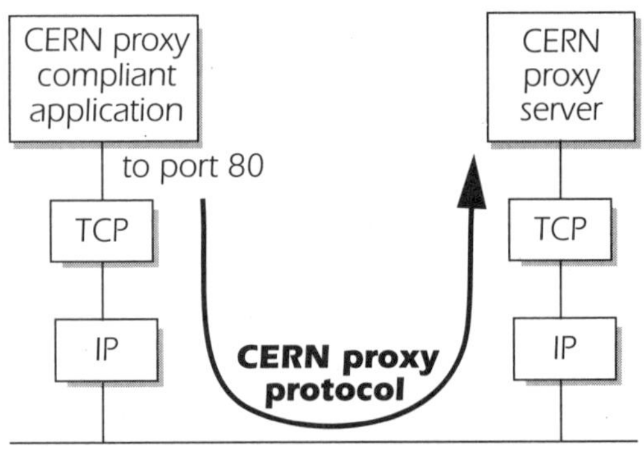

Figure 12.26 The CERN proxy protocol is used by CERN-proxy compliant browsers.

Figure 12.26 demonstrates the use of the CERN proxy protocol from a CERN proxy compliant browser to a CERN proxy server. The destination port for these packets will be port 80. Note that it is the client application that has been modified to support the CERN proxy protocol.

Internet Explorer is an example of a CERN-compliant browser, and will use the CERN proxy protocol if the box *Connect through a proxy server* is checked (Figure 12.22).

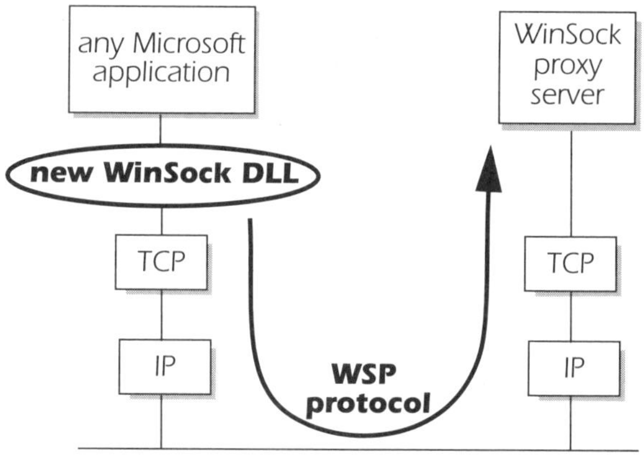

Figure 12.27 The WinSock Proxy (WSP) protocol can be used by all network applications that run on NT.

Figure 12.27 shows the WSP protocol in use between a NT workstation and the Microsoft proxy server. The advantage to this method, as opposed to CERN proxy, is that new applications don't need to be installed in order to work with the proxy server. When the NT machine is configured to be a WSP client (using the WSP Client control panel shown in Figure 12.25), all networked applications will use the WSP protocol.

The WSP protocol is implemented on the client workstation by installing a new WinSock DLL. This new DLL implements the WSP protocol, thus removing that burden from the application.

The initial WSP connection to the proxy server uses port 1055. After the initial handshake, a random port number is used.

If Internet Explorer is not explicitly configured to use a proxy server (Figure 12.22), yet the WSP control panel enables the WSP protocol, then IE will still operate with the proxy server. In this case, IE will use the WSP protocol to connect to the proxy server.

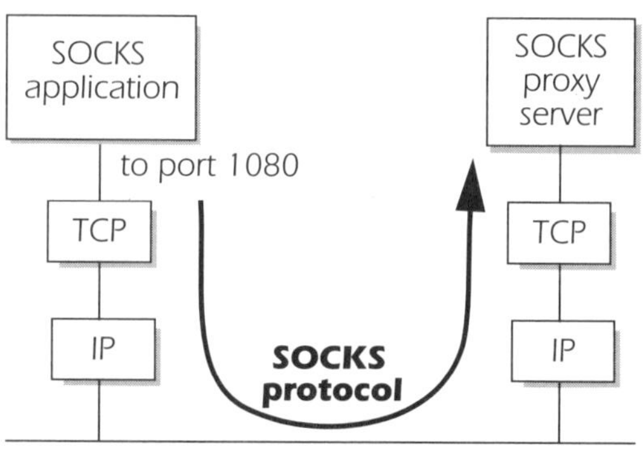

Figure 12.28 The SOCKS protocol is used by applications that support SOCKS.

Figure 12.28 shows the use of the SOCKS protocol between a SOCKSified application and a SOCKS proxy server. The client sends TCP packets to port 1080.

In this example, the application has been modified to support the SOCKS protocol. A few third-party vendors have created a SOCKS DLL to work with NT. A SOCKS DLL operates much like the new WinSock DLL. Thus if you use the SOCKS DLL, you do not need SOCKSified clients.

Understanding Proxy through Packet Traces

There are many references on the normal datagram exchanges which are used by services such as FTP and HTTP. When faced with the need to troubleshoot a problem with these services, it helps to understand what message flow is normal and what is unusual.

When dealing with proxy services, understanding them (let alone verifying that they're actually working correctly) can be even more exciting than dealing with the unaltered traditional services. In order to get a grasp on what is going on with all of this proxying, let's take a walk through some actual packet traces for a few proxy scenarios.

- First we'll see the startup script that is loaded when the web browser starts.
- Next we'll look at a simple Web Proxy example of access to a web page.
- Then we'll examine a Telnet session that uses WinSock proxy.

In order to understand what we're looking at, let's see the network from which these captures were taken. Figure 12.29 shows roadrunner on the left, which is the client. The proxy server, proxy, and primary DNS server, pri_dns, are shown on the right.

The address database for the examples used in this chapter is called proxy_ch.adr on the CD. The source filenames of the capture files are indicated in the diagram.

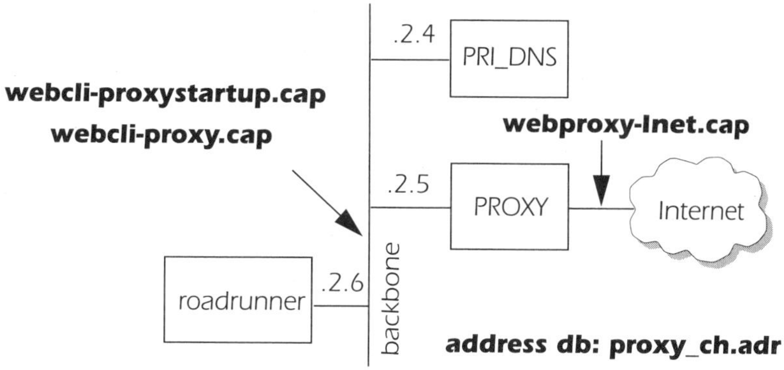

Figure 12.29 A fragment of the network which shows the machines involved in the captures.

Automatic Configuration Using a Startup Script

Internet Explorer on roadrunner is configured to use automatic configuration when it starts up. Therefore, when IE starts up, it requests the automatic configuration startup script from the proxy server. The script contains information regarding whether requests should be directed to the proxy server or to the actual servers. The request is sent using a regular HTTP request, as shown in Figure 12.30.

Figure 12.30 The client fetches the configuration script from the proxy server.

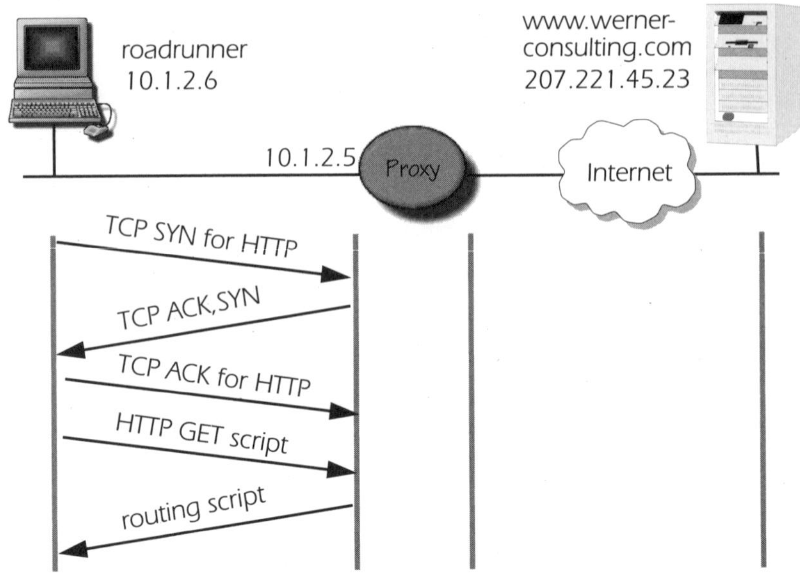

The HTTP response actually requires several TCP segments due to the way which the proxy server presents the data to TCP, and due to the relative size of the file with respect to the MSS/MTU over Ethernet.

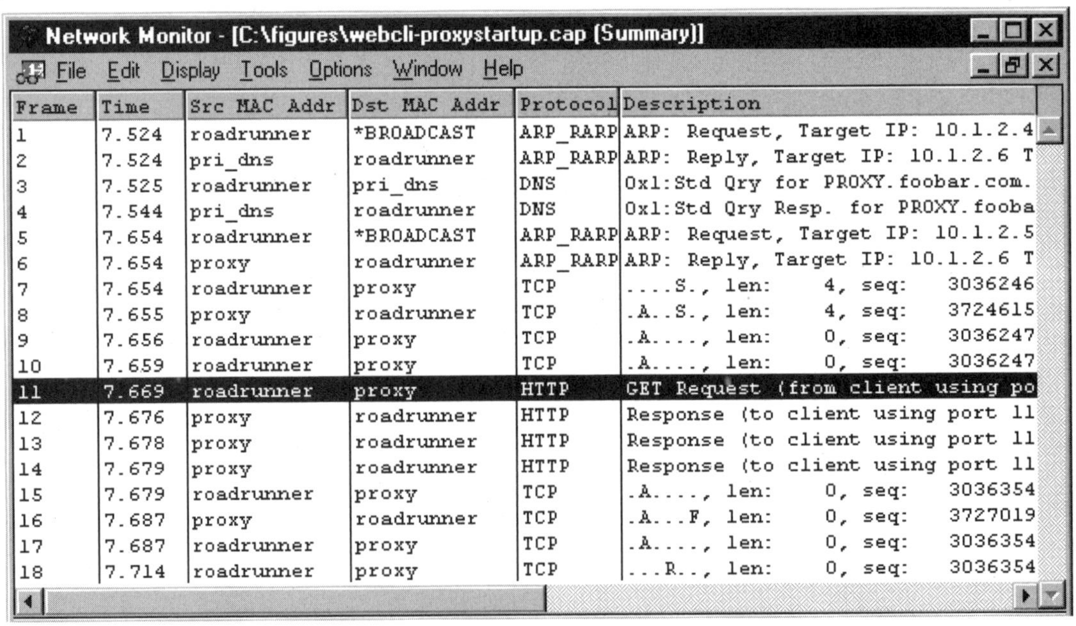

Network Monitor - [C:\figures\webcli-proxystartup.cap (Summary)]

File Edit Display Tools Options Window Help

Frame	Time	Src MAC Addr	Dst MAC Addr	Protocol	Description
1	7.524	roadrunner	*BROADCAST	ARP_RARP	ARP: Request, Target IP: 10.1.2.4
2	7.524	pri_dns	roadrunner	ARP_RARP	ARP: Reply, Target IP: 10.1.2.6 T
3	7.525	roadrunner	pri_dns	DNS	0x1:Std Qry for PROXY.foobar.com.
4	7.544	pri_dns	roadrunner	DNS	0x1:Std Qry Resp. for PROXY.fooba
5	7.654	roadrunner	*BROADCAST	ARP_RARP	ARP: Request, Target IP: 10.1.2.5
6	7.654	proxy	roadrunner	ARP_RARP	ARP: Reply, Target IP: 10.1.2.6 T
7	7.654	roadrunner	proxy	TCP	....S., len: 4, seq: 3036246
8	7.655	proxy	roadrunner	TCP	.A..S., len: 4, seq: 3724615
9	7.656	roadrunner	proxy	TCP	.A...., len: 0, seq: 3036247
10	7.659	roadrunner	proxy	TCP	.A...., len: 0, seq: 3036247
11	7.669	roadrunner	proxy	HTTP	GET Request (from client using po
12	7.676	proxy	roadrunner	HTTP	Response (to client using port 11
13	7.678	proxy	roadrunner	HTTP	Response (to client using port 11
14	7.679	proxy	roadrunner	HTTP	Response (to client using port 11
15	7.679	roadrunner	proxy	TCP	.A...., len: 0, seq: 3036354
16	7.687	proxy	roadrunner	TCP	.A...F, len: 0, seq: 3727019
17	7.687	roadrunner	proxy	TCP	.A...., len: 0, seq: 3036354
18	7.714	roadrunner	proxy	TCP	...R.., len: 0, seq: 3036354

Figure 12.31 Web client startup fetches the configuration script from the proxy server.

Figure 12.31 is a packet capture of the initial connection between Internet Explorer and the proxy server. It contains the transfer of the startup script. Here's a play-by-play of the packet capture in Figure 12.31.

webcli-proxy startup.cap

Frame 1: The client (roadrunner) was configured with the name of the proxy server (proxy), thus it must use DNS to resolve the name into an IP address. Yet roadrunner doesn't have the MAC address of the DNS server (pri_dns). Frame one is an ARP request from roadrunner to find the address of pri_dns.

Frame 2: Pri_dns's ARP software replies with its MAC address.

Frame 3: Roadrunner issues a DNS query to pri_dns requesting the IP address for proxy.foobar.com.

Frame 4: Pri_dns replies to roadrunner with a standard query response containing the IP address of proxy.

Frame 5: Now that roadrunner has proxy's IP address, it needs its MAC address. Roadrunner issues an ARP request to find proxy.

Frame 6: Proxy replies with an ARP response to roadrunner.

Frame 7: Roadrunner issues a TCP SYN to port 80 (HTTP) on proxy. This is the first step of a TCP handshake.

Frame 8: Proxy responds with an ACK,SYN to roadrunner.

Frame 9: Roadrunner ACKs proxy. The HTTP connection is set up.

Frame 10: Roadrunner ACKs proxy again to adjust its window size.

Frame 11: Roadrunner sends the HTTP GET request to proxy. Because the URL in the GET request specifies no service or hostname, this is not a CERN-compatible proxy request, but a request directly of the proxy server. Recall that the implementation of Proxy Server is based on IIS.

Frame 12: The response code and headers of the HTTP response are sent from proxy back to roadrunner.

Frame 13: The first 1480 octets of the body of the response (i.e. routing script) are sent back from proxy to roadrunner.

Frame 14: The remainder of the file is sent from proxy to roadrunner.

Frame 15: Roadrunner ACKs that it got all octets from 12, 13, and 14.

Frame 16: Proxy has finished sending to roadrunner on this connection, so it sends a TCP FIN.

Frame 17: Roadrunner ACKs the FIN.

Frame 18: In a "normal" TCP connection teardown, roadrunner would send a FIN to say it's finished sending and then proxy would ACK that. Instead, Internet Explorer pulls the plug on the connection and issues a RST from roadrunner.

The request in frame 11 and the response in frame 12, followed by the contents of the file in frames 13 and 14, are the essential parts of this trace. The rest is incidental. In the remaining traces throughout this chapter, the commentary will focus in on the salient points. Refer back to this annotation as a guide.

The routing script represents an example of a standard HTTP request/response. The information provided allows the client to determine what should be proxied and what should be sent directly to the proper actual servers. Now let's look at some proxied communications.

What Does Web Proxy Really Look Like?

A web proxy request (CERN-proxy request) is essentially a normal HTTP request in which the URL specified still includes the service and domain name. When a proxy server receives such a request, it initiates the proxying process.

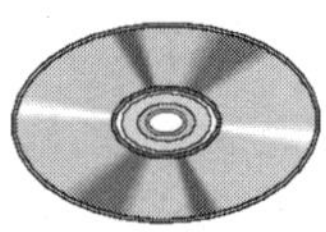

webcli-proxy.cap

An HTTP request was issued from roadrunner for the web page of www.wernerconsulting.com. Figure 12.32 shows the interaction between roadrunner and proxy as captured in the file webcli-proxy.cap.

The first three frames are setting up a TCP connection from a random port on roadrunner to port 80 on proxy. Frame four shows the HTTP GET request which contains a complete URL. This complete URL will be parsed by proxy and set up an independent connection. When proxy parses the request, it finds:

- http is the requested protocol

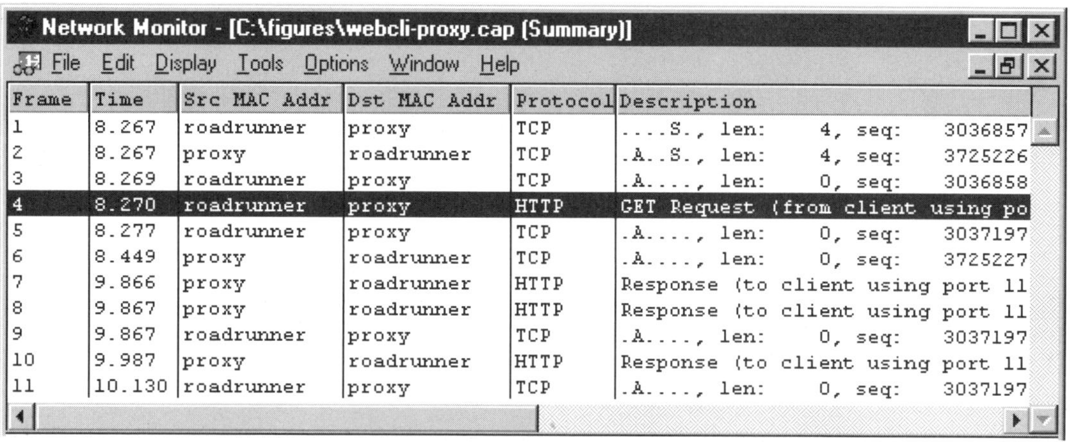

Network Monitor - [C:\figures\webcli-proxy.cap (Summary)]

File Edit Display Tools Options Window Help

Frame	Time	Src MAC Addr	Dst MAC Addr	Protocol	Description
1	8.267	roadrunner	proxy	TCP	....S., len: 4, seq: 3036857
2	8.267	proxy	roadrunner	TCP	.A..S., len: 4, seq: 3725226
3	8.269	roadrunner	proxy	TCP	.A...., len: 0, seq: 3036858
4	8.270	roadrunner	proxy	HTTP	GET Request (from client using po
5	8.277	roadrunner	proxy	TCP	.A...., len: 0, seq: 3037197
6	8.449	proxy	roadrunner	TCP	.A...., len: 0, seq: 3725227
7	9.866	proxy	roadrunner	HTTP	Response (to client using port 11
8	9.867	proxy	roadrunner	HTTP	Response (to client using port 11
9	9.867	roadrunner	proxy	TCP	.A...., len: 0, seq: 3037197
10	9.987	proxy	roadrunner	HTTP	Response (to client using port 11
11	10.130	roadrunner	proxy	TCP	.A...., len: 0, seq: 3037197

Figure 12.32 The interaction between the client (roadrunner) and the proxy server.

- www.wernerconsulting.com is the server to contact
- / (slash) is the resource to be retrieved (default page)

Thus, proxy will note that the connection from roadrunner is still in progress, and sets up a partial entry in the mapping table.

In order to set up a connection to the actual server, proxy must resolve the domain name www.wernerconsulting.com. Figure 12.33 shows a DNS query and response (frames 1 & 2) to the DNS server which proxy is using.

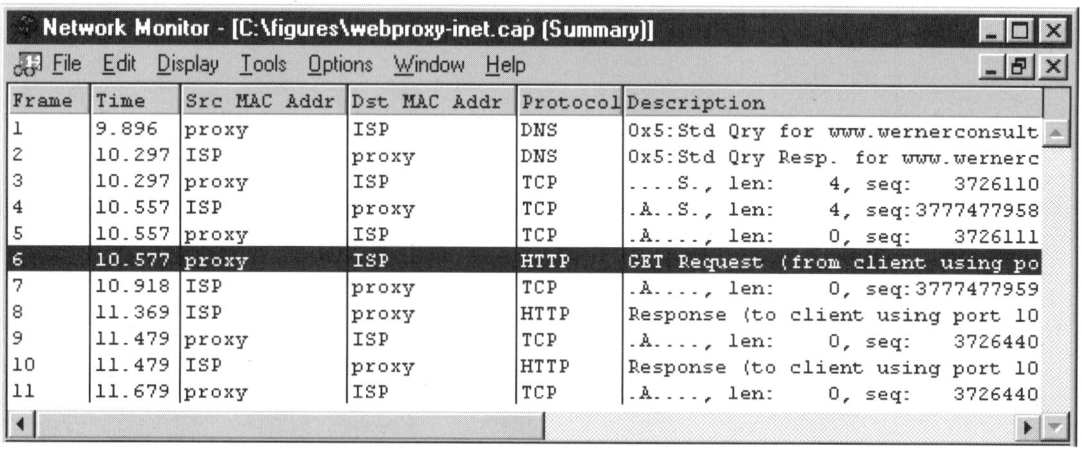

Network Monitor - [C:\figures\webproxy-inet.cap (Summary)]

File Edit Display Tools Options Window Help

Frame	Time	Src MAC Addr	Dst MAC Addr	Protocol	Description
1	9.896	proxy	ISP	DNS	0x5:Std Qry for www.wernerconsult
2	10.297	ISP	proxy	DNS	0x5:Std Qry Resp. for www.wernerc
3	10.297	proxy	ISP	TCP	....S., len: 4, seq: 3726110
4	10.557	ISP	proxy	TCP	.A..S., len: 4, seq:3777477958
5	10.557	proxy	ISP	TCP	.A...., len: 0, seq: 3726111
6	10.577	proxy	ISP	HTTP	GET Request (from client using po
7	10.918	ISP	proxy	TCP	.A...., len: 0, seq:3777477959
8	11.369	ISP	proxy	HTTP	Response (to client using port 10
9	11.479	proxy	ISP	TCP	.A...., len: 0, seq: 3726440
10	11.479	ISP	proxy	HTTP	Response (to client using port 10
11	11.679	proxy	ISP	TCP	.A...., len: 0, seq: 3726440

Figure 12.33 The interaction between the proxy server and the outside world (through an ISP).

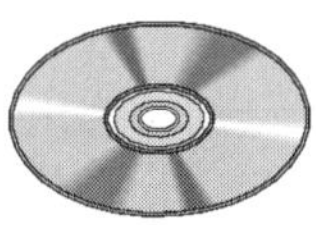

webproxy-inet.cap

Then in frames 3-5, proxy sets up a connection to the web server, and in frame 6, forwards a GET request which is based on the one in Figure 12.32's frame 4.

Figure 12.34
The client sends an HTTP request to the server and sever relays it.

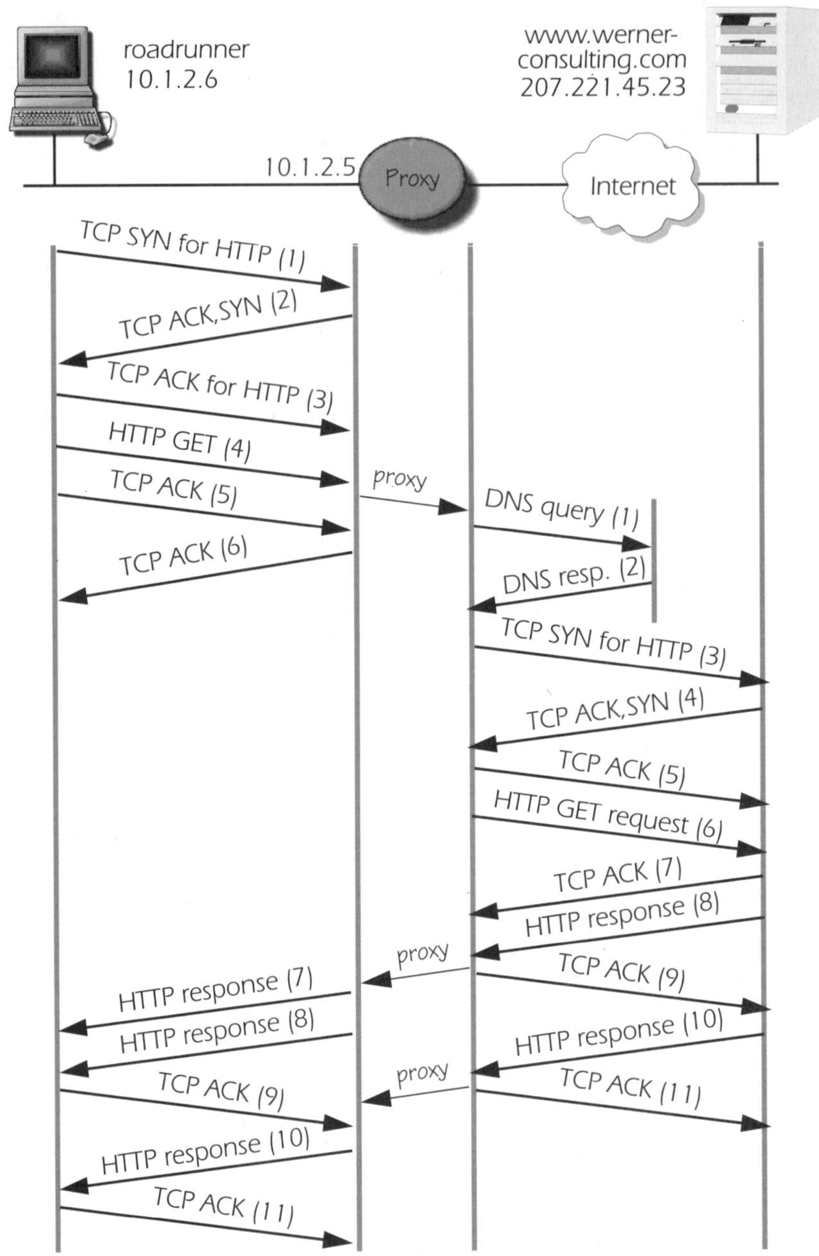

This is a very important aspect of the proxying process. The fact that the GET request is *rewritten* by the proxy server provides a method for hiding the details of the actual client which may have been revealed by the headers in the original HTTP request. Thus, the proxy server not only hides the identity of the actual client from an IP address standpoint, but also from an application layer standpoint as well.

Another example of how a proxy server may modify the information transferred is shown in this example as well. Note that frame 8 on the Internet side (Figure 12.33) is actually transferred onto the client side (Figure 12.32) as two frames: 7 and 8.

Figure 12.34 shows this in a run-down of the whole conversation which may be correlated to the two packet captures. So why is there not a one-to-one correspondence among the response messages? The first response frame from the Internet side (frame 8) is a TCP segment containing 1460 octets of HTTP information. When the proxy server edits the HTTP headers prior to passing this message back to the client side, it adds additional octets to the message. The proxy then passes this message to TCP on the connection to the client, yet the maximum segment size on that connection is also 1460, thus two segments are sent to the client (frames 7 and 8). The second response segment is passed intact on the client side connection (frame 10).

Figure 12.35 shows a simplified rendition of the HTTP proxy process.

Figure 12.35 Summary of HTTP proxy.

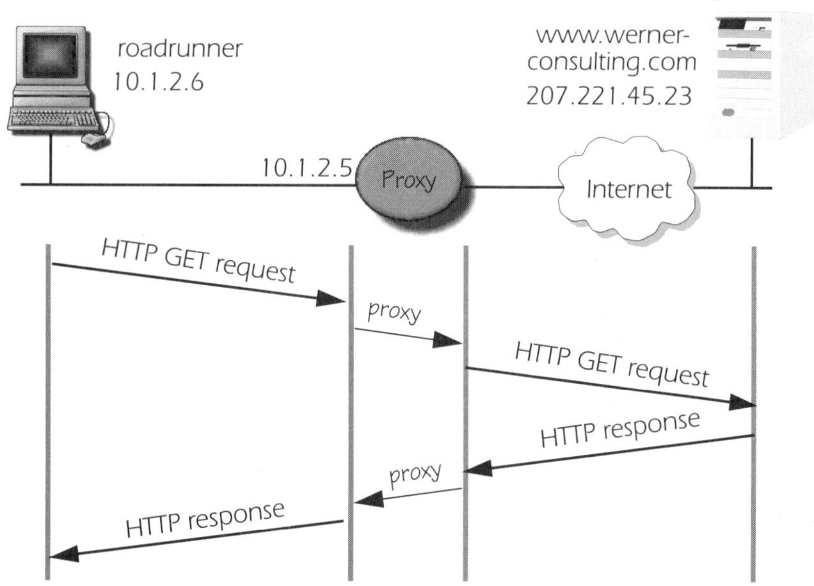

The Web Proxy method may be used for HTTP, FTP, and Gopher resources. The client to proxy access is always with HTTP and a fully qualified URL. The proxy server handles the adaptation between the client's HTTP session and whichever session type is required to the actual server.

How Are Non-Web Clients (e.g. Telnet) Proxied?

Many protocols do not fit into the near-HTTP paradigm as FTP and Gopher do. Therefore, different methods for proxying the other protocols are required. Rather than develop a different proxy mechanism for each other protocol, a common method may be employed. In this section, we'll look at an example of Telnet supported by Proxy Server with the WinSock Proxy service. Figure 12.36 shows the point at which packet captures were obtained in the network for this example.

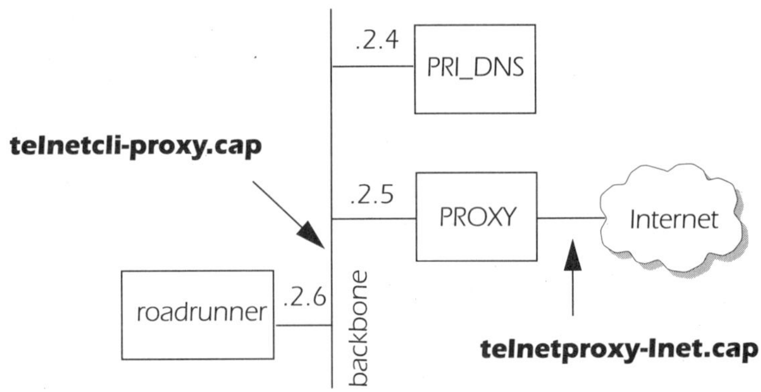

Figure 12.36 The network layout for the telnet example.

We started up a Telnet client on roadrunner and issued a connect request to netcom.com. Figure 12.37 shows the communications between roadrunner and proxy.

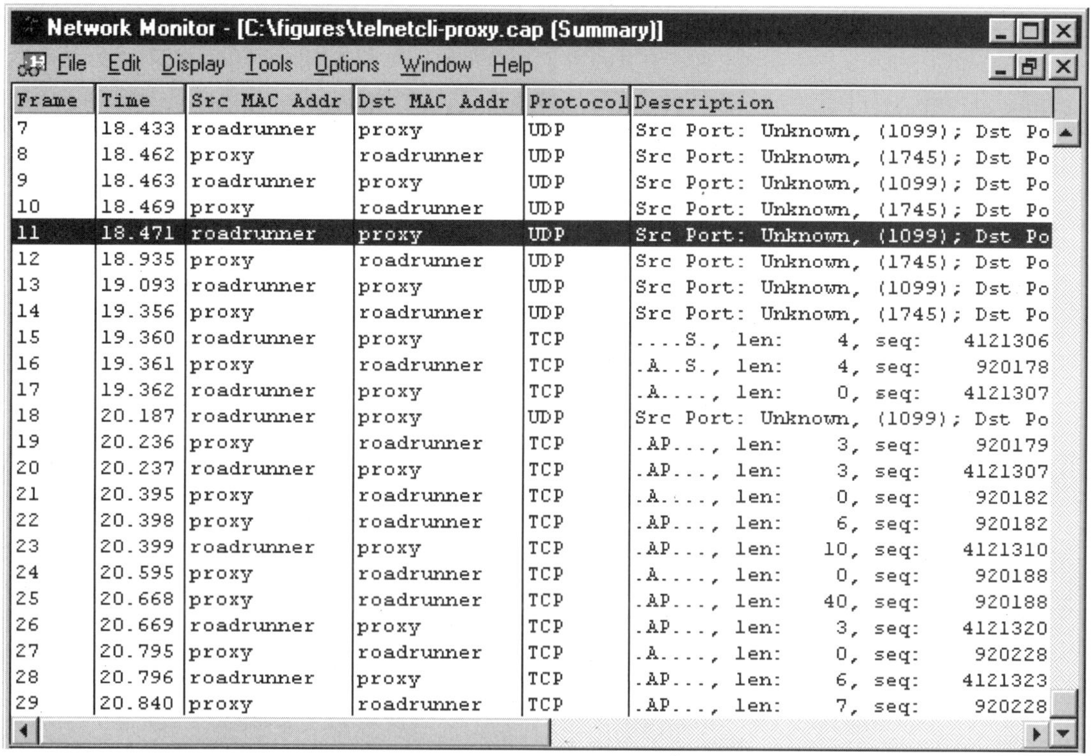

Frame	Time	Src MAC Addr	Dst MAC Addr	Protocol	Description
7	18.433	roadrunner	proxy	UDP	Src Port: Unknown, (1099); Dst Po
8	18.462	proxy	roadrunner	UDP	Src Port: Unknown, (1745); Dst Po
9	18.463	roadrunner	proxy	UDP	Src Port: Unknown, (1099); Dst Po
10	18.469	proxy	roadrunner	UDP	Src Port: Unknown, (1745); Dst Po
11	18.471	roadrunner	proxy	UDP	Src Port: Unknown, (1099); Dst Po
12	18.935	proxy	roadrunner	UDP	Src Port: Unknown, (1745); Dst Po
13	19.093	roadrunner	proxy	UDP	Src Port: Unknown, (1099); Dst Po
14	19.356	proxy	roadrunner	UDP	Src Port: Unknown, (1745); Dst Po
15	19.360	roadrunner	proxy	TCP	....S., len: 4, seq: 4121306
16	19.361	proxy	roadrunner	TCP	.A..S., len: 4, seq: 920178
17	19.362	roadrunner	proxy	TCP	.A...., len: 0, seq: 4121307
18	20.187	roadrunner	proxy	UDP	Src Port: Unknown, (1099); Dst Po
19	20.236	proxy	roadrunner	TCP	.AP..., len: 3, seq: 920179
20	20.237	roadrunner	proxy	TCP	.AP..., len: 3, seq: 4121307
21	20.395	proxy	roadrunner	TCP	.A...., len: 0, seq: 920182
22	20.398	proxy	roadrunner	TCP	.AP..., len: 6, seq: 920182
23	20.399	roadrunner	proxy	TCP	.AP..., len: 10, seq: 4121310
24	20.595	proxy	roadrunner	TCP	.A...., len: 0, seq: 920188
25	20.668	proxy	roadrunner	TCP	.AP..., len: 40, seq: 920188
26	20.669	roadrunner	proxy	TCP	.AP..., len: 3, seq: 4121320
27	20.795	proxy	roadrunner	TCP	.A...., len: 0, seq: 920228
28	20.796	roadrunner	proxy	TCP	.AP..., len: 6, seq: 4121323
29	20.840	proxy	roadrunner	TCP	.AP..., len: 7, seq: 920228

Figure 12.37 Client side telnet proxy capture.

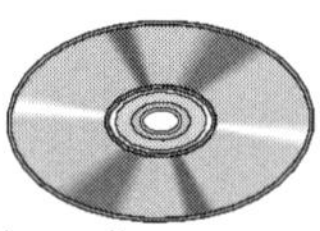
telnetcli-proxy.cap

Frame 7 shows a UDP datagram from roadrunner's port 1099 to port 1745 on proxy's 10.1.2.5 interface.[6] Recall from the discussion of Proxy Server's services that UDP port 1745 is used for WinSock Proxy negotiation. The contents of frame 7 include the username, encrypted password, application name, and machine name of the client.

The next three frames are also used to exchange authentication information between the client and the proxy.

In frame 11, roadrunner passes proxy the domain name netcom.com to be resolved. This is acknowledged in frame 12.

Next, the port number that roadrunner's Telnet client will use (1101) is sent to proxy in frame 13. Then in frame 14 proxy passes back the port number (1035) and IP address (10.1.2.5) it will use for proxying the Telnet connection. At this point, the proxy server has completed the following:

---

6. Frames 1-6 of this capture are ARP request/response to DNS, DNS query/response, then ARP request/response to proxy.

- Resolved the name netcom.com into an IP address.
- Selected a port number to use on the Internet side: 1034.
- Selected the port number to use on the client side: 1035.
- Establishes a map table entry between its client side socket and its Internet side socket.
- Has just told the client the socket address to connect to.
- Listens for a connection request on the client side socket.

Now any TCP segments coming from roadrunner's port 1101 to port 1035 on proxy's interface 1035 will be proxied (i.e. forwarded) over to proxy's Internet interface at port 1034 to be sent to netcom.com at port 23 and vice versa. This is due to the mapping table entry. Figure 12.38 shows the communication between proxy and netcom.com's Telnet server.

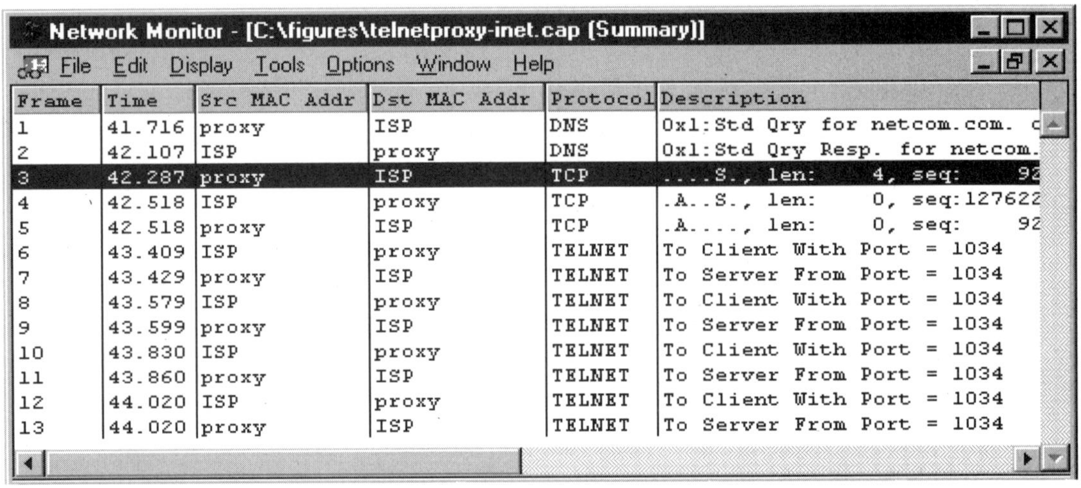

Frame	Time	Src MAC Addr	Dst MAC Addr	Protocol	Description
1	41.716	proxy	ISP	DNS	0x1:Std Qry for netcom.com. c
2	42.107	ISP	proxy	DNS	0x1:Std Qry Resp. for netcom.
3	42.287	proxy	ISP	TCP	....S., len: 4, seq: 92
4	42.518	ISP	proxy	TCP	.A..S., len: 0, seq:127622
5	42.518	proxy	ISP	TCP	.A...., len: 0, seq: 92
6	43.409	ISP	proxy	TELNET	To Client With Port = 1034
7	43.429	proxy	ISP	TELNET	To Server From Port = 1034
8	43.579	ISP	proxy	TELNET	To Client With Port = 1034
9	43.599	proxy	ISP	TELNET	To Server From Port = 1034
10	43.830	ISP	proxy	TELNET	To Client With Port = 1034
11	43.860	proxy	ISP	TELNET	To Server From Port = 1034
12	44.020	ISP	proxy	TELNET	To Client With Port = 1034
13	44.020	proxy	ISP	TELNET	To Server From Port = 1034

Figure 12.38 Internet side telnet proxy capture.

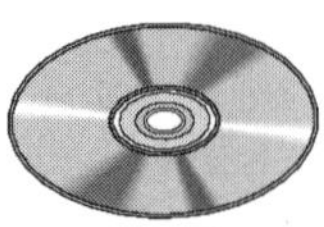

telnetproxy-inet.cap

Frames 1 and 2 on the Internet side show the DNS query and response with which proxy obtains the IP address of the Telnet server.

Note the timing of the TCP handshakes in the two captures. These connection establishments are independent of each other from a TCP perspective. When WinSock Proxy handles TCP connections, the proxy maintains state information about the connection on each side, yet lets TCP do its work normally. A ladder diagram correlating the two captures is shown in Figure 12.39.

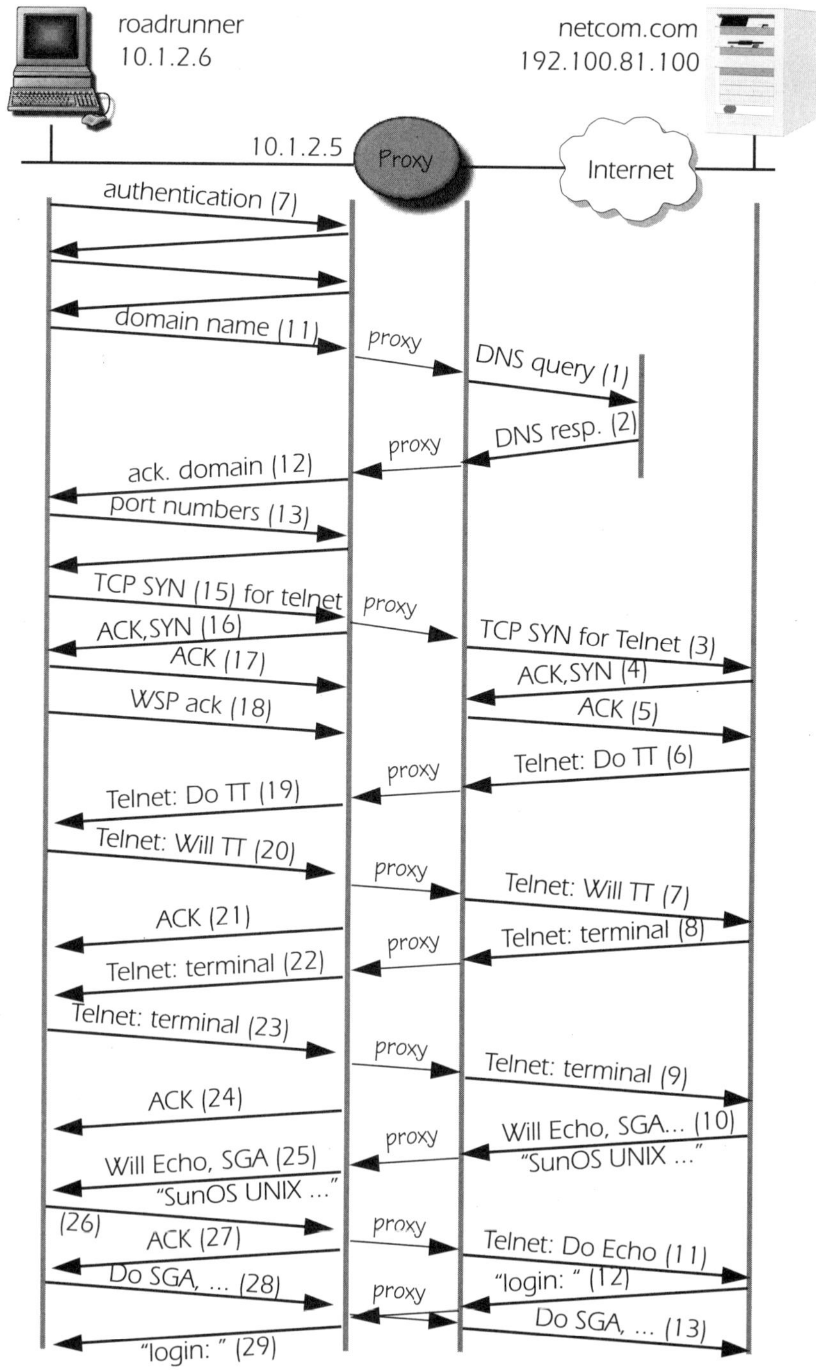

Figure 12.39 An exchange of WinSock proxy UDP messages take place before the Telnet traffic is started.

The actual Telnet messages are passed end-to-end through the proxy, yet because the connections on each side of the proxy are independent, TCP may add "extra" acknowledgments as necessary. Examples of this are seen in frames 21, 24, and 27 on the client side.

In the HTTP proxy example, the exchange of messages followed the request and response nature of HTTP. There was a long delay on the client side while a whole request/response cycle took place on the Internet side. With protocols such as Telnet however, each side is asynchronous to the other[7], thus several messages may be in transit end-to-end in each direction simultaneously. This is depicted where we've ended the captures (and ladder diagram) with the responses to the options that travelled with the system banner (server frame 10) go back (in server frame 11) at the same time that the login prompt (server frame 12) is also in transit. Table 12.1 shows which frames on the Internet (server) side match up with the frames on the client side.

Table 12.1 Frame correlations for the Telnet example.

Client frame	Direction	Internet frame
19	inbound	6
20	outbound	7
22	inbound	8
23	outbound	9
25	inbound	10
26	outbound	11
29	inbound	12
28	outbound	13

7. Telnet's initial option negotiation phase is request / response in nature, but when the virtual terminal service phase is entered, it becomes less synchronous. Note also that in this phase, options may still be passed.

Summary

We've seen several things in this chapter.

- HTTP operation is simplistic— it consists of Get request packets, and Response packets.
- Firewalls are devices that are used to keep network traffic separate.
- Filtering routers are often simplistic firewalls in that they filter packets based upon some property of the packet, such as port numbers.
- Stateful firewalls keep track of the state of TCP connections and use this information to determine which packets are dropped and which packets are forwarded.
- Address translation allows a company to have only one (or a few) InterNIC-assigned IP addresses, yet still be able to connect the company's intranet with the Internet.
- Non-intrusive firewalls are much easier to install than intrusive firewalls, but are more complex and usually more expensive.
- A proxy server acts as a server to a client trying to access an Internet server. A proxy server also simultaneously acts as a client to an Internet server. Two separate connections are established, yet the to the client operation appears to be normal.
- Microsoft Proxy Server 2.0 is a caching proxy that can handle requests from not only NT and Windows 95 machines, but Unix and Macintoshes as well (using CERN-proxy and SOCKS proxy).

Further Reading

The following sources can be used to research further information on HTTP, SOCKS, CERN-proxy, and firewalls in general.

[Berners-Lee1996] Berners-Lee, T., Fielding, R., Frystyk, H., *Hypertext Transfer Protocol – HTTP/1.0,* 1996, IETF RFC 1945

[Chapman1995] Chapman, D. Brent, Zwicky, Elizabeth D., *Building Internet Firewalls,* 1995, O'Reilly and Associates

[Cheswick1994] Cheswick, William R., Bellovin, Steven M., *Firewalls and Internet Security: Repelling the Wily Hacker,* 1994, Addison-Wesley

[Kaufman1995] Kaufman, Charlie, Perlman, Radia, Speciner, Mike, *Network Security: Private Communication in a Public World,* 1995, Prentice Hall

[Leech1996] Leech, M., Ganis, M., Lee, Y., Kuris, R., Koblas, D., Jones, L., *SOCKS Protocol Version 5,* 1996, IETF RFC 1928

[Rubin1997] Rubin, Aviel D., Geer, Daniel, Ranum, Marcus J., *Web Security Sourcebook,* 1997, Wiley Computer Publishing

[Rutstein1997] Rustein, Charles B., *Guide to Windows NT Security,* 1997, Mc-Graw Hill

13

Advanced DNS Configuration

In the "Domain Name Resolution" chapter, fundamental DNS configuration issues were addressed. This chapter focuses on some of the more advanced issues of DNS configuration on NT, including the following topics:

- Forwarding DNS requests to other DNS servers
- Forwarding DNS requests to WINS servers
- Transferring zone information between primaries and secondaries
- Configuring multihomed DNS servers
- Configuring DNS to load from the boot file
- Configuring a cache-only DNS
- Configuring a caching DNS server with Microsoft's Proxy Server

There are two screens that will be used throughout this chapter. First is the *Server Properties* screen. The *Server Properties* screen is obtained by highlighting the server's IP address, right clicking, and selecting *Properties*, as shown in Figure 13.1. The tabs (subscreens) of *Server Properties* are shown in Figure 13.2.

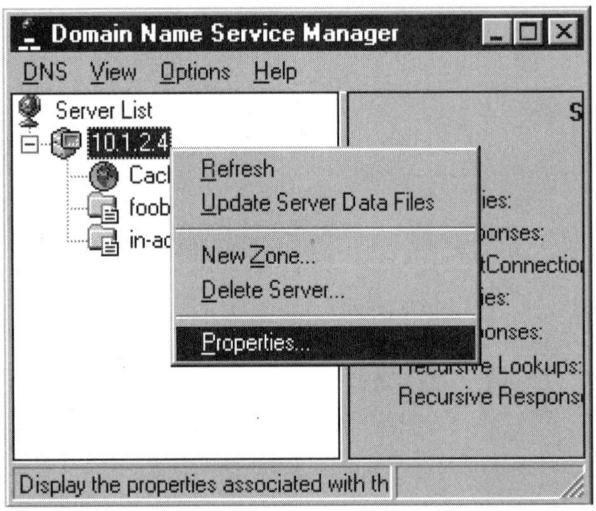

Figure 13.1
The DNS server's properties may be accessed with the pop-up menu from the server's IP address.

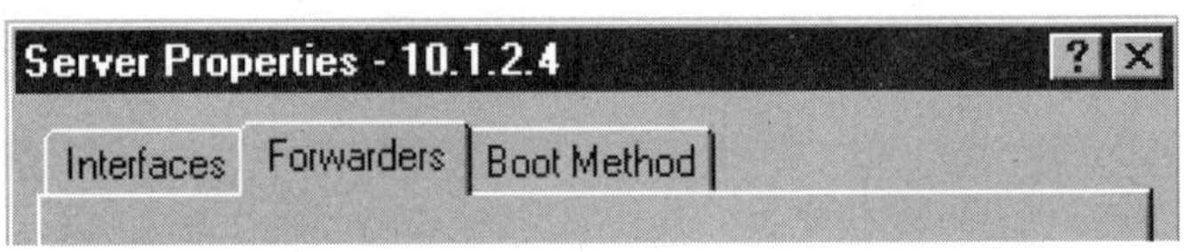

Figure 13.2
The DNS server properties dialog has three tabs.

The second screen discussed within this chapter is the *Zone Properties* screen. It is obtained by right-clicking the zone name, and selecting *Properties*, as shown in Figure 13.3. The tabs (subscreens) of *Zone Properties* for a primary DNS are shown in Figure 13.4.

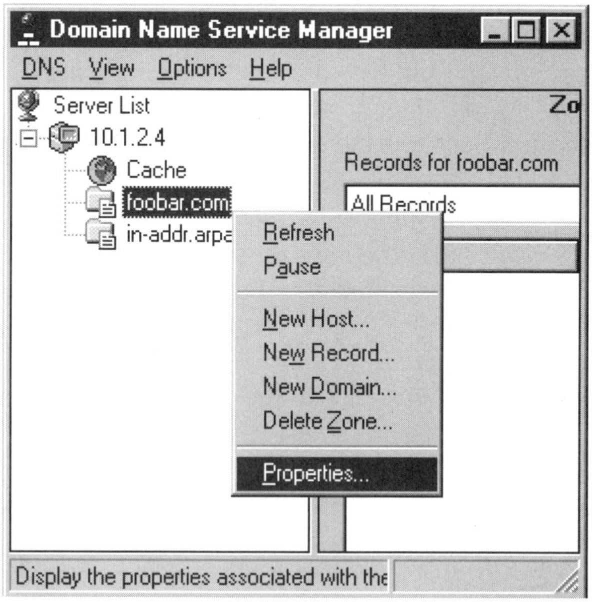

Figure 13.3
The properties for a zone may be accessed using this pop-up menu from the zone name.

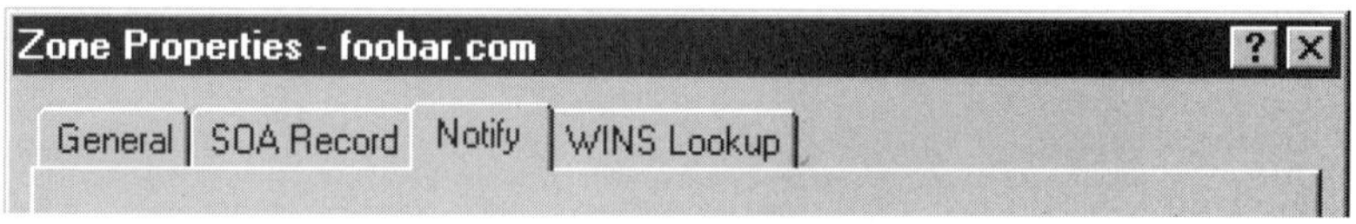

Figure 13.4
DNS zone properties are split into four tabs.

Forwarding DNS Queries to Other DNS Servers

Before discussing how to configure the Microsoft DNS server to forward queries, let's review some details of name resolution.

Review of Name Resolution

In order to understand some of the advanced concepts of the operation of DNS, a clear picture of name resolution is required. The name resolution process is described in the following 6 steps.

Step 1. Client application issues request.

A client application passes a request to the DNS resolver (Figure 13.5). Because this resolver is quite simple (e.g. is not authoritative for a zone, and does not cache any information), it is called a *stub resolver*. The DNS stub resolver resides on a client system.

Step 2. Client system sends query to DNS server.

The client DNS resolver formulates a query to the domain name server which it has been configured to contact (Figure 13.5). A part of the formulation involves appending a suffix to the domain name. If this query fails, the resolver may retry the query with other suffixes, or may send the request to other servers.

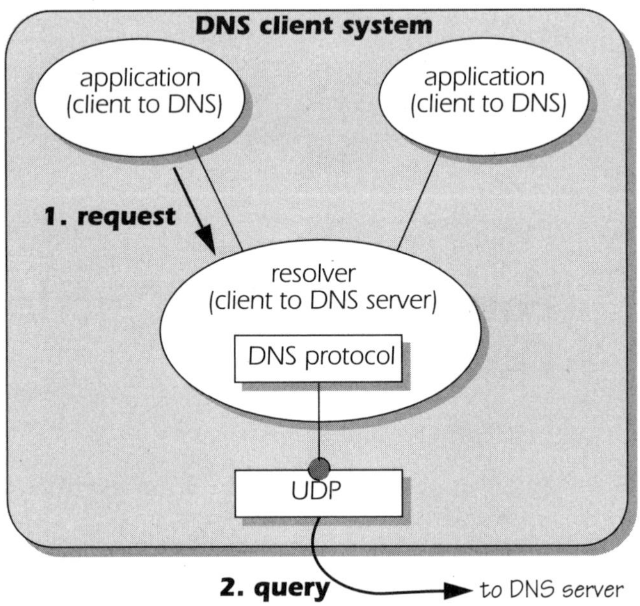

Figure 13.5 DNS client performs step 1 (request) and step 2 (query DNS server).

Step 3. DNS server consults local database.

The DNS server receives the DNS query. The DNS server checks to see if it is authoritative for the question asked in the query. The server is authoritative for that domain if it is a primary or a secondary server for the queried domain. If it is not authoritative, is proceeds with the next step.

Figure 13.6 shows the DNS server consulting its zone files. The zone file could be on this DNS server machine if the server is acting as a primary server for the zone. A copy of the zone file (i.e. a zone image) could be stored on the server if it is acting as a secondary server for the zone.

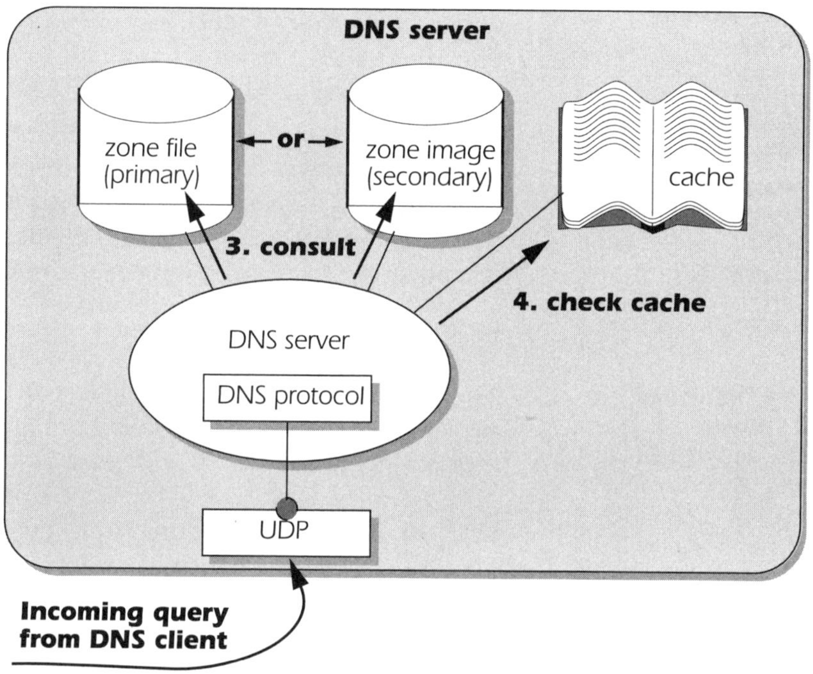

Figure 13.6
In step 3, the DNS server consults its database. In step 4, the DNS server checks its cache.

If the server finds an answer in its database, it sends the answer back to the client. Otherwise, it continues with the next step.

Step 4. DNS server checks its cache.

Next, the domain server checks its cache (Figure 13.6). The cache contains records of recently-resolved names. If the cache contains the answer to the query, the server will use this cached information to answer the query. Otherwise it continues with the next step.

Step 5. DNS server queries another DNS server.

recursive query: the requestor wants the receiving DNS to check all possible resources for an answer to the query.

iterative query: the requestor is asking the receiving DNS to check its database and cache for an answer, but not to query any other DNS servers.

forwarder: a DNS server that forwards queries to other DNS servers.

Two terms need to be defined here: recursive queries and iterative queries. **Recursive queries** are queries sent to a DNS server that is asking the receiving DNS server to use all its resources to answer the request. The DNS server will check its database, cache, other DNS servers, and a root server in order to find the final answer to the query.

Contrast this with an **iterative query**. With an iterative query, the requestor wants the receiving DNS to only check its database and cache— no other DNS servers should be queried by the receiver of the iterative query.

Back to the example, if the DNS server has been set up to forward queries to a specific higher authority, a recursive query[1] is sent to the specified DNS server (Figure 13.7). In this case, the DNS server that is querying another DNS server is called a **forwarder.**

If the DNS server receives an answer from the DNS it queried, it returns the answer to the client. If this server doesn't hear back from the DNS it queried in a short period of time, it will try the next DNS server in its list. After all specified DNS servers have been queried, the server proceeds with step 6.

Step 6. DNS server queries a root server.

cache file: a file that contains a list of root servers and their IP addresses.

The DNS server sends the query to one of the *root servers* specified in a file called a **cache file**. The cache file contains a list of root servers and their IP addresses. Note that the cache file is poorly named, and is NOT the same thing as the cache used by DNS to retain information from previous queries. Refer to Figure 13.10 on page 502 for an example of this file.

A root server will reply with a partial answer- an answer that the DNS server can use to obtain the answer to the original query. The partial answer will contain the IP addresses of the primary and secondary servers for the queried domain. Thus the original DNS server can then direct a query to the authoritative DNS server, and receive back a reply the client can use.

1. Recursive forwarding can be disabled by setting the registry parameter NoRecursion to 1 (true). NoRecursion is found under HKLM\System\CCS\Services\DNS\Parameters, and is type REG_DWORD.

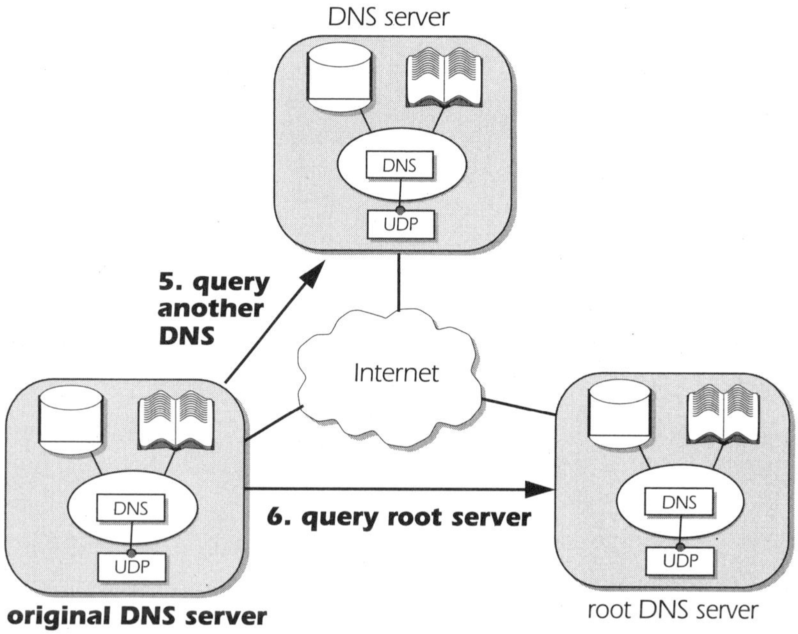

Figure 13.7
In step 5, the DNS server queries one or more other DNS servers. In step 6, the DNS server queries a root server.

Step 7. If all of the above steps do not provide an answer, the DNS server sends back an error message to the client.

Forwarding Queries

One of the options for sending queries on to another server is called forwarding. With forwarding, the server which doesn't know the answer to the query must be configured with a list of DNS servers it should forward requests to (Figure 13.8).

Figure 13.8
When a server doesn't know an answer for a query, it may forward the query to another DNS server for resolution.

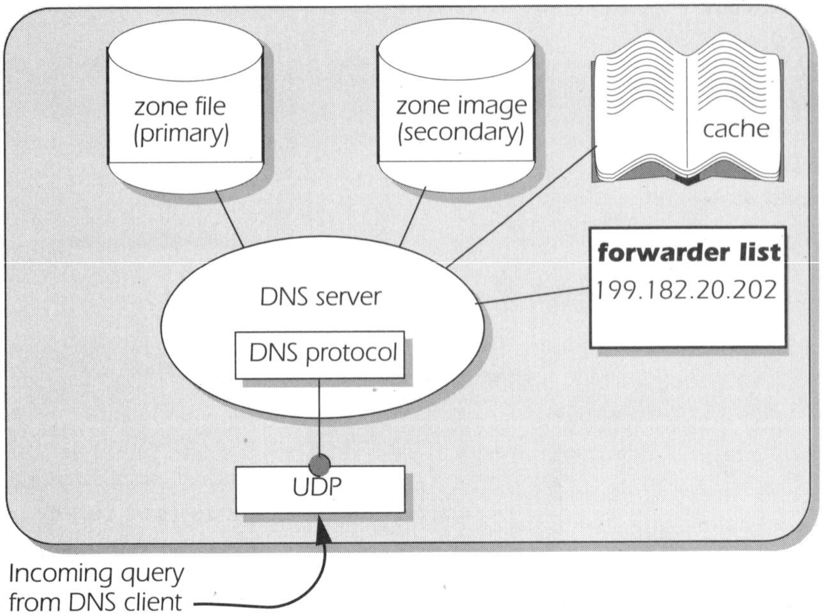

The list of forwarders may be configured using the *DNS Server Property* dialog, *Forwarders tab* (Figure 13.9). Use this screen on the DNS server that you want to have forward unresolvable DNS requests. Here you may enter the IP address of the DNS server or servers you wish requests to be forwarded to.

Figure 13.9
DNS forwarders tab is used to specify the next DNS server to query.

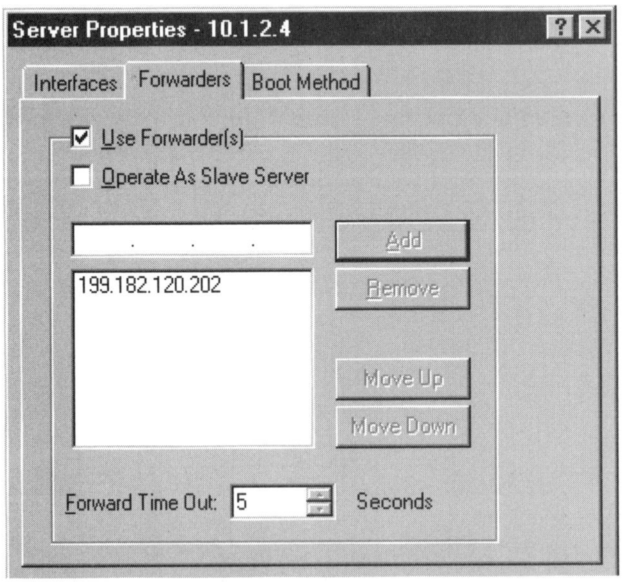

slave DNS server: a server that does not query any other DNS servers other than the ones listed on the DNS Forwarders screen.

When the original server receives a query which it can't resolve using its database or cache, it selects the first forwarder from the list, and sends the query on to that server. If that server doesn't respond within the *forward time-out* specified (5 seconds in Figure 13.9), this server will try the next forwarder in the list. If none of the DNS servers on the list answer the request, one of two conditions may occur, depending upon if this server is a **slave DNS server**.

- If the *Operate As Slave Server* box has been checked, then this server will not send a query to root servers.
- If this server is not configured as a slave, then the server attempts to contact a root server. Resolution through root servers is discussed next.

Sending Queries to the Root Servers

When a server has determined that it is not authoritative for the name in a query, that it doesn't have an entry in cache, and all the DNS servers it queried didn't have an answer, the server will (unless it's a slave server) query a root server.

Each server contains a *cache file*.[2] The cache file contains a list of all the root servers and their IP addresses, as shown in Figure 13.10. Since the root servers are used by all Internet hosts, they don't change IP addresses often. Therefore the cache file is fairly static, and is identical for all DNS servers on the Internet. The NT DNS cache file, cache.dns, is found in the DNS directory under %systemroot%\system32.

2. This file is NOT the same things as the DNS cache (table of recently learned translations). The DNS cache is stored in memory only.

```
;   Cache file:
;
.                       IN      NS      A.ROOT-SERVERS.NET.
A.ROOT-SERVERS.NET.     IN      A       198.41.0.4
.                       IN      NS      B.ROOT-SERVERS.NET.
B.ROOT-SERVERS.NET.     IN      A       128.9.0.107
.                       IN      NS      C.ROOT-SERVERS.NET.
C.ROOT-SERVERS.NET.     IN      A       192.33.4.12
.                       IN      NS      D.ROOT-SERVERS.NET.
D.ROOT-SERVERS.NET.     IN      A       128.8.10.90
.                       IN      NS      E.ROOT-SERVERS.NET.
E.ROOT-SERVERS.NET.     IN      A       192.203.230.10
.                       IN      NS      F.ROOT-SERVERS.NET.
F.ROOT-SERVERS.NET.     IN      A       39.13.229.241
.                       IN      NS      G.ROOT-SERVERS.NET.
G.ROOT-SERVERS.NET.     IN      A       192.112.36.4
.                       IN      NS      H.ROOT-SERVERS.NET.
H.ROOT-SERVERS.NET.     IN      A       128.63.2.53
.                       IN      NS      I.ROOT-SERVERS.NET.
I.ROOT-SERVERS.NET.     IN      A       192.36.148.17
```

Figure 13.10 An example of the %systemroot%\system32\dns\cache.dns file

The NS resource record specifies a name server which is authoritative for the zone listed in the first column. Thus, A.ROOT-SERVERS.NET. is authoritative for ".", which is the root of the DNS tree. The next record in the file lists the IP address of this server. Eight other root servers are listed in this file.

The query will be passed from this server to a root server as non-recursive query, meaning that the root server is expected to pass only the best information it has. For instance, if queried for a resolution of www.microsoft.com., a root server would respond with name server information (NS records) for microsoft.com.

The server doing the iteration would take this partial resolution and cache the name server record(s). Then it would query that name server to resolve the name. If the response to that query again contains partial results, those too will be cached and the server will iterate. When the server gets a response, it will cache the result and return the response to the original client (i.e. resolver).

Forwarding Resolution Requests to WINS Servers

Microsoft's Windows Internet Name Service (WINS) is used for translation of NetBIOS computer names into IP addresses. For sites which use WINS servers for NetBIOS name resolution, it may be useful to have Microsoft DNS server consult a WINS server. Refer to chapter 16, "NetBIOS Name Resolution", for discussion of this implementation.

Zone Transfers

In any well-designed network, there will be at least one backup server for every primary server. In the case of DNS, primary servers are backed up by secondary DNS servers.

A server which is primary for a zone is often called a primary server, but that nomenclature is sometimes confusing, since a server may be authoritative for more than one zone. For example, a server may be a primary for two zones and a secondary for three others. Whether this server is a primary or secondary server depends on the zone that you're referring to.

When querying a DNS server, it doesn't matter whether a secondary or primary is queried. Either type is authoritative for the domain and will give just as good an answer as the other. In fact, it often makes sense for most clients to be configured to query servers which are secondary for a zone.

zone transfer: the process of copying the primary's zone database to the secondary.

The reason behind this practice stems from the nature of the primary to secondary relationship. The primary and secondary servers exchange database information (found in the primary) using a process called a **zone transfer**. If the primary is spending processing time transferring zone information to one or more secondaries, it may not have as much free time as a given secondary to answer queries. Zone transfers occur regularly, such that if a primary goes down, the secondary will answer requests.

Note that a secondary server can request a zone transfer from the primary server for a zone, as well as from any secondaries for that zone. Be aware that the propagation time for resource records from the primary to a second or third generation secondary may cause stale information to linger in your network longer than if all secondaries transfer from the primary. Thus, use of multiple generations of secondaries are recommended only when necessary.

In our example network of foobar.com, we are now adding a secondary DNS server, called SEC_DNS, with IP address 10.1.2.7. A depiction of a zone transfer is shown in Figure 13.11.

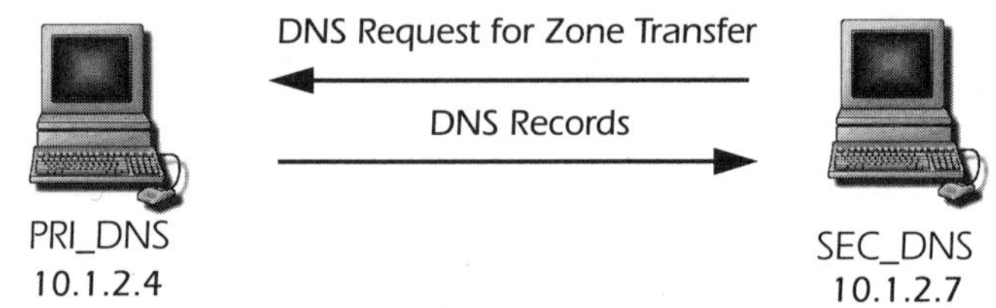

Figure 13.11
A server which is acting as a secondary for a zone may request a zone transfer from the primary.

Configuration of a Secondary DNS Server

Configuration parameters relating to secondaries and zone transfers are found on two dialogs: *Zone Properties: General* (Figure 13.12) and *Zone Properties: Notify* (Figure 13.13). The general properties are used for configuring a primary server for a zone as well. Now let's look at the details of secondary server configuration.

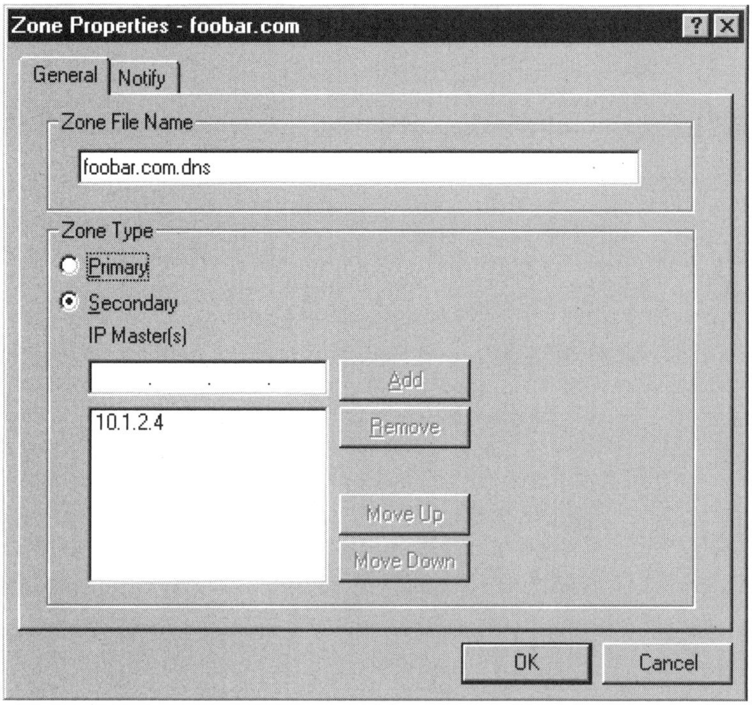

Figure 13.12
The zone file name and type of zone may be configured in the General Zone Properties dialog.

At the top of the dialog in Figure 13.12 is the name of the zone database. This file is found in the directory %systemroot%\system32\dns. If you show the contents of this file, you will see that its format is the same format as other DNS zone files.

The bottom of the dialog shows the type of zone, either primary or secondary. Recall that a primary zone is one where the database records are created and permanently stored on that server. A secondary zone only receives copies of records from other authoritative servers (either the primary, or a secondary), and keeps those records in memory for a limited amount of time — typically 1 hour.

Figure 13.12 was captured from a DNS server (SEC_DNS) acting as a secondary for the foobar.com. zone. Upon service startup, the DNS server will request a zone transfer from the IP Master for that zone. An *IP Master* is another name for the source of the zone transfer, often the primary DNS server for that zone. Note that in this example, the IP Master for the secondary is the IP address of PRI_DNS (10.1.2.4), which is the primary for this zone.

When the IP Master (or simply "master") receives a zone transfer request from a secondary, it will send the resource records for the zone to the secondary via a TCP connection.

Traditionally, the secondaries would request a transfer of the entire zone database, as described in the following steps.

Zone Transfer Process

The following are the steps that occur in the zone transfer process between a secondary and the IP Master.

Step 1. The secondary queries the master for the zone's SOA record.

Step 2. The master responds with the contents of the SOA record.

Step 3. The secondary checks the serial number in the SOA record. If the serial number is greater than the last serial number it received, new records have been created, thus a zone transfer should occur. If the serial number has not changed, no zone transfer is necessary.

Step 4. The secondary sets up a TCP connection to the master.

Step 5. The secondary requests a zone transfer over this connection.

Step 6. The transfer of the zone is sent from the master to the secondary on this connection.

Step 7. The connection is torn down when the transfer is complete.

Notify Lists and Restricting Zone Transfers

Two questions may have come to mind when looking at the zone transfer process:

- Can updates (rather than the whole file) be sent to a secondary?
- Can any machine request a zone transfer from a DNS server?

incremental zone transfer: zone transfer in which only the changed records are transmitted.

A recent addition called **incremental zone transfer** has been added to the DNS capabilities. Figure 13.13 was captured from a primary DNS server, PRI_DNS. The *Notify tab* lists the IP addresses of secondary DNS servers for this zone. These secondary servers will be informed of changes in the primary server's database.[3] In our example network, SEC_DNS will act as a secondary to PRI_DNS. Therefore the screen in Figure 13.13 will be used on PRI_DNS to tell it to send updates to SEC_DNS (10.1.2.7).

Figure 13.13 A list of secondary servers for this primary zone.

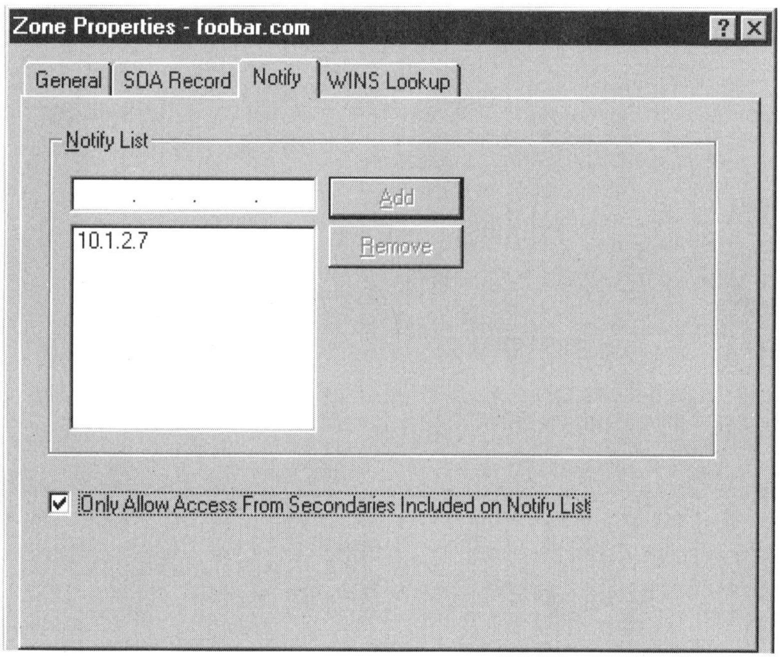

3. The first zone transfer occurs when you enter an IP address in the dialog in Figure 13.13 and hit "ok." Subsequent updates occurs when the primary server's DNS files are updated. Files are updated when the DNS service is shut down, or when the user selects the menu option DNS-> Update Server Data Files.

In order to prevent random, potentially insecure DNS servers on the Internet from downloading your DNS database, it is recommended you check the box at the bottom of the dialog. This checkbox will prevent servers that are not on the list from performing a zone transfer.

Note: to force a zone transfer, the ***nslookup ls*** (i.e. "list") command can be used to initiate a zone transfer from the server specified in the command.

Zone Transfer Packet Captures

zonetransfer.cap

An example of a zone transfer is shown in the packet capture in Figure 13.14. The capture file is called zonetransfer.cap, and the address file is dns_ch.adr. Frames 3 and 4 are the query and response for the SOA record. Packet 8 (highlighted) shows the request for the zone transfer. Packet nine shows the transfer itself. These are sent over a TCP connection.

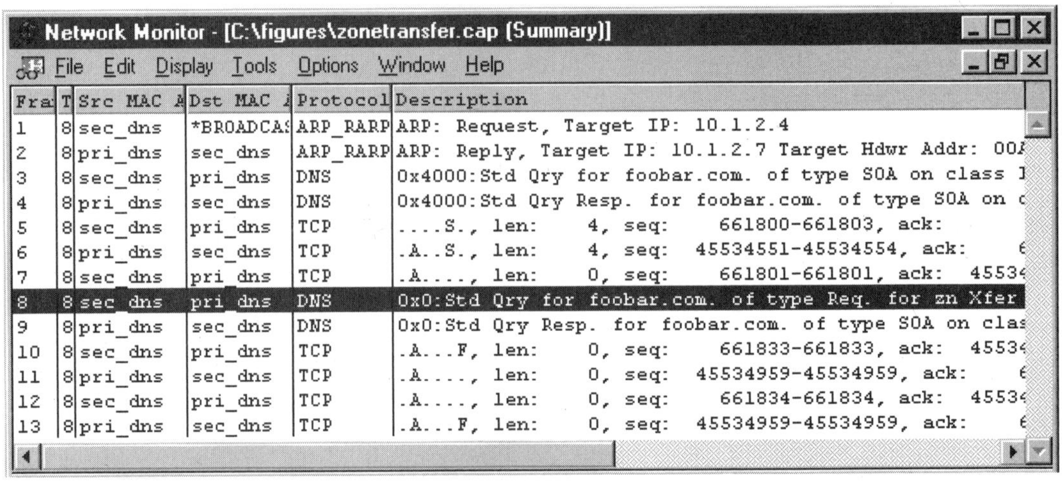

Fra	T	Src MAC A	Dst MAC A	Protocol	Description
1	8	sec_dns	*BROADCAS	ARP_RARP	ARP: Request, Target IP: 10.1.2.4
2	8	pri_dns	sec_dns	ARP_RARP	ARP: Reply, Target IP: 10.1.2.7 Target Hdwr Addr: 00A
3	8	sec_dns	pri_dns	DNS	0x4000:Std Qry for foobar.com. of type SOA on class I
4	8	pri_dns	sec_dns	DNS	0x4000:Std Qry Resp. for foobar.com. of type SOA on c
5	8	sec_dns	pri_dns	TCP	....S., len: 4, seq: 661800-661803, ack:
6	8	pri_dns	sec_dns	TCP	.A..S., len: 4, seq: 45534551-45534554, ack: 6
7	8	sec_dns	pri_dns	TCP	.A...., len: 0, seq: 661801-661801, ack: 45534
8	8	sec_dns	pri_dns	DNS	0x0:Std Qry for foobar.com. of type Req. for zn Xfer
9	8	pri_dns	sec_dns	DNS	0x0:Std Qry Resp. for foobar.com. of type SOA on clas
10	8	sec_dns	pri_dns	TCP	.A...F, len: 0, seq: 661833-661833, ack: 45534
11	8	pri_dns	sec_dns	TCP	.A...., len: 0, seq: 45534959-45534959, ack: 6
12	8	sec_dns	pri_dns	TCP	.A...., len: 0, seq: 661834-661834, ack: 45534
13	8	pri_dns	sec_dns	TCP	.A...F, len: 0, seq: 45534959-45534959, ack: 6

Figure 13.14 A packet capture of a zone transfer.

zonedenial.cap

Now consider another example for which the master has been configured to only allow access from secondaries listed in the *Notify tab* of the *Zone Properties* configuration. For this example, the address of the potential secondary has been removed from the list of IP addresses allowed to transfer from the master. Figure 13.15 shows a packet capture of the zone denial which occurs when SEC_DNS attempts to perform a zone transfer. The capture file for this example is zonedenial.cap. Notice that packet 10 shows the denial of the zone transfer.

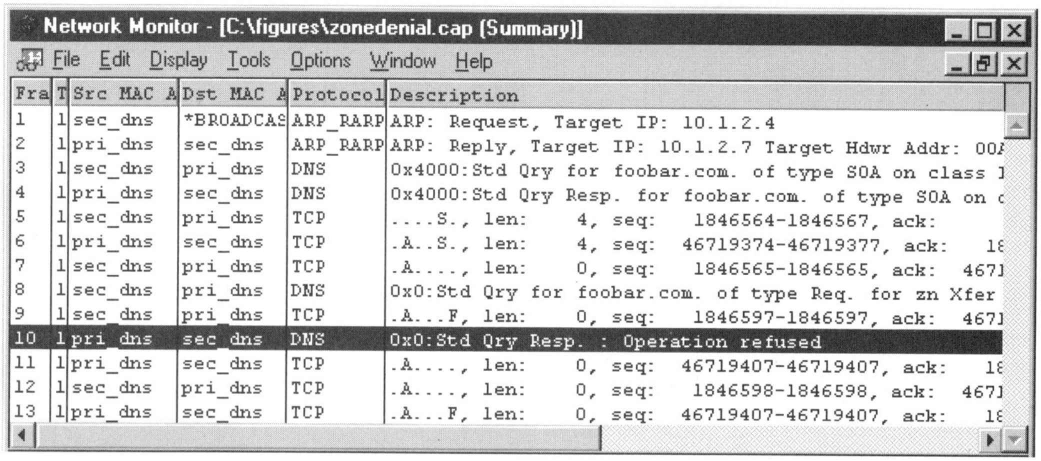

Figure 13.15 An example of zone denial. The zone transfer was prevented by the master.

Configuring Zone Transfer and Cache Timers

The *Zone Properties-> SOA Record* screen is used to configure zone transfer and cache parameters. This screen is shown in Figure 13.16.

The following is a list of the parameters found on this screen and their meanings:

- Primary DNS name— Specifies FQDN of the machine on which the database was created.
- Responsible person— The complete email address of the user who is responsible for its maintenance. Note that the email address should be indicated in DNS form, with the @ sign replaced with a dot.
- Serial number— This is the serial number of the zone database file. This integer is automatically increased whenever the file is changed.

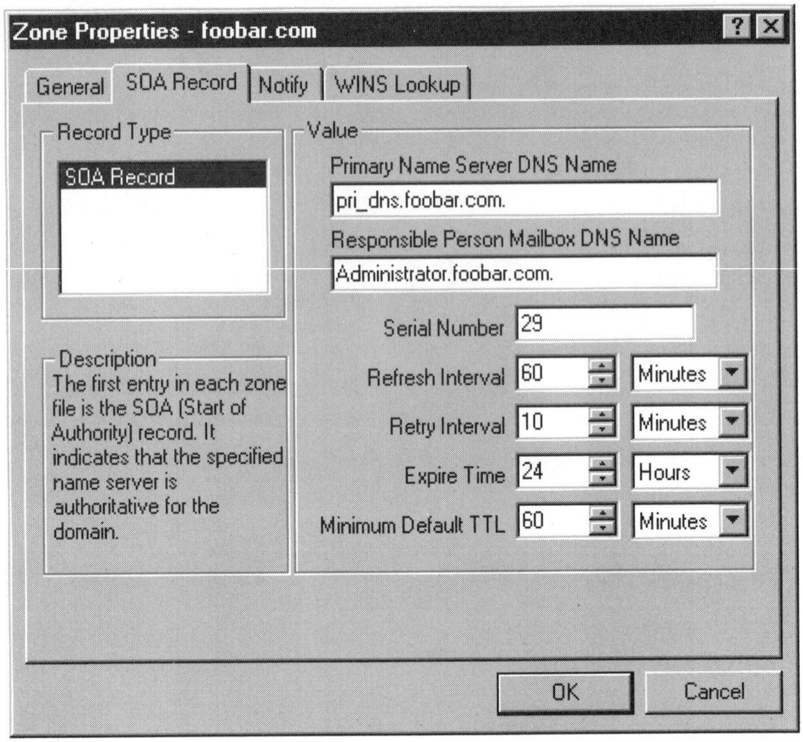

Figure 13.16
A number of parameters are specified in the Start of Zone Authority record, such as caching properties.

- The next three values are used by secondary servers to govern updates of information from the primary.

  - Refresh interval— The number of seconds that may elapse before a secondary server will request an update of the zone information.

  - Retry interval— The number of seconds that a secondary will wait if it failed to get a response from the primary at the refresh interval. After this time, the secondary will attempt another update request. If this update fails as well, it will repeat the process again after the retry interval.

  - Expire time— This timer bounds the refresh/retry process. If after this amount of time, the secondary has still not been able to refresh the zone from its primary, then the zone data will become expired (i.e. forgotten).

  - Minimum default TTL— This timer governs how long a DNS server may cache information learned from this zone.

Configuring Multihomed DNS Servers

When a DNS server has more than one interface (i.e. multihomed), should it answer DNS queries on all interfaces? The *Server Properties* dialog *Interface tab*, as shown in Figure 13.17, allows you to select which of your multiple interfaces you want the DNS server to answer queries on.

Figure 13.17
DNS can operate on multiple interfaces.

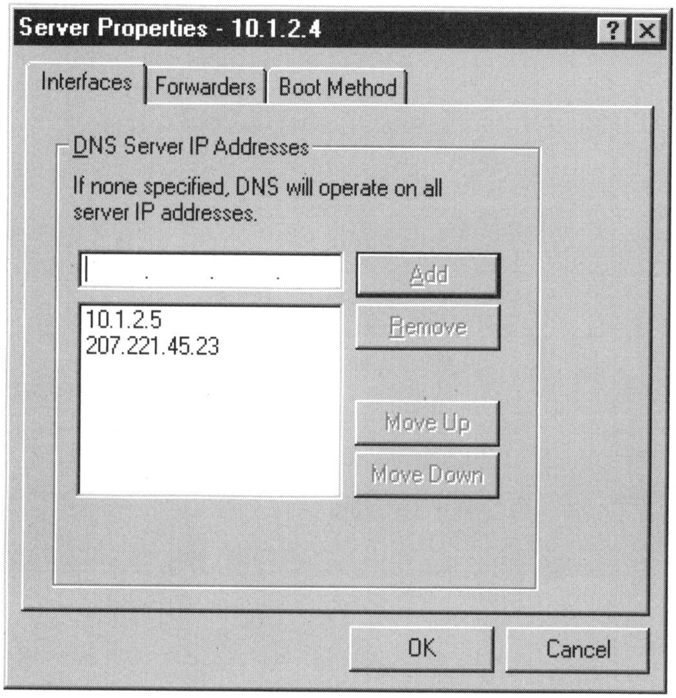

Restricting a DNS server to answer queries only on certain interfaces may be useful when running a proxy server on the same machine as the DNS service.

Configuring DNS to Load From the Boot File

DNS servers on the Internet, since their invention, have been run on UNIX machines without a windowing interface. Therefore, configuration of DNS servers up to this point has usually involved editing text files manually. Microsoft has added a GUI for their version of DNS — the DNS Manager.

The most common implementation of DNS (BIND) not only uses the standard DNS zone files, but also a configuration file used to bootstrap the server. The BIND boot file is called named.boot. The boot file supplies the following information to the server:

- The directory in which to store the DNS configuration files.
- A line for each zone file to be loaded into the server, specifying:
    - An indication of whether the server is a primary or secondary for the zone.
    - The domain name of the zone.
    - The list of IP masters if the server is a secondary for the zone.
    - The filename of the zone database.
- A list of forwarders to be used.
- Whether the server is a slave, or if it can query root servers.

This is a simple text file in the BIND implementations. The DNS Manager on the other hand, stores some of the DNS server information in the Windows NT registry by default. It is possible to have the DNS Manager boot from the BIND compatible boot file instead of the registry. To do that, you must delete the *EnableRegistryBoot* registry entry shown in Table 13.1.

Table 13.1
EnableRegistryBoot registry parameter.

Hive:	HKEY_LOCAL_MACHINE
Key:	\System\CurrentControlSet\Services\DNS\Parameters
Name:	EnableRegistryBoot
Type:	REG_DWORD
Value:	1 (true)

After deleting that entry, you must put your desired boot file into the directory %systemroot%\system32\dns. However, if you do this, all zone creations that were done through the DNS Manager will be lost. To fix this, add the appropriate entries to the NT DNS boot file. The NT boot file is called boot and is found in %systemroot%\system32\dns directory.

If you have added any zones through DNS Manager, use a registry editor to view the \System\CurrentControlSet\Services\DNS\Zones key in the registry. For each zone, you will see a registry entry named after each zone. The registry rendition of the BIND boot file is stored under the following registry parameters under the key for each zone.

The *DatabaseFile* parameter holds the file name of the DNS configuration file for the zone, such as cache.dns or foobar.com.dns, shown in Table 13.2.

Table 13.2 DatabaseFile registry parameter.

Hive:	HKEY_LOCAL_MACHINE
Key:	\System\CurrentControlSet\Services\DNS\Zones\<zoneName>
Name:	DatabaseFile
Type:	REG_SZ
Value:	"foobar.com.dns"

The next parameter for each zone specifies the *Type* of the zone, cache, primary, or secondary as shown in Table 13.3.

Table 13.3 Type registry parameter.

Hive:	HKEY_LOCAL_MACHINE
Key:	\System\CurrentControlSet\Services\DNS\Zones\<zoneName>
Name:	Type
Type:	REG_DWORD
Value:	0 (cache), 1 (primary), 2 (secondary)

If the server performs a secondary role for the zone, an additional registry parameter exists called *MasterServers*. The value for this parameter is a list of IP addresses of the masters (10.1.2.4), with the first entry in the list being the number of masters (1), as shown in Table 13.4.

Table 13.4 MasterServers registry parameter.

Hive:	HKEY_LOCAL_MACHINE
Key:	\System\CurrentControlSet\Services\DNS\Zones\<zoneName>
Name:	MasterServers
Type:	REG_MULTI_SZ
Value:	1, { 10.1.2.4 }

When converting each zone from the registry to a BIND-compatible boot file, create one line for each zone. On each line, write the keyword for the zone type, then the zone name, followed by the list of master servers for a secondary and finally the database filename.

After these zone configuration lines, write a list of forwarders on a "forwarders" line based on the *Forwarders* registry parameter. This registry parameter again is a list of IP addresses of the DNS servers to forward requests to, with the very first entry in the list being the number of IP addresses.

Table 13.5 Forwarders registry parameter.

Hive:	HKEY_LOCAL_MACHINE
Key:	\System\CurrentControlSet\Services\DNS\Parameters
Name:	Forwarders
Type:	REG_DWORD
Value:	1, { 10.1.2.7 }

Finally, write "slave" line to the boot file if the *IsSlave* registry parameter has a value of one (Table 13.6).

Table 13.6 IsSlave registry parameter.

Hive:	HKEY_LOCAL_MACHINE
Key:	\System\CurrentControlSet\Services\DNS
Name:	IsSlave
Type:	REG_DWORD
Value:	0

And for you die-hard UNIX fans, you don't have to use the GUI to make configuration changes to the Microsoft DNS server. You can make the above changes, and all future changes, by editing the files found in the %systemroot%\system32\dns directory. If you've converted the registry parameters to a boot file, make all zone additions to the boot file.

Cache-Only DNS

Small offices, workgroups, or departments may benefit from having a DNS server which is not authoritative for any zones, but can cache information learned by querying other DNS servers. A DNS server without any primary or secondary zones is called a *cache-only* DNS server (Figure 13.18). Caching DNS servers can help balance network load by being placed at strategic points in the network. Caching DNS servers can also reduce the amount of time it takes to resolve a DNS query.[4]

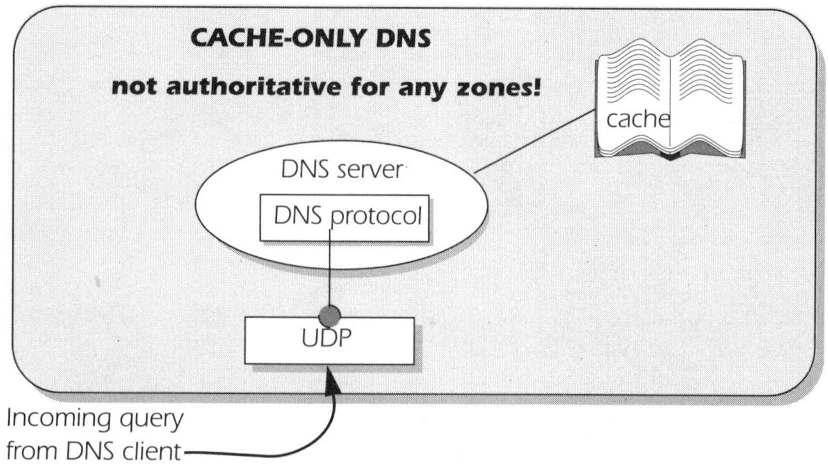

Figure 13.18 A cache-only DNS is not authoritative for any zones, but may be used to hold information from queries of other servers.

To view the DNS cache with DNS Manager, double click on cache icon. Note that sometimes the view of the cache isn't updated immediately even when the refresh screen option is used, yet ***nslookup*** tests indicate that the information has indeed been cached.

Figure 13.19 shows a view of the cache with the root server entries which were loaded from the cache file. Again, don't confuse the two. The file is simply a list of IP addresses of root servers which are preloaded into the cache. The cache-only server will learn information from other servers via the normal query process.

4. Cache-only DNS servers are also called caching-only DNS servers.

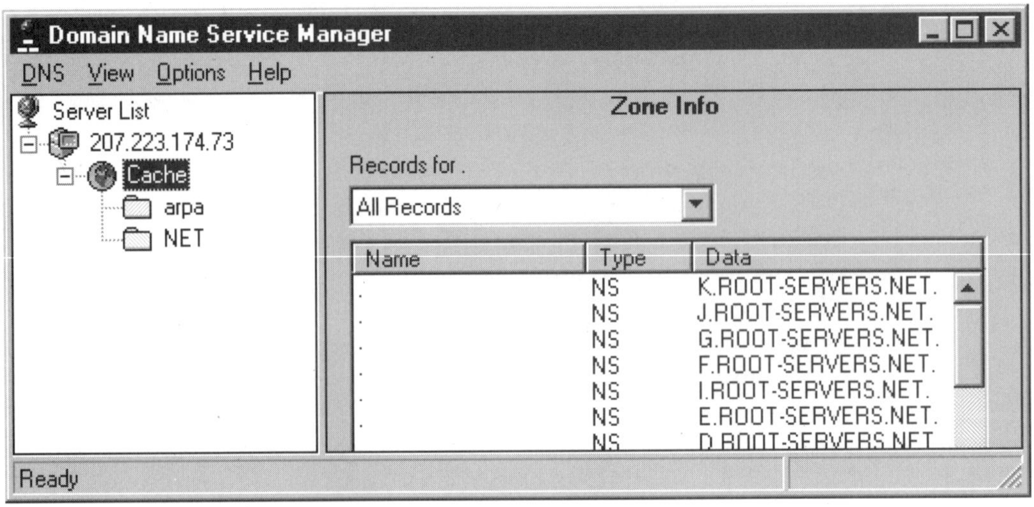

Figure 13.19 The cache contains the root server entries from the cache file.

The address records for the root servers are shown in Figure 13.20. Notice that while all of these servers are in the ROOT-SERVERS.NET. zone, they have different IP networks. This may be true of your zones as well.

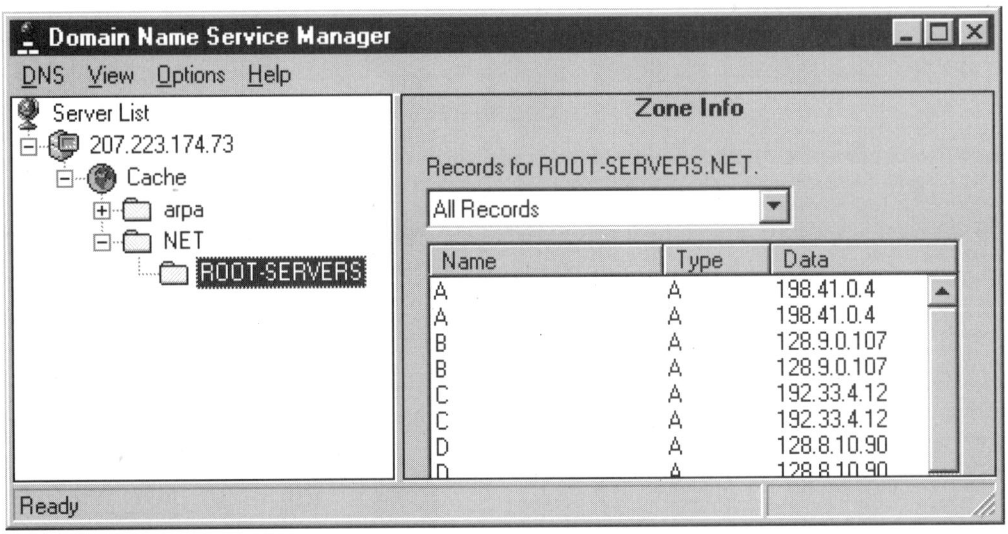

Figure 13.20 The address records for the root servers are in the cache.

Once some queries have been placed to the server, it will have resolved the addresses of its forwarders and other queried name servers as shown in Figure 13.21.

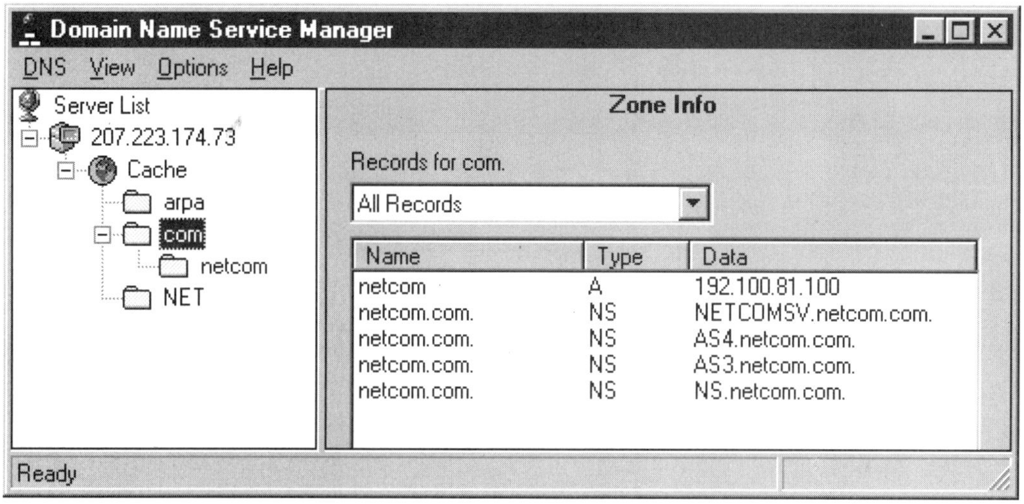

Figure 13.21 *After a few queries, the server has cached some name server entries.*

When addresses in another domain, such as microsoft.com have been queried of the root servers, the cache-only DNS caches the name server entries for the other DNS servers as shown in Figure 13.22.

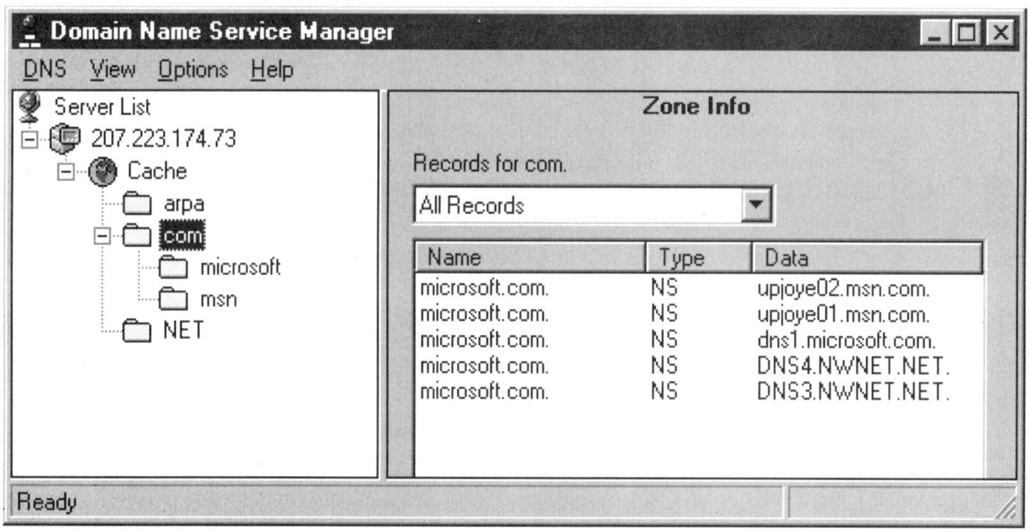

Figure 13.22 The cache following the query of the root servers for microsoft.com.

Then, once the cache-only DNS server has been able to query one of these DNS servers at microsoft.com, the name www.microsoft.com has been resolved, as shown in the cache in Figure 13.23.

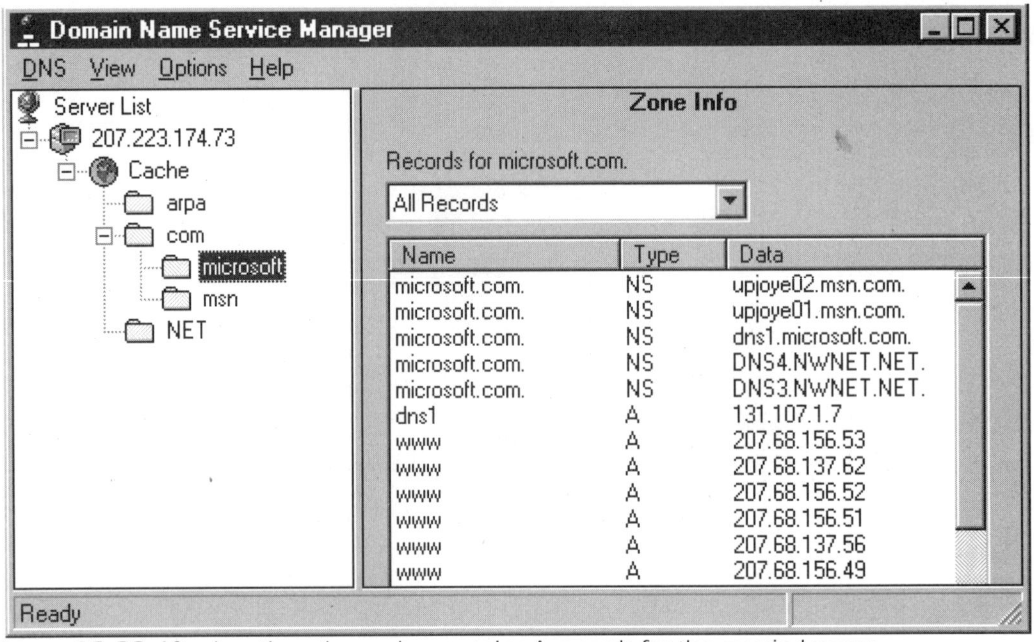

Figure 13.23 After iteration, the cache contains A records for the queried name.

Configuring a Caching DNS for Use by Proxy Server

It may be advantageous to configure a cache-only DNS on the same machine as your proxy server, as shown in Figure 13.24. This configuration would provide quicker response times for name resolution queries.

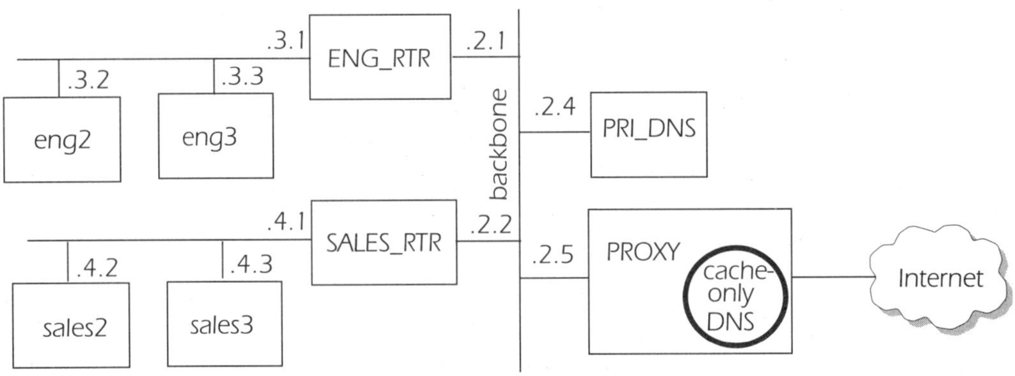

Figure 13.24 Network diagram showing a cache-only DNS on the proxy server.

Note that this DNS would not define any records for the corporate network, and would not be advertised to anyone as a potential DNS to query. It would strictly be used by the proxy server

It is a simple process to do, once your proxy server is running.[5] To install a caching-only DNS on your proxy server, perform the following steps:

- Install DNS service on the Proxy machine.
- Enable DNS for the external interface only (Figure 13.25).
- Configure Proxy Server to use that DNS using *Network Control Panel-> TCP/IP Properties -> DNS tab.*

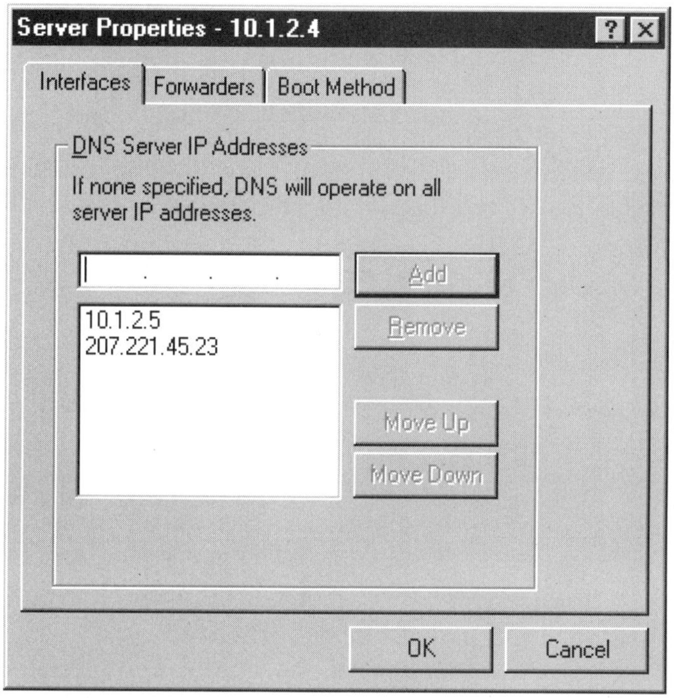

Figure 13.25 Here, both the internal interface and the Internet interface are shown. Remove the internal interface entry for use with proxy server.

You can use ***nslookup*** and Network Monitor to determine if answers are actually being cached on the server.

5. Refer to Chapter 12, "Internet Access Using Proxy Server" for how to do this.

Summary

Here's a summary of the items which have been addressed in this chapter.

- DNS servers use multiple sources to resolve requests: local database, local cache, other DNS servers, as well as DNS root servers.
- Secondary DNS servers obtain copies of the zone information from the primary DNS for that zone, or other secondary servers for that zone. This process is called a zone transfer.
- A caching-only DNS can be created to decrease resolution time as well as lessen the load on other DNS servers.

Further Reading

Additional information on DNS may be found in the following references.

[Albitz1994] Albitz, Paul and Lui, Cricket, *DNS and Bind,* 1994, O'Reilly & Associates, Inc.

[Mockapetris1987a] Mockapetris, P.V., *Domain Names — Concepts and Facilities,* 1987, IETF RFC 1034

[Mockapetris1987b] Mockapetris, P.V., *Domain Names — Implementation and Specification,* 1987, IETF RFC 1035

[Mockapetris1989] Mockapetris, P.V., *DNS Encoding of Network Names and Other Types,* 1989, IETF RFC 1101

14

Securing Web Traffic using SSL and IIS

Microsoft's Internet Information Server (IIS) provides services which allow you to deliver information either to a small organization or the world-wide community. So whether you plan to publish information for a small work-group or special interest group, or to millions and millions of readers, or even if you want to develop a framework for collaboration among all of these participants, read on.

This chapter is divided into two major parts. The first part is more theoretical, and covers a background of cryptography and the Secure Socket Layer (SSL). The second part focuses on configuration and management of security in IIS.

Cryptography Concepts

Cryptography[1] is a branch of theoretical and applied mathematics which is well beyond the scope of this book. What we focus on here is the use of cryptography for web-type communications.

The basic aspects of security which need to be addressed for web communication are:

- Privacy (or Confidentiality) — keeping something secret. The primary way to keep something secret is to use *encryption* to transform data into some unreadable format, and *decryption* to convert encrypted data back to its original format (Figure 14.1).
- Integrity — ensuring the message is the same as when it left the sender. That it, confirming the message was not changed during the transmission process.
- Authenticity — ensuring the message is from who we think it is from. **Authentication** is the process of accurately identifying a user, machine, or organization. This may involve a certificate of authenticity. The primary goal of authentication is protecting against fakes or forgeries.

Authentication: the process of accurately identifying a user, machine, or organization.

1. Cryptology is the study of writing (cryptography) and reading (cryptanalysis) ciphers.

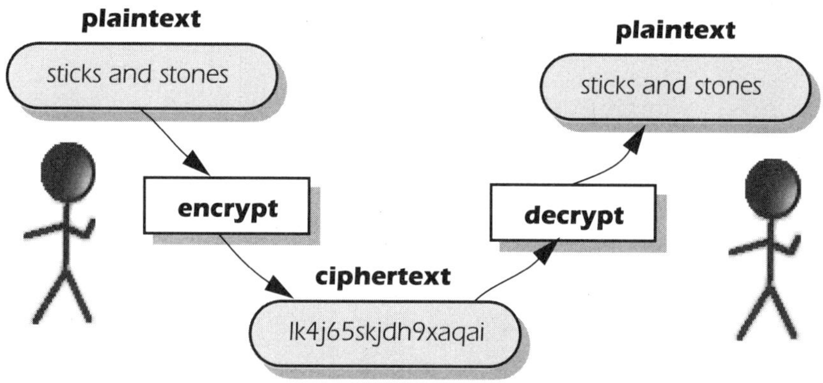

Figure 14.1
A plaintext message may be encrypted into an unreadable ciphertext message. Decryption is the reverse process, revealing plaintext for the recipient.

Depending on the application, only integrity may be a concern. In other cases, privacy, integrity, and authentication are necessary. Let's consider a few examples from everyday life.

- You are watching television. Do you care where the news or movie came from (authenticity), whether anyone else sees it (privacy), or whether anything critical has been edited out (integrity)?
- You go to a cash machine in a supermarket and withdraw $20 from your checking account. Did the money come from your account (authenticity)? Can you withdraw money from someone else's account (privacy)?
- While travelling through an airport, you call a colleague from a payphone using your calling card. Did someone see or hear your calling card number as you entered it (privacy)?
- You visit a web page to check the airfare to visit relatives for a holiday. Within one week you receive email trying to convince you that you should take a vacation to far-off lands (privacy).

Two of the basic guidelines of security are:

1. Don't spend more on security than what you're trying to protect is worth. But be careful in estimating value.
2. There is no absolute security or cryptography. Encryption methods that have not been cracked before today may be cracked tomorrow.

Hashes

A *hash* is a transformation of information into a mathematical summary which may be used as a short-hand of the original (Figure 14.2). Another name for a hash is a *message digest (MD)*. Most hashes are fixed length, regardless of message length. Because they are condensed with respect to the original message, hashes are not unique.

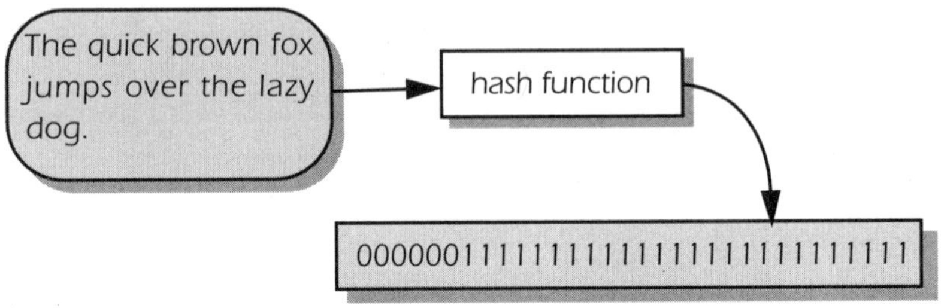

Figure 14.2 Hashing summarizes a message. This example shows which letters are present in the message.

The following lists a few ways that hashes are used.

- Hashing is used in information systems for speeding up table lookups, such as in a database management system.
- A form of hashing is used for checksums and cyclic redundancy checks (CRCs) to protect against bit errors in recording and transmission of information. Some typical checksums and CRCs are between eight and 32 bits in length.
- Longer hashes are used to protect messages from tampering. These are often called cryptographic hashes or **message integrity checks (MICs)**.

message integrity check (MIC): a summary of a message which is not prone to defeat by simple attack.

Of these three uses, the one that we'll be discussing here is the last one, where MICs are used to ensure integrity. An example of a MIC is shown in Figure 14.3.

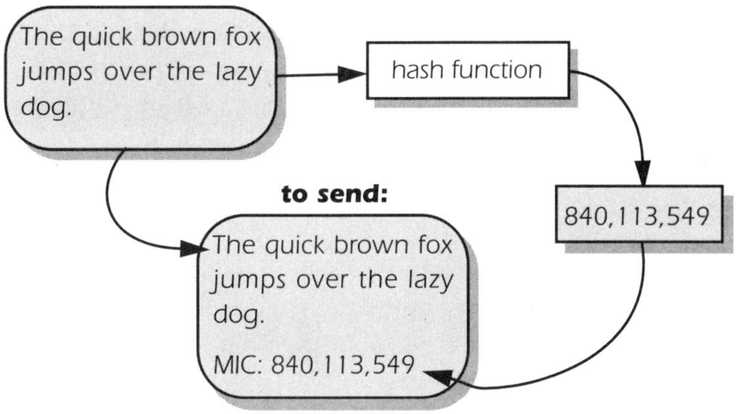

Figure 14.3 Message integrity may be checked by sending a good hash at the end of the message.

Two more terms need to be defined while we are talking about MICs. A *digital signature* is a MIC appended to a message which can be used along with an authentication scheme to confirm that the message came from whomever it was supposed to, and that it did not get modified in transmission. *Signature verification* is the process of using the digital signature to accurately determine the senders identity, and that the message was unaltered in transit (Figure 14.4).

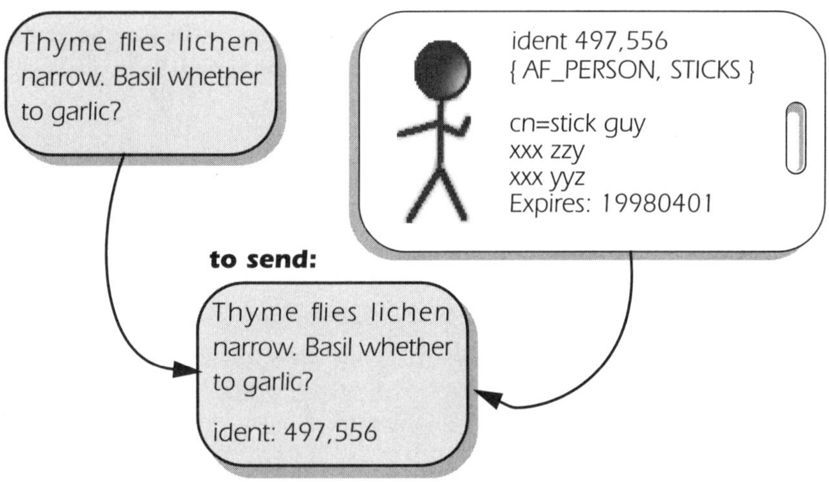

Figure 14.4 Authentication information may be added to a message. The recipient must be able to confirm or deny the identity in some way.

In cryptographic hashes, particular algorithms and hash lengths are chosen so that another message with the same hash can't easily be found within a reasonable amount of time. Typical lengths of cryptographic hashes are 64 to 2048 bits in length.

An example of a weak hash is the simplistic function shown in Figure 14.5. Simply rearranging letters in the message may result in a similar but different message, thus any integrity based on a weak hash is prone to simple attacks. A decent hash function must at least make it difficult to guess another message which results in the same hash. The amount of time to find a hash by brute force should well exceed the lifetime of the desired privacy or integrity.

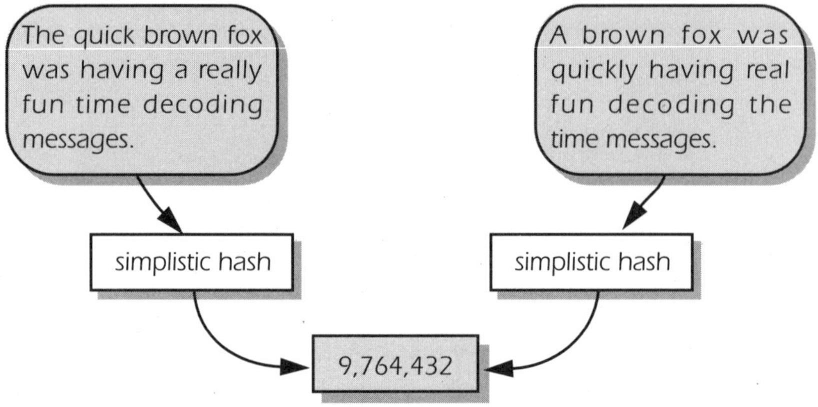

Figure 14.5
A good hash must not make it easy for someone to guess another message which results in the same hash.

challenge/response: an authentication method in which a party challenges the suspect party and expects a response which only the expected party could return.

Seeding the hash function with random numbers[2] or varying initialization vectors may help improve an already good hash function. Seeding the hash of a message with part of (or a hash of) a previous message may be used to produce a different hash for the same message based on the sequence or context of the message. Later we'll see that this may be used for **challenge/response**.

Message Digest Types

Recall that another term for a hash is a Message Digest (MD). Specifically, Ron Rivest of RSA fame developed a Message Digest algorithm called MD. This was followed by other kinds of MDs called MD2, MD3, MD4, and MD5. Of these, the MD2, MD4, and MD5 specifications are pub-

2. Actual random numbers are essential to real cryptography. It has been said that pseudo random numbers result in pseudo security.

lished as IETF RFCs[3]. The U.S. National Institute for Standards and Technology (NIST) also developed an MD function called the Secure Hash Algorithm (SHA), as a part of the Secure Hash Specification (SHS).

Of particular interest here is MD5, which breaks messages into 512 bit blocks and runs the hashing function to generate a 128 bit digest regardless of the length of the message. The message must be padded so that the length field, as shown in Figure 14.6, is aligned to the end of a 512 bit block. The length field is 64 bits, which specifies the number of bits in the message. The padding must be at least one bit (with a value of 1), followed by up to 511 zero bits as necessary to properly align the length field. The MD5 function seeds the message digest with a constant initialization vector. It then takes 512 bits of the padded message and runs four passes of mathematical manipulation to yield a message digest. This process is repeated for as many remaining blocks as are in the message. For example, for messages between 960 and 1471 bits (inclusive) in length, three blocks are necessary. When the last block has been manipulated, the resulting digest is used as the digest of the whole message.

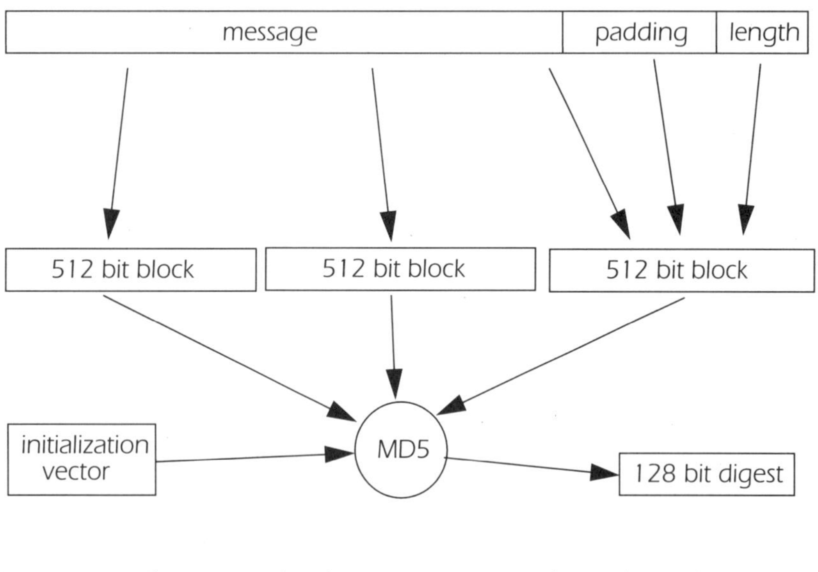

Figure 14.6 An example of a MD5 digest for a message of 960 through 1471 bits in length.

The message digest function is a *one-way hash*. It is not invertible. In other words, you can't take the hash and reveal the original message.

3. RFC1319 describes MD2. RFC1320 describes MD4, and MD5 is detailed in RFC1321.

Checking Message Integrity

Now let's look at how a message digest may be used as a message integrity check (MIC). With a well known hash function, anyone could generate the proper hash for a message. In other words, if simply a hash of the message is appended to the end of the message, it is easy to intercept the message and send a substitute, or even send a complete forgery. Therefore, a hash alone only provides for protection against accidental errors, not intentional ones.

When a secret key is appended to the message to be hashed, the digest may provide some protection against tampering. Figure 14.7 shows an example of a secret key being used to generate a MIC.

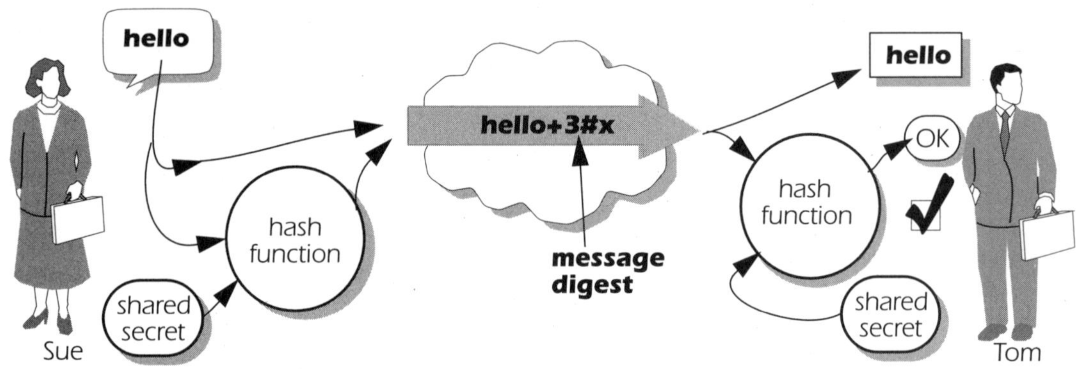

Figure 14.7 Example of a message integrity check.

secret key/ shared secret: a string of text shared between the sender and receiver that is used to encode/ decode messages.

Sue wants to send a message to Tom. She takes a message "hello" and catenates it with the **secret key**. Then she runs the combined key and message through the hash function and appends the resulting message digest to a copy of the original message (without the key). She sends the combined message and MD to Tom.

Tom may read the plaintext message, but needs to know the key that Sue used to confirm the MIC, thus the key is referred to as a **shared secret**. Tom will take the secret key and the body of the message (without the MIC) and hash it. If the resulting MD matches the MIC, then the message was sent by someone who knows the shared secret. It could have been sent by Sue, Tom himself, or anyone else who knows the key, thus this kind of a MIC is not really a digital signature.

An essential requirement for this kind of MIC to be useful is that the key is kept secret.

Is Your Cryptography Symmetric?

The concept of a digital key is similar to the workings of a physical key. Both are used to gain access to an object, such as a car or a message. In the case of a physical key, the same key is used to both lock and unlock a car. The same is true of *symmetric key cryptography* in which the same key is used to encode and decode the message.

However, in certain cases, it is more appropriate to have one key to lock the door, and another key to unlock the door. In *public key cryptography,* there are two keys: one key to encrypt the message (the public key), and another key to decrypt the message (the private key). Thus, the key pair is asymmetric.

Symmetric Key Cryptography (a.k.a Secret Key Cryptography)

The more traditional form of cryptography is based on the notion that the sender and receiver share a secret key.

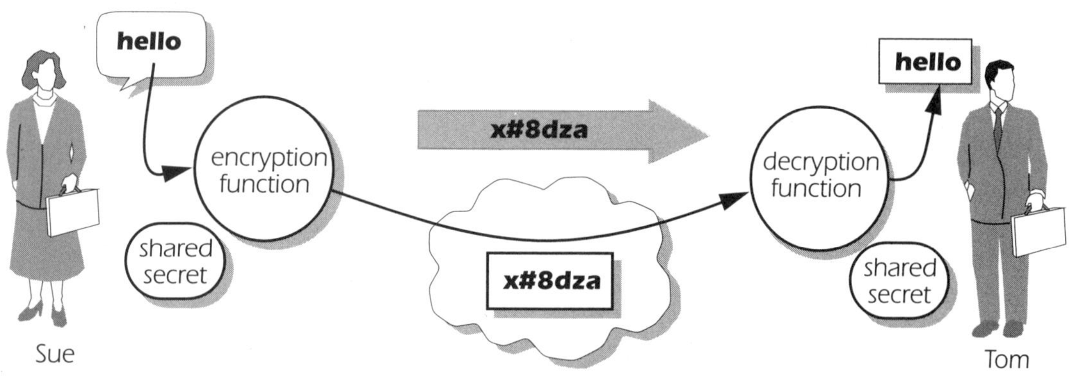

Figure 14.8 Example of symmetric key (secret key) encryption.

symmetric key cryptography: cryptography in which the same key is used to encode and decode the message.

Figure 14.8 shows two people who wish to communicate with one another. If they share a secret key, either party may encrypt messages with the key and send them to the other person. The receiver may use the shared key to decrypt the message. The same key is used to encrypt and decrypt messages, and the same key may be used to send messages in either direction, thus this shared key method is called **symmetric key cryptography**.

Two common symmetric key methods are *Data Encryption Standard (DES)* and *International Data Encryption Algorithm (IDEA)*.

DES has been in use since the late 1970s. It uses a 56 bit key on 64 bit blocks of data. Sixteen rounds are performed on the block. There are several methods of encrypting successive blocks. The simplest is electronic code book (ECB) mode. Another more secure mode is called cipher block chaining (CBC) in which the results of one block affect the next. Furthermore, to vary the encryption of the same message sent at different times (or by different sources), a random initialization vector is used.

IDEA was published in the early 1990s. It uses a 128 bit key on 64 bit blocks of data. Seventeen rounds are performed on the block.

With these methods of symmetric key cryptography, the sender and receiver must both know the secret key. The distribution of keys must be maintained very carefully.

Public Key Cryptography

Rather than maintaining a shared secret, two communicating parties could each have a published key, called their *public keys*. Yet with each of their public keys available, no security would be provided if symmetric key algorithms are used.

If each party maintains a real secret we may have security, but how can we have communication? If a private and public key are coupled so that one inverts the other, then we have something interesting. Figure 14.9 shows an example of how these could be used.

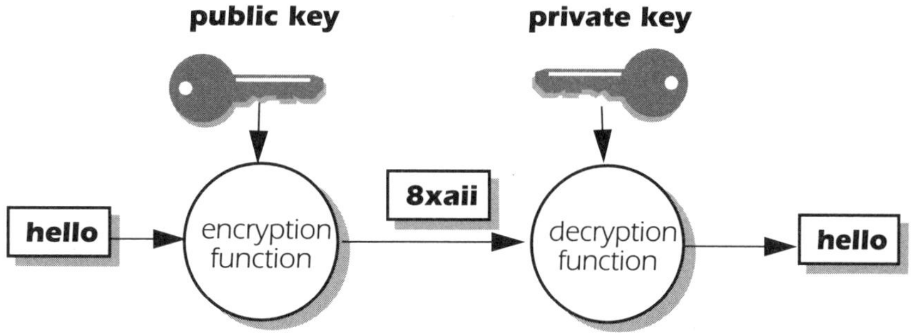

Figure 14.9
Asymmetric keys.

The key pair is designed so that if one key of this pair is used to encrypt (i.e. confidentially lock) a plaintext message, the other key may be used to decrypt (i.e. confidentially unlock) the resulting ciphertext message.

You may use one of these keys as a public key, shared with everyone. The other key must be kept secret, thus it is a private key. Which key should be used for encryption and which for decryption? If you use the private key for encryption, anyone (i.e. everyone) with the public key may decrypt the message, which isn't very confidential[4]. If however anyone who sends you a message uses your public key to encrypt it, then only your private key (i.e. you) may decrypt it. No one with your public key (including the sender) may decrypt the ciphertext.

public key cryptography: cryptography in which two different keys are used to encode and decode the message. These keys are called the public key and private key.

Public key cryptography has the following features:

- What's locked with the public key may only be unlocked with the corresponding private key.
- What's locked with the private key may only be unlocked with the corresponding public key.

These properties are quite a feat. As an example of public key cryptography, recall our friends Sue and Tom[5]. In Figure 14.10, Sue is sending a message to Tom using his public key. Only Tom may decrypt the message using his private key[6].

4. Encrypting messages with your public key is one method of signing messages.
5. Sue and Tom are actually close friends of Alice and Bob.
6. Assuming that the key system is cryptographically strong and that Tom has in no way revealed his private key.

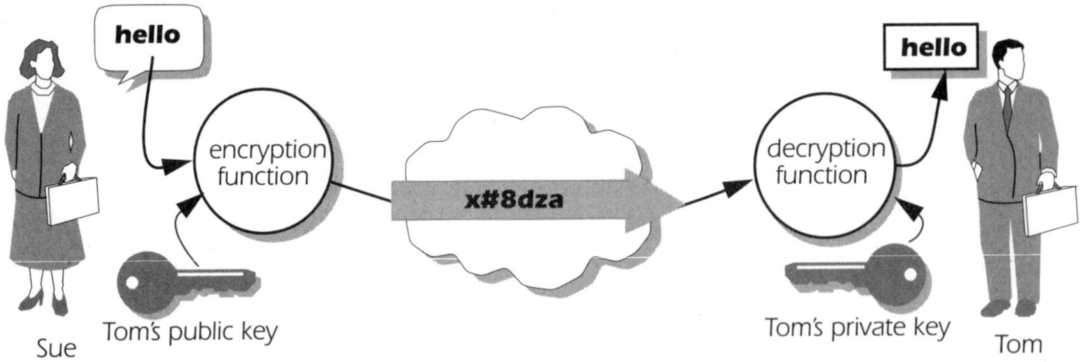

Figure 14.10 Example of public key encryption.

If Tom wants to send a message to Sue, he would encrypt it with her public key, and Sue would decrypt it with her private key. One of the classic problems with encryption is how to exchange keys. One method is to use a public key server.

Consider the example of the use of public/private keys shown in Figure 14.11. The steps used to transmit encrypted data using public key cryptography are outlined below.

1. Tom creates both a public and a private key for himself, using a predefined key-generating algorithm.
2. Tom registers his public key with a public key server on the Internet. Tom does not tell *anyone* what his private key is. If he did, then they could decrypt messages sent to him.
3. Sue wants to send a message to Tom. She creates the message. In order to encrypt the message, she must obtain Tom's public key from the public key server.
4. The encryption function can now encrypt the message using Tom's public key. The encrypted message is sent over the Internet.
5. Tom receives the encrypted message. He decrypts the message using his private key. Now that the message is readable, he can act upon the message as he decides.

Note that the above process only shows messages going from Sue to Tom. What if Tom wanted to reply to the message? The reverse of the above process would have to occur, but using Sue's public and private keys. Therefore in order to have a two-way encrypted conversation using public key cryptography, four keys are involved: the sender's public and private key, and the receiver's public and private key.

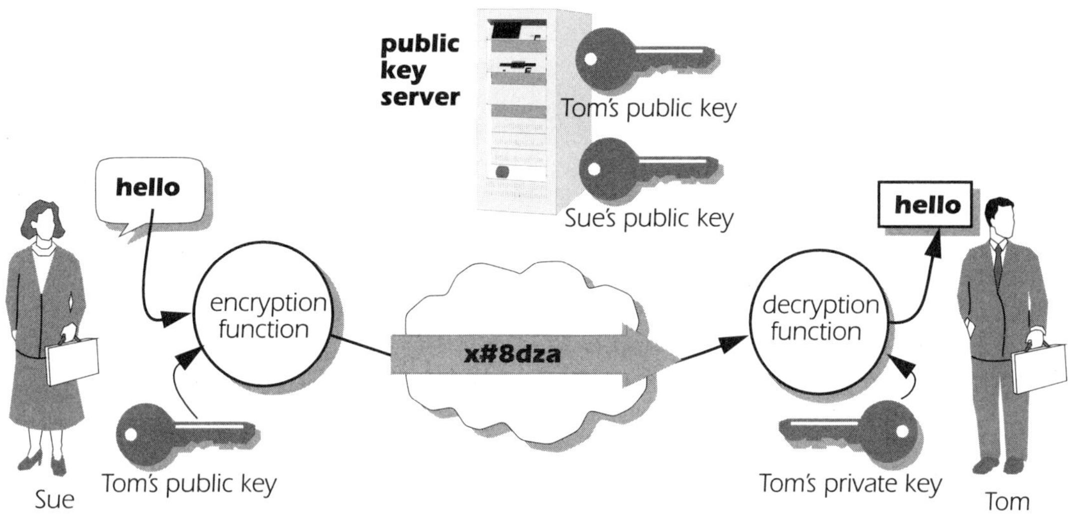

Figure 14.11 A public key server may be used as a key distribution center.

Authenticating a Message

We've seen that private key cryptography may be used for confidentiality, and that message digests may be used to check message integrity. Recall that the message integrity check (MIC) was a hash using a shared secret password. We may use public key cryptography as a *message authentication check (MAC)*. The whole message could be encrypted with the sender's private key, thus decrypting with the corresponding public key confirms not only the integrity of the message, but also the authenticity as it could only have been encrypted with the sender's private key.

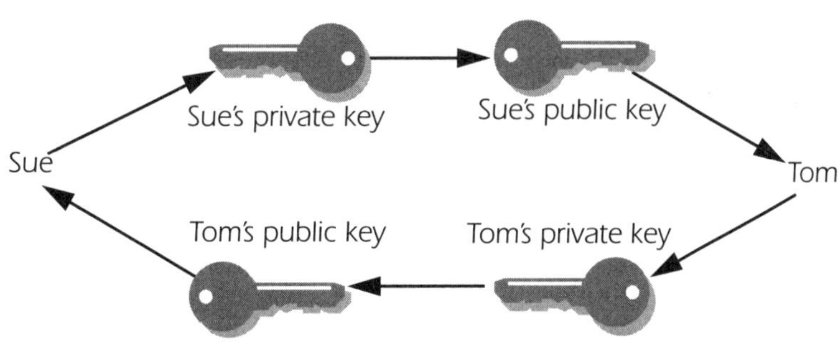

Figure 14.12 Authentication may be performed by signing with the sender's private key, and checked using the sender's public key.

When both confidentiality and authenticity are required, the message may be signed with a MAC as just described, and then the message may be encrypted using the recipient's public key.

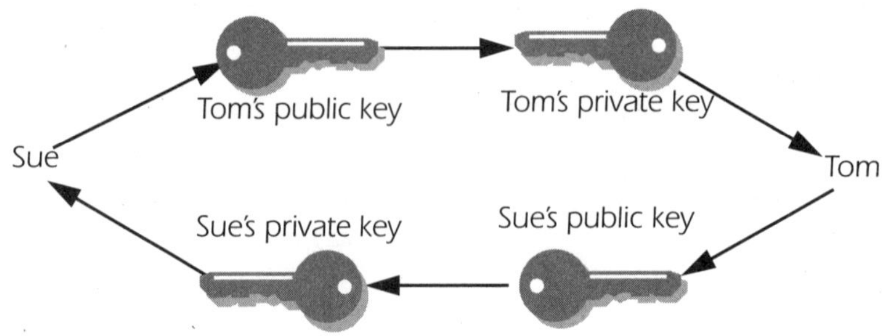

Figure 14.13 Confidentiality may be achieved by using encryption with the recipient's public key and decryption using the recipient's private key.

Hybrid Key Cryptography

While there are more applications of public key technology than secret key technology, the more complex mathematics of the key pairs makes public key cryptography significantly slower to use on current computers. Could a combination of the secret and public methods be used for both speed and flexibility? The answer is yes.

You can use public key cryptography to perform authentication and key exchange. The result of the key exchange is a shared secret (a.k.a. *session key*). This symmetric session key is then used to encrypt the data that is sent during the session. The advantages to using this combined method is that:

- You can securely exchange keys.
- Symmetric key encryption/decryption is faster than public key encryption/decryption.

An example of using this combined method is shown in Figure 14.14.

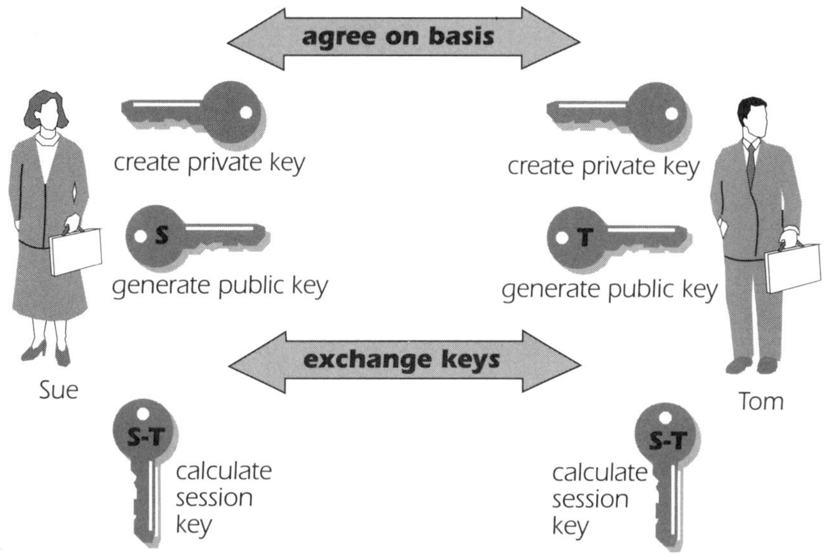

Figure 14.14 Using both public key and secret key encryption to exchange data.

The steps to obtain a session key are described below.

1. Agree on the basis for the key calculations. Typically two numbers, a prime number and a generator, are chosen and exchanged. These two numbers will serve as the foundation for the keys which are used throughout the rest of the process.
2. Each of the two parties independently selects a private key. These private keys are random numbers which may be unique for each conversation the two parties have.
3. Each party generates a public key from their private key and the generator and prime number.
4. The two parties exchange public keys. This may occur simultaneously, or with one party responding to the receipt of the other's public key.
5. Based on the private key and the other party's public key, calculate a shared secret key to be used for this session (i.e. session key). Because the public keys are based on the same generator and prime, the cross-pollination of your private key with your peer's public key will result in the same session key for both parties.

In summary, public key cryptography is used for the key exchange. Following this exchange, the two parties share a secret session key. The two parties may use the session key for a conversation using symmetric key cryptography, which is faster than public key cryptography.

Because this hybrid of public key and secret key cryptography is quite effective, it has recently come into common use. In fact, many schemes which are called public key systems really just use pure public key cryptography for the key exchange and then use a symmetric session key for bulk data transfer. An example of this is the protocol Secure Sockets Layer (SSL). SSL will be discussed shortly.

Digital Certificates

Rather than picking new generators, primes, and private and public key pairs to generate every session key, if we use fairly strong cryptography (e.g. long key length with fairly random pattern insensitive algorithms) then we may select public and private keys once in a great while[7]. Having the same public key for a prolonged period of time has a benefit of being possible to associate a public key with your identity.

If you have exchanged public keys with someone whom you have met in person, and also happen to trust, this establishment of trust may be used to leverage other trust relationships. You may sign a third person's public key with yours, and the person who trusts you may accept that third party's signature based on that trust. Eventually, a web of trust may be established. Then you may communicate with these people and be able to confirm their identities based on their digital signatures.

certificate authority (CA): an organization that provides the service of assigning certificates to organizations or individuals.

A **certificate authority** (CA) is an organization that provides the service of assigning certificates to anyone who requests them. When you request a certificate, the certificate authority uses various methods to determine if you are who you say you are. A table of certificate authorities is shown in Table 14.1.

7. As long as the cryptography with which we select the session key is not prone to quick attack.

Table 14.1 Public certificate authorities (current and potential).

CA Organization	Web site	Notes
BelSign	www.belsign.be	Belgium
CertCo	www.certco.com	CA for banking industry
CertiSign	www.certisign.com.br	Brazil
Cost	www.cost.se	Stockholm, SE
CyberTrust	www.cybertrust.com	GTE
Entrust	www.nortel.com	Nortel
Key Witness	www.keywitness.ca	Canada
Thawte Consulting	www.thawte.com	Cape Town, ZA
US Postal Service	www.usps.gov	to be run by Cylink Corp.
VeriSign	www.verisign.com	RSA

digital certificate: a data file that contains information that uniquely identifies a person or an organization.

A **digital certificate** is a data file that contains information that uniquely identifies a person or an organization. Digital certificates are also called digital IDs or public key certificates. One of the most common forms of digital certificates are defined by an ITU standard called X.509. An example certificate is shown in Figure 14.15.

```
subjects distinguished name
        C=US, O=Werner Consulting, OU=MIS,CN=www.wernerconsulting.com

issuers distinguished name
        C=US, O=VeriSign, CN=Verisign

subjects public key (public key algorithm = RSA encryption)
        85:32:a4:c3:b8:76:9f:45:08:43:85:46:83:98:45

issuers signature (signature algorithm = md5 with RSA encryption)
        4c:9e:46:83:98:45:08:43:85:32:a4:c3:b8:76:9f

validity period
        1/1/97-12/31/98
```

Figure 14.15 Example contents of an X.509 certificate.

The fields in an X.509 certificate are listed below.

- subject's distinguished name (DN) — a name that uniquely identifies the owner of the certificate. Note that the web server domain name is used here because this is a web site certificate.

- issuer's distinguished name — a name that uniquely identifies the certificate authority that signed the certificate
- subject's public key — the owner's public key
- issuer's signature — the certificate authority's digital signature
- validity period — dates between which the certificate is valid
- serial number — a unique number generated by the certificate authority for administrative purposes.

Note that the certificate has a validity period which implies an expiration of the certificate. Some CAs may have a means of enforcing certificate revocation, in the case that you or the issuer decide to cancel the certificate prior to this expiration.

Identifying Users and Resources

distinguished name (DN): the fully qualified identification of a particular object or attribute.

X.509 certificates and other OSI functions and protocols use a concept called a **distinguished name (DN)**. In the X.509 certificate, one DN is used to identify the subject of the certificate, and another is used to identify the issuer of the certificate. What can be identified by these DNs? The origins of DNs lie in object oriented modeling.

At the top level of our model we may identify political objects — countries (Figure 14.16). Each country has a number of attributes, such as population, area, location, name, gross national product, etc. In order to identify a given country, we may use the values of some attributes which distinguish it from other countries.

Figure 14.16
The top level of the containment hierarchy contains countries. A few examples are shown here.

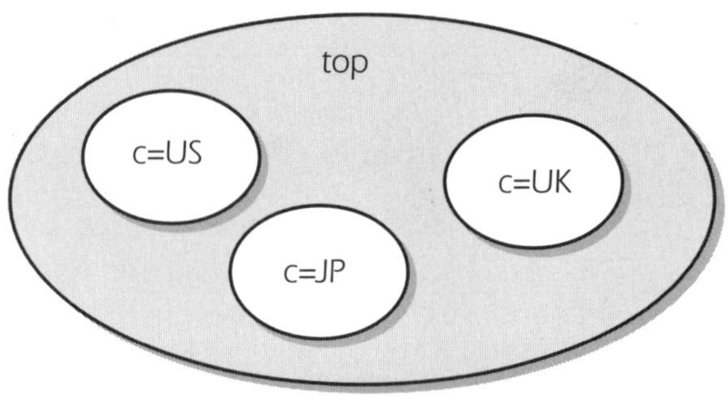

attribute value assertion (AVA): the statement of the name of a characteristic of an object and the actual value of that characteristic.

relative distinguished name (RDN): a set of one or more distinguished attributes of an object.

It would be a good idea to pick attribute values for the country which don't often change, such as the name. Luckily, the ISO has defined a number of country codes, which are two letter codes. Thus if we want to identify the country called The United States of America, we may assert that the object we're talking about is c=US, where the c is an abbreviation for country code. This **attribute value assertion (AVA)** may be used as a **relative distinguished name (RDN)** for the U.S. because it is unique relative to the other top level objects on the planet earth (the context). If we specify an object relative to the root, we turn the RDN into a fully qualified distinguished name, or simply a distinguished name (DN), such as the DN /c=US.

Let's say that you wanted to call someone on the phone. How would you use this scheme to identify a person? In the traditional world, you might look up their number in a paper-based phone book (a.k.a. directory). But what phone book do you look in? If this is a personal (i.e. residential) number, you would need to know the person's locality (i.e. city, town), which may be within a state or province within a country. Another method is to call directory assistance, and request that someone look it up for you. You'll need to give the directory operator specific information about the person you're trying to call.

If you're making a business call, you'd need the name of the organization where that person works. In many organizations, you'd need to know the division, department, or organizational unit in which they work. If we're looking up this person not by job title or role, but by common name, we'd need to specify that as well. For instance,

```
/c=US/o=Werner Consulting/ou=Engineering/cn=Brad Werner
```

would be a way to refer to a specific person. One of the attributes of that person may be their phone number. We could use a DN to look up any of this person's attributes in a directory.

Figure 14.17 shows an example of the nesting of objects within one another. The DN is simply the sequence of RDNs from the outside in. While we may call this a containment hierarchy, the word containment is used in a conceptual, not necessarily a physical sense. For countries, their name is expected to change fairly infrequently, thus the country name was chosen as the AVA for the RDN. For organizations, the name of the organization is spelled out as their RDN.

Figure 14.17
A DN is composed of the sequence of RDNs from the outside in.

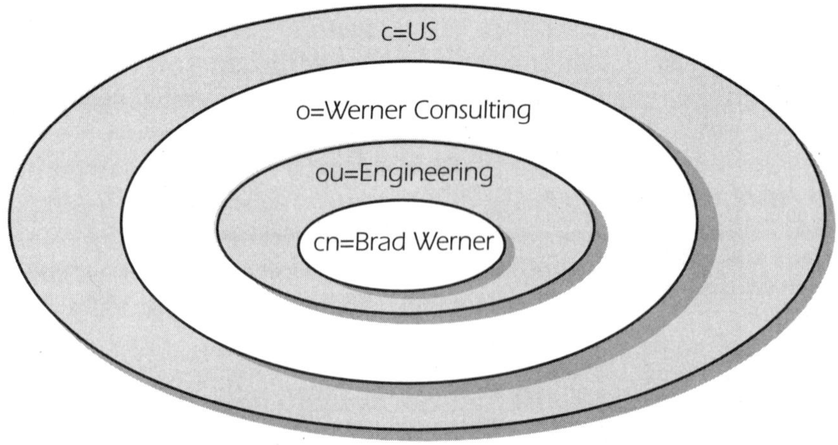

The Directory: the X.500 distributed database which maintains a reference of useful information.

A directory is being built based on the ITU's X.500 series of recommendations, called **The Directory**. But The Directory may be used to identify (and store attributes for) not only people, but also organizations, systems, computers, conceptually anything. It uses the object model and distinguished name hierarchy to identify objects. Members of the IETF are developing a Lightweight Directory Access Protocol (LDAP) for access to systems supporting the (potentially) globally distributed directory. LDAP is a method of registering and querying The Directory using Internet protocols.

Implementations of LDAP and other portions of directory services are being developed in products such as Microsoft's Active Directory.

Secure Sockets Layer (SSL) Operation

The Secure Sockets Layer (SSL) protocol was created by Netscape to provide a way to send encrypted web data over the Internet. SSL can encrypt higher-level protocols such as HTTP and FTP (Figure 14.18). In order for the client and the server to send and receive encrypted data, both sides must know the secret to decrypting the data. This is where public and private keys come in. SSL uses both symmetric key and public key cryptography to ensure data integrity and confidentiality.

Figure 14.18
The Secure Sockets Layer (SSL) protocol provides encryption and authentication between a client and server.

SSL provides three fundamental security services:

- *Message privacy,* using symmetric and public-key encryption. All traffic between an SSL client and an SSL server is encrypted using a key and encryption algorithm. The key and encryption algorithm are negotiated during the initial SSL connection setup.
- *Message integrity,* using message authentication codes. Message integrity tells the receiver if the message was tampered with after it has left the sender.
- *Mutual authentication,* using X.509 certificates. The SSL server proves its identity to the client, and (optionally) the client can prove its identity to the server. Mutual authentication occurs during the initial SSL handshake.

Note that SSL connections are slower than non-encrypted connections. Therefore, you should use SSL only for content that you desire encrypted, not necessarily for your entire site.

SSL Handshake

Each SSL connection begins with a specific sequence of packets. This sequence is called the *SSL handshake.* SSL uses TCP port 443 for incoming server connections. The following is a list of the handshake steps that occur during SSL startup (Figure 14.19).

1. The client attempts to connect to the SSL port (TCP port 443) on the web server. The client sends a client hello message to the server which provides information regarding its SSL capabilities.

2. The server sends the client its X.509 certificate. Recall that this certificate contains the server's public key. Optionally, the client sends its certificate to the server. Certificates are verified by checking the validity dates and verifying the certificate has the certification authority's correct signature. The certificate exchange is a part of the server hello sequence[8].
3. The client randomly generates a session key to be used for this connection. This session key is encrypted using the SSL server's public key (which it obtained in the previous step) and sent to the SSL server.

   After the server receives the session key, it is able to send encrypted data to the client. The client will also use the session key to encrypt data sent to the server. Thus, public key encryption is used for the key exchange and authentication, yet symmetric key encryption based on the session key is used for the application data.
4. The client and server negotiate which encryption algorithm will be used (for example, RSA encryption). Typically the client tells the server all of the algorithms that it can support in the client hello message.
5. The server selects the most secure algorithm from the list of client supported encryption algorithms, and notifies the client.

From this point on, until the teardown of the connection, all data will be encrypted and decrypted using the session key, and the encryption and MAC algorithms selected by the client and server.

8. If the server doesn't have a certificate, it may provide a key instead. Also, as a part of the server hello sequence, the server may request a certificate from the client.

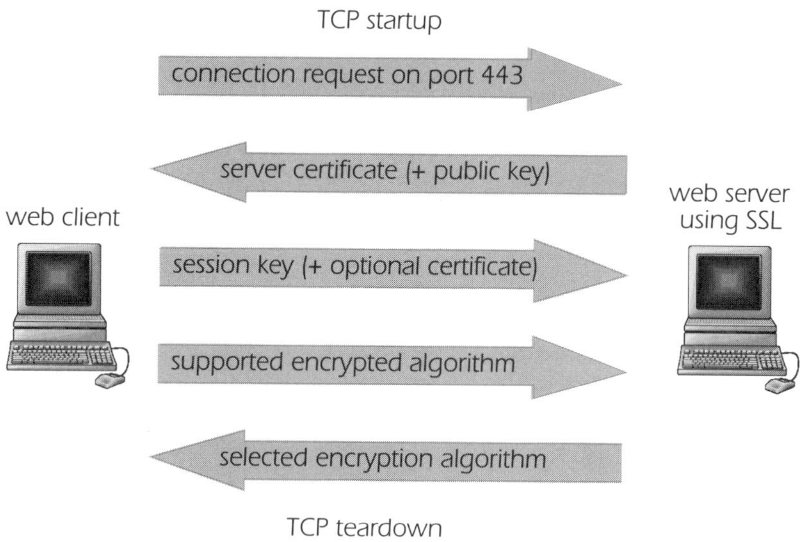

Figure 14.19
The SSL handshake involves exchanging public keys and certificates.

SSL Packet Trace

sslstartup.cap

The SSL packets in Figure 14.20 are between roadrunner (10.1.2.6) and webserver (10.1.2.8). A new directory was created on the webserver, called /private, and a default.htm file was placed in that directory. The client used the command line:

https://10.1.2.8/private

to start the SSL session. This packet capture, sslstartup.cap, shows the frames depicted in Figure 14.19 being exchanged. The address database for this capture is ssl_ch.adr.

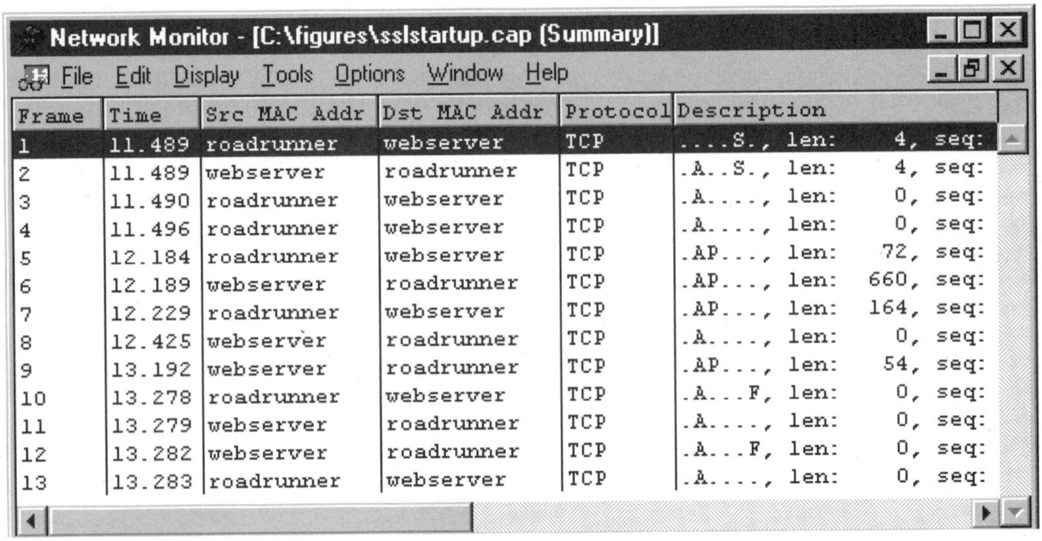

Frame	Time	Src MAC Addr	Dst MAC Addr	Protocol	Description
1	11.489	roadrunner	webserver	TCP	....S., len: 4, seq:
2	11.489	webserver	roadrunner	TCP	.A..S., len: 4, seq:
3	11.490	roadrunner	webserver	TCP	.A...., len: 0, seq:
4	11.496	roadrunner	webserver	TCP	.A...., len: 0, seq:
5	12.184	roadrunner	webserver	TCP	.AP..., len: 72, seq:
6	12.189	webserver	roadrunner	TCP	.AP..., len: 660, seq:
7	12.229	roadrunner	webserver	TCP	.AP..., len: 164, seq:
8	12.425	webserver	roadrunner	TCP	.A...., len: 0, seq:
9	13.192	webserver	roadrunner	TCP	.AP..., len: 54, seq:
10	13.278	roadrunner	webserver	TCP	.A...F, len: 0, seq:
11	13.279	webserver	roadrunner	TCP	.A...., len: 0, seq:
12	13.282	webserver	roadrunner	TCP	.A...F, len: 0, seq:
13	13.283	roadrunner	webserver	TCP	.A...., len: 0, seq:

Figure 14.20 SSL startup handshake — frames 5,6,7 & 9.

Frames one through four are the three step TCP connection handshake and a window readjustment. Frame 5 carries the client hello message. The server responds in frame 6 with the server hello along with the server certificate. Frame 7 contains the supported encryption algorithms, and frame 9 is the server informing the client which encryption algorithm to use.

When you use a protocol analyzer to decode an SSL session, you of course will not be able to decrypt the data. Unfortunately Network Monitor doesn't decode the SSL startup packets, or identify those packets as SSL.

IIS Management

Recall that Chapter 12, "Internet Access Using Proxy Server", covered the operation of HTTP. The remainder of this chapter focuses on the security features of IIS, including implementing SSL.

Configuring IIS 4.0 Using the Microsoft Management Console

The application used to configure the web server in version 3.0 of IIS is called the Internet Service Manager. In IIS version 4.0, the functionality found in ISM is now available though the IIS snap-in for the Microsoft Management Console (MMC). Shown in Figure 14.21 is the management console for IIS 4.0.

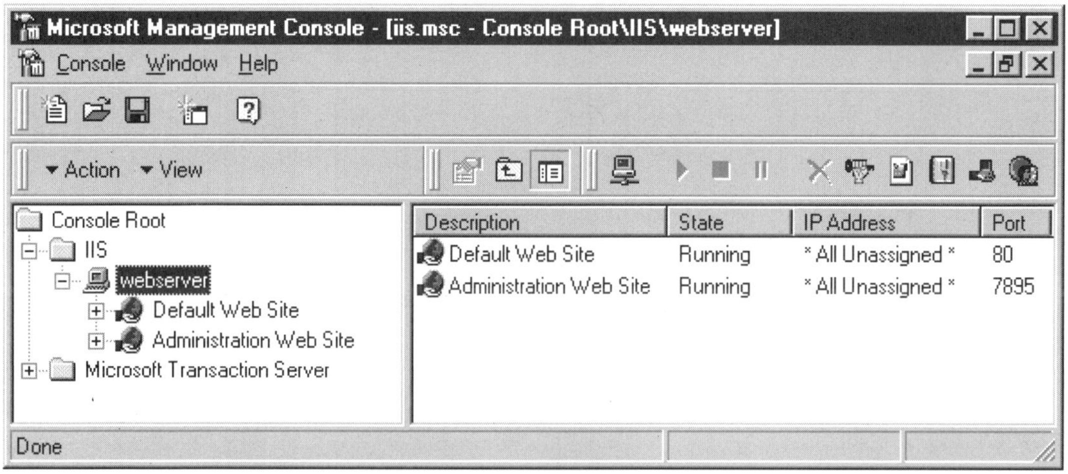

Figure 14.21 IIS is configured using the IIS snap-in for the Microsoft Management Console.

The directories in Figure 14.22 are the directories that will be used to store the HTML files for the Default Web Server. The full path is shown on the left, and the alias is shown on the right.

Notice that there are two web sites on this machine. The default web site, as well as the Administration web site. The Administration web site is used by remote administrators to manage the web server using their browser. In order to connect to the administration web site, HTTP requests must go to port 7895.

The file default.htm, found in the Inetpub\wwwroot directory, is the default file that will be displayed if users do not specify a file on the browser URL line.

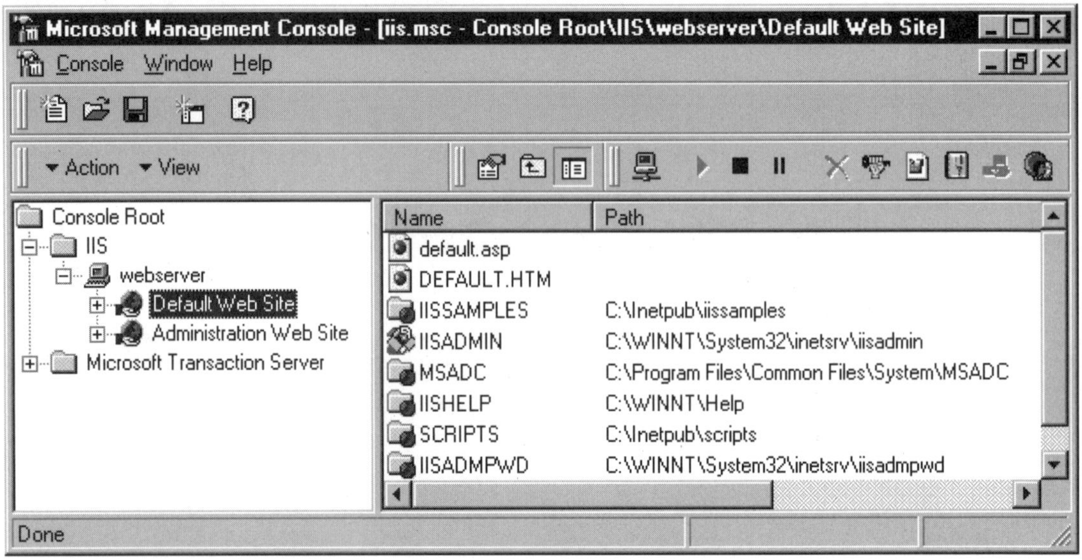

Figure 14.22 The web page directories and their aliases are shown when selecting the web site name. Shown here are the aliases and directories that are created when IIS is installed.

IIS Security Checks

There are a series of security tests that any incoming IIS request must pass before access is granted. The four conditions that are checked are:

1. IP address — Is a request from the source IP address permitted?
2. username — Is a request from this username permitted?
3. directory access — Do IIS permission allow access?
4. NTFS file/folder access — Do NTFS permissions allow access?

If any of these checks fail, access is denied to that client.

IIS Anonymous User

When IIS is installed, a new user account is created on the local server, even if the machine is a member of a domain. This account will be used by incoming Web and anonymous FTP connections. The default account name contains the machine's current computer name, and is preceded by the letters *IUSR_*. Therefore the format of the anonymous username is:

IUSR_MACHINENAME

For the example in Figure 14.23, the anonymous account is called IUSR_WEBSERVER, since Webserver is the name of the machine. Note that the anonymous logon user account must be a valid NT user account on the web server, and it must have the *Log on Locally* right. (Don't give it any other rights!)

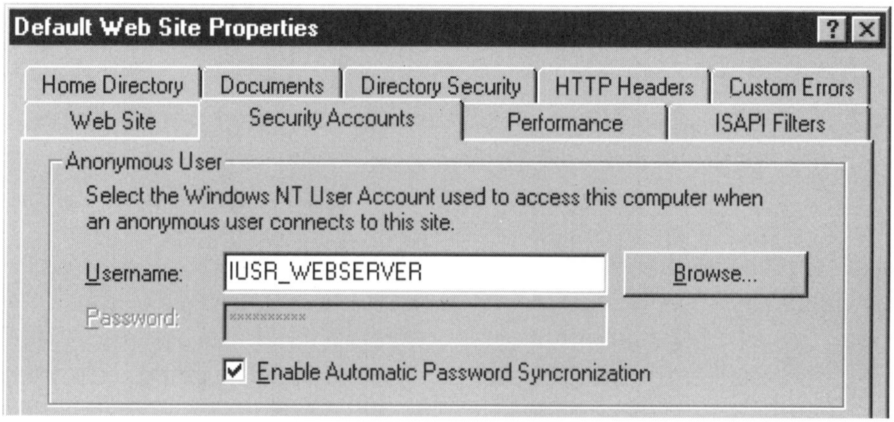

Figure 14.23 The Web Site Properties screen, Security Accounts tab is used to configure the NT user account that will be used when the web user is trying to access NTFS files.

When the account is created, it is created with a randomly generated password, which no one will know. Thus no one will be able to log into the machine locally using IUSR_MACHINENAME account since they will not know the password. Only the FTP and web services will have access to that account. In IIS 3.0, if you wanted to change the anonymous account password, you had to change it in two places — the ISM configuration screen, and User Manager. Now in IIS 4.0 you can synchronize the passwords between IIS and User Manager using the checkbox *Enable Automatic Password Synchronization.*

Upon creation, the IUSR_MACHINENAME account is added to the Guests group. So be careful if you change settings to that group, as they affect the anonymous account as well.

NT Challenge Response

Before we discuss NT challenge/response, the Security Accounts Manager (SAM) needs to be described. SAM is an NT process that maintains all the user and group accounts. SAM stores user account information in the SAM database. Thus the SAM database contains all user IDs, passwords, and other user account information.

For user account verification, there are two scenarios that are possible:

- SAM database exists on local machine.
- SAM database exists on remote machine (the domain controller).

Local User Authentication

Local user authentication occurs when the user is logging in to a local account- a user account found in the SAM database of the local machine. This also occurs when the local machine is a Primary Domain Controller (PDC) or Backup Domain Controller (BDC). In local user authentication, the LSA[9] encrypts the user/password information and contacts SAM for account verification. SAM returns to LSA the user ID and group IDs. This is shown in Figure 14.24.

9. Local Security Authority (LSA) is the process used during logon that creates the user's shell.

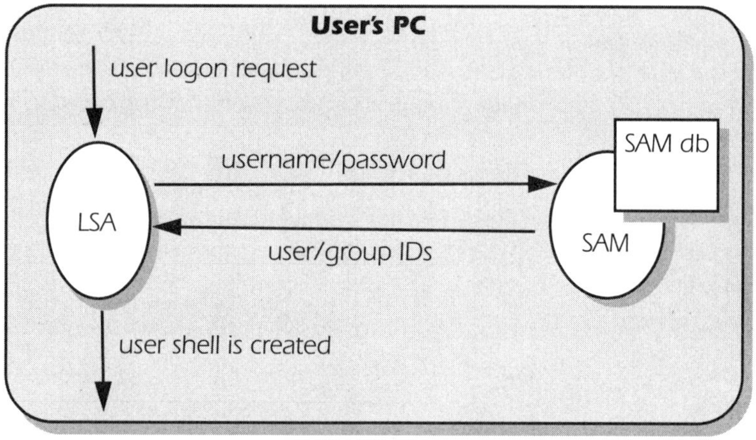

Figure 14.24 Logon using a local user account.

User Authentication using a Remote SAM Database

User authentication using a remote SAM database is performed when the client machine is part of a Microsoft domain. In this scenario, the PDCs and the BDCs contain the SAM database. The method that is used to verify the account validity is called NT Challenge-Response.

NT Challenge-Response[10] is a sequence of packets that are exchanged between a client workstation and a server. These packets are used to authenticate the client. Figure 14.25 illustrates these packets. The following describes those steps:

1. The user enters the username and password at the client machine. A login request message is sent to the domain controller, containing only the username.
2. The domain controller sends back a 16-byte challenge message which it has just generated. The challenge message is unique from one login request to the next.
3. The client receives this challenge, and combines that message with the encrypted password to create the response message.

10. NT Challenge/Response is also called **NTLM**.

4. The domain controller receives the client response. The original challenge message is combined with the encrypted password (from the SAM database) to create the expected response message. The domain controller compares the received response with the calculated response, and if the two match, the login is successful. If they don't match, the user cannot log in. The login status is then sent back to the client machine.

Figure 14.25
Challenge response packets.

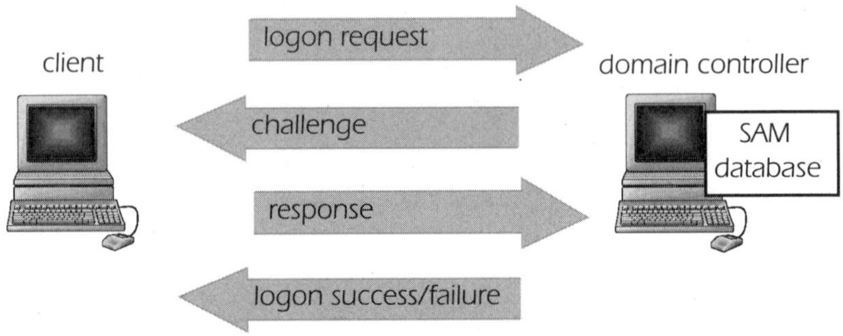

We can combine Figure 14.24 with Figure 14.25 to obtain the detailed NT command/response packet sequence shown in Figure 14.26. Notice there is a new process involved: the netlogon process.

The netlogon process runs on every NT computer that is part of a domain. For each logon request, the netlogon process:

- Sets up a secure channel with a domain controller.
- Exchanges the challenge/response packets.
- Tears down the secure channel.

After the LSA receives the user and group IDs, it then creates the user's access token and shell.

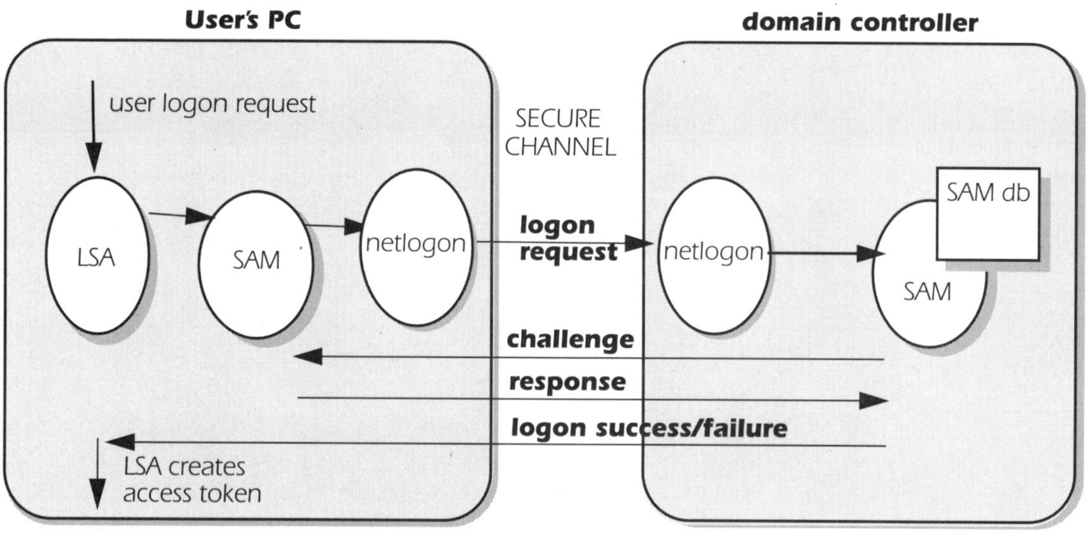

Figure 14.26 Logon to an account found on the domain controller

Controlling IIS Access by User or Group

With IIS 4.0, there are multiple ways to authenticate the user. The screen used to configure authentication methods is brought up using the *Directory Security tab* in the *Web Site Properties* screen (Figure 14.27).

Figure 14.27 Press Edit to bring up the screen to configure IIS user authentication.

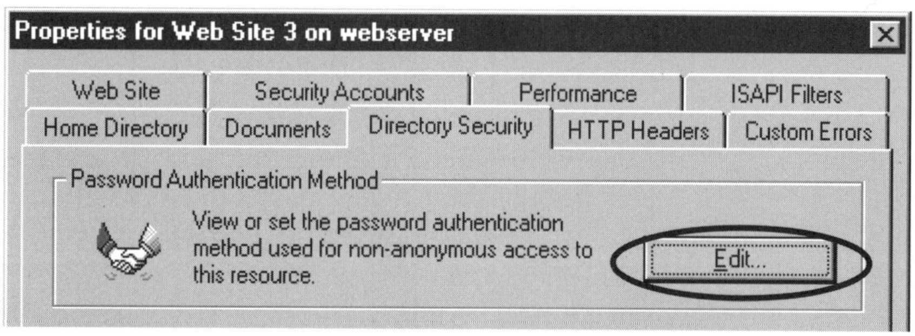

Pressing Edit results in the screen shown in Figure 14.28.

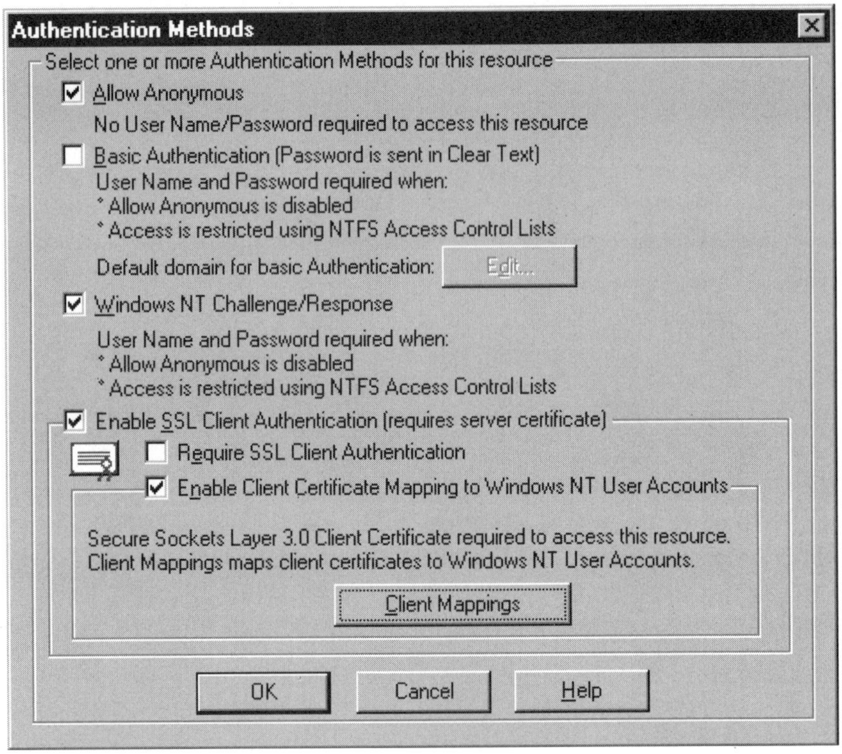

Figure 14.28 The possible methods for password authentication are shown here.

Notice in Figure 14.28 that there are multiple authentication methods possible. These methods are described below.

- Allow anonymous— This was discussed in the section "IIS Anonymous User" on page 547.
- Basic authentication — The username and password is sent in clear text. The security problem with basic authentication is that the username and password can be captured by a protocol analyzer attached to the LAN. The user will have to have a valid name and password on the web server (a local NT account) in order to view the web pages.
- NT Challenge/Response authentication— The clear-text password is never sent over the network, and thus this authentication is more secure. Again, the user will have to have a valid name and password on the local web server in order to view the web pages.

- Enable SSL client authentication— Clients can use their X.509 certificate to authenticate with the web server. Client certificates can be mapped to NT user accounts using the *Client Mappings* button.

Configuring IIS to Use Multiple IP Addresses

Assume that you already have a web server set up, as was shown in Figure 14.21 on page 545. Now the engineering department wants their own web site. Rather than buy another machine, use the current company web server, but make it look like it is an independent web server. What is needed is a web server setup as shown in Figure 14.29.

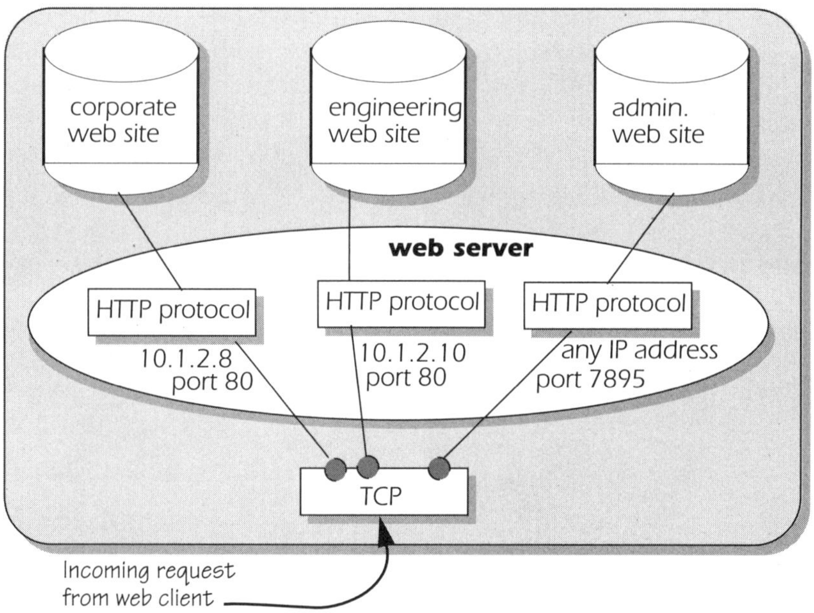

Figure 14.29 The one web server handles three web sites, distinguished by the IP address and port number to which the requests are destined.

IIS supports several web sites on the same web server. This is useful not only for internal web sites, but also for providing web sites for other organizations (e.g. if you run an ISP). If the traffic load increases to the point where you need a dedicated box for the web site, there is minimal disruption in moving the web site at that time.

The first step toward creating a virtual web server for the engineering department is to add another IP address to the existing NIC. *Network Control Panel -> TCP/IP Properties->Advanced IP Addressing* screen is used to configure additional IP addresses (Figure 14.30). For our webserver, there are now two IP addresses bound to the NIC: 10.1.2.8 and 10.1.2.10.

Figure 14.30 Configuring multiple IP addresses on one NIC.

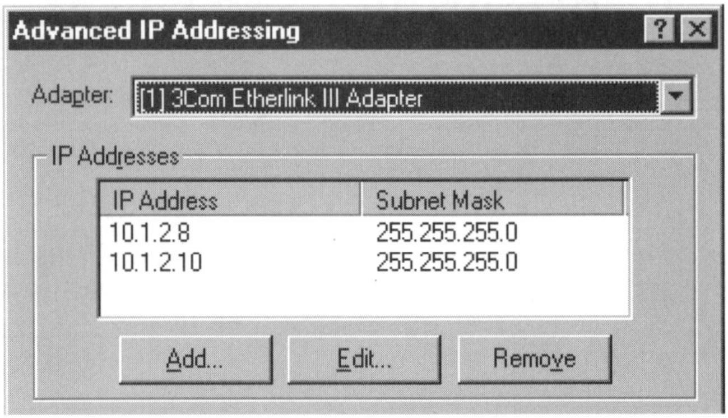

Next, use the IIS plug-in to MMC to add the engineering web site to the web server. Figure 14.31 shows the property dialog for the default web site, which we'll continue to use for the corporate web information. Use this dialog to select the address for the corporate web site. In our example, the address to be chosen is 10.1.2.8. This will cause the web server to respond to calls to the corporate web site at this address.

Figure 14.31 Selecting the IP address for which this web site responds

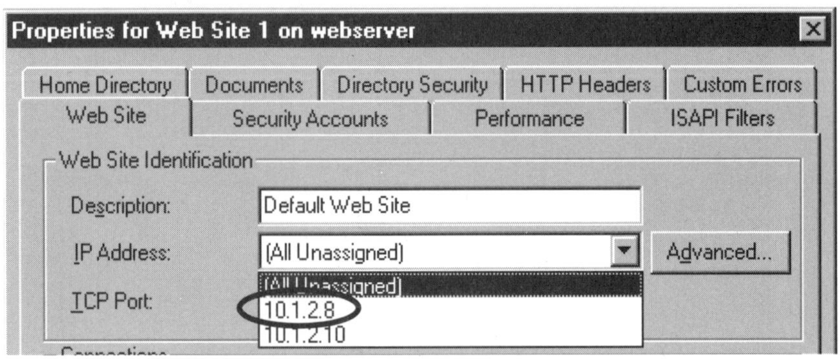

Now the engineering web site may be added. Use the pop-up menu option from the MMC IIS dialog shown in Figure 14.32. This will start the *New Web Site Wizard*.

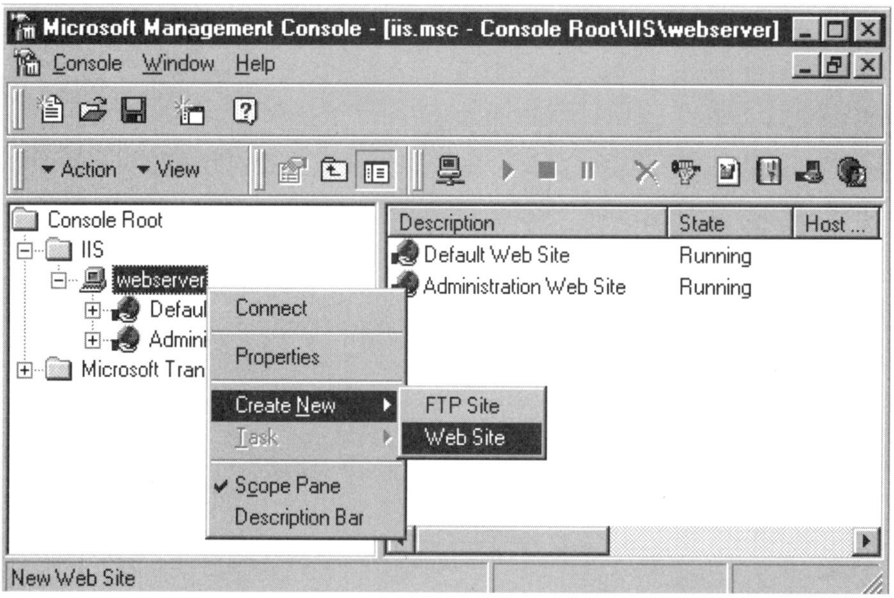

Figure 14.32 Use this pop-up menu to create a new web site.

Figure 14.33 shows the first dialog of the wizard, in which the IP address for the engineering web site, 10.1.2.10 is selected. When the web server receives HTTP requests with 10.1.2.10 as the target IP address, the requests will be referred to the engineering web site. As we had configured back in Figure 14.31, requests with 10.1.2.8 as the target IP address will be referred to the corporate web site.

Figure 14.33 Creating a new web site — selecting the IP address.

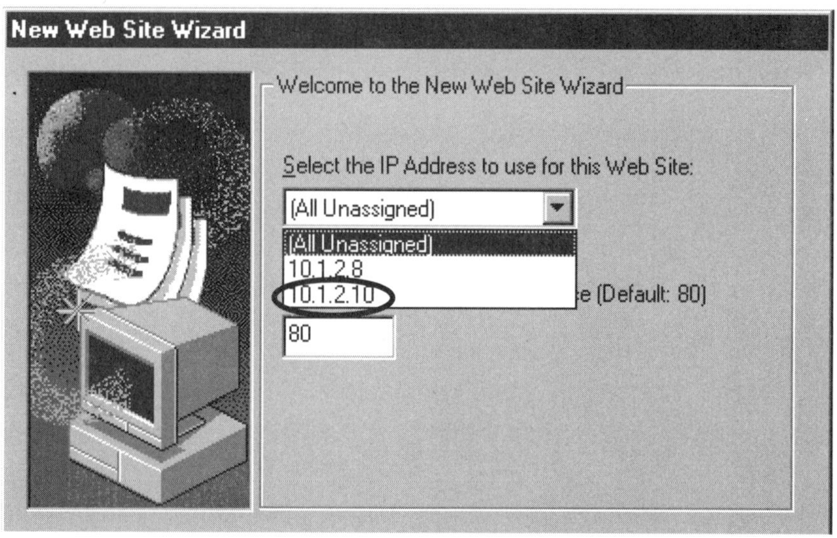

In order to have several web sites on the same web server, each must have its own root directory. Figure 14.34 shows the path which is used for our engineering web site.

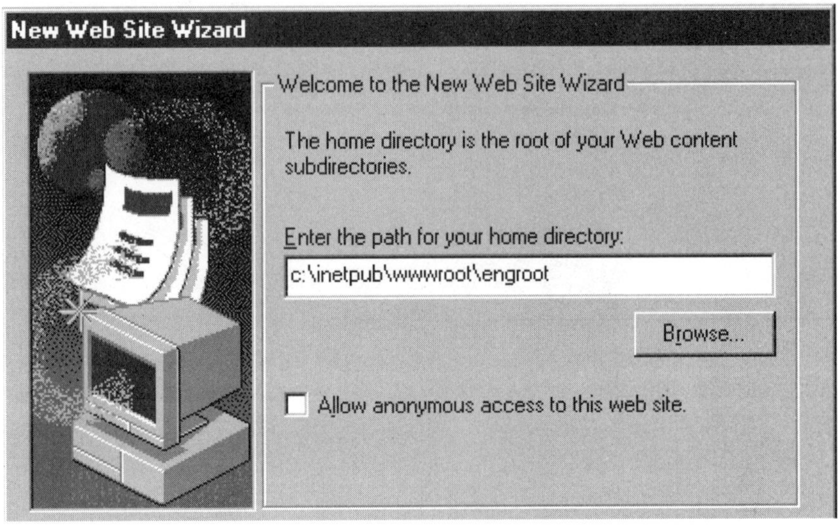

Figure 14.34 The root directory of the web site is entered.

Figure 14.35 shows the resultant paths to the web site data files. Notice the paths to the default (corporate) web site and engineering web site are under c:\Inetpub\wwwroot, which is the default directory when IIS is installed. The files for the Administration web site are in WINNT\System32\inetsrv\iisadmin.

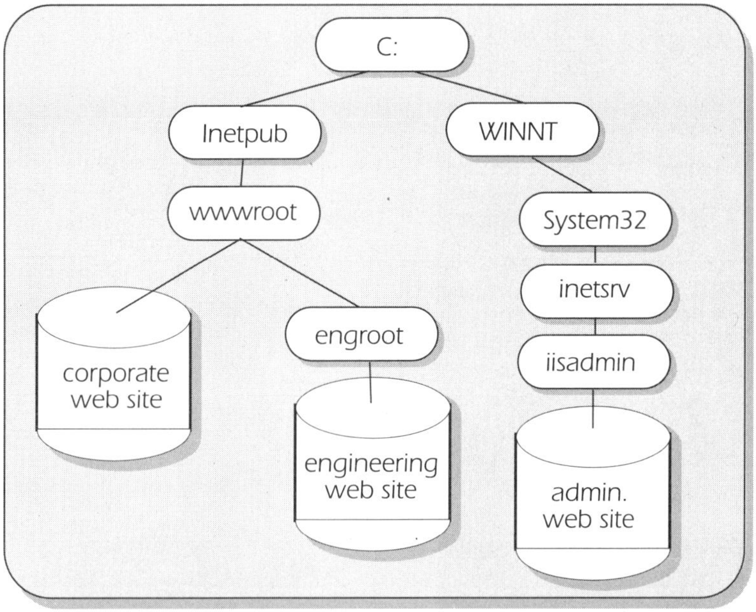

Figure 14.35 Each web site fits into the directory tree of the web server according to IIS configuration.

Because we only want clients to view information from the engineering server, we've selected only read access in the dialog shown in Figure 14.36

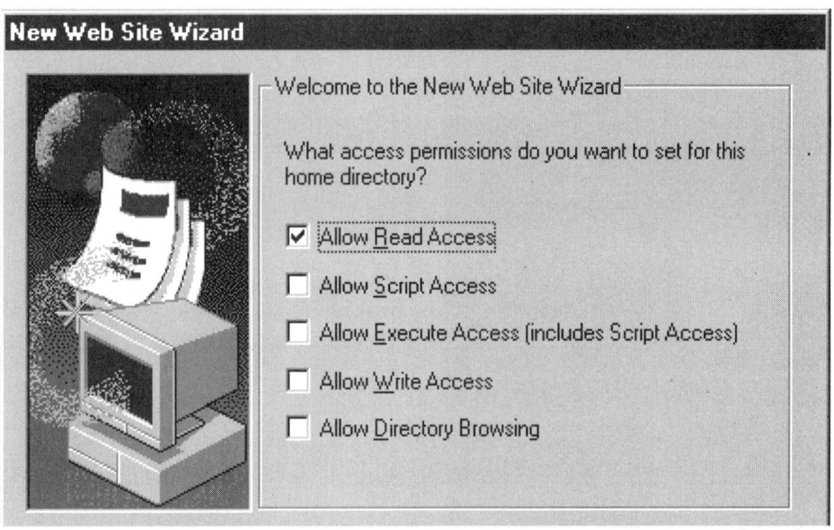

Figure 14.36 Permissions on the root directory of the web site are established with this dialog.

After we've finished adding the new engineering web site, the main dialog of the MMC IIS plug-in shows all three web sites on this server (Figure 14.37). Detailed configuration information for each web site may be obtained by selecting the web site of interest and using the properties item in the pop-up menu.

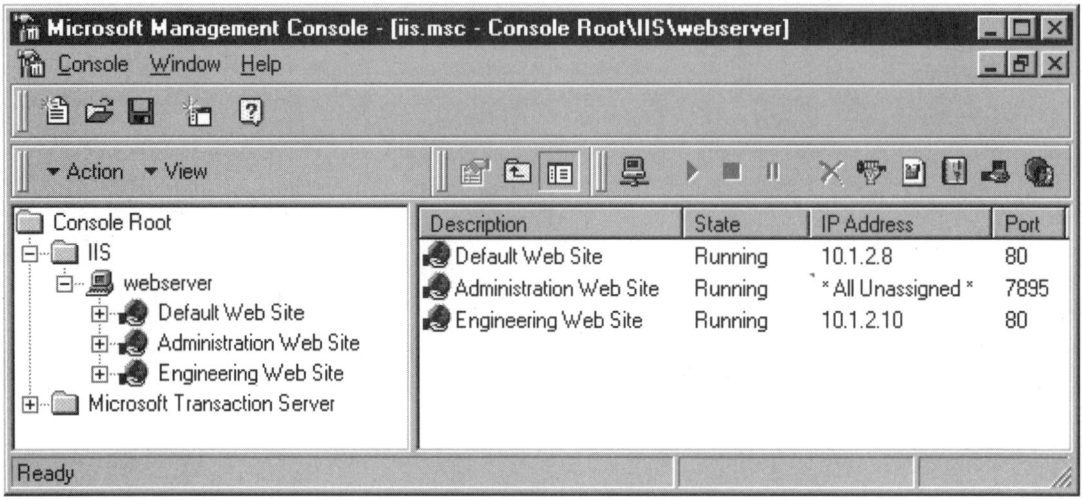

Figure 14.37 Three web sites are running on the web server.

We now have the following configuration.

- Default corporate web server on IP address 10.1.2.8 (Figure 14.38).
- Engineering web server on IP address 10.1.2.10 (Figure 14.39).

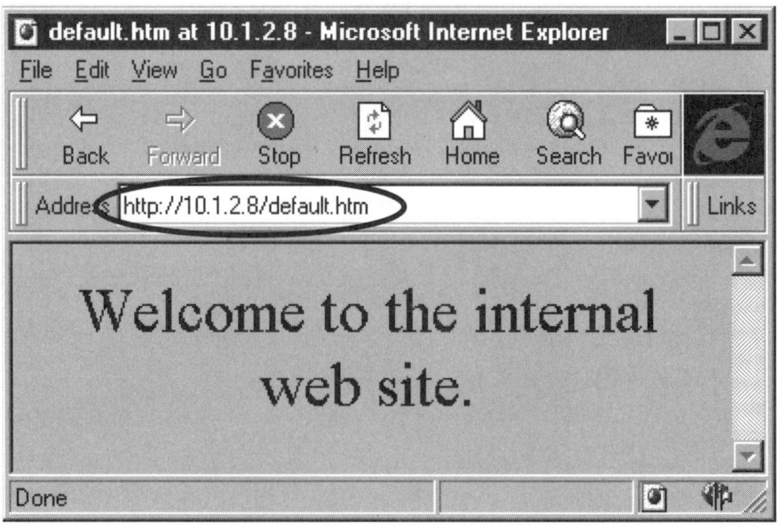

Figure 14.38 Testing access to the corporate web site.

In Figure 14.39, access to the new engineering web site shows that indeed, a different root directory is used for that virtual server.

Figure 14.39
Testing access to the new engineering web site.

Another typical configuration step at this point is to assign a useful domain name to the IP address 10.1.2.10. Configure that name and IP address in the DNS server for the organization.

Steps to Enable SSL on IIS

Now that the engineering web site has been established, normal access with HTTP may be disabled, and clients can be forced to use the Secure Socket Layer (SSL) to access that web site. The corporate web site will be unaffected, because the two sites are independently configured.

The following are the four steps required to configure IIS to use SSL for data transmission:

1. Generate a key pair file and certificate request file using Key Manager.
2. Request a certificate from a certificate authority.
3. Install the certificate on your IIS server.
4. Activate SSL security on WWW directories that you select.

Key Manager icon

Each of these steps will be described shortly. But first, bring up the Key Manager application (Figure 14.40). Key Manager can be obtained by pressing the Key Manager icon button in the MMC IIS tool bar.

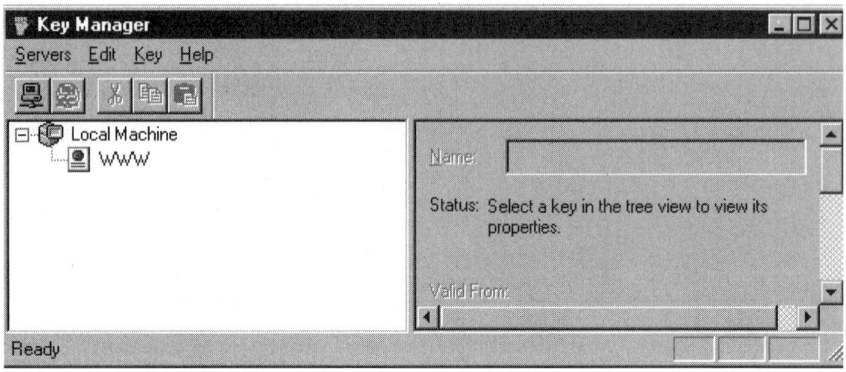

Figure 14.40
The Key Manager may be used to configure SSL keys to use in IIS.

Step 1: Creating a New Key and Certificate Request

From the *Key Manager -> Key* menu, select *Create New Key.* The *Create New Key Wizard* will appear. You will be asked to enter the following information:

- request file name
- key name
- password
- key bit length
- organization name (O)
- organizational unit (OU)
- web server fully-qualified domain name (CN)
- country (C)
- state (ST)
- locality (L)
- your name and email address

This information will then be stored in the request file you specified. When you enter the requested information in the dialog, you may want to record certain parameters. For instance, the password will be needed again when the reply comes back from the CA.

Figure 14.41 shows the DN of the X.509 certificate that was generated using this last step. Compare this with the contents of the certificate request, as shown in Figure 14.42.

Figure 14.41 The DN of the X.509 certificate.

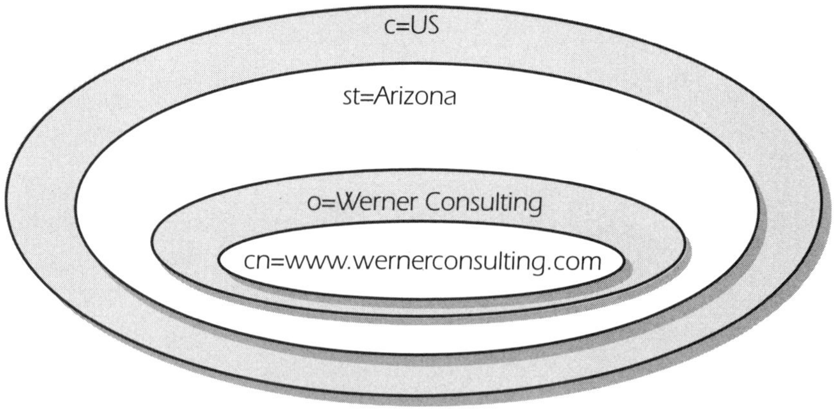


```
Webmaster: brad@wernerconsulting.com
Phone:
Server: Microsoft Key Manager for IIS 4.0

Common-name: www.wernerconsulting.com
Organization Unit:
Organization: Werner Consulting
Locality: Phoenix
State: Arizona
Country: US

-----BEGIN NEW CERTIFICATE REQUEST-----
MIIBrzCCARgCAQAwcDELMAkGA1UEBhMCVVMxEDAOBgNVBAgTB0FyaXpvbmExEDAO
BgNVBAcTB1Bob2VuaXgxGjAYBgNVBAoTEVdlcm5lciBDb25zdWx0aW5nMSEwHwYD
VQQDFBh3d3cud2VybmVyY29uc3VsdGluZy5jb20wgZ4wDQYJKoZIhvcNAQEBBQAD
gYwAMIGIAoGAahOW9rJ2HdVB8VbhyxjtFK4OLnAIBJ/p9MTNNa2Cu9VXG6alY/PF
0Cplz+FYQIGb1BudIbkbIDLVPz4IWtcTns0vDSaXvvJzvkOnuf2wn4zaC7mqhLht
HTmCCbeC03Cty91EjxuRftEhQWMa1SDtJWt1aGG3Moa2UrWeG4KRuS8CAwEAAaAA
MA0GCSqGSIb3DQEBBAUAA4GBABgZYxaElOJs5aGJQIrkwkcVKZzR4rJYIrZuNlYR
VWSiGJvwMgPhdHVbh8CV7n94ZFzUHQfD4luo0vDXUCkEv27XbBo547GWnDFCo8kv
9xwe2TwfyAouaHsjfWoCNIpHQ9Yz8N2zcGw2IERO0pxK86rOEQ7CTLh1F94vsXpa
-----END NEW CERTIFICATE REQUEST-----
```

Figure 14.42 Contents of certificate request file.

Note that the keys you generated are only valid on that particular web server. If you have more than one web server, you must obtain additional certificates.

Step 2: Send the Request to a Certificate Authority

Take the request file that was created in the previous step and send it to a certificate authority. Recall that Table 14.1 on page 537 listed a few public CAs.

If you choose to obtain your certificate from VeriSign, for instance, connect to their web site to obtain detailed instructions. Organizational certificates and personal certificates are available for a fee[11] on an annual basis.

After a few days of processing, you will receive a certificate back by email, signed by the CA. You then use Key Manager to install the certificate on the server (see the next step.)

Standard formats have been specified for the certificate request and reply messages so that you may choose a CA independent of your choice of web server or browser. The format of the certificate request is a PKCS #10 message.[12] The reply is a PKCS #7 message.

Step 3: Install Certificate Using Key Manager

When the certificate authority sends you your web server certificate, it will look similar to Figure 14.43.

11. Annual fees may be in the range of hundreds of dollars for an organizational certificate, and tens of dollars for a personal certificate. The prices may change over the coming years as the popularity of electronic transactions increases.
12. Public Key Cryptography Standards (PKCS) define various aspects of public key security. Documents on PKCS can be found at www.rsa.com.

```
-----BEGIN CERTIFICATE-----
MIICVjCCAgACEHCoZK5Wmx3j9SNy8s+eISUwDQYJKoZIhvcNAQEEBQAwgakxFjAU
BgNVBAoTDVZlcmlTaWduLCBJbmMxRzBFBgNVBAsTPnd3dy52ZXJpc2lnbi5jb20v
cmVwb3NpdG9yeS9UZXN0Q1BTIEluY29ycC4gQnkgUmVmLiBMaWFiLiBMVEQuMUYw
RAYDVQQLEz1Gb3IgVmVyaVNpZ24gYXV0aG9yaXplZCB0ZXN0aW5nIG9ubHkuIE5v
IGFzc3VyYW5jZXMgKEMpVlMxOTk3MB4XDTk3MDkwNjAwMDAwMFoXDTk3MDkyMDIz
NTk1OVowcDELMAkGA1UEBhMCVVMxEDAOBgNVBAgTB0FyaXpvbmExEDAOBgNVBAcU
B1Bob2VuaXgxGjAYBgNVBAoUEVdlcm5lciBDb25zdWx0aW5nMSEwHwYDVQQDFBh3
d3cud2VybmVyY29uc3VsdGluZy5jb20wgZ4wDQYJKoZIhvcNAQEBBQADgYwAMIGI
AoGAahOW9rJ2HdVB8VbhyxjtFK4OLnAIBJ/p9MTNNa2Cu9VXG6alY/PF0Cplz+FY
QIGb1BudIbkbIDLVPz4IWtcTns0vDSaXvvJzvkOnuf2wn4zaC7mqhLhtHTmCCbeC
03Cty91EjxuRftEhQWMa1SDtJWt1aGG3Moa2UrWeG4KRuS8CAwEAATANBgkqhkiG
9w0BAQQFAANBAGyBAyeaol77PCWi8COqOWNfYNJ+dTjqyhv5QZuuy1VeO1i7+96U
M+zPtqjUPU/rX63k7oxihr0v1t2fS/Rbds8=
-----END CERTIFICATE-----
```


Figure 14.43 Certificate reply from a certificate authority.

Use the *Install Key Certificate* option in Key Manager, as shown in Figure 14.44, to install the key you received. The Key Manager will store the information in the registry.

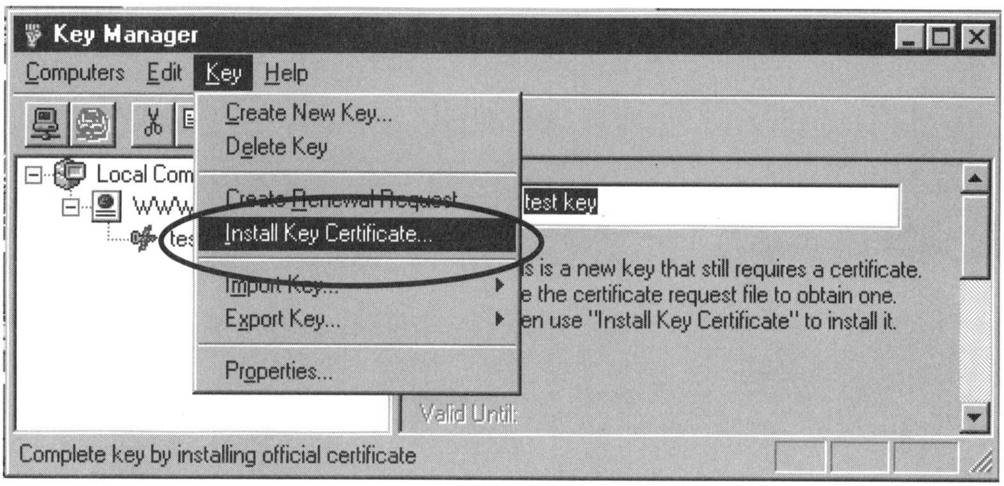

Figure 14.44 Installing a certificate once the certificate reply has been received.

You're then asked what server to apply the certificate to. Notice that in Figure 14.45, the engineering web site (10.1.2.10) is selected. After key installation, SSL can now be used by that web site.

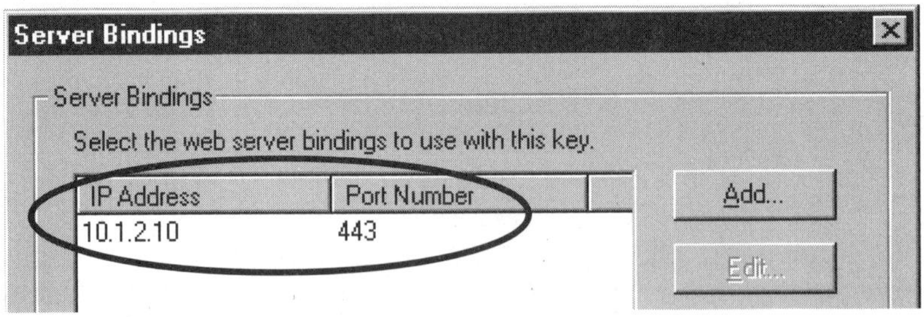

Figure 14.45 Selecting a server to enable SSL upon.

In our case, the engineering web site is for internal use only. If your SSL activity is only internal, and your organization is fairly large, and you have experience with certificate authority operations, you may consider setting up your own internal CA server. Certificate server software can be obtained from various companies, including Netscape and Microsoft.

Keep a copy of the key reply. It is also a very good idea to back up the key to a floppy disk. Use *Key Manager -> Export Key -> Backup File* to write a copy of the certificate to disk. Make sure to keep the password that goes with that certificate in a safe place as well.

Verify that the information displayed in the Key Manager is correct. In Figure 14.46, a test certificate is displayed.

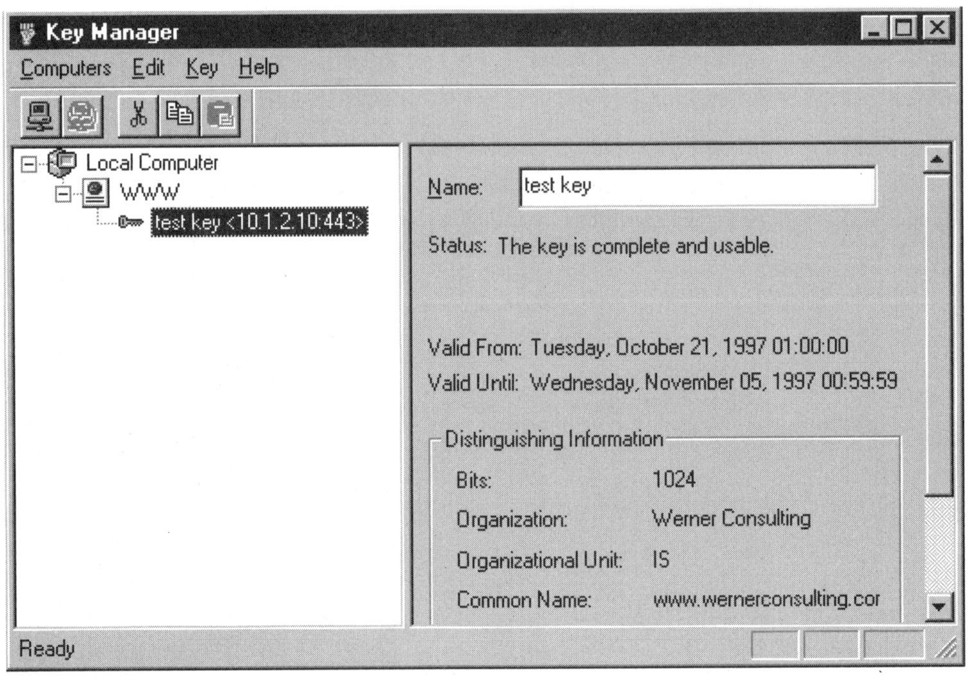

Figure 14.46 A test key has been successfully installed.

Step 4: Select the Directories Which Will Use SSL

Once the server certificate has been installed, directories can be enabled to use SSL. In the IIS management console, select the web server and directory that you want to configure to use SSL. Bring up the *Properties* screen for that directory. Under the *Directory Security tab*, edit the *Secure Communications* settings. (Alternately you may specify the directory security settings for the root of a web site.) The dialog shown in Figure 14.47 will appear.

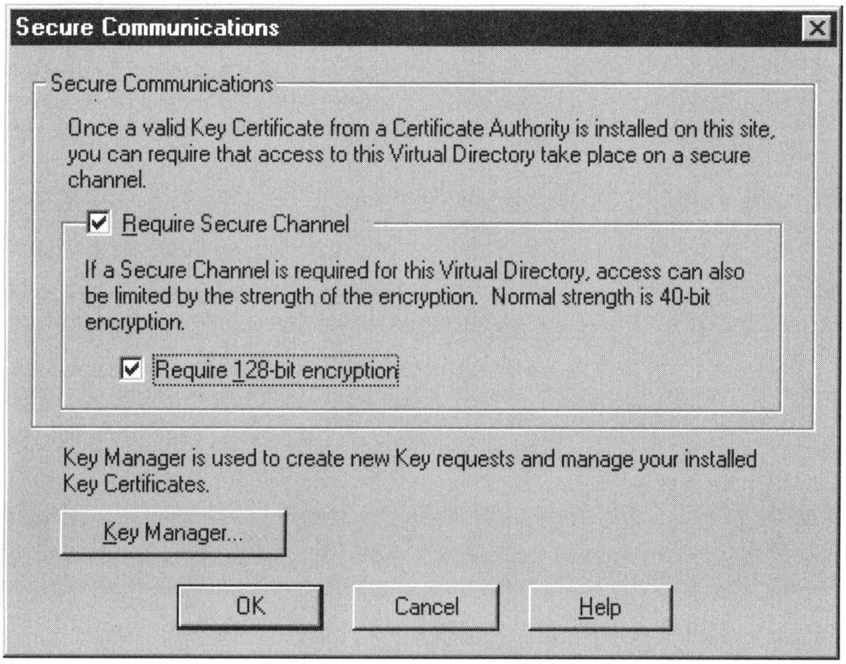

Figure 14.47 Use of 128 bit encryption is recommended whenever possible, as 40 bit encryption is now considered fairly weak.

Check the box *Require Secure Channel* to enable SSL for that directory. Also, use of strong encryption (128-bit) may be required of the web site clients if the second check box is checked. Otherwise, strong encryption is optional, at the discretion of the client. Once a directory has been marked as SSL, the only way for clients to access that directory is by using SSL. Connection requests to a URL beginning with "http://" will not work any longer, clients must use "https://". For example, if the engineering web site requires SSL, this site may only be accessed with the URL "https://10.1.2.10".

Security

There is a problem in the way in which we have configured the engineering web site such that when we supposedly made it secure with SSL, we left open a back door.

Recall the directory structure of the web server shown in Figure 14.35 on page 557. The wwwroot directory contains the engroot directory. While access to the engroot directory is now protected with SSL for the 10.1.2.10 web site, the 10.1.2.8 web site is rooted with plain old HTTP access to the wwwroot directory and its contents, including engroot. Thus, engroot may be accessed with SSL as https://10.1.2.10 or without SSL as http://10.1.2.8/engroot! Be careful when planning your virtual servers so that one web site does not "contain" another.

Testing SSL Access

The web server for foobar.com now has the default web site on IP address 10.1.2.8. Also, the engineering web site is using IP address 10.1.2.10 with SSL-only access (assuming we close the back-door by moving the directory to a different location).

Figure 14.48 shows a failed access attempt to the engineering web site, since https is not used in the URL. A successful access of the engineering web site using SSL is displayed in Figure 14.49.

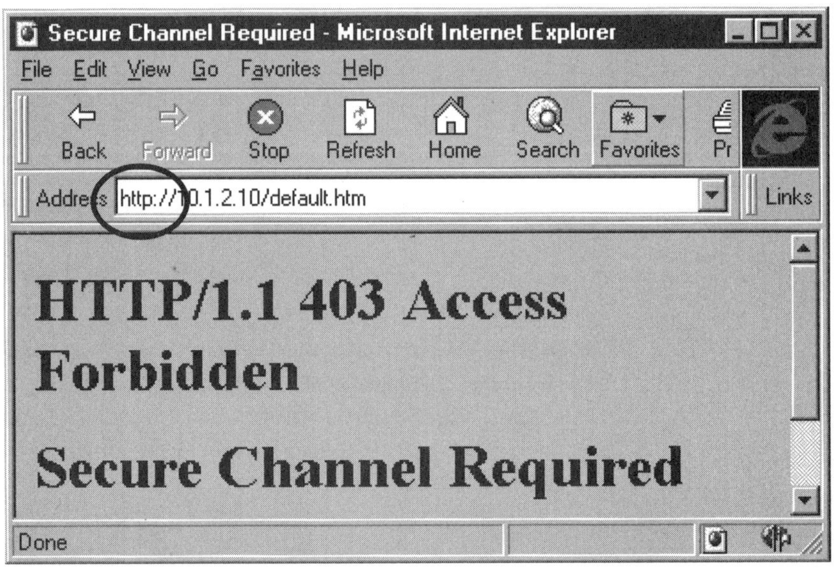

Figure 14.48 Attempted insecure access to a secure web site.

Figure 14.49
Secure access with https to the engineering web site.

This kind of brief test should only be the first steps which you should take when testing if SSL is doing its job. Check subdirectories and aliases under the root directory of the web site. Also, check for methods of access without use of SSL, such as the bad design of the directory structure for the engineering web site in our example.

Summary

Here is a brief summary of the items addressed in this chapter.

- Three aspects of security are privacy, integrity and authenticity.
- Three schemes of cryptography may be used:
  - Symmetric (secret) key cryptography
  - Asymmetric (public) key cryptography
  - Hybrid key cryptography (public key with a secret session key)

- NT Challenge/Response is a method use to authenticate NT users. It involves the server sending a challenge message to the client, and the client using the challenge to encrypt the password to be sent over the network.
- Key Manager is used to create and install certificates to enable SSL on IIS.
- Secure Sockets Layer (SLL) is a protocol used to encrypt web data. SSL creates a TCP connection on port 443 for HTTP.

Further Reading

Here is information about various books and magazines in which to look for further information on the subject.

[Berners-Lee1996] Berners-Lee, T., Fielding, R., Frystyk, H., *Hypertext Transfer Protocol – HTTP/1.0,* 1996, IETF RFC 1945

[Huitema1996] Huitema, Christian, *IPv6: The New Internet Protocol,* 1996, Prentice Hall

[Kaliski1992] Kaliski, B., *The MD2 Message-Digest Algorithm,* 1992, IETF RFC 1319

[Kaufman1995] Kaufman, Charlie, Perlman, Radia, Speciner, Mike, *Network Security — Private Communication in a Public World,* 1995, Prentice-Hall

[Rivest1992a] Rivest, R., *The MD4 Message-Digest Algorithm,* 1992, IETF RFC 1320

[Rivest1992b] Rivest, R., *The MD5 Message-Digest Algorithm,* 1992, IETF RFC 1321

[Rubin1997] Rubin, Aviel D., Geer, Daniel, and Ranum, Marcus J., *Web Security Sourcebook — A Complete Guide to Web Security Threats and Solutions,* 1997 Wiley

[Schneier1996] Schneier, Bruce, *Applied Cryptography: Protocols, Algorithms, and Source Code in C,* 1996, Wiley

15

DHCP

Chapter 5, "Installing and Configuring TCP/IP on NT," showed the steps needed to configure a Windows NT machine to be a part of a TCP/IP network. Using that manual (a.k.a. static) configuration method, you would have to physically visit each machine in the network and repeat the configuration procedure. Consider the following:

- Do users in your network move from one office to another?
- Does your network experience any growth?
- Do you sometimes change default router, WINS server, or DNS server addresses?
- Are new machines used temporarily in your network?

Manually configuring each machine in your network can become a tedious and time consuming process. Several techniques may be used to automate the configuration process. A common trait of these techniques is that each time a computer starts up, it will request an IP address and other configuration information.

Methods of IP Address Assignment

There are three protocols that can be used to automatically assign IP addresses to devices running TCP/IP. These protocols are called Reverse Address Resolution Protocol (RARP), Bootstrap Protocol (BootP), and Dynamic Host Configuration Protocol (DHCP). Let's examine each of these methods.

Reverse Address Resolution Protocol (RARP)

Reverse Address Resolution Protocol (RARP) is used to answer incoming requests for IP address assignment. These RARP requests contain the MAC address of the requesting client. The requests are answered by a RARP server, which contains a configuration file of mappings. The mappings are from MAC address to IP address (Figure 15.1).

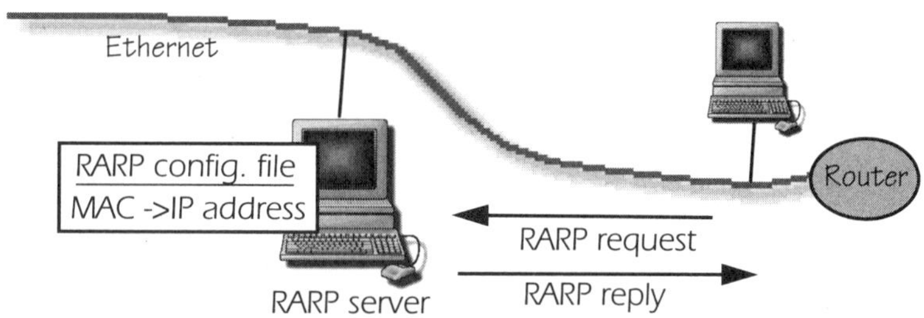

Figure 15.1 A RARP server assigns IP addresses based upon the requestor's MAC address.

One drawback of RARP is that the RARP configuration file must be updated whenever machines are added to the network. Another problem is that the client requests are sent as an MAC-layer broadcast; therefore the packets will not pass though routers. Additionally, the only configuration information supplied to the client is the IP address. Other parameters, such as a subnet mask and default gateway, must be obtained using other protocols.[1] RARP simplifies network configuration, yet not as much as it could.

Bootstrap Protocol (BootP)

Bootstrap Protocol (BootP) extends the concepts introduced in RARP. BootP answers client requests for IP address assignment. Routers may be configured to forward BootP requests and replies between subnets. BootP can also assign other configuration information at the same time as the address, such as a subnet mask and a default gateway address (Figure 15.2).

1. Subnet masks can be obtained using ICMP subnet request/reply message. The default gateways would be first set to the address of the RARP server, and then set to the appropriate gateway address using ICMP redirect messages.

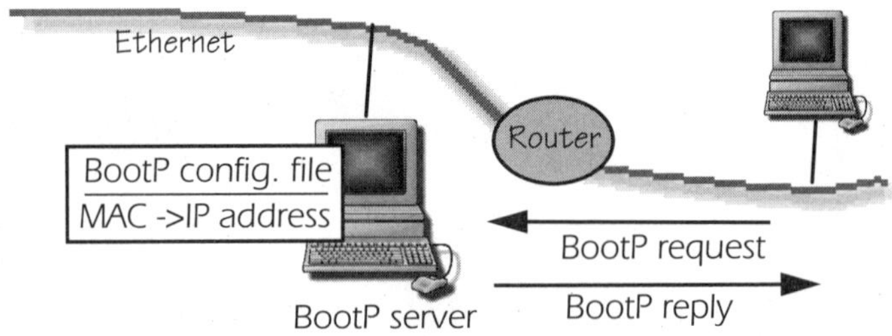

Figure 15.2
A BootP server assigns IP addresses based upon the requestor's MAC address.

A BootP configuration file contains a static list of mappings of MAC addresses to IP addresses. Additional parameters, such as subnet masks, may be specified in this file. Thus, the BootP server centralizes address administration on a network. Whenever you add a new BootP client machine to the network, you must edit the BootP configuration file on the BootP server.[2]

BootP can also be used to inform the client of a configuration file that it should download using Trivial File Transfer Protocol (TFTP). It is common for diskless workstations, dataless workstations, and X terminals to use BootP to download configuration information.

Dynamic Host Configuration Protocol (DHCP)

Dynamic Host Configuration Protocol (DHCP) is based upon BootP; in fact, it uses the same message format, and the same UDP ports: 67 and 68. The main advantage DHCP over BootP is the dynamic nature of address assignment.

The improvement over BootP is that the DHCP server does not need to be configured with the hardware addresses of all potential DHCP clients. Addresses may be "leased" from a general pool of IP addresses which will work within a certain subnet or network (Figure 15.3). The assignment obtained from the server is valid only for a certain period of time, the *lease time.* Should a lease expire, the DHCP client may receive a different IP address when it requests its new lease. This adds a degree of variability

2. When you change a NIC in a BootP client, the BootP configuration file must also be changed to reflect the new MAC address.

in the network which wasn't present with the fixed addressing of manual configuration, RARP, and BootP.

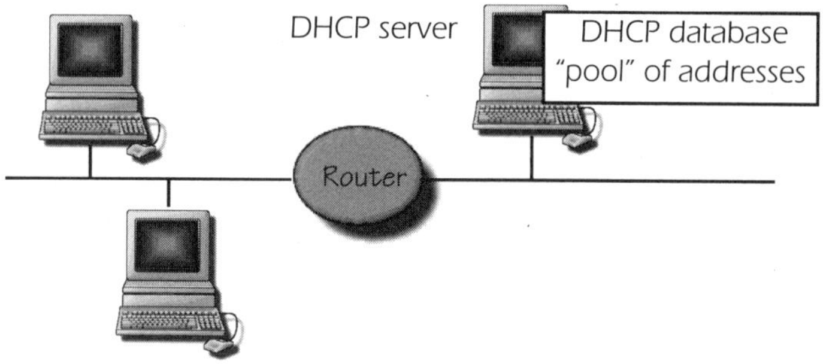

Figure 15.3 A DHCP server contains a pool of IP addresses from which it assigns.

It is not recommended to have IP addresses dynamically assigned to servers or routers. Typically client machines are configured with the fixed IP addresses of the WINS and DNS servers, and a default router or gateway. If the IP address of the servers changed every few days, communication between the clients and servers would require an additional degree of constant client reconfiguration and service interruptions.

Configuring Clients to Use DHCP

To configure a machine to use DHCP, there is only one step. Open the *TCP/IP Configuration* dialog on the client, and click on the radio button *Obtain an IP address from a DHCP server* (see Figure 15.4).

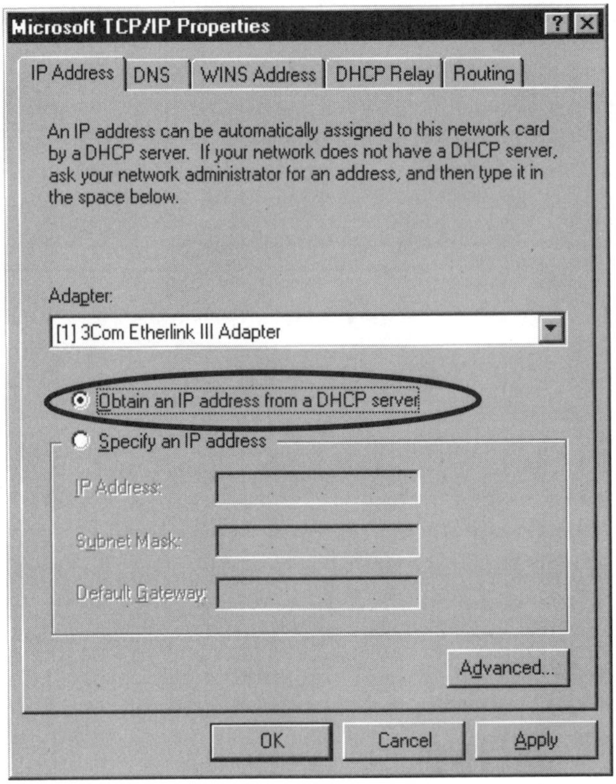

Figure 15.4 The Windows NT DHCP client configuration.

Once you select OK, that machine will transmit a DHCP discover message on the network. Assuming a lease is successfully obtained, TCP/IP transmissions can proceed normally. If there is no response to the discover message, the message will be transmitted at five minute intervals until it receives a successful lease.

DHCP can be used to assign configuration information to NT, Windows 95, and other clients such as Macintosh and Unix machines.

Confirming the Dynamic Assignment: ipconfig /all

To confirm that an IP address has been obtained, at the NT command prompt use the command ***ipconfig /all.*** This will show the currently assigned IP address (and other parameters) being used on the current machine (Figure 15.5).

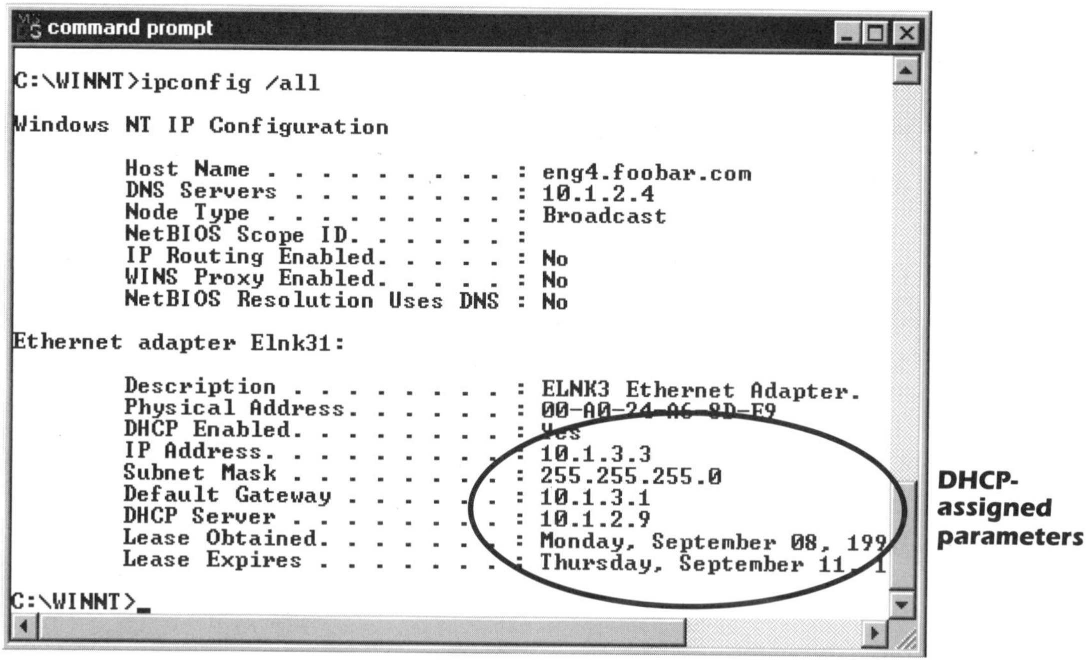

Figure 15.5 Viewing DHCP-assigned parameters using ipconfig.

Testing Tool: ipconfig /release and /renew

There are two additional ***ipconfig*** options: ***/renew*** and ***/release***. These options can be used to test DHCP. They are shown in Figure 15.6.

The ***ipconfig /release*** command frees up the IP address which had been assigned to this NIC. A release message is sent to the DHCP server and the local IP address is set to 0.0.0.0. Use this command when you want to remove a computer from the network or move a computer to another network.[3]

The ***ipconfig /renew*** command requests one of the following:

- Renew a current lease.
- Obtain a new lease when there is no current lease.

3. Note that a DHCP server cannot force a client to release its current lease. Thus in order to immediately release a client address, you must execute ipconfig /release on the client machine.

```
command prompt

C:\WINNT>ipconfig /release

Windows NT IP Configuration

IP address 10.1.3.3 successfully released for adapter "Elnk31"

C:\WINNT>ipconfig /renew

Windows NT IP Configuration

Ethernet adapter Elnk31:

        IP Address. . . . . . . . . : 10.1.3.6
        Subnet Mask . . . . . . . . : 255.255.255.0
        Default Gateway . . . . . . : 10.1.3.1

C:\WINNT>
```

Figure 15.6 Examples of the ipconfig command with the /release and /renew options.

Either way, a renew request message is sent to the server. The server sends an acknowledgment to the client noting that the lease has been renewed. This ACK will also contain all of the current DHCP options, which may be different from the last renewal.

If the address is not renewed, the client will still use the IP address until the lease time has expired.

Note: an additional way to release and renew a current lease is to use the tool ***wntipcfg.exe***. Buttons on the resulting dialog allow you to renew and release. Refer to Figure 5.22 on page 193 for an example of this dialog.

DHCP Scopes and Options

scope:
range of IP addresses that can be assigned to DHCP clients.

A DHCP **scope** is a range of IP addresses with a set of configuration options that will apply to the clients. A scope is typically a subnet, or a part of a subnet. A scope will never contain addresses for more than one subnet!

A scope is configured with:

- a subnet mask.
- a lease duration (3 days default).
- excluded addresses — ones that are manually assigned.
- reserved addresses — certain hardware addresses that receive certain IP addresses.

options: configuration parameters that are assigned by DHCP at the same time as an IP address.

DHCP **options** are additional configuration parameters that can be assigned along with the IP address. Possible options include default router address, DNS address, and WINS server address. Options can be set globally, for a group of systems (scope), or on an individual basis. Option details are discussed in the next section.

Installing and Managing DHCP Server

The DHCP Server is installed using the dialog shown in Figure 15.7. That dialog is obtained using *Network Control Panel -> Services -> Add.*

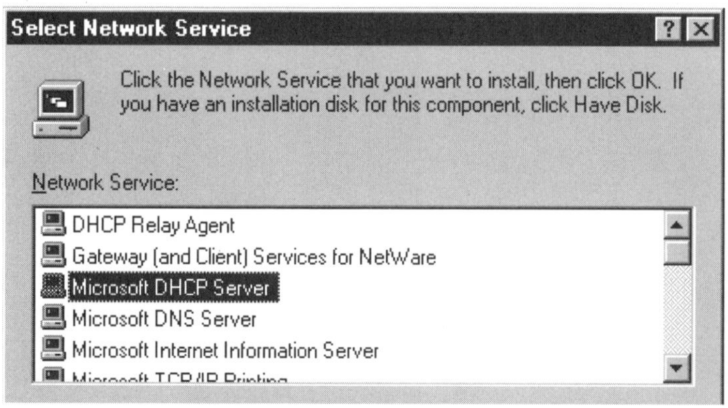

Figure 15.7 Add the DHCP Server service.

After installation, a new application will be found under the menu *Start -> Programs -> Administrative Tools:* DHCP Manager. DHCP Manager is used for all configuration changes to the DHCP server. The main dialog for the DHCP Manager is shown in Figure 15.8.

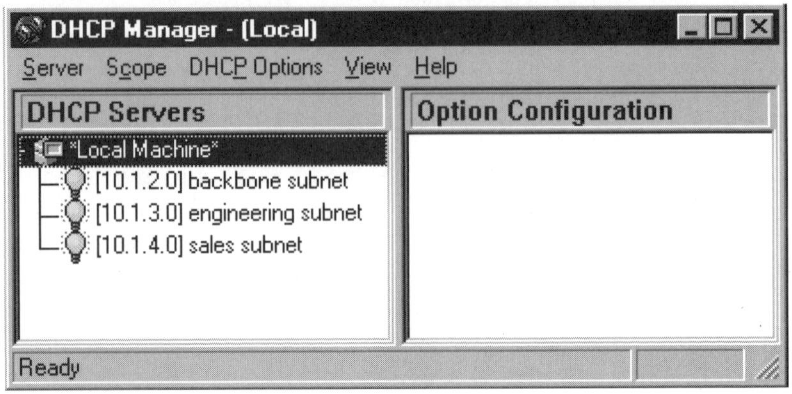

Figure 15.8 DHCP Manager is used to configure the DHCP Server.

The DHCP Manager application can be run from machines other than the DHCP server. The executable file, dhcpadmn.exe, as well as certain other files, must be copied to the other machine. Assuming you are in the same directory as the executable, you can start the DHCP Manager using the following command:

dhcpadmn.exe

You can then connect to a DHCP server using *Server-> Add* menu option. You will be able to connect to the DHCP server only if your local username is part of the administrator group on the DHCP server you connect to. Once you are connected, you can remotely control and configure the DHCP server.

DHCP Scope Properties

Figure 15.9 shows the dialog used to configure scope properties. Each scope will have a range of IP addresses which the server can assign. The DHCP server also assigns the subnet mask. It is possible to exclude certain IP addresses from this address pool — that is done using the *Exclusion Range* boxes. Also configured on this dialog are the lease duration, scope name, and scope comment.

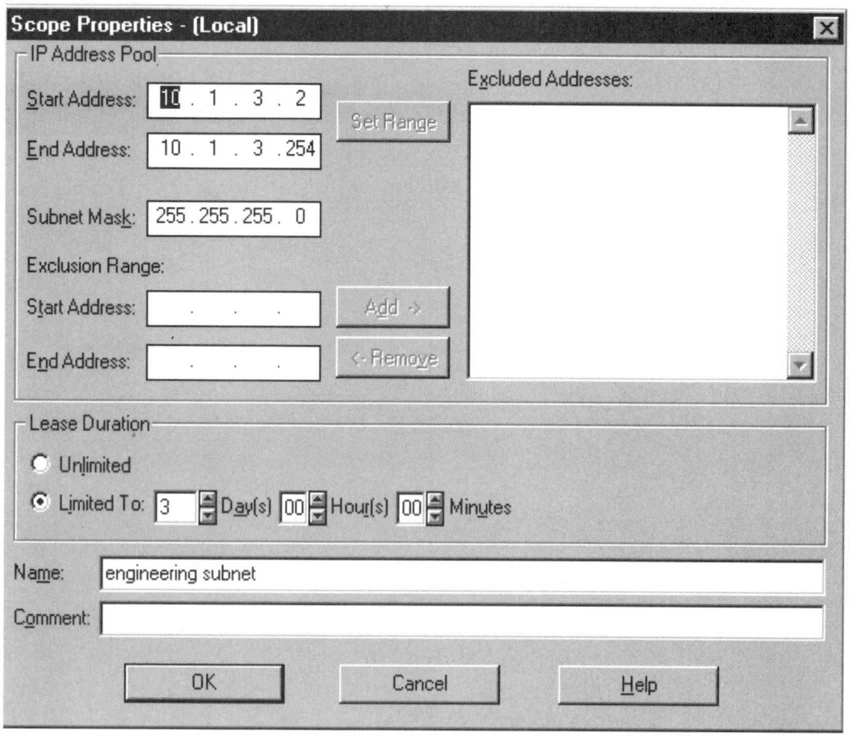

Figure 15.9 Scope properties include the range of IP addresses as well as length of lease time.

We want to convert a portion of the foobar.com network to use DHCP. In particular, we want the engineering subnet and sales subnet to use DHCP. Also, some devices on the backbone subnet will use DHCP. Each one of those subnets will have its own scope. Figure 15.10 illustrates the location of each of the three scopes.

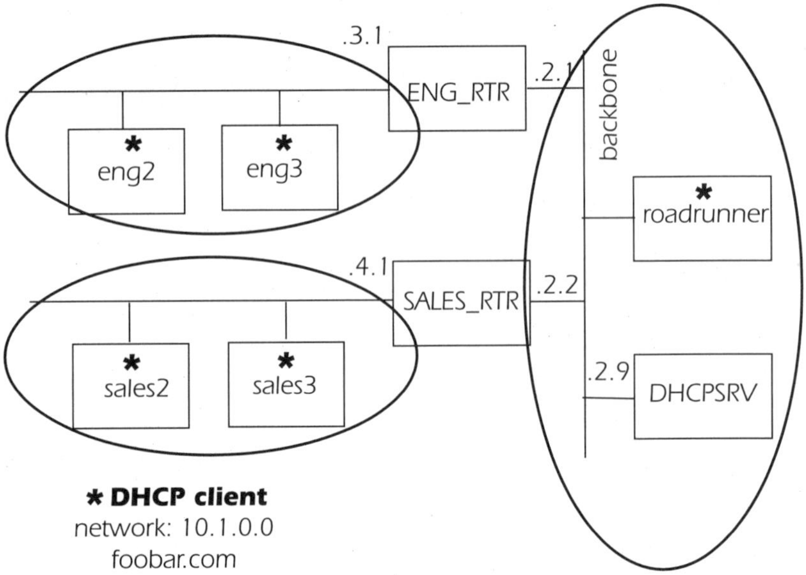

Figure 15.10 Three subnets that will be using DHCP. Each subnet will have its own DHCP scope.

We will create three scopes, one for each subnet. The scopes will have the properties shown in Table 15.1. Note that address 10.1.3.1 and 10.1.4.1 cannot be part of the scope, as they are already assigned to ENG_RTR and SALES_RTR. Also note that the backbone subnet[4] begins with the last byte being 10, as addresses 1-9 in that subnet have been assigned to other devices already.

Table 15.1 Scopes for foobar.com.

Scope name	Starting IP address	Ending IP address
engineering	10.1.3.2	10.1.3.254
sales	10.1.4.2	10.1.4.254
backbone	10.1.2.10	10.1.2.254

The resulting scopes are listed in DHCP Manager, as shown in Figure 15.11.

4. Devices attached to the backbone in most cases should have a fixed address, as most will be servers or routers. However, for the sake of example, a backbone scope is being created, with one potential client shown: roadrunner.

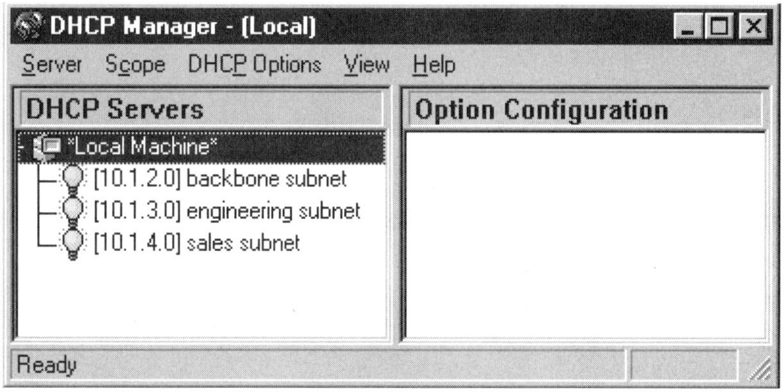

Figure 15.11 DHCP Manager application may be used to configure scope information.

Notice that the scopes are identified by name as well as subnet address. Recall from the subnetting chapter that a subnet address consists of the network field and the subnet field with the appropriate values to identify the subnet, and the interface field set to all zeros binary. If you are using a subnet mask that does not end on an octet boundary, the subnet addresses shown in DHCP manager may cause you some confusion at first as to where they came from. However, what is listed in DHCP manager is the *subnet address*.

Viewing Active DHCP Leases

The *Active Leases* dialog (Figure 15.12) shows all of the active IP addresses leased from this scope on this server. The buttons on this dialog include:

- Properties— Shows the IP address, computer name, and MAC address of the selected entry.

Warning

- Delete— Deletes the selected lease. WARNING: this button should be used very carefully. When you delete a lease, you only delete it from the DHCP database; the client is *not* told to give up that IP address! Thus the next time the DHCP server needs a "free" IP address to assign, it could select this "free" address that is still in use.
- Reconcile— Ensures that the DHCP database is consistent with leases recorded in the registry.
- Refresh— Refreshes the display to show the current list of leases.

Figure 15.12
Viewing active DHCP leases.

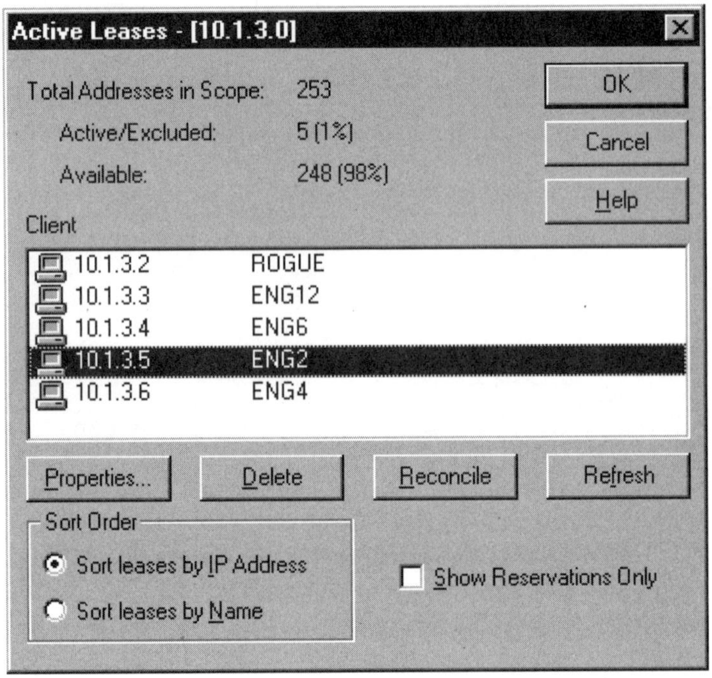

If you change the computer name on a machine that has a current DHCP lease, the name will be updated in the database the next time the client renews.

Security

One disadvantage of DHCP is the lack of security as to what machines obtain IP addresses. If you run DHCP on your network, anyone can attach to your LAN and obtain a valid IP address. (Notice the machine named ROGUE in Figure 15.12.) This person could then proceed to obtain information about your network, resources, or use your printing services. The concept of authenticating DHCP clients is not currently implemented in this DHCP server.

Selecting *Properties* on the *Active Leases* dialog will display the *Client Properties* dialog (Figure 15.13).

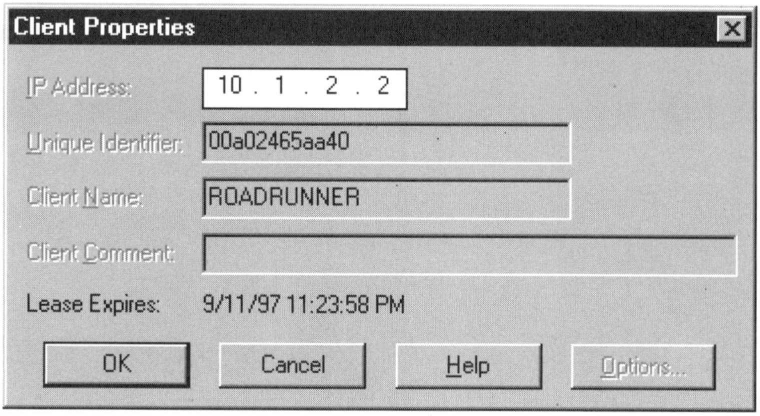

Figure 15.13
The Client Properties dialog displays the IP address assigned to a particular MAC address.

This information may be useful for certain kinds of troubleshooting, such as the security issues which have just been mentioned. The unique identifier (MAC address in 802 LANs) and lease expiration time may help to track down the unexpected lessee.

Client Reservation in DHCP

You can configure a DHCP server to use *client reservation* so that the same IP address will always be assigned to a certain client[5]. Recall that it is not a good idea to assign a dynamic address to a server or a printer. One way to prevent a server that uses DHCP from receiving a changing IP address is to reserve a specific IP address using the *Add Reserved Clients* dialog (Figure 15.14).

The *Add Reserved Clients* dialog is found in the scope pull-down menu in the DHCP Manager. Enter in the IP address to assign to the client. Also enter the MAC address of the client in the *Unique Identifier* field. If this value does not match the MAC address of the device, the device will not receive the reserved IP address.

5. If you have multiple DHCP servers you must add this reservation to each server.

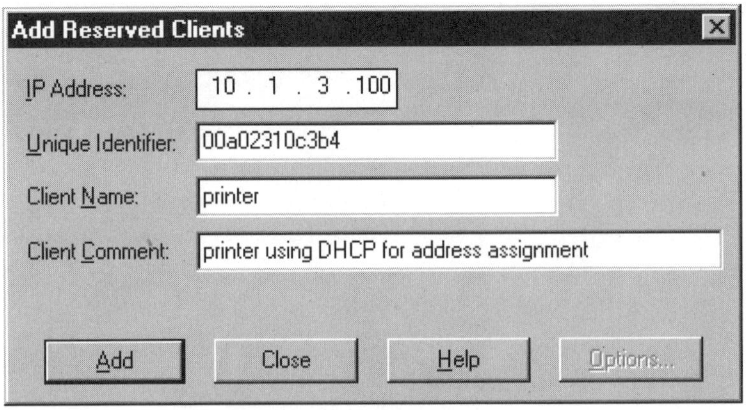

Figure 15.14 Setting up reserved client information.

After the reservation has been added, options can be assigned to that client on an individual basis. The *Client Properties* dialog for an existing reservation will have the *Options* button in bold, meaning it can be used to assign options to that one client.

Assigning DHCP Options

Recall that DHCP options are configuration values to be downloaded to the DHCP client. As an administrator, you can assign options to three different groups: everyone (global options), a subnet (scope options), or to individuals.

- Global options — assigned to every client that receives an IP address from this server.
- Scope options — assigned to every client within that particular scope.
- Individual options — assigned to only one machine. Individual options are assigned by first creating a reservation for that client, and then assigning the option using the *Client Properties-> Options* button (as seen in Figure 15.13).

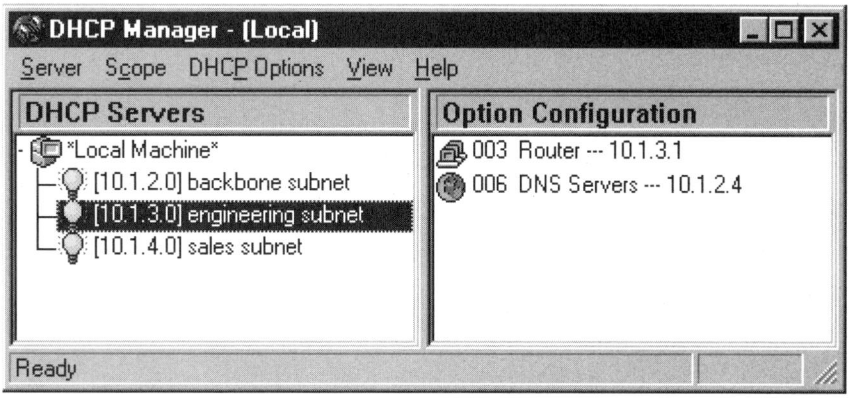

Figure 15.15 Options can be assigned on a global, scope, or individual basis.

In Figure 15.15, there are two options assigned to the engineering subnet: the router option and the DNS server option. The different icons in front of the option name identify whether the option is a scope option (three small PCs) or a global option (a globe). The DNS option is a global option as all requests should go to this one machine. The router option is a scope option, as the default router for each subnet will be different.

If you have configured multiple DHCP options, you should note that there is an order in which they are applied, called *option precedence*. The following is the ranking of options:

- Global options are overridden by scope options.
- Scope options are overridden by individual options.
- Any DHCP option is overridden by a value configured manually at the machine.

Be careful of this ordering system, as it may cause you hours of frustration if you assign options at the DHCP server, but find out that the values are already manually configured at the machine!

Selecting Options to Configure

Figure 15.16 shows the dialog used to select the options to configure. On the left there is a list of all of the available DHCP options. Options can be added to this list, as we will see shortly. Selecting an option on the left and clicking *Add* will move the option to the right. Clicking on *Value* will display the bottom half of the dialog that shows the array of values for that option. In order to configure the option you must click on *Edit Array*, which will bring up the dialog shown in Figure 15.17.

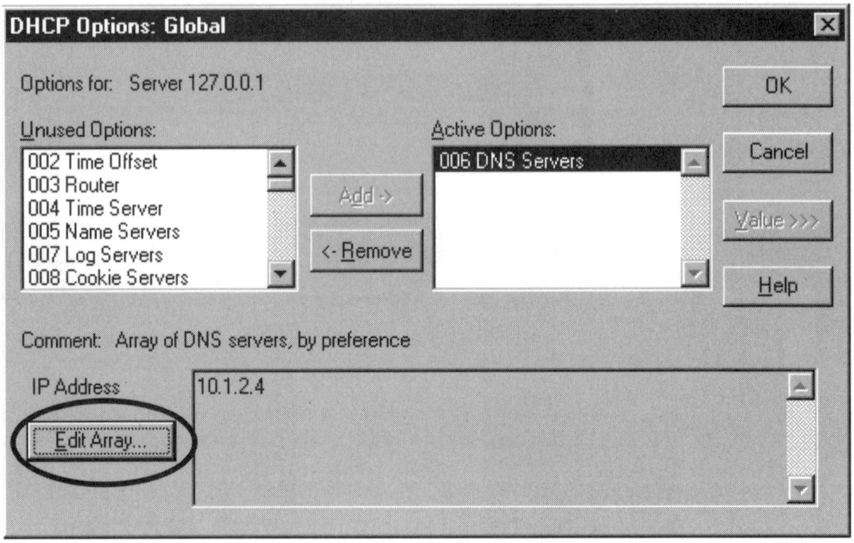

Figure 15.16 Options are configured using this dialog.

Note that *Microsoft clients support only certain options.* These are:

- 003 Router
- 006 DNS Server
- 015 Domain name
- 044 WINS/NBNS (IP address of WINS server)
- 046 WINS/NetBT node type (b-node, p-node, m-node, h-node)[6]
- 047 NetBIOS scope ID

If options not in the above list are assigned and sent to Microsoft clients, those additional options will be ignored.

You can use the DHCP server to configure options to be used by non-Microsoft DHCP clients, assuming those clients will support those options.

6. Refer to Chapter 16, "NetBIOS Name Resolution", for a description of NetBT node types.

Assigning Values to Options

The *IP Address Array Editor* dialog is one of the dialogs used to configure the value for a particular option. In Figure 15.17, the DNS Server option is being set to IP address 10.1.2.4.

The *Resolve* button can be used if you know the name of the machine, but not the IP address. After entering the server name and clicking on Resolve, NT will obtain the IP address for the server, using one of the typical NetBIOS name resolution methods[7]. NT will put the "resolved" IP address in the *New IP Address* box. You would then have to click on *Add* to move the address to the right column.

Figure 15.17
Assigning values to options.

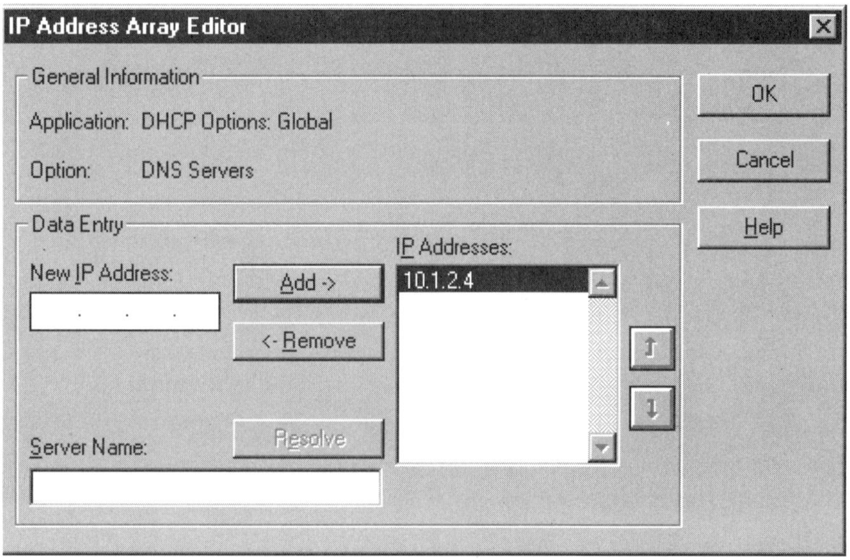

You can assign multiple IP addresses to a specific DHCP option. All of the configured IP addresses will be sent to the DHCP client in the DHCP message. The order of use of the IP addresses is set using the up and down arrows (shown on the right side of the dialog). The order selects which IP address the client tries first, before moving to the next address in the list.

7. Refer to Chapter 16, "NetBIOS Name Resolution" for a discussion of the NetBIOS name resolution methods.

Adding a New DHCP Option Type

Over time, new DHCP options are defined in the specification, and implemented by certain vendors. These new option types can be added to your DHCP server, and can be downloaded to the clients. To add a new DHCP option type, from the main menu of DHCP Manager, select *DHCP Options->Default Values*. Figure 15.18 shows the pull-down list of currently-available DHCP options.

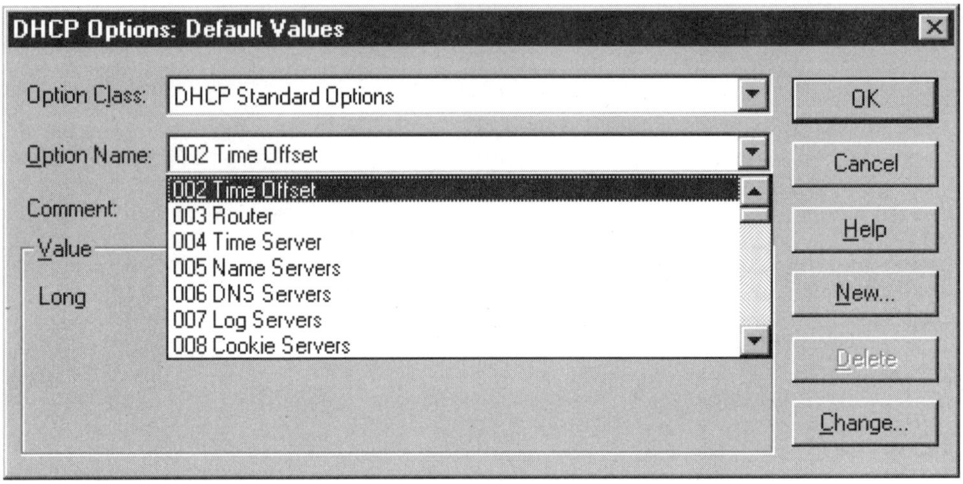

Figure 15.18 Displaying the list of currently available DHCP options.

To add a new option to this list, click on *New*. The *Add Option Type* dialog will appear (Figure 15.19).

Figure 15.19 Adding a new option type.

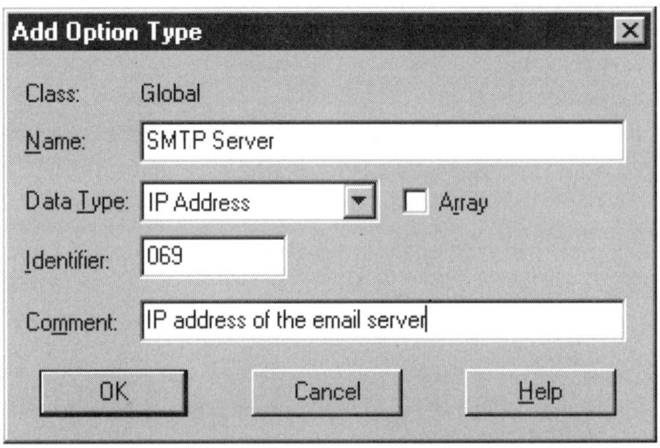

Use the *Add Option Type* dialog to add any DHCP option that you wish. Once you create this new option type, it will be in the pull-down list of available options.

DHCP Logging

The *Server Properties* dialog shown in Figure 15.20 is used to configure DHCP logging and IP address conflicts. These features were added with the release of NT 4.0 service pack 2. This dialog is obtained by selecting the IP address of the DHCP server, and then selecting *Server->Properties*.

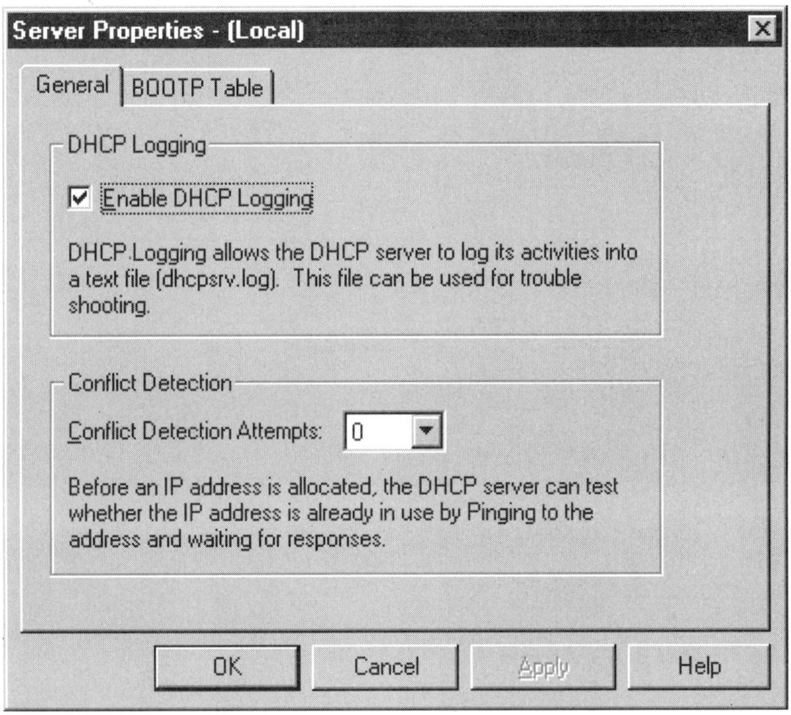

Figure 15.20 The Server Properties dialog is used to enable logging and configure IP address conflict detection.

When the *Enable DHCP Logging* box is checked, DHCP activities will be logged to the file dhcpsrv.log, found in %systemroot%\system32\dhcp. An example of the file is shown in Figure 15.21.

```
                         Microsoft DHCP Server Activity Log
Event ID  Meaning
00        The log was started.
01        The log was stopped.
02        The log was temporarily paused due to low disk space.
10        A new IP address was leased to a client.
11        A lease was renewed by a client.
12        A lease was released by a client.
13        An IP address was found to be in use on the network.
14        A lease request could not be satisfied because the scope's
          address pool was exhausted.
15        A lease was denied.
20        A BOOTP address was leased to a client.

ID Date,Time,Description,IP Address,Host Name,MAC Address

10,12/08/97,22:53:11,Assign,10.1.3.3,ENG4,00A024A68DE9
12,12/08/97,23:01:21,Release,10.1.3.3,ENG4,00A024A68DE9
10,12/08/97,23:03:21,Assign,10.1.3.2,ROGUE,00A02465AA43
10,12/08/97,23:07:36,Assign,10.1.3.3,ENG12,0080C7C76BB9
10,12/08/97,23:08:40,Assign,10.1.3.6,ENG4,00A024A68DE9
10,12/08/97,23:09:17,Assign,10.1.3.5,ENG2,0080C77CDC96
```

Figure 15.21 Example dhcpsrv.log file.

Notice that the first few lines of text are a description of each of the event codes that may occur. The bottom six lines show assigned and released IP addresses, as well as which machines received the addresses.

IP Address Conflict Detection

The bottom half of the *Server Properties* dialog is used to configure IP address conflict detection (Figure 15.20).

When the DHCP server receives a request for a new IP address, it searches the database for an "available" IP address. Before Service Pack 2, the DHCP server would take the first available address and assign it to the client. When the client then continues the booting process, it may find that IP address is already in use by another machine. An error message would appear on the screen, and the TCP/IP stack would be disabled. The only way to fix that problem is manual intervention.

To prevent the above problem from occurring, the DHCP server now has the ability to detect if an IP address it is about to assign is already in use. Before assigning a particular address, the server will attempt to ***ping*** that address. If in the dialog shown in Figure 15.20 the number of attempts is set to three, the DHCP server will send out three ICMP echo request messages (or three ARP request messages). If there is no reply to these queries, that IP address will be assigned to the client. If there is a reply, the address will be marked as a BAD ADDRESS, and the next "available" address in the scope be will tried (see Figure 15.22). This process continues until either a free address is found or there are no further addresses in the scope.

Figure 15.22
The DHCP server tried to assign 10.1.3.5, but found it was already in use.

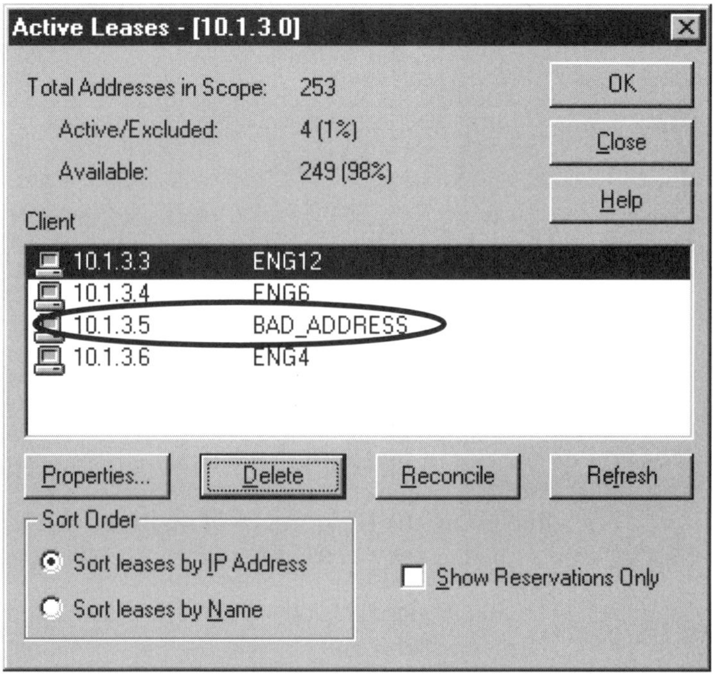

Clients also have the ability to detect duplicate IP addresses. If a client is assigned an IP address that is already in use[8], it will send a DHCP Decline message to the server and then request a new IP address.

8. As any IP stack will do (with static or dynamic address assignment), the client, upon receiving an IP address, will send out a gratuitous ARP — an ARP request addressed to itself (the IP address it was just assigned). If there is a reply to that ARP, then another machine has that IP address, and a new address should be requested.

DHCP Database Record States

The DHCP server maintains a database to keep track of the current scopes of available addresses, and current DHCP leases. Entries in the DHCP database go through various states, as shown in Figure 15.23. The first state is the *active state* — when a particular IP address has been assigned to a particular DHCP client. The record stays in that state for a certain period of time — the lease time. If the lease is renewed, the record will stay in the active state.

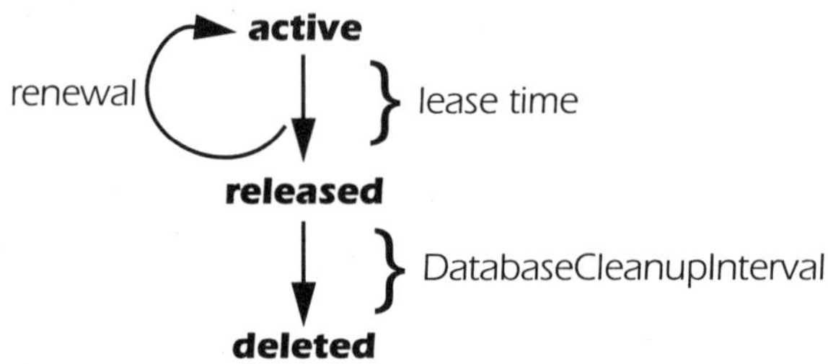

Figure 15.23 The stages of a IP address record DHCP lease.

How Records are Released

At some point, the IP address will go into the released state, either by the lease expiring or by being released by the client.

- Explicit client release — The client has issued the command ***ipconfig /release***.
- Implicit client release — The client configured a static address on the interface which had a lease.
- Lease expiration caused by the client — A DHCP client *does not* release its IP address when shutting down. Therefore the lease is still in the active state immediately after shutdown. If the client is not available to renew the lease within the remainder of the lease time, the server will expire the lease because the client was not present. The client may not be present because the client is still powered off, or it has been moved to another network.

- Lease expiration caused by the server — Another form of lease expiration occurs when the client cannot renew a lease with the server. The server may not respond to a lease renewal for the following reasons.
    - The server is powered down, or the DHCP server service has been stopped.
    - The server has been reconfigured. If a network administrator changes the definition of a scope so that the leased address is no longer in the scope, the server will deny the client's attempts to renew the lease.

After Lease Release

When the lease is released, the IP address is not immediately available to be assigned to a new client: the IP address is "on hold" for a period of time. The database record is now in the *released state*. If the same DHCP client[9] requests an IP address when the record is in the released state, the same IP address will be assigned to the client, and the record will go back into the active state.

The record stays in the released state for 24 hours by default. This period of time is configurable using the registry variable *DatabaseCleanupInterval* (Table 15.2).

Table 15.2 DatabaseCleanup Interval registry parameter.

Hive:	HKEY_LOCAL_MACHINE
Key:	\System\CurrentControlSet\Services\DHCPServer\Parameters
Name:	DatabaseCleanupInterval
Type:	REG_DWORD
Value:	1440 minutes (default)

After the *DatabaseCleanupInterval* time period has passed, the database record will be deleted. The IP address is now available to be assigned to a DHCP client.

9. "Same DHCP client" can be defined as an incoming request that has a client MAC address that matches the MAC address in the released record.

Obtaining a Lease

A DHCP client will go through the initial leasing process to obtain a new IP address. The initial leasing process will be invoked for various reasons, including:

- the client is initializing TCP/IP for the first time with DHCP.
- the client has been denied a specific IP address, usually due to the server dropping/not renewing the lease.
- the client released its previous lease and needs a new IP address.

Let's look at the packets involved in the initial leasing process.

Four-Step Initial Leasing Process

The initial leasing of an IP address with DHCP is a four step process. Each step involves the transmission of a message between the DHCP client and DHCP server. The four packets exchanged are shown in Figure 15.24. An acronym is sometimes used to remember the order of the packets. The acronym DORA represents the discover, offer, request, and ack packets that are sent.

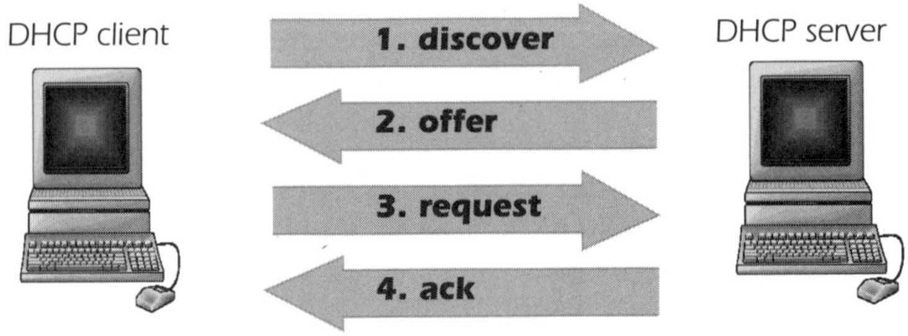

Figure 15.24 There are four packets exchanged in DHCP's initial leasing process: discover, offer, request, ack.

There are two things to note about all of these messages: they are all IP broadcasts, and they are sent between UDP ports 67 and 68.

Figure 15.25 shows a Network Monitor packet capture of a successful initial lease. This capture is found in the file dhcpinit.cap, and the address database is found in dhcp_ch.adr.

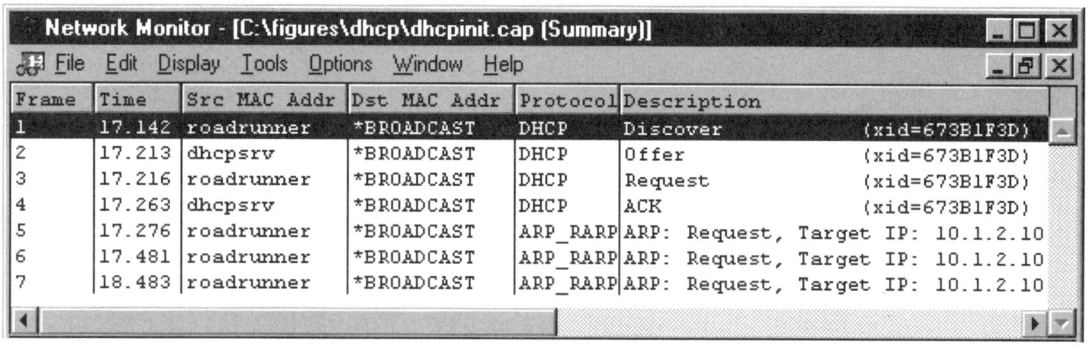

Figure 15.25 *Four message lease sequence plus 3 ARP requests.*

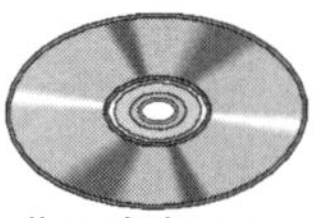

dhcpinit.cap

The first four messages are the discover, offer, request, and acknowledge as expected for the DHCP lease. Once the client configures the IP address onto its network interface, it will issue a gratuitous ARP to detect any other machines on the LAN with the same IP address. So why are there three ARP requests here? The gratuitous ARP seen here is no different than any regular ARP would be. If there is no reply to the first request, ARP retries after a brief timeout (about a fifth of a second in this example) by issuing a second request. When there is no reply to the second attempt, ARP again times out (after about a second this time) and issues a third attempt. The increased time is normal. When there is no reply at all after three attempts, ARP gives up, assuming that there is no (other) machine with that IP address.[10]

As was mentioned during the description of conflict detection, if the client had received an ARP reply, it would have given up the address and issued a Decline message to the DHCP server to request another address.

Example Lease Scenario

In order to describe the details, we'll step through an example lease. For this example, the client and server will both be in the same subnet, the

10. Refer to chapter 2, or RFCs 826 and 1122 for further information on ARP.

foobar.com backbone subnet, 10.1.2.0. Figure 15.26 shows the initial configuration — before an IP address has ever been assigned to the client.

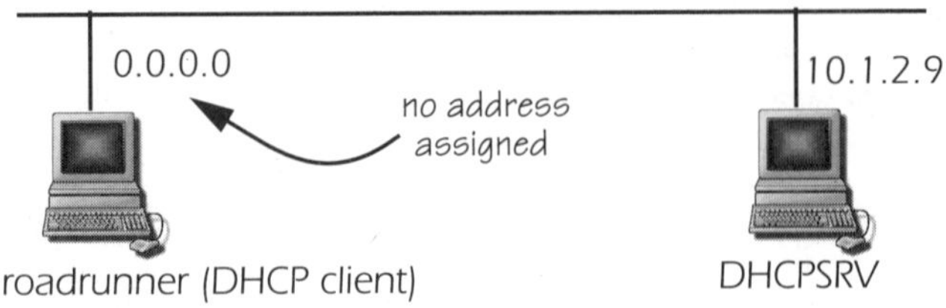

Figure 15.26 The DHCP client and server are both attached to the foobar.com backbone, subnet 10.1.2.0.

Upon boot of the DHCP client, a DHCP discover message will be transmitted.

DHCP Discover

A *DHCP discover* packet is shown in Figure 15.28. It contains the client's hardware address. The message is sent to IP address 255.255.255.255 and from 0.0.0.0 since the DHCP client does not yet have an IP address. The source port is 68 (BootP client) and destination port is 67 (BootP server).

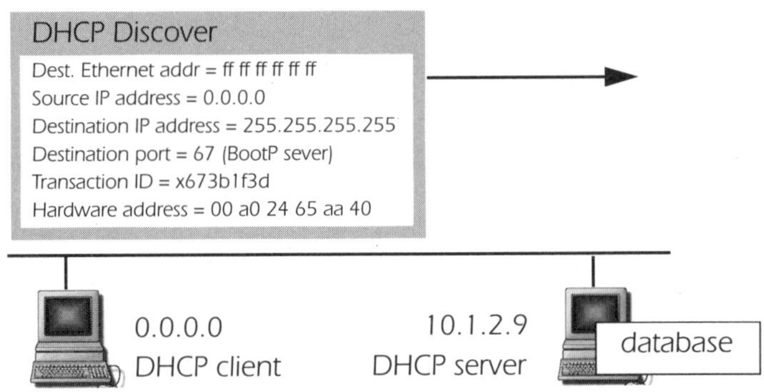

Figure 15.27 The DHCP client broadcasts a discover message.

If there is no reply to the discover packet, the client retransmits four times within the first few minutes. If there is still no response, a message is displayed on the client screen, and the DHCP client sends a discover message every five minutes from then on.

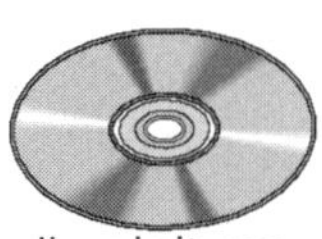

dhcpinit.cap frame #1

The complete contents of a DHCP discover message is shown in Figure 15.28. This capture file is called dhcpinit.cap on the CD.

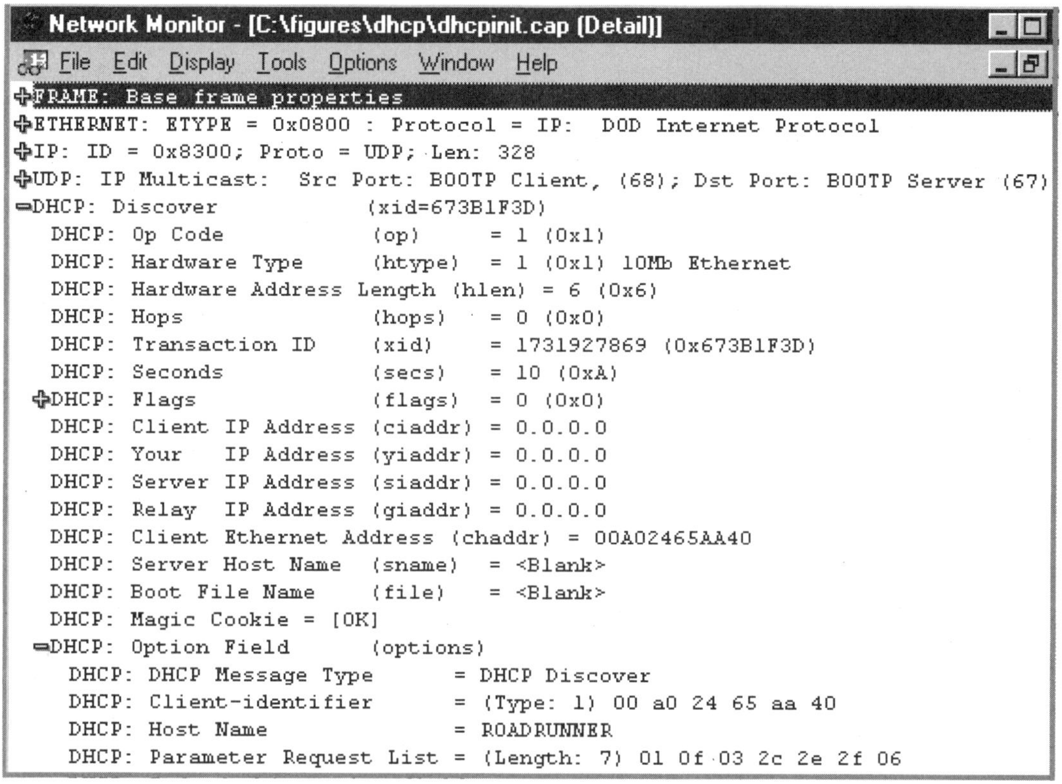

Figure 15.28 Contents of a DHCP discover message.

Note that the operation code has a value of one, which identifies this message as a BootP request. As was mentioned earlier, the format of DHCP messages is the same as BootP messages. There is a difference in the messages — DHCP places added information in what BootP called the options field. The actual type of DHCP message (a discover in this case) is specified in the options area.

DHCP Offer

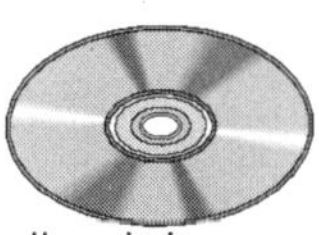

dhcpinit.cap
frame #2

The second message is *DHCP offer* message, sent from all DHCP servers that received the discover message. If the client receives multiple DHCP offers, the first of those offers will be the address it requests.

Figure 15.29 and Figure 15.30 both show the contents of a DHCP offer message. Note that the client cannot use the offered IP address until the DHCP ACK is received.

Figure 15.29
The DHCP server broadcasts an offer message.

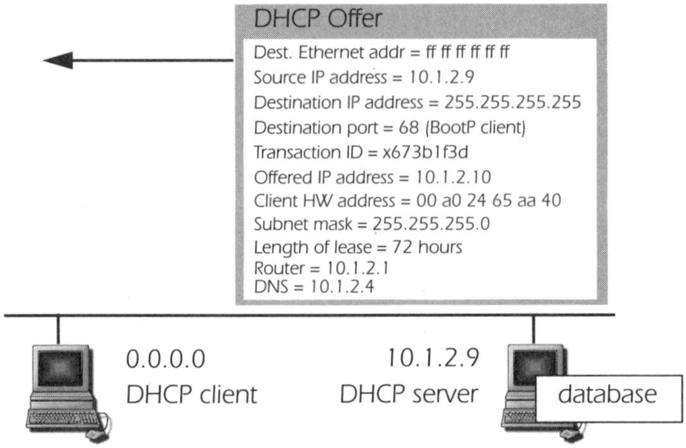

Figure 15.30
Contents of DHCP offer message (file dhcpinit.cap)

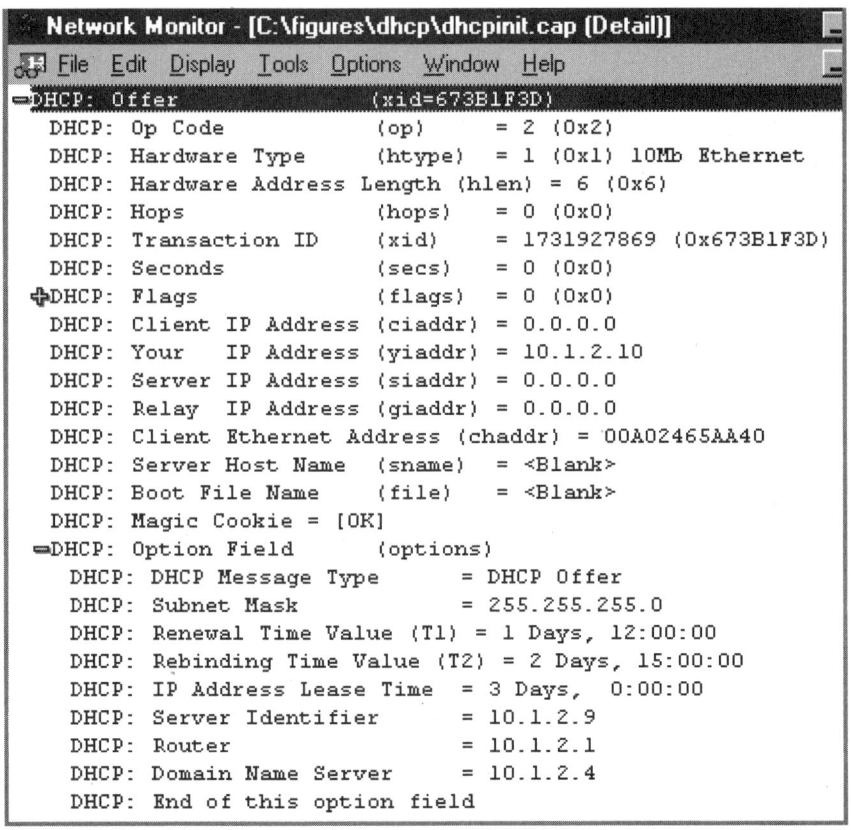

```
Network Monitor - [C:\figures\dhcp\dhcpinit.cap (Detail)]
File  Edit  Display  Tools  Options  Window  Help
-DHCP: Offer                  (xid=673B1F3D)
  DHCP: Op Code               (op)      = 2 (0x2)
  DHCP: Hardware Type         (htype)   = 1 (0x1) 10Mb Ethernet
  DHCP: Hardware Address Length (hlen) = 6 (0x6)
  DHCP: Hops                  (hops)    = 0 (0x0)
  DHCP: Transaction ID        (xid)     = 1731927869 (0x673B1F3D)
  DHCP: Seconds               (secs)    = 0 (0x0)
 +DHCP: Flags                 (flags)   = 0 (0x0)
  DHCP: Client IP Address (ciaddr) = 0.0.0.0
  DHCP: Your   IP Address (yiaddr) = 10.1.2.10
  DHCP: Server IP Address (siaddr) = 0.0.0.0
  DHCP: Relay  IP Address (giaddr) = 0.0.0.0
  DHCP: Client Ethernet Address (chaddr) = 00A02465AA40
  DHCP: Server Host Name  (sname)  = <Blank>
  DHCP: Boot File Name    (file)   = <Blank>
  DHCP: Magic Cookie = [OK]
 -DHCP: Option Field      (options)
    DHCP: DHCP Message Type       = DHCP Offer
    DHCP: Subnet Mask             = 255.255.255.0
    DHCP: Renewal Time Value (T1) = 1 Days, 12:00:00
    DHCP: Rebinding Time Value (T2) = 2 Days, 15:00:00
    DHCP: IP Address Lease Time  = 3 Days,  0:00:00
    DHCP: Server Identifier       = 10.1.2.9
    DHCP: Router                  = 10.1.2.1
    DHCP: Domain Name Server      = 10.1.2.4
    DHCP: End of this option field
```

DHCP Request

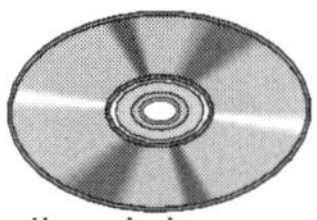

dhcpinit.cap
frame #3

The client now sends a *DHCP request* to the first server it received an offer from. It is essentially a repeat of the information in the offer message. The DHCP request is sent as a IP and MAC-layer broadcast, such that other DHCP servers who offered that client an address will know that the client chose another server. Figure 15.31 and Figure 15.32 show the contents of a DHCP request.

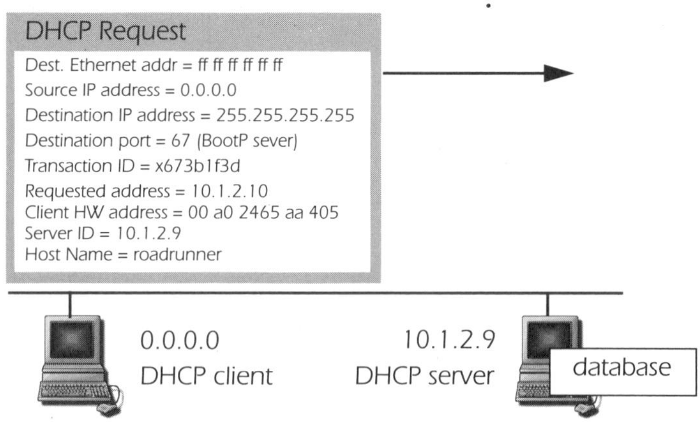

Figure 15.31
The DHCP client broadcasts a request message intended for the DHCP server.

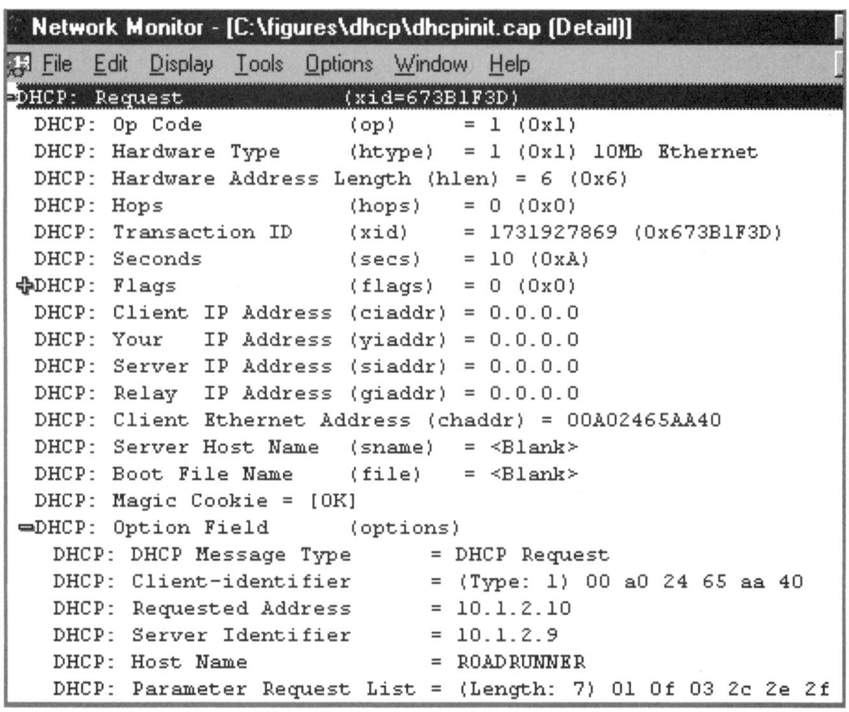

```
Network Monitor - [C:\figures\dhcp\dhcpinit.cap (Detail)]
File  Edit  Display  Tools  Options  Window  Help
DHCP: Request                  (xid=673B1F3D)
  DHCP: Op Code               (op)      = 1 (0x1)
  DHCP: Hardware Type         (htype)   = 1 (0x1) 10Mb Ethernet
  DHCP: Hardware Address Length (hlen) = 6 (0x6)
  DHCP: Hops                  (hops)    = 0 (0x0)
  DHCP: Transaction ID        (xid)     = 1731927869 (0x673B1F3D)
  DHCP: Seconds               (secs)    = 10 (0xA)
 +DHCP: Flags                 (flags)   = 0 (0x0)
  DHCP: Client IP Address (ciaddr) = 0.0.0.0
  DHCP: Your   IP Address (yiaddr) = 0.0.0.0
  DHCP: Server IP Address (siaddr) = 0.0.0.0
  DHCP: Relay  IP Address (giaddr) = 0.0.0.0
  DHCP: Client Ethernet Address (chaddr) = 00A02465AA40
  DHCP: Server Host Name  (sname)   = <Blank>
  DHCP: Boot File Name    (file)    = <Blank>
  DHCP: Magic Cookie = [OK]
 -DHCP: Option Field        (options)
    DHCP: DHCP Message Type       = DHCP Request
    DHCP: Client-identifier       = (Type: 1) 00 a0 24 65 aa 40
    DHCP: Requested Address       = 10.1.2.10
    DHCP: Server Identifier       = 10.1.2.9
    DHCP: Host Name               = ROADRUNNER
    DHCP: Parameter Request List = (Length: 7) 01 0f 03 2c 2e 2f
```

Figure 15.32
Contents of DHCP request message.

DHCP Acknowledgment

In step 4 the server sends a DHCP acknowledgment (ACK) to the client (Figure 15.33 and Figure 15.34). After the ACK has been received, the client may use its address until the lease expires.

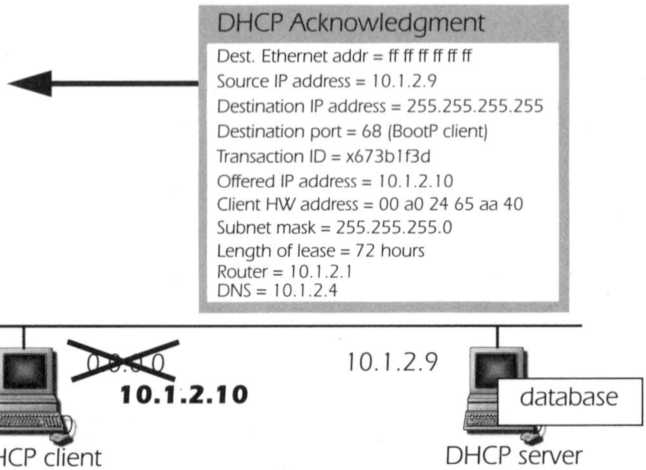

Figure 15.33 The DHCP server broadcasts an acknowledgment message which the DHCP client should hear.

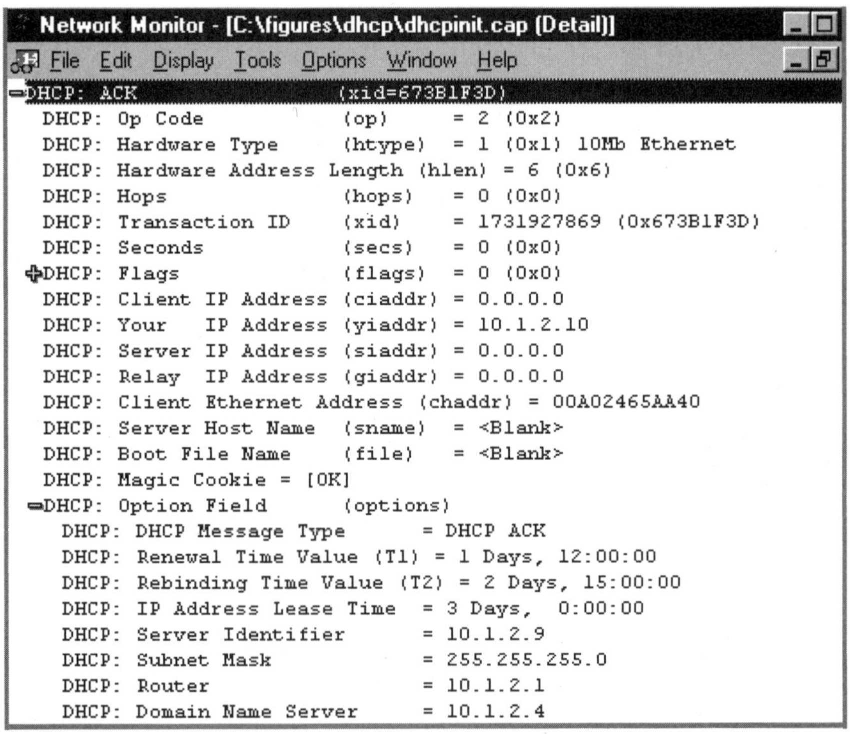

Figure 15.34 Contents of DHCP acknowledgment message (file dhcpinit.cap)

dhcpinit.cap
frame #4

The IP address and subnet mask are stored locally in the registry in

HKLM\SYSTEM\CurrentControlSet\Services\nic\Parameters\Tcpip

where nic is the name of the network interface card.

Extending Lease Time

After half of the lease time has expired, the client sends a request to extend the lease. This message is the same message as was sent in step three of the initial leasing process, with one change: this message is sent to the IP address of the DHCP server, instead of being sent as a broadcast.

dhcprenew.cap

The DHCP server should then reply with a DHCP ACK message directed to the client. This message is the same message as was sent in step four of the initial leasing process. These two messages are illustrated in Figure 15.35. For more details on the contents of these messages, examine the file dhcprenew.cap found on the CD.

Figure 15.35
A lease renewal request is issued to extend a lease.

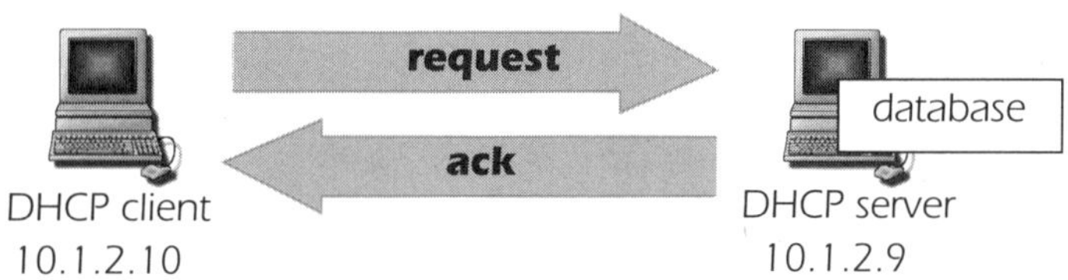

If the client could not renew its lease at 1/2 of the lease time-to-live, it will again try at 7/8 of time-to-live. If this does not succeed, the client will resort to broadcasting its request, trying to obtain an ACK from any DHCP server.

In the event that the client's lease expires, the IP address is forfeited. The lease may expire normally when the time is up or may be forced to expire if the client receives a DHCP negative acknowledgment (NACK) rather than a DHCP ACK in response to its DHCP request message.

DHCP Reboot Sequence

When a DHCP client boots up, and it had a previously assigned IP address, it will send a request message in order to ensure that its IP address is still valid (Figure 15.36). This request message will contain the IP address it was last assigned. Note that this request is sent as both an Ethernet and IP broadcast!

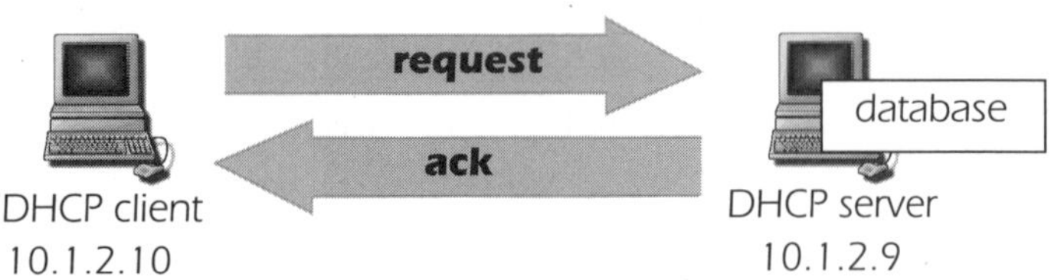

Figure 15.36
Upon reboot, a client will issue a request to re-acquire a lease.

The advantage to the message being a broadcast is that if this machine was moved to a different subnet when powered off, this broadcasted DHCP request will ensure that it receives a valid IP address fairly quickly. The local DHCP server, when receiving a renew for an IP address not assigned by it, will reply with a DHCP NACK. The client will then begin the initial leasing process to obtain an IP address valid on the new subnet.

The disadvantage of this method is the same with any broadcast message — each machine attached to that LAN will spend a slight bit more amount of time in processing that message, a message that was likely not destined for it.

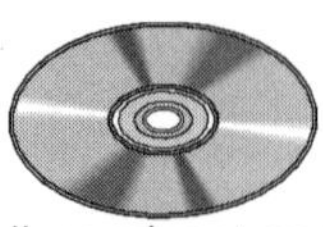

dhcpreboot.cap

Figure 15.37 shows both the request and ACK messages sent as a broadcast. For more details on the contents of these messages, examine the capture file dhcpreboot.cap, found on the CD.

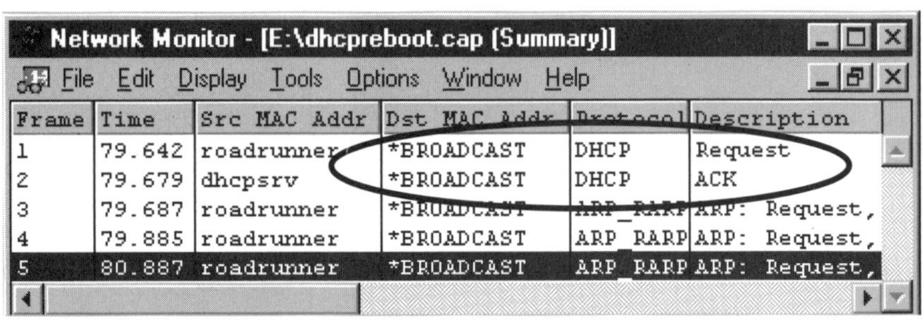

Figure 15.37
The DHCP request and ACK after client reboot is sent as an IP and Ethernet broadcast.

Using DHCP in Routed Networks

The case where the client and server are on the same subnet is the simplest case for DHCP operation. DHCP operation becomes more complicated when routers are involved. Recall that broadcast packets (whether they're IP or Ethernet) *are not* forwarded by routers. The advantage is that broadcasts are not propagated throughout a network. The disadvantage, in the case of DHCP (and BootP) is that most DHCP messages are sent as broadcasts. If the routers do not forward the messages, you would need a DHCP server on every subnet.

Since having a DHCP server on every subnet is often not practical, another solution was created. Why not configure the routers to forward the DHCP messages? That solution was originally described in RFC 1542, "Clarifications and Extensions for the Bootstrap Protocol." Let's look at this method.

DHCP Relay Agent

If there will not be a DHCP server on every subnet in your network, the routers in your network must be configured to pass BootP/DHCP messages through to the other segment. Both BootP and DHCP messages use UDP ports 67 and 68, therefore the router will pass messages sent as IP broadcasts to those ports. This router is now acting as a DHCP relay agent.[11]

Recall our the network design for foobar.com was to create three DHCP scopes, as shown in Figure 15.38. In order for the DHCP clients eng2, eng3, sales2, sales3, etc. to obtain IP addresses using DHCP, the routers connecting the subnets to the subnet containing the DHCP server must be configured to be DHCP relay agents. Therefore both ENG_RTR and SALES_RTR must be configured as a relay agent.

11. Depending on who you ask, the terminology changes. In NT, it is called a DHCP relay agent, but in RFC 1542, it is called a BootP relay agent. To configure Cisco routers to pass DHCP and BootP traffic, you use the command "iphelper".

Figure 15.38 Two DHCP scopes require DHCP relay agent software to operate on the attached routers.

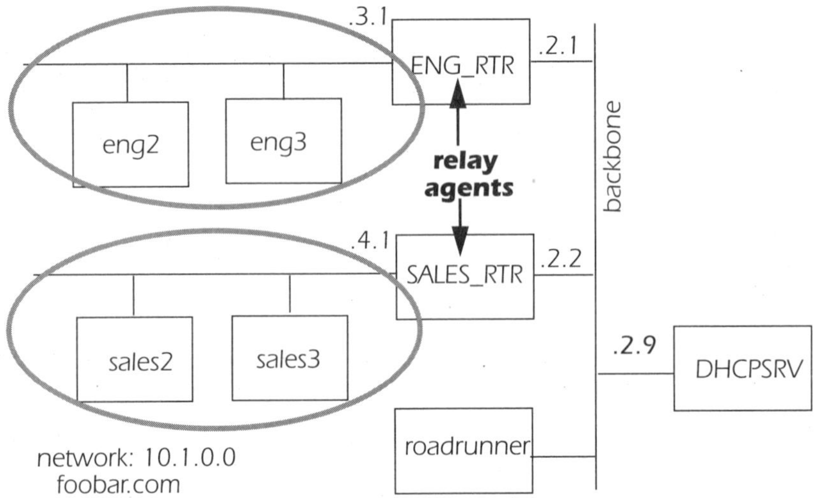

The dialog used to configure the DHCP relay agent in NT 4.0 is the *Microsoft TCP/IP Properties* dialog, *DHCP Relay tab.* (Recall this dialog is obtained using the *Network Control Panel.*) Figure 15.39 shows this dialog as it is configured on the machine ENG_RTR. The IP address of the DHCP server (10.1.2.9) has been entered in that dialog.

Figure 15.39 The DHCP relay configuration dialog allows specification of DHCP servers to contact.

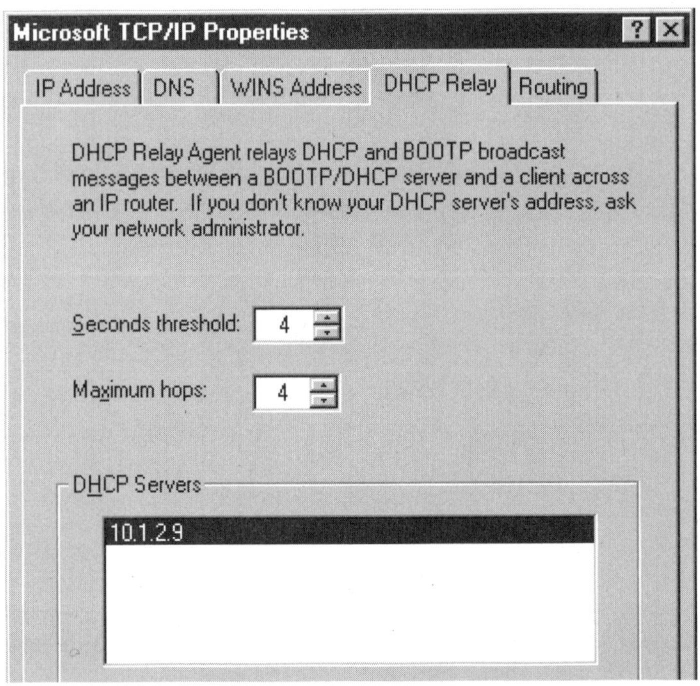

We'll see how the seconds threshold and maximum hops parameters are used shortly.

Configuring DHCP Relay Agent Using Steelhead

Steelhead can also act as a DHCP relay. The DHCP relay software is added as a "protocol" under IP. Configure it using a dialog similar to Figure 15.39, then assign it interfaces to operate upon. Figure 15.40 shows the RRAS Manager with the DHCP relay agent configured to operate upon the 3Com Ethernet interface.

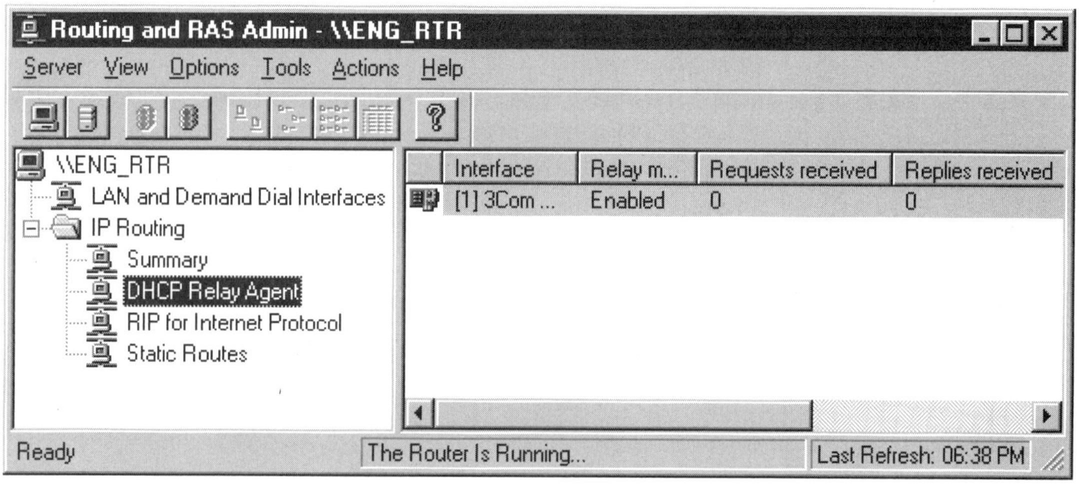

Figure 15.40 A Steelhead router can also function as a DHCP relay agent.

Relay Agent Operation

Recall that a DHCP client sends a discover message as an IP broadcast. Also recall that all DHCP messages are sent either to or from port 67 and port 68.

A DHCP relay agent looks for two properties in an incoming message:

- Destination IP address of 255.255.255.255 and target port number of 67 (messages from client to server).
- Destination IP address of one of its interfaces and a target port number of 68 (messages from server to client).

If either of these two cases hold true, that message is sent to the relay agent software to be processed further.

Consider ENG_RTR with the DHCP Relay configuration shown in Figure 15.39. When ENG_RTR sees DHCP discover messages from the engineering subnet, it may conditionally forward them to the DHCP server at 10.1.2.9.

If the discover message's seconds field is greater than the relay agent's (ENG_RTR) seconds threshold, then the relay agent assumes that the DHCP client has been attempting to obtain a lease for more than four seconds without having a server respond. In this case, the DHCP relay agent will forward to the DHCP server. As was shown in the DHCP packet captures earlier (Figure 15.28 and Figure 15.32), the Windows NT DHCP client specifies a seconds parameter of ten seconds. Because this is greater than our threshold on ENG_RTR (four seconds), such discover messages will be forwarded on.

Router operation involves forwarding messages with no modification to the original message. However, the relay agent will change the DHCP messages in a few ways. Once the DHCP relay agent decides that it should pay attention to a discover or request message, it performs the following:

- Increments the hop count field (which the client initially sets to zero).
- Fills in the IP address of the interface on which it received the message into the gateway address (giaddr) field.
- Sends the message as a directed (IP unicast) message to the DHCP server.

If the hop count exceeds the hop count limit in the relay, the message will not be forwarded. Note that the DHCP hop count will be the number of DHCP relays which the message has gone through, not the number of IP routers. Because the DHCP relay forwards the messages on with the DHCP server IP address as the target, one DHCP hop may be one or more IP hops.

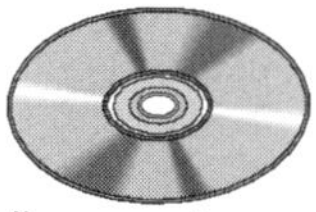

dhcpsrv-rtr.cap
frame #1

An example of this message manipulation is shown in Figure 15.41. The giaddr is used by the DHCP server to determine what subnet the client is on, so that it can assign an appropriate IP address to the client. The giaddr is also useful when sending from the server back to the relay, as giaddr will be the destination IP address in the DHCP server's response packet.

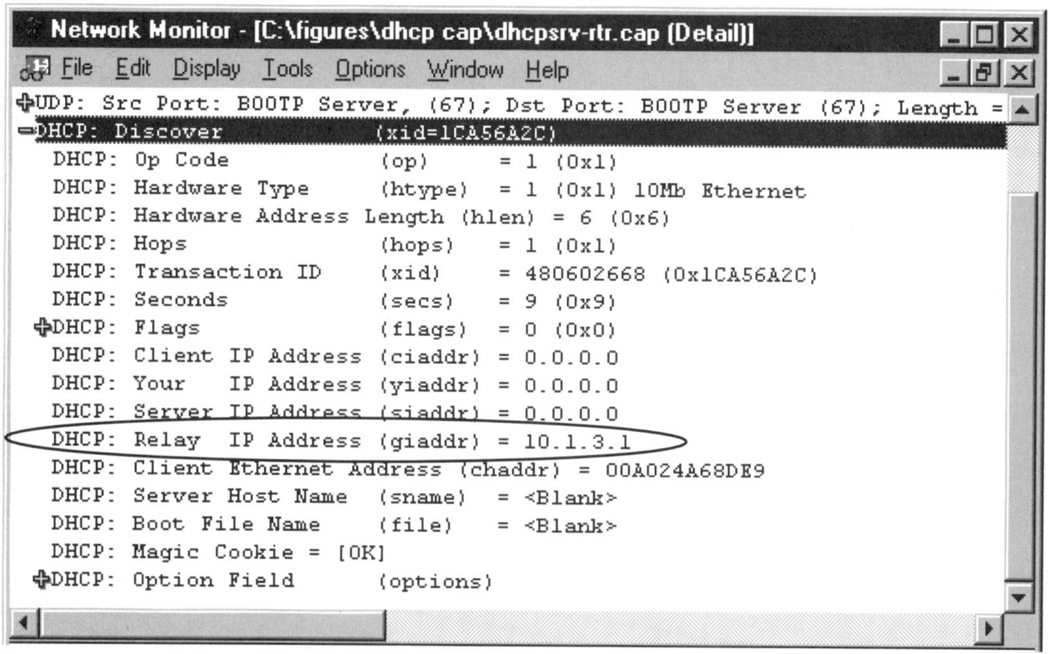

Figure 15.41 Discover message after it went through the relay agent.

We've described what happens with discover and request messages travelling from a client through a relay to a server. How are offer and acknowledgment messages transmitted from the server through the relay to the client? The server sends offer and ACK messages back to the relay, which sends them out its gateway interface to the client.

Figure 15.42 is a ladder diagram of the message exchange between the client, router and server.

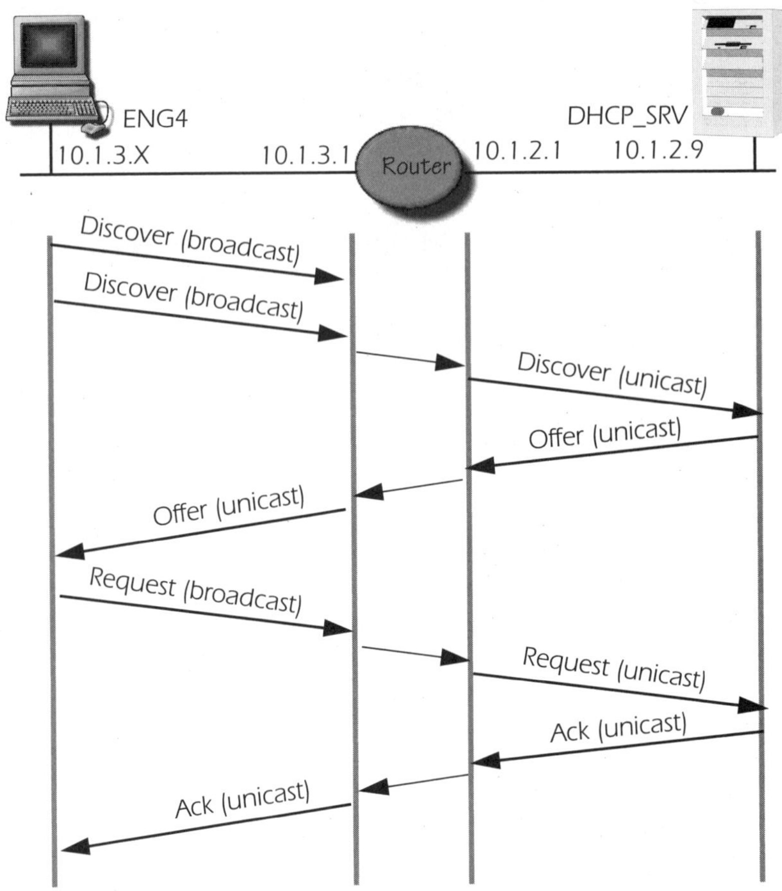

Figure 15.42 DHCP message exchange through a relay agent.

Recall that the DHCP relay agent inspects the seconds field in the discover messages, and compares it to the seconds threshold shown in Figure 15.39 on page 604. The first discover message in this example (Figure 15.42) has a lower seconds field than the seconds threshold configured in the relay agent, therefore it is ignored. The second discover message has a higher seconds value than the threshold, thus it is relayed to the server.

dhcpcli-rtr.cap
dhcpsrv-rtr.cap

Figure 15.43 and Figure 15.44 show the packet captures for this exchange. Each of these captures were recorded from a different perspective. The first vantage point captured the messages between the DHCP client and the relay agent on the router. The second vantage point recorded the exchange between the relay agent on the router and DHCP server. These capture files are called dhcpcli-rtr.cap and dhcpsrv-rtr.cap.

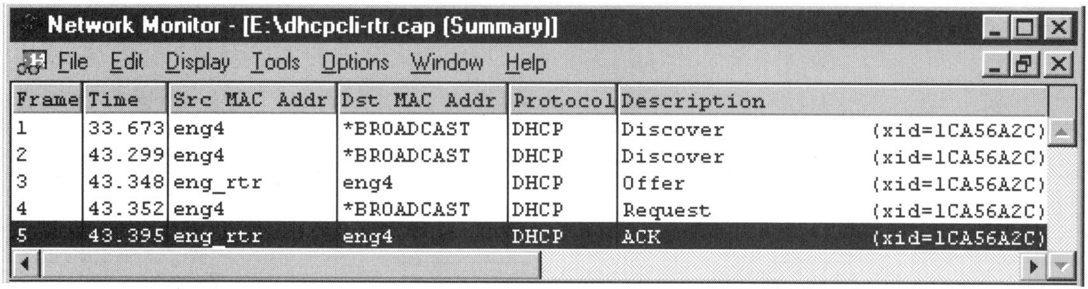

Network Monitor - [E:\dhcpcli-rtr.cap (Summary)]

File Edit Display Tools Options Window Help

Frame	Time	Src MAC Addr	Dst MAC Addr	Protocol	Description
1	33.673	eng4	*BROADCAST	DHCP	Discover (xid=1CA56A2C)
2	43.299	eng4	*BROADCAST	DHCP	Discover (xid=1CA56A2C)
3	43.348	eng_rtr	eng4	DHCP	Offer (xid=1CA56A2C)
4	43.352	eng4	*BROADCAST	DHCP	Request (xid=1CA56A2C)
5	43.395	eng_rtr	eng4	DHCP	ACK (xid=1CA56A2C)

Figure 15.43 DHCP messages between the client and router.

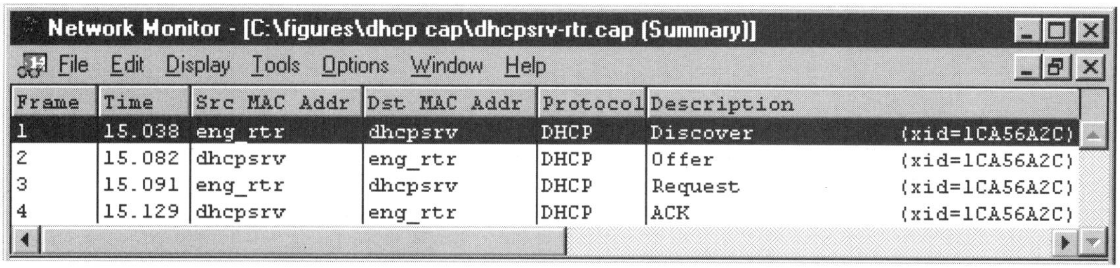

Network Monitor - [C:\figures\dhcp cap\dhcpsrv-rtr.cap (Summary)]

File Edit Display Tools Options Window Help

Frame	Time	Src MAC Addr	Dst MAC Addr	Protocol	Description
1	15.038	eng_rtr	dhcpsrv	DHCP	Discover (xid=1CA56A2C)
2	15.082	dhcpsrv	eng_rtr	DHCP	Offer (xid=1CA56A2C)
3	15.091	eng_rtr	dhcpsrv	DHCP	Request (xid=1CA56A2C)
4	15.129	dhcpsrv	eng_rtr	DHCP	ACK (xid=1CA56A2C)

Figure 15.44 DHCP messages between the router and DHCP server.

Note that only the first relay agent will modify the contents of the DHCP message. The first relay agent is the router that is on the same subnet as the client. DHCP messages that are unicast will not be modified by any further routers between the relay agent and the server.Routers between the first DHCP relay agent and the DHCP server will of course leave the DHCP message untouched (just changing lower layer headers as necessary).

If there is a need for another DHCP relay agent, it will not change the gateway address, but will increase the DHCP hop count to protect against relay agent loops.

Backing Up and Restoring the DHCP Database

The DHCP database is automatically backed up on a regular basis. The registry entry *BackupInterval* parameter specifies the number of minutes to periodically back up the database (default: 60 minutes). The database will be backed up in the directory *BackupDatabasePath*\jet\new, to the file dhcp.mdb. This parameter is described in Table 15.3.

Table 15.3 BackupInterval registry parameter.

Hive:	HKEY_LOCAL_MACHINE
Key:	\System\CurrentControlSet\Services\DHCPServer\Parameters
Name:	BackupInterval
Type:	REG_DWORD
Value:	60 (default)

The *BackupDatabasePath* registry parameter is used to specify the path to the backup database (Table 15.4). The backup files will be kept in this directory under the subdirectory \jet\new.

Table 15.4 BackupDatabase Path registry parameter.

Hive:	HKEY_LOCAL_MACHINE
Key:	\System\CurrentControlSet\Services\DHCPServer\Parameters
Name:	BackupDatabasePath
Type:	REG_MULTI_SZ
Value:	%SystemRoot%\system32\dhcp\backup (default)

The DHCP database can be restored from the backup either manually or automatically. If the DHCP server detects a corrupt database upon service startup, it will begin restoring from the backup database. If it becomes necessary to manually restore the DHCP database, set the registry entry *RestoreFlag* to 1 to start the restoration process (Table 15.5).

Table 15.5 RestoreFlag registry parameter.

Hive:	HKEY_LOCAL_MACHINE
Key:	\System\CurrentControlSet\Services\DHCPServer\Parameters
Name:	RestoreFlag
Type:	REG_DWORD
Value:	0 (default)

Note that after restoring the database, make sure to bring the database up to date on active leases not recorded on the backup copy of the database. In DHCP Manager, select a scope, bring up the *Active Leases* dialog (Figure 15.22), and click on the *Reconcile* button to reconcile the database.

Backing up the DHCP Servers

There is no intercommunication between multiple DHCP servers in a network. Therefore each DHCP server needs to be configured with its own unique range of addresses. If there is an overlapping of scope, then there can potentially be clients with duplicate IP addresses — a big problem.

However, it is a good idea to have a DHCP server that could handle DHCP requests in case another DHCP server goes down (Figure 15.45). If a DHCP server is going to backup the primary DHCP server, it is suggested that only 3/4 of the addresses be assigned to the primary server. Assign the remaining 1/4 addresses of that subnet to the backup DHCP server. Additionally, you may choose to assign the first server 1/4 of the second server's addresses so that the servers may cooperatively back each other up.

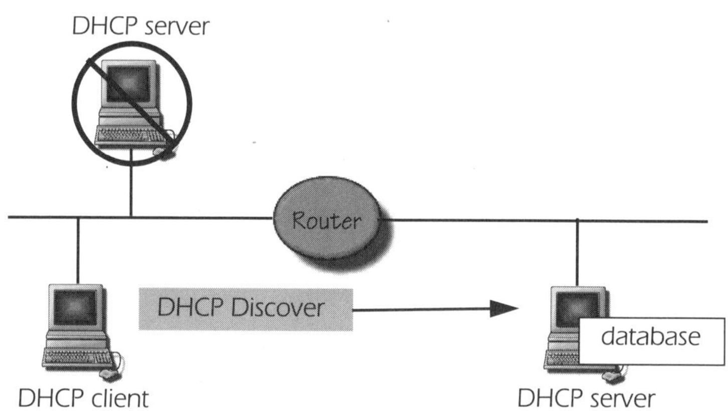

Figure 15.45 When the local DHCP server is down, there must be another DHCP server which has a scope for addresses in the client's subnet.

Make sure the router in between forwards DHCP messages as was described in the DHCP relay section.

Summary

Here's a summary of the items which have been addressed in this chapter.

- Dynamic assignment of IP addresses to clients may ease address management. RARP, BootP, and DHCP provide various kinds of dynamic assignment.
- The command ***ipconfig /release*** will release the current DHCP lease. The command ***ipconfig /renew*** will attempt to renew the current DHCP lease or obtain a new lease. The tool ***wntipcfg.exe*** can also perform these functions.
- A DHCP scope is a range of IP addresses that can be assigned to clients. The address ranges within a scope will fall within one subnet.
- DHCP Manager is used to configure the DHCP server, as well as determine which clients have which IP addresses.
- DHCP options are pieces of configuration information that are assigned along with the IP address.
- The initial client leasing process consists of four packets summarized by the acronym DORA: discover, offer, request, ack. All of these packets are sent as IP broadcasts, except when relay agents are involved.
- The client renewal process consists of two packets: request and ack.
- A DHCP relay agent is used to forward the broadcasted DHCP packets between networks. Both NT 4.0 and NT 4.0 with Steelhead software can be configured to be a DHCP relay agent.

Further Reading

Here is information about various books and magazines in which to look for further information on the subject.

[Alexander1997] Alexander, S., Droms, R., *DHCP Options and BOOTP Vendor Extensions,* 1997, IETF RFC 2132

[Croft1985] Croft, W.J., Gilmore, J., *Bootstrap Protocol,* 1985, IETF RFC 951

[Droms1993] Droms, R., *Interoperation Between DHCP and BOOTP,* 1993, IETF RFC 1534

[Droms1997] Droms, R., *Dynamic Host Configuration Protocol,* 1997, IETF RFC 2131

[Finlayson1984a] Finlayson, R., Mann, T., Mogul, J.C., Theimer, M., *Reverse Address Resolution Protocol,* 1984, IETF RFC 903

[Finlayson1984b] Finlayson, R., *Bootstrap loading using TFTP,* 1984, IETF RFC 906

[MSPress1997] Microsoft Press, *Microsoft Windows NT Resource Kit,* 1997, Microsoft Press

[Wimer1993] Wimer, W., *Clarifications and Extensions for the Bootstrap Protocol,* 1993, IETF RFC 1542

16

NetBIOS Name Resolution

In Chapter 11, "Domain Name Resolution", we described the process of obtaining IP addresses for Internet domain names. The two typical methods are to either use a host file, or query a DNS server.

In this chapter, we'll describe the various methods NT uses to resolve NetBIOS computer names to IP addresses. One of the most popular of those methods is to query the Windows Internet Name Server (WINS). Operation of the WINS server will be discussed, as well as the contents of WINS packets.

Why We Need NetBIOS Name Resolution

With traditional NetBIOS networking, there are no IP addresses, there is no internetworking, there are no routers. NetBIOS network layer addresses are known as NetBIOS computer names. NetBIOS computer names are not hierarchical. They support the NetBIOS model of one flat network.

Traditionally, in order for machines running NetBIOS to communicate, they must resolve computer names into MAC addresses. This NetBIOS name resolution is analogous to ARP for IP. Figure 16.1 shows that NetBIOS computer names are used by the NetBEUI Frame protocol (NBF), whereas IP addresses are used by IP. Applications which use IP may use domain names as a user-friendly aliases for IP addresses.

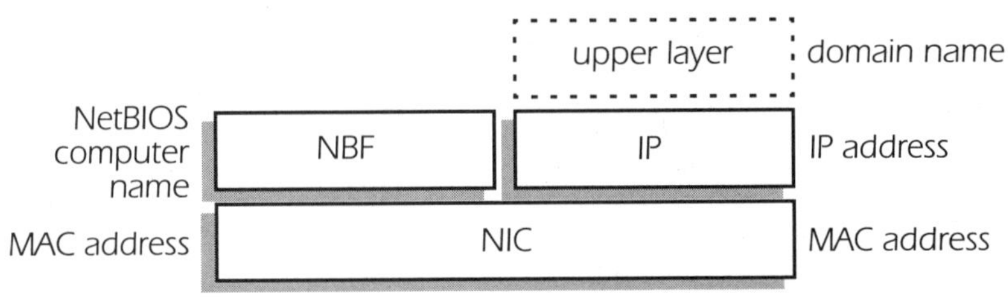

Figure 16.1 NetBIOS uses computer names, while IP uses IP addresses.

When NetBIOS is run over an internetworking protocol such as IP, name resolution becomes more interesting. Recall that NetBIOS over TCP/IP (NetBT) was created to run NetBIOS networking over IP networks. With NetBT, NetBIOS computer names need to be resolved into IP addresses.

If you do not run NetBIOS applications, then NetBIOS name resolution is not needed. If you run NetBIOS applications (e.g. browsing) on NetBEUI, NetBIOS names do not need to be translated to IP addresses, since NetBEUI doesn't use IP addresses.

In order to still use traditional NetBIOS applications which weren't designed for internetworks, we need name resolution to convert from NetBIOS computer names to IP address.

Because this modern form of NetBIOS name resolution allows NetBIOS to be used in IP internetworks, one of the techniques of name resolution used for Microsoft Windows networking is called the Windows Internet Name Service (WINS).

Two things to note about WINS:

- WINS does not necessarily have anything to do with The Internet other than the fact that IP is being used.
- WINS is used for flat NetBIOS computer names. While it answers name queries like DNS, it is not as sophisticated as DNS, partially because of the flat name space.

How Long Will NetBIOS Be Used?

If we accept the fact that NetBIOS was designed for small LANs, and most new applications are designed for internetworking (and specifically, IP networks) the following questions may come to mind.

- How long will NetBIOS be around?
- Do we need NetBIOS name resolution without NetBIOS?

Depending on your situation (i.e. how dependent you are on NetBIOS applications), the answers may simply be "not long," and "no."

Even if NetBIOS does persist, the current name resolution methods may be short-lived. The methods discussed in this chapter may be replaced by various extensions to DNS, and/or technologies such as The Directory and the Light-weight Directory Access Protocol (LDAP).

Browsing

Many current NetBIOS applications are based on LAN Manager and Server Message Block (SMB) communications. Applications such as browsing and mapping network drives are NetBIOS-based.

browsing: the process of obtaining a list of available resources on the LAN.

Browsing is the process of obtaining a list of all of the available resources on the LAN. Resources include other PCs, file servers, and printers. You browse the network when you:

- view the Network Neighborhood (Figure 16.2)
- use the command ***net view*** (Figure 16.3)
- map a network drive (Figure 16.4)

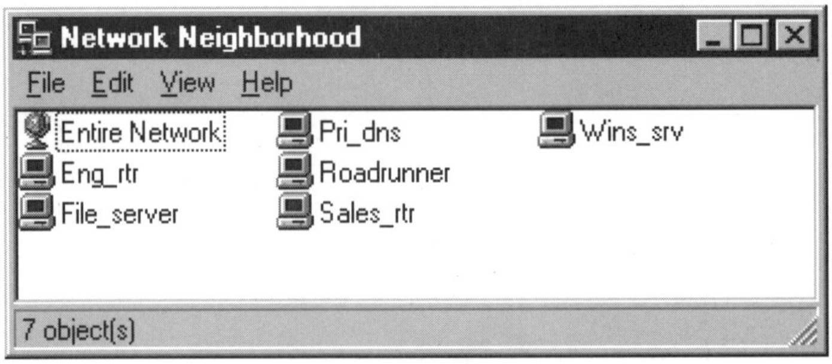

Figure 16.2 Browsing with the Network Neighborhood application.

The browsing software was written using the NetBIOS API, originally running over the NetBEUI transport. To keep this functionality in NT, browsing can now also use the transport protocol NetBT.

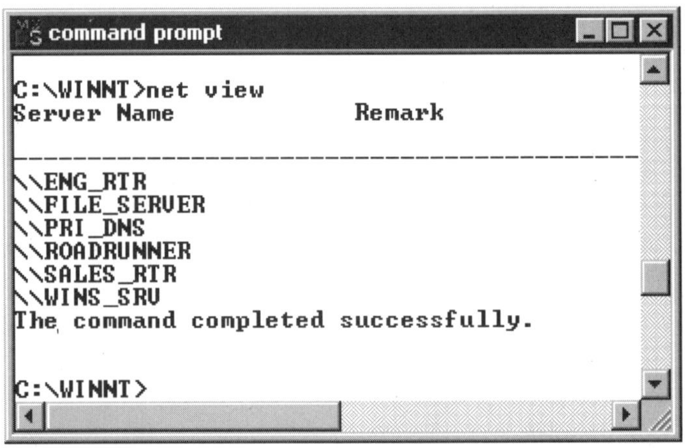

Figure 16.3 Browsing using the command net view.

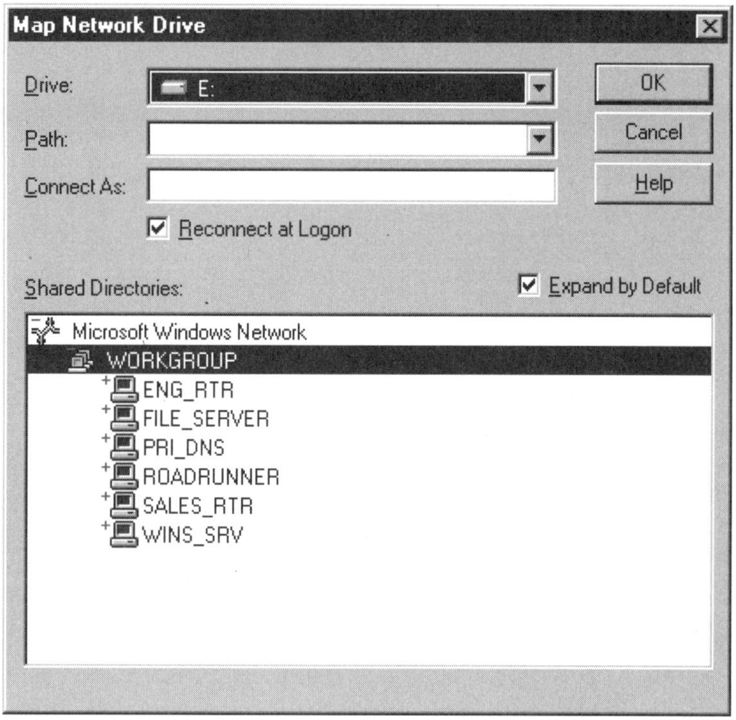

Figure 16.4 Mapping a network drive.

Current Network Diagram for Foobar.com

Throughout the book, the network for foobar.com has been expanding. We've described each component that was added. For this chapter, two new devices have been added to the network a file server called FILE_SRV, and a WINS server called WINS_SRV. We'll be referring to both of those machines, as well as roadrunner, in the remainder of this chapter. Figure 16.5 shows the current network diagram.

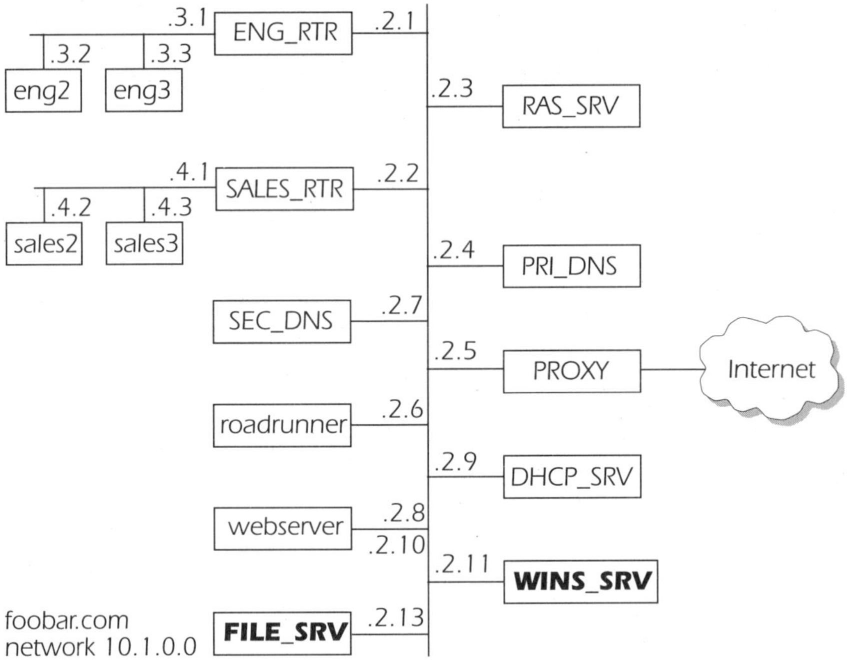

Figure 16.5
Current network map of foobar.com. The machines shown in bold are newly added.

You can compare this network map with the list of machines in Network Neighborhood (Figure 16.2) to see that we were browsing the backbone subnet.

NetBIOS Over TCP/IP (NetBT)

In order to allow Windows applications to run over large networks, a new protocol was created to process data between the NetBIOS API and TCP/IP. This new protocol is called NetBIOS over TCP/IP (NetBT). In particular, NetBT uses both UDP and TCP to send its packets (Figure 16.6).

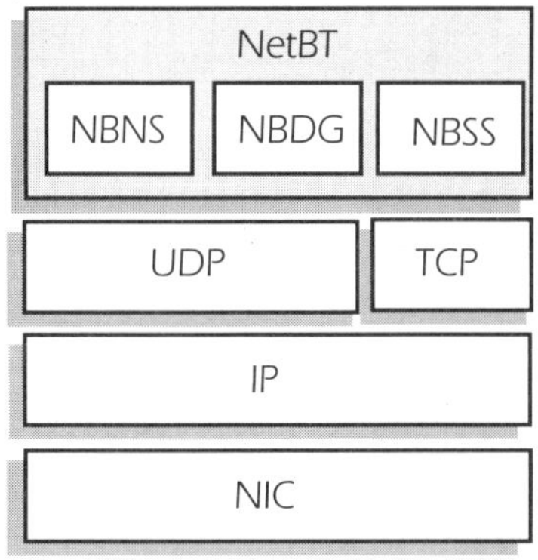

Figure 16.6
NetBIOS over TCP/IP (NetBT) runs over both TCP and UDP.

The NetBIOS session service (NBSS) runs over TCP, while the NetBIOS datagram service (NBDG) runs over UDP. The NetBIOS Name Service (NBNS) also runs over UDP. WINS is an implementation of the NBNS. NetBT sends name queries and name registrations to the IP address of the WINS server. In particular, the WINS server service listens on UDP port 137. NetBT uses other TCP and UDP ports for certain applications, shown in Table 16.1.

Table 16.1
Port numbers used for NetBIOS over TCP/IP services.

Port number	Description
UDP port 137	NetBIOS name service
UDP port 138	NetBIOS datagram service
TCP port 139	NetBIOS session service

Microsoft NetBIOS Names

NetBIOS resource type: 16th character of a NetBIOS name that represents a particular service or user on that machine.

Each computer within a Microsoft network must have a unique name, called a NetBIOS computer name. NetBIOS names are a maximum of 15 user-assigned characters in length. The 16th character is reserved: it will contain a **resource type** — essentially a number associated with a particular service. These names will be registered dynamically when a particular service starts, or when a user logs in.

Figure 16.7 shows a list of the various NetBIOS names that are found on the machine roadrunner. The command ***nbtstat -n*** was used to obtain the local name table.

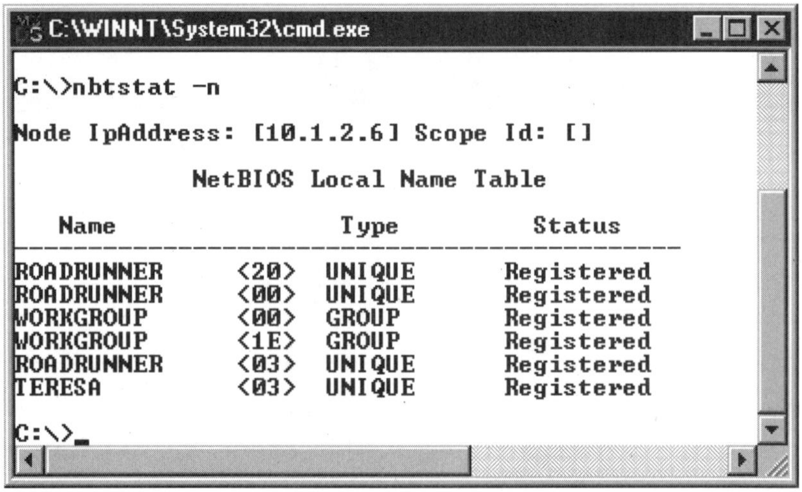

Figure 16.7 Nbtstat -n is used to view the local NetBIOS names being used on roadrunner.

Notice that each of the names in Figure 16.7 are followed by a column that represents the NetBIOS service type. Table 16.2 describes the names and the codes for these service types.

Table 16.2 Interpretation of a local NetBIOS name table on the machine roadrunner.

ROADRUNNER[00h]	The workstation service started on ROADRUNNER.
ROADRUNNER[03h]	The messenger service started on ROADRUNNER.
ROADRUNNER[20h]	The server service started on ROADRUNNER.
TERESA[03h]	The user TERESA logged into ROADRUNNER. This information is used by the messenger service to send messages to particular users.
WORKGROUP[00]	The group name WORKGROUP has been registered by the workstation service.
WORKGROUP[1E]	The group name WORKGROUP has been registered, and will be used to elect a master browser.

The third column in Figure 16.7, labelled "Type", lists one of two possibilities: unique names or group names. *Unique NetBIOS names* have one IP address associated with a name. *Group NetBIOS names* have more than one IP address mapped to a name. In this case, only one IP address is assigned to the group name WORKGROUP.

The reason why we are concerned with these codes is that when we examine the WINS database in detail, we will see each of these names and codes entered in the database. Each of the names shown above will be registered with the WINS server.

You may see other NetBIOS service types listed in the WINS database as well as in other documentation. Some of the most popular NetBIOS service types are listed in Table 16.3.

Table 16.3 NetBIOS unique name service numbers.

Service number (hex)	Service name
00	workstation
03	messenger
06	RAS server
20	server
21	RAS client
BE	network monitoring agent
BF	network monitoring utility

For a complete listing of NetBIOS names, refer to [MSPress1996].

Methods of Resolution

There are six possible methods of NetBIOS name resolution:

- a local file called LMHOSTS is searched
- a WINS server is queried for the IP address
- the name query is broadcast on the local LAN
- the IP address is found in the NetBIOS name cache (it was already resolved, or configured as a static entry in the name cache)
- a local file called hosts is searched (as seen in the DNS chapter)
- a DNS server is queried

One or more of these methods can be attempted by a client. The order in which these methods is tried is configurable— to a degree. First let's discuss each of these methods, and then we'll see how they can be combined.

The LMHOSTS File

The LMHOSTS (LAN Manager HOSTS) is an ASCII file, found in %systemroot%\system32\drivers\etc. This file is very similar in function and content to the DNS hosts file. It maps NetBIOS names to IP addresses, as shown in the example in Figure 16.8.

Figure 16.8
An example LMHOSTS file.

```
#Example LMHOSTS file
10.1.2.13      FILE_SRV   #PRE
10.1.3.2       ENG2
10.1.4.2       SALES2
```

Each machine may have an LMHOSTS file which lists a mapping for every other machine in the network. When a new machine is added to the network, a new mapping would have to be added to the LMHOSTS file on every machine in the network, and a copy of the file should be placed on the new machine.

Options may be listed at the end of a line. The #DOM option may be placed at the end of a line to associate an entry with a domain.

A #INCLUDE directive can be used to include another file. This may be used to bring in another local file which has been distributed to each machine, or to reference a file on a remote machine; for example: #INCLUDE \\FILE_SRV\PUBLIC\LMHOSTS states that the contents of the LMHOSTS file from another host, FILE_SRV, are to be included at the point of the #INCLUDE in the local LMHOSTS file.

NetBT can preload a certain number of entries into NetBIOS name cache from the LMHOSTS file, using the #PRE option. The *MaxPreload* registry parameter specifies the maximum number of entries loaded from the LMHOSTS file. The default is 100 entries. Entries included in the cache due to the #PRE option remain in the cache until it is reloaded. Their life is shown as -1.

Use LMHOSTS files under the following conditions:

- You have a small number of nodes. If you have a large number of nodes, it will be a lot of work to keep the LMHOSTS files updated on each machine.

- You are not using WINS to resolve name queries. If all your machines are WINS clients, there is no need to place entries into the LMHOSTS file.

You shouldn't use LMHOSTS files if:

- You are using WINS. WINS will provide the same functionality as the LMHOSTS file, but with less hassle.
- You are using DHCP to assign IP addresses. It would be impossible to keep updating the LMHOSTS files for every newly assigned IP address.

Windows Internet Name Service (WINS) Operation

The Windows Internet Name Service (WINS) was created to provide NetBIOS name to IP address mapping. WINS is a specific implementation of a NBNS. The WINS server receives and replies to requests for IP addresses as shown in Figure 16.9.

Figure 16.9
NetBIOS name to IP address resolution using a WINS server.

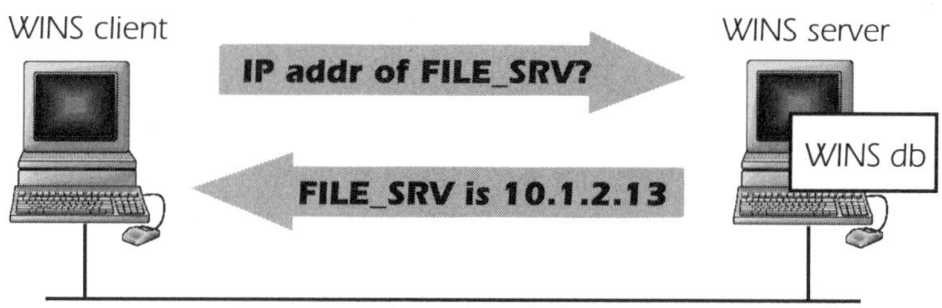

Some of the benefits to running WINS include:

- Fewer NetBIOS application broadcasts.
- Names and addresses are updated dynamically at one central location: the WINS server.
- WINS is scalable — it can easily accommodate increases in the number of nodes in your network.

A WINS client will query a WINS server multiple times if the WINS server doesn't respond. The number of times the client will send a name query request to the WINS server is three by default. This value is configurable using the registry parameter *NameSrvQueryCount,* shown in Table 16.4. The *NameSrvQueryCount* parameter specifies the total number of attempts which NetBT will make before failing.

Table 16.4 NameSrvQuery Count registry parameter.

Hive:	HKEY_LOCAL_MACHINE
Key:	\System\CurrentControlSet\Services\NetBT\Parameters
Name:	NameSrvQueryCount
Type:	REG_DWORD
Value:	3 attempts (default)

The time in between the WINS queries is by default 1.5 seconds. This value is configurable using the registry value *NameSrvQueryTimeout,* shown in Table 16.5. The *NameSrvQueryTimeout* parameter specifies the number of milliseconds that NetBT will wait before a re-attempt.

Table 16.5 NameSrvQuery Timeout registry parameter.

Hive:	HKEY_LOCAL_MACHINE
Key:	\System\CurrentControlSet\Services\NetBT\Parameters
Name:	NameSrvQueryTimeout
Type:	REG_DWORD
Value:	1500 milliseconds (default)

Packet Decode of Name Queries

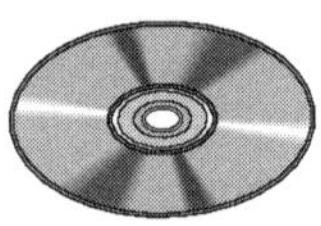

querysuccess.cap

Here is an example of a WINS query sent from roadrunner to WINS_SRV, trying to resolve the name FILE_SRV into an IP address. The packet capture of this request is in the file querysuccess.cap on the CD. The address database is called wins_ch.adr.

Note that the query request shown in Figure 16.9 is sent as an IP unicast message from roadrunner to WINS_SRV. Recall that WINS uses UDP port 137 (Table 16.1).

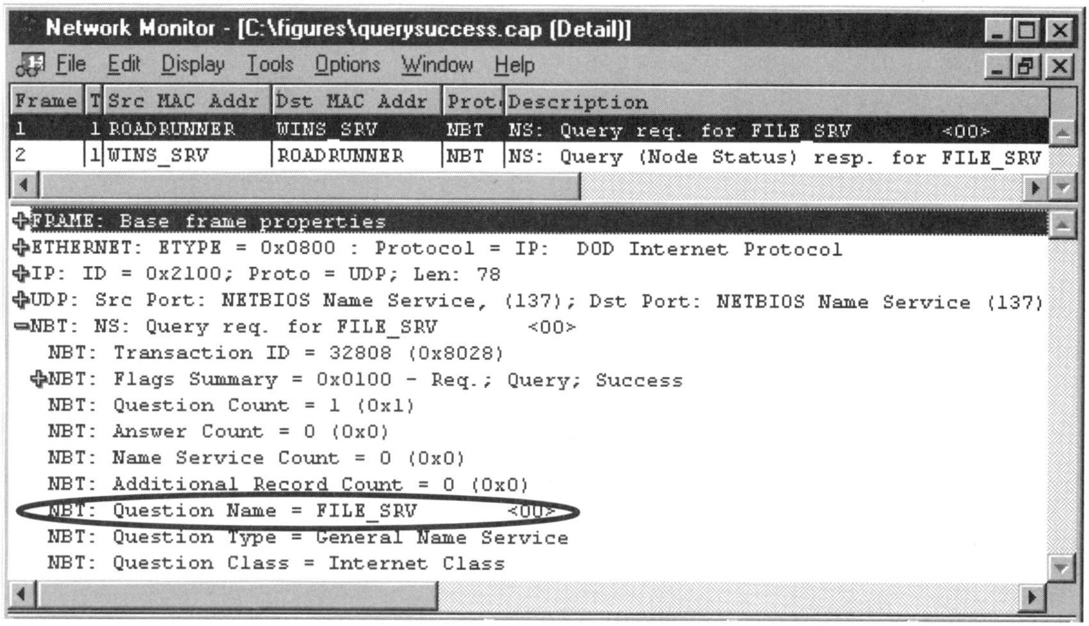

Figure 16.10 *WINS query request from roadrunner to WINS_SRV.*

Note that like DNS, WINS has question and answer sections of the message. The name being queried is a 16 octet NetBIOS name. The first 15 octets are the name FILE_SRV padded with spaces. The sixteenth octet identifies the resource type (00 = workstation service).

When WINS_SRV receives this query, it looks in its database of mappings. In our example, WINS_SRV finds a mapping for the workstation service on FILE_SRV to the IP address 10.1.2.13. A WINS query response is sent back to roadrunner, as shown in Figure 16.11.

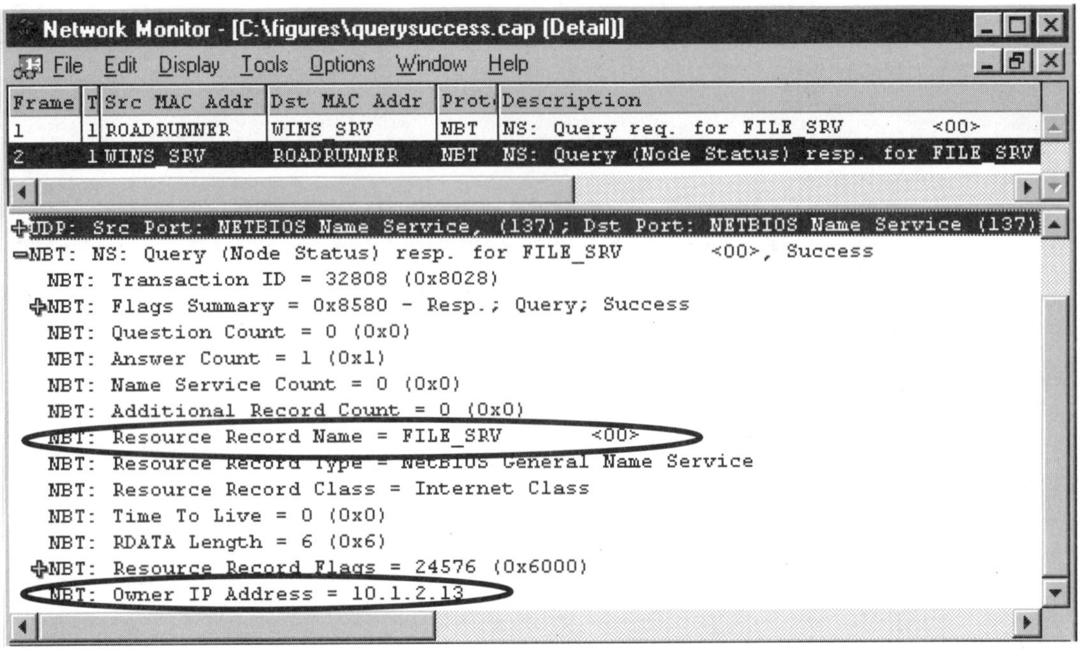

Figure 16.11 WINS query response from WINS_SRV to roadrunner.

After roadrunner receives this response, roadrunner can send NetBT messages over the IP network to FILE_SRV using the IP address 10.1.2.13. The normal rules of IP apply, thus roadrunner has to resolve the IP address into a MAC address.

If the machines in the engineering and sales subnets are known by the WINS server, roadrunner would be able to resolve their names into IP addresses. Thus, when WINS is used for NetBIOS name resolution, NetBT may treat an IP internet as a tunnel for a virtual NetBIOS network.

Broadcast Query Packets

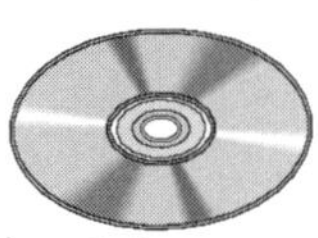

queryfailure.cap

Another NetBIOS name resolution method is broadcasting the name query. Like ARP, this method will only work if the machine named in the packet is on the local LAN. For this example, roadrunner has been configured to try the broadcast resolution method if attempts to use WINS fail. Figure 16.12 shows a packet capture of roadrunner's attempt to resolve the name BOGUS, a name which isn't registered with WINS_SRV.

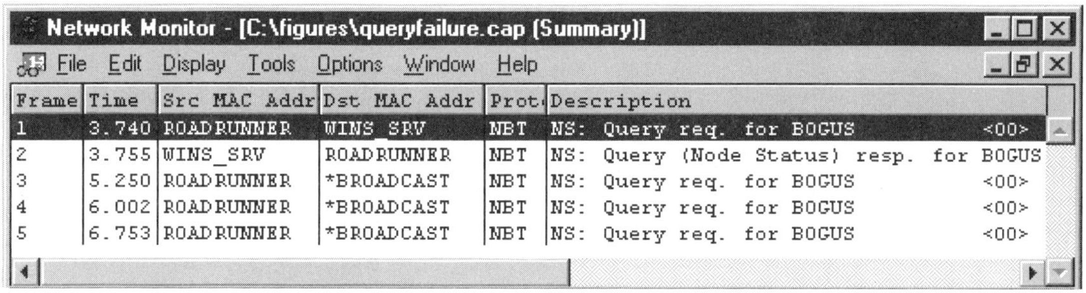

Figure 16.12 WINS name query, failure response, and broadcast queries for BOGUS.

The query in this case is like the query for FILE_SRV in the previous example. Because the WINS server doesn't know about the name BOGUS, it replies with a query response indicating that BOGUS does not exist in the WINS database. See Figure 16.13 for the details of the response.

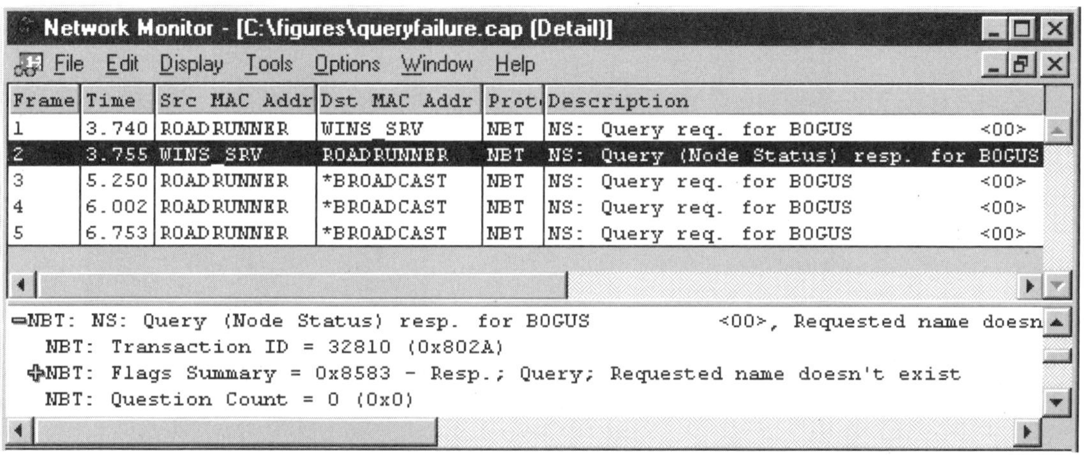

Figure 16.13 WINS query response reporting that BOGUS is not known.

Because roadrunner was configured to attempt the broadcast method in the event of a failure to resolve with WINS, roadrunner now sends another query request as a subnet broadcast in frame three of the capture.

If a response has not been received in a certain amount of time, another attempt may be made (see BcastNameQueryCount). The *BcastQueryTimeout* parameter (Table 16.6) specifies the number of milliseconds that NetBT will time out after sending a broadcast name query if it has not received a response.

Table 16.6
BcastQueryTimeout registry parameter.

Hive:	HKEY_LOCAL_MACHINE
Key:	\System\CurrentControlSet\Services\NetBT\Parameters
Name:	BcastQueryTimeout
Type:	REG_DWORD
Value:	750 milliseconds (default)

Note the timeouts between frames 3 and 4, and again between frames 4 and 5 in the example in queryfailure.cap (Figure 16.13). They are very close to the configured timeout value of 750 milliseconds.

When a response to a NetBT name query broadcast has not been received, NetBT will repeat the broadcast. The *BcastNameQueryCount* registry parameter, described in Table 16.7, specifies the maximum number of times an NetBT name query will be broadcast without receiving a response.

Table 16.7
BcastNameQuery Count registry parameter.

Hive:	HKEY_LOCAL_MACHINE
Key:	\System\CurrentControlSet\Services\NetBT\Parameters
Name:	BcastNameQueryCount
Type:	REG_DWORD
Value:	3 attempts (default)

NetBIOS Name Cache

The NetBIOS name cache contains a list of the recently-used computer names and their IP addresses. The cache can be viewed using the command ***nbtstat* -c**. An example of viewing the name cache on WINS_SRV is shown in Figure 16.14.

```
C:\WINNT>nbtstat -c

No names in cache

C:\WINNT>ping roadrunner

Pinging roadrunner [10.1.2.6] with 32 bytes of data:

Reply from 10.1.2.6: bytes=32 time<10ms TTL=128
Reply from 10.1.2.6: bytes=32 time<10ms TTL=128
Reply from 10.1.2.6: bytes=32 time<10ms TTL=128
Reply from 10.1.2.6: bytes=32 time<10ms TTL=128

C:\WINNT>nbtstat -c

Node IpAddress: [10.1.2.11] Scope Id: []

              NetBIOS Remote Cache Name Table

    Name              Type       Host Address    Life [sec]
-------------------------------------------------------------
ROADRUNNER     <00>  UNIQUE      10.1.2.6           660

C:\WINNT>
```

Figure 16.14 The nbtstat command shows that the name roadrunner was resolved and entered into the NetBIOS name cache.

Recall that the NetBIOS name table (see Figure 16.7 on page 622) contains mappings which are local to a machine. The NetBIOS name cache contains entries which are for other (i.e. remote) machines. Note that this use of the words local/remote do not refer to LAN vs. internetwork mappings, but rather mappings for this machine and for other machines.

The name cache is checked every time a NetBIOS name needs to be resolved into an IP address. If an entry is found in the name cache for that computer name, the NetBT packet can be sent immediately. Otherwise, some other method (e.g. WINS or broadcast query) must be used to obtain the IP address.

The results of name queries are held for a certain time in the name cache. The *CacheTimeout* registry parameter (Table 16.8) specifies the number of milliseconds which entries are to be cached in the name cache. The default value is 600000 milliseconds (10 minutes).

Table 16.8
CacheTimeout registry parameter.

Hive:	HKEY_LOCAL_MACHINE
Key:	\System\CurrentControlSet\Services\NetBT\Parameters
Name:	CacheTimeout
Type:	REG_DWORD
Value:	600000 milliseconds (default)

Using the Hosts File to Resolve NetBIOS Name Queries

Another technique which is similar to using the LMHOSTS file may be used to resolve NetBIOS names. The hosts file, normally used to resolve domain names into IP addresses, may also be used to resolve NetBIOS computer names into IP addresses.

Using DNS to Resolve NetBIOS Name Queries

For all of the same reasons that maintaining a DNS server may be preferable to maintaining a host file on each machine for domain name resolution, using DNS to resolve NetBIOS computer names may be a method of choice.

If you maintain one or more DNS servers for domain name resolution, you may use them to resolve NetBIOS computer name queries. We'll see how to configure this option in the section called "Client Configuration" on page 634.

NetBT Node Types

In certain cases, network devices are called nodes. The NetBIOS name resolution methods can be used in varying order, and are based upon the *type* of node requesting the resolution — b-node, p-node, p-node, or m-node. A brief list of the NetBIOS node types is shown in Table 16.9.

Table 16.9 Meaning of NetBIOS node types.

Node type	WINS and/or broadcast method used
b-node	uses broadcast, but doesn't use WINS
p-node	uses WINS, but doesn't use broadcast
h-node	uses WINS, and then uses broadcast
m-node	uses broadcast, and then uses WINS

The most basic of the NetBT name resolution modes is *b-node*, which is short for broadcast-node. A node that is a b-node broadcasts UDP datagrams for name resolution. By default, NT machines are b-nodes. Because b-node uses broadcasts, large networks of b-node clients may suffer from an increased network load. Additionally, most routers do not pass broadcasts so b-node will usually only work within one network segment.

An alternative to b-node uses directed or "peer-to-peer" communications rather than broadcasts for name resolution and is called *p-node*. This has an advantage over b-node because the name server for b-node clients may be on the far side of a router. Also, the network load is less than with b-node because only the name server will receive the query and only the requester will receive the response. Each p-node host must be configured with the IP address of the name server.

The b-node method requires no configuration, but is wasteful of network resources, and is restricted to one subnet. While the p-node method is less wasteful and can span subnets, it requires that a server be configured, and that each client be configured with the address of the server. Because there are limitations to each b-node and p-node, two combination modes were created.

The "hybrid" of p-node and b-node is called *h-node*. With h-node, the client attempts to use WINS to resolve a name; if that fails, the client sends a broadcast name resolution request.

In "mixed" mode, or *m-node*, the client first tries broadcast and then tries WINS.

Clients can be configured to be a h-node or a m-node using DHCP to assign the NetBT Node type. option. The following are the possible settings for node type:

- 0x1 b-node
- 0x2 p-node
- 0x4 m-node
- 0x8 h-node

The Complete Search List

The NetBIOS node type determines if WINS or a broadcast is going to be used, and the order to use them, to resolve names. Name resolution can also take advantage of other methods, such as searching a local file (LMHOSTS, hosts) or sending a request to the DNS. These methods can be used by the client if configured using the *TCP/IP Configuration* screen. Table 16.10 shows the order of the search methods for each of the NetBIOS node types.

Table 16.10
Complete search list order by method.

Node type	Search methods and the order used
b-node	NetBIOS cache, broadcast, LMHOSTS, hosts, DNS
p-node	NetBIOS cache, WINS, LMHOSTS, hosts, DNS
h-node	NetBIOS cache, WINS, broadcast, LMHOSTS, hosts, DNS
m-node	NetBIOS cache, broadcast, WINS, LMHOSTS, hosts, DNS

Shown in Figure 16.15 is the order of name resolution queries for h-node, which was used on roadrunner in the examples for FILE_SRV and BOGUS.

Figure 16.15
Order of NetBIOS name resolution methods for h-node.

1. NetBIOS name cache
2. NetBIOS name server (WINS)
3. Broadcast
4. LMHOSTS file
5. hosts file
6. Domain Name Service (DNS)

Client Configuration

The dialog in Figure 16.9 is used to configure name resolution methods. A *primary WINS server* is the WINS server that this machine will register with and query. In case the primary WINS server is down, the *secondary*

WINS server can answer requests. Once you enter in one or two IP addresses of WINS servers, your machine is configured to be a WINS client, and is a h-node.

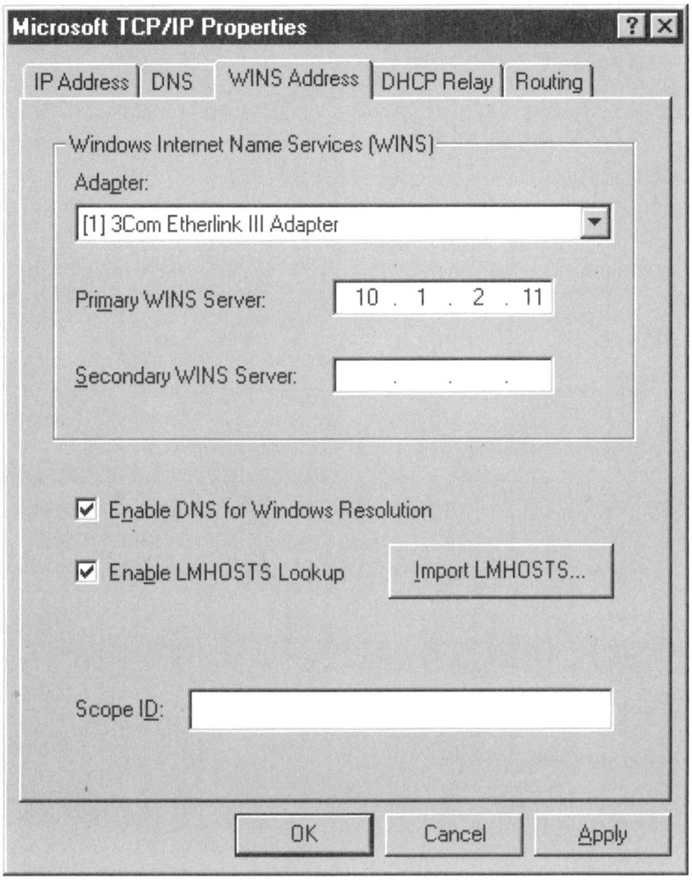

Figure 16.16 Client configuration to use WINS.

Other configuration possibilities include sending name resolution requests to the DNS server, and/or checking the local LMHOSTS file. Note that if the box for LMHOSTS is *not* checked, the LMHOSTS file will not be scanned for entries to be preloaded (with #PRE).

The node type is shown in the output of the ***ipconfig /all*** command (Figure 16.17). The default node type on Windows NT is b-node, because WINS is not configured and the broadcast method must be used.

```
C:\WINNT>ipconfig /all

Windows NT IP Configuration

        Host Name . . . . . . . . . : roadrunner.foobar.com
        DNS Servers . . . . . . . . : 10.1.2.11
        Node Type . . . . . . . . . : Broadcast
        NetBIOS Scope ID. . . . . . :
        IP Routing Enabled. . . . . : No
        WINS Proxy Enabled. . . . . : No
        NetBIOS Resolution Uses DNS : Yes

Ethernet adapter Elnk31:

        Description . . . . . . . . : ELNK3 Ethernet Adapter.
        Physical Address. . . . . . : 00-A0-24-A6-8D-E9
        DHCP Enabled. . . . . . . . : No
        IP Address. . . . . . . . . : 10.1.2.6
        Subnet Mask . . . . . . . . : 255.255.255.0
        Default Gateway . . . . . . : 10.1.2.1

C:\WINNT>
```

Figure 16.17 Without configuration as a WINS client, the client is a b-node.

```
C:\WINNT>ipconfig /all

Windows NT IP Configuration

        Host Name . . . . . . . . . : roadrunner.foobar.com
        DNS Servers . . . . . . . . : 10.1.2.11
        Node Type . . . . . . . . . : Hybrid
        NetBIOS Scope ID. . . . . . :
        IP Routing Enabled. . . . . : No
        WINS Proxy Enabled. . . . . : No
        NetBIOS Resolution Uses DNS : Yes

Ethernet adapter Elnk31:

        Description . . . . . . . . : ELNK3 Ethernet Adapter.
        Physical Address. . . . . . : 00-A0-24-A6-8D-E9
        DHCP Enabled. . . . . . . . : No
        IP Address. . . . . . . . . : 10.1.2.6
        Subnet Mask . . . . . . . . : 255.255.255.0
        Default Gateway . . . . . . : 10.1.2.1
        Primary WINS Server . . . . : 10.1.2.11

C:\WINNT>
```

Figure 16.18 A hybrid node (h-node) first tries to contact the WINS server, then broadcast.

When the client is configured with a WINS server address, name resolution operates in hybrid mode, as shown in Figure 16.18. When a name translation is not in the client's NetBIOS name cache, the h-node method first attempts to use the WINS server (10.1.2.11 in the figure) to resolve the name. If this fails, the client next sends a broadcast query. If this too fails, the client tries LMHOSTS, hosts, and finally DNS. Notice the "NetBIOS Resolution Uses DNS" option in the ***ipconfig /all*** output.

WINS Proxy

In general, WINS allows NetBT to treat a collection of machines on various subnets as one NetBIOS network neighborhood when all machines in that neighborhood use the WINS server.

Some older Microsoft operating systems support NetBT but not WINS, and other operating systems may also support NetBT but not WINS. When some of the machines that you want to be in the same neighborhood can't be WINS clients, something special must be done.

non-WINS enabled: a machine that does not (cannot) register with the WINS server.

The broadcast (b-node) method of resolution is more traditional than p-node, h-node, or m-node. Figure 16.19 shows a client without WINS enabled. This client is called **non-WINS enabled**. If this client is configured as a b-node, it will send broadcast messages for name resolution. The router typically will not pass these broadcasts. Thus the WINS server, on the other side of the router, will not receive them.

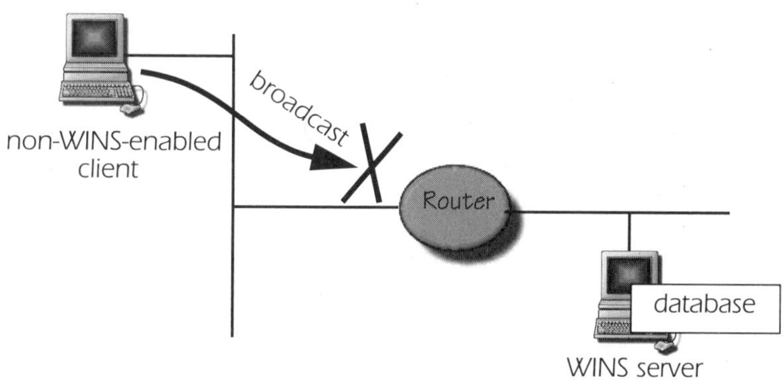

Figure 16.19 Broadcasts from a b-node will not be forwarded by a router, thus a WINS server on another subnet will not hear the name queries from the b-node.

WINS proxy agent: a WINS client that will forward name queries to the WINS server.

A Windows NT or Windows for Workgroups machine on the same network as the non-WINS-enabled client may be configured to act as a WINS proxy. The **WINS proxy agent** is a server or highly-available workstation which is a WINS client. This computer can be made to act as a WINS proxy agent by changing the registry value *EnableProxy* (see Table 16.11) to 1 (true).

Table 16.11
EnableProxy registry parameter.

Hive:	HKEY_LOCAL_MACHINE
Key:	\System\CurrentControlSet\Services\NetBT\Parameters
Name:	EnableProxy
Type:	REG_DWORD
Value:	0 (false- default)

When configured as a WINS proxy, any broadcast name requests received by this computer will be converted to p-node queries and directed to its WINS server, as shown in Figure 16.20. The WINS server replies to the WINS proxy, and the WINS proxy then unicasts the response. In this way, a WINS proxy may serve many non-WINS-enabled clients on its network when the WINS server is on a different network.

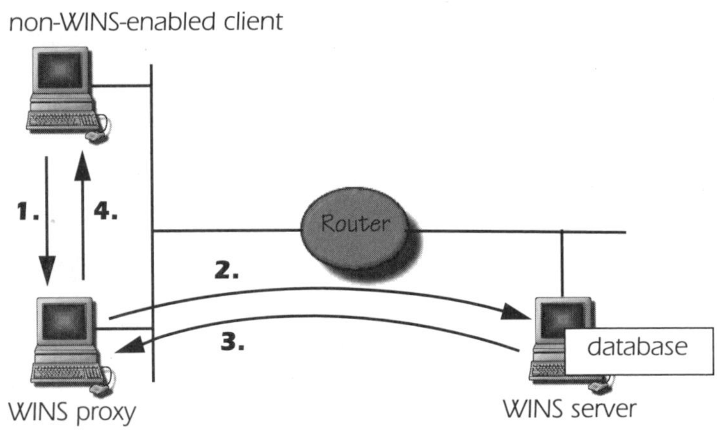

Figure 16.20
A WINS proxy forwards name resolution queries to the WINS server.

Note that you should only have one machine on a subnet as a proxy, as each proxy will forward requests, thus unnecessarily increasing network traffic. This however leaves the WINS proxy as a single point of failure for non-WINS-enabled clients.

Even if you have a WINS server on the same subnet as the non-WINS enabled client, it *will not* answer the broadcast name resolution requests. Thus you need a WINS proxy on every subnet that has non-WINS-enabled clients.

WINS Manager

The WINS Server is installed using *Network Control Panel -> Services -> Add.* The resulting dialog (Figure 16.21) lists possible services to add. After selecting the Microsoft WINS Server and clicking OK, you will be asked to reboot the computer.

Figure 16.21
Add the WINS server service.

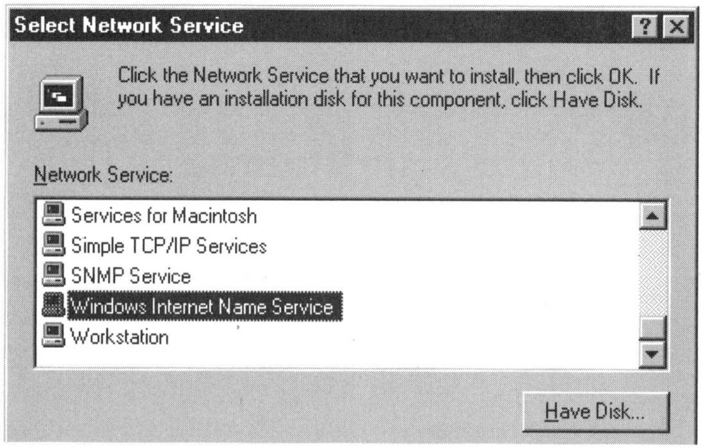

After reboot, a new application will be found under the menu *Start -> Programs -> Administrative Tools -> WINS Manager.* WINS Manager is used for all configuration changes to the WINS server. The main dialog for the WINS Manager is shown in Figure 16.22.

Figure 16.22
The WINS Manager may be used to view and configure the operation of WINS servers.

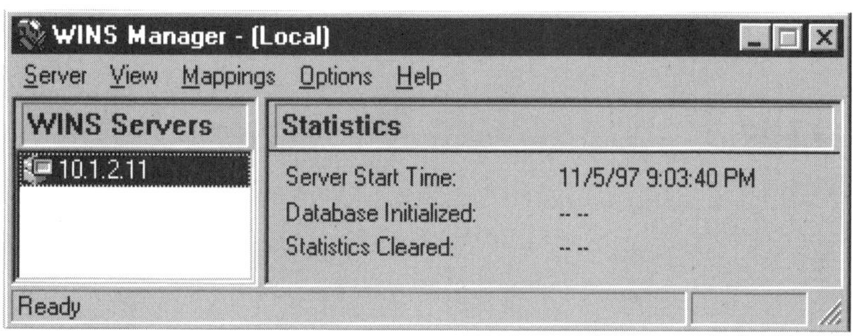

The WINS Manager application can be run from another NT machine after copying the executable file, ***winsadmn.exe***, as well as the associated DLLs to the remote machine. Assuming you are in the same directory as the executable, you can start the WINS Manager using the command ***winsadmn.exe***.

Once the application starts, you use *Add Server* to connect to a remote WINS server. In the *Add Server* window, you can specify an IP address to use TCP/IP to connect, or if you specify a NetBIOS name, it will connect using NetBEUI.

You will be able to connect to the remote WINS server only if your local username is part of the administrator group on the remote WINS server. Once you are connected you can remotely control and configure the WINS server.

Understanding the WINS Database

The broadcast method (b-node) of NetBIOS name resolution effectively uses a distributed database of computer name to IP address bindings. Each machine which is running NetBT has a NetBIOS computer name bound to an IP address. When a query is broadcast onto the LAN, the NetBT software on each node is responsible for responding to queries for its own name.

The WINS method (p-node) has a centralized database of computer name to IP address bindings. Each machine querying the WINS server gets a query response from the WINS sever without bothering the other nodes in the neighborhood.

How is the WINS Database Populated?

Somehow, the WINS database must be populated with all of the appropriate NetBIOS computer name to IP address mappings.

Recall that DNS is one of the options which may be used to resolve NetBIOS names. DNS provides a centralized database per zone (distributed for the whole domain name system) with central administration. Therefore, WINS must logically provide something which DNS does not, otherwise why would it exist?

At the time when WINS was developed, DNS did not provide a means of dynamic client registration.[1] The added value which WINS provides is that clients may dynamically register with the WINS server. WINS has a centralized database, yet with the dynamic client registration, the administration is decentralized. The ease of administration that goes along with dynamic registration is considered to outweigh any added complexity or added security risk due to decentralized administration.

NetBIOS Name Registration

When a machine that is configured to use WINS boots, it sends a Name Registration request to the WINS server, as both roadrunner and FILE_SRV are doing in Figure 16.23. This name registration will enter into the WINS database the computer name and the associated IP address. Thus other machines that want to communicate with that machine will query the WINS server for the appropriate IP address to use.

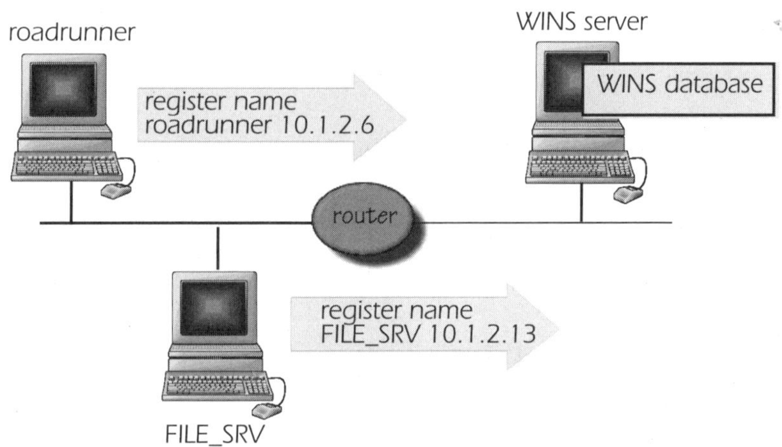

Figure 16.23 Each machine registers its NetBIOS computer and IP address with the WINS server.

Note that also registered in the WINS database will be service numbers — numbers associated with a particular service (application) that is running on the WINS client.

1. Dynamic DNS is now available for UNIX systems, and will be shortly for Windows NT. Security issues with both WINS and traditional DNS are also being addressed in recently proposed extensions to DNS.

Recall that clients that cannot or do not register with WINS in this way are called non-WINS enabled. Older applications are often non-WINS enabled, and will have to be treated differently in order for name resolution to work.

When a WINS client initializes, it registers its NetBIOS name by sending a name registration request directly to the configured WINS server. An example of this is depicted in Figure 16.24. NetBIOS names are registered when services or applications start, such as the redirector, server, and messenger. Recall that the 16th octet of a NetBIOS name is the resource type: a number associated with a particular application.

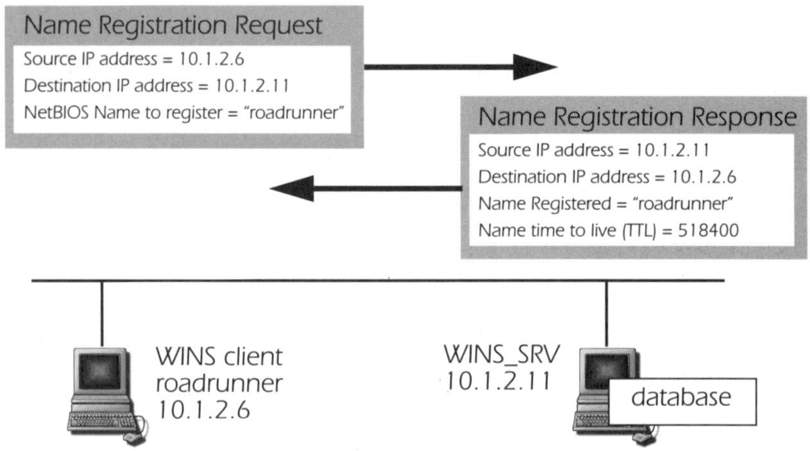

Figure 16.24 The WINS client issues a name registration request and the WINS server replies with a name registration response.

The service that sends the name registration/release requests to the WINS server is the Workstation service. These requests are sent to UDP port 137.

If the WINS server is available and the name is not already registered by another WINS client, a successful registration message is returned to the client. This message contains the amount of time the NetBIOS name is registered to the client, specified as the Time to Live (TTL). The default TTL is six days. Note that 518,400 seconds, as shown in Figure 16.24, is six days.

Name Registration Packet Decode

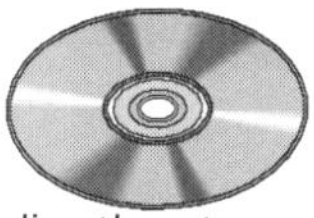

clientboot.cap

Figure 16.25 shows a packet capture of several registration requests and responses between roadrunner and WINS_SRV. This capture file is called clientboot.cap on the CD. The address database is called wins_ch.adr.

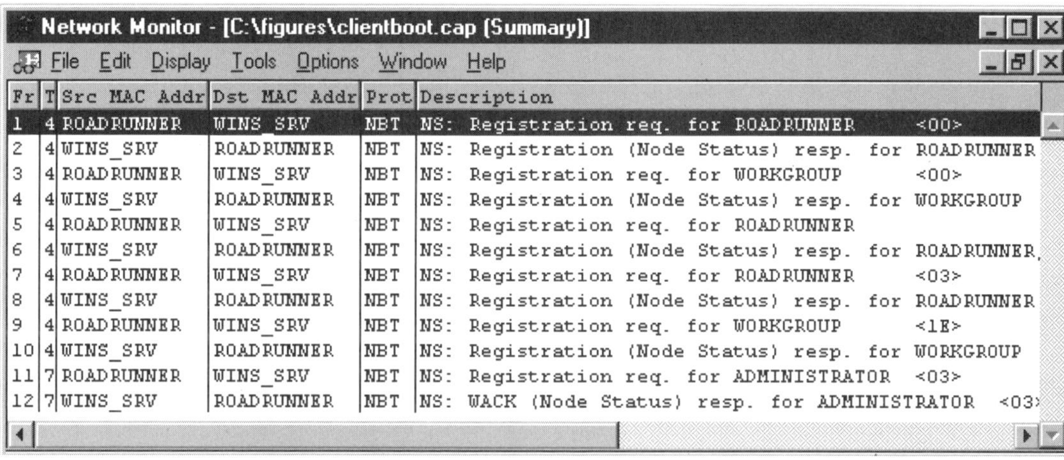

Network Monitor - [C:\figures\clientboot.cap (Summary)]

File Edit Display Tools Options Window Help

Fr	T	Src MAC Addr	Dst MAC Addr	Prot	Description
1	4	ROADRUNNER	WINS_SRV	NBT	NS: Registration req. for ROADRUNNER <00>
2	4	WINS_SRV	ROADRUNNER	NBT	NS: Registration (Node Status) resp. for ROADRUNNER
3	4	ROADRUNNER	WINS_SRV	NBT	NS: Registration req. for WORKGROUP <00>
4	4	WINS_SRV	ROADRUNNER	NBT	NS: Registration (Node Status) resp. for WORKGROUP
5	4	ROADRUNNER	WINS_SRV	NBT	NS: Registration req. for ROADRUNNER
6	4	WINS_SRV	ROADRUNNER	NBT	NS: Registration (Node Status) resp. for ROADRUNNER
7	4	ROADRUNNER	WINS_SRV	NBT	NS: Registration req. for ROADRUNNER <03>
8	4	WINS_SRV	ROADRUNNER	NBT	NS: Registration (Node Status) resp. for ROADRUNNER
9	4	ROADRUNNER	WINS_SRV	NBT	NS: Registration req. for WORKGROUP <1E>
10	4	WINS_SRV	ROADRUNNER	NBT	NS: Registration (Node Status) resp. for WORKGROUP
11	7	ROADRUNNER	WINS_SRV	NBT	NS: Registration req. for ADMINISTRATOR <03>
12	7	WINS_SRV	ROADRUNNER	NBT	NS: WACK (Node Status) resp. for ADMINISTRATOR <03

Figure 16.25 Name registrations for several resources on roadrunner.

The following is a description of each of the packets.

- Frame 1 is a registration for the workstation service (type 0) on roadrunner. Frame 2 is the reply from the WINS server stating that the name was registered successfully.
- Frame 3 is a registration for the group name WORKGROUP, type 0. Frame 4 is the WINS server reply.
- Frame 5 is a registration for the server service (type 20) on roadrunner. Note that the code <20> is not shown because the hex value 20 is printable as a space. Frame 6 is the WINS server response.
- Frame 7 is the registration for the messenger service (type 3) on roadrunner. Frame 8 is the WINS server reply.
- Frame 9 is a registration for the group name WORKGROUP, type 1E. Frame 10 is the WINS server reply.

- Frame 11 is the registration of the username Administrator for the machine roadrunner. Frame 12 is a Wait for Acknowledgment (WACK) from the WINS server. A WACK is sent when the name is already registered by someone else.

Immediately following a WACK, the server will try to confirm or deny the presence of the machine which currently has the name registered. If that machine responds to a name query, the WINS server sends the new registrant a negative registration response as a follow-up to the WACK. If the original registrant doesn't respond to three successive queries from the WINS server, the server sends a positive name registration response to the new registrant it had just WACKed.

Not shown in the figure is frame 13, where the WINS server sent a negative name registration response to roadrunner. This implies that another user was already logged on as Administrator somewhere in the network.

Viewing the WINS Database

Shown in Figure 16.26 is the WINS database on WINS_SRV after the WINS server service has just been installed. Since it is newly installed, no other machines are aware of its existence— therefore the only entries in the database will be from the local machine.

The first column lists the names that are registered. The associated IP address is listed in the second column. The registered names shown in Figure 16.26 are summarized in Table 16.12. Each of these entries has a specific use in NT networking and name resolution.

Table 16.12 The local names registered by the services on the WINS server.

WINS_SRV[00h]	the workstation service started on WINS_SRV
WINS_SRV[03h]	the messenger service started on WINS_SRV
WINS_SRV[20h]	the server service started on WINS_SRV
WORKGROUP[00h]	the group name WORKGROUP has been registered, and will be used to receive browser broadcasts
WORKGROUP[1Eh]	the group name WORKGROUP has been registered, and will be used to elect a master browser

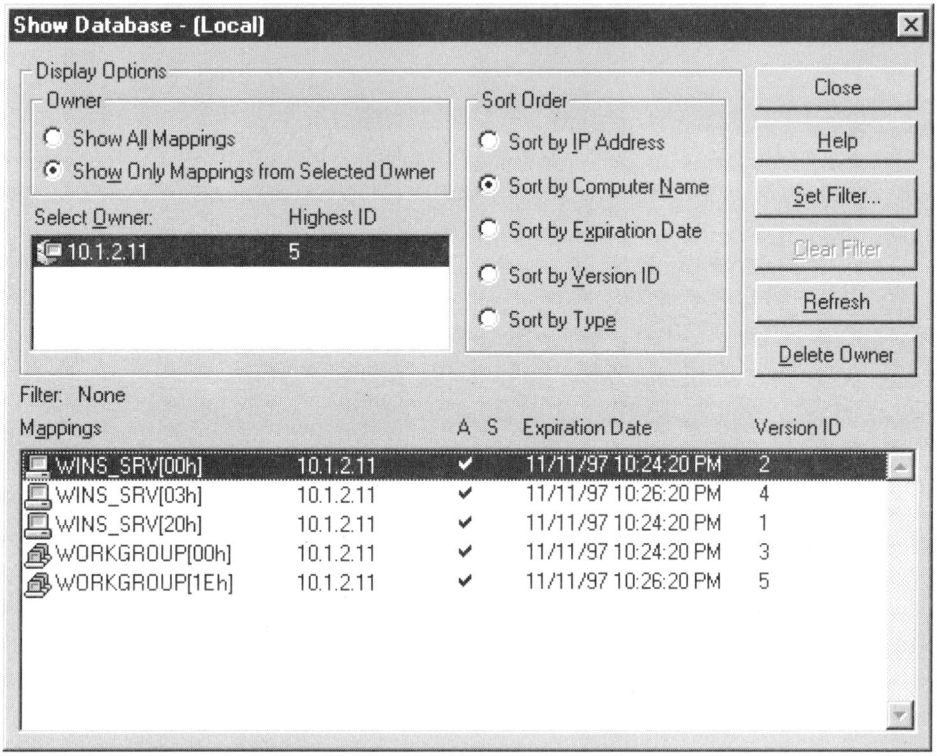

Figure 16.26 The Show Database dialog displays the mappings in the current database.

The A and S columns show the state of the record entry. The A column, short for Active, will contain a symbol that represents the status of that record. Possible record statuses are active, released, and expired. These will be discussed in a few pages. The S column, short for Static, will contain a checkmark if that entry is a static entry in the database.

After the expiration date column, there is a column labelled version ID. The version ID is actually a record number associated with each record. These record numbers are used when WINS servers exchange data with each other. Notice that since this screen is from a newly-installed WINS server, the record number starts out with the value 1.

One other thing to note about this screen. The *Delete Owner* button will delete the highlighted records from the database on the WINS server in the Select Owner box. Be careful with this! To delete a single record from the database, use the Delete Name (DN) option to the command ***winscl.exe.*** The ***winscl.exe*** command and its readme file, winscl.txt, is found in the NT resource kit.

Viewing the WINS Database with Client Records

Now that we saw what the WINS database looked like after the WINS server booted, let's see what happens when a client boots. The machine roadrunner was configured to be a WINS client and was rebooted. Upon reboot, it sent multiple name registration packets to the WINS server. The result of these name registration packets is shown in Figure 16.27. Records (version ID) 6, 7, 8, and 9 have been added. The names that were registered are shown in Table 16.13.

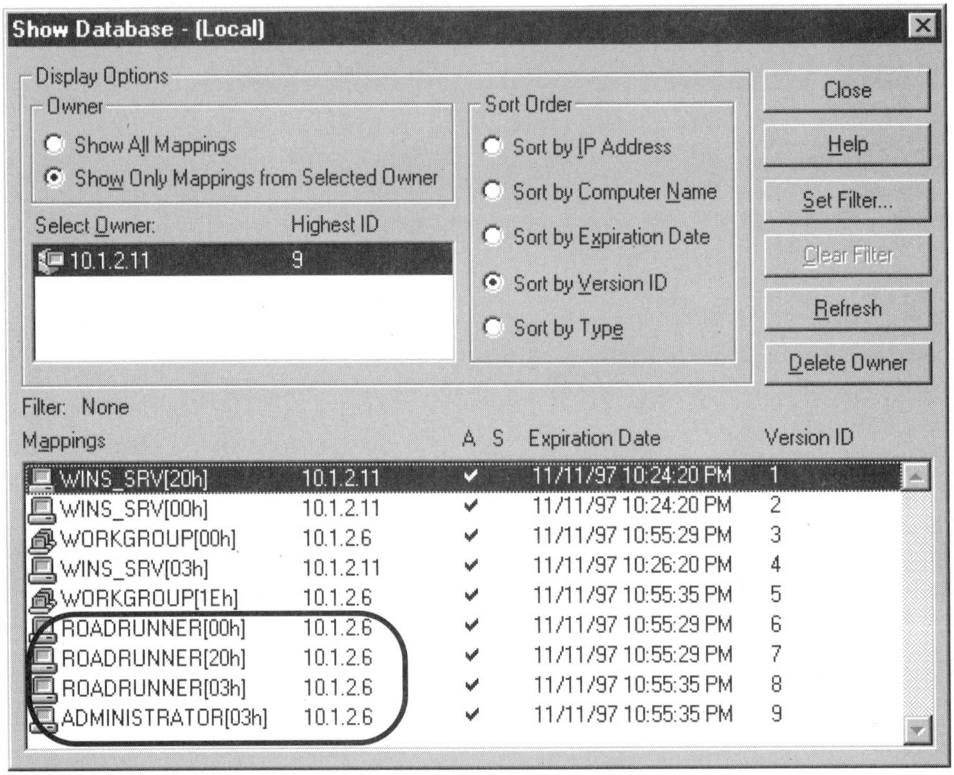

Figure 16.27 The registration entries for roadrunner have been added to the WINS database.

The name WORKGROUP, with resource types <00> and <1E> has also been registered by roadrunner. Recall that in Table 16.12 these resources for WORKGROUP were mapped to WINS_SRV (10.1.2.11) rather than roadrunner (10.1.2.6). Both roadrunner and WINS_SRV are part of the WORKGROUP.

Table 16.13 Names registered with WINS_SRV by roadrunner.

ROADRUNNER[00h]	the workstation service started on ROADRUNNER
ROADRUNNER[03h]	the messenger service started on ROADRUNNER
ROADRUNNER[20h]	the server service started on ROADRUNNER
Administrator[03h]	the user Administrator logged into ROADRUNNER. This information is used by the messenger service to send messages to particular users.

WINS Database Records

Entries in the WINS database go through various states, as shown in Figure 16.28. Upon boot, the name and IP address is registered with the WINS server. The name and IP address is renewed over time, according to the renewal interval. If the name has not been renewed, the record is considered to be *released*. A record will be in the released state for a period of time (the extinction interval). The next state will be the *extinct* state, also called *tombstone* state. After the extinction timeout, the record will finally be deleted from the database.

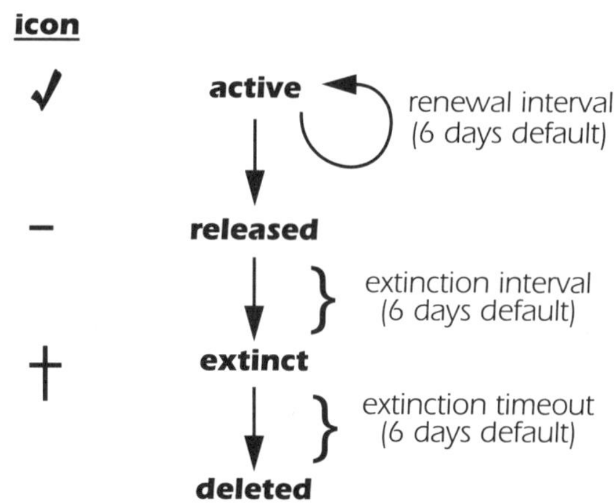

Figure 16.28 The lifeline of a WINS name registration record, as well as the associated icons.

Each record has an associated version ID, better described as a record number. Version IDs are used by the WINS servers to determine what records need to be replicated to other WINS servers.

Each record can be in one of the states shown in Figure 16.28 (active, released, extinct/tombstone, or deleted). The icon for that state (i.e. check, dash, cross) is shown in the *active* (A) column in the *Show Database* dialog (e.g. Figure 16.27).

Why are there two separate states, released and extinct? The reason is related to replication of the records between WINS servers. Released records are *not* replicated regardless of their version IDs, whereas extinct records are replicated to the other WINS servers. (Since records are released after every clean shutdown, there could be a lot of traffic if released records were replicated.)

The *WINS Server Configuration* dialog, shown in Figure 16.29, may be used to configure the timer intervals between the states. Use the *Server -> Configuration...* menu item to get this dialog. All dynamic (not static) records are subject to these timers.

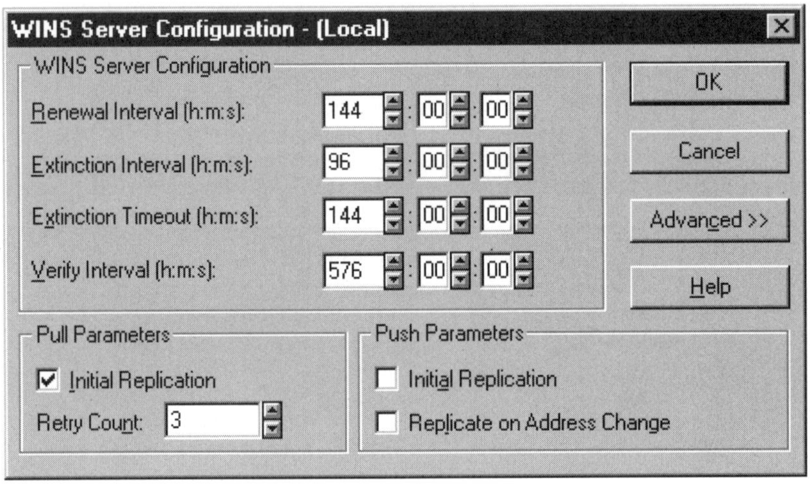

Figure 16.29 The WINS server configuration dialog allows the time intervals to be adjusted to your needs.

WINS Name Renewal

To continue using the same NetBIOS name, a client must renew its lease before it expires. If a client does not renew the lease, the WINS server makes it available for another WINS client.

When one half of the lease (TTL) has expired, a WINS client sends a name refresh request directly to the primary WINS server asking to refresh its registration. The request includes its IP address and NetBIOS name, as shown in Figure 16.30.

Figure 16.30
The WINS client issues a name refresh request and the WINS server replies with a name refresh response.

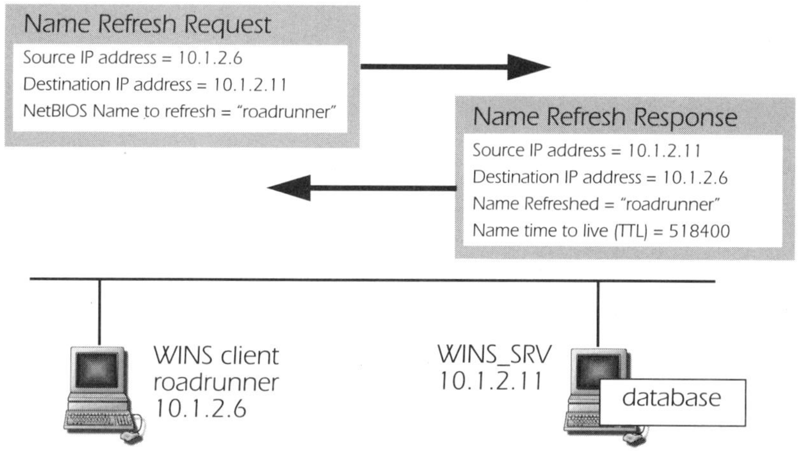

Once a refresh request is successful, the client starts the refresh process again when one half of the new lease has expired. When a WINS server receives the name refresh request, it sends the client a name refresh response with a new TTL.

WINS Name Release

When a WINS client is properly shut down, it sends a name release request directly to the WINS server for each registered name. The name release request includes the client's IP address and the NetBIOS name to be removed from the WINS database.

When the WINS server receives the name release request, it checks its database for the specified name. If the WINS server encounters a database error, or if a different IP address maps the registered name, it sends a negative name release to the WINS client.

Otherwise, the WINS server sends a positive name release and then designates the specified name as inactive in its database. The name release response contains the released NetBIOS name and a TTL value of zero, as shown in Figure 16.31.

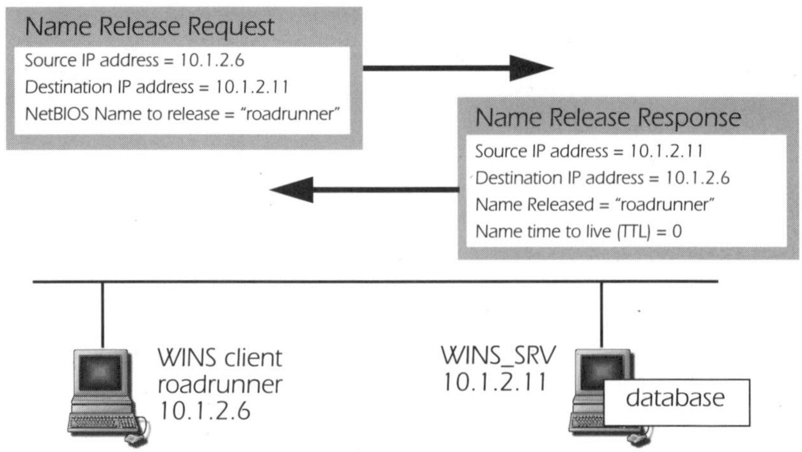

Figure 16.31 The WINS client issues a name release request and the WINS server replies with a name release response.

clientshutdown.cap

Figure 16.32 shows an example of roadrunner issuing a name release request when it shuts down. WINS_SRV replies with a positive name release response. The name released here is the one with resource type <20> (which is displayed as a space, not in hex), which is the *server* resource code.

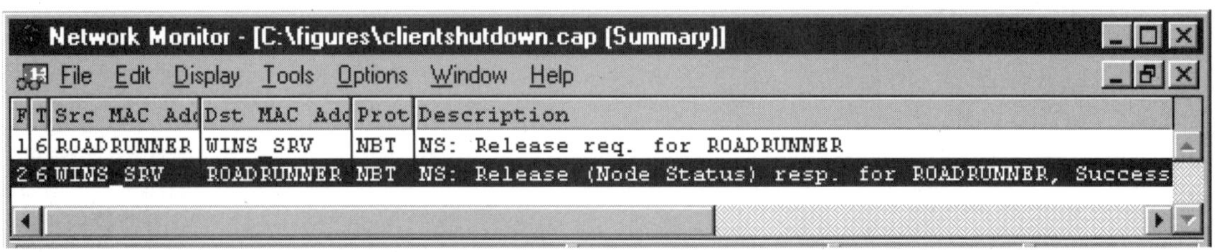

Figure 16.32 A WINS name release exchange from a client shutdown.

After this name release has completed, WINS Manager's *Show Database* command will indicate the state of the entry in the active (A) column with a dash, which represents the *released* state.

Backing up and Restoring the WINS Database

The database is backed up automatically every 24 hours to a directory you specify using WINS Manager, using the dialog in Figure 16.33. There is no default for this entry — if you don't give a path, the WINS server won't back your database up. The *Select Backup Directory* dialog is obtained by *WINS Manager -> Mappings -> Backup Database.*

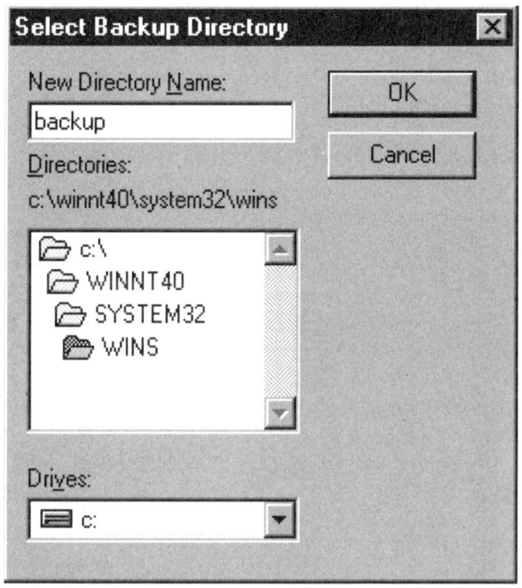

Figure 16.33 Use this dialog to specify the directory which you want your WINS database backed up into.

Make a backup copy of your WINS database. One of the reasons to do this is shown in Figure 16.34 — a missing or corrupt WINS database. Note that the first step recommended in this error dialog is to restore the database from a backup copy.

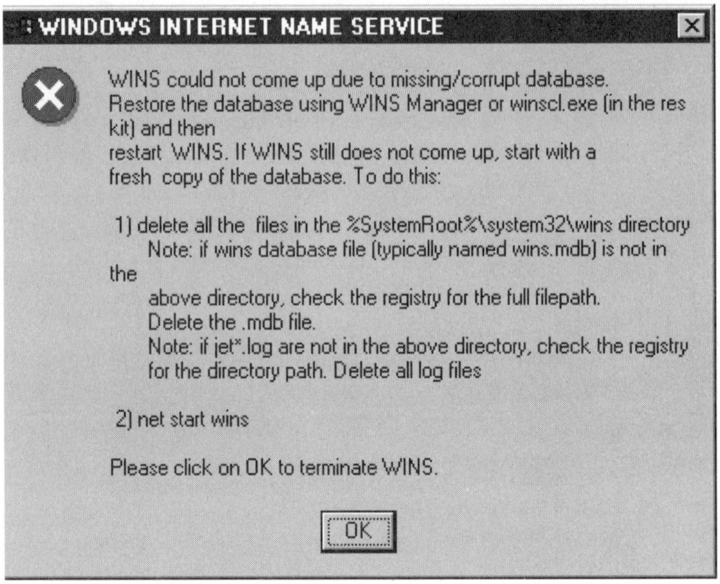

Figure 16.34 WINS database failures are one reason why making backups of the WINS database is a good idea.

Restoring the database from a backup copy is initiated manually using *WINS Manager -> Mappings -> Restore Local Database.*

The database file name is specified in the registry under the WINS registry parameter *DbFileNm* (Table 16.14).

Table 16.14 DbFileNm registry parameter.

Hive:	HKEY_LOCAL_MACHINE
Key:	\System\CurrentControlSet\Services\WINS\Parameters
Name:	DbFileNm
Type:	REG_MULTI_SZ
Value:	%systemroot%\system32\wins\wins.mdb

DNS and WINS Integration

WINS and DNS perform similar but different functions. WINS handles registration and resolution of NetBIOS computer names into IP addresses for NetBT. DNS performs resolution of domain names and IP addresses.

Forwarding Requests from DNS to WINS Servers

The Microsoft DNS service can forward name queries to a WINS server in order to resolve that name to an IP address. This is configured using DNS Manager, under the *Zone Properties -> WINS lookup* tab, shown in Figure 16.35.

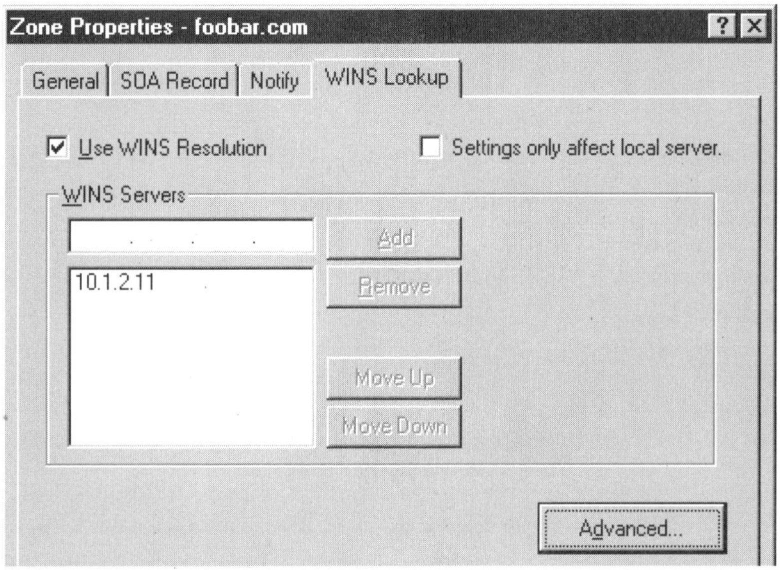

Figure 16.35 Microsoft DNS servers may be configured to use WINS resolution for a zone.

Note that the "Use WINS Resolution" configuration option pertains to a a zone on the DNS server, not necessarily the server as a whole.

It is possible for this DNS server to forward name query requests that it cannot answer to one or more WINS servers. The *WINS Lookup* tab lists the IP addresses of the WINS servers that will be tried in order to resolve the query. The *Advanced...* button at the bottom of the *WINS Lookup* tab (Figure 16.35) brings up the dialog shown in Figure 16.36.

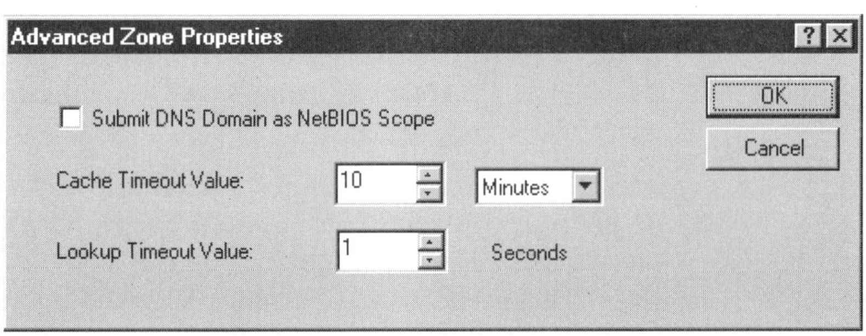

Figure 16.36 Cache timeout values may be specified for the WINS server interactions.

The *Cache Timeout Value* is the length of time the DNS server will cache the information received from WINS. The *Lookup Timeout Value* is the amount of time the DNS server should wait for a response from the WINS server before returning an error to the requester.

Consider the following example. Someone is working with a colleague at the main office of wernerconsulting.com. This person at the main office has put up an FTP server on their workstation, called coyote. The remote user issues the command ***ftp coyote.wernerconsulting.com*** to fetch some files from this FTP server at the main office, as shown in Figure 16.37.

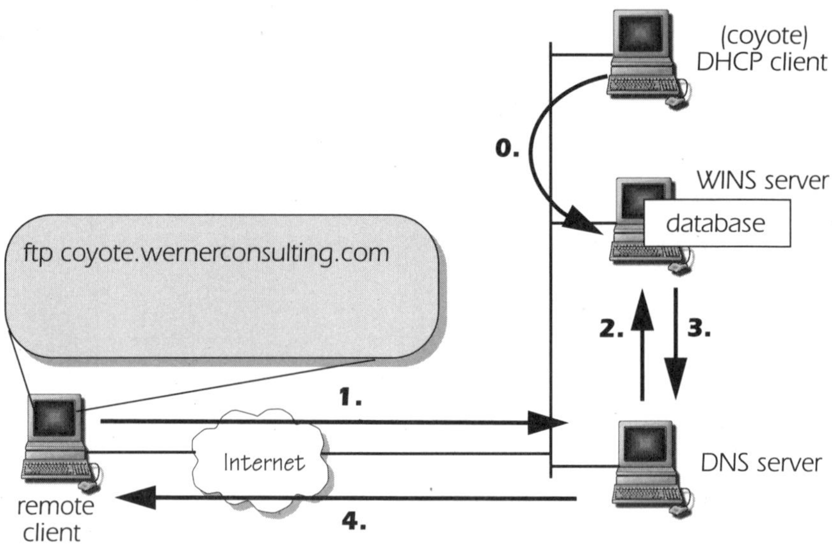

Figure 16.37
A remote client uses the DNS server in the main office, which uses the WINS server to resolve the address of a workstation in the main office.

Once the remote client finds the DNS server authoritative for wernerconsulting.com, the client queries that server for the name coyote (step 1). Assuming that user workstations at this site don't have entries in the zone database on the DNS server, then DNS is not authoritative for the name coyote in the normal sense.

Client workstations at this site use DHCP to obtain IP addresses. For instance, at the beginning of the day, coyote obtained an IP address from a DHCP server. Then coyote registered its name and that IP address with the WINS server (step 0).

The DNS server was configured to refer to WINS when the zone database doesn't have an entry. This was done by checking the *Use WINS Resolution* box on the *WINS Lookup* tab in the *Zone Properties* dialog (Figure 16.35 on page 653). Therefore, the DNS server takes the DNS name query from step one and translates this into a NetBIOS name query which it sends to the WINS server (step 2).

The WINS server receives the name query request and processes it just as if it had come from the actual client. The DNS server is effectively the client of the WINS server in this case. Because coyote had registered its DHCP assigned IP address with the WINS server, the server sends back a NetBIOS name query response to the DNS server (step 3).

The DNS server takes the NetBIOS name query response and translates the results into a DNS name query response and ships this off to the remote client (step 4).

The remote client now has the IP address of coyote.wernerconsulting.com, and may start the FTP session with coyote's FTP server.

This example shows that this form of DNS and WINS integration provides a method of allowing DNS to resolve names to DHCP assigned addresses. When implementations of the standardized dynamic DNS are available, the use of WINS may not be necessary.

Summary

Here's a summary of the items which have been addressed in this chapter.

- NetBT is useful for running NetBIOS applications over IP networks.
- NetBIOS name resolution was originally done via broadcasts, similar to the way ARP is used over 802 LANs.
- NetBIOS name resolution with NetBT may still be done with broadcasts if the NetBIOS network is on a single LAN. An alternate method may be used on NetBT internets, called NetBIOS Name Service (NBNS). An implementation of an NBNS is the Windows Internet Name Service (WINS).
- There are several different ways which a NetBIOS name may be resolved. Four combinations of these different methods are defined. Each of these combinations first checks a NetBIOS name cache.

- Broadcast nodes (b-node) next use the traditional broadcast method.
- Peer nodes (p-node) next try to contact a WINS server.
- Hybrid nodes (h-node) attempts the WINS method and then the broadcast method if necessary.
- Mixed nodes (m-node) use the broadcast method and then the WINS method if necessary.

All of these methods may then consult local files (LMHOSTS, hosts) and then a DNS server if previous methods have not resolved the name.

- WINS maintains a database of current registrations. Clients may register with the server directly, or by proxy. Each registration has a time to live (TTL), and may be renewed within that period.
- Microsoft DNS servers may be configured to refer to WINS servers to resolve names not listed in the DNS zone database. This is useful for resolution of names associated with dynamically assigned IP addresses (e.g. with DHCP).

Further Reading

Here is information about various books and magazines in which to look for further information on the subject.

[MSPress1996] *Microsoft Windows NT Server 4.0 Resource Kit Networking Guide*, 1996, MSPress

[NetBIOS1987a] NetBIOS Working Group, *Protocol Standard for a NetBIOS Service on a TCP/UDP Transport: Concepts and Methods*, 1987, IETF RFC 1001

[NetBIOS1987b] NetBIOS Working Group, *Protocol Standard for a NetBIOS Service on a TCP/UDP Transport: Detailed Specifications*, 1987, IETF RFC 1002

17

Monitoring Using SNMP

As networks have become more and more complex, the maintenance of internetworking devices has become more difficult. Network management tools and techniques have been formalized in order to deal with this increasing difficulty.

This chapter first discusses the concepts behind network management. It then goes into detail on the use of the Simple Network Management Protocol (SNMP) to monitor and configure devices that use TCP/IP.

Network Management Concepts

Monitoring and control of a network can be complex. Dividing the issues of network management into several areas can help to make a complex job more manageable.

Management Areas

There are many techniques which you may use manage your network. Management of networks may be broken down into five functional areas as listed below, and are shown in Figure 17.1.

- Fault management — the process of detecting and isolating faults and error conditions in your network
- Configuration management — dealing with the set-up and configuration of network parameters
- Accounting management — keeping track of the users and groups making use of particular network resources
- Performance management — assessing how well your network is meeting its expected goals
- Security management — finding and preventing of breaches of data, resource, and physical security

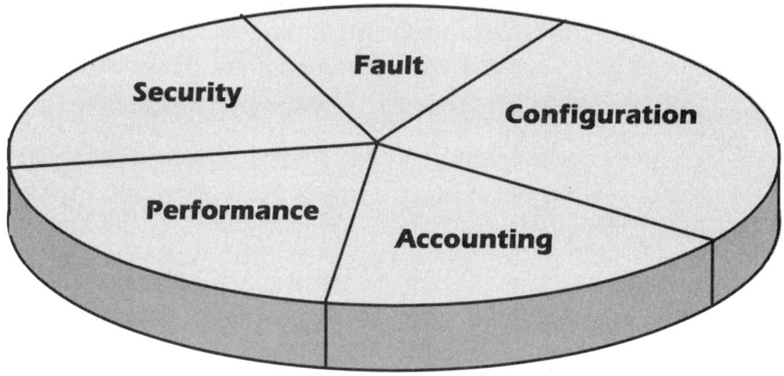

Figure 17.1 Five functional areas of systems and network management.

This division of network management functions into the five areas is a part of the Open Systems Interconnect (OSI) network management framework. Each of these five functional areas of management apply to several levels of management, as shown in Figure 17.2.

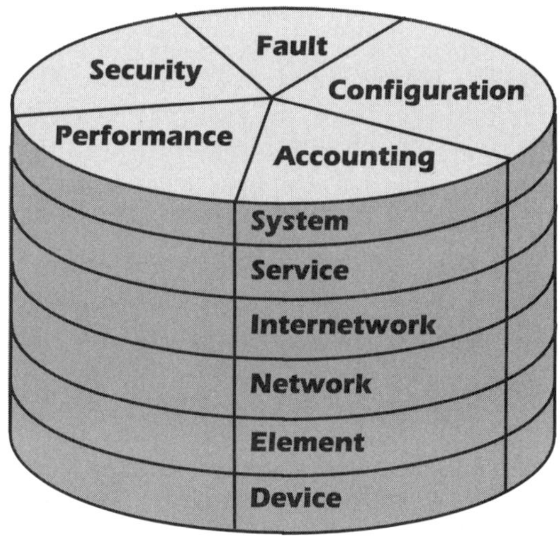

Figure 17.2 The five functional areas of management apply to each of six levels of management.

At the most basic level of management, activities of control and monitoring may focus on a given device, thus this is called *device management.* Several devices which act together as one for performance or fault tolerance purposes are called a network element. *Element management* is similar to device management, yet deals with one network element at a time.

When the operation of one network of devices and elements are managed, this is called *network management.* Sometimes the distinction of *internetwork management* is used to clarify a larger scope when managing several connected networks, yet this too is often termed network management. When management activities focus on the services themselves, this is called *service management*. Management of the services and the infrastructure together is *system management*.

Another related focus of management activity is *desktop management*, which deals with device management, and service management of workstations.

The general term network management is often used to apply to all of these focuses.

Managing Networks with SNMP

The Simple Network Management Protocol (SNMP) is an Internet standard which may be used to manage your network. Here are some of the tasks that SNMP can help with:

- configuring network devices, including workstations, servers, routers, switches
- examining the current state of your network devices
- real-time alerts of problems in the network such as congestion and outages
- proactively monitor the network to prevent problems and accommodate growth

Essentially, SNMP can help you to maintain control of your network. So what does it take to make use of SNMP in your network? There are two basic requirements:

SNMP manageable: a quality of a device which accepts SNMP management requests.

1. Network devices must speak SNMP. This is called being **SNMP manageable**. If you have devices which are not directly SNMP manageable, you may be able to manage them with an SNMP proxy agent.

2. Obtain network management tools which use SNMP. You need software which will talk to all of the SNMP manageable devices and allow you to monitor and control them.

SNMP Operations

Classical information services often have two types of applications that play two different roles: that of client and server. For instance, with HTTP, there are two types of applications: web servers and web browsers (a.k.a. clients).

Two different types of applications use SNMP. The kind of application used on a given piece of equipment depends on that device's role for management:

SNMP agent: application software on a managed device which provides access to management information.

- Devices which are to be managed run an SNMP application called an **SNMP agent**.
- The workstation or server which is used to monitor and control other devices runs a **SNMP manager** application.

An SNMP manager and multiple devices running SNMP agents are shown in Figure 17.3.

Figure 17.3 One SNMP manager may support many managed devices.

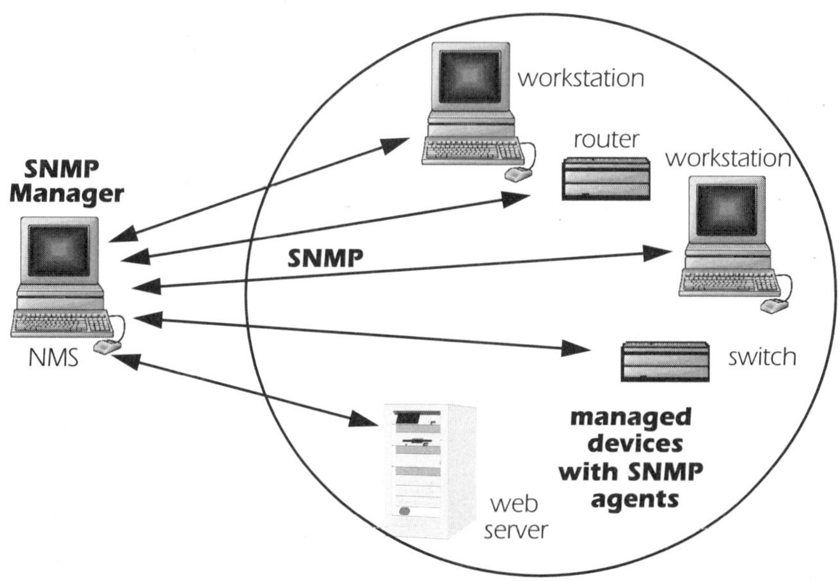

SNMP manager: application software which uses SNMP to query SNMP agents to manage a network.

Both the agent and manager applications may be run on the same machine, when both roles need to be played. If the SNMP manager application is the main application which a workstation is used for, the workstation is commonly called a *Network Management Station* (NMS).

How do the agent and manager used for network management relate to the familiar model of information services? Agents actually perform the duties of a management information server, because they actually carry out the direct monitoring and control operations. Managers are actually the clients in this model, as they query agents for information, or request that agents perform some operation (Figure 17.4).[1]

Figure 17.4 In most SNMP operations, the manager requests information from an agent.

Rather than operating on files as FTP does, or hypertext documents as HTTP does, SNMP allows operations on individual pieces of management information. An SNMP manager may send the following messages to any SNMP agent:

- *set-request* — allows the manager to configure parameters on the agent
- *get-request* — fetches configuration, status, or statistics from the agent
- *get-next-request* — fetches the next piece of data from the agent (note that the manager maintains the context)

These messages are shown in Figure 17.5.

As a reply to any of these requests, the SNMP agent should send back a *get-response* indicating success or failure. These messages are sent as UDP datagrams. The manager uses a random port number, and the agent listens and responds on port 161.

When an SNMP agent feels that it has something important to tell an SNMP manager, it may send a trap message (again, as a UDP datagram).

1. Some vendors have developed an alternate management technique to SNMP — they use web browsers (cheap or free) as the manager, and provide agents which can be accessed with HTTP as though they were web servers.

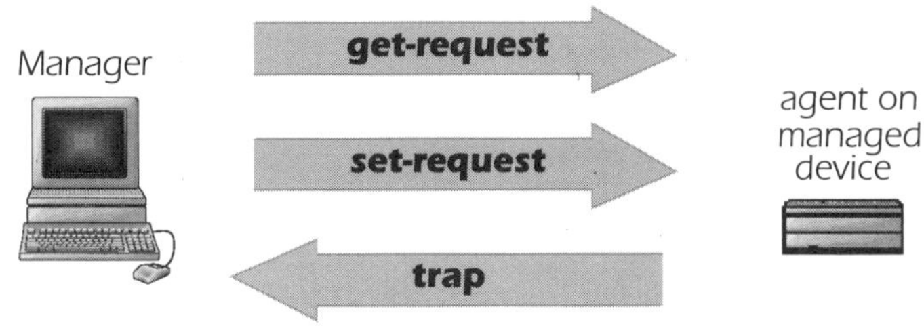

Figure 17.5
An SNMP manager may initiate get or set requests. Agents may generate traps to send unsolicited notifications to managers.

- *trap* — sends unsolicited notification from the agent to the manager.

Traps are sent from a random port on the agent to port 162 on a management station. SNMP traps do not contain a lot of information. SNMP relies on "trap-directed-polling", i.e. when a manager gets a trap it should perform some get-requests for detail.

SNMP Simplicity

When managing multiple networks, there are often several devices which each have a few small pieces of information for the management puzzle you are trying to solve.

SNMP itself does not correlate the information which comes from different devices, it merely provides access to individual pieces of information. The management application using SNMP must perform the correlation itself.

Some advanced agents have the ability to perform more complex tasks. An example of this is an agent which supports the standard *remote monitoring (RMON)* set of management information. Even with advanced agents, the manager is still responsible for deciding what to monitor and control.

The basic SNMP operations are simple one time requests for a parameter or a collection of a few parameters. If a manager wants periodic update of a parameter from a device every minute, it is entirely up to the manager to send a get-request to that device's agent every minute.

What if a manager wants a parameter from twenty routers every minute? Remember that the name of the protocol is the *Simple* Network Management Protocol. The manager would issue twenty independent

SNMP get-requests, one to each device's agent. Hopefully, twenty get-responses are returned, one from each agent. After a minute, the manager is responsible to repeat the process. Request, response, repeat.

Before getting into the details of SNMP operations, along with some examples, we must lay the foundations with a discussion of management information.

SNMP Managed Information

What kinds of management information can SNMP deal with, and how is this information identified?

There are different kinds of devices that can be managed with SNMP. A router would have a different set of parameters than a workstation. Even though two different kinds of routers may have common parameters, there may be vendor-specific parameters. Different kinds of workstations may have vendor-specific parameters as well.

A manager would send a get-request for a specific piece of information to a specific agent as shown in Figure 17.6. The parameter requested is mentioned in the get-request by identifier, such as sysDescr.0[2] in this example.

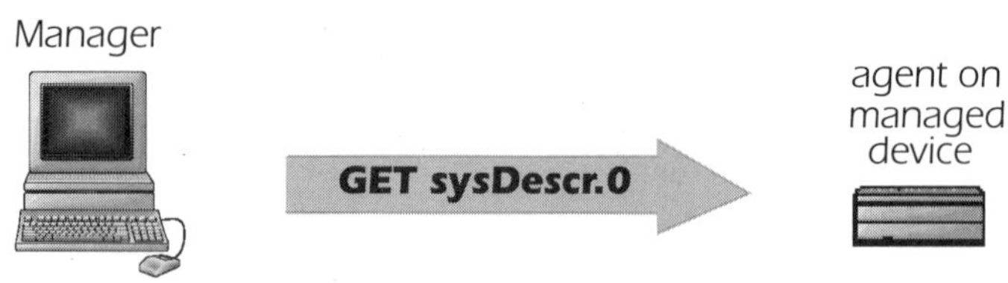

Figure 17.6 The manager requests a specific piece of information from a device.

To keep all of the different sets of parameters straight, they have been organized into standard sets of parameters and vendor-specific sets. When a network equipment manufacturer supplies an SNMP agent for

2. By the end of this section, you'll see that such identifiers are only written in the form like sysDescr.0 as a human convenience. These identifiers will actually look more like 1.3.6.1.2.1.1.1.0 when SNMP sees them.

their device, they publish information on both the standard parameter sets and the proprietary parameter sets which are implemented.

Management Information Base (MIB): a database of management information which is accessed with SNMP.

Because these parameters are used for managing devices, a set of parameters is called a **Management Information Base (MIB)**.[3] A MIB is a database of management information which is accessed with SNMP.

Each parameter in a MIB is called a MIB variable. MIB variables may be categorized into the five areas of network management: fault, configuration, accounting, performance, and security. Some MIB variables are used for control and some are used for monitoring. When vendors publish information on the parameters sets which an agent supports, they are providing standard and vendor-specific MIBs.

Remember, a MIB is just the specification of a set of parameters — simply a schema of what you can view for monitoring and what you can control.

An SNMP agent may support multiple MIBs. Typically, an SNMP agent supports one or more MIBs for each function a machine provides, or each module which makes up the machine. For example, a router is a communications system, so a router's agent should support the standard communications MIB. Many routers also have more complex routing tables than hosts, thus these routers' agents should allow you to access the extended information. Some routers may also support other standard or proprietary functions and/or protocols, and should allow management of these functions by supporting corresponding MIBs in their agents.

Figure 17.7 shows an example of a few of the MIBs which are installed by Steelhead into NT's SNMP agent.

3. Although a MIB is essentially a database of management information, the word "database" is explicitly not used by the SNMP designers. This is so that people do not associate traditional database concepts, such as disks and SQL, with MIBs.

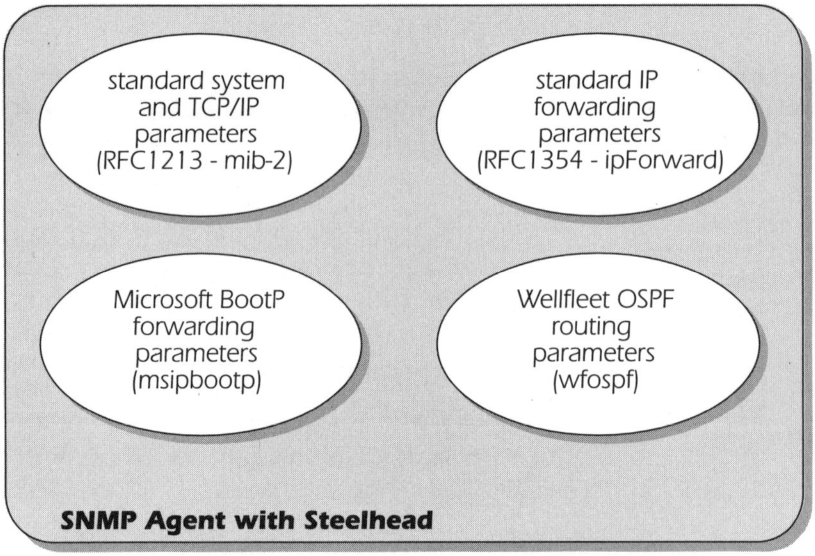

Figure 17.7
An SNMP agent may support one or more MIBs. Each MIB describes several parameters. A few of the MIBs supported by Steelhead are shown here.

Structure of Management Information

There is a standard language which MIBs are written in, which is called the *Structure of Management Information (SMI)*. It is essentially a very basic set of guidelines for the syntax of defining MIB variables. In keeping with the simple nature of SNMP, much of the detail of semantics guidelines for the definition of MIBs was left to MIB authors, and the practice has evolved over the years.

The SMI is based on an even more basic notation for describing abstract syntaxes, called the *Abstract Syntax Notation One (ASN.1)*. ASN.1 was developed by as a part of the OSI standardization process, but is recently becoming more popular in Internet related technologies. Being a general notation for information notation and protocol, ASN.1 has been used for many networking standards, such as X.509 certificates, LDAP, Kerberos V5, and of course OSI protocols such as CMIP and ROSE. ASN.1 is not only used as the foundations for SMI, but also for the SNMP protocol itself.

A correlation between MIB/SMI/ASN.1 and another language is shown in Figure 17.8.

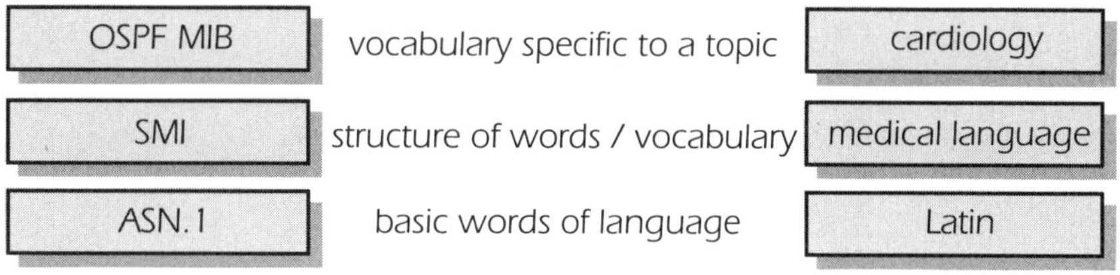

Figure 17.8 MIBs are written in the language of SMI, which has ASN.1 as its basis.

Each MIB describes a certain topic of conversation which a manager may have with each agent.

Loading MIBs

When an SNMP manager deals with a new kind of device, the manager must load the device's MIB (or MIBs) to gain knowledge of the variables which the device supports. Once the MIB has been loaded, the manager may get the values for MIB variables and may set those variables which are not read-only.

MIB file: a text file (written in SMI format) which defines a collection of MIB variables.

Each MIB is defined in a human-readable text file which describes the schema of the MIB. This is called a **MIB file**, and is written according to the SMI.

Figure 17.9 shows an example of an SNMP manager which initially only has knowledge of the standard MIB (mib_ii.mib).[4] In order to effectively manage the functions of a device such as the Steelhead router shown in the figure, the manager must learn about the additional kinds of parameters that a Steelhead router supports. Most SNMP management applications may learn about new MIBs through a process called *compiling the MIB*. In order to install new MIBs, we must:

- Get a copy of the files which define each of the MIBs that the manager doesn't currently know about. Usually the vendor of the hardware or software which contains the agent will supply the necessary files.
- Load ("compile") each MIB file into your management application.

4. SNMP agents will already have the standard Internet MIB, called MIB2, installed upon agent startup.

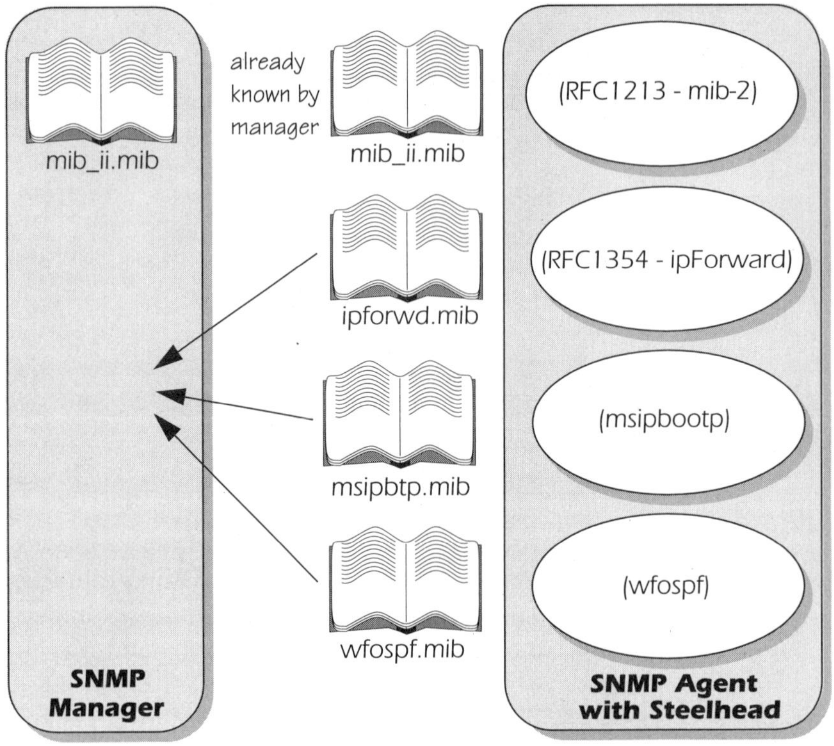

Figure 17.9 Managers must be capable of dealing with all of the MIBs which agents support.

Now the manager knows the identifiers for the new MIB variables, like learning new vocabulary. That's the simple part. Then the human using the SNMP manager needs to learn (or get a specific management application which automates) how to speak in the new vocabulary intelligently and productively.

The bottom line is that having SNMP or an agent with a snazzy MIB doesn't mean that you have a managed network, it simply means that you're standing there with a hammer and a pile of lumber and you want a house. You need to become a carpenter. The alternative is to hire a carpenter and work with them to convey your plan for a house.

The next sections are not intended to teach you how to be an SNMP carpenter, but to understand how to nail wood together. If you want to be a carpenter, start with books such as [Leinwand1996] and [Rose1995].

How to Select Information — Object Identifiers (OIDs)

In managing information systems, a consistent addressing scheme is required for accessing configuration and status information.

There are many functions that a piece of equipment may perform, such as:

- physical and data link operations for network interfaces
- routing, and exchange of routing information
- dynamic address assignment, and address resolutions
- running applications

We can create a tree which provides addressing for every type of management information we may have in any kind of system. We then overlay this tree on top of the actual system. The result is a consistent way of managing systems which is independent from the vendor or model of the equipment. Figure 17.10 shows a model of five devices, each with a tree used to address its MIB variables.

Figure 17.10
Each device may have different MIBs, yet all MIB trees are based upon a common model.

Object Identifier (OID): a unique path into a object tree.

Each MIB variable may be accessed independently using its unique identifier, called an **Object Identifier (OID)**. An OID specifies a unique path into a tree of object registrations. Object identifiers were designed by ISO to be a way of identifying the registration of object definitions in an object oriented hierarchy.

For example, a kid climbs a tree and hides something under a leaf. He wants to know the path he took so that he can either get back there later and retrieve it, or tell a friend where to find it. The object identifier tells him the path from the root of the tree to the leaf. Any kid will always put the same kind of object under that leaf, not only in that tree but in any tree. Figure 17.11 shows an example of a consistent addressing scheme for identifying leaves in a tree.

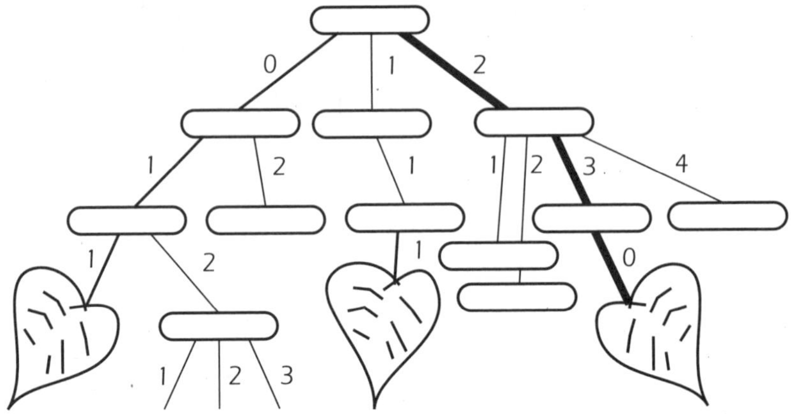

Figure 17.11
The path to this leaf is 2.3.0, which may be used to uniquely identify the object hidden under the leaf. The same kind of object will be under leaf 2.3.0 in any tree.

The object identifier was designed to specify a unique path into a registration hierarchy. Object identifiers are written in dotted decimal notation, such as 2.3.0 to identify the object under the right-most leaf in Figure 17.11. Before we look at some example OIDs, let's first discuss some important issues.

Object Class and Instance

An object identifier (OID) can specify a path from the root of a registration tree, to a leaf which identifies the kind of object we're dealing with. For network management, this means that we can specify the kind of parameter we want to monitor or control. There are two very important issues which the OID doesn't address:

1. How do we find the proper tree? In other words, how do we specify the SNMP agent we're trying to send a request to?
2. If there can be more than one instance of a given kind of information per agent, how do we specify which one we're referring to?

Before discussing how SNMP addresses these issues, here's a bit of the history of how they are solved in other systems which use object identifiers.

When SNMP was first developed, it was intended to be a stepping stone to another management protocol which would be general enough to address management not just of simple network devices, but of systems, networks and individual devices. The idea is that the differences in those different scopes of management can be embodied in definitions of the managed objects. Thus, there could be a common protocol for doing device, network, service, or systems management. It is called the *Common Management Information Protocol (CMIP).*

While CMIP is used for certain kinds of systems management in certain parts of the world, it has not caught on as quickly as SNMP. In fact, because of its simpler form, SNMP has become much more wide-spread than envisioned. But for involved management operations, the management system built around SNMP can become very complex due to its simplistic nature. Yet the developers of SNMP products have found some very good ways of keeping SNMP alive.

CMIP was designed as the protocol piece of the OSI management framework — an object oriented model of systems and network management, defined in the X.700 series of recommendations from the ITU.

object class: the kind of object you're dealing with.

In object oriented modeling, there is a basic distinction between the *kind* of an object and the *actual* object of that kind you're dealing with. The kind of object you're dealing with is called an **object class**. The particular object of a class is called the **object instance.** Figure 17.12 shows that these two concepts are used to identify the kind, and which one of that kind of object you're dealing with.

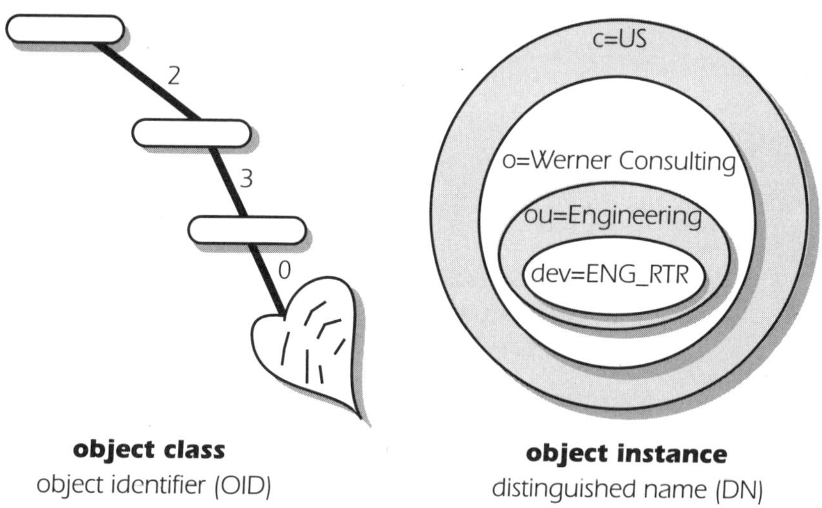

Figure 17.12 The object class is identified with an OID, and the object instance is identified with a distinguished name (DN).

objectinstance: an actual implementation of an object class.

For management purposes, the thing that you're trying to manage has an object class and an object instance. The object class is specified with an object identifier (OID). This implies that when a vendor or standards organization develops a new kind of thing (e.g. router, switch, server, browser, protocol) and they register that thing with the standards bodies, they are assigned an object identifier to use as the object class.

The object instance addresses both of our problems which the object identifier didn't address. Figure 17.13 shows an example of an object instance. It identifies the machine as well as the particular instance of the object on that machine.

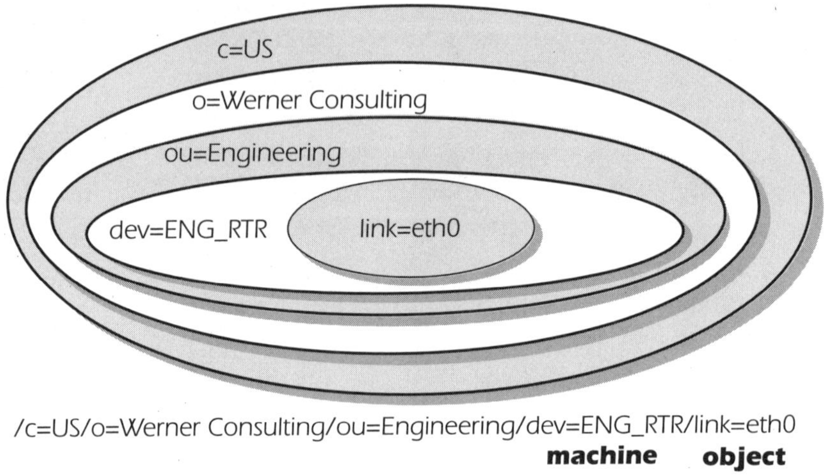

Figure 17.13 An object instance DN may be used to specify a machine and an object (e.g. software or hardware module) within that machine. This DN represents an Ethernet card in the router ENG_RTR.

Object instances are written as distinguished names (DNs). Recall the DNs which were used in X.509 certificates in Chapter 14. Recall that a DN is simply the sequence of relative DNs, and an relative distinguished name (RDN) is simply a set of attribute value assertions.

Each object (specified by object class and object instance) may have many attributes. Each object may have many attributes beyond those used to form its RDN. Each attribute of an object is specified with an *attribute identifier.* An attribute identifier is simply another object identifier. The CMIP set and get operations allow changing or reading attribute values of an object anywhere in the distributed system.

Simplifying Class and Instance for SNMP

The SNMP designers saw a few problems with the CMIP design of network management. These problems are listed below.

- CMIP was dependent upon The Directory, which in the early 80s, was not well defined.
- CMIP was based upon object-oriented modeling techniques, which vendors at that time were unfamiliar with.
- CMIP did not draw a line between the machine and the service on that machine being managed.

Given these motivations, the SNMP solution to identifying a piece of management information was to do the following:

- Don't specify the machine you're talking to in SNMP itself. Simply use a lower-layer protocol to address the machine.
- Combine the specification of the object class, attribute identifier, and object instance into one object identifier. (However, this mangles the whole object oriented concept and makes SNMP confusing to some people.)

Figure 17.14 shows the combination of object class, attribute type, and object instance into one object identifier. There may be several branches in the object class portion and several more branches in the object instance portion. For simple variables there is usually one branch for the attribute type. Simple variables usually have an instance number of zero for the last twig of their object identifier.

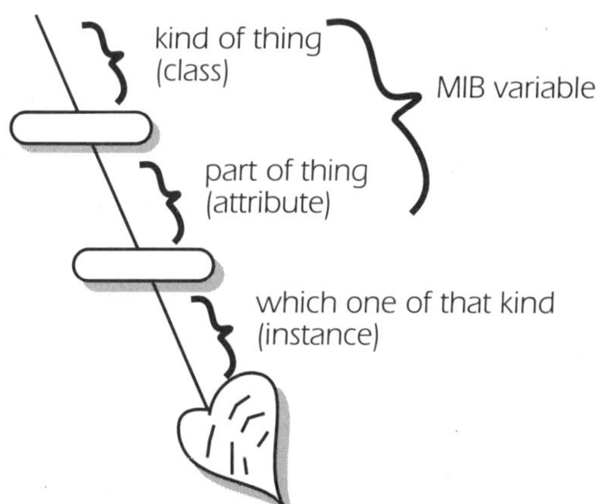

Figure 17.14
In SNMP the class, attribute, and instance of a managed object are specified with one object identifier.

Some MIB variables have multiple instances. Figure 17.15 shows an example of this.

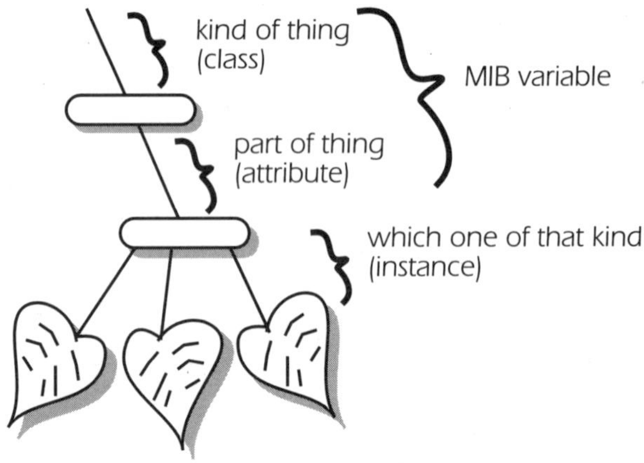

Figure 17.15
A MIB variable with multiple instances. The last twigs to the leaf uniquely identify the instance.

It is usually the case that when there are multiple instances of an object, there are also multiple attributes of that object. To keep these different attributes together and distinguish them from the neighboring simple variables, the various attributes of an object are collected together in a table. Each attribute is a column of the table, and each instance is a row in the table. How does this affect the object identifier? Tables of information are collected together as twigs on a on common branch as shown in Figure 17.16.

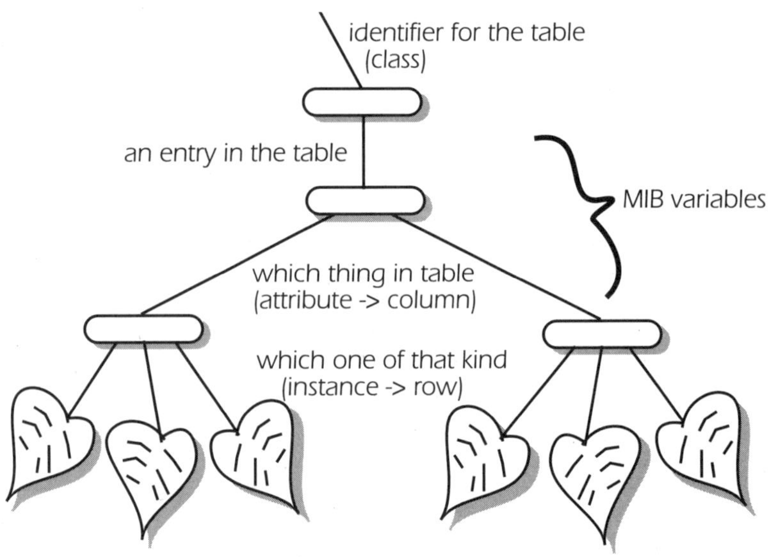

Figure 17.16
Several attributes may be collected into a table. The object identifiers specify a table, attribute, and instance in this way.

The first several branches of the object identifier (OID) gets you down to the root of the table. Common practice is to put a branch which is number 1 next. This branch is used to specify that an entry of the table is being addressed (but the particular entry is not yet identified). Next, a branch identifies the attribute (i.e. column) in the table. Finally, the last one or more twigs to the leaf identify the instance (i.e. row or entry) of that in the table.

Get Next

A get-request may be used to retrieve any MIB variable from an SNMP agent. With a get-request, the explicit object identifier including object class, attribute type, and object instance must be specified. In some cases, it is difficult to know what the actual instance portion of the object identifier is supposed to be. Also, it is sometimes convenient to not even have to know what the attribute type portion is.

The SNMP get-next-request provides an operation that allows us to specify either:

- A partial object identifier.
    - For instance, the object class and attribute type may be specified without a specific object instance. The agent receiving such a get-next-request responds with the first instance if that attribute.
    - The OID may actually be so vague as to only specify a just a group (e.g. IP), or a MIB, or the whole OID tree. The first instance of the first MIB variable in that group, MIB, or the whole OID tree will be selected for the response.
- A fully specific object identifier.
    - For a scalar variable, the next variable in the MIB will be selected for the response.
    - The next instance of a table variable will be selected. If the last instance of that attribute was identified then the first instance of the next attribute in the table is selected. If the last instance of the last attribute in the table is identified, then the next MIB variable is selected.

Figure 17.17 shows a manager sending a get-next-request to an agent. When the agent receives the get-next-request with the OID of ipFowarding.0, it must determine the next MIB variable for the response. The next variable after ipFowarding is the ipDefaultTTL. The agent's get-response contains the OID of ipDefaultTTL.0 and the integer value 128.

Figure 17.17 For get-next, the agent must determine what the next variable it knows about is.

How does the agent know what variable comes next? Figure 17.18 shows that the agent uses the tree structure of the object identifiers to its advantage.

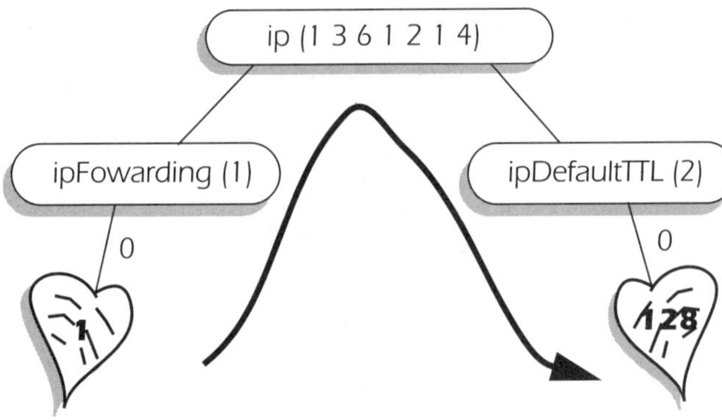

Figure 17.18 The agent determines which variable is next based on the object identifiers.

All of the actual MIB variable instances are at the leaves of the tree. The whole OID tree has a specific lexicographical ordering associated with it. This ordering is a numerical ascending sort on the hierarchy of subidentifiers. The get-next operation is based on this ordering, which the agent maintains. The next instance is determined by the following procedure from the OID supplied to get-next.

1. Go down and left as far as you can.
2. If you were already at a leaf, go up and over to the right.
3. If there are no other leaves directly to the right, go up until there is another branch and go to step 1.
4. If there wasn't another branch in step 3, there are no more leaves, so get-next must report an error.

The manager could use the OID returned in the response to the get-next of ipForwarding.0 when issuing a subsequent get-next-request. The get-next of ipDefaultTTL.0 would give the response with ipInReceives.0 the appropriate value at the current time. Thus the manager is responsible for keeping track of the context for requesting a series of MIB variable instances.

How the Tree Was Built

Thus far, the structure of the tree toward the leaves has been described. Let's examine the tree starting with the root and working our way down.

There are three main trunks off of the root of the object identifier tree, each identifying an organization responsible for assignments in the tree. (Recall that object identifiers are a part of the OSI standards, which were developed by the ITU-T and ISO.) These trunks are:

- ITU-T assignments (0)
- ISO assignments (1)
- Joint assignments (2)

Every object identifier begins with one of these trunks. The object identifier tree is used for more than network management. For instance, OSI management information is defined by a joint effort of the ITU-T (formerly referred to as CCITT) and ISO, thus the trunk number is two.

Recall (from Figure 17.11) that object identifiers are written as the sequence of numbers of the path down the trunk, branches, and twigs to a leaf. The generic term for a trunk, branch, or twig is arc, and the generic term for an arc number is sub-identifier. Therefore an object identifier is simply a sequence of sub-identifiers.

The ITU-T and ISO don't want to be directly responsible for defining each sub-identifier in the whole OID tree. They delegate registration responsibility for various subtrees to certain other organizations. Figure 17.19 shows the three arcs from the root as well as the two of the arcs beneath ISO[5]. Each member organization is defined under the 1.2 arc, such as 1.2.840 which is the United States. ISO delegates registration authority to that organization. For instance, the American National Standards Institute (ANSI) registers organizations under the US arc 1.2.840.

5. OIDs actually identify arc numbers, yet we've labelled the nodes (joints between arcs) with the numbers.

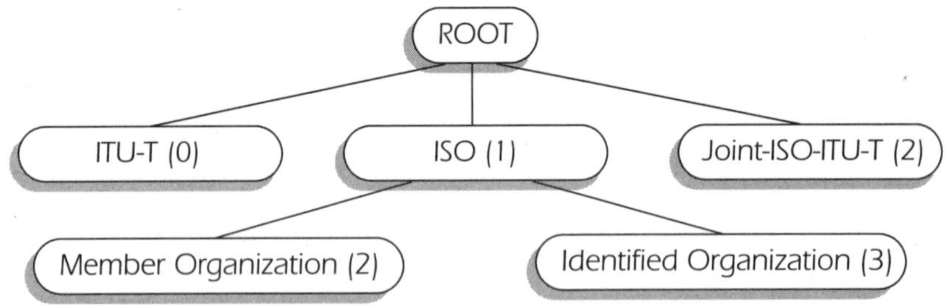

Figure 17.19 The three trunks of the object identifier tree, and two of the branches beneath ISO.

Similarly, ISO also delegates registration authority to organizations which the ISO has registered under as identified organizations, such as the United States Department of Defense (U.S. DoD) with arc 1.3.6. These organizations may in turn delegate registrations for subtrees as they see fit. One organization of particular interest is the Internet Architecture Board, registered as 1.3.6.1, because the origins of Internet (actually ARPAnet) had its roots in the DoD.

Figure 17.20 depicts two of the assignments beneath 1.3.6.1, which are Internet assignments. Management information defined by Internet standards is defined underneath 1.3.6.1.2.1. The IAB delegates responsibility for subtrees under the private enterprises arc to private enterprises.

If you wanted to find standard network management information, you would find it under 2.9.3.2 if it is an OSI management standard, or 1.3.6.1.2.1 if it is an Internet standard. Similarly, directory information may be found under 2.5.4 (attributes) for the OSI directory, or 1.3.6.1.1 for the Internet directory.

Each organization which defines object identifiers could technically register information under any arcs it has been assigned, however it is recommended that OSI related information be registered under an arc from a direct OSI delegated authority such as ANSI (1.2.840), and information relating to Internet technologies be registered under the organization's private enterprise arc (under 1.3.6.1.4.1). If your organization does not have an assignment, contact the proper authority.

The object identifier tree is actually quite a bit larger than that used for SNMP, as management information is just one type of information which needs to be identified.

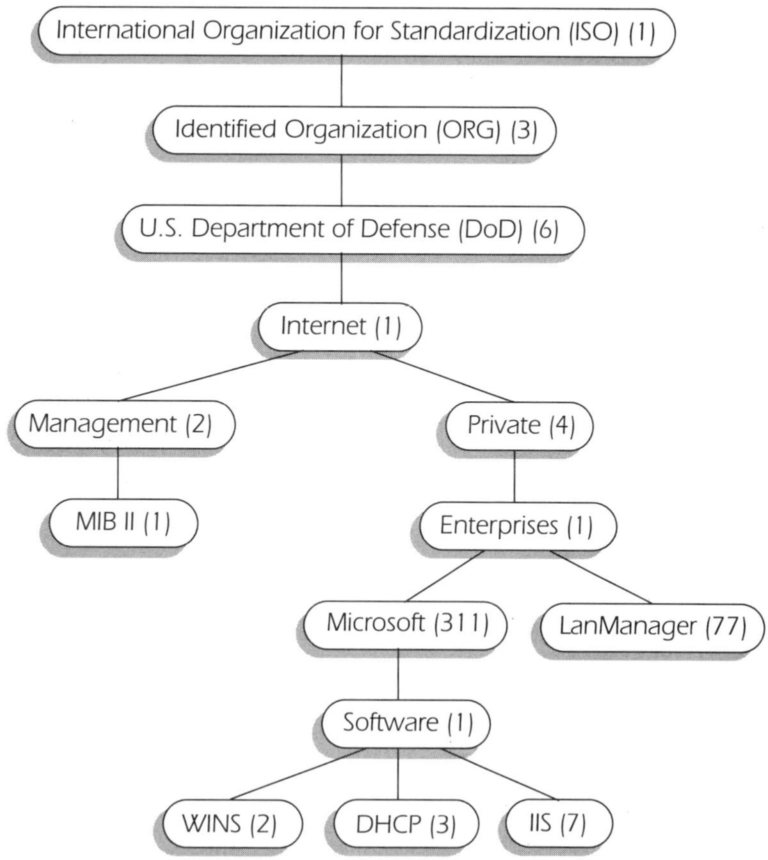

Figure 17.20 Management Information is registered in a "tree of knowledge" for uniqueness.

Grafting onto the Tree

Once a number of parameters have been defined together as a MIB, that whole MIB must be grafted onto the object identifier tree. MIBs are usually defined as a wholly contained subtree, thus there is typically one graft point for a given MIB. The graft point is actually specified as a part of the MIB. For instance, Microsoft's Internet Server MIB (inetsrv.mib)[6] grafts itself into the OID tree at 1.3.6.1.4.1.311.1.7 by using the definitions shown in Figure 17.21.

6. The file shown is a simplified version of the actual inetsrv.mib.

```
InternetServer-MIB DEFINITIONS ::= BEGIN

        IMPORTS
                enterprises,
                OBJECT-TYPE,
                Counter
                        FROM RFC1155-SMI;

        microsoft       OBJECT IDENTIFIER ::= { enterprises 311 }
        software        OBJECT IDENTIFIER ::= { microsoft 1 }
        internetServer  OBJECT IDENTIFIER ::= { software 7 }
        inetSrvCommon   OBJECT IDENTIFIER ::= { internetServer 1 }
        inetSrvStats    OBJECT IDENTIFIER ::= { inetSrvCommon 1 }

-- Internet Server Common Statistics

END
```

Figure 17.21 Microsoft's Internet Server MIB grafts itself into the OID tree at 1.3.6.1.4.1.311.1.7.

Other MIBs may import the definition of internetServer from this MIB and use it as a part of their grafting point, just as inetsrv.mib imported the definition of enterprises from the SMI.

There is one "tree of knowledge", because it is a global registry used as a model for identifying information. Each SNMP agent maintains a collection of actual information which matches a portion of the model. Depending on kind of device which the agent is running on, certain arcs will have nothing actually in them (actually there are no arcs there), while others will be present that weren't in another kind of agent. For instance, a router may not have the same kind of information that a web server would.

One tree model is used to keep the OIDs unique, but each device doesn't implement all of the features of networking, thus doesn't have all of the branches in the tree. Because the unique scheme is used though, functions may be added to a device without conflict, and you can get at the same kind of information on any devices in the same way.

Installing the SNMP Agent on NT

SNMP agent software may be installed on Windows NT using the *Network Control Panel* (Figure 17.22).

Figure 17.22
Installing the SNMP (agent) service.

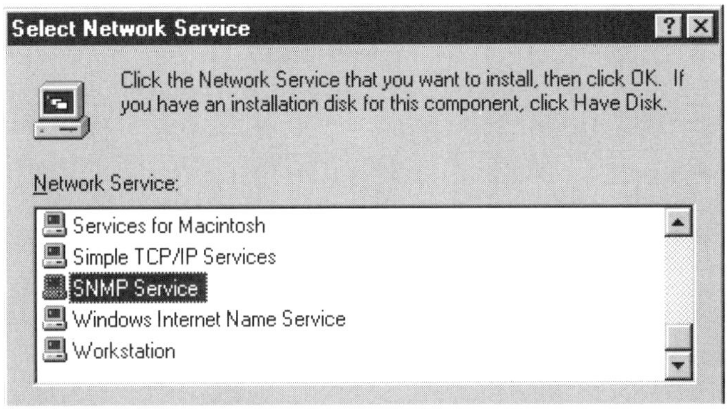

Installing the SNMP agent software installs five MIBs on the local machine. These default MIBs are listed in Table 17.1.

Table 17.1
The five MIBs installed with the Microsoft SNMP agent software.

Name	OID	Description
Internet MIB-II	.1.3.6.1.2.1	IP configuration or fault analysis objects (as defined in RFC1213).
LanManager MIB	.1.3.6.1.4.1.77	Session, logon, share, and statistics objects in LanManager.
WINS Server MIB	.1.3.6.1.4.1.311.1.2	WINS server statistics, database information, and push and pull data.
DHCP Server MIB	.1.3.6.1.4.1.311.1.3	DHCP server statistics and scope information.
Microsoft IIS	.1.3.6.1.4.1.311.1.7	Internet Information Server objects, including FTP, gopher, and HTTP.

The Object Identifiers (OIDs) shown in the middle column of Table 17.1 identify the address in the MIB tree where information about a particular module can be found. Figure 17.20 showed how these MIBs are grafted onto the OID tree.

Recall the actual definitions shown in Figure 17.21 which are used to graft the internetServer MIB (shown as IIS in Figure 17.20) onto the tree at

1.3.6.1.4.1.311.1.7. Similar definitions are used to graft the WINS, DHCP, and LAN Manager MIBs onto the tree.

Each MIB file specifies a schema[7] for a certain MIB. The MIB files are used as a human-readable reference and index to the MIB, and as a standard format for compiling knowledge of MIB variables into manager software.

The agent must be able to actually implement each MIB described in these specifications. The Windows NT SNMP agent (installed as in Figure 17.22) is an example of an extensible agent. This means that a core piece of software, ***snmp.exe***, implements the basic ability to respond to SNMP queries but doesn't know about any MIB variables. This core agent may be extended with one or more subagents. Each subagent is implemented as a dynamically linked library (DLL). For instance, the file mib_ii.mib is the standard specification of the MIB-2 schema, and the file mib2util.dll is the Microsoft subagent implementation. Microsoft's proprietary DHCP MIB is specified in dhcp.mib and its subagent is implemented in dhcpmib.dll.

When additional software is added to the machine, additional subagents and corresponding MIBs may also be added automatically. There is not always a one to one correspondence of MIB files to subagents. For instance, the MIB variables in mib_ii.mib and ipforwd.mib (IP forwarding MIB used for Steelhead) may both be supported by mib2util.dll.

Several MIBs are supported by Steelhead and Proxy Server. One of the MIBs supported by Steelhead is the IP forwarding table MIB which is defined in RFC 1354. This MIB is registered under the MIB-2 IP group with an OID of 1.3.6.1.2.1.4.24. Many of the other MIBs in Steelhead are private (i.e. proprietary) MIBs, and are therefore registered under the private enterprises branch of the OID tree.

Figure 17.23 depicts the MIB installed with the NT SNMP agent, as well as the Steelhead and Proxy Server MIBs.

Note that some of the private MIBs implemented in these Microsoft products were defined by other organizations. This is typical of many products which reuse (e.g. license) existing technologies. For example, the implementation of OSPF in Steelhead is a port of Wellfleet's (i.e. Bay Networks') OSPF software.

7. The schema defined in the MIB files is essentially like source code, or an interface specification for the MIB.

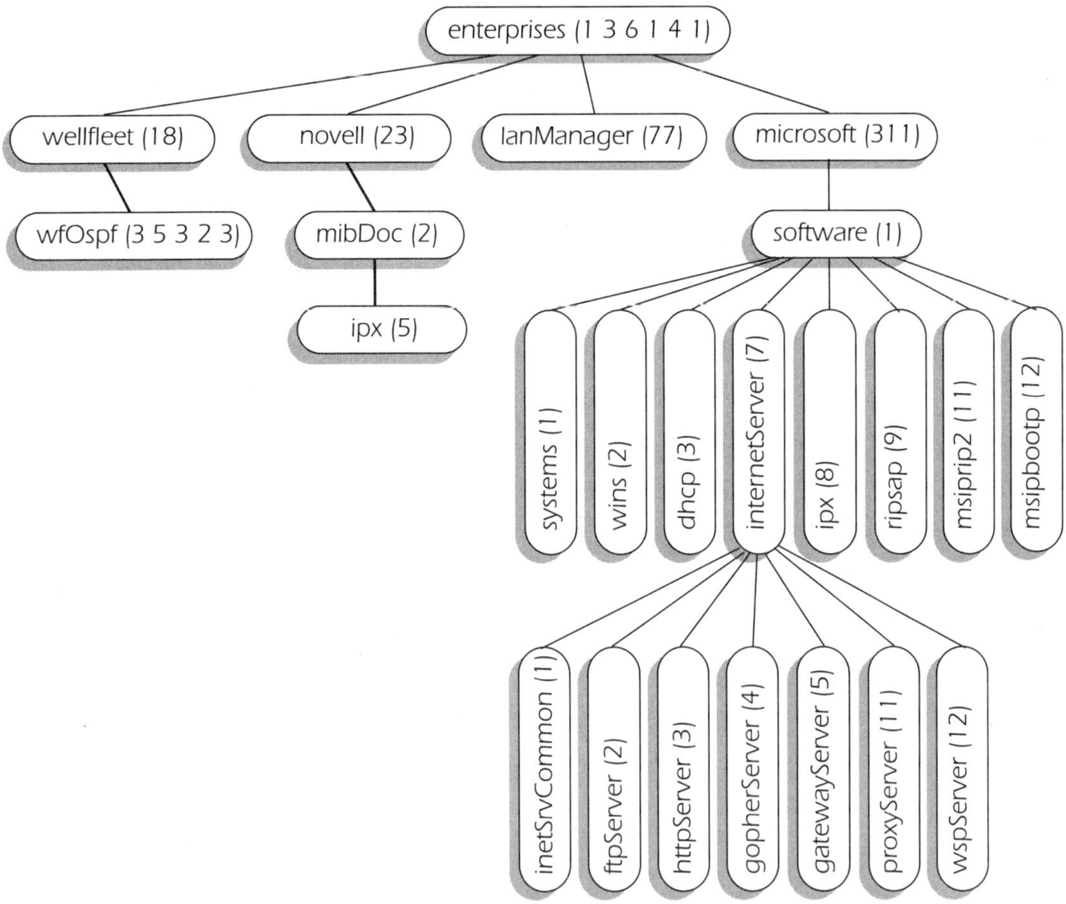

Figure 17.23 Core Microsoft MIBs as well as Steelhead and Proxy Server MIBs.

The names of these MIB files and the OIDs at which they are registered are shown in Table 17.2

Table 17.2
Complete list of NT MIB file names and the OIDs of the NT MIB grafting points.

Name	OID	Description
mib_ii.mib	.1.3.6.1.2.1	Internet MIB-II
ipforwd.mib	.1.3.6.1.2.1.4.24	IP Forwarding Table MIB
wospf.mib	.1.3.6.1.4.1.18.3.5.3.2.3	Wellfleet (Bay) OSPF MIB
nipx.mib	.1.3.6.1.4.1.23.2.5	Novell IPX MIB
lmmib2.mib	.1.3.6.1.4.1.77	LAN Manager MIB
wins.mib	.1.3.6.1.4.1.311.1.2	WINS server MIB
dhcp.mib	.1.3.6.1.4.1.311.1.3	DHCP server MIB
inetsrv.mib	.1.3.6.1.4.1.311.1.7	IIS MIBs
ftp.mib	.1.3.6.1.4.1.311.1.7.2	FTP server MIB
http.mib	.1.3.6.1.4.1.311.1.7.3	Web server MIB
gopherd.mib	.1.3.6.1.4.1.311.1.7.4	Gopher daemon MIB
gateway.mib	.1.3.6.1.4.1.311.1.7.5	Gateway MIB
w3p.mib	.1.3.6.1.4.1.311.1.7.11	WWW (CERN) proxy MIB
wsp.mib	.1.3.6.1.4.1.311.1.7.12	WinSock proxy MIB
mipx.mib	.1.3.6.1.4.1.311.8	MS NWLink IPX MIB
mripsap.mib	.1.3.6.1.4.1.311.9	MS NWLink RIP/SAP MIB
msiprip2.mib	.1.3.6.1.4.1.311.11	MS RIPv2 MIB
msipbtp.mib	.1.3.6.1.4.1.311.12	MS BootP relay MIB

SNMP Agent Properties

The agent properties dialog for SNMP (Figure 17.24) allows you to configure the SNMP agent software on this computer. This information is then available on the SNMP management station when it queries this machine's agent.

If there is a problem with this workstation or server, a network manager may look up the contact information to determine who to call. Put in a name, phone or pager number for the system administrator responsible for this system.

The location field should be filled in with detailed enough information so that a network administrator could send a technician to the server in the event of problems.

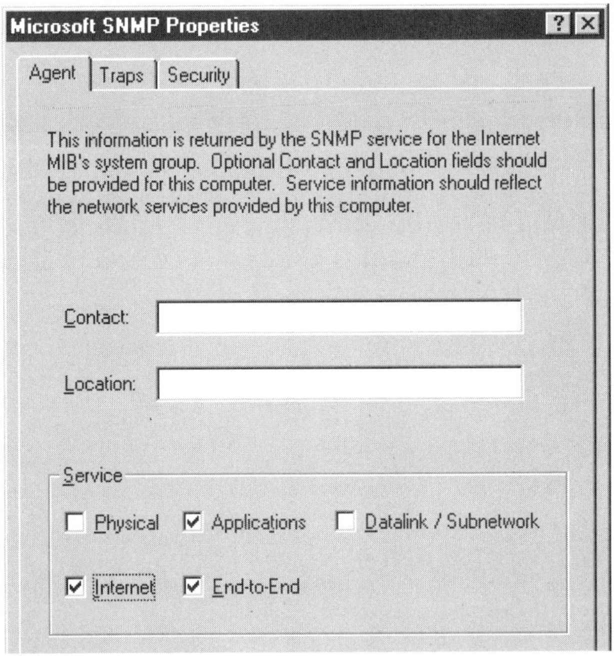

Figure 17.24 The SNMP agent properties are the contact person, location, and services provided on the system.

The service fields should contain indications of what layers of services are performed by the computer. These five layers associated with the TCP/IP layers. If the computer supports applications, then the "Applications" box should be checked. End-to-end services refer to the host-to-host or transport layer.

SNMP Communities

Several people (or whole departments) may be responsible for managing various routers, servers, and other devices in a network. The collection of devices which a manager is responsible for is called a management community.

community name: a logical name assigned to a group of SNMP agents. It is used to provide security.

Each management station and SNMP agent in a community may be configured to use a common **community name** for authorization purposes.

An SNMP manager would use the appropriate community name for requests sent to agents in a given community. The community name is used by agents to determine if incoming requests should be honored. It is a plaintext string that is used to provide security among SNMP devices.

Because the community name is a text string, it is also called the *community string*. Note that tools such as Network Monitor may allow other people on your network to reveal your plaintext community name. Even without this risk, this name should be regarded as a password, and should be set to a word not found in the dictionary. It should *not* be the word "public", as this allows any incoming SNMP requests with that default name to be processed.

Note

Treat SNMP community names as passwords which allow full monitoring and a great degree of control over (potentially) every device in your network!

SNMP Trap Configuration

Trap messages may be sent from this computer to the network management station in the event of problems or failures. You must configure a community name for the traps and one or more addresses of your management stations (Figure 17.25).

The community name entered on this control panel will be included in each trap message sent by the SNMP agent on this machine. You may want to use a different community name here than the one which will be used in the SNMP Security tab. The trap community name may be used by a trap manager as a quick check of the agent's identity. Many trap managers don't check the trap community.

A trap destination may be an IP address or a domain name. For example, put the IP address of your management station in this field. If several management stations should receive traps from this machine, add the IP address (or hostname) of each management station to the list.

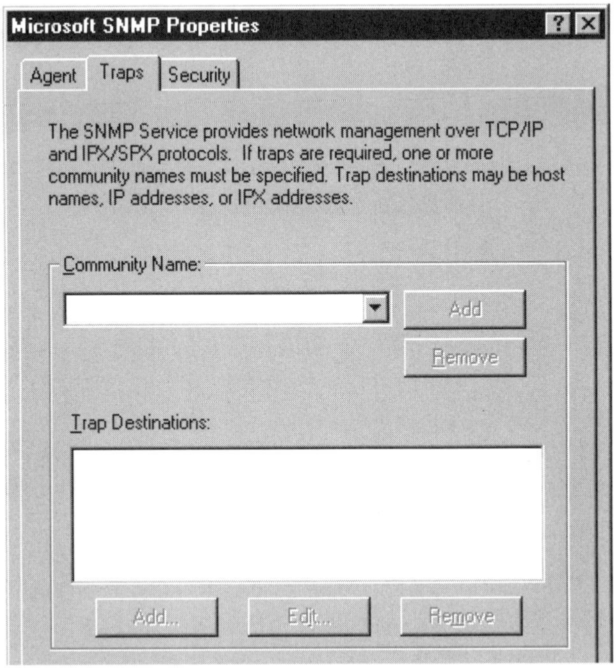

Figure 17.25 Trap messages may be sent by the SNMP agent. This configuration dialog allows you to specify the community name used in these traps as well as the destinations to which the traps will be sent.

SNMP Security

The security properties allow you to restrict access to your computer from certain network management stations. This may be useful because there is a wealth of information which users may retrieve from your computer with SNMP. Figure 17.26 shows the security properties.

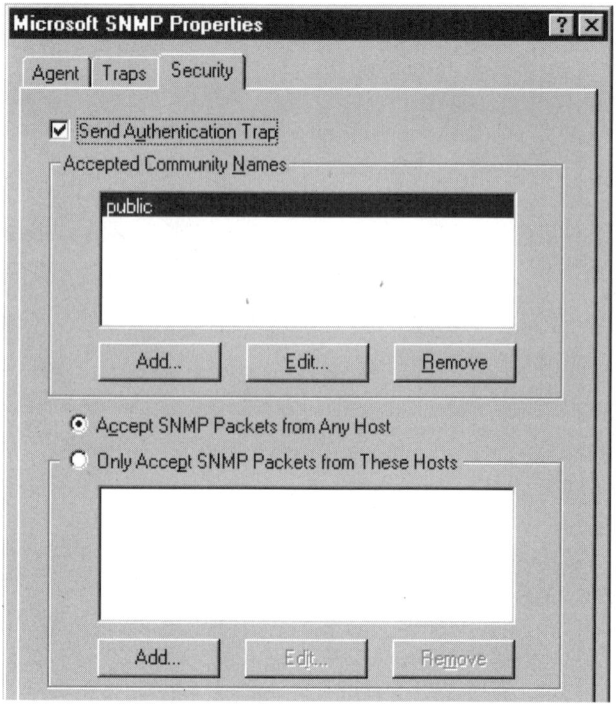

Figure 17.26
This dialog allows configuration of community names which may be used to talk with this machine's SNMP agent, as well as machine restrictions (source IP address).

It is common for all devices in a network to accept the community string "public," however it is advised that you change this from the default on computers which must be protected in your network. The community names entered in this agent's configuration should be kept secret.

If a user attempts to access information on this computer via SNMP and they use an incorrect community string, an authentication trap can be generated to the actual management station, as shown in Figure 17.27.

Machine A, acting as a SNMP manager attempts to perform a set request to machine B. The agent on machine B doesn't accept the community string which A used in the request (e.g. "public"), so it sends an authentication trap to the manager(s) it has been configured to send traps to.

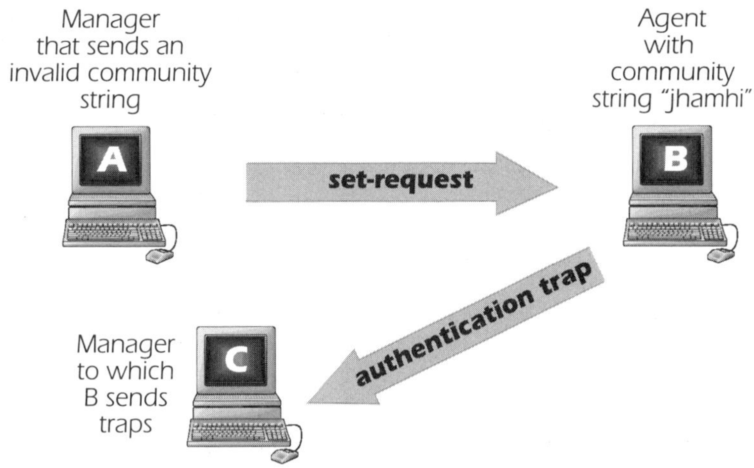

Figure 17.27 An SNMP agent which receives a request with a bad community string (or from a manager not on the accepted manager list) will send a trap to its configured manager(s).

SNMP Utilities and Files

Several SNMP-related files are located in the NT 4.0 Resource Kit CD. The MIB files are in the directory \common\netdiag. The SNMP utilities are in the directory \i386\netdiag.

SNMP MIB Files

The files shown in Table 17.3 are installed on the SNMP Manager to inform the manager of the MIB variables that the agents use. Additional files which are installed with other software are listed in Table 17.2. If you are managing equipment which supports other MIBs, obtain the appropriate MIB files from the vendor or a third party.

Table 17.3
SNMP MIB Files

MIB name	description
dhcp.mib	DHCP server objects
wins.mib	WINS server object
inetsrv.mib	Internet Information Server objects
ftp.mib	FTP server objects
gopherd.mib	gopher server objects
http.mib	HTTP server objects
Lmmib2.mib	LAN Manager MIB 2 objects
mib_ii.mib	MIB-II objects
smi.mib	structure of the manager information MIB: global definitions used to define the objects in the other MIBs (see RFC 1155)

SNMP Utilities

The utilities listed in Table 17.4 allow you to work with management information from Windows NT.

Table 17.4
SNMP Utilities for Windows NT

utility	description
mibcc.exe	MIB compiler.
perf2mib.exe	MIB builder tool used to create a new MIB file based on certain performance monitor counters.
snmputil.exe	Test utility that implements the SNMP commands get, get next, walk and trap.
snmpmon.exe	Monitors MIB objects on remote hosts.

SNMP Utility (snmputil.exe)

To test the SNMP agent, you may use the utility called ***snmputil***. As shown in the usage line in Figure 17.28, ***snmputil*** allows you to issue SNMP commands to an SNMP agent, such as the one you just installed.

```
cmd
C:\>snmputil
Error:   Incorrect number of arguments specified.

usage:   snmputil [get|getnext|walk] agent community oid [oid ...]
         snmputil trap

C:\>snmputil get 10.1.2.8 public .1.3.6.1.2.1.1.2.0
Variable = system.sysObjectID.0
Value    = OBJECT IDENTIFIER - .1.3.6.1.4.1.311.1.1.3.1.2


C:\>snmputil get 10.1.2.8 public .1.3.6.1.2.1.1.3.0
Variable = system.sysUpTime.0
Value    = TimeTicks - 4315644


C:\>snmputil get 10.1.2.8 public .1.3.6.1.4.1.311.1.3.1.2.0
Variable = .iso.org.dod.internet.private.enterprises.microsoft.software.
dhcp.dhcpPar.parDhcpTotalNoOfDiscovers.0
Value    = Counter - 0


C:\>
```

Figure 17.28 Example output of the snmputil command.

Following the usage line in Figure 17.28, the command "get" is sent to the agent at IP address 10.1.2.8, with community name "public." The request contains an object identifier of 1.3.6.1.2.1.1.1.2.0 which identifies the information to get from the agent (an identifier of the kind of system that the agent is running on). The output of the command shows the registered name for the object identifier (OID) (system.sysObjectID) and that instance zero (0) was retrieved, as requested. The value is of type OBJECT IDENTIFIER, a common SNMP type, and the OID value is 1.3.6.1.4.1.311.1.1.3.1.2.

Next, another "get" command is sent to the same agent with the same community name. The requested piece of information is identified with OID 1.3.6.1.2.1.1.3.0. The agent sends back a get-response which ***snmputil*** (the simple manager) displays. The ***snmputil*** command interprets the meaning of the OID to be system.sysUpTime.0, where "system" is a group (number 1) in the MIB-II (1.3.6.1.2.1). Within the system group, parameter (or attribute) number 3 is the amount of time that the system has been up and running. Because a given system can only be up for one certain amount of time, there is only one instance of this MIB variable, thus we specified instance zero in the request. The value returned by the agent is of type TimeTicks, another common SNMP type which specifies time in hundredths of seconds (centiseconds). The actual value was (at the time which the agent responded) 4,315,644 centiseconds. This is nearly 12 hours (11:59:16.44).

Finally, the value which the agent has at OID 1.3.6.1.4.1.311.1.3.1.2.0 is requested. From the output of ***snmputil***, we see that this identifies a MIB variable called parDhcpTotalNoOfDiscovers which Microsoft defined and registered.

Summary

Here's a summary of the items which have been addressed in this chapter.

- Systems and network management is a broad topic with many dimensions. Management activities may focus on fault, configuration, accounting, performance, and security management. Each of these focuses may be applied to various scopes, from managing a single machine to a large network system which provides many services.

- The Simple Network Management Protocol (SNMP) may be used for management of devices and services. SNMP provides basic operations to retrieve configuration and status information, and to control the behavior of devices and services.

- Groups of management parameters are defined in Management Information Bases (MIBs). There are many rules for how information is defined in MIBs.

- Management applications can be run on a Network Management Station (NMS) for centralized control of a network. These management tools may be custom or generalized applications. Microsoft provides a utility called ***snmputil*** for rudimentary testing. Third party tools can be used for any substantial management, as Microsoft management applications don't currently make use of standards-based SNMP management techniques.

Further Reading

Here is information about various books and magazines in which to look for further information on the subject.

[Baker1992] Baker, F., *IP Forwarding Table MIB,* 1992, IETF RFC 1354

[Case1990] Case, J., *A Simple Network Management Protocol (SNMP),* 1990, IETF RFC 1157

[Leinwand1996] Leinwand, Allan, Conroy, Karen Fang, *Network Management — A Practical Perspective,* 1996, Addison Wesley

[McCloghrie1991] McCloghrie, K., *Management Information Base for Network Management of TCP/IP-based Internets: MIB-II,* 1991, IETF RFC 1213

[Rose1990] Rose, M., *Structure and Identification of Management Information for TCP/IP-based Internets,* 1990, IETF RFC 1155

[Rose1994] Rose, Marshall T., *The Simple Book — An Introduction to Internet Management/2e,* 1994, Prentice-Hall

[Rose1995] Rose, Marshall, T., McCloghrie, Keith, *How to Manage Your Network Using SNMP — The Network Management Practicum,* 1995, Prentice-Hall

[Sloman1994] Sloman, Morris, ed., *Network and Distributed Systems Management,* 1994, Addison Wesley

[Stallings1996] Stallings, William, *SNMP, SNMPv2, and RMON — Practical Network Management/2e,* 1996, Addison Wesley

Index

A

acknowledgment
  indicator. *See* TCP - ACK
  number. *See* TCP - acknowledgment number
address
  broadcast 60, 257
  broadcast, general 60
  database, Netmon 218
  family 145, 274, 302
    AF_INET 145, 166
    AF_IPX 145
    AF_NETBIOS 145, 166
  IP 49, 54—95, 147, 174, 388
    configuration 181
    multiple per NIC 183
  loopback 61
  MAC 153, 209, 219
  mapping 458, 463, 467
  multicast 60, 257, 297, 299, 326
  network 59, 122, 274, 302
  network broadcast 122
  non-routable 66
  private 66
  socket 145
  subnet 110, 122, 257
  subnet broadcast 110, 123
  table, local 467
  translation 458, 463, 467
  unicast 60
address family
  AF_INET 166
  AF_NETBIOS 166
Address Resolution Protocol. *See* ARP
AFS 162
agent
  Network Monitor 221, 236
  SNMP 661
ALOHA 32
Andrew File System. *See* AFS
anonymous user. *See* IIS
  anonymous user
answer, the 42
API 142
  mail slot 143
  named pipe 143
  NetBIOS 143, 152
  RPC 143
  SMB 143
  WinsockWindows Sockets
    library. *See* socket - library
  WNet 143
AppleTalk 165
Application Programming Interface. *See* API
ARP 29, 47, 67, 73, 249, 591, 595
  cache 73, 153
  cache life. *See* ARP - TTL
  in a routed network 78
  ladder diagram 78
  registry parameters 76, 197
  reply 73, 215
  request 73, 214
  TTL 74
Assigned Numbers RFC 40
asymmetric key. *See* cryptography - public key
ATM 169
attribute value assertion (AVA) 539
authentication
  basic 552
  definition 522
  message check. *See* Message Authentication Check
  NT challenge/response. *See* challenge/response - NT
  PPP 343
  SSL 553
authoritative
  for a domain. *See* DNS - authoritative

B

BGP 252
BIND 420, 512, 513, 514
binding 39, 55
  dynamic, software 143
  socket 147
  static, software 143
BIOS 152
BootP 11, 43, 571
  relay agent. *See* DHCP - relay agent
Bootstrap Protocol. *See* BootP
broadcast
  address. *See* address - broadcast
  network 122

packets not forwarded 77, 249
RIPv2 advertisement 299
subnet address. *See* address - subnet broadcast
browsing 155, 618

C

cache 439
caching DNS 515, 518
caching proxy 462
Callback Control Protocol. *See* PPP - CBCP
CBC, mode of DES 530
CBCP. *See* PPP - CBCP
CCP. *See* PPP - CCP
CERN proxy. *See* proxy - CERN
certificate
authority 536, 562
digital 537
server software 564
X.509 537, 553, 561, 666, 672
Challenge Handshake Authentication Protocol. *See* PPP - CHAP
challenge/response 526
NT 548, 549, 552
PPP CHAP 344, 377
CHAP. *See* PPP - CHAP
checksum
ICMP 90
IP 86
TCP 15
CIFS 154
ciphertext 523
client
RAS 349
SMB 155
CMIP 666, 671, 672, 673
Common Internet File System. *See* CIFS
Common Management Information Protocol. *See* CMIP
Compression Control Protocol. *See* PPP - CCP
computer name. *See* NetBIOS - computer name
configuration
default gateway 181
DNS client 187
IP address 181
subnet mask 181
WINS client 188
connection
-less 26, 146, 153, 157
-oriented 26, 146, 153
setup. *See* PPTP - connection setup
setup. *See* TCP - connection establishment
teardown. *See* TCP - connection termination
cryptography 522—540
asymmetric key. *See* cryptography - public key
hybrid key 534
public key 529, 530, 531
server 532
symmetric key 529, 530
CSMA/CD 32

D

Data Encryption Standard. *See* DES
datagram 146, 153, 157
identifier 84
UDP 26
dead gateway detection 183
decapsulation 46
DECnet 165
decryption 522, 523, 529, 530, 531, 532, 534, 540, 544
default
gateway 67, 175, 183, 251, 257
configuration 181
subnet mask 112, 117
default router. *See* default - gateway
demilitarized zone. *See* DMZ
DES 530
destination unreachable. *See* ICMP - destination unreachable
detunnel 372, 375
DHCP 8, 47, 175, 250, 358, 570—613
ack 600
backing up servers 611
client
configuration 573
reboot 602
reservation 583

conflict detection 590
database
backup 610
records 592
discover 596
initial leasing process 594
lease renewal 601
logging 589
MIB 681, 684
NetBT node type option 633
offer 597
options 577, 584—589
relay agent 603—609
MIB 684
request 599
scope 576, 578
security 582
server installation 577
dialup
access using RAS 334
connections using RAS 348
monitoring using Network Monitor 235
digital certificate 537
See Also certificate - X.509
digital signature 525
directory
access protocol, lightweight. *See* LDAP
Directory, The 540, 673
distinguished name 672
definition 538
issuer 538
relative 539, 672
subject 537, 561
Distributed Computing Environment (DCE) 150
distributed software 150
DLL 143, 682
DMZ 464
DNS 8, 47, 147, 406—444, 494—520
A record 426, 432
adding hosts 428
authoritative 409, 497, 502
boot file 512
cache 414, 415, 416, 426, 439, 496, 497, 498, 501, 502, 509, 515
cache file. *See* DNS - file - cache
cache-only server 515, 518
CNAME record 426
configuration, client 187, 419, 436
configuration, server 422—435, 437
file
boot 512
cache 498, 501, 515
in-addr.arpa 434
updating 433, 434, 507
zone 424, 425, 434, 505, 509, 513
forwarder
definition 498
list 500
registry entry 514
IP master 505, 513
multihomed server 511
NS record 425, 426, 502
packet capture 416—418
primary server 408, 424, 497, 503
proxy server use 467
PTR record 426, 432
query 409, 412, 414, 416—418, 435—442
iterative 498, 502
non-recursive. *See* DNS - query - iterative
recursive 498
resolver 496
definition 406
reverse lookup
definition 429
root server 498, 501
searchlist 439
secondary server 409, 497, 503, 504
server installation 420
slave server 501
registry entry 514
SOA record 425, 426, 506, 508
update server data files 433
WINS and DNS 503, 623, 632, 634, 635, 640, 652—655
zone
default TTL 510
definition 423
file 497
file name 424
image 497
IP master 505, 513
refresh interval 510
retry interval 510
serial number 509
transfer 503—510
transfer, incremental 507

transfer, packet capture 508
domain name 147, 388
definition 406
fully qualified. *See* FQDN
in-addr.arpa 429—435, 438
label
definition 412
resolution
definition 406
resolver. *See* DNS — resolver
tree 411
Domain Name System. *See* DNS
DOS 152
dynamic binding 143
Dynamic Host Configuration Protocol. *See* DHCP
dynamic routing. *See* routing - dynamic
dynamically linked library. *See* DLL

E

ECB, mode of DES 530
echo request
ICMP. *See* ICMP - echo request
EGP 252
EIGRP 252
emulator
NetBIOS 160, 161
WinSock 160, 161
encapsulation 44
generic routing. *See* GRE
PPTP 371
encryption 334, 369, 522—535, 540—544, 548, 565
in PPTP 370, 392
Ethernet 169
802.3 33
DIX 33
protocol type. *See* EtherType
EtherType 33, 37, 42, 214, 229, 230
exterior routing protocol 252

F

FDDI 169
file system
Andrew. *See* AFS
Common Internet. *See* CIFS
Network. *See* NFS
File Transfer Protocol. *See* FTP
filtering
by port number 185
FTP 228
Netmon
by address during capture 231
by address during display 225
by pattern during capture 231
by protocol property during display 227
by protocol type during display 226
by SAP or ETYPE during capture 230
PPTP 184, 381
router 455, 457
definition 456
stateful 457
final data indication. *See* TCP - FIN
firewall 50, 455—467
definition 455
filtering router 455
gateway 458
hybrid 463
non-intrusive 458
stateless 457
transparent 458
fnord 206
FQDN 388, 412, 422, 434, 435, 437, 439, 509
definition 412
fragmentation. *See* IP - fragmentation
FTP 6, 47, 141, 155
filtering 228
MIB 684
fully qualified domain name. *See* FQDN

G

gateway 66
default 67, 183, 251
detection, dead 183
-firewall 458
definition 459
Generic Routing Encapsulation. *See* GRE
GRE 369, 377
packet capture 379
packet format 377

H

handshake
  CHAP. *See* PPP - CHAP
  SSL 541
  three step. *See* TCP - connection establishment 18
hardware routing 294
hash 524
  one-way 527
hop count. *See* routing - metric
hop-by-hop transmission 70
host file
  definition 407
host route. *See* routing - host route
hostname 187
  definition 406
HTML 446, 447, 448, 469, 545
HTTP 6, 148, 446—449
  get 447, 456, 484
  packet capture 449
  packet exchange 448
  response 447
HTTPS 565
  See Also SSL
hybrid firewall 463
HyperText Markup Language (HTML). *See* HTML
HyperText Transfer Protocol. *See* HTTP

I

ICMP 29, 47, 90
  destination unreachable 91
  echo request 93, 193, 211, 217, 591
  message code 90
  message type 90
  time exceeded 92, 286, 289
IGMP 65
IGRP 252
IIS 540—568
  anonymous user 547
  authentication 548—553
  Internet Service Manager 545
  MIB 681, 684
  multiple IP addresses 553
  security checks 546
  SSL configuration 559—566
in-addr.arpa. *See* domain name - in-addr.arpa
installation
  DHCP server 577
  DNS server 420
  PPTP 382, 389
  RAS client 351—353
  RAS server 355—358
  RIP 277
  RIPv2 307
  Steelhead 305, 395
  TCP/IP 174—203
integrity check, message. *See* MIC
interior routing protocol 252
International Data Encryption Algorithm (IDEA) 530
Internet
  control message protocol. *See* ICMP
  protocol. *See* IP
Internet Architecture Board (IAB) 47
Internet Assigned Numbers Authority (IANA) 48
Internet Control Message Protocol. *See* ICMP
Internet Engineering Task Force (IETF) 48
Internet Explorer
  automatic configuration 473, 479
  proxy configuration 473
Internet Group Management Protocol. *See* IGMP
Internet Information Server. *See* IIS
Internet Network Information Center. *See* InterNIC
Internet Protocol Control Protocol. *See* PPP - IPCP
Internet Research Task Force (IRTF) 48
Internet Society 47
InterNIC 46, 48, 49, 50, 62, 63, 411, 450, 453, 463
IP 27, 47
  address 147, 174, 388
    configuration 181
    multiple per NIC 183
  addressing 54—95
  checksum 86
  datagram identifier 84
  fragmentation 84, 88

failure 92
header length 81
precedence 82
protocol field 85
raw interface 164, 167, 185
reassembly 88, 89
routing 246—291, 294—331
subnetting. *See* subnet, subnetting
total length 83
TTL 72, 85, 286—290
type of service 83
version number 81
ipconfig.exe 190, 192, 298, 398, 400, 401, 574—575, 592, 635, 637
graphical interface 192
IPCP. *See* PPP - IPCP
IPSEC 366
IPX 144, 145, 152, 161, 164, 168, 369
iterative query. *See* DNS - query - iterative

K

Kerberos 666
kernel routing table 296—298
kernrout.exe 296, 297, 397, 398, 401
interface numbers 298, 400
key pair. *See* cryptography - public key
key. *See* cryptography

L

L2TP 366
ladder diagram 21
ARP 78
ping 195
PPP 346, 378
PPTP 378
proxy server 461, 484, 485, 489
tracert 288
LAN Manager 155, 624
LCP. *See* PPP - LCP
LDAP 540, 666
library 143
dynamically linked 143
mail slot 143, 157
named pipe 143, 156
NetBIOS 143, 152
provider 157, 159
shared 143
socket 143
Lightweight Directory Access Protocol (LDAP). *See* LDAP
Link Control Protocol. *See* PPP - LCP
Link Service Access Point. *See* SAP - LSAP
LLC 31, 35, 42, 44
LMHOSTS 238, 623, 624—625
local address table (LAT) 467
See Also address - translation
Logical Link Control. *See* LLC
loopback
address 61
interface 257, 298
network 61
LSAP 41
LSAP. *See* SAP - LSAP

M

MAC 31, 153, 583
See Also Message Authentication Check
magic cookie
PPTP 372
magic word
xyzzy 106
mail slot library 143, 157
Management Information Base. *See* SNMP — MIB
mask
network. *See* subnet - mask, routing
maximum segment size. *See* TCP - MSS
maximum transmission unit. *See* IP - MTU
MD 524, 526
MD5 526, 527
Medium Access Control. *See* MAC
Message Authentication Check (MAC) 533
message digest. *See* MD
message integrity check. *See* MIC
metric
routing. *See* routing - metric
MIC 524, 528, 533
Microsoft Management Console (MMC) 545

MPR 162
MPR. *See* Multi-Provider Router or Multiple Protocol Router
MS-Net 157
  provider library 159
  redirector 159
MTU 24
  default 87
multicast
  address. *See* address - multicast
  packet 65, 299
multihomed 251, 253, 258
  DNS server 511
multi-layer inspection 462
Multiple Protocol Router (MPR) 305
Multiple UNC Provider. *See* MUP
Multi-Provider Router (MPR) 157, 162
MUP 160, 162

N

named pipe library 143, 156
NBF 154, 164, 167, 168
NBNS 142, 153, 621, 625, 655
NBNWLink 164
NBT 8, 47, 164, 166, 167, 616, 618, 620, 621, 624, 626, 628, 630, 631, 632, 633, 637, 640, 652
nbtstat.exe 621, 630
NDIS 39, 139, 165, 169, 295
neighbor
  RIP 319
NetBEUI 152, 164, 168, 369
NetBEUI Frame. *See* NBF
NetBIOS 8, 144, 152
  computer name 153, 178, 187
  emulator 160, 161
  library 143, 152
  name table 153
NetBIOS Enhanced User Interface. *See* NetBEUI
NetBIOS Name Service. *See* NBNS
NetBIOS over TCP/IP. *See* NBT
NetBT. *See* NBT
netlogon
  service 550
network
  loopback 61
  neighborhood 141, 618, 620, 637, 640
  non-routable 66
  virtual private. *See* VPN
network address. *See* address - network
Network Device Interface Specification. *See* NDIS
Network File System. *See* NFS
Network Information Center (NIC) 48
network interface
  layer 30
Network Interface Card. *See* NIC
Network Management Station.*See* SNMP NMS
network mask. *See* subnet - mask, routing
Network Monitor 208—243, 376, 393
  address database 218, 220
  agent 221, 236
  configuration file 239, 376
  installation 208
  monitoring a dialup connection 235
  monitoring a remote network 236
  NIC description 222
  selecting the NIC to use 234
Network Service Access Point. *See* SAP - NSAP
NFS 154, 162
NIC 209, 233, 295
  multiple 182, 191
  multiple addresses 183, 554
  multiport 296
  See Also Network Information Center
non-intrusive firewall 458
non-routable networks 66
non-transparent
  proxy 461
non-WINS enabled 638
nslookup.exe 435, 508, 515, 519
  -debug 438
NTLM 549
NWLink 164, 168

O

object identifiers. *See* SNMP

OID
one-way hash 527
Open Group 150
Open Systems Interconnect. *See* OSI
Organizationally Unique Identifiers 37
OS/2 156, 157
OSI 4, 144
OSPF 252, 299

P

packet capture
- ARP 211, 213, 214, 216, 595
- DHCP 595—600, 602, 607, 609
- DNS, name query 416—418, 442
- DNS, zone transfer 508
- GRE 379
- HTTP 449
- ICMP echo 211, 217, 287
- PPP 343, 345, 379
- PPTP 376, 379
- proxy server 478—490
- RIP 279—284
- RIPv2 325—329
- SSL 543
- tracert 287
- WINS 627, 629, 643

packet format
- Ethernet 34, 38, 79
- GRE 377
- ICMP 90
  - diagnostic 93
  - exception 91
- IP 79, 80
- LLC 36, 38
- PPP 339
- PPTP 372, 374
- RIPv1 273
- RIPv2 300, 301
- SNAP 37, 38
- TCP 14
- UDP 27

Password Authentication Protocol. *See* PPP - PAP
persistent route
- definition. *See* RIP - persistent route - definition

persistent route. *See* RIP - persistent route
phonebook entry 386
ping.exe 29, 93, 141, 164, 167, 193, 210
PKCS 562
plaintext 523
point-to-point
- protocol. *See* PPP
- tunneling protocol. *See* PPTP

poison reverse 282, 300, 322, 328
- definition 275

port
- ephemeral 11
- named 11, 43
- number 43, 147, 448, 456, 457, 458, 464, 465, 469, 553
- randomly assigned 11, 470, 487
- source ..., TCP 15
- target ..., TCP 15
- well-known 11, 43, 469, 470, 471, 487, 541, 545

PPP 169, 334, 338—363, 366, 369—379
- authentication 343
- CBCP 345, 378
- CCP 345, 377, 378
- CHAP 343, 377
- IPCP 345, 378
- ladder diagram 346, 378
- LCP 342, 377
- link establishment 342
- link phase 341—347
- network control protocol 345
- packet capture 379
- packet format 339
- PAP 343, 377
- protocol type 340

PPTP 184, 239, 334, 336, 337, 366—404
- bearer type 375
- call identifier 375
- client 390
- connection setup 373
- encapsulation 371
- encryption 370, 392
- establishing a session 380
- filtering 184, 381
- installation 382, 389
- ladder diagram 378
- magic cookie 372
- outgoing call reply 375
- outgoing call request 374
- packet capture 379

packet format 372, 374
phonebook entry 386
receive window size 375
server 389, 393
start session reply 373
start session request 373
tunnel 368—379
programming
RPC 151
socket 144, 151
protocol
analyzer 208
field, IP 42, 85
host-to-host layer 9
internet layer 27
network interface layer 30
process layer 5
routing, exterior 252
routing, interior 252
type, Ethernet. *See* EtherType
type, PPP 340
provider library 157
proxy 446—492
caching 462
CERN 468, 482
MIB 684
client configuration 466
definition 459
DNS and proxy 467, 518
ladder diagram 461, 485
telnet traffic 489
web traffic 484
multi-layer inspection 462
non-transparent 461
operation 460
packet capture 478—490
server 50, 66
SOCKS 471
client configuration 474
transparent 461
web 468, 482
client configuration 472
WinSock 470
client configuration 474
MIB 684
WSP client control panel 475
PSTN 335, 348, 349
public key cryptography. *See* cryptography - public key

R

RARP 571
RAS 334—363, 366, 380, 395
client 349, 382, 390, 394
installation 351—353
server 349, 388, 389, 393, 397, 401
installation 355—358
raw IP interface 164, 167
filtering 185
raw socket 167
reassembly. *See* IP - reassembly
recursive query. *See* DNS - query - recursive
redirector 158, 160, 162
MS-Net 159
refresh interval
DNS 510
registry 195
adding parameters 199
ARP cache 76
editor, regedit.exe 196, 199
editor, regedt32.exe 196
RIP values 278
relative distinguished name 539
remote access
encrypted 334
service. *See* RAS
Remote Access Service. *See* RAS
Remote Procedure Call. *See* RPC
Request for Comments. *See* RFC
resolver. *See* domain name - resolver
Reverse Address Resolution Protocol. *See* RARP
RFC
Assigned Numbers 40, 85
Host Requirements 123
Private Addressing 66
rights
NT user 547
RIP 252, 294
infinite distance 316, 322
metric for directly attached networks 281
neighbor 318
neighbor list 320
operation 264
packet capture 279—284
persistent route 261

definition 255
problem with NT implementation 281
registry entries 278
route tag 302, 304, 316
silent RIP 278, 315
unreachable network 316
v1
disadvantages 282
installation 277
packet format 273
v2
improvements upon v1 299
installation 307
MIB 684
operation 300
packet capture 325—329
packet format 300
root server. *See* DNS - root server
route tag. *See* RIP - route tag
route.exe 254, 260, 296, 324
router
default. *See* default - gateway
definition 246
filtering 455, 457
definition 456
routing 246—291, 294—331
accepting routes 317
advertisement 311, 314, 316
announcing routes 317
domain 311
dynamic 251, 264
enabling on NT 253
hardware 294
hop count 256
host route 297, 322
kernel routing table 296—298
metric 255, 256, 265, 274, 303, 304, 316, 322
neighbor 318, 319
periodic announcement 321
protocol (definition) 251
protocol, exterior 252
protocol, interior 252
route expiration 322
route removal 322
stateful inspection 457
static 251, 253, 255, 259
subnet route 247, 297
table 250, 254, 256, 257, 259, 268, 270, 304, 397, 398, 401
convergence 276, 300
multihomed machine 258
triggered update 309
Routing and Remote Access Service. *See* Steelhead
RPC 143, 150
RRAS. *See* Steelhead

S

SAM database 548
samba 155
SAP 39, 41, 229, 230
LSAP 35, 41
NSAP 41
TSAP 41
scope. *See* DHCP — scope
secret key. *See* cryptography - symmetric key
Secure Sockets Layer. *See* SSL
security
IIS checks 546
Network Monitor 221
RIPv2 configuration 310
SAM database 548
user rights, IIS 547
security problems
DHCP 582
FTP 228
protocol analyzers 209
RAS 350
RIP 251, 311
war dialing 350
segment. *See* TCP - segment
sequence number
initial 17
segment 15
synchronization indication. *See* TCP - SYN
serial number
DNS zone 509
X.509 certificate 538
server
public key 532
service 161
SMB 155
Server Message Block. *See* SMB
service
/etc/services 148, 186
netlogon 550

remote access. *See* RAS
server 161
workstation 159, 161
Service Access Point. *See* SAP
session key 535
SHA 527
shared library 143
shared secret. *See* cryptography - symmetric key
SHS 527
signature verification 525
Simple Mail Transfer Protocol. *See* SMTP
Simple Network Management Protocol. *See* SNMP
slave server. *See* DNS - slave server
SMB 143, 154, 161
SMS 208
SMTP 6
SNAP 36, 42, 44
SNMP 8, 658—693
agent
definition 661
ASN.1 666
CMIP. *See* CMIP
community 685, 688
manager
definition 662
messages 662
MIB 665—692
definition 665
file 667
Steelhead 665, 667, 684
MIB compiling 667
NMS 662
object class 670, 671
object instance 670, 671
OID 669
RMON 663
SMI 666, 667
trap 663, 686
snmputil.exe 690
socket
address 145
bound 147
descriptor 144
emulator 160, 161
library 143
programming 144, 151
raw 164, 167
type 146
socket types
SOCK_DGRAM 146, 166
SOCK_STREAM 146, 166
SOCKS
proxy. *See* proxy - SOCKS
split horizon 300, 322
definition 275
SPX 164
SSL 536, 540—568
handshake 541
packet capture 543
state, firewall
stateful filtering 457
stateful inspection 457
stateless firewall 457
static binding 143
static routing 251, 253, 255, 259
Steelhead 246, 294—331, 337, 394, 395, 451
administration tool 396
DHCP relay agent 605
installation 305, 395
SNMP MIBs 665, 667, 684
viewing the routing table 323
STREAMS 165, 169
subject's distinguished name 537
subnet
address 110, 122, 257
broadcast address 110, 123
mask 99, 112, 115, 174
configuration 181
mask, default 112, 117
mask, routing 255
route. *See* routing - subnet route
table (precalculated) 119
subnetting 98—135
constant width 116, 302
rules of 122
variable width 116, 300, 302
SubNetwork Access Protocol. *See* SNAP
Sun Microsystems 150, 154, 162, 165
symmetric key cryptography. *See* cryptography - symmetric key
SYN. *See* TCP - SYN
synchronization indication. *See* TCP - SYN
Systems Management Server. *See* SMS

T

TCP 12, 13, 47, 145, 164, 166
  ACK 16
  acknowledgment
    indicator. *See* TCP - ACK
    number 15
  connection establishment 18
  connection termination 24
  EOL 18
  filtering 185
  FIN 17, 25
  flag 16
  header fields 14
  header length 15
  MSS 18, 23
  options 17, 18
  port. *See* port
  PSH 16
  RST 17
  segment 14
  SYN 17, 21, 148
  URG 16
  urgent
    data size 15
    mode indication. *See* TCP - URG
  window size 15
TCP/IP 4—52
  installation 174—203
TDI 139, 161, 163, 164, 165
teardown
  four step. *See* TCP - connection termination
Telnet 6, 7, 47, 141, 486
  as a terminal emulator 7
time exceeded. *See* ICMP - time exceeded
time to live (TTL) 92, 286
  ARP cache 74
  DNS 510
  in tracert 286—290
  IP datagram. *See* IP - TTL
Token Ring 169
tracert.exe 167, 284—290
transmission
  hop-by-hop 70
Transmission Control Protocol. *See* TCP
transparent
  firewall 458
  proxy 461
Transport Driver Interface. *See* TDI
Transport Service Access Point. *See* SAP - TSAP
triggered update 309, 322
tunnel 367, 372, 375, 377, 401
  definition 367
  PPTP 368—379
type of service. *See* IP - type of service

U

UDP 12, 26, 47, 145, 164, 166, 267
  datagram 26
  filtering 185
  port. *See* port
UNC 162
unicast address. *See* address - unicast
Uniform Resource Locator. *See* URL
Universal Naming Convention. *See* UNC
UNIX 144, 154, 156, 165, 512
  socket API 11
  use of process model in TCP/IP 5
URL 147, 162, 447, 482, 545
User Datagram Protocol. *See* UDP

V

VINES 157, 165
virtual host 183
virtual network 367
virtual private network. *See* VPN
virtual wire 377
VPN 334, 367, 382, 390
  interface 369, 383, 390, 401

W

WAN 400
web proxy. *See* proxy - web
web site 544—567
  administration 545
  create new 555
  default 545
window size. *See* TCP - window

size
WINS 142, 238, 616—655
configuration, client 188
database backup 651
delete record using winscl.exe 645
DNS and WINS 503, 623, 632, 634, 635, 640, 652—655
MIB 681, 684
name release 649
name renewal 648
node types 633
non-WINS enabled 637, 638
proxy 637
winscl.exe 645
WinSock
emulator 160, 161
library. *See* socket - library
proxy. *See* proxy - WinSock
WNet 143, 157
wntipcfg.exe 192, 576
workstation
service 159, 161
WSP. *See* proxy server - WinSock

X

X.509. *See* certificate
X.509
X/Open 154
XNS 144
xyzzy 106

Z

zone. *See* DNS — zone

Network Diagram

Here is a diagram of the foobar.com network used in many of the examples throughout the book.

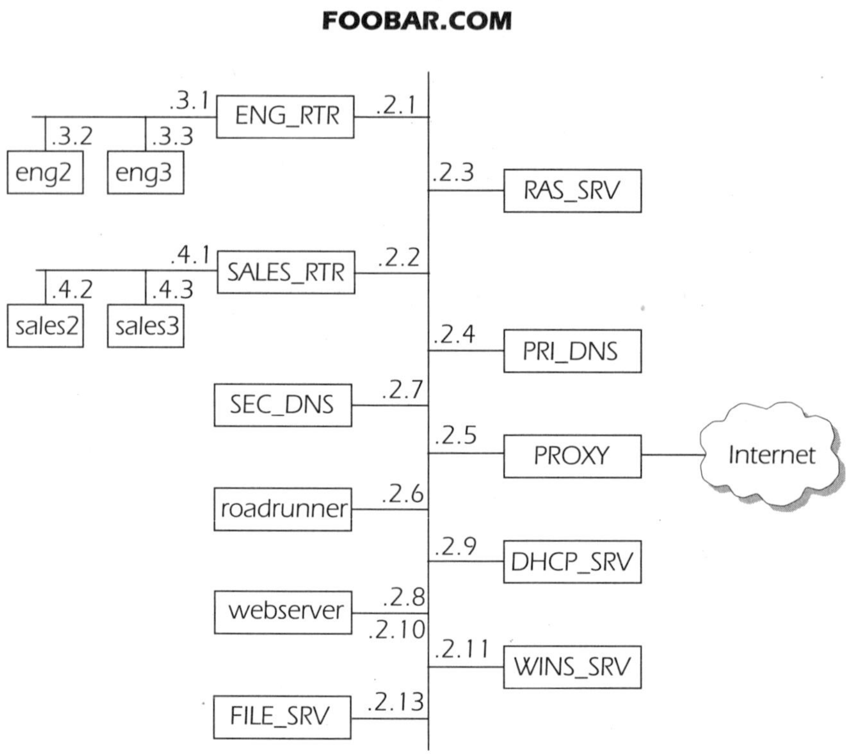

Contents of the Companion CD

The TCP/IP with Windows NT Companion CD contains reference information to complement the material printed in this book. Thanks to John Bisaillon for designing the web pages and mastering the CD.

Where to Begin

Use a web browser to open the file default.htm on the CD. To start Network Monitor when opening a .cap file, configure your browser to associate .cap files with Network Monitor.

RFCs

The CD contains Internet RFCs which may be used for further reading. It is best to use a fixed width font when viewing RFCs. For additional RFCs or Internet drafts, refer to one of the RFC mirror sites such as ftp://ftp.isi.edu and ftp://ds.internic.net.

Packet Captures

The Network Monitor capture files which are discussed throughout the book are included on the CD. Use Network Monitor to load these capture files and examine the packets as you refer to the examples in the book.

SOFTWARE AND INFORMATION LICENSE

The software and information on this diskette (collectively referred to as the "Product") are the property of The McGraw-Hill Companies, Inc. ("McGraw-Hill") and are protected by both United States copyright law and international copyright treaty provision. You must treat this Product just like a book, except that you may copy it into a computer to be used and you may make archival copies of the Products for the sole purpose of backing up our software and protecting your investment from loss.

By saying "just like a book," McGraw-Hill means, for example, that the Product may be used by any number of people and may be freely moved from one computer location to another, so long as there is no possibility of the Product (or any part of the Product) being used at one location or on one computer while it is being used at another. Just as a book cannot be read by two different people in two different places at the same time, neither can the Product be used by two different people in two different places at the same time (unless, of course, McGraw-Hill's rights are being violated).

McGraw-Hill reserves the right to alter or modify the contents of the Product at any time.

This agreement is effective until terminated. The Agreement will terminate automatically without notice if you fail to comply with any provisions of this Agreement. In the event of termination by reason of your breach, you will destroy or erase all copies of the Product installed on any computer system or made for backup purposes and shall expunge the Product from your data storage facilities.

LIMITED WARRANTY

McGraw-Hill warrants the physical diskette(s) enclosed herein to be free of defects in materials and workmanship for a period of sixty days from the purchase date. If McGraw-Hill receives written notification within the warranty period of defects in materials or workmanship, and such notification is determined by McGraw-Hill to be correct, McGraw-Hill will replace the defective diskette(s). Send request to:

Customer Service
McGraw-Hill
Gahanna Industrial Park
860 Taylor Station Road
Blacklick, OH 43004-9615

The entire and exclusive liability and remedy for breach of this Limited Warranty shall be limited to replacement of defective diskette(s) and shall not include or extend to any claim for or right to cover any other damages, including but not limited to, loss of profit, data, or use of the software, or special, incidental, or consequential damages or other similar claims, even if McGraw-Hill has been specifically advised as to the possibility of such damages. In no event will McGraw-Hill's liability for any damages to you or any other person ever exceed the lower of suggested list price or actual price paid for the license to use the Product, regardless of any form of the claim.

THE McGRAW-HILL COMPANIES, INC. SPECIFICALLY DISCLAIMS ALL OTHER WARRANTIES, EXPRESS OR IMPLIED, INCLUDING BUT NOT LIMITED TO, ANY IMPLIED WARRANTY OF MERCHANTABILITY OR FITNESS FOR A PARTICULAR PURPOSE. Specifically, McGraw-Hill makes no representation or warranty that the Product is fit for any particular purpose and any implied warranty of merchantability is limited to the sixty day duration of the Limited Warranty covering the physical diskette(s) only (and not the software or in-formation) and is otherwise expressly and specifically disclaimed.

This Limited Warranty gives you specific legal rights; you may have others which may vary from state to state. Some states do not allow the exclusion of incidental or consequential damages, or the limitation on how long an implied warranty lasts, so some of the above may not apply to you.

This Agreement constitutes the entire agreement between the parties relating to use of the Product. The terms of any purchase order shall have no effect on the terms of this Agreement. Failure of McGraw-Hill to insist at any time on strict compliance with this Agreement shall not constitute a waiver of any rights under this Agreement. This Agreement shall be construed and governed in accordance with the laws of New York. If any provision of this Agreement is held to be contrary to law, that provision will be enforced to the maximum extent permissible and the remaining provisions will remain in force and effect.